MO[illegible] ATLAS

GREAT BRITAIN AND IRELAND

RV VERLAG

MOTORING ATLAS

GREAT BRITAIN AND IRELAND

Cover photos:
Front cover (from above left to below rigth): Castle Stalker on Loch Linnhe, Scottand (Bavaria – Manfred Thonig). Lincoln Cathedral (W. Klammet). Beefeater at the Tower of London (Mauritius – Phipp). London – Tower Bridge (IFA – Aberham). Stonehenge (Bavaria – Günter Becker). Dartmouth Harbour (Klammet/ E.Nägele).
Spine: East Loch Tabert (Mauritius – Thonig). London – Big Ben (IFA – TPC). Cliffs near Dover (IFA – TPL).
Back cover: Cliffs of Dover (Bavaria – The Telegraph).

Title page: Crummock Water, Cumbria (Images/BAVARIA). Hampton Court (PhotoPress/Rothhahn). Eildon Hills and River Tweed in Roxboroughshire, Scotland (Tony Stone Worldwide – Colin Prior).

P. 10/11: Toft Harbour, Shetland. Stromness, waterfront.
P. 58/59: Dorset Heritage Coast. Bargate, Southampton.
P. 134/135: Ruined Llanthony Priory. Fishguard Harbour.
P. 154/155: Cattle grazing in the Antrim Hills. Musicians in one of Belfast's public houses.
P. 176/177: London: The Thames from Waterloo. The Edinburgh Tattoo.
P. 234/235: Denventwater, Cumbria. Rievaulx Abbey, Yorkshire.

Picture Credits
Aberdeen Tourist Board: p. 178(4). Marius Alexander: pp. 12, 13(5), 21(2), 26-27, 35, 41(2), 42(2), 180(5), 182(2), 183(2), 184(4), 187(5). David Ball, Bavaria: pp. 60, 202. Barry Beattie: pp. 176-177, 217, 218, 219, 220, 221, 224, 225(2), 226, 227. Borders Regional Council: pp. 238, 239. Cardiff City Council: pp. 210(2), 211(2). Chester City Council: p. 203. Dumfries and Galloway Tourist Board: pp. 50(2), 52(2). Paul Felix: pp. 42(2), 43(1), 50, 51, 84(2), 85(2), 90, 91(3), 100(3),101(2), 114(3), 126(2), 127 (2), 128(2), 129, 133(2), 134-135(2), 137, 149(1), 153, 204(3), 206(3), 212(2), 216(3), 217, 218, 245(2). Suzanne and Nick Geary/Tony Stone Worldwide: p. 196. Colin Iles: pp. 94, 208-209(4), 233(2). Images Bavaria: pp. 2-3. Irish Tourist Board: pp. 250(2), 251(3). Island Photographics: pp. 60(3), p. 66(3). Geoff Johnson/Tony Stone Worldwide: p. 212. John Kinory: pp. 80(3), 81(2), 90, 100, 142, 143(3), 226(2), 227, 244(2). Lincolnshire County Council: pp. 200(2), 201(2), 246(2). Gunnie Moberg: pp. 10, 13, 27. Werner Neumeister: p. 238. Northern Ireland Tourist Board: pp. 154(2), 156(3), 157(2), 162, 163(2), 166, 167(4), 188(3), 189(2), 190(2), 236, 237(2). Perthshire Tourist Board: pp. 34, 35(2). PhotoPress/Rothhahn: pp. 2-3. Colin Prior/Tony Stone Worldwide: pp. 2-3, 196, 238. David Sellman: pp. 74(3), 75(3), 94, 95(3), 106(2), 107(3), 110(2), 111(3), 115(2), 118, 119(3), 122(2), 123(3), 148, 149, 214(3), 218, 221, 222-223(3), 228, 229(2). Kit Snedaker: pp. 136 (2), 137, 225, 232, 246. Southern Tourist Board: p. 58(2). Charles Tait: pp. 10, 11(1), 21, 22(2), 43(1), 176, 218, 219, 220, 221(2), 227, 246(2). Southern Tourist Board: pp. 58(2), 59. Stratford-upon-Avon District Council: pp. 242(2), 243. Peter Titmuss Photography: p. 119. Unichrome (Bath) Limited: p. 214. West Country Tourist Board: pp. 128 (2), 133(2), 230-231(4). Bill Wilkinson: pp. 234/235(2), 240(3), 241(2). Yorkshire and Humberside Tourist Board: pp. 68(4), 69(3), 192-193(4). Zefa-U.K.: pp. 196, 203. The Borough of Berwick upon Tweed: 60(3).

First published in the U.K. by GeoCenter International U.K. Limited

Text: Josephine Bacon
Editing: Myra Hackman
The author wishes to acknowledge the assistance of the following in the preparation of the text: Colin Iles, Olivier Mirwasser, Hanna Bacon, Gunnie Moberg.

Cartography: RV Reise- und Verkehrsverlag GmbH, Berlin • Gütersloh • Leipzig • Munich • Potsdam • Stuttgart
Design, coordination: Prisma Verlag GmbH, Munich
Cover design: Prisma Verlag GmbH, Munich
Typography, layout: Micropress GmbH, Taufkirchen/Munich
Reproduction: Worldscan, Munich

Distributed in the United Kingdom by: GeoCenter International U.K. Limited, The Viables Centre, Harrow Way, Basingstoke, Hants. RG22 4BJ.
Tel. (0256) 817 987.

Printed and produced by Mohndruck Graphische Betriebe, Gütersloh
Printed in Germany
ISBN 3-575-26031-1

Contents

Great Britain
Map Scale 1:300,000

Great Britain Key to Maps

TRAFFIC

- 20 21 — Motorway with junction - Half junction - Filling station - with snackbar - Restaurant - with motel
- Motorway under construction
- Road with four or more lanes, single or dual carriageway - under construction
- National or federal road - under construction
- Major main road - under construction
- Main road
- Secondary road
- Practicable road (restricted passage)
- 429 4553 M 5 — Road numbering
- E 30 — Number of main european route
- 10% — Gradient
- X - IV — Mountain pass closed in winter (from - to)
- Not suitable - closed for caravans
- 75 30 45 — Distances on motorways in miles
- 35 25 10 — Distances on other roads in miles
- Main railway - Other railway with station
- Railway (freight haulage only)
- Rackrailway or cabin lift
- Cable lift
- Chair lift or T-bar
- Railway ferry for cars
- Shipping route
- Car ferry route - Car ferry on river
- Tourist road
- Scenic road
- Toll - Toll road
- Road closed for motor traffic
- Airport - Airfield
- Gliding field - Heliport

PLACES OF INTEREST

- CAMBRIDGE — Place of particular interest
- BRIGHTON — Place of interest
- Westminster Abbey — Building of particular interest
- Bayham Abbey — Interesting building
- The Needles — Natural object of particular interest
- STONEHENGE, Sheffield Park — Other object of interest
- Botanical gardens
- Zoological gardens - Game park
- Nature park
- Viewpoint
- Castle - Monastery - Ruins
- Church, chapel - Monument
- Tower - Radio- or TV tower
- Lighthouse - Lightship - Windmill
- Limes with castellum (roman)

OTHER INFORMATION

- Youth hostel - Motel
- Isolated hotel or inn - Mountain hut
- Camping site, permanent - seasonal
- Caravan site (not allowed for tents)
- Recommended beach
- Bathing place - Swimming pool - Spa
- International boundary - Border crossing point
- Administrative boundary
- Tidal flat - Sand and dunes
- Forest - Heath
- Glacier - Restricted area

Distances in miles

Altitude reading in feet

1 Mile ≙ 1,6 km; 1 km ≙ 0,62 mi

1 Foot ≙ 0,3 m; 1 m ≙ 3,28 ft

- Motorway
- Road with four lanes
- Through road
- Main road
- Other roads
- Pedestrian zone
- Main railway with station
- Other railways
- Rapid city railway
- Underground
- Parking
- Information
- Hospital
- Monument
- Youth hostel
- Police station - Post office
- Church - Church of interest
- Built-up area - Public building
- Industrial area
- Park, forest

Föroyar
Færøerne
(Danmark)
Streymoy
Nordhuroyar
Eysturoy
Vágar
Tórshavn
Sandoy
Tvöroyri
Sudhuroy
Island
Lerwick
Hanstholm,
Esbjerg
Shetland Islands
Yell
Hillswick
Tórshavn
Lerwick
Mainland
Bergen
Shetland
Islands
Mainland
Kirkwall
Orkney
Islands
Hoy
Pentland Firth
Thurso
Duncansby Hd
Wick
Durness
Outer Hebrides
Isle of
Lewis
Stornoway
Harris
Tarbert
North Minch
North
Uist
Lochmaddy
Little Minch
Ullapool
Dornoch
Uig
Skye
Kyle of
Lochalsh
Dingwall
Inverness
Moray Firth
Elgin
Fraserburgh
South
Uist
Lochboisdale
Barra
Sea
of the
Hebrides
Rhum
Mallaig
Loch
Ness
Kingussie
Invergarry
1343
Fort B. Nevis
William
North West Highlands
Grampian Mts.
Braemar
ABERDEEN
N
Coll
Tiree
Salen
Mull
Fingal's Cave
Iona
Oban
Tyndrum
Firth of Lorne
Perth
DUNDEE
St. Andrews
Jura
Islay
Greenock
Firth of Forth
EDINBURGH
GLASGOW
MOTHERWELL
AND W.
Port
Ellen
Ardrossan
Brodick
Ayr
Kilmarnock
Abington
Tweed
Berwick-u.-Tw.
Galashiels
Alnwick
Hawick
North Channel
Campbeltown
Firth of Clyde
Southern Uplands
Galloway
Malin Hd
Giant's
Causeway
Coleraine
Londonderry
Strabane
Ballymena
Larne
Northern Ireland
L. Neagh
Lough Erne
Stranraer
Kirkcudbright
Dumfries
Solway Firth
Carlisle
Cumbria
Penrith
NEWCASTLE U.T.
SOUTH SHIELDS
SUNDERLAND
Erris Hd
Donegal Bay
Ballyshannon
Ballygawley
Dungannon
Bangor
BELFAST
Workington
Darlington
Hartlepool
MIDDLES-
BROUGH
GREAT
BRITAIN
Belmullet
Ballina
Sligo
Enniskillen
Armagh
Newry
Achill
Castlebar
Boyle
Cavan
Isle of
Man
Douglas
Kendal
Barrow-
in-Furness
Morecambe &
Heysham
Thirsk
Scarborough
Bridlington
Westport
Connaught
Longford
Dundalk
Lancaster
Yorkshire
Skipton
YORK
Clifden
Roscommon
Kells
Drogheda
Irish Sea
Fleetwood
BLACKPOOL
Burnley
BRADFORD
LEEDS
Lough Corrib
Galway
Mullingar
Athlone
Lough Ree
Kinnegad
Royal Can.
DUBLIN
BAILE ATHA CLIATH
PRESTON
BOLTON
MAN-
CHESTER
KINGSTON UPON
HULL
Galway Bay
Aran Is
Cliffs
of Moher
Grand Canal
Naas
Kingstown
Dún Laoghaire
Anglesey
Holyhead
LIVERPOOL
BIRKENHEAD
Doncaster
Grimsby
Humber
IRELAND
(EIRE)
Ennis
Lough Derg
Port Laoise
Wicklow Mts.
Caernafon
Bangor
Snowdon
Chester
Corwen
SHEFFIELD
Lincoln
Skegness
Limerick
Luimneach
Roscrea
Shannon
Arklow
Newark
KINGDOM
Tralee
Cahir
Cashel
Kilkenny
Enniscorthy
Dolgellau
Shrewsbury
STOKE
O.TR.
DERBY
NOTTINGHAM
Boston
The Wash
King's Lynn
NORWICH
Slea Hd
Dingle B.
Mallow
Clonmel
Waterford
Wexford
Rosslare
Cardigan Bay
Aberystwyth
Welshpool
WOLVER-
HAMPTON
WALSALL
LEICESTER
Kettering
Peterborough
Lowestoft
Killarney
CORK
CORCAIGH
Llanguria
BIRMINGHAM
COVENTRY
NORTHAMPTON
Newmarket
Cambrian Mountains
Builth
Wells
Worcester
Stratford
on Avon
CAMBRIDGE
St. George's Channel
Bantry B.
Bantry
Fishguard &
Goodwick
Cardigan
Carmarthen
Brecon
Hereford
Cheltenham
Bedford
LUTON
IPSWICH
St. David's
Milford Haven
Pembroke
Merthyr Tydfil
Gloucester
OXFORD
Colchester
SWANSEA
NEWPORT
CARDIFF
SWINDON
BRISTOL
READING
Thames
SOUTHEND-ON-SEA
Bristol Channel
Severn
Bath
Weston-
s.-M.
Newbury
Windsor
LONDON
Barnstaple
Taunton
Stonehenge
Basingstoke
Guildford
Maidstone
Canterbury
Kent
Winchester
Salisbury
Devon
Yeovil
Sussex
Worthing
Folkestone
Hastings
Eastbourne
Exeter
Dorchester
Weymouth
SOUTHAMPTON
PORTSMOUTH
BRIGHTON
Newhaven
Boulogne-
s.-M.
Bodmin
Cornwall
PLYMOUTH
TORBAY
Lyme Bay
POOLE
BOURNEMOUTH
I. of
Wight
Penzance
Land's End
Falmouth
Isles of Scilly
English Channel
La Manche
Dieppe
Cap de
la Hague
Cherbourg
Baie de la Seine
LE HAVRE
Seine
ROUEN
Guernsey
St. Peter Port
Channel Islands
Jersey
St. Helier
Deauville
Bayeux
CAEN
Coutances
St.-Lô
Granville
Normandie
Flers
Argentan
Evreux
Santander
Roscoff
Lannion
Paimpol
Golfe de St. Malo
Le Mont-St.-Michel
Avranches
Pontorson
Morlaix
Guingamp
St.-Malo
St.-Brieuc
Dreux
BREST
Pte. d'Ouessant

OSLO
N O R G E
S V E R I G E
D A N M A R K
D E U T S C H L A N D
N E D E R L A N D
B E L G I Q U E
F R A N C E
NORDSEE
OSTSEE
Skagerrak
Kattegat
Stavanger
Haugesund
Kristiansand
Göteborg
Örebro
Norrköping
Linköping
Jönköping
Borås
Helsingborg
Malmö
København
Odense
Århus
Ålborg
Esbjerg
Kiel
Lübeck
Rostock
Hamburg
Bremen
Bremerhaven
Berlin
Hannover
Magdeburg
Leipzig
Dresden
Amsterdam
Rotterdam
'S-Gravenhage
Den Haag
Utrecht
Bruxelles/Brussel
Antwerpen
Liège
Köln
Düsseldorf
Essen
Dortmund
Frankfurt a.M.
Würzburg
Nürnberg
Mannheim
Karlsruhe
Saarbrücken
Metz
Reims
Paris
Nancy
Strasbourg
Basel
Stuttgart
Ulm
München
Stockholm
Kalmar
Gdansk Bydgoszcz
Frankf./O.
Cottbus
Görlitz
Praha
Linz

SCOTLAND

Wild, rugged scenery, great tracts of forest, treeless moors and small, friendly villages are typical of northern Scotland, from the far islands of Orkney and Shetland, the Highlands north and south of the Great Glen that splits the land in two. The Lowlands landscape is gentler. The romance of Scotland's history is captured in the picturesque glens and lochs from Bridge of Allen and Water of Leith to the Rhinns and the Mull of Kintyre.

The Islands and the North Highlands

The far north of the British Isles, including the tip of the Scottish mainland and the 600 or so islands that drift away to the north and west, the Orkney and Shetland Islands and the Outer Hebrides. Wild and rugged with an ancient heritage.

This is most northerly and the least populated part of the British Isles. Orkney and Shetland have only 46,000 inhabitants between them and the largest mainland towns of Thurso and Wick have populations of 10,000 each, the size of a large village in southern England. The islands have a wild beauty all their own, and even in the height of the summer they are unspoilt and uncrowded. They also benefit from a great deal of sunshine. The summer weather is surprisingly warm in the Inner Hebrides and western Highlands, due to the presence of the Gulf Stream. The winters are long and dark, but in Shetland, in the summer months of June and July, there is a constant glow on the horizon throughout the night, known as the "simmer dim" , which gives an eerie phosphorescence to the surrounding landscape – the Islands' version of the Midnight Sun.

Fair Isle

This island is the largest of the 20 or so that dot the sea between Shetland and Orkney. It lies midway between the two groups of islands but is considered part of Shetland. It is famous mainly for the Fairisle sweaters, knitted to a pattern which is probably of Scandinavian origin. The island is now administered by the National Trust for Scotland. It has two lighthouses and a bird sanctuary.

The North Highlands

The jagged coastline along the top of the Highlands is full of sea lochs and rocky promontories. The western side is probably the remotest part of Britain, not served by any major road. It is a magnificent drive to take the A836 from John O'Groats, supposedly the most northerly point in Britain, via Thurso to Tongue, where it becomes the A838. Inland there are the mountain ranges of the Reay Forest, dotted with lochs, and traversed by foaming mountain streams. It is worth visiting Cape Wrath, at the very north-westernmost tip of the mainland. If you start in the east, as most people do, since they have come north on the A9, the first town in the region you will come to is Wick, in Caithness. It has a picturesque harbour sprinkled with castles and an unusual rock formation offshore known as the Brig 'o Tram. There are also many brochs. The only other large town in the area is Thurso, also in Caithness. It has a long bay and was once the centre for exporting Caithness stone, the blue-grey stone used to pave the streets of many European cities. Now the main export is oil and gas. Travelling west, you will soon encounter the silver dome of Doonreay, a nuclear power station which was the first fast-breeder reactor in the world. It is open to the public for visits. But this whole area is famous not for the townscapes but for the magnificent scenery – the lochs, the mountains, the waterfalls and the ever-changing skies.

Orkney

The Orkney Islands divide themselves into three groups, the South Isles, Mainland and the North Isles. Mainland has half the land area and contains the major town, Kirkwall, which has five thousand inhabitants. There are about 68 islands in all, of which 29 are still inhabited. The houses of Kirkwall are painted in pretty pastel shades The Cathedral of St. Magnus is at Kirkwall and the saint is buried in it. The only other large town is Stromness on the south-west tip of the island, built in the 18th century and hardly changed. The Pier Arts Centre in Victoria Street has the best collection of modern art in the Highlands area. The Orkneys are strewn with mysterious monuments to their pre-Viking inhabitants, who left no written record. These include great burial mound of Maeshowe near the Harray and Stenness lochs, the Standing Stones of Stenness and the Ring of Brodgar. There is a ruined 16th-century Earl's Palace at Birsay on Mainland. The South Isles, south of Mainland are part of the sea channel called Scapa Flow, famous in British naval history in so many wars, since it has provided a safe

haven for the British fleet. A pile of naval detritus partially blocks the entrance to Scapa Flow which is now an oil port. Hoy, the second-largest island, is very rocky and has gigantic cliffs. The most spectacular rock formation is known as the Old Man of Hoy. It is a perpendicular column of red sandstone which stands just offshore by the cliffs of Rora Head. At St. Mary's, Lamb Holm, near the causeway that links Mainland to Burray and South Ronaldsay, there is a Roman Catholic chapel built by Italian prisoners-of-war from a Nissen hut, much to the admiration of the local population, who have lovingly preserved it.

The Outer Hebrides and the Far Isles

The Outer Hebrides, also known as The Western Isles is a 140-mile long chain of islands, of which the main ones are South Uist, North Uist, Benbecula, Harris and Lewis. The southernmost islands are known as the Barra Group. All have magnificent landscapes, few inhabitants and a unique culture. These islands were once ruled by the Vikings, but only for 200 years. The Gaelic tradition is strong here, and this is one of the few places in Scotland where Gaelic is still spoken as a first language, though everyone speaks English. There is also strong Sabbath observance which means that there is no transport on Sundays and very little entertainment. South Uist has gigantic cliffs rising to a height of over 2,000 feet (610 metres), which are favourites with rock-climbers. Bonnie Prince Charlie landed here and it is here that his companion, Flora Macdonald, was born. The island has a large Catholic population, who have erected a gigantic statue, Our Lady of the Isles, which is a useful navigation landmark to sailors. There are ruined crofts everywhere, evidence of the cruel Highland Clearances, when the local laird packed off his tenants to Canada to make way for sheep-farming. North Uist and Benbecula are very popular with anglers, because it has many fresh-water lochs. The island is famous for its prehistoric sites, including burial chambers and fortresses and there is the 13th-century ruined Trinity Temple at Carinish. Harris and Lewis are actually one landmass, sixty miles long, connected by an isthmus. However, they differ considerably because Harris is rather mountainous whereas Lewis consists mainly of moorland. The church of St. Clement at Rodel on Harris dates from

The Strath of Kildonan, looking towards Sutherland (opposite).

Stornoway Harbour, Isle of Lewis (top left).

Duncansby Head lighthouse, Caithness (centre left).

Gvinig Castle, Caithness (below left).

The Stones of Stenness (top).

The Standing Stones of Callanish, Lewis (above).

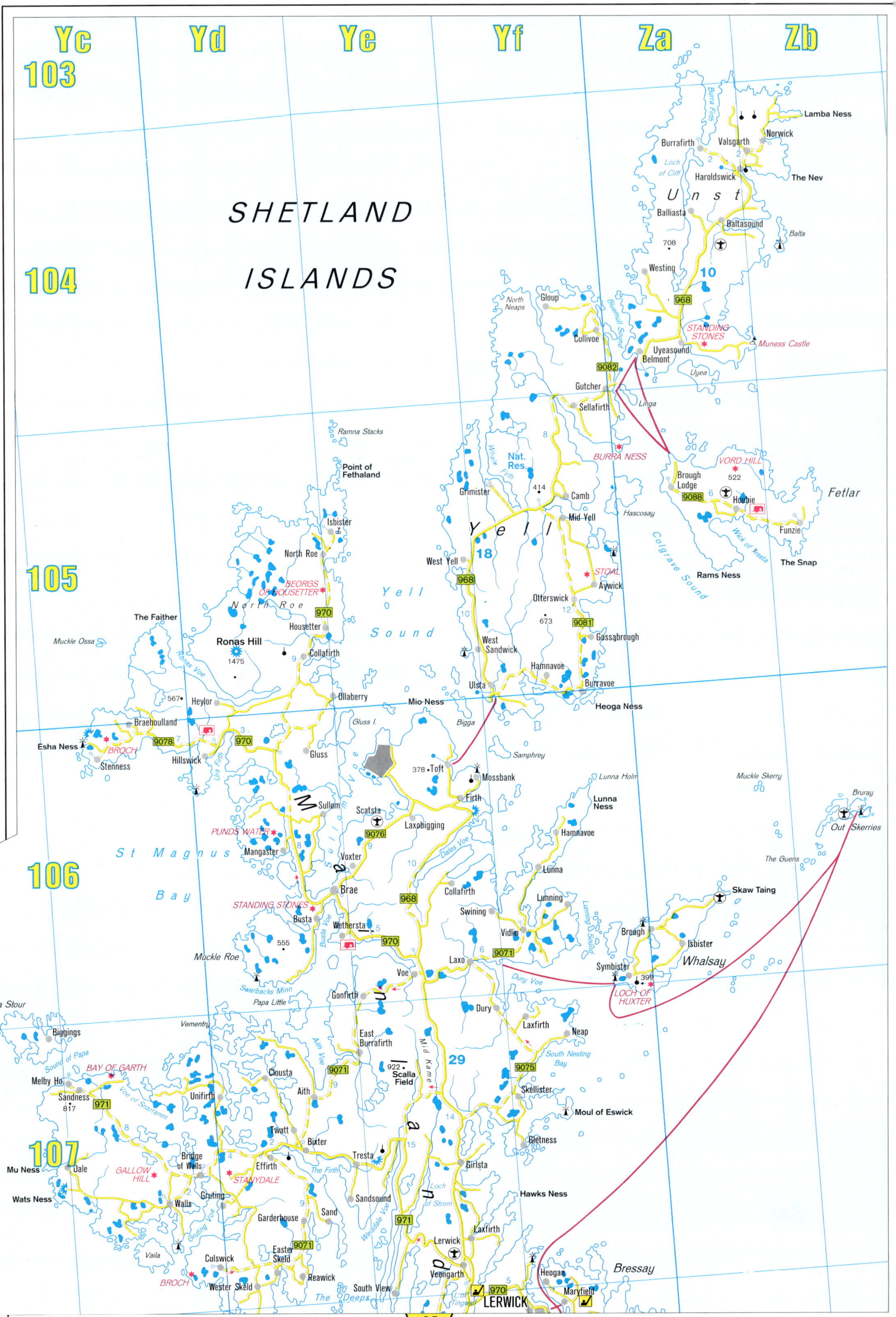
Yc
Yd
Ye
Yf
Za
Zb
103
104
105
106
107
SHETLAND
ISLANDS
Lamba Ness
Norwick
Burrafirth
Valsgarth
Loch of Cliff
Haroldswick
The Nev
Unst
Balliasta
Baltasound
Balta
708
Westing
10
968
Gloup
North Neaps
Bluemull Sound
Cullivoe
STANDING STONES
Uyeasound
Belmont
Muness Castle
Uyea
9082
Gutcher
Sellafirth
Linga
Ramna Stacks
Point of Fethaland
Whale Firth
Nat. Res.
BURRA NESS
VORD HILL
522
Brough Lodge
9088
Houbie
Fetlar
Grimister
414
Camb
Mid Yell
Hascosay
Funzie
Isbister
Yell
North Roe
West Yell
18
Colgrave Sound
Wick of Tresta
The Snap
Rams Ness
BEORGS OF HOUSETTER
STOAL
Aywick
968
Yell Sound
North Roe
970
Otterswick
673
9081
The Faither
Housetter
Gossabrough
Muckle Ossa
Ronas Hill
1475
Collafirth
West Sandwick
Ronas Voe
Hamnavoe
567
Heylor
Ollaberry
Ulsta
Burravoe
Mio Ness
Heoga Ness
Braehoulland
Gluss I.
Bigga
Esha Ness
BROCH
9078
Hillswick
970
Stenness
Ura Firth
Gluss
Samphrey
378
Toft
Mossbank
Lunna Holm
Muckle Skerry
Firth
Lunna Ness
Bruray
Sullom
Scatsta
Laxobigging
Out Skerries
PUNDS WATER
9076
Hamnavoe
Mangaster
St Magnus Bay
Voxter
Dales Voe
The Guens
Lunna
Mainland
Skaw Taing
Brae
Collafirth
STANDING STONES
Lunning
Busta
968
Swining
Busta Voe
Brough
Wetherstal
Vidlin
Isbister
555
970
Lunning Sound
Whalsay
Muckle Roe
9071
Symbister
Laxo
Voe
399
Dury Voe
LOCH OF HUXTER
Swarbacks Minn
Gonfirth
Papa Little
Papa Stour
Dury
Vementry
Laxfirth
Neap
Biggings
East Burrafirth
Mid Kame
South Nesting Bay
Sound of Papa
Alith Voe
29
BAY OF GARTH
9071
922
Scalla Field
9075
Clousta
Melby
Sandness
Aith
Skellister
817
971
Unifirth
Voe of Snarraness
Moul of Eswick
Twatt
Bixter
Gletness
107
Bridge of Walls
Tresta
Mu Ness
Dale
Effirth
GALLOW HILL
STANYDALE
The Firth
Girlsta
Loch of Strom
Hawks Ness
Wats Ness
Walls
Gruting
Sandsound
Gruting Voe
Garderhouse
Sand
Weisdale Voe
971
Laxfirth
Vaila
Easter Skeld
9071
Lerwick
Bressay
Culswick
BROCH
Wester Skeld
Reawick
South View
Veensgarth
Heogan
The Deeps
Loch of Tingwall
970
LERWICK
Maryfield
15

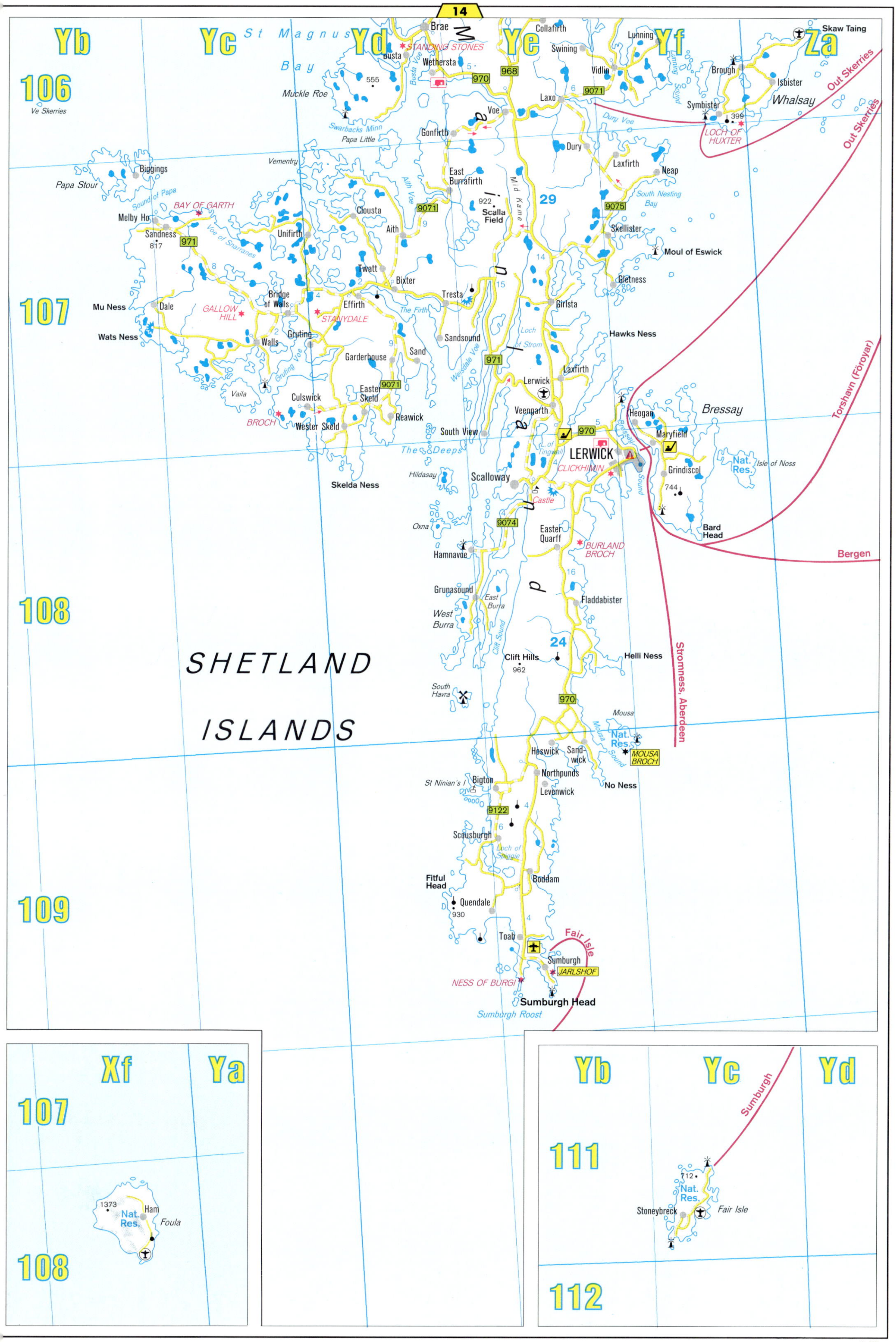
14
Yb
Yc
Yd
Ye
Yf
Za
106
107
108
109
St Magnus Bay
Mainland
SHETLAND
ISLANDS
Ve Skerries
Papa Stour
Biggings
Sound of Papa
BAY OF GARTH
Melby Ho
Sandness
817
971
Voe of Snarranes
Muckle Roe
555
Swarbacks Minn
Papa Little
Vementry
Brae
STANDING STONES
Busta
Busta Voe
Wetherста
Wethersta
970
968
Collafirth
Swining
Lunning
Lunning Sound
Vidlin
9071
Laxo
Skaw Taing
Brough
Isbister
Whalsay
Symbister
399
LOCH OF HUXTER
Out Skerries
Dury Voe
Voe
Gonfirth
Dury
Laxfirth
Neap
South Nesting Bay
East Burrafirth
Aith Voe
Mid Kame
922
Scalla Field
29
9075
Clousta
Aith
Unifirth
Skellister
Moul of Eswick
Twatt
Bixter
Gletness
Mu Ness
Dale
GALLOW HILL
Bridge of Walls
Effirth
STANYDALE
Tresta
The Firth
Girlsta
Loch of Strom
Wats Ness
Walls
Gruting
Gruting Voe
Sandsound
Hawks Ness
Garderhouse
Sand
Weisdale Voe
971
Laxfirth
Lerwick
Vaila
Culswick
Easter Skeld
9071
Reawick
Veensgarth
Heogan
Bressay
BROCH
Wester Skeld
South View
970
Maryfield
The Deeps
L. of Tingwall
LERWICK
CLICKHIMIN
Bressay Sound
Nat. Res.
Isle of Noss
Grindiscol
Skelda Ness
Hildasay
Scalloway
Castle
744
Torshavn (Föroyar)
Oxna
9074
Easter Quarff
Bard Head
Hamnavoe
BURLAND BROCH
Bergen
16
Grunasound
East Burra
West Burra
Fladdabister
Cliff Sound
24
Stromness, Aberdeen
Clift Hills
962
Helli Ness
South Havra
970
Mousa
Mousa Sound
Nat. Res.
MOUSA BROCH
Hoswick
Sandwick
Northpunds
No Ness
St Ninian's I
Bigton
Levenwick
9122
Scousburgh
Loch of Spiggie
Boddam
Fitful Head
Quendale
930
Toab
Fair Isle
Sumburgh
JARLSHOF
NESS OF BURGI
Sumburgh Head
Sumburgh Roost
Xf
Ya
107
108
1373
Ham
Nat. Res.
Foula
Yb
Yc
Yd
111
112
Sumburgh
712
Nat. Res.
Stoneybreck
Fair Isle

Ud
Ue
Uf
Va
Vb
114
115
116
117
118
V
Cape Wrath
Kearvaig
The Parbh
984
Inshore
Fashven
1498
Achiemore
Fareid Head
Balnakeil Bay
Balnakeil
Durness
Caves of Smoo
Keoldale
Kyle of Durness
Whiten Head or An Ceann Geal
Eilean Hoan
Rispond
Sangobeg
Sarsgrum
Meall Meadhonach
1387
Loch Eriboll
Portnancon
Heilam
Hope
Eilean Choraidh
Eriboll
Polla
Cranstackie
2630
Strath Dionard
Loch Dionard
Am Balg
Sandwood Loch
Strath Shinary
Creag Riabhach
1592
Grudie
Balchrick
Droman
Oldshore Beg
Oldshoremore
Eilean an Ròin Mòr
Loch Clash
Kinlochbervie
Badcall
Achriesgill
Loch Inchard
Rhiconich
838
801
20
31
Ardmore Point
Ardmore
Fanagmore
Tarbet
Foindle
Loch Laxford
Laxford Bridge
Handa Island
403
Nat. Res.
Folinaven
2980
Arkle
2580
Ben Hope
3040
Loch Hope
Strathmore
Altnacailich
23

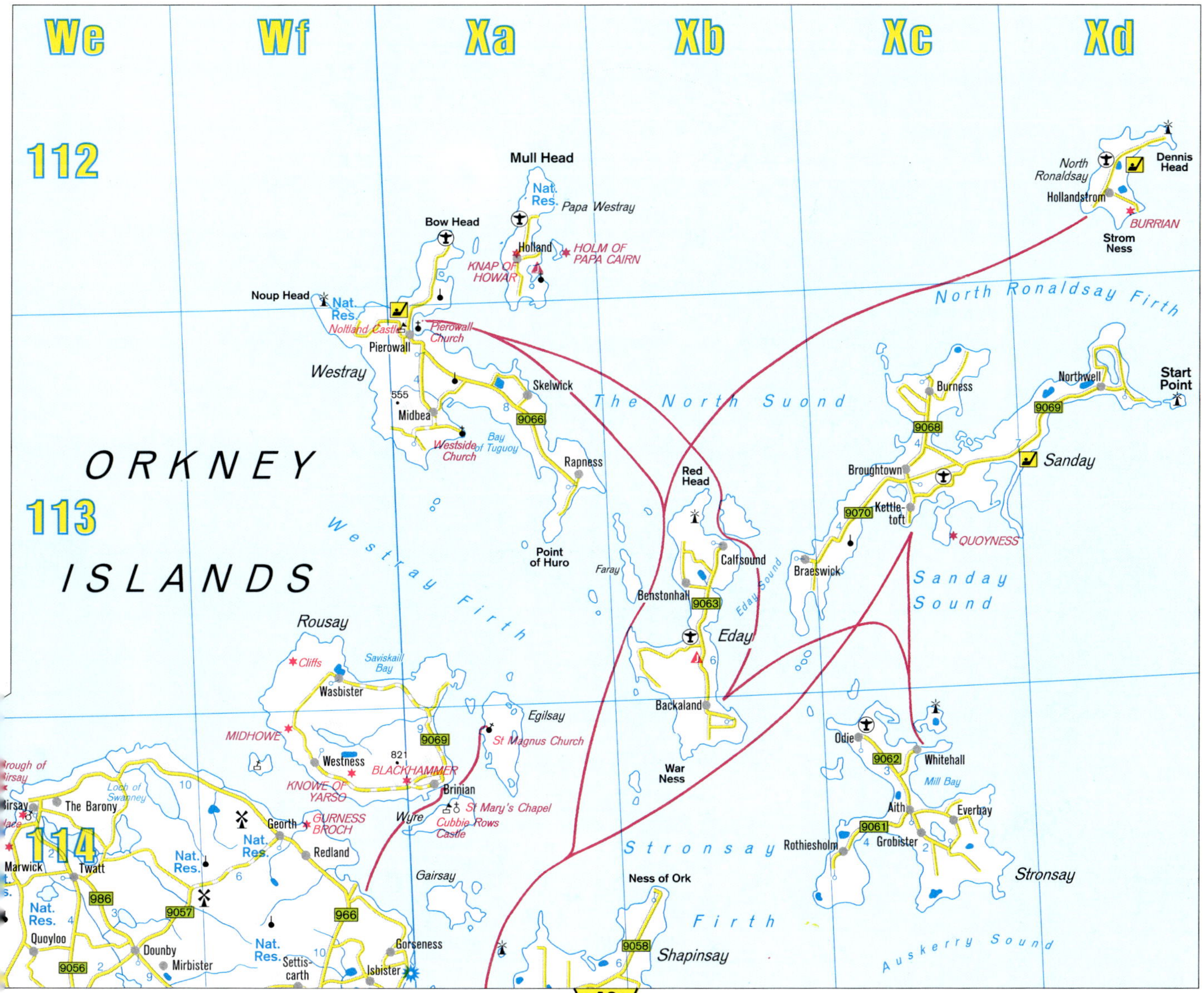

We Wf Xa Xb Xc Xd
112
113
114
ORKNEY ISLANDS
Mull Head
Nat. Res.
Papa Westray
Bow Head
Holland
KNAP OF HOWAR
HOLM OF PAPA CAIRN
Noup Head
Noltland Castle
Pierowall Church
Pierowall
Westray
555
Midbea
Westside Church
Bay of Tuguoy
Skelwick
9066
Rapness
Point of Huro
North Ronaldsay
Hollandstrom
Dennis Head
BURRIAN
Strom Ness
North Ronaldsay Firth
The North Suond
Burness
Northwall
Start Point
9069
9068
Sanday
Broughtown
Kettletoft
9070
QUOYNESS
Braeswick
Sanday Sound
Red Head
Calfsound
Faray
Benstonhall
9063
Eday Sound
Eday
Backaland
War Ness
Westray Firth
Rousay
Cliffs
Saviskaill Bay
Wasbister
MIDHOWE
Westness
821
9069
BLACKHAMMER
KNOWE OF YARSO
Brinian
Egilsay
St Magnus Church
St Mary's Chapel
Cubbie Rows Castle
Wyre
Gairsay
Brough of Birsay
Birsay
The Barony
Loch of Swannay
Marwick
Twatt
Georth
GURNESS BROCH
Nat. Res.
Redland
986
9057
Quoyloo
Dounby
Mirbister
9056
Settiscarth
966
Gorseness
Isbister
Odie
9062
Whitehall
Mill Bay
Aith
Everbay
9061
Rothiesholm
Grobister
Stronsay
Stronsay Firth
Ness of Ork
9058
Shapinsay
Auskerry Sound
18

Vd Ve Vf Wa Wb Wc
Brims Ness
Strathy Point
Scrabster
St Mary's
Crosskirk
836
Bridge of Forss
Viewfield
Dounreay
Buldoo
Lythmore
Newlands of Geise
Achreamie
CNOC FREICEADAIN CAIRNS
Westfield
Shebster
Forss W
Loch Calder
Calder Mains
Broubster
Shurrery
Brawlbin
Totegan
Baligill
Melvich Bay
836
Portskerra
Red Point
Fresgoe
Isauld
Reay
Bighouse
Melvich
Eilean nan Ròn
Armadale Bay
Brawl
Strathy
Cave
Armadale
Strathy Forest
Farr Point
Neave or Coomb Island
Rabbit Islands
Torrisdale Bay
Midfield
Talmine
Skullomie
Skerray
Torrisdale
Farr
Kirtomy
Bettyhill
Achina
Loch Meadie
Bowside Lodge
Achridigill Loch
Golval
Loch Akran
897
Loch na Seilge
Coldbackie
Borgie
Leckfurin
Kyle of Tongue
838
Coldrach
Tongue
836
Skelpick
Loch Buidhe Mòr
751
Beinn nam Bò
Upper Bighouse
Achiemore
953
Beinn nam Bad Mòr
Loch Scye
Loch Shurrery
Dorrery
801
Borgie
Borgie Forest
Achargary
Strathy
Dalhalvaig
Trantlemore
Loch Tuim Ghlais
Loch Caluim
Kinloch Lodge
2509
Ben Loyal
Lettermore
Loch Loyal
Loch an Dherue
Loch Loyal Lodge
Strathnaver
Rhifail
Naver
Skail
Loch nam Breac
Loch Strathy
Halladale
Strath Halladale
Forsinain
Loch Sletill
Loch Meadie
Loch More
24
25

17
Wd
We
Wf
Xa
Xb
Xc
114
115
116
117
118
Main-land
Marwick
Nat. Res.
Twatt
Quoyloo
Dounby
Mirbister
Skaill
SKARA BRAE
Yesnaby
Vey
Bimbister
Settiscarth
Gorseness
Isbister
Gairsay
Loch of Harray
Finstown
RENNIBISTER
RING OF BRODGAR
STENNESS
MAES HOWE
Clouston
CAIRN
Wideford Hill
GRAINBANK
KIRKWALL
Cathedral
Bishop's Palace
Outertown
STROMNESS
Ireland
Kirbister
Ward Hill
Clestrain
Orphir
Earl's Bu and Church
Nat. Res.
Scapa Bay
Kirkwall (Grimsetter)
Ness of Ork
Stronsay Firth
Stronsay
Shapinsay
Balfour Castle
Balfour
Newlot
Wide Firth
Shapinsay Sound
Rerwick Head
Mull Head
The Gloup
Deer Sound
Skaill
Toab
Gritley
Upper Sanday
Nat. Res. Copinsay
Lerwick
Scrabster
Aberdeen
Gramsay
Linksness
Moness
Ward Hill
Nat. Res.
DWARFIE STANE
Old Man of Hoy
Rackwick
Rora Head
Hoy
Cava
Scapa Flow
Rysa Little
Fara
Calf of Flotta
Flotta
Sound of Hoxa
Howe of Hoxa
Lyness
Crockness
Bow
Longhope
Hackness Martello Tower
Tor Ness
Brims
South Walls
St Mary's
Italian Chapel
Canseway
Burray
Southtown
St Margaret's Hope
Herston
Widewall
Lythes
South Ronaldsay
Burwick
Old Head
Swona
Pentland Firth
Island of Stroma
Nethertown
Uppertown
Pentland Skerries
Dunnet Head
St John's Point
Castle of Mey
Scarfskerry
Ham
Brough
Hunspow
St John's Loch
Loch of Mey
Gills Bay
Gills
Huna
John o'Groats
Duncansby Head
Stacks of Duncansby
Rattar
Canisbay
Barrock
Dunnet
Inkstack
Brabster
Everley
Skirza
Skirza Head
Holborn Head
Dunnet Bay
Thurso Bay
Bishop's Palace
Clardon
Stitley
THURSO
Castletown
Greenland
Loch Heilen
Lochend
Freswick
Freswick Bay
Ness Head
Bucholie Castle
Tain
Slickly
Reaster
Alterwall
Auckengill
Weydale
Hilliclay
Durran
Bower-madden
Lyth
Nybster
Achingills
Sortat
Howe
Keiss
Sordale
Knockdee
Stemster Ho
Halcro
Hastigrow
Mireland
Braal Castle
Roadside
Clayock
Halkirk
Loch Scarmclate
North Watten
Kirk
Loch of Wester
Sinclair's Bay
Killimster
Ackergill Tower
Noss Head
Castle Girnigoe a Sinclair
Olgrinmore
Old Hall
Loch Watten
Reiss
Winless
Spittal
Mybster
Watten
Backlass
Ackergill
Staxigoe
Loch of Toftingall
Bilbster
Wick
Milton
North Head
WICK
Westerdale
Thurso
Achairn Burn
Newton
Castle of Old Wick
Whiterow
Badlipster
Loch Hempriggs
Tannach
Hempriggs House
GREY CAIRNS OF CAMSTER
Thrumster
25
Inverness
Inverness

Rb
Rc
Rd
Re
114
Sula Sgeir
Rona
Rb
Rc
Rd
3
4
Boreray
1245
Soay
1225
St Kilda or Hirta
1234
Dun
Sb
Sc
Sd
2
3
Haskeir Island
Haskeir Eagach
Heisker or Monach Islands
Shillay
Hearnish
Ceann Ear
Stockay
Causamul
Sound of Monach
Se
Sf
Ta
20
120
1
Crowlista
Camas Uig
Timsgarry
Miavaig
Reef
Loch Roag
Ard More Mangersta
Mangersta
Ardroil
Carishader
B8011
Geshader
16
Little Loch Roag
Loch Suainaval
Loch Grunavat
Enaclete
Islivig
Aird Brenish
Brenish
1625
Gisla
20
1303
Mealasta Island
Caolas an Eilein
Loch Tamanavay
Loch Benisval
Kearstay
Loch Resort
Morsgail Forest
Braigh Mòr
Ulladale
1012
Scarp
Hushinish
Tirga Mòr
2257
Gasker
Hushinish Point
2165
13
Govig
B887
Amhuinnsuidhe
2392
Arda Mora
Forest of Harris
Meavaig
North Harris
Taransay Glorigs
Cliasmol
Meavaig
Bunavoneadar
Soay Mor
West Loch Tarbert
Ardhasaig
Isay
877
Taransay
1661
Aird Vanish
Paible
Sound of Taransay
Luskentyre
South Harris Forest
Rubha Sgeirigin
Seilebost
24
16
Toe Head
Borve
South Harris
Harris
Ardvey
Coppay
1207
Scarastavore
1305
1267
Likisto
13
Geocrab
Loch Langavat
Manish
Shillay
Sound of Shillay
Northon
Fiodabay
Brenish Point
642
Ardvey
Loch Flodabay
Pabbay
Leverburgh
Finsbay
Quidnish
Ensay
1507
Lingarabay
Sound of Pabbay
Carminish
Lingarabay Island
Spuir
Killegray
Sound of Harris
St Clements Church
Rodel
Berneray
Langay
Ruisgarry
Renish Point
Borve
Baile
Boreray
Groay
Gilsay
Caolas a' Mhorain
Sound of Berneray
Lingay
Newton-ferry
Torogay
Scaravay
Lingay
Veilish Point
Valley
Newton
Sursay
Griminish Point
Oronsay
624
Stromay
Tahay
B893
Trumisgarry
Grenitote
Hermetray
Valley Strand
11
B865
Sollas
25
Balmartin
Loch nan Geireann
B865
Tarbert
735
NORTH UIST
Houghary
Nat. Res.
756
Loch Scadavay
Loch Maddy
Weaver's Point
Uig
Balmarand
Bayhead
Lochmaddy
Rubha nam Pléac
17
Loch Hunа
Rubha Raouill
Paible
Claddach Kirkibost
BARPA LANGASS
South Lee
920
Kirkibost Island
Vorogai
Locheport
Loch Eport
Sidinish
Teanamachar
Samala
Loch Caravat
B865
Baleshare
Bail Uachdraich
1139
Eaval
Temple of Carinish
Carinish
Floddaybeg
Floddaymore
14
Grimsay
379
Uachdar
Balivanich
B892
Flodda
Ronay
28

Sf
Ta
Tb
Tc
Td
Te
118
119
120
1
2
OUTER HEBRIDES
Isle of Lewis
Harris
Butt of Lewis
Europie
Five Penny Ness
Lionel
Port of Ness
Aird Dell
Dell
Cross
Skigersta
Ness
North Galson
South Galson
857
Cellar Head
Melbost Borve
Five Penny Borve
Loch Langavat
Shader
STONE CIRCLE
Ballantrushal
Loch Mòr Sandavat
Black House
Brue
Barvas
Labost
Bragar
Arnol
Muirneag
813
New Tolsta
Fivig
North Tolsta
Tolsta Head
37
Glen Mòr Barvas
28
Shawbost
Loch Urrahag
Glen Tolsta
Dalberg
Dalmore
Garenin
Carloway
856
Campay
Griais
Bac
DUN CARLOWAY BROCH
Kirlvick
858
Little Bernera
Croir
Loch na Scaravat
Beinn Mholach
955
895
Breivig
Rubha an Trumpain
Gallan Head
West Loch Roag
East Loch Roag
Pabay Mòr
Tobson
Great Bernera
Vacsay
Tolsta Chaolais
Breaclete
Loch Laxavat Ard
Tunga
Broad Bay
Cnoc Amhlaigh
Aird Uig
Valtos
Aird Tunga
Port Mholair
Newmarket
Shulishader
Aird
Miavaig
Vuia Mòr
Barraglom
Kirkibost
Breasclete
Loch A' Tuath
Timsgarry
Reef
Hacklete
STORNOWAY
866
Seisiadar
Crowlista
Carishader
Loch Roag
Callanish
STANDING STONES
Lewis Castle
Melbost
Aignish
Garrabost
Ardroil
Cruliviig
8059
Linshader
Garynahine
An Cnoc
Eye Peninsula
Holm
Pabail Uarach
Geshader
8011
858
Achmore
14
Arnish Head
Pabail Iarach
Chicken Head
Loch Suainaval
Loch Grunavat
Enaclete
Little Loch Roag
Loch Tungavat
Loch Orasay
Grimshader
8011
Loch nam Falcag
Leurbost
897
Ben Casgro
Loch Trealaval
Ranish
Gisla
Crossbost
Barkin Isles
1303
20
Loch Airigh nah Airde
859
Tabhaidh Mhòr
Eilean Chaluim Chille
Keose
Cromore
Eilean Orasaidh
922
Laxay
Ullaport
Balallan
Loch Erisort
Garyvard
Caversta
Habost
Eilean Thoraidh
Shiltenish
Kershader
Marvig
Loch Tamanavay
Loch Benisvat
8060
Kintarvie
36
Arivruaich
Seaforth Head
Loch Scibacleit
Calbost
Loch Resort
Morsgail Forest
Loch Langavat
Glenside
Gravir
Uladale
L. Odhairn
Kebock Head
859
Park or Pairc
1611
Orinsay
Stulaval
1901
Aline Lodge
Lemreway
Eishken
Tirga Mòr
2257
Seaforth Island
Loch Shell or Loch Seaforth
Ardvourlie
Beinn Mhòr
1874
Eilean Iubhard
2165
Amhuinnsuidhe
2392
Clisham
2621
1217
Forest of Harris
887
Meavaig
Maaruig
Crionaig
1532
Mol Truisg
Cliasmol
North Harris
Loch Seaforth
Soay Mor
Bunavoneadar
1473
Loch Claidh
Loch Bhrollum
West Loch Tarbert
1829
Taransay
Isay
Ardhasaig
Rhenigidale
877
Loch Trollamarig
Tarbert
1661
Eilean Mòr a' Bhaigh
Sound of Shiant
Paible
Sound of Taransay
South Harris Forest
Eilean Mhuire
Luskentyre
Urgha
Carragreich
Shiant Islands
Loch Ceann Dibig
Scotasay
Kyles Scalpay
Carnach
Seilebost
24
East Loch Tarbert
341
Scalpay
859
Meavag
South Harris
Borve
Drinishader
Ceann-na Cleithe
Ardvey
Grosebay
Likisto
1267
Lackalee
Scadabay
Geocrab
Cluer
Grosebay
Lochmaddy
Uig
Loch Langavat
Stockinish
13
Manish
Stockinish Island
Flodabay
19

c. 1500 but was heavily restored in 1873; it has magnificent stone carvings. Harris is world-famous for the woolen cloth known as Harris tweed, which can be bought on the island or at Stornoway in Lewis. Stornoway is the only town in the Outer Hebrides. On the A858 west of Stornoway is one of the greatest monuments in Britain, the Standing Stones of Callanish, which are the Stonehenge of the north. Dun Carloway Broch is an Iron Age tower that is well-preserved. The Shawbost Museum and Mill at Stornoway contain exhibits from Lewis life, and a Lewis clachan is open to public.

The Far Isles are those remote dots of land west of the Outer Hebrides, which are the closest part of Britain to the coast of North America. Many of them are inaccessible, Sula Sgeir is the only to which there is regular access by ship. Boats sail from Lewis, because the men of Ness have the right to harvest the gannets, which are among the wild birds that populate the island. The boned, smoked young bird, known as "guga" is a delicacy that is widely exported to expatriate Lewis men all ove the world. Sula Sgeir now belongs to the Nature Conservancy Council. The St. Kilda group, 50 miles west of Harris, consists of four islands – Hirta, Boreray, Dun and Soay. The cliffs of Hirta have the highest sheer drop in the United Kingdom. All the islands were bequeathed by their owner, the Marquess of Bute, to the National Trust for Scotland in 1957, and all are now wildlife refuges.The islands have been uninhabited since the 1930s.

Shetland

Fewer than 20 of the 100 or so Shetland Islands are inhabited. The largest is simply called Mainland and has the capital, Lerwick. The Shetlanders consider themselves to be more Scandinavian than Scottish and this is not surprising since for five centuries they were under Norse rule, only becoming part of Scotland in 1469. The biggest industries used to be fishing and farming, the latter consisting mainly of sheep-rearing, but the oil-and-gas industry is now very important and has brought much prosperity to the islands. The oil terminal at Sullom Voe, the deep sea loch that almost splits Mainland in half, is the largest in Britain. Lerwick is a good place to buy sealskin clothing and bags and fine woolens spun and woven locally. The Shetland shawl is so fine that it can be drawn through a wedding ring, yet it is amazingly warm. Another traditional export is the Shetland pony. Once used mainly as pit ponies, these tiny horses are still sent all over the world and are often to be seen in circuses. The next-largest islands after Mainland are Yell and Unst. The 16th-century Mu Ness Castle is on Unst There are many ancient ruins on the islands, one of the most impressive being the prehistoric subterranean village at Jarlshof at the southern tip of Mainland. St. Ninian's Isle, joined to the west coast of Mainland by a thin sand bar west of the village of Bigton, is the site of one of the earliest Celtic churches in Shetland, which was excavated by archaeologists from Aberdeen University in 1958. During the excavations, magnificent treasures were dug up from under a stone slab. They had probably been hidden from the invading Vikings by the monks. To the north are the island of South Havra, which was inhabited early in the century and the twin islands of Burra, now joined by a bridge. Most of the population of these islands live in the lovely fishing village of Hamnavoe. The Shetlands are full of mysterious "standing stones", some of which are obviously of Christian significance. There are also many stone towers, known as brochs, built as fortresses by the Picts. The broch on the island of Mousa is considered to be one of the best in Scotland. It is estimated to be about 1800 years old and is slightly different from other brochs because its round wall overhangs at the top, making it almost impossible to climb. Burra is famous for its knitwear; the sweaters are handknitted by fishermen's wives to support the meagre family income. Papa Stour is an island famous for its sea caves, especially the one called Francie's Hole which has mysterious red and green caverns. Vementry is an uninhabited island that bears many signs of human habitation, including gun emplacements from World War I which still point menacingly out across St. Magnus Bay.

Information
Shetland Tourist Organisation
Market Cross
Lerwick, Shetland Islands
ZE1 0LU
Tel: (0595) 3434

Events
Up-Helly-Aa is a traditional Viking festival held in Lerwick in late January to celebrate the winter solstice. Each year, a Viking long ship is built and transported by 900 Shetlanders in traditional dress to a park, where it is set ablaze.
The Shetland Folk Festival is held in early April and draws musicians from Britain and all over the world.
The Orkney Traditional Folk Festival is based on the main island but has spread to other islands. There are many events for children.
Feis Bharraigh is a celebration of all things Gaelic, including language, drama, music and the visual arts.

Tips
In this part of the world, accommodation is scarce and it is essential to book ahead, several months in advance if possible, especially on the islands.

The Stacks of Duncansby, Caithness (top left).

Stornoway Castle, Lewis (left).

Haroldswick Post Office on Unst in the Shetlands, the most northerly P. O. in the British Isles (above).

The north-west Highlands

This most romantic part of the Highlands takes in Sutherland and the County of Ross, divided into Wester Ross and Easter Ross. The scenic beauty of this area of the Highlands is probably unrivalled, at least in Scotland, though the Irish would make a claim to match it.

Dornoch
Dornoch is the county town of Sutherland. Dornoch Castle, on the main street, was the medieval palace of the Bishops of Caithness. It is now a hotel, which can be visited by non-residents. The garden has lovely views of Dornoch Firth. Dornoch Golf Course is a particularly fine one, highly recommended by professionals.

Dunbeath
This village clings to a cliff, with a torrent racing by it and a ruined castle perched precariously on the cliff edge. The castle, a fortress of the Sinclairs, is not open to the public. Just outside the village is the Laidhey Croft, a museum of crofting life.

Dunrobin Castle
Seat of the Dukes of Sutherland on plateau overlooking the sea, Dunrobin (pronounced "Dun-Roe-bin") was begun in the Middle Ages, but only completed in 1921. It resembles a huge white-turreted French château, and has lovely interiors. The grounds are extensive and are now a leisure centre. The road from here runs over the moors to Kildonan, once a gold-prospecting town.

Golspie
This little seaside resort is the administrative headquarters of Sutherland. It is dominated by Ben Vraggie, a two-thousand foot mountain on the top of which is a huge statue of the first Duke of Sutherland. Since he was responsible for the notorious Clearances which made so many Highlanders homeless it is surprising that the statue has not been torn down! There are many woods and hills and it is a lovely centre for walks. The most popular ramble is to the Big Burn waterfall in Dunrobin Glen. The Sutherlands always regarded Golspie as their personal property. The railway station is called Dunrobin Castle rather than Golspie, and the 17th-century St. Andrew's Church has a special Sutherland Loft complete with a retiring room for the Earl.

Lochinver
This busy fishing port is the main centre for the north-west coast. It is a good place from which to take a boat trip to view the local wildlife, including seals. There are also interesting mountain walks, rock-climbs and sea-angling. At Baddidarroch, just west of Lochinver, the Highland Stoneware Pottery exhibits and sells its wares.

Loch Maree
This is the most picturesque loch in the region, whose northern edge is ringed with mountains. The area around the Bridge of Grudie is a nature reserve. Isle Maree, one of the many islets in the lake off Talladale, has an ancient graveyard and ruined chapel. The Slattadale Forest contains the Victoria Falls reached by a log footpath.

Tain
This little town is said to be the birthplace of St. Duthoc, an 11th-century bishop of the Celtic church. The ruined St. Duthus Chapel and the Collegiate church are dedicated to him, and were places of pilgrimage. The latter is famous for its stained glass. Castle Brae contains the Tain Museum which is dedicated to the relics of the clan Ross. The 16th-century Tollbooth is in perfect condition and the bell is still rung. There is a Mercat Cross in front of it. A rose garden has been planted with 900 roses to mark the town's 900th anniversary. Nearby Morangie Forest is of great interest to nature-lovers.

Ullapool
This quaint little fishing village and holiday resort is the ferry terminal for Stornoway. It is a lively centre for sporting activities, and is a good place to stay. The Loch Broom Museum is full of local curiosities.

Quinog from Ullapool (above).

Sunset over the Braes (above right).

Ullapool, the Harbour (right).

Information
For information about Sutherland and Easter Ross:
Inverness Tourist Office
23 Church Street
Inverness
Tel: (0463) 234353

For information about Wester Ross:
Ullapool Tourist Centre
Shore Street
Tel: (0854) 2135

Events
The Sutherland County Show is held in Dornoch in late July and the Highland Games are held here in August.

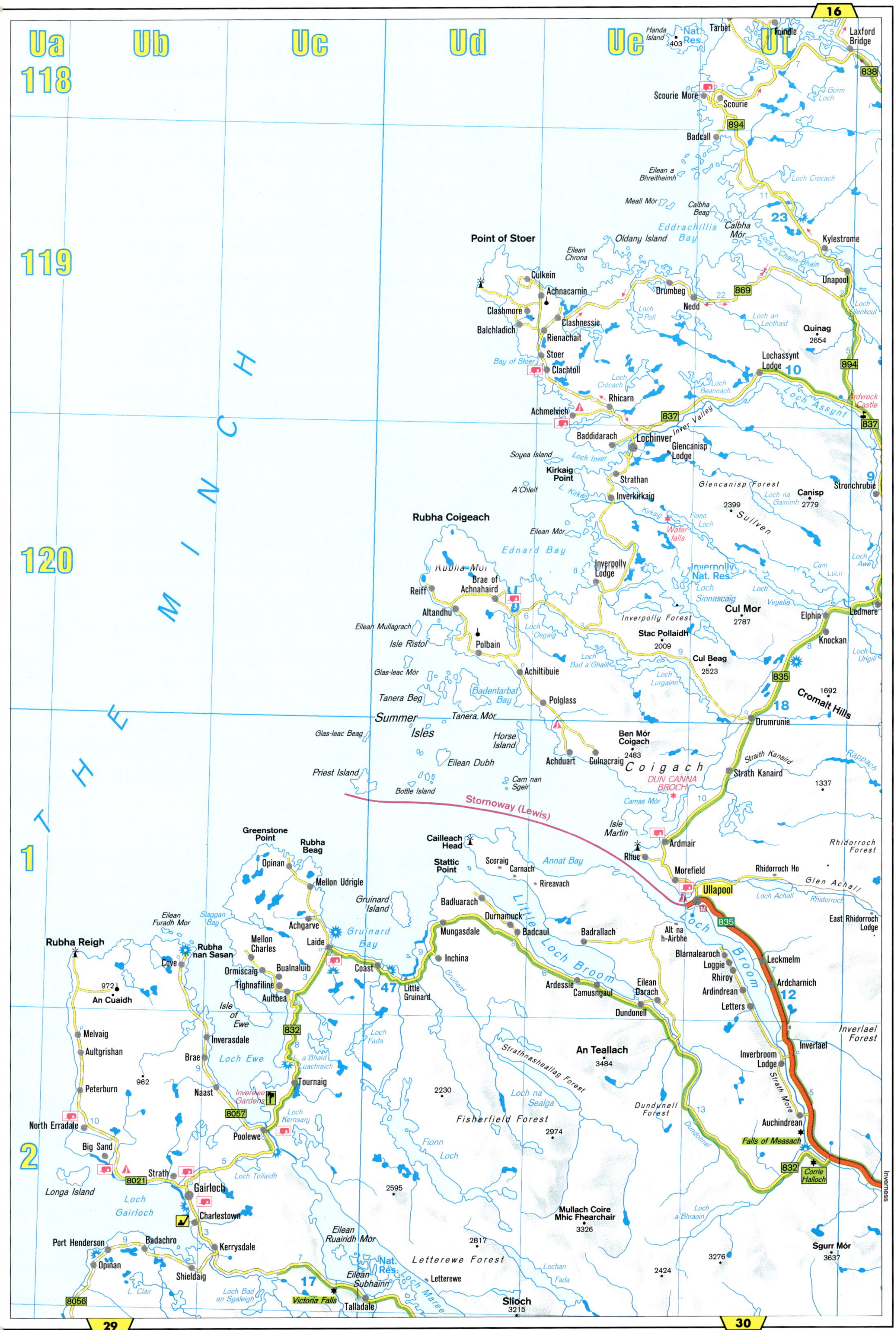
Ua
Ub
Uc
Ud
Ue
Uf
118
119
120
1
2
16
29
30
Handa Island
403
Nat. Res.
Tarbet
Foindle
Laxford Bridge
838
Scourie More
Scourie
Gorm Loch
894
Badcall
Eilean a Bhreitheimh
Loch Crócach
Meall Mór
Calbha Beag
Eddrachillis Bay
Calbha Mór
23
Loch a Chàirn Bhàin
Kylestrome
Point of Stoer
Oldany Island
Eilean Chrona
Culkein
Achnacarnin
Drumbeg
Nedd
869
Unapool
Loch Glenkoul
Clashmore
Clashnessie
Loch Poll
Loch an Leothaid
Quinag
2654
Balchladich
Rienachait
Stoer
Bay of Stoer
Clachtoll
Lochassynt Lodge
10
894
Loch Crócach
Loch Beannach
Loch Assynt
Ardvreck Castle
Rhicarn
Achmelvich
837
Inver Valley
Baddidarach
Lochinver
Glencanisp Lodge
837
Soyea Island
Loch Inver
Kirkaig Point
Strathan
Glencanisp Forest
Loch na Gainimh
Canisp
2779
Stronchrubie
9
A'Chleit
L. Kirkaig
Inverkirkaig
2399
Suilven
Rubha Coigeach
Kirkaig
Water falls
Fionn Loch
Eilean Mór
Edrnard Bay
Inverpolly Lodge
Inverpolly Nat. Res.
Loch Awe
Cam Loch
Rubha Mór
Brae of Achnahaird
Reiff
Loch Sionascaig
Loch Veyatie
Altandhu
Inverpolly Forest
Cul Mor
2787
Elphin
Ledmore
Eilean Mullagrach
Polbain
Loch Osgaig
Stac Pollaidh
2009
Knockan
Isle Ristol
Loch Bad a' Ghaill
Cul Beag
2523
Loch Urigill
Glas-leac Mór
Achiltibuie
Loch Lurgainn
835
Tanera Beg
Badentarbat Bay
Polglass
1692
Cromalt Hills
18
Summer Isles
Tanera Mór
Drumrunie
Glas-leac Beag
Horse Island
Ben Mór Coigach
2483
Straith Kanaird
Rappach
Eilean Dubh
Achduart
Culnacraig
Coigach
Strath Kanaird
Priest Island
Carn nan Sgeir
DUN CANNA BROCH
1337
Bottle Island
Camas Mór
Stornoway (Lewis)
Isle Martin
Rhidorroch Forest
Greenstone Point
Rubha Beag
Cailleach Head
Ardmair
Opinan
Scoraig
Annat Bay
Rhue
Static Point
Carnach
Morefield
Rhidorroch Ho
Mellon Udrigle
Rireavach
Ullapool
Glen Achall
Loch Achall
Rhidorroch
Gruinard Island
Badluarach
Eilean Furadh Mor
Slaggan Bay
Achgarve
Dumamuck
Little Loch Broom
East Rhidorroch Lodge
835
Gruinard Bay
Mungasdale
Badcaul
Badrallach
Alt na h-Airbhe
Rubha Reigh
Rubha nan Sasan
Mellon Charles
Laide
Loch Broom
Cove
Inchina
Blarnalearoch
Leckmelm
Coast
Loggie
Ormiscaig
Bualnaluib
Rhiroy
Ardcharnich
972
47
Gruinard
Aultbea
Little Gruinard
Ardessie
Camusnagaul
Eilean Darach
Ardindrean
12
An Cuaidh
Tighnafiline
Letters
Isle of Ewe
Dundonell
832
Loch Fada
Inverlael Forest
Melvaig
Inverasdale
Inverlael
Aultgrishan
Brae
Loch Ewe
Loch a' Bhaid Luachraich
An Teallach
3484
Strathnasheallag Forest
Inverbroom Lodge
962
Tournaig
Strath More
Peterburn
Naast
Inverewe Gardens
2230
Loch na Sealga
Dundunell Forest
8057
Loch Kernsary
Fisherfield Forest
North Erradale
Poolewe
2974
Auchindrean
Falls of Measach
Big Sand
Fionn Loch
Dundonnel
832
Corrie Halloch
Inverness
Strath
8021
Gairloch
Loch Tollaidh
2595
Longa Island
Loch Gairloch
Charlestown
Mullach Coire Mhic Fhearchair
3326
Loch a' Bhraoin
Eilean Ruairidh Mór
2817
3276
Sgurr Mór
3637
Port Henderson
Badachro
Kerrysdale
Nat. Res.
Letterewe Forest
Opinan
Shieldaig
Eilean Subhainn
Loch Maree
Letterewe
Loch Fada
2424
L. Clair
Loch Bad an Sgalaigh
17
Victoria Falls
Talladale
Slioch
3215
8056

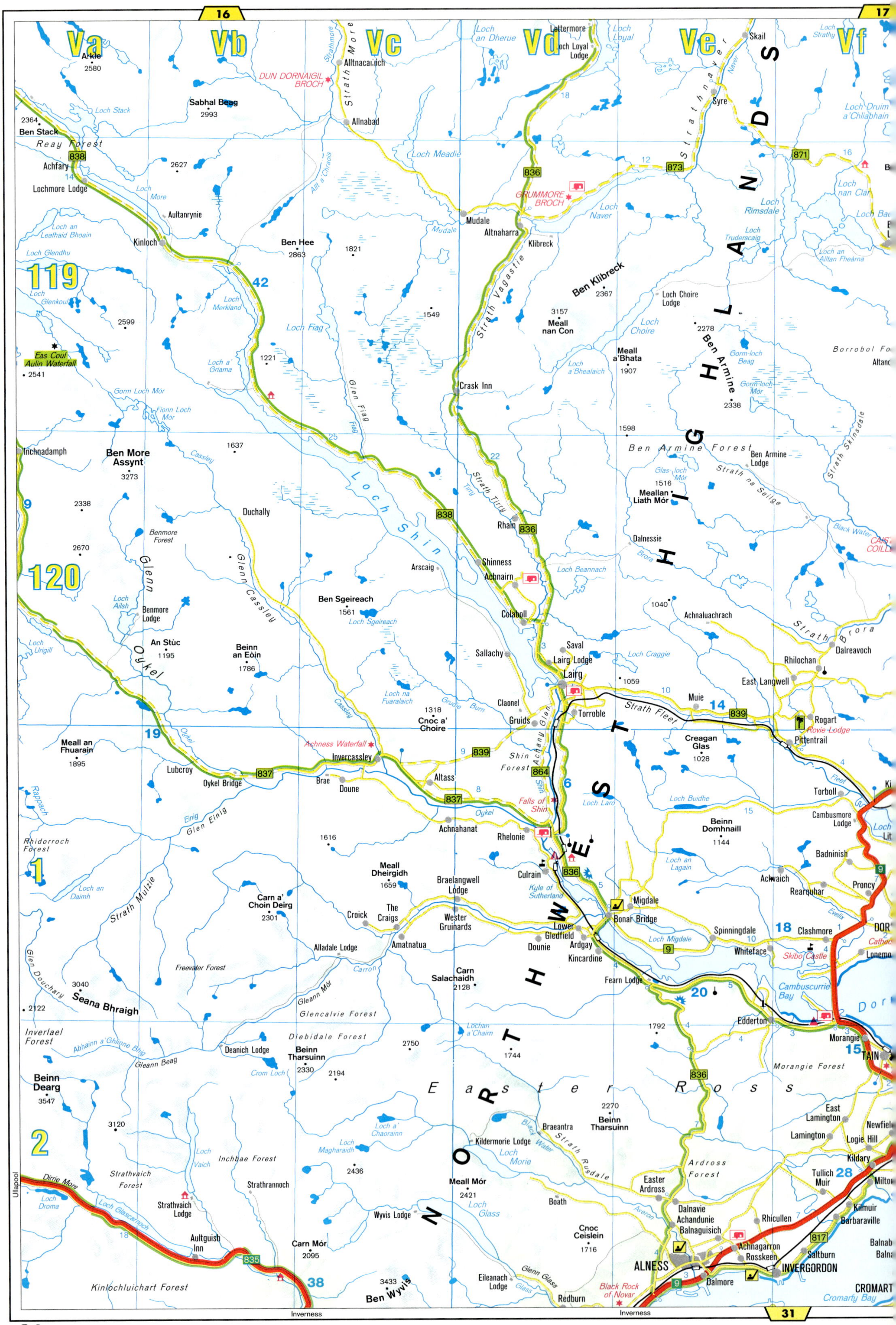
16
17
31
Va
Vb
Vc
Vd
Ve
Vf
119
120
1
2
A'Mhaighdean
Arkle
2580
Sabhal Beag
2993
Alltnacaillich
DUN DORNAIGIL BROCH
Strathmore
Strath More
Allnabad
Loch Stack
2364
Ben Stack
Reay Forest
838
Achfary
Lochmore Lodge
2627
Loch More
Aultanrynie
Loch an Leathaid Bhoain
Kinloch
Loch Glendhu
Loch Glencoul
2599
Eas Coul Aulin Waterfall
2541
Loch Merkland
Loch a' Griama
1221
Ben Hee
2863
1821
1549
Loch Fiag
Glen Fiag
Allt a' Chraois
Loch Meadie
Mudale
Altnaharra
Klibreck
Lettermore
Loch an Dherue
Loch Loyal
Loch Loyal Lodge
836
GRUMMORE BROCH
Loch Naver
Strath Vagastie
Ben Klibreck
2367
3157
Meall nan Con
Loch Choire Lodge
Loch Choire
Meall a' Bhata
1907
Loch a' Bhealaich
Crask Inn
Skail
Syre
Strathnaver
Naver
873
871
Loch Rimsdale
Loch Truderscaig
Loch an Alltan Fhearna
Loch Druim a' Chliabhain
Loch nan Clar
Loch Badanloch
2278
Ben Armine
Gorm-loch Beag
Gorm-loch Mòr
2338
Borrobol Forest
Altanduin
1598
Ben Armine Forest
Ben Armine Lodge
Strath Skinsdale
Strath na Seilge
Glas-loch Mòr
1516
Meallan Liath Mòr
Dalnessie
Brora
Black Water
1040
Achnaluachrach
Strath Brora
Dalreavoch
Rhilochan
East Langwell
Gorm Loch Mòr
Fionn Loch Mòr
Inchnadamph
Ben More Assynt
3273
1637
Cassley
2338
Duchally
2670
Benmore Forest
Glen Oykel
Glen Cassley
Loch Ailsh
Benmore Lodge
An Stùc
1195
Beinn an Eòin
1786
Loch Urigill
Loch Shin
Strath Tirry
Rhaoin
Shinness
Achnairn
Arscaig
Ben Sgeireach
1561
Loch Sgeireach
Colaboll
Sallachy
Saval
Lairg Lodge
Lairg
Loch Beannach
Loch Craggie
1059
Muie
Strath Fleet
839
Rogart
Rovie Lodge
Pittentrail
Loch na Fuaralaich
Grudie Burn
1318
Cnoc a' Choire
Claonel
Gruids
Achany Glen
Torroble
Creagan Glas
1028
Meall an Fhuarain
1895
Lubcroy
Oykel Bridge
837
Achness Waterfall
Invercassley
Brae
Doune
Altass
864
Shin Forest
Falls of Shin
Loch Laro
Loch Buidhe
Torboll
Rappach
Rhidorroch Forest
Einig
Glen Einig
Achnahanat
Rhelonie
Beinn Domhnaill
1144
Cambusmore Lodge
Badninish
Loch an Daimh
Strath Mulzie
1616
Meall Dheirgidh
1659
Carn a' Choin Deirg
2301
Croick
The Craigs
Braelangwell Lodge
Culrain
Kyle of Sutherland
Migdale
Bonar Bridge
Loch an Lagain
Achvaich
Rearquhar
Proncy
Evelix
Spinningdale
Loch Migdale
Clashmore
Skibo Castle
Whiteface
Lonemore
Glen Douchary
Freevater Forest
Alladale Lodge
Amatnatua
Wester Gruinards
Lower Gledfield
Ardgay
Kincardine
Dounie
Carron
Carn Salachaidh
2128
Fearn Lodge
20
Cambuscurrie Bay
Dornoch Firth
Edderton
Morangie
Tain
3040
Seana Bhraigh
2122
Glean Mòr
Glencalvie Forest
Inverlael Forest
Abhainn a' Ghlinne Bhig
Gleann Beag
Deanich Lodge
Diebidale Forest
Beinn Tharsuinn
2330
Crom Loch
2194
2750
Lochan a' Chairn
1744
1792
Morangie Forest
Easter Ross
Beinn Dearg
3547
3120
2270
Beinn Tharsuinn
Black Water
Braeantra
Strath Rusdale
East Lamington
Lamington
Newfield
Logie Hill
Kildary
Loch a' Chaorainn
Loch Magharaidh
Kildermorie Lodge
Loch Morie
Ardross Forest
Tullich Muir
Milton
Loch Vaich
Inchbae Forest
2436
Meall Mòr
2421
Easter Ardross
Strathvaich Forest
Strathvaich Lodge
Strathrannoch
Loch Glass
Boath
Dalnavie
Achandunie
Balnaguisich
Rhicullen
Kilmuir
Barbaraville
Dirrie More
Loch Droma
Loch Glascarnoch
Ullapool
Aultguish Inn
835
Wyvis Lodge
Carn Mòr
2095
Cnoc Ceislein
1716
Averon
Achnagarron
Rosskeen
817
Saltburn
Balnabruach
Balnapaling
Alness
Invergordon
Dalmore
38
Kinlochluichart Forest
3433
Ben Wyvis
Eileanach Lodge
Glenn Glass
Redburn
Black Rock of Novar
Cromarty
Cromarty Bay
Inverness
NORTHWEST HIGHLANDS

18
Thurso
Wick
Wa
Wb
Wc
Wd
We
Wf
Forsinard
Loch More
Loch Ruard
Loch Sand
Lochan Thulachan
Loch Rangag
Achavanich
895
815
Stemster Hill
GREY CAIRNS OF CAMSTER
Camster
Thrumster
Sarclet
Loch of Yarrows
Ulbster
HILL O'MANY STONES
Bruan
Roster
STONE ROWS
Halberry Head
Dalganachar
Forest
1144
Ben Alisky
Loch Dubh
741
Rumster Forest
44
CAIRN O'GET
Swiney
37
Occumster
Lybster
Houstry
STONE
Forse
Latheron
Smerral
Janetstown
Lochside
1437
Knockfin Heights
953
Achentoul
Kinbrace
Dunbeath Water
Braemore
Berriedale Water
Dunbeath
Broch
Dunbeath Castle
1434
2313
Morven
897
1699
2055
Scaraben
Borgue
Newport
LEARABLE HILL CAIRNS
1819
Cnoe na Maoile
1305
Langwell W
Kildonan Lodge
Berriedale
Ousdale
BROCH
Craggie
Strath of Kildonan
or Strath Ullie
Kilphedir
1134
1581
2060
Beinn Dhorain
1940
West Helmsdale
Helmsdale
Gartymore
Portgower
Glen Loth
Lothmore
Lothbeg
Col-bheinn
1765
Gordonbush
21
Kintradwell
KINTRADWELL BROCH
Loch Brora
West Clyne
Doll
Brora
Backies
CAIRN LIATH
Dunrobin Castle
NORTH SEA
Tarbat Ness
Wilkhaven
Innis Mhór
Portmahomack
Innis Bheag
Inver Bay
Rockfield
Inver
Arboll
Tarrel
Lochslin
9165
Rhynie
Loans of Tullich
Hilton of Cadboll Chapel
Hilton of Cadboll
Balintore
Shandwick
Moray Firth
King's Cave
Sutor
Halliman Skerries
Covesea Skerries
BRANDERBURGH
LOSSIEMOUTH
9040
Lossiemouth
BURGHEAD
Burghead Well
Burghead Bay
Hopeman
Duffus
Gordonstoun
Cummingstown
St Peter
Roseisle
9012
Duffus Castle
9013
9103
Loch Spynie
941
Spynie Palace
Lossie Forest
Spey Bay
Kingston
Spey Bay
32

The Inner Hebrides and the Highlands

The Isle of Skye, the Great Glen, Speyside, the Cairngorms, the Grampians and the Heart of the Highlands are favourite destinations for anyone seeking the true Highlands. The north-east, known as the Grampians, has more castles than any other part of the British Isles.

Aberdeen

See "Historic Cities"

Cairngorm Mountains

The Cairngorms National Nature Reserve contain the highest range of mountains in Britain, though none are more than 4,300 feet. They are popular with climbers and hikers. The forests that once covered the mountains in thick vegetation have been decimated for their wood, but are still attractive. Abernethy is a tourist attraction for its wild birds, including ospreys. Aviemore is the biggest ski resort in Britain and has a rather continental flavour. It has a Santa Claus Land Amusement Park for children. Only three miles away is one of the loveliest lochs in Scotland, Loch-na-Eilean. The ruined castle on an island in the centre is supposed to have been the headquarters of the wicked "Wolf of Badenoch", who terrorised the Grampians and the Cairngorms.

Elgin

This Royal Burgh and market town is the second-largest in the Grampian region after Aberdeen. It is best known for its ruined cathedral, founded in 1224 and one of the finest in Scotland. Although badly damaged in 1390 by Alexander Stewart, the Wolf of Badenoch, and later stripped of lead from the roof, much of it was restored in the 19th century. The Panns Port or east gate still stands, as does the Bishop's Palace, also in ruins, which dates from 1406. The Elgin Museum contains local artefacts and archaeological finds from Elgin and Moray.

Forres

This is the setting for the opening scenes of Macbeth. Although there are many genuinely medieval buildings in the town, the Tollbooth and Mercat Cross are both 19th-century Gothic Revival creations, modelled after the Scott Monument in Edinburgh. Nearby, Brodie Castle has been the home of the Brodie family since 1160. It is open to the public and in addition to the usual attractions, it has an adventure playground. Darnaway Castle in the Findhorn Valley was the seat of the Earls of Moray and has a splendid 15th century hammerbeam roof and portraits of the Stuarts. The Findhorn Foundation near Forres is a community of people wanting to pursue an alternative lifestyle who welcome visitors. It is famous for the profusion of flowers, fruit and vegetables grown by the community members.

Glenlivet

This village in the Grampians is far more famous than its size would suggest, due to the fine malt whisky distilled here. The distillery has been modernised but the distilling is still practised in the same old way. Visitors are welcome.

Inverness

Inverness is often referred to as the Capital of the Highlands. It is in a magnificent setting between two firths and commands the entrance to the Great Glen. The oldest building in the town is the 16th century Queen Mary's House. The Abertarff house, the headquarters of the Highland Association, An Comunn Gaidhealach. was built in 1593 for Lord Lovat and features a turnpike staircase. There is a permanent exhibition of the origins and history of the Gaelic peoples. Inverness Castle is a 19th-century building, which stands on the site of two earlier fortresses. The main road to Nairn passes by Culloden Moor where Bonnie Prince Charlie's armies were routed on 16 April, 1746 by the English forces of the Duke of Cumberland, who proceeded to revenge himself further by massacring Highlanders who had supported the Young Pretender. The site, now owned by the National Trust for Scotland, is covered with graves of fallen Highlanders, grouped by their clans.

Information
Scottish Tourist Board
Meall House
Portree, Skye
Tel: (0478) 2137

Forres Tourist Information Centre
Falconer Museum
Tollbooth Street
Forres
Tel: (0309) 72938

Events
Skye Week, a celebration of Hebridean and Scottish culture, is held in May.

Duntulm Castle on the Isle of Skye (above left).

Looking towards Glen Afric, north of Inverness (right).

Dunvegan Castle on Skye (above right).

The Five Sisters of Kintail (above far right).

Gardenstown on the coast of the Moray Firth (far right).

Kyle of Lochalsh

This is the tourist centre for visiting Skye as well as the Applecross Peninsula and the Five Sisters which tower over Glen Shiel. Most of the Lochalsh Peninsula belongs to the Balmacara Estate, owned by the National Trust for Scotland. There is an information centre just outside the town. Visitors will be surprised at the exotic vegetation that grows here, thanks to the warming effects of the Gulf Stream.

Loch Ness

This long, narrow strip of water is remarkable in many ways - not just for the Loch Ness Monster. It is fed by eight rivers and is deeper than the North Sea and much of the Atlantic Ocean. It has never been known to freeze over. A drive around the lake is a 70-mile trip. The north shore is flat and rather uninteresting but the south side, where the military road was built by General Wade, is much more varied. Fort Augustus, at the southern end of the Loch, contains the Great Glen Exhibition, an audio-visual display of the region's colourful history.

Nairn

This is a popular seaside resort with sandy beaches, lots of sunshine and a championship golf course. It was also once a herring port; though those days are gone, they are commemorated in the Fishertown Museum. Cawdor Castle, south of Nairn, is famous for its connections with Macbeth, who became Thane of Cawdor. The castle is 15th-century with 17th-century additions. Another 15th-century castle, Kilravock, two miles west of Cawdor, overlooks the River Nairn. The grounds are open to the public, but not the castle itself.

Skye

This large island, 50 miles in length, with its six peninsulas and jagged coastline with sea lochs has the most glorious scenery. Parts of Skye are so close to the mainland that cattle herders used to make their cows swim across from the Kyle of Lochalsh. The boat trip to Kyleakin only takes five minutes. The ruins of medieval Moil Castle across the sound is so close that one owner, nicknamed Saucy Mary for her impudence, is alleged to have trapped passing ships with a long chain and demanded a toll from them! Skye is famous for the Coolins or Cuilins, a range of jagged black mountains, celebrated in the song, The Road to the Isles. The largest community on the island, and the place where you are most likely to find accommodation, is Portree. The name means "The King's Harbour", to commemorate a visit by James V. St. Columba's Episcopal Church contains a Flora Macdonald Memorial Window. Prince Charlie's cave is five miles away by boat, and is alleged to have been visited by the Young Pretender while on the island. Dunvegan Castle, the ancestral home of the McLeods, was founded in the 9th century. It has been visited over the years by every dignitary who ever set foot on the island, including Queen Elizabeth I and Sir Walter Scott. The Sleat Peninsula in the far south has an interesting topography, something like the Giant's Causeway in Northern Ireland, due to the same lava flows of black basalt rock.

19

Sd
Se
Sf
Ta
Tb
Tc
NORTH UIST
Balmartin
Sollas
Loch nan Geireann
735
756
Loch Scadavay
Weaver's Point
Tarbert
Lochmaddy
Loch Maddy
Rubha nam Pléac
Balmarand
Bayhead
Loch Hunà
17
Paible
Claddach Kirkibost
LANGASS BARPA
South Lee
920
Kirkibost Island
Vorogai
Locheport
Loch Eport
Sidinish
Teanamachar
Samala
Loch Caravat
Bail Uachdraich
1139
Eaval
Baleshare
Temple of Carinish
Carinish
Floddaybeg
Floddaymore
Benbecula
Balivanich
14
Uachdar
Grimsay
379
Flodda
Ronay
Nunton
Rueval
408
Maragay Mór
Griminish
Torlum
Loch Uiskevagh
Maaey Riabhach
Liniclate
Hornish Point
Creagorry
Ardivachar Point
Ardivachar
Eochar
334
Loch a' Laip
Wiay
Bag nam Faoileann
Loch Bee
Lochcarnan
Sandwick
West Gerinish
Lochskipport
Loch Skipport
Stilligary
Loch Druidibeg
Mol a' Tuath
Usinish
Verran Island
Howmore
Hecla
1988
Stoneybridge
23
SOUTH UIST
Beinn Mhór
2033
Ormiclate Castle
Loch Ollay
Loch Kildonan
730
Loch Eynort
Mingary
Loch Snigiscleit
Stulaval
1228
Stuley
Askernish House
Loch Stulaval
Daliburgh
Crossdougal
Kilpheder
Lochboisdale
Boisdale
Loch Boisdale
Calvay
Orosay
South Lochboisdale
Garrynamonie
Pollachar
Rubha na h-Ordaig
Oban
661
Kilbride
Ludag
Sound of Eriskay
Sgeir a' Mhill
Lingay
Balla
610
Eriskay
Fiaray
Scurrival Point
Sound of Fuday
Sound of Barra
291
Fuday
Stack Islands
Eoligary
Orosay
Oitir Mhór
Gighay
Cleat
Cuier
Sound of Hellisay
Hellisay
Bruernish
Flodday
Balnabodach
Fuiay
Bruernish Point
Heaval
1260
Earsary
Barra
Castlebay
Kiessimul Castle
Mallaig
Oban
Muldoanich
HEBRIDES OR
WESTERN ISLES
THE LITTLE MINCH
SEA OF THE
HEBRI
Waterish Point
Waternish
Trumpan
Ardmore Point
Halistra
Hallin
Dunvegan Head
Mingay
Isay
Loch Dunvegan
Claigan
Galtrigill
Borreraig
Uig
L. Pooltiel
Feriniquarrie
Totaig
Dunvegan Castle
Oisgill Bay
Milovaig
Lephin
Colbost
Skinidin
Neist
Moonen bay
Hamara
1538
Ramasaig
Macleod's Tables
Hoe Rape
Orbost
1601
Hoe Point
1207
An Dubh Sgeir
Idrigill Point
Sb
Sc
Sd
6
Fiaray
Scurrival Point
Eoligary
Greian Head
Cleat
Cuier
Barra
Borve
Doirlinn Head
1090
Heaval
Earsary
Castlebay
1260
Kiessimul Castle
Caolis
624
7
Vatersay
Vatersay Bay
Muldoanich
Flodday
Sound of Sandray
678
Sandray
Lingay
Greanamul
Sound of Pabbay
Pabbay
561
Rosinish
Sound of Mingulay
Heiskers
Mingulay
Mingulay Bay
8
896
Sound of Berneray
Berneray
Barra Head
Rubha Langanes
Garrisdale Point
Canna
Humla
Oigh-sgeir
3
4
5
6
7
865
888
892
891
890
884

23
Td
Te
Tf
Ua
Ub
Uc
Kilmaluag Bay
Lub Score
Kilmaluag
Duntulm Castle
Flodigarry
Eilean Flodigarry
Tarbert
Borneskitaig
Flora Macdonald Monument
1781
Kilvaxter
Quiraing
Staffin Bay
Staffin Island
Balgown
Rha
Staffin
Linicro
Kilt Rock Waterfall
Ellishader
855
Valtos
Mealt
Idrigill
Uig
Uig Bay
Marishader
Garros
Rubha nam Brathairean
Beinn Edra
2006
Culnaknock
Balnaknock
Earlish
Lealt
856
1995
Tote
34
Peinlich
Lyndale Point
Greshornish Point
Hinnisdal
Rigg
Kingsburgh
Lyndale Ho
The Storr
2358
Old Man of Storr
Treaslane
16
Eyre
Greshornish
Flashader
Trotternish
24
Kensaleyre
Edinbane
Cairn Liath
Bernisdale
8036
856
Carbost
Borve
Loch Leathan
Loch Fada
855
Glen Bernisdale
Skeabost
Prince Charles's Cave
872
Uigshader
Drumuie
Achachork
850
Torvaig
Glengrasco
Portree
1367
Penifiler
1355
885
Ose
Glenmore
883
Camastianavaig
Mugeary
Loch Duagrich
863
Dun Beag
Struan
Ullinish
Conordan
Ollach
Gedintailor
10
Glen Varragill
1442
Portnalong
The Braes
Peinchorran
Fernilea
Loch Harport
8009
Carbost
Drynoch
863
Loch Sligachan
Sconser
830
Glamaig
2542
850
Talisker
Sligachan
Glen Brittle Forest
Eynort
Minginish
3167
17
Loch Eynort
Glen Brittle
Sgurr a'Ghreadaidh
3197
Cuillin Hills
Sgurr Alasdair
3257
Bualintur
Glenbrittle House
Sgurr nan Eag
3037
Loch Brittle
Cairn
Rubh' an Dùnain
Soay Sound
464
Soay
Loch Scavaig
Cuillin Sound
Rubha Shamhnan Insir
Kilmory
997
Kinloch Castle
Rubha na Roinne
Nat. Res.
Kinloch Castle
Loch Scresort
Harris
2663
Askival
2552
Rubha nam Meirleach
36
Isle of Rona
410
Eilean Garbh
Sound of Raasay
Eilean Tigh
Garbh Eilean
Eilean Raddy
833
Torran
Manish Point
Arnish
Brochel
Island of Raasay
Inner Sound
Glame
Balachuirn
Balmeanach
Dùn Caan
1455
Uskaig
North Fearns
Chlachan
Inverarish
Eyre Point
Caol Mòr
Scalpay
1298
Mullach na Càrn
Loch Ainort
Dunan
Luib
Caolas Scalpay
2649
Bla Bheinn
3046
Loch na Creitheach
Camasunary
Strathaird
Kilmarie
Dun Ringill
Loch Slapin
Torrin
Beinn na Caillich
2403
881
Broadford
Broadford Bay
Corry
Breakish
Harrapool
Elgol
Glasnakille
Dun Grugaig
Eilean na h-Airde
Rubha na h-Easgainne
Rubha Suisnish
Tarskavaig Point
Loch Eishort
908
983
Heast
Eilean Heast
Castle Dungaith
Nat. Res.
Ord
Tokavaig
981
Tarskavaig
Achnacloich
Teangue
Kilmore
Kilbeg
Knock Castle
Knock Bay
Sleat
Inver Dalavil
Armadale Castle
Armadale Bay
Ardvasar
Calligarry
920
Aird of Sleat
Point of Sleat
Sound of Sleat
Castlebay (Barra)
Mallaig
1796
830
Morar
Glenancross
Traigh Ho
Fort William
Eilean Mòr
Crowlin Islands
Longay
Pabay
Kyleakin
Kyle of Lochalsh
Skulamus
Drochaid Lusa
Sgurr na Coinnich
2424
Ben Aslak
2424
Kyleakea
1984
851
Kinloch
Drumfearn
Duisdalemore
Isleornsay or Eilean Iarmain
Ornsay
17
Eilean Meadhonach
Eilean Beag
Eilean na Bà
Caolas Mòr
Uags
Toscaig
Culduie
Ard-dhubh
Camusterrach
Camusteel
Applecross
Applecross Ho
2053
Lonbain
Kalnakill
Cuaig
Fearnbeg
Fearnmore
Rubha na Fearn
Loch Torridon
Red Point
Redpoint
8056
L. Clàir
Loch Bad an Sgalaigh
Shieldaig Forest
Loch a'Bhealaich
Craig
Lower Diabaig
Alligin Shuas
Rechullin
Inveralligin
Upper Loch Torridon
Arinacrinachd
Kenmore
Ardheslaig
Loch Shieldaig
Balsy
Shieldaig
34
1613
Loch Lundie
896
Beinn Bhan
2938
2539
2328
Meall Gorm
Ardarroch
Achintraid
Loch Kishorn
Plockton
Achmore
Duirinish
Drumbuie
Erbusaig
Badicaul
Kirkton
Balmacara
87
Inverness
Loch Alsh
Bernera
Galltair
Glenelg Bay
Gleneig
Eilanreach
Gleneig Brochs
2421
Sandaig Islands
Beinn Sgritheall
3194
Loch Hourn
Arnisdale
Rubh' Ard Slisneach
Inverguseran
Beinn na Caillich
2573
Airor
Ladhar Bheinn
3343
Knoydart
Sandaig
Aultvoulin
2612
Inverie
Inverie Bay
Glas Eilean
Rubha Raonill
Loch Nevis
Beinn Bhuidhe
2805
North Morar
Stoul
Bracora
Bracorina
Brinacory
Tarbet
Kylesmorar
Swordland
37
Isle of Skye
Rum

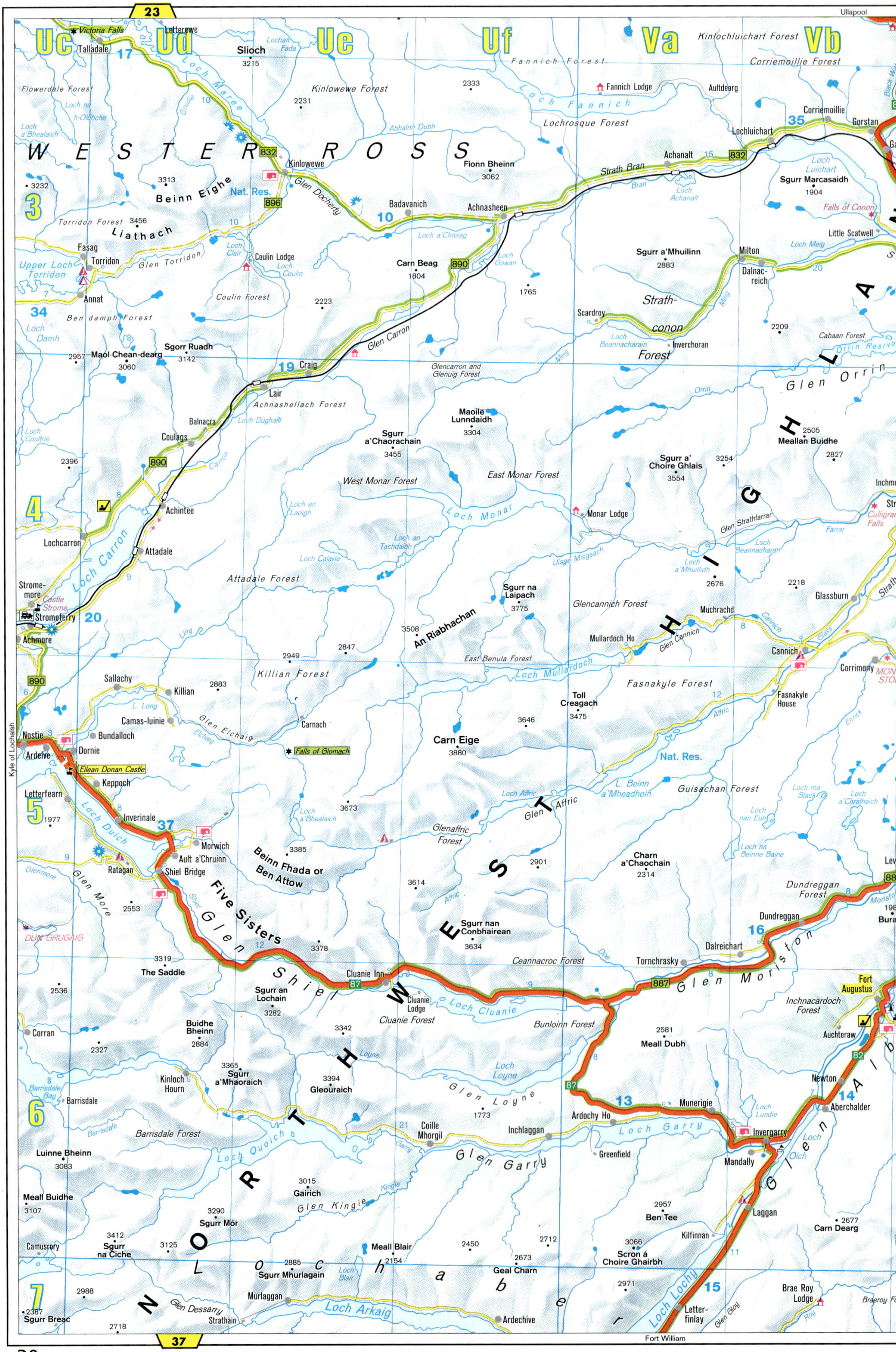

23
Uc
Ud
Ue
Uf
Va
Vb
Victoria Falls
Letterewe
Talladale
Slioch
3215
Loch Maree
Lochan Fada
Kinlochluichart Forest
Corriemoillie Forest
Fannich Forest
Ullapool
Flowerdale Forest
Kinlowewe Forest
2333
2231
Fannich Lodge
Aultdearg
Loch Fannich
Lochrosque Forest
Abhainn Dubh
Corriemoillie
Gorstan
Lochluichart
WESTER ROSS
Kinlowewe
Glen Docherty
Achanalt
Strath Bran
Loch Luichart
Sgurr Marcasaidh
1904
Fionn Bheinn
3062
3232
3313
Beinn Eighe
Nat. Res.
Badavanich
Achnasheen
Loch Achanalt
Falls of Conon
Torridon Forest
3456
Liathach
Loch a' Chroisg
Little Scatwell
Loch Meig
Fasag
Torridon
Upper Loch Torridon
Glen Torridon
Loch Clair
Coulin Lodge
Loch Coulin
Carn Beag
1804
Loch Gowan
Sgurr a'Mhuilinn
2883
Milton
Dalnacreich
Annat
Coulin Forest
2223
1765
Strathconon Forest
34
Ben-damph Forest
Scardroy
Loch Beannacharain
Inverchoran
2209
Cabaan Forest
Loch Damh
Glen Carron
Orrin Reservoir
2957
Maol Chean-dearg
3060
Sgorr Ruadh
3142
Craig
Glencarron and Glenuig Forest
Glen Orrin
Lair
Achnashellach Forest
Loch Dughaill
Maoile Lunndaidh
3304
Balnacra
Coulags
Sgurr a'Chaorachain
3455
2505
Meallan Buidhe
Loch Coultrie
2396
Carron
Sgurr a' Choire Ghlais
3554
3254
2827
West Monar Forest
East Monar Forest
Inchmore
Achintee
Loch an Laoigh
Loch Monar
Monar Lodge
Glen Strathfarrar
Culligran Falls
Farrar
Lochcarron
Loch Carron
Attadale
Loch an Tachdaidh
Loch Beannacharan
Loch Calavie
Uisge Misgeach
Loch a' Mhuillidh
2676
2218
Strome-more
Castle Strome
Stromeferry
Attadale Forest
Sgurr na Lapaich
3775
Glencannich Forest
Glassburn
20
Achmore
3508
An Riabhachan
Muchrachd
Mullardoch Ho
Glen Cannich
Cannich
Ling
2949
2847
East Benula Forest
Loch Mullardoch
Corrimony
Sallachy
Killian
2883
Killian Forest
Fasnakyle Forest
Fasnakyle House
Camas-luinie
Toll Creagach
3475
L. Long
Glen Elchaig
Carnach
3646
Nostie
Bundalloch
Ardelve
Dornie
Falls of Glomach
Carn Eige
3880
Nat. Res.
Eilean Donan Castle
Keppoch
L. Beinn a'Mheadhoin
Guisachan Forest
Loch Affric
Loch ma Stack
Loch a'Chrathaich
Letterfearn
1977
Loch a' Bhealaich
3673
Glen Affric
Loch nan Eun
Inverinale
Loch Duich
37
Morwich
Glenaffric Forest
Loch na Beinne Baine
Aullt a'Chruinn
3385
Charn a'Chaochain
2314
Ratagan
Shiel Bridge
Beinn Fhada or Ben Attow
2901
Glenmore
Glen More
Five Sisters
3614
Dundreggan Forest
Moriston
2553
Affric
Dundreggan
DUN GRUGAIG
Sgurr nan Conbhairean
3634
NORTHWEST HIGHLANDS
Glen Shiel
3378
3319
The Saddle
Ceannacroc Forest
Tornchrasky
Dalreichart
Glen Moriston
Cluanie Inn
2536
Sgurr an Lochain
3282
Cluanie Lodge
Loch Cluanie
Cluanie Forest
Fort Augustus
Inchnacardoch Forest
Bunloinn Forest
Corran
Buidhe Bheinn
2884
2327
3342
2581
Meall Dubh
Auchteraw
Loyne
Loch Loyne
3365
Sgurr a'Mhaoraich
Kinloch Hourn
Newton
Barrisdale Bay
Barrisdale
3394
Gleouraich
Glen Loyne
1773
Glen Albyn
13
Munerigie
Aberchalder
Ardochy Ho
Barrisdale Forest
Coille Mhorgil
Inchlaggan
Loch Garry
Invergarry
Loch Lundie
Loch Oich
Luinne Bheinn
3083
Loch Quoich
Greenfield
Glen Garry
Mandally
3015
Gairich
Meall Buidhe
3107
Glen Kingie
Kingie
2957
Ben Tee
Laggan
3290
Sgurr Mòr
2677
Carn Dearg
3412
Sgurr na Ciche
3125
2450
2712
Kilfinnan
Camusrory
Meall Blair
2885
2154
2673
3066
Sron a Choire Ghairbh
Sgurr Mhurlagain
Loch Blair
Geal Charn
Lochaber
2971
Brae Roy Lodge
Braeroy Forest
2988
2387
Sgurr Breac
Murlaggan
Loch Arkaig
Glen Dessarry
Strathain
Loch Lochy
15
Letterfinlay
Glen Gloy
Roy
Ardechive
2718
37
Fort William
Kyle of Lochalsh
3
4
5
6
7

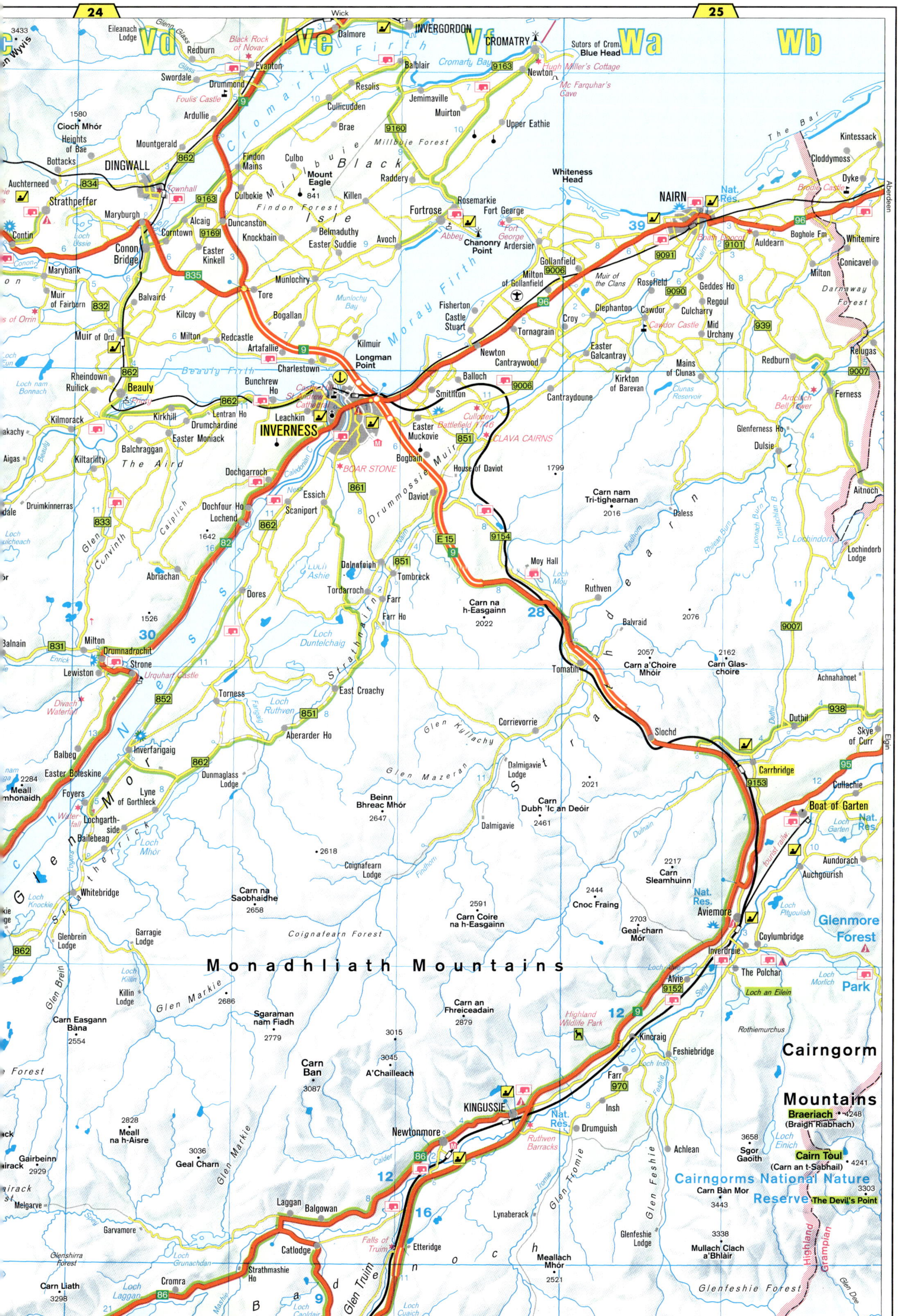
24
25
38
39
Vd
Ve
Vf
Wa
Wb
Wick
INVERGORDON
CROMATRY
Dalmore
Black Rock of Novar
Evanton
Redburn
Swordale
Drummond
Foulis Castle
Ardullie
Eileanach Lodge
Cromarty Firth
Cromarty Bay
Balblair
Resolis
Cullicudden
Jemimaville
Muirton
Brae
Newton
Hugh Miller's Cottage
Mc Farquhar's Cave
Sutors of Cromarty
Blue Head
Upper Eathie
Millbuie Forest
Black Isle
Cioch Mhór
Heights of Bae
Mountgerald
Bottacks
DINGWALL
Townhall
Findon Mains
Culbo
Mount Eagle
Raddery
Auchterneed
Strathpeffer
Culbokie
Findon Forest
Killen
Fortrose
Rosemarkie
Fort George
Whiteness Head
NAIRN
Nat. Res.
Maryburgh
Alcaig
Duncanston
Belmaduthy
Avoch
Chanonry Point
Ardersier
Contin
Conon Bridge
Corntown
Knockbain
Easter Kinkell
Easter Suddie
Abbey
Marybank
Munlochy
Milton of Gollanfield
Gollanfield
Rosefield
Geddes Ho
Auldearn
Boghole Fm
Whitemire
Conicavel
Muir of Fairburn
Balvaird
Tore
Munlochy Bay
Moray Firth
Fisherton
Castle Stuart
Croy
Clephanton
Cawdor
Cawdor Castle
Culcharry
Regoul
Mid Urchany
Darnaway Forest
Kilcoy
Bogallan
Tornagrain
Milton
Redcastle
Artafallie
Kilmuir
Newton
Cantraywood
Easter Galcantray
Redburn
Relugas
Muir of Ord
Beauly Firth
Charlestown
Longman Point
Mains of Clunas
Rheindown
Ruilick
Beauly
Priory
Bunchrew Ho
Balloch
Smithton
Kirkton of Barevan
Cantraydoune
Ferness
Ardclach Bell Tower
Kilmorack
Kirkhill
Lentran Ho
Drumchardine
Leachkin
INVERNESS
Easter Muckovie
Culloden Battlefield 1746
Clava Cairns
Glenferness Ho
Dulsie
Aigas
Kiltarlity
Balchraggan
Easter Moniack
The Aird
Dochgarroch
Boar Stone
Bogbain
House of Daviot
Daviot
Drummossie Muir
Carn nam Tri-tighearnan
2016
1799
Daless
Aitnoch
Druimkinnerras
Dochfour Ho
Lochend
Essich
Scaniport
Glen Convinth
Caiplich
Abriachan
Loch Ashie
Dalnafoich
Tombreck
Moy Hall
Loch Moy
Ruthven
Lochindorb
Lochindorb Lodge
Dores
Tordarroch
Farr
Farr Ho
Carn na h-Easgainn
2022
Balvraid
2076
Milton
Drumnadrochit
Strone
Lewiston
Urquhart Castle
Loch Duntelchaig
Strathnairn
Loch Ness
Tomatin
Carn a'Choire Mhòir
2057
Carn Glas-choire
2162
Achnahannet
Divach Waterfall
Torness
Loch Ruthven
East Croachy
Aberarder Ho
Glen Kyllachy
Corrievorrie
Slochd
Duthil
Skye of Curr
Balbeg
Inverfarigaig
Dunmaglass Lodge
Glen Mazeran
Dalmigavie Lodge
Carrbridge
Cullachie
Easter Boleskine
Meall mhonaidh
Foyers
Lyne of Gorthleck
Beinn Bhreac Mhór
2647
Carn Dubh 'Ic an Deóir
2461
Dalmigavie
Boat of Garten
Loch Garten
Lochgarth-side
Bailebeag
Stratherrick
Loch Mhór
2618
Coignafearn Lodge
Carn Sleamhuinn
2217
Aundorach
Auchgourish
Whitebridge
Carn na Saobhaidhe
2658
Carn Coire na h-Easgainn
2591
Cnoc Fraing
2444
Aviemore
Geal-charn Mór
2703
Glenmore Forest
Coylumbridge
Glenbrein Lodge
Garragie Lodge
Coignafearn Forest
Inverdruie
The Polchar
Loch Morlich
Park
Monadhliath Mountains
Loch an Eilein
Killin Lodge
Glen Markie
2686
Carn an Fhreiceadain
2879
Highland Wildlife Park
Rothiemurchus
Carn Easgann Bana
2554
Sgaraman nam Fiadh
2779
3015
Kincraig
Feshiebridge
Cairngorm Mountains
Carn Ban
3087
3045
A'Chailleach
Farr
Insh
KINGUSSIE
Braeriach
4248
(Braigh Riabhach)
Meall na h-Aisre
2828
Newtonmore
Drumguish
Ruthven Barracks
Achlean
Sgor Gaoith
3658
Loch Einich
Cairn Toul
4241
(Carn an t-Sabhail)
Gairbeinn
2929
Geal Charn
3036
Glen Tromie
Glen Feshie
Cairngorms National Nature Reserve
Carn Bàn Mor
3443
3303
The Devil's Point
Melgarve
Laggan
Balgowan
Lynaberack
Garvamore
Catlodge
Falls of Truim
Etteridge
Glenfeshie Lodge
Mullach Clach a'Bhlàir
3338
Meallach Mhór
2521
Strathmashie Ho
Badenoch
Glenfeshie Forest
Highland
Grampian
Carn Liath
3298
Cromra
Loch Laggan
Loch Caoldair
Loch Cuaich
Glen Truim
Fort William
Perth
Aberdeen
Elgin

25
Wc
Wd
We
Wf
Xa
Burghead Well
Burghead Bay
Roseisle
Duffus Castle
Loch Spynie
Spynie Palace
Lossie Forest
Spey Bay
Bay
Kingston
Lochhill
Leuchars Ho
Innes House
BUCKIE
PORTKNOCKIE
FINDOCHTY
Portessie
Bauds of Cullen
Cullen House
Cullen
Cullen Bay
Lintmill
Rathven
Portgordon
Spey Bay
Garmouth
Findhorn
Culbin Forest
Findhorn Bay
Kincorth Ho
Kinloss
Kinloss Abbey
Hempriggs
Coltfield
Alves
Newton
Quarrydood
ELGIN
Urquhart
Muir of Lochs
Bogmoor
Nether Dallachy
Auchenhalrig
Sackhead
Drybridge
Broadley
Clochan
Lhanbryde
Miltonduff
Pittendreich
Cloddach
Moss of Barmuckity
Mosstodloch
Fochabers
Dipple
Ordiquish
Speymouth Forest
Inchberry
Longmorn
Whitewreath
Moy Ho
SVENO'S STONE
FORRES
Rafford
Califer
Pluscarden Abbey
Black Burn
Barnhill
Thomshill
Briach
Hill of the Wangie
1046
Kellas
Altyre Woods
Phorb
Branchill
Dallas
Glenlatterach Reservoir
1164
1197
Glen of Rothes
474
Teindland Forest
Newlands
Boat o Brig
Mulben
Rosarie Forest
Hill of Towie
1111
Towiemore
250
Forgie
Aultmore
Glen of Newmill
Newmill
Davoch of Grange
Bracobrae
KEITH
Strathisla
Black-hillock
Little Pitlurg
Knock
Drumnagorrach
Farmtown
The Balloch
1200
Ruthven
Cairnie
The Bin Forest
Huntly Castle
HUNTLY
Kirktown of Deskford
Deskford Church
Berryhillock
Craibstone
1028
Deerhill
Grange Crossroads
Crannoch
Gordonstown
Knock Hill
Sillyearn
Milton
1051
987
Aultmore
Inverness
1129
Hill of Tomechole
Loch Dallas
Beachans
1324
Carn na Cailliche
Elchies Forest
Whiteacen
ROTHES
Archiestown
Nether Ringorm
Craigellachie
Maggieknocktar
Kininvie Ho
Drummuir Castle
Upper Knockando
Cardow
CHARLESTOWN OF ABERLOUR
Daugh of Kinermony
Knockando
Carron
Milltown of Edinville
Balvenie Castle
DUFFTOWN
Fiddich
Milltown of Auchindoun
Auchindoun Castle
Cainborrow
Torry
Haugh of Glass
Strathbogie
Bailiesward
Beldorney Castle
Succoth
Tillathrowie
Bridgend
Coynachie
Culdrain
Gartly
Tomnaven
Clashindarroch
Inverharroch
Bridgend
Milton of Lesmore
Kennethmont
Rhynie
Cottown
Wheedlemont
Craig Castle
St Mary's Kirk
Knockespock Ho
1599
Correen Hills
Clova
Lumsden
1699
Mossat
Kildrummy
Kildrummy Castle
Milltown
Auchintoul
Howe
Carn Kitty
1712
Grampian
Highland
1783
Larig Hill
Dava
1800
Carn na Lòine
Marypark
Belleheiglash
Ben Rinnes
2759
Glen Rinnes
Glen Fiddich
Favillar
Glenfiddich Lodge
Spey
Bridge of Avon
Advie
Upper Derraid
Auchnagallin
Lettoch
Mains of Davey
Dellefure
Cottartown
GRANTOWN-ON-SPEY
Cromdale
Hills of Cromdale
Drumin
Shenval
Glenlivet
2561
Corryhabbie Hill
1872
Aldunie
Cabrach
Blackwater Forest
Tomnavoulin
Glen Livet
Strath Avon
Bulnain Bridge
Fort William
2369
Creagan a'Chaise
Knockandhu
2065
Hill of Three Stones
The Buck
2366
Nethy Bridge
Siemone
Lettoch
Fodderletter
Chapeltown
Ladder Hills
Badenyon
2073
Creag an Eunan
Dell Lodge
Abernethy Forest
Dorback Lodge
Milton
Tomintoul
Carn Mór
2639
Moss Hill
2159
Water of Nochty
Rinmore
Belnacraig
Kirkton of Glenbuchat
Glenbuchat Castle
Glenkindie
Towie
Sinnahard
Forest Lodge
Dorback Burn
2257
Carn na Farraidh
Conglass Water
Blairnamarrow
2598
2356
The Socach
Bellabeg
Strathdon
Milltown of Towie
Milton of Cushnie
Leochel-Cushnie
Carn Ealasaid
2600
Heugh-head
Boultenstone
Geal Charn
2692
2337
2332
Cock Bridge
2207
Hillockhead
An Lurg
2463
Corgarff
Corgarff Castle
Colnabaichin
East Davoch
Big Garvoun
2431
Delnadamph Lodge
Migvie
Douneside
Craskins
Bynack More
3574
Glen Avon
Mona Gowan
2456
Coynach
Tarland
CULSH SOUTERRAIN
Cairngorm
Cairn Gorm
4084
Loch Avon
Beinn Mheadhoin
3883
2721
2442
Morven
2861
Logie Coldstone
Cromar
Loch Builg
Ben Avon
3843
Glendavan Ho
Ordie
STONE CIRCLE
Loch Davan
Coull
Gairnshiel Lodge
Lary
Glen Gairn
Mountains
3924
Beinn a'Bhuird
L. Etachan
4296
Ben Macdui
(Beinn Macduibh)
3556
Càrn Eàs
2953
Culardoch
Geallaig Hill
2438
Coilarich
Milton of Tullich
Loch Kinord
Dinnet
3051
2830
Bush Crathie
Crathie
Balmoral Castle
Abergeldie Castle
BALLATER
Glascorrie
Inver
Easter Balmoral
Birkhall
Water of Tanar
Forest of Glen Tanar
Forest of
Ballochan
Braemar Castle
Linn of Quoich
Invercauld Bridge
Allanaquoich
Braemar
Bridge of Dee
Falls of Garbh Allt
Glen Gelder
Aucholzie
2293
Cairn Leuchan
Glen Tanar
2081
Sgòr Mór
2266
Cleybokie
Tomintoul
Forest of Mar
Linn of Dee
Muir
Inverey
Linn of Corriemulzie
Auchallater
Balmoral Forest
Glen Muick
3080
Mount Keen
2387
Cock Cairn
Mudlee Bracks
2259
Perth
GRAMPIAN MOUNTAINS
39

FRASERBURGH
Kinnaird Head
Sealch's Hole
ROSEHEARTY
Pitsligo Castle
Sandhaven
Troup Head
Pennan Head
Pennan
Aberdour Bay
Gamrie Bay
Crovie
Gardenstown
Xc
Xd
Xe
Xf
Ya
Yb
Whitehills
Easter Whyn
BANFF
MACDUFF
Boyndie
Mid Culbeuchly
Duff House
Greenskares
Longmanhill
Minnonie
Silverford
Dubford
New Aberdour
759
Windyheads Hill
Boyndlie
Peathill
Mid Ardlaw
Memsie
Burial Cairn
Rathen
Fraserburgh Bay
Cairnbulg Point
Inverallochy
St Combs
Cairnbulg Castle
Gowanhill
Loch of Strathbeg
Strathbeg Bay
Crimonmogate
Rattray Head
Old Rattray
Blackhill
Ladysford
Hillhead of Auchentumb
Mormond Hill
768
763
Strichen
Glasslaw
Netherbrae
745
Keilhill
Kirktown of Alvah
Fattahead
Eden Castle
Gorrachie
Oldtown of Ord
Weachyburn
The Pole of Itlaw
Milltown of Craigston
Craigston Castle
Fintry
Muirden
Finnygaud
Cranna
ABERCHIRDER
Bogton
Clunie
Kirkton
TURRIFF
Muiryfold
Delgatie Castle
Colp
Darra
Hatton Castle
Birkenhills
Inverkeithny
Yonder Bognie
Auchininna
Fortrie
New Pitsligo
New Byth
Garmond
Balthangie
Cuminestown
Bonnykelly
Ironside
North Ugie
New Leeds
Leys
Backfolds
St Fergus
Scotstown Head
Kirkton Head
Kirktown
Rora
Denhead
Fetterangus
Toux
Buchan
Deer Abbey
South Ugie
Mintlaw
Longside
Torterston
Inverugie
PETERHEAD
Flushing
Federate
Culsh
New Deer
Maud
Backhill of Clackriach
Old Deer
Stuartfield
Howe of Teuchar
Drymuir
Millbreck
Nether Kinmundy
Hillhead of Cocklaw
Peterhead Bay
Burnhaven
Sandford Bay
Buchan Ness
Boddam
Crofts of Inverthernie
Towie Barclay Castle
Nethermuir
Crichie
Kinnadie
Clola
Little Dens
Moss of Cruden
Blackhill
Sandfordhill
Drumblair
Steinmanhill
Millbrex
Knaven
Annochie
Skelmuir
Newton
Smallburn
Kinknockie
Auchnagatt
Fortrie
Stoneygate
Coldwells
Corse
Aucharnie
Balgaveny
Kirkton of Auchterless
Gourdas
Lethenty
Monkshill
Cottown
Brownhill
Backhill
Logie Newton
Gordonstown
Rothiebrisbane
Fyvie Castle
Tifty
Backhill
Woodhead
Fyvie
Crofts of Haddo
Methlick
Skelmonae
Quilquox
Milton Coldwells
Muirtack
Hatton
Bullers of Buchan
Ythanwells
Badenscoth
Drumwhindle
Arthrath
Toll of Birness
Cruden Bay
Slains Castle
Rothienorman
Fisherford
Petty
Bogbrae
Chapel Hill
Bay of Cruden
Barthol Chapel
Haddo House
Ythanbank
Hilton
Birness
St Katharines
Folla Rule
Kirkton of Culsalmond
Largie
Cairnhill
Colpy
Tocher
Meikle Wartle
Cross of Jackston
Balgove
Earls-ford
Wedderlairs
Inverebrie
Broomfield
Leask
Whinnyfold
Jackstown
Craigdam
Medieval Tomb
Tarves
Kinharrachie
ELLON
Artrochie
Auchmacoy
Wrangham
Kirkton of Rayne
Formartine
Ythsie
Esslemont
Auquhorthies
Aulton
Insch
Loanhead of Daviot
Daviot
OLDMELDRUM
Tolquhon Castle
Pitmedden Garden
Pitmedden
Kirkton of Logie Buchan
Collieston
Old Rayne
Durno
Meikle Tarty
Tipperty
Sands of Forvie
Hackley Head or Forvie Ness
Oyne
Whiteford
Fingask
Hill of Barra
Udny Green
Tarty Burn
Newburgh
Kirkton
Leslie
Garioch
Pitcaple
Harlaw Ho
Cairnbrogie
Hattoncrook
Pettymuick
Coltercullen
Newburgh Bar
Auchleven
Lickleyhead Castle
Pittodrie Ho
Maiden Stone
Chapel of Garioch
Kirkton of Bourtie
Whiterashes
Affleck
Tillycorthie
Minnes
Bennachie
1733
East Aquhorthies Stone Circle
Balhalgardy
Hillbrae
Tillygreig
Drums
1698
Keith Hall
Nether Crimond
Middlemuir
Delfrigs
INVERURIE
Port Elphinstone
Causeyend
Glenton
Burnhervie
Middleton
Kinmuck
Craigie
Keig
Castle Forbes
Bograxie
Newmacher
Whitecairns
Balmedie
Rorandle
Blairdaff
Kinkell Church
Balbithan
Balbithan Ho
Kinmundy
Belhelvie
1468
Pitfichie
Grantlodge
Kemnay
KINTORE
Hatton of Fintray
Cothall
Drumligair
Potterton
Skelly Rock
Pitmunie
Wester Fintray
Symbol Stones
Corby Loch
Whitehouse
Cottown
Town House
Overton
DYCE
Blackdog
Lerwick, Stromness
Kirkton of Tough
Monymusk
Craigearn
Leylodge
Tyrebagger Hill
Aberdeen (Dyce)
Blackdog Rock
Castle Fraser
Tillyfourie
Lauchintilly
Blackburn
Bankhead
Ordhead
Sauchen
Achath
Clinterty
Craibstone
BRIDGE OF DON
Corrennie Forest
Lyne of Skene
Don
St Machar's Cathedral
Dunecht
BUCKSBURN
874
King's College
1621
Corsindae
Old Kinnernie
Kirkton of Skene
Westhill
ABERDEEN
Bankhead
Comers
Loch of Skene
Marischal College
St Nicholas
Girdle Ness
Tornaveen
Echt
Carnie
Elrick
(869)
Nigg Bay
Lumphanan
Drumlassie
South Kirkton
Garlogie
Cullerlie Stone Circle
Easter Ord
Greg Ness
Midmar Castle
Redhill
Blacktop
CULTS
Landerberry
1545
Hill of Fare
Schoolhill
Contlaw
Charlestown
Cove Bay
Torphins
Milton of Campfield
Dee
Bieldside
Kincardine O'Neil
Hardgate
Banchory Devenick
Mid Beltie
Brathens
Hirnfield
Drum Castle
Peterculter
Mains of Drum
Auchlunies
Kirkton of Maryculter
Hillside
Drumoak
Findon
Bridge of Canny
East Mains
Upper Lochton
The Neuk
Crathes Castle
Auchlee
Potarch
BANCHORY
Bridge of Feugh
Crathes
Kirkton of Durris
Denside
Muirskie
Portlethen
Portlethen Village
Blackhall Forest
Auchattie
Crossroads
Woodlands
Upper Burnhaugh
Cammachmore
Downies
Finzean
Whitestone
Netherley
Cockney
Borrowfield
Newtonhill
Muchalls Castle
Muchalls
Water of Feugh
Lochton
1241
Cairn-mon-earn
Union Cottage
Bridge of Muchalls
1232
Mongour
Rickarton
Mowtie
Water of Dye
Water of Aven
1754
Kerloch
Mergie
Garron Point
Hill of Edendocher
1944
Bridge of Dye
1052
Hill of Trusta
Cowie Water
Kirktown of Fetteresso
STONEHAVEN
40

The Inner Hebrides and Sutherland

The southern Highlands, below the Great Glen, is an area of farms and forests, industry and prosperity. It escaped the Highland Clearances and is now a thriving community, with mixed farming and small manufacturing.

Aberfeldy
Aberfeldy's most famous sight is the Wade Bridge over the Tay, built in 1733 by General Sir George Wade, who was Scotland's great road-builder. Wade lived nearby in Weem, and there is a monument to him near Dalnacardoch. Aberfeldy is a handy spot from which to visit the local beauty spot, the Falls of Moness, on the Tay.

Arbroath
It was at Abroath Abbey that Robert the Bruce signed Scotland's Declaration of Independence in 1302. The Abbey is now in ruins. The city is a fishing port, famous for the delicacy known as "Arbroath smoakies", haddock smoked over oakwood. Signal Tower Museum is inside the lighthouse built by Robert Louis Stevenson's grandson.

Blair Atholl
Blair Castle, ancient home of the Murrays of Atholl, is surrounded by acres of primæval forest and the fertile farmland of Perthshire, seven miles north of Pitlochry. The huge, white, 13th-century castle stands in 300,000 acres of grounds. It is the last castle to have been laid siege to, an event which happened when the owner, Lord George Murray, returned home from battle to find strangers in possession. The Laird has the right to own the only private army left in Britain, the Atholl Highlanders. A few miles to the north-west is the lovely waterfall known as Bruar Falls. This area was once owned by members of the Clan Donaghaid, the Robertsons, now the biggest landless clan in the Highlands. A little museum by the roadside at the beginning of the path to the Falls documents the clan history.

Blairgowrie
This is a resort centre for climbers who want to ascend Glenshee, especially the twisting section called the Devil's Elbow. Four miles south of the village, at Meikelour, there is an extraordinary beech hedge. It is over 100 feet high and still growing, and is said to have been planted by Bonnie Prince Charlie in 1745.

Dundee
This city on the Firth of Tay has always been famous for "jam, jute and journalism". It is the place where marmalade was invented. Jute was another raw material imported and processed here, and the journalism comes from D.C. Thomson, the magazine and newspaper publishers whose headquarters are here. The Caird Hall is an ancient civic building attesting to the prosperity of the town. St. Mary's Tower is now a museum. Camperdown House contains a golfing museum.

Fort William
This little town is named after the fort, erected in 1655, which was dismantled to make way for the West Highland Railway; only the gates remain. The West Highland Museum contains a replica of the Governor's Room in which the order for the Massacre of Glencoe was signed in 1692. There are many other fascinating historic exhibits. Fort William is an important rail and road junction, the terminal of the Caledonian Canal and a leading tourist centre. There is a big hydroelectric plant here in the shadow of Ben Nevis, Scotland's

highest mountain (4406 feet). Climbers use several routes up the mountain, the most popular one starts only two miles outside the town.

Glamis Castle

Glamis is one of the great historic homes of Scotland, the scene of the murder of King Duncan, so vividly recalled in *Macbeth* . The room in which the murder took place can be visited. This 14th-century stone castle, with some 17th century additions, has panelled rooms, and beautiful paintings and tapestries. It is the seat of the Earls of Strathmore and was the birthplace of Princess Margaret.

Iona

This tiny island, three miles by one mile, is where St. Columba landed in 563 on his journey from Ireland to spread Christianity throughout northern Scotland. The Cathedral and monastic buildings, which now belong to the Church of Scotland, have largely been restored by the Iona Community, founded in 1938. The ecclesiastical buildings are on the shore, and many visitors never go further inland. The rest of the island has white, sandy beaches and is sparsely populated.

Mull

This beautiful island is the third-largest in the Hebrides. The climate is very humid and the landscape beautiful, though treeless. Tobermory, the main community, attracts increasing numbers of visitors, who also use Mull as a starting point for trips to the neighbouring islands of Iona (see above), Staffa (see below) and the Trenish Isles. Tobermory is set in a lovely bay, sheltered by Calve Island. Somewhere in this bay lies the wreck of a Spanish ship which foundered during the Armada. Several objects have been retrieved from the wreck, but most of the treasure it carried still lies beneath the sea. Tobermory has many recreational facilities, including the Aros Forest Park, which has gardens as well as woods and a play area for children. The northern end of Mull is bleak and deserted but there is an interesting castle, Glengorm, on the Mishnish headland. Dervaig is a charming village in the north, which is home to the Little Theatre of Mull. Nearby there is the Old Byre Heritage Centre, a reconstruction of Scottish farming life, with rebuilt crofts. Ben More, the island's highest mountain (3169 feet) is a two-and-a-half hour climb. From Gribun there are good views of Inch Kenneth, a privately-owned island. Mackinnon's Cave, below the Gribun Cliffs, is the subject of many local legends. At Croig there are superb views of the islands of Eigg and Rhum and the Moun-

The Perthshine Hills in spring (opposite).

The Palace of Scone (above left).

Perth from the River Tay, famous for its salmon (left).

The beech hedge at Meikelour, allegedly planted by Bonnie Prince Charlie (above).

29

Ta
Tb
Td
Te
Tf
Ua
TIREE
Vaul
Caolas
Ruaig
Clachan Mór
Belephetrish Bay
Balevullin
Kenovay
Gott Bay
8069
8068
Scarinish
Heanish
Arinagour (Coll)
Kilkenneth
Moss
Heylipol
Middleton
8065
Barrapol
Crossapol
Hynish Bay
8067
Balemartine
Balephuil
Mannal
Balephuil Bay
Hynish
RHUM
Rubha nam Meirleach
Sound of Rhum
Bay of Laig
Cleadale
Eigg
Rubha an Fhasaidh
Kildonnan
1292
An Sgurr
Galmisdale
Rubha na Crannaig
Eilean Chathasteil
Sound of Eigg
Godag
Eilean nan Each
452
Port Mór
Muck
Eilean Ighe
Luinga Bheag
Luinga Mhór
Rubh' Arisaig
INNER HEBRIDES
Lochboisdale (South Uist)
Rubha Aird Druimnich
Farquhar Point
Kilmory
Fascadale
Ockle
Sanna
Branault
Sanna Bay
Achnaha
1433
Meall nan Con
Ardnamurchan
1171
Point of Ardnamurchan
Portuairk
Achosnich
Loch Mudle
Kilchoan
Ormsaigmore
Mingary Castle
Ben Hiant
1731
Glenbeg
Glenborrodale
Kilchoan Bay
Scròn Bheag
(seasonal)
Ardslignish
Oronsay
Risga
Eilean Mór
Sorisdale
Bousd
8072
Gallanach
Arnabost
Grishipoll
Loch Cliad
8071
Hogh Bay
Ballyhaugh
Arinagour
COLL
Totronald
8070
Arileod
Loch Eatharna
Peall Bay
Acha
Breachacha Castle
Caolas Ban
Crossapol Bay
Ardmore Point
Auliston Point
Glengorm Castle
Bloody Bay
Quinish Point
Rubha nan Gall
Mishnish
TOBERMORY
Drimnin House
Caliach Point
Quinish
Calve Island
Drimnin
8073
1481
Mornish
Dervaig
Calgary
Achnadrish
Rhemore
Calgary Bay
Loch Frisa
1458
Aros
Lettermore
Ardnacross
Killundine
Treshnish Point
Ensay
342
Carn Mor
Kengharair Farm
Sound of Mull
849
Haunn
Salen Forest
Kilninian
Aros Mains
Burg
Achleck
Fanmore
ISLAND
Rubha Mór
848
Ballygown
Salen
Pennyghael
Cairn na Burgh Beg
Treshnish Islands
Fladda
Loch Tuath
1939
Waterfall
Killiechronan
8035
Corry
Lagganulva
Kellan
Laggan Bay
Gruline
Chreag
Lunga
Geometra
1026
Ulva
Killiemor
Macquarie Mausoleum
Gruline Ho
Ulva House
Sound of Ulva
Eorsa
Loch Bà
Knock
Maisgeir
Eilean na Creiche
Loch na Keal
Bac Mór or Dutchman's Cap
1939
Bac Beag
Staffa
Fingal's Cave
Little Colonsay
Inch Kenneth
Derryguaig
Balnahard
2311
3171
1837
Ben More
8035
MULL
Erisgeir
1704
Balevulin
Uluvalt
Coladoir
1613
Ardmeanach
Aird of Kinloch
Rubha na h-Uamha
Ben Bui
2354
Lochbui
Loch Fuaran
1649
STONE CIRCLE
Loch Scridain
Rubha nan Cearc
Abbey, Cross-slabs, Chapel
333
Reidh Eilean
Pennycross
Aird Fada
Torrans
Iona
Baile Mór
Fionnphort
Aridhglas
Bun an Leoib
Ardtun
Brolass
Beinn Chreagach
Carsaig
Loch Buie
Loch Poit na h-I
849
1232
1235
Carsaig Bay
Rubha Dubh
Sound of Iona
Fidden
Bunessan
Ross of Mull
Erraid
Loch Assapol
Ardchiavaig
Scoor
Soa Island
Ardalanish
411
Ardalanish Bay
Rubha nam Bràithrean
Malcolms Point
Eilean a'Chalmain
Rubh' Ardalanish
Torrain
Rocks
Lockw

44

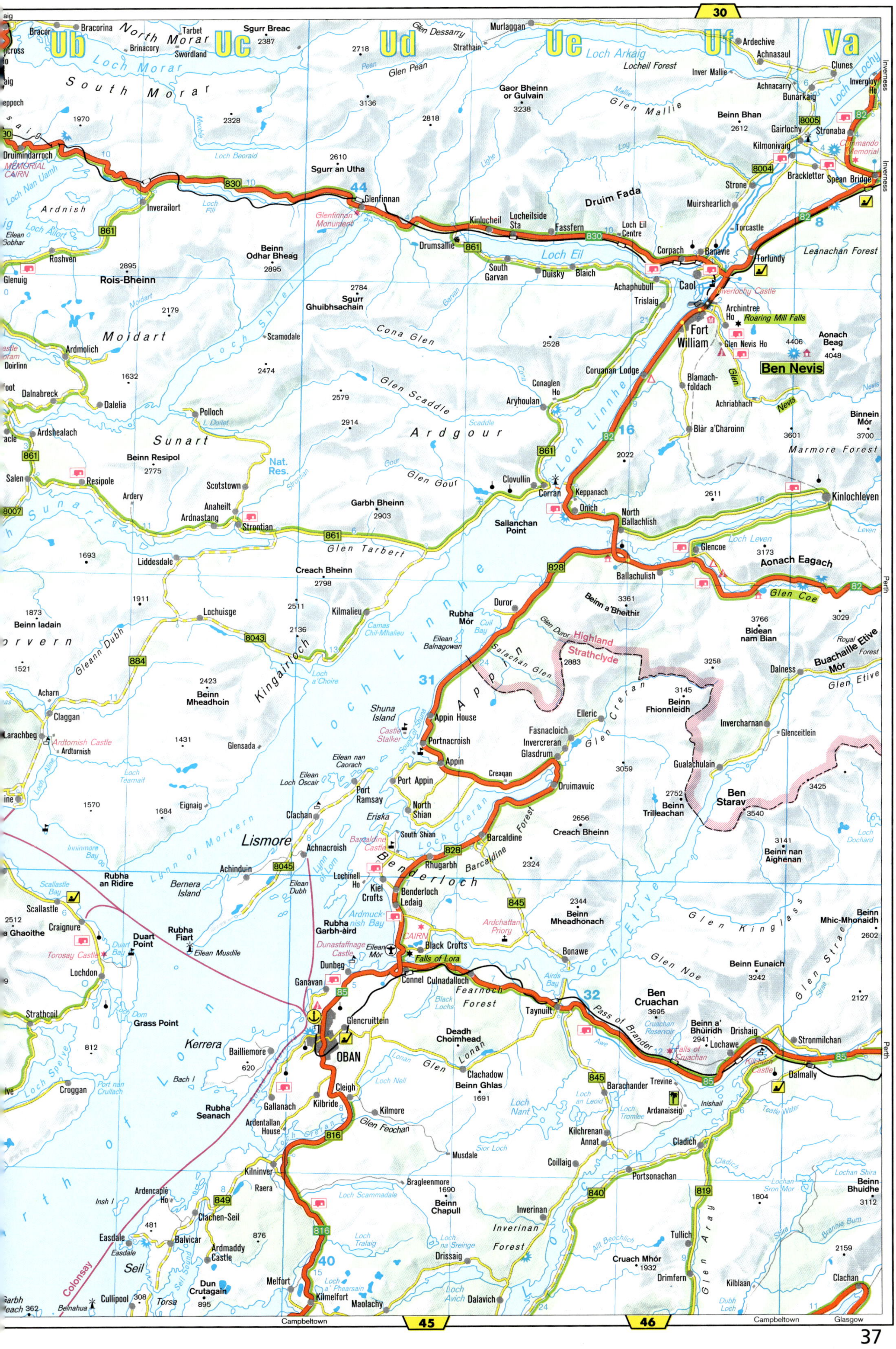
30
Ub
Uc
Ud
Ue
Uf
Va
Bracorina
North Morar
Tarbet
Sgurr Breac
2387
Brinacory
Swordland
Loch Morar
South Morar
Glen Dessarry
Murlaggan
Strathain
Glen Pean
Loch Arkaig
Locheil Forest
Ardechive
Achnasaul
Clunes
Inver Mallie
Achnacarry
Bunarkaig
Loch Lochy
Invergloy Ho
Inverness
Gaor Bheinn or Gulvain
3238
Glen Mallie
Beinn Bhan
2612
Gairlochy
Stronaba
Kilmonivaig
Commando Memorial
Spean Bridge
Brackletter
Strone
Muirshearlich
Druimindarroch
MEMORIAL CAIRN
Loch Nan Uamh
Ardnish
Inverailort
Loch Ailort
Loch Beoraid
Sgurr an Utha
2610
Glenfinnan
Glenfinnan Monument
Kinlocheil
Locheilside Sta
Fassfern
Loch Eil Centre
Druim Fada
Torcastle
Banavie
Corpach
Drumsallie
Loch Eil
South Garvan
Duisky
Blaich
Achaphubuil
Caol
Inverlochy Castle
Torlundy
Leanachan Forest
Roshven
Glenuig
Beinn Odhar Bheag
2895
Rois-Bheinn
Sgurr Ghuibhsachain
2784
Cona Glen
Trislaig
Archintree Ho
Roaring Mill Falls
Fort William
Glen Nevis Ho
Aonach Beag
4048
4406
Ben Nevis
Moidart
Loch Shiel
Scamodale
Ardmolich
Doirlinn
Dalnabreck
Dalelia
Glen Scaddle
Conaglen Ho
Aryhoulan
Corrunan Lodge
Blamach-foldach
Achriabhach
Glen Nevis
Binnein Mór
3700
3601
Marmore Forest
Polloch
Sunart
Ardshealach
Ardgour
Loch Linnhe
Blàr a'Charoinn
2022
Beinn Resipol
2775
Resipole
Salen
Nat. Res.
Scotstown
Glen Gour
Clovullin
Corran
Keppanach
Onich
2611
Kinlochleven
Ardery
Anaheilt
Ardnastang
Strontian
Garbh Bheinn
2903
Sallanchan Point
North Ballachlish
Loch Sunart
Glen Tarbert
Glencoe
Loch Leven
3173
Aonach Eagach
Liddesdale
Creach Bheinn
2798
Ballachulish
Glen Coe
Perth
Lochuisge
Kilmalieu
Duror
Rubha Mór
Cuil Bay
Beinn a'Bheithir
3361
Beinn Iadain
Morvern
Kingairloch
Eilean Balnagowan
Glen Duror
Highland
Strathclyde
2883
3766
Bidean nam Bian
3029
Royal Forest
Buachaille Etive Mór
Gleann Dubh
Salachan Glen
Appin
3258
Dalness
Glen Etive
Acharn
Beinn Mheadhoin
2423
31
Loch a'Choire
3145
Beinn Fhionnleidh
Glen Creran
Claggan
Shuna Island
Castle Stalker
Appin House
Elleric
Inverchannan
Glenceitlein
Larachbeg
Ardtornish Castle
Ardtornish
Glensanda
Portnacroish
Fasnacloich
Invercreran
Glasdrum
Creagan
Druimavuic
Gualachulain
Eilean nan Caorach
Eilean Loch Oscair
Port Appin
Port Ramsay
North Shian
Eriska
South Shian
Ben Starav
3540
3425
Eignaig
Clachan
Lismore
Achnacroish
Barcaldine Castle
Loch Creran
Barcaldine
Creach Bheinn
2656
Beinn Trilleachan
2752
Beinn nan Aighenan
3141
Loch Dochard
Lynn of Morvern
Achinduin
Bernera Island
Lynn of Lorn
Eilean Dubh
Lochnell Ho
Rhugarbh
Benderloch
Barcaldine Forest
2324
Kiel Crofts
Ledaig
Rubha an Ridire
Scallastle Bay
Scallastle
Craignure
Duart Point
Duart Bay
Torosay Castle
Rubha Fiart
Eilean Musdile
Rubha Garbh-àird
Ardmucknish Bay
CAIRN
Ardchattan Priory
Beinn Mheadhonach
2344
Glen Kinglass
Beinn Mhic-Mhonaidh
2602
Dunstaffnage Castle
Eilean Mór
Black Crofts
Falls of Lora
Connel
Bonawe
Loch Etive
Glen Noe
Beinn Eunaich
3242
Glen Strae
Lochdon
Dunbeg
Ganavan
Culnadalloch
Fearnoch Forest
Black Lochs
Taynuilt
Airds Bay
32
Ben Cruachan
3695
Pass of Brander
Cruachan Reservoir
Falls of Cruachan
Beinn a' Bhuiridh
2941
Drishaig
Lochawe
Kilchurn Castle
Stronmilchan
Dalmally
Strathcoil
Grass Point
Glencruittein
Deadh Choimhead
Kerrera
Bailliemore
OBAN
Glen Lonan
Clachadow
Beinn Ghlas
1691
Loch Nell
Cleigh
Gallanach
Kilbride
Kilmore
Glen Feochan
Loch Spelve
Port nan Crullach
Croggan
Rubha Seanach
Ardentallan House
Barachander
Trevine
Inishail
Ardanaiseig
Loch Nant
Loch Tromlee
Kilchrenan
Annat
Cladich
Coillaig
Portsonachan
Musdale
Sior Loch
Firth of Lorn
Kilninver
Raera
Bragleenmore
1690
Beinn Chapull
Loch Scammadale
Ardencaple Ho
Inverinan
Inverinan Forest
Loch Awe
Lochan Shira
Beinn Bhuidhe
3112
Clachan-Seil
Easdale
Balvicar
Ardmaddy Castle
Seil
Dun Crutagain
Torsa
Cullipool
Belnahua
Melfort
Kilmelfort
Maolachy
Loch Avich
Dalavich
Drissaig
Cruach Mhór
1932
Drimfern
Tullich
Glen Aray
Kilblaan
Clachan
Colonsay
Campbeltown
Glasgow
45
46

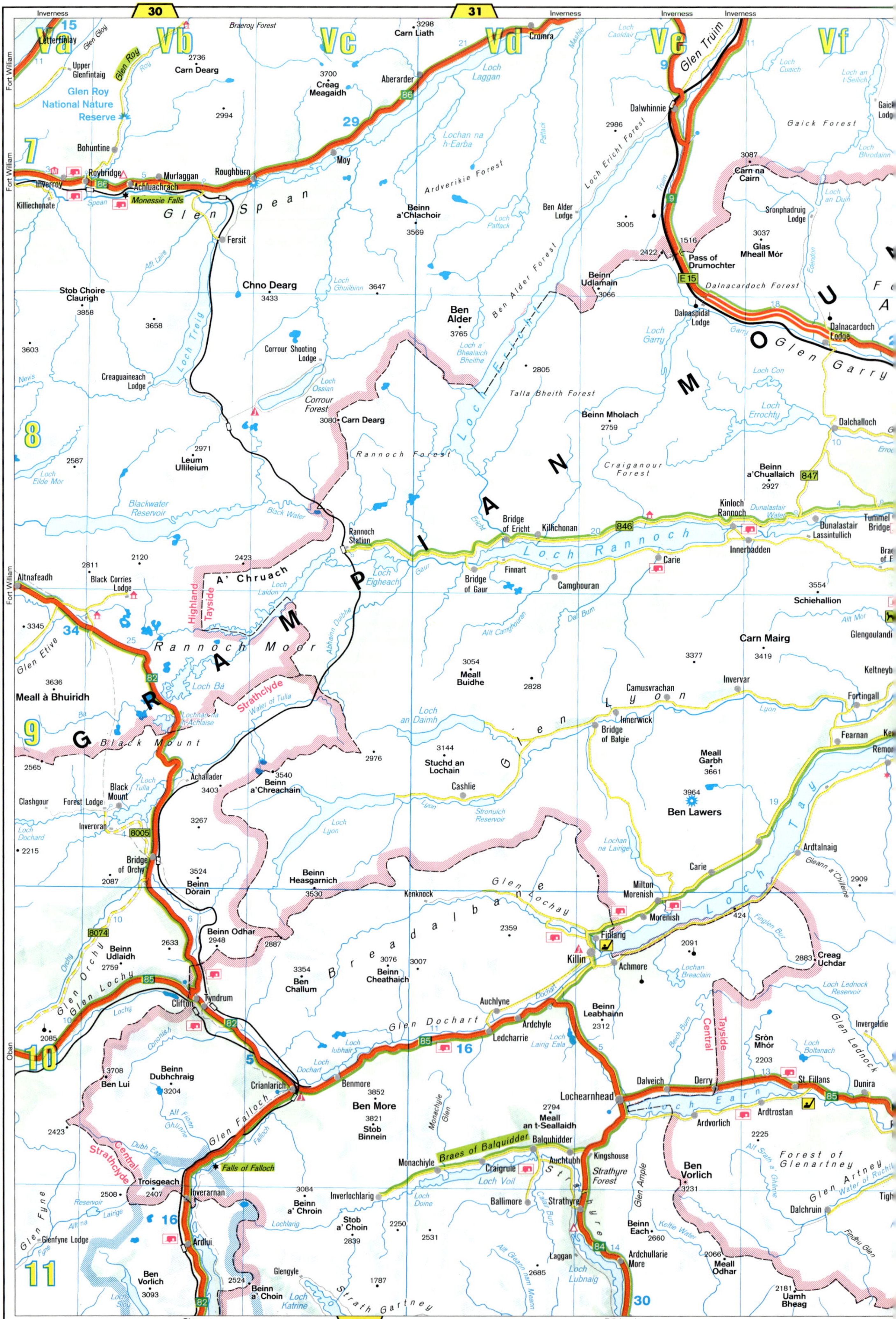

30
31
46
Inverness
Fort William
Oban
Glasgow
Edinburgh
Va
Vb
Vc
Vd
Ve
Vf
7
8
9
10
11
Letterfinlay
Glen Gloy
Upper Glenfintaig
Glen Roy
Glen Roy National Nature Reserve
Braeroy Forest
2736
Carn Dearg
2994
3298
Carn Liath
3700
Creag Meagaidh
Aberarder
Cromra
Loch Laggan
Loch Caoldair
Glen Truim
Loch Cuaich
Loch an t-Seilich
Dalwhinnie
2986
Gaick Forest
Bohuntine
Roybridge
Inverroy
Murlaggan
Achluachrach
Monessie Falls
Roughburn
Moy
Killiechonate
Spean
Glen Spean
Fersit
Lochan na h-Earba
Ardverikie Forest
Beinn a'Chlachoir
3569
Loch Pattack
Ben Alder Lodge
Loch Ericht Forest
3005
3087
Carn na Cairn
Sronphadruig Lodge
Loch an Duin
3037
Glas Mheall Mór
2422
1516
Pass of Drumochter
Dalnacardoch Forest
E15
Beinn Udlamain
3066
Ben Alder Forest
Stob Choire Claurigh
3858
3658
3603
Chno Dearg
3433
Loch Ghuilbinn
3647
Ben Alder
3765
Loch a' Bhealaich Bheithe
Loch Ericht
Dalnaspidal Lodge
Loch Garry
Dalnacardoch Lodge
Glen Garry
Nevis
Loch Treig
Corrour Shooting Lodge
Creaguaineach Lodge
Loch Ossian
Corrour Forest
2805
Talla Bheith Forest
Loch Con
Loch Errochty
Beinn Mholach
2759
Dalchalloch
3080
Carn Dearg
2971
Leum Ullileium
2587
Loch Eilde Mór
Rannoch Forest
Craiganour Forest
Beinn a'Chuallaich
2927
847
Blackwater Reservoir
Black Water
Rannoch Station
Bridge of Ericht
Killichonan
846
Loch Rannoch
Kinloch Rannoch
Dunalastair Water
Dunalastair
Lassintullich
Tummel Bridge
Innerhadden
Carie
Finnart
Camghouran
Bridge of Gaur
Gaur
Loch Eigheach
Loch Laidon
2811
2120
2423
Altnafeadh
Black Corries Lodge
A' Chruach
Highland
Tayside
3554
Schiehallion
Glengoulandie
3345
34
Glen Etive
Rannoch Moor
Abhainn Duibhe
Dall Burn
Allt Camghouran
3054
Meall Buidhe
2828
3377
Carn Mairg
3419
Keltneyburn
3636
Meall à Bhuiridh
Loch Bà
Strathclyde
Water of Tulla
Lochan na h-Achlaise
Camusvrachan
Invervar
Fortingall
Glen Lyon
Loch an Daimh
Innerwick
Bridge of Balgie
Black Mount
G R A M P I A N
M O U N
2565
2976
3144
Stuchd an Lochain
Cashlie
Meall Garbh
3661
Fearnan
3964
Ben Lawers
Achallader
3540
Beinn a'Chreachain
Clashgour
Forest Lodge
Black Mount
Loch Tulla
3403
Loch Lyon
Stronuich Reservoir
Lyon
19
Loch Dochard
Inveroran
8005
2215
3267
Bridge of Orchy
2087
3524
Beinn Dorain
Beinn Heasgarnich
3530
Kenknock
Glen Lochay
Lochan na Lairige
Milton Morenish
Carie
Ardtalnaig
2909
Gleann a'Chilleine
8074
Beinn Udlaidh
2759
2633
Beinn Odhar
2948
2887
Breadalbane
2359
Morenish
Finlarig
424
Loch Tay
Finglen Burn
Glen Orchy
Glen Lochy
3354
Ben Challum
3076
Beinn Cheathaich
3007
Killin
Achmore
2091
Lochan Breaclain
2883
Creag Uchdar
Loch Lednock Reservoir
85
Tyndrum
Clifton
82
Auchlyne
Dochart
Beinn Leabhainn
2312
Glen Dochart
Ardchyle
Ledcharrie
Loch Lairig Eala
Loch Iubhair
16
Sròn Mhór
2203
Loch Boltanach
Invergeldie
Glen Lednock
2085
3708
Ben Lui
Beinn Dubhchraig
3204
Crianlarich
Loch Dochart
Benmore
3852
Ben More
3821
Stob Binnein
Monachyle Glen
2794
Meall an t-Seallaidh
Lochearnhead
Dalveich
Derry
Loch Earn
St. Fillans
Dunira
Ardtrostan
Ardvorlich
Central
Tayside
2423
Glen Falloch
Falloch
Dubh Eas
Allt Fionn Ghlinne
Braes of Balquidder
Balquhidder
Auchtubh
Kingshouse
Strathyre Forest
2225
Forest of Glenartney
Central
Strathclyde
Troisgeach
2407
2508
Falls of Falloch
Inverarnan
3084
Beinn a' Chroin
Inverlochlarig
Monachyle
Craigruie
Loch Voil
Loch Doine
Ballimore
Strathyre
Glen Ample
Ben Vorlich
3231
Glen Artney
Water of Ruchill
Dalchruin
Glen Fyne
Reservoir
Glenfyne Lodge
Ardlui
16
Lochlarig
Stob a' Choin
2839
2250
2531
Allt Gleann nam Meann
Laggan
Beinn Each
2660
Keltie Water
Ardchullarie More
2066
Meall Odhar
Findhu Glen
Ben Vorlich
3093
Glengyle
2524
Beinn a' Choin
Loch Katrine
1787
Strath Gartney
Loch Lubnaig
Loch Sloy
84
30
2181
Uamh Bheag

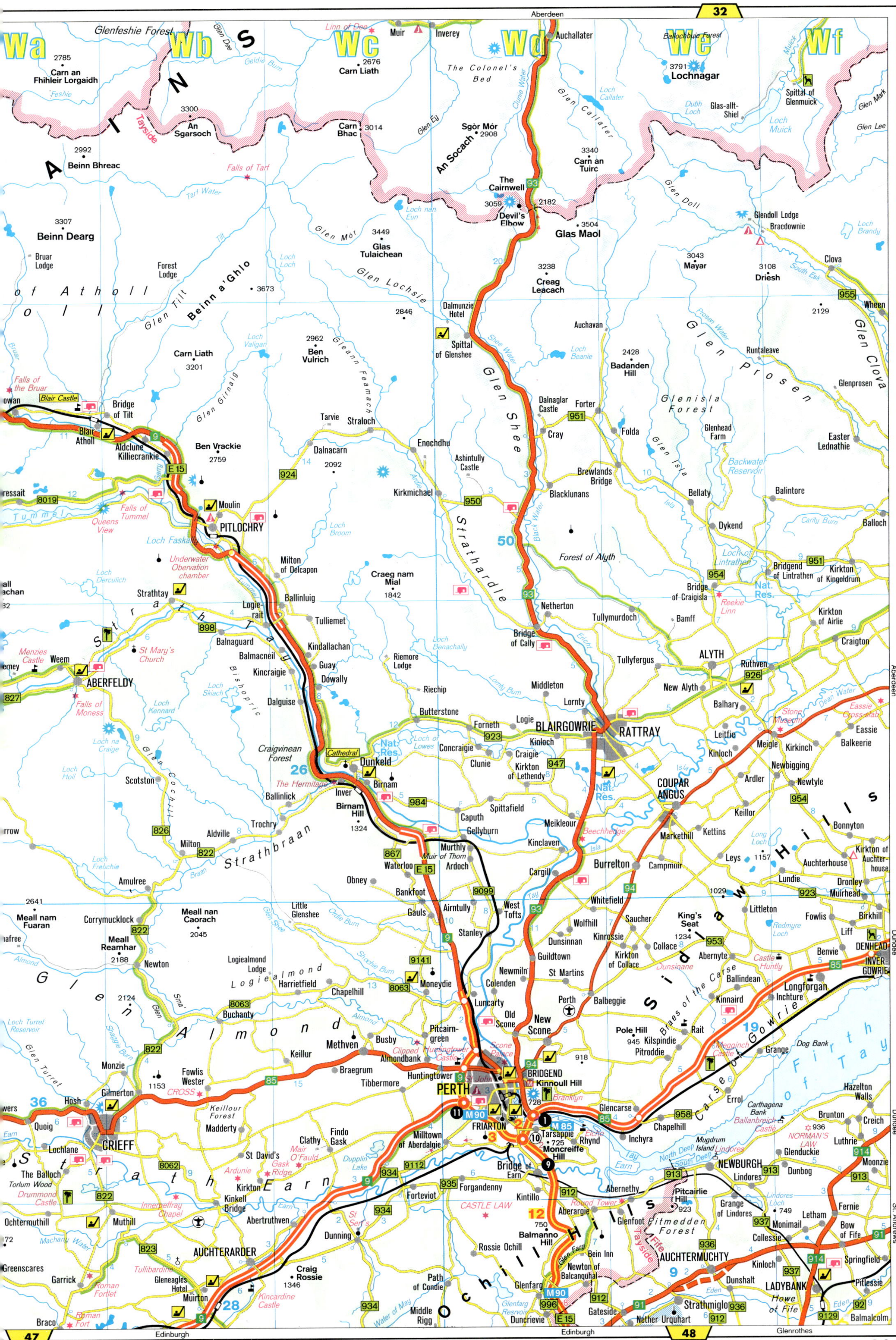
Aberdeen
32
Wa
Wb
Wc
Wd
We
Wf
Glenfeshie Forest
Carn an Fhihleir Lorgaidh
Carn Liath
Inverey
Auchallater
Lochnagar
The Colonel's Bed
Spittal of Glenmuick
An Sgarsoch
Carn Bhac
Sgòr Mór
An Socach
Carn an Tuirc
Beinn Bhreac
Falls of Tarf
The Cairnwell
Devil's Elbow
Glas Maol
Glendoll Lodge
Beinn Dearg
Glas Tulaichean
Mayar
Driesh
Clova
Bruar Lodge
Forest Lodge
Beinn a'Ghlo
Creag Leacach
Glen Lochsie
Dalmunzie Hotel
Wheen
Carn Liath
Ben Vulrich
Spittal of Glenshee
Auchavan
Badanden Hill
Runtaleave
Glen Prosen
Glen Clova
Glenprosen
Falls of the Bruar
Blair Castle
Bridge of Tilt
Tarvie
Straloch
Dalnaglar Castle
Forter
Glen Shee
Glenisla Forest
Blair Atholl
Aldclune
Killiecrankie
Ben Vrackie
Dalnacarn
Enochdhu
Cray
Folda
Glenhead Farm
Easter Lednathie
Ashintully Castle
Brewlands Bridge
Backwater Reservoir
Moulin
Kirkmichael
Blacklunans
Bellaty
Balintore
Falls of Tummel
Queens View
PITLOCHRY
Loch Faskally
Strathardle
Dykend
Balloch
Underwater Observation chamber
Milton of Delcapon
Craeg nam Mial
Forest of Alyth
Bridgend of Lintrathen
Kirkton of Kingoldrum
Strathtay
Logierait
Ballinluig
Netherton
Bridge of Craigisla
Reekie Linn
Bamff
Kirkton of Airlie
Tulliemet
Tullymurdoch
Menzies Castle
Weem
Balnaguard
Kindallachan
Balmacneil
St Mary's Church
Riemore Lodge
Bridge of Cally
Craigton
ABERFELDY
Kincraigie
Guay
Dowally
Tullyfergus
ALYTH
Ruthven
New Alyth
Falls of Moness
Dalguise
Riechip
Middleton
Lornty
Balhary
Butterstone
Forneth
Logie
BLAIRGOWRIE
RATTRAY
Stone Museum
Eassie Cross slab
Eassie
Craigvinean Forest
Cathedral
Dunkeld
Concraigie
Kinloch
Craigie
Leitfie
Meigle
Kirkinch
Balkeerie
Scotston
The Hermitage
Birnam
Clunie
Kirkton of Lethendy
Kinloch
Newbigging
Ardler
COUPAR ANGUS
Newtyle
Ballinlick
Inver
Birnam Hill
Spittaffield
Keillor
Bonnyton
Trochry
Caputh
Meikleour
Aldville
Gellyburn
Kettins
Milton
Murthly
Kinclaven
Beechhedge
Markethill
Strathbraan
Muir of Thorn
Ardoch
Burrelton
Campmuir
Leys
Kirkton of Auchterhouse
Auchterhouse
Amulree
Waterloo
Cargill
Obney
Lundie
Dronley
Bankfoot
Muirhead
Meall nan Fuaran
Corrymucklock
Meall nan Caorach
Little Glenshee
Gauls
Airntully
West Tofts
Whitefield
Littleton
Fowlis
Birkhill
Wolfhill
Saucher
King's Seat
Meall Reamhar
Stanley
Dunsinnan
Kinrossie
Collace
Liff
DENHEAD
Abernyte
Newton
Logiealmond Lodge
Guildtown
Kirkton of Collace
Dunsinane
Castle Huntly
Benvie
INVERGOWRIE
Harrietfield
Newmiln
St Martins
Ballindean
Longforgan
Moneydie
Chapelhill
Colenden
Perth
Inchture
Kinnaird
Buchanty
Luncarty
Balbeggie
Old Scone
New Scone
Pitcairngreen
Pole Hill
Kilspindie
Rait
Braes of the Carse
Sidlaw Hills
Almond
Busby
Methven
Clipped Huntingtower
Scone Palace
Pitroddie
Megginch Castle
Grange
Dog Bank
Firth of Tay
Keillur
Almondbank
Huntingtower Castle
Monzie
Fowlis Wester
Braegrum
Tibbermore
BRIDGEND
Kinnoull Hill
Hazelton Walls
Gilmerton
CROSS
PERTH
Branklyn
Errol
Carse of Gowrie
Keillour Forest
Carthagena Bank
Ballanbreich Castle
Hosh
Quoig
Madderty
Glencarse
Chapelhill
Brunton
Creich
CRIEFF
Clathy
Findo Gask
Milltown of Aberdalgie
FRIARTON
Tarsappie
Moncreiffe Hill
Rhynd
Elcho
Inchyra
Mugdrum Island
NORMAN'S LAW
Luthrie
Lochlane
St David's
Mair O'Fauld
Gask Ridge
Dupplin Lake
Bridge of Earn
North Deep
South Deep
Lindores
Glenduckie
NEWBURGH
Moonzie
The Balloch
Torlum Wood
Drummond Castle
Ardunie
Kirkton
Strathearn
Forteviot
Forgandenny
Kintillo
Abernethy
Pitcairlie Hill
Dunbog
Lindores Loch
Innerpeffray Chapel
Kinkell Bridge
Abertruthven
CASTLE LAW
Aberargie
Round Tower
Glenfoot
Pitmedden Forest
Grange of Lindores
Letham
Fernie
Ochtermuthill
Muthill
St Serf's
Dunning
Balmanno Hill
Monimail
Collessie
Bow of Fife
Machany Water
AUCHTERARDER
Rossie Ochill
Ochill Hills
Bein Inn
Glen Farg
Newton of Balcanquhal
AUCHTERMUCHTY
Kinloch
Springfield
Greenscares
Tullibardine
Gleneagles Hotel
Craig Rossie
Kincardine Castle
Path of Condie
Glenfarg
Glenfarg Reservoir
Dunshalt
LADYBANK
Pitlessie
Garrick
Roman Fortlet
Muirton
Middle Rigg
Gateside
Strathmiglo
Howe of Fife
Braco
Roman Fort
Duncrievie
Nether Urquhart
Balmalcolm
47
Edinburgh
Edinburgh
48
Glenrothes
Dundee
St. Andrews
Tayside
Fife

32
33

Xa
Xb
Xc
Xd
Xe
7
8
9
10
11
Aberdeen
Mount Keen
3080
Mudlee Bracks
2259
Mount Battock
2554
Hill of Edendocher
1944
Bridge of Dye
Kerloch
1754
Hill of Trusta
1052
Kirktown of Fetteresso
Garron Point
STONEHAVEN
Fetteresso Forest
Carmont
Glen Dye
Goyle Hill
1526
Mains of Dellavaird
Glenfarquhar Lodge
Drumlithie
Glen Lee
Auchronie
Grampian
Tayside
Cairn Mount
1488
Drumtochty Forest
Glenbervie
Fiddes
Barras
Bruxie Hill
711
Crawton
Tarfside
Cairncross
Millden Lodge
Loch Lee
Inchgrundle
Glen Esk
1785
Clatterin Brig
Drumtochty Castle
Glensaugh
Auchenblae
Pitforthie
Roadside of Catterline
Catterline
Todhead Point
Fasque House
Fasque
Fordoun
Roadside of Kinneff
White Hill
2424
West Knock
2273
1986
Auchmull
Thainston
Arbuthnott House
Allardice Castle
Arbuthnott
Kinneff
Little John's Haven
Ben Tirran
2941
Hill of Wirren
2224
2544
Water of Saughs
Fettercairn
Howe of the Mearns
INVERBERVIE
Bervie Bay
Dalbog
The Burn
Meikle Strath
Mains of Thornton
LAURENCEKIRK
Tulloch
Gourdon
Doolie Ness
Hunthill Lodge
Gannochy
Edzell Castle
Sauchieburn
Luthermuir
Benholm
Rottal
Dog Hillock
2410
Balfield
Edzell
910
Johnshaven
Peat Hill
1578
1900
Bridgend
Dunlappie
Tillyarblet
WHITE CATERTHUN FORT
BROWN CATERTHUN FORT
Inchbare
Ecclesgreig
Marykirk
Craigo
Lochside
St Cyrus
Milton Ness
Pert
Kirkton of Menmuir
Tigerton
Newton-mill
Logie Pert
Logie
Glenmoy
Auchnacree
Redheugh
Belliehill
Muirton of Ballochy
Hillside
Horniehaugh
Glenquiech
Falls of Drumly Harry
Mains of Balhall
South Esk
Little Brechin
Trinity
Kirkhill
Ogil
Fern
West Muir
BRECHIN
Dun
Dykehead
Newmill of Inshewan
Noranside
Careston
Strathmore
Maison Dieu Chapel
Round Tower
Bridge of Dun
MONTROSE
Montrose Basin
Pearsie
Memus
Tannadice
Scurdie Ness
Cortachy
Murthill
Netherton
Middle Drums
Barnhead
Maryton
Ferryden
Inverquharity
Shielhill
Oathlaw
Finavon
Cross Stones
Mains of Melgund
Long Craig
Kinnordy
Northmuir
Finavon Castle
Aberlemno
Farnell
Bonnyton
Kirkton of Craig
Boddin Point
Barrie's House
Westerton
503
KIRRIEMUIR
Carse Gray
Westmuir
Mosside
Lunanhead
Restenneth Priory
Balgavies
Glasterlaw
Bolshan
Braehead
Lunan
Mains of Ballindarg
Padanaram
Reswallie
Nat. Res.
Guthrie
Kinnell
Redcastle
Lunan Bay
Drumgley
St Orland's Stone
FORFAR
Burnside
Letham
Pitmuies
Friockheim
Inverkeilor
Lang Craig
Ethie Mains
Leys of Cossans
Glamis Castle
Kingsmuir
Dunnichen
Chapelton
Ethie Castle
Glamis
Douglastown
Lownie Moor
Craichie
Idvies
Leysmill
Cauldcots
Kirkton
Thornton
822
Tulloes
Drunkendub
Charleston
Foffarty
Inverarity
Whigstreet
Mosston
Colliston
Auchmithie
Gateside
Kirkbuddo
Greystone
Redford
Marywell
Milton
Denhead of Arbirlot
St Vigeans
Carlingheugh Bay
Nether Handwick
Gallowfauld
Hayhillock
Crombie
Carmyllie
ARBROATH
Arbirlot
Abbey
Bonnington
Smiddy
Crombie Reservoir
Coldstream
1492
Balgray
Sweet Burn
Monikie
Kirkton of Monikie
Affleck Castle
Monikie Reservoir
Craigton
Salmond's Muir
TEALING DOVECOT
Wellbank
Upper Victoria
Muirdrum
Leoch
Bucklerheads
Newbigging
Bridgefoot
Burnside of Duntrune
Kellas
Drumsturdy
CARLUNGIE
Barry
Claypotts Castle
DUNDEE
Mains of Ardestie
CARNOUSTIE
DOWNFIELD
DOUGLAS AND ANGUS
Barry Links
BROUGHTY FERRY
MONIFIETH
Dudhope Castle
Camperdown Park
Mills Observatory
LOCHEE
INVERGOWRIE
Broughty Castle
Buddon Ness
Firth of Tay
TAYPORT
Tentsmuir Point
Abertay
Dundee
Tay Road Bridge
Tay Bridge
NEWPORT-ON-TAY
NORTH SEA
Tentsmuir
Wormit
Forest
Bottomcraig
Balmerino
Gauldry
Lucklawhill
624
Leuchars
Earlshall
Kilmany
Balmullo
Norman Church
Eden Mouth
Rathillet
Logie
Leuchars
Out Head
Nat. Res.
St Andrews Bay
Dairsie or Osnaburgh
Kincaple
Castle
SAINT ANDREWS
Eden
Strathkinness
Botanic Gardens
Cathedral
Kinkell Ness
CUPAR
Buddo Ness
Blebocraigs
Craigtoun
Boarhills
Kemback
Babbet Ness
Prior Muir
Pitscottie
716
Denhead
Kingsbarns
Cambo Ness
Bridgend
Cameron Burn
Kenly Burn
Hill of Tarvit
Cameron Reservoir
Ceres
Baldinnie
Stravithie
Carr Brigs
Balcomie
Fife Ness
Scotstarvit Tower
Craigrothie
Peat Inn
Kinaldy Burn
Kippo Burn
Clatto Reservoir
New Gilston
Backmuir of New Gilston
Lathones
Lochty
CRAIL
Perth
Edinburgh

48

tains of Skye. The 13th-century Duart Castle, the home of the Mcleans, dominates the Sound of Mull. It was fully restored in 1912 and is open to the public. The rooms are furnished with relics of the clan. Torosay Castle is really a 19th-century mansion, and has Victorian furniture. The gardens are in the Italian style.

Oban

Oban is the most popular resort in the West Highlands, and the port for the Hebrides. It is surrounded by beautiful countryside, including Loch Etive. The Cruachan Dam hydro-electric project in the Argyll Hills is worth visiting. There are two castles nearby, the ruined Dunmollie Castle, on a headland outside the bay and Dunstaffnage Castle, three miles to the north. There are magnificent views of the hills of Argyll from the castle. MacCaig's Folly, on the clifftop, was built by a 19th-century philanthropist to give work to local unemployed fishermen, but it is only half-finished.

Information
Arbroath Tourist Information Centre
Marketgate
Arbroath
Tel: (0241)72609

Perth Tourist Association
The Round House
Marshall Place, Perth
Perthshire, PH2 8NS
Tel: (0738)38353

Events
The Pitlochry Festival centres mainly around events staged at the Theatre in the Hills, from May to October. Perth Festival of the Arts is held in the last half of May and lasts for two weeks. Details from Perth Tourist Association.

Perth

"The Fair City", once Scotland's capital, is a sea port on Tayside, the river being navigable to this point. It has always been famous for curing and smoking the salmon found in the river. The river occasionally yields up the rare white river pearls. The Tay floods regularly, which is why the lovely parklands outside the city are known as the Inches (islands). Perth is a commercial centre especially for the liquor trade, since not only whisky distilleries but Sandeman's Port have made it their headquarters. The house of the Fair Maid of Perth, immortalised in the story by Sir Walter Scott, which was made into an opera, can be visited. The belfry of St. John's Church contains eight of the oldest church bells in Britain. The city has some fascinating alleyways called vennels, down which two of the city's most famous public houses lie. These are the Salutation, at which Bonnie Prince Charlie once lodged and the Royal George, still used as a hotel, which is famous for its substantial breakfasts.

Pitlochry

This little town is taken to be the centre of Scotland, though the true geographical centre lies a few miles away. It is a popular holiday resort with a Festival Theatre, two whisky distilleries and a tweed mill. It is surrounded by magnificent countryside. The Pitlochry Dam contains a fish ladder where visitors can watch the salmon leaping upstream to spawn. Just north of Pitlochry, on the A9, is Killiecrankie, the site of one of Scotland's most famous battles. This is where Graham of Claverhouse, known as "Bonnie Dundee" defeated King William of Orange, whose forces were greatly superior, while fighting the cause of the exiled King James II of England, the Old Pretender. The story is told in the Scottish song "Bonnie Dundee". The National Trust for Scotland has a Visitors' Centre at Killiecrankie.

St. Andrews

This "Little City Worn and Grey" as the poet Andrew Lang (1844-1912) described it was the first bishopric in Scotland. It stands on a wide bay and has a bracing climate, exposed as it is to the winds of the North Sea. St. Andrews is world-famous for its golf course, the Royal and Ancient, which dates from the late 14th century, but which is only one of five at St. Andrews. The manufacture of golf balls and other golfing equipment is a local industry. St. Andrews' other claim to fame is the university, the oldest in Scotland, founded in 1411. The two original colleges were in the town centre, but the 15th-century college of St. Leonard's has now been turned into a girls' school. The city has suffered considerably from the religious wars which plagued the Scots. The cathedral is a ruin, as are the town walls, due to the battles between Catholics and Protestants. In 1547, Cardinal-bishop Beaton was murdered and John Knox, the Protestant reformer, came to show his solidarity with the murderers. French galleys stormed the city walls and transported Knox to France where he spent 18 months in the prison ships.

Staffa

This strangely-shaped black block of basalt, just off the Isle of Mull, can be visited though it is uninhabited. It consists of columns stacked one on another, just like the Giant's Causeway which faces it across the Irish Sea. They are, of course, part of the same geological formation. The very name Staffa means "island of staves", due to the staveshape of the columns. The island is uninhabited, but can be visited. It was unknown until in 1772, the famous botanist Sir Joseph Banks ran aground on it while on a journey to Iceland. It was visited by several literary figures in the 19th century, including John Keats, who wrote of it, "For solemnity and grandeur it surpasses the finest cathedral". Of course, it is most famous as the inspiration for Mendelssohn's *Hebrides Concerto* which includes the passage *Fingal's Cave.* Mendelssohn also referred to the cathedral-like quality of the Cave, which is known as the Musical Cave, for the strange, eerie sound made by the wind blowing through the basalt columns.

St. Andrews' ruined cathedral (above).

St. Andrews, a view over the bay (left).

Between Islay and Edinburgh

This central part of Scotland, often ignored by tourists, has all the romantic ingredients of the Scottish landscape, and is easily accessible from Scotland's great cities. The scenery is as lovely as any in the Highlands.

Ardrossan

This port on the Argyll coast was conceived by Hugh Montgomerie, 12th Earl of Eglinton (1739-1819). The harbour was laid out in 1806 to a design by Peter Nicholson of Glasgow. The ruined 12th-century Ardrossan Castle, overlooking the sandy beaches south of the port, stands on the hillside above the town. From here there are good views of Ailsa Craig, the island which was a refuge for Catholics during the Reformation and which is now a bird sanctuary.

Arran, Isle of

The dramatic peaks of this island are visible from many parts of the mainland. It is very popular with Scottish holidaymakers. Brodick Castle is one of the few in this part of Scotland not to have been attacked by Cromwell, and remains the seat of the Hamiltons. It has an elegant interior and remarkably fine grounds. Further south on the island there are the ruins of Kildonan Castle, from which there is a good view of Ailsa Craig. The Standing Stones of Tormore are the remains of an impressive prehistoric site on Machrie Moor.

Bannockburn

Just south of Stirling is the site of the historic Battle of Bannockburn, fought in 1314. The Scottish footsoldiers, led by Robert the Bruce, routed the English knights in armour who rode powerful warhorses. It was the first time in history that this had happened. Although the actual site of the battleground has long since disappeared beneath urban development, the Bannockburn Heritage Centre is nearby, which contains a Kingdom of the Scots exhibition.

Bute

Just south of Cowall and separated from it by the narrow channel known as the Kyles of Bute, the Isle of Bute is a popular destination for Glaswegians. The main town is Rothesay, a resort dominated by its ruined castle, partly restored in the 19th century, which has a unique circular design.
The Bute Museum, opposite the castle, has displays on the island's natural history. St. Ninian's Bay, also known as Cockle Shore from the profusion of shells, has a wide sandy beach. .

Culzean (pronounced "Kú-lane") Castle

This is Scotland's most popular castle with visitors because it is situated within a 560 -acre country park. It is the ancestral home of the Kennedy family, and was designed by Robert Adam in 1777. It was a favourite haunt of General Eisenhower who used to stay here on his frequent trips to Scotland. The curving turrets overlook the Atlantic and offer spectacular views. The gardens include a walled garden, orangery, aviary and camellia house. The farm buildings are now used for lectures. There are conducted nature walks.

Cowall

The Cowall Peninsula looks very much like an island since there is only one road to it, along the eastern shore of Loch Fyne (famous for its kippers). It is actually most accessible by sea. Cowall has suffered from the incessant feuding between the two clans that ruled the peninsula, the Lamonts and the Campbells. Both the Campbell Castle and Carrick Castle, home of the Lamonts, are in ruins. Dunoon, the largest town, is a popular holiday resort for Glaswegians. Puck's Glen in central Cowal is a famous beauty spot of streams and waterfalls. The Younger Botanic Garden has a magnificent collection of trees and shrubs, including California redwoods which are still mere saplings at 100 years old, and what is supposed to be the finest rhododendron collection in the world. The Forestry Commission has an arboretum on Cowall on

Floors Castle (above).

Dawyck, Botanical Gardens in the Borders (top right).

Castle Sween overlooking the Loch on the West Coast of Kintyre (middle right).

Ardrishaig, the Crinan Canal (bottom right).

The Old Bridge over the Forth at Stirling (opposite above).

Looking across the harbour at Tarkert (opposite below).

the shores of Holy Loch. This Loch is used for testing nuclear submarines.

Edinburgh
See "Historic Cities"

Glasgow
See "Historic Cities"

Irvine
This town on the Argyll Coast is the beginning of the area known as the Burns Country. The poet was sent here in 1781 to learn linen-dressing. Seagate Castle, where Mary Queen of Scots stayed on her visit to the town in 1563, is now in ruins.

Islay
Islay has some of the finest Celtic Christian remains in Britain. Kildalton Cross, which stands a few miles south of the ferry terminal at Port Ellen, dates from the 9th century. The island has many dairy farms and eight whisky distilleries, supporting a population of only 4,000.

Jura
This rugged island has a population of only about 200. It is the ideal destination for the true nature-lover and rock-climber. The west coast, exposed to the Atlantic is wild but the eastern coast is sheltered and there are many gardens.

Falkirk and the Roman Wall
This typical Scottish industrial city contains sections of the Antonine Wall, also known as Graham's Dyke, built by the Romans in 140 A.D. The Falkirk Museum traces its line. The wall runs from the Clyde to Bo'ness on the Forth, to link the line of forts built by Agricola in 80 A.D. The best preserved forts on the line are at Kirkintilloch and Rough Castle. Sections of the wall can be seen in the grounds of Callendar House, and near Bearsden.

Lanark
This little town has some major attractions. The 12th century church of St. Kentigern still stands, the only relic of the castle built by David I. The parish church has a statue of the Scottish hero, Sir William Wallace, over the porch. To the south is New Lanark, the model town built by the great socialist reformer, Robert Owen. Further south are the Cora Linn Falls and the ruins of Cora Castle.

Linlithgow
The chief town of West Lothian is dominated by Linlithgow Palace, once the home of Scottish royalty, which burned down accidentally in 1746, though large parts have survived. There is a magnificent Renaissance fountain in the Great Quadrangle. The adjoining St. Michael's Church is the largest pre-Reformation church in Scotland, though the spire is modern and rather controversial. The Binns is a historic house built by Sir Tam Dalyell (pronounced "Dée-ell") whose descendant sits as a Labour M. P. at Westminster. The house is now owned by the National Trust for Scotland.

Saltcoats
This village is named after the saltworks established here in the reign of King James V. It is home to the North Ayrshire Museum which contains relics of everyday life in this part of Scotland. When the tide is low, 26 fossilised tree-trunks are revealed in the harbour.

Stirling
"The Gateway to the Highlands" controlled the north from the castle on the top of Stirling Hill. Castle Rock is in the most natural place for a fortification, and there has been one on this site for well over 1,000 years. The present castle was begun in the 13th century and completed in the 17th. James II was born here in 1430. James IV added towers to the castle, and James V was responsible for the magnificent Renaissance interior. The castle museum is devoted to the history of the Argyll and Sutherland Highlanders and contains many portraits of the Scottish kings. The view from the ramparts over the cliff is spectacular. The road leading up to the castle passes the Church of the Holy Rood where King James VI was crowned, at the age of 13 months. Argyll's Lodging is a magnificent mansion once owned by the Earl of Argyll. High on Abbey Craig, north-east of the town and visible for miles around, is the Wallace Monument, a large tower, looking as if it had fallen off a French château. It was erected in the 1860s as a tribute to Sir William Wallace who defeated the superior forces of the English at the Battle of Stirling Bridge in 1297. The busts of other famous Scotsmen are inside in the Hall of Fame.

Information

The Mid Argyll, Kintyre and Islay Tourist Board
The Pier
Campbelltown
Argyll
PA28 6EF
Tel: (0586) 52056

The Dunoon and Cowal Tourist Information Centre
7 Alexandra Parade,
Dunoon
Argyll
PA23 7HL

Arran Tourist Information Centre
Brodick Pier
Isle of Arran
Tel: (0770) 2401

Events

At Irvine, there is a week of festivities, known as the Marymass Celebration, in honour of Mary Queen of Scots' visit to the town in 1565.
Events include the Marymass Races, a pageant and the crowning of a queen of the festivities.
Dunoon holds a Highland Gathering on the last weekend of August.
So many events are held on the Isle of Arran that there is no room to list them here. Details from the Tourist Information Office.

36
Sf
Ta
Tb
Tc
Td
Te
11
12
13
14
15
Kilchattan
An Rubha
870
Mach
Garvar
Dubh Eilean
Priory
Eilean nan Ròn
Nave Island
Ardnave Point
Gortantaoid Point
Gortantaoi
940
Ardnave
An Clachan
Sanaigmore
Kilnave
Loch Gruinart
8018
Ballinaby
Carnduncan
Aoradh
Craigens
Saligo Bay
STANDING STONES
Loch Gorm
8017
Abhainn Ghlas
Coul Point
Aruadh
8018
I
S
L
Kilchoman
Machir Bay
Blackrock
Bridgend
Conisby
Bruichladdich
Kilchiaran
Bowmore
Tormisdale
Port Charlotte
CAIRN
Loch Indaal
Gartbreck
Rhinns of Islay
790
847
Lossit
Nerabus
Laggan Point
Laggan
Lossit Bay
Rubha na Faing
Duich
8016
Portnahaven
Port Wemyss
Orsay
Rhinns Point
Laggan Bay
Knockangle Point
Glenegedale
846
Rubha Mór
Kintra
Cornabus
Glenastle
The Oa
Risabus
Lower Killeyan
Loch Kinnabus
Inerval
Mull of Oa
661
Rubha nan Leacan
160

Oban
37
Tf
Ua
Ub
Uc
Ud
Ue
Garbh Eileach
362
Garvellachs
Belnahua
Cullipool
308
Torsa
895
Dun Crutagain
Melfort
Kilmelfort
Maolachy
Dalavich
Eileach an Naoimh
Eilean Dubh Mór
Lunga
Luing
Sound of Luing
Shuna Sound
FORT
DUN
Arduaine Point
Shuna
Loch Melford
Arduaine
Kames
Garraron
40
1610
Carn Duchara
Loch
Inverliever Forest
Kilmaha
Eredine
Durran
Awe
Eredine Forest
Toberonochy
296
Craobh Haven
Barravullin
Lunga
816
CAIRNS, STANDING STONE
Inverliever
Kintraw
Torran
Scarba
Kilmory Lodge
Ban Rubha
1474
Cruach Scarba
Rubha nam Faoilean
Ardfern
Eilean Mhic Chrion
Ford
840
Fincharn
Corranmore
8022
Tibertich
Loch Ederline
Carnassarie Castle
Strait of Corryvreckan
Rèisa Mhic Phaidean
Eilean Rìgh
Craignish
Loch Gaineanhach
1503
Aird
1048
Rèisa an t-Sruith
Kinuachdrachd
Craignish Point
I Macaskin
CAIRNS
Kilmartin
Garbh Rèisa
Slockavullin
Loch Leathan
Poltalloch
STANDING STONES
Rubh' a' Geodha
Colonsay
Oban
Loch a' Bhùrra
Rubh' a' Bhacain
DUNTRUNE CASTLE
Balameanach
Kilmichael Glassary
Ardnoe Point
Loch Crinan
1198
8025
Crinan
Dunadd
A
R
G
Y
L
L
Loch Glashan
Inverness
83
Bridgend
Lussa
Corpach Bay
Ruadh Sgeir
Bellanoch
DRUIM AN DUIN
Arichonan
841
Crinan Canal
816
ACHNABRECK
784
Asknish
Lochgair
Beinn Bhreac
1532
Cairnbaan
Goirtein
Cam Loch
Lochgilphead
Kilmory Castle
Carrick
Port Ann
Largiemore
1487
Rainberg Mór
Ardlussa
Shian Bay
Eilean Dubh
Tayvallich
Achnamara
1180
Port Askeig
Lussagiven
8025
Kilmichael of Inverlussa
Ardrishaig
Castleton
Otter Ferry
Loch Righ Mór
Barrahormid
Rubha Caolard
Ballimore
1530
Cruach Lusach
Rubh' an t-Sàilean
846
425
Achabraid
Tarbert
Loch Sween
Keills Cross
Keillmore
Dunrostan
Inverneill
Rubh' a' Chrois-aoinidh
927
New Ulva
1247
8024
Loch Tarbert
Rubh' a' Mhail
Lagg
Castle Sween
Lochead
Kilfinan
8000
1439
Beinn Bhreac
Loch an Aircill
Achahoish
Drum
Ellary
1564
Achamore
Melldalloch
Eilean Mór
St Cormac's Chapel
Clachbreck
Erines
Beinn an Oir
2576
2477
Paps of Jura
Kilmory
1843
Sliabh Gaoil
Auchalick Bay
Loch a' Chnuic Bhric
Corran
Baile Boidheach
872
Loch an t-Siob
Jura Forest
Lowlandman's Bay
Skervuile Lighthouse
Point of Knap
Loch Caolisport
Loch Chaorainn
Asgog Loch
Leargybreck
Knockrome
Druimdrishaig
1574
1079
8024
Millhouse
Glas Bheinn
1839
Loch na Mile
Dubh Chreag
Tarbert
East Loch Tarbert
Portavadie
Feolin Ferry
Keils
Small Isles
1000
Loch nan Torran
Dubhchladach
Mealdarroch Point
Craighouse
West Tarbert
Cretshengan
Loch a' Chaorainn
Asgog Bay
Askeig
Cabrach
846
DUN BHORARAIC
Kilberry Head
Kilberry
DUN A' CHOIN DUIBH
Achadacaie
Cnoc a' Bhaile-shios
1383
8024
Jura Ho
Am Fraoch Eilean
Brosdale I
Rubha na Tràille
Carse House
Dunmore
FORT
Kennacraig
Whitehouse
Ardpatrick
Kilchamaig
834
Loch Stornoway
Culindrach
Glas Bheinn
1544
McArthur's Head
Ardpatrick Ho
Gartnagrenach
8001
Ardpatrick Point
Portachoillan
83
Skipness
Skipness Point
West Loch Tarbert
DUN SKEIG
Dunskeig Bay
Claonaig
Skipness Bay
Beinn Bheigier
1612
886
Clachan
842
Carraig Mhór
Rubh' a' Chàirn Bhàin
Loch Ciaran
CORRIECHREVIE
Escairt
(seasonal)
Rubha Creagan Dubha
Proaig
Claggain Bay
West Tarbert Bay
Fast Tarbert Bay
Ballochroy
North Newton
South Newton
Tarbert
Gigha Island
331
Rhunahaorine Point
50
Crossaig
Lochranza
Catacol
Catacol Bay
Kintour
Kildalton Cross
Ardmore Point
Loch Garasdale
Ardminish
Achamore
Eilean a' Chuirn
Rhunahaorine
Cour
1870
Thundergay
Kildalton House
Eilean Bhride
Leim
Sound of Gigha
31
Rubha na Gainmhich
Gigalum I
Tayinloan
Sunadale Cott
Grogport
Killean
CAIRN, STANDING STONE
185
Cara Island
Whitefarland Point
Pirnmill
2366
Beinn Bharrain
Loch Tanna
Beacharr
ARRAN
Imachar
Carradale Water
Kilbrannan Sound
1196
Muasdale
Clachaig Water
Iorsa Water
Balliekine
842
1398
Glenacardoch Point
Carradale
Belloch
Arnicle
Bridgend
Carradale Point
High Dougarie
Barr Water
Fort
1490
Beinn an Tuirc
83
841
Glenbarr
CAIRN
Machrie Bay
Auchagallon
Machrie Water
Carradale Bay
Cleongart
880
Campbeltown
53

37
38
Perth, Fort William

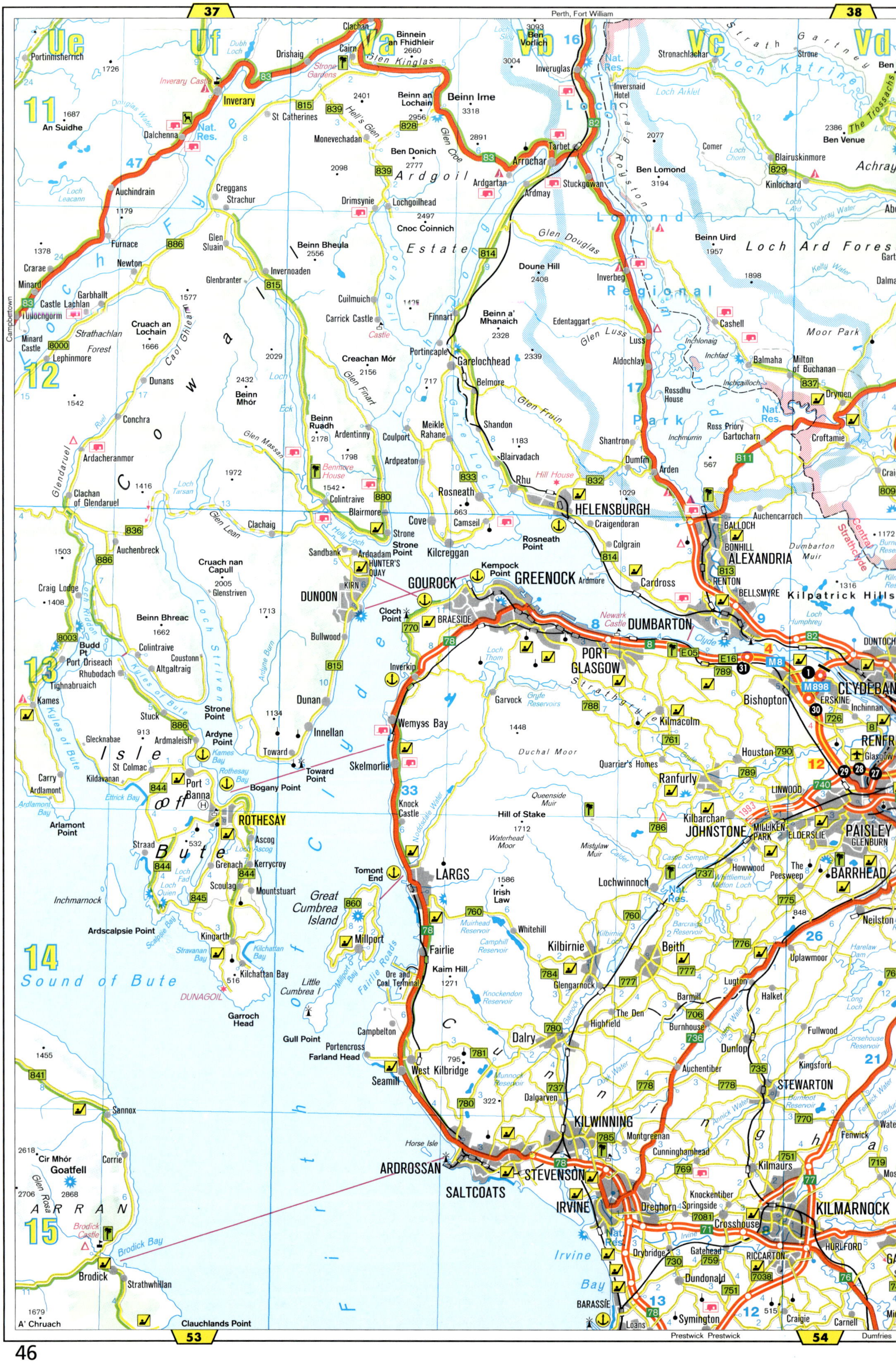

53
54

39
55
Perth
Edinburgh
Carlisle
Prestwick
CALLANDER
DUNBLANE
Doune
STIRLING
ALVA
TILLICOULTRY
DOLLAR
ALLOA
Tullibody
Clackmannan
Kincardine
DUNFERMLINE
Rosyth
GRANGEMOUTH
BO'NESS
FALKIRK
Stenhousemuir
Denny
Polmont
LINLITHGOW
KILSYTH
CUMBERNAULD
KIRKINTILLOCH
Lennoxtown
Bishopbriggs
Muirhead
Stepps
GLASGOW
Rutherglen
Cambuslang
Uddington
Viewpark
COATBRIDGE
AIRDRIE
Bellshill
MOTHERWELL
WISHAW
HAMILTON
EAST KILBRIDE
Blantyre
Larkhall
Strathaven
Carluke
LANARK
Lesmahagow
Douglas
BIGGAR
ARMADALE
BATHGATE
LIVINGSTON
WHITBURN
Harthill
Shotts
Fauldhouse
Blackburn
West Calder
Broxburn
Uphall
Forth
Carnwath
Carstairs
Ochil Hills
Campsie Fells
Kilsyth Hills
Tinto Hills
Central
Tayside
Fife
Lothian
Strathclyde
Borders

39 40

Perth
Dundee
St. William
Wd
We
Wf
Xa
Xb
Xc
Fife
Lomond Hills
FALKLAND
Strathmiglo
Freuchie
Kettlebridge
Balmalcolm
Clatto Hill
Montrave
Largo Law
Lower Largo
Largo Bay
Wester Newburn
Colinsburgh
Lathones
Largoward
Arncroach
Kellie Law
Carnbee
CRAIL
KILRENNY
ANSTRUTHER
PITTENWEEM
ST MONANCE
ELIE
EARLSFERRY
Ruddons Point
Chapel Ness
Sauchar Point
Kilconquhar
Drumeldrie
Kennoway
MARKINCH
LESLIE
GLENROTHES
Thornton
LEVEN
INNERLEVEN
METHIL
BUCKHAFEN
East Wemyss
Coaltown of Wemyss
West Wemyss
DYSART
GALLATOWN
KIRKCALDY
LINKTOWN
KINROSS
Loch Leven
Milnathort
Scotlandwell
Kinglassie
Ballingry
Lochore
Cardenden
Auchterderran
LOCHGELLY
COWDENBEATH
Kelty
Auchtertool
DUNFERMLINE
Dalgety Bay
Aberdour
BURNTISLAND
KINGHORN
Pettycur
INVERKEITHING
Rosyth
North Queensferry
QUEENSFERRY
Dalmeny
Inchkeith
Inchcolm
Oxcars
Firth of Forth
Fidra
Eyebroughy
Craigleith
Bass Rock
NORTH BERWICK
Dirleton
Gullane
Gullane Point
Aberlady
Drem
EAST LINTON
Athelstaneford
Ballencreiff
Longniddry
HADDINGTON
Garleton Hills
Traprain
Tyninghame
Whitekirk
Kingston
Auldhame
Scoughall
St Baldred's Boat
EDINBURGH
LEITH
CRAMOND
Cramond Island
BLACKHALL
CORSTORPHINE
MORNINGSIDE
CRAIGLOCKHART
COLINTON
FAIRMILEHEAD
LIBERTON
Braid Hills
PORTOBELLO
JOPPA
MUSSELBURGH
INVERESK
DUDDINGSTON
NIDDRIE
GILMERTON
Danderhall
KAIMES
LASSWADE
DALKEITH
BONNYRIGG
LOANHEAD
Roslin
COCKENZIE AND PORT SETON
PRESTONPANS
TRANENT
Elphinstone
Ormiston
Pencaitland
Macmerry
Gladsmuir
Samuelston
Bolton
Gifford
Longyester
East Saltoun
West Saltoun
Gilchrist
Humbie
Fala
Fala Dam
EASTHOUSES
MAYFIELD
Newtongrange
Gorebridge
Arniston Engine
North Middleton
Middleton
Temple
Carrington
Rosewell
PENICUIK
Howgate
Leadburn
Kirkliston
Ratho
Ratho Station
Newbridge
Hermiston
Currie
Balerno
Wilkieston
Kirknewton
Pentland Hills
Allermuir Hill
Black Hill
Scald Law
Silverburn
West Cairn Hill
The Mount
Carlops
West Linton
Mendick Hill
Dolphinton
Blyth Bridge
Romannobridge
Eddleston
Cringletie
PEEBLES
KINGS MUIR
Cardrona
INNERLEITHEN
Walkerburn
Traquair
Kirkhouse
Minch Moor
Clovenfords
Caddonfoot
GALASHIELS
MELROSE
Darnick
Eildon Hills
Newstead
Newtown St Boswells
St Boswells
Bowden
Maxton
Earlston
Redpath
Bemersyde
Clintmains
Smailholm
Fans
Legerwood
LAUDER
Thirlestane
Carfraemill Hotel
Oxton
Westruther
Lammermuir Hills
Lammer Law
Meikle Says Law
Crib Law
Hunt Law
Hogs Law
Collie Law
Moorfoot Hills
Heriot
Torfichen Hill
Blackhope Scar
Dun Law
Fountainhall
Torquhan
Stow
Bowland
Buckholm
Meigle Hill
Great Law
Windlestraw Law
Priesthope Hill
Whitehope Law
Dunslair Heights
Black Law
Lee Pen
Glentress
Blackhaugh
Broughton
Brougton Height
Trahenna Hill
Drumelzier
Bellspool
Stobo
Kirkton Manor
Whitelaw Hill
Stob Law
Dun Rig
Pykestone Hill
Blakehope Head
Stanhope
Broadmeadows
Upper Tweeddale
Carlisle
Newcastle-upon-Tyne
Glasgow
Stirling
Motherwell
Edinburgh

55 56

Xd
Xe
Xf
Ya
Yb
Yc
N O R T H
S E A
Barns Ness
Skateraw
Skateraw Harbour
Thorntonloch
Innerwick
Bilsdean
Collegiate Church
Reed Point
Pease Bay
Siccar Point
Wheat Stack
Fast Castle
Telegraph Hill
Lumsdaine
EARN'S HEUGH
St Abb's Head
Nat. Res.
Northfield
St Abbs
Coldingham Loch
Coldingham Moor
Coldingham Bay
Buss Craig
Coldingham
Press
Cockburnspath
Ecelaw
Lothian
Borders
Meickle Black Law
Blackburn Rig
Grantshouse
Houndwood
Eye Water
Cairncross
Reston
Ayton
EYEMOUTH
Burnmouth
Horseley Hill
Abbey St Bathans
Ellemford
Marygold
Auchencrow
EDIN'S HALL BROCH
COCKBURN LAW
Lamberton Beach
Lamberton
Marshall Meadows Bay
Lintlaw
Preston
Chirnside
Halidon Hill 1333
Clappers
Foulden
Whiteadder Water
Needles Eye
Sharper's Head
Duns Law
Duns Castle
Manderston House
Edrom
Allanton
Hutton
Paxton
Elizab. Ramparts
BERWICK-UPON-TWEED
Nat. Res.
DUNS
Blackadder
Blackadder Water
TWEEDMOUTH
EAST ORD
Royal Border Bridge
SPITTAL
Tweed
Redshin Cove
Gavinton
Whitsome
Horncliffe
Greenlaw Moor
Polwarth
Hule Moss
Fogo
New Horndean
Murton
Scremerston
Thornton
Cheswick Black Rocks
Swinton
Ladykirk
Norham Castle
Norham
Cheswick
Greenlaw
Swintonmill
Simprim
Shoreswood
Grindon
Shoresdean
West Allerdean
Allerdean Burn
Ancroft
Causeway flooded at high tide
Goswick
Keel Head
Emmanuel Head
Holy Island or Lindisfarne
Leitholm
Northumberland
Felkington
Haydon Dean
Berrington
Haggerston
Beal
Causeway
Nat. Res.
Holy Island
Holy Island Sands
Lindisfarne Castle
Lindisfarne Priory
Castle Point
Lambden
Duddo
Bowsden
Eccles
Hume Castle
The Hirsel
Lennel
Kyloe
Guile Point
Fenham Flats
Longstone
Farne Nat. Res.
COLDSTREAM
Bridge
Pallinsburn Ho
Etal
Fenwick
Buckton
Lowick
Kyloe Hills
Birgham
Crookham
Ford
Elwick
Ross
Farn Island
Staple Sound
Islands
Stichill
Carham
Wark
Learmouth
Branxton
Inner Sound
Bamburgh Castle
Ednam
Flodden Field 1513
Flodden
Kimmerston
Holburn
Detchant
Budle Bay
Budle
Bamburgh
Monks House Rocks
Hadden
Pressen
St Cuthbert's Cave
Easington
Waren Mill
Burton
Belford
KELSO
Sprouston
Downham
Fenton
Spindlestone
Seahouses
MAXWELLHEUGH
Housedon Hill
Milfield
Nesbit
Doddington
DODDINGTON MOOR
North Sunderland
Bellshill
Elford
Pawston
Kilham
Lanton
Glen
Horton
Adderstone
Lucker
Hoselaw Loch
Heiton
Coupland
Warenton
Beadnell
West Fleetham
Bowmont Forest
Linton Hill
Town Yetholm
Kirk Yetholm
Hethpool
Kirknewton
YEAVERING BELL
Akeld
Humbleton
WOOLER
Chatton
Greendykes
Warenford
Newstead
Newham
Swinhoe
Beadnell Bay
Nat. Res.
Chathill
Newcastle-upon-Tyne
57
Newcastle-upon-Tyne

The Southwestern Lowlands

The little-explored area of Dumfries and Galloway has many tourist attractions. The scenery of the Mull of Kintyre,the Rhinns and Galloway is spectacular, at least as beautiful as the Highlands, and nearer to the main centres of population.

South-western Scotland is an area that is largely unvisited by foreign tourists, except those in search of Burns memorabilia, though it has many resorts that are popular with the Scots themselves. The routes from England to Stranraer and Cairn Ryan are busy as these are the points from which the ferry route to Ireland is the shortest. The main road from England leads north from Carlisle and passes through Gretna Green, once famous for elopements.

Ayr

This attractive little town whose "twa brigs" (two bridges) over the River Ayr are immortalised in *The Brigs of Ayr* by Robert Burns, is the county town of Ayrshire. It is to Scotland what Stratford-upon-Avon is to England, since it is Burns' birthplace and his childhood home. The poet was born in 1759 in an "auld clay biggin" built by his father at Alloway, two miles south of the town. This is now the Burns Cottage Museum. The Land o' Burns Visitor Centre is part of the same complex. It provides a Burns Heritage Trail, tracking the life of the poet through two counties. The church, a ruin in Burn's day, and the Brig o'Doon, both feature in Burn's poem *Tam o'Shanter.* Ayr was Oliver Cromwell's main fortress and port in south-western Scotland but little remains of the fortifications except a rampart wall. Ayr has Scotland's leading racecourse, on which the Scottish Grand National and the Scottish Gold Cup are run. Belleisle Park south of the town has a zoo, nature trail and the lush gardens that are typical of this part of Scotland. It is fun to take a trip on the *Waverley*, the last sea-going paddle steamer in the world, which sails down the west coast in summer. Ayr has grown considerably since the international airport at neighbouring Prestwick was opened.

Dumfries

Anyone familiar with football will know that this city, like its football team, is known as the "Queen of the South". It was granted a royal charter in 1395 but the Old Bridge, the first bridge over the Nith, is even older. It was built by Devorgilla, mother of John Balliol, king of Scotland, in 1273 and it is still used as a footbridge. Dumfries is famous not just for its football but for its literary connections. Three of Scotland's most famous writers, Robert Burns, J.M. Barrie and Thomas Carlyle, have links with the town. Robert Burns spent the last five years of his life here, and his house, in what is now called Burns Street, is a museum. He is buried in the churchyard of St. Michael's church. The Robert Burns Centre, on the banks of the River Nith, a converted 18th-century mill, tells the story of his life. Burns' first house in the Wee Vennel (now Bank Street) is privately-owned,

Bruce's Stone, Lower Troon (above).

The Neolithic caverns at Cairnholy, Gatehouse of Fleet (above right).

Ruins of an old farmhouse in the hills near Campbelltown, on the Mull of Kintyre (right).

Blackfare ram, a typical breed in this area (opposite above).

South Kintyre, looking towards Arran (opposite below).

but his second home may be visited. The farm at Ellisland, six miles outside the town by the River Nith, has been turned into a living museum to show what farming was like in Burns' time. J.M. Barrie spent his childhood in Victoria Terrace, Dumfries and attended Dumfries Academy. The garden of his home at Moat Brae House is where he dreamed up the story of Peter Pan. Thomas Carlyle (1795-1881), the great interpreter of German Romanticism, famous for his *Life of Schiller* (1825) and his translation of Goethe's *Wilhelm Meister* (1824), was born at nearby Ecclefechan. Dumfries has a memorial to him.

Galloway

This is the western section of the county of Dumfries and Galloway. It has a small population and its scenery is reminiscent of the Highlands. It is known for its thick forests, including the Cairn Edward Forest, the Kirroughtree Forest and the Glentrool Forest to the west, a national forest park. The land is mountainous and many of the streams and lochs are part of hydroelectric projects.

Gatehouse of Fleet

The largest town in Galloway. There are small chambered cairns of the Neolithic period (2000 b.c.) at Cairnholy near this town, which is a good centre from which to explore the Water of Fleet and the castles in the area. Cardoness Castle, overlooking Fleet Bay, has associations with Young Lochinvar, made famous in the poem about his deeds. Another ruined castle, Rusco, in the vicinity, is also associated with the Gordons of Lochinvar.

Gretna

This little village just over the border from Carlisle is still famous for the blacksmith's shop where couples eloping from England were wed. In Scotland, it was legal to marry merely by making a declaration before witnesses. This practice was abolished in 1939, but couples continued to come here because the age of consent in Britain was 21, whereas it was only 18 in Scotland. The whole flourishing wedding trade stopped in 1966, when the age of consent was reduced to 18 all over Britain, though mock weddings are still performed at the forge for the benefit of tourists.

Kirkcudbright (pronounced "Kirkudbree")

Once the capital of the county of Kirkcudbrightshire, Kirkcudbright is in an area known as the Stewartry. While on a visit to Galloway, Robert Burns wrote the grace now recited at Burns Night Suppers. This attractive town of mainly Georgian architecture stands on the estuary of the River Dee. The town was surrounded by a wall. All that is left of the great gate, Meikle Yat, is two marks in the road. The Stewartry Museum contains exhibits by local craftsmen and the history of local regiments. The ruined 16th-century McLellan's Castle features the "laird's lug", a secret listening post within the huge drawing-room mantlepiece, through which the lord ("laird") could evesdrop on conversations.

A few miles east of the town stands Dundrennan Abbey, found-

Information

Tourist Information Centre
39 Sandgate
Ayr KA7 1BG
Tel:(0292)284196

Tourist Information Centre
Harbour Square
Kirkcudbright
Tel:(0557) 30494

Events

The Scottish Grand National is run at Ayr racecourse in April. In May, Ayr has a Youth Football Tournament. In May there is the Burns Festival. The Ayrshire Arts Festival and Golf Week are in June. The Scottish Gold Cup is run at Ayr racecourse in September. Lockerbie holds the Lamb Fair on Lamb Hill, an event that dates back to 1680.

ed in 1142. This is where Mary Queen of Scots spent her last night in Scotland. At Port Mary, a mile away, there is the stone from which she stepped into a boat on her fateful journey to England, imprisonment and eventual execution.

Lockerbie

This little town is unfortunately famous for the Locherbie Disaster, the plane that crashed into the town in 1990 after a bomb had been planted on board. It is the heart of the area known as the Western Dales. Castle Milk is three miles to the south and has lovely grounds. There is a Roman camp nearby. Many of Lockerbie's houses are built of stone from the Corncockle Quarry which contains footprints of dynosaurs.

Lochmaben

This lovely holiday centre has a ruined castle which is one of the reputed birthplaces of Robert the Bruce (1274-1329). He certainly lived in the town, and there is a statue to him in front of the Town Hall. The Castle Loch is the only lake in the British Isles to contain the freshwater fish known as vendace. They are reputed to have been introduced by Mary Queen of Scots and are traditionally netted in August.

Moffat

This spa has been famous since the 18th century for its healing waters. The old Bath House can still be visited, and the saline and sulphur waters sampled. Five miles north of the town, there is huge hollow, 500 feet deep, known as the Devil's Beef Tub.

Mull of Kintyre

This 70-mile long peninsula runs north to south through a variety of landscapes. The Crinan area is famous for its canal, built in 1801 and still in use. The area has a wealth of prehistoric monuments, standing stones and cairns. Dunadd Fort, the ancient capital of Dalriada, the kingdom of western Scotland, dominates the area. Campbelltown, the chief town on the peninsula, is famous for its whisky and locally-made cheeses. From the tip of the Mull of Kintyre, there are spectacular views of the coast of Antrim, Northern Ireland and Rathlin Island where there is one of the caves identified as the place where Robert the Bruce saw the spider.

New Abbey

The ruins of New or Sweetheart Abbey, founded in 1273 by Devorgilla, mother of the Scottish king John Balliol, dominate this village on the Pow Burn. The Abbey is called Sweetheart because Devorgilla ordered that her husband's heart be buried before the high altar.

Newton Stewart

This is the largest town in western Galloway and was once a thriving spinning and weaving centre. Now it is more of a tourist resort, an excellent base for visiting the forests of Galloway and the surrounding area. There are plenty of golfing and angling facilities.

The Rhinns

The Rhinns of Galloway are on a T-shaped peninsula of rich farmland, well sheltered and warmed by the Gulf Stream. The ruins of the chapel at Kirkmandrine contain stones with early Christian inscriptions. The Rhinns are famous for their beautiful gardens, especially that of Castle Kennedy near Stranraer. Ardwell House, south of Sandhead and the Logan Botanic Gardens near Port Logan have rival displays. At Port Logan, the tidal basin contains a fishpond where sea fish have become tame enough to feed out of the visitors' hands. Kirkmaiden Church with its picturesque sculpted stones is the southwesternmost church in Scotland.

Stranraer

The largest town in the Rhinns is also an important ferry terminal for boats to the Isle of Man and Larne, Northern Ireland; neighbouring Cairn Ryan also has sailings to Ireland. Irish currency is accepted in these ports, but not elsewhere in Scotland, so it is important to ensure you do not get given it by mistake. Furthermore, it is also worth less than Scottish currency. The ruined 15th-century castle in the town centre was once the stronghold of "Bluidy" (bloody) Claverhouse, scourge of the Covenanters in the 17th century.

Whithorn

This little peninsula, almost an island, in a relatively remote region of the Lowlands, is a historic place of pilgrimage. This is because it is the location of the 4th-century chapel built by St. Ninian, his so-called "candida casa" (white house). Despite rival claims, archæologists findings show that the saint did indeed settle at Whithorn. There is also a 12th-century priory on Whithorn, adorned with the arms of Scotland.

Statue of Robert the Bruce, Lochmaker (left).

The Devil's Beeftub near Moffat (above).

45
46
Inverness
Ub
Uc
Ud
Ue
Uf
Va
15
16
17
18
19
20
21
Cleongart
Bellochantuy Bay
Bellochantuy
Killocraw
Lussa Loch
Tangy Loch
Sgreadán
1302
1228
Abbey
Saddell
Saddell Bay
Ugadale
Ugadale Point
KILDONAN
Skeroblingarry
CAIRN
Kilchenzie
Peninver
Ardnacross Bay
Darlochan
Machrihanish Bay
CAMPBELTOWN
Campbeltown Loch
Island Davaar
Machrihanish
Drumlemble
Knocknaha
Beinn Ghuilean
1155
Kildalloig
Chiscan Water
Killellan
1263
Moy
908
Breakerie Water
Conieglen Water
Feochaig
788
CHAMBERED CAIRN
Carrine
Southend
Machariоch
Lice
Carskiey
Keil
Carskey Bay
Sanda Sound
Sheep Island
Sanda Island
K I N T Y R E
Kilbrannan Sound
Machrie Bay
Auchagallon
1679
A' Chruach
Tormore
STONE CIRCLES
Ballymichael
1649
BURIAL CHAMBER
Torbeg
Shiskine
Drumadoon Point
Blackwaterfoot
Drumadoon Bay
Kilpatrick
A R R A N
Tighvein
1503
CAIRN
Sliddery Water
Bennecarrigan
TORR A' CHAISTEIL
Sliddery
Lagg
Kilmory Water
Torrylinn
Bennan
Bennan Head
CHAMBERED CAIRN
Clauchlands Point
Margnaheglish
Lamlash
Lamlash Bay
Holy Island
1030
Kingscross Point
Knockenkelly
Kingscross
Whiting Bay
Largymore
Largybeg
GIANT'S GRAVES
Dippen
Dippen Head
Kildonan
Pladda
1109
Ailsa Craig
Prestwick
Lendalfoot
Bennane Head
Colmonell
871
Stinchar
Ballantrae Bay
Water of Tig
Ballantrae
Cosses
Balkissock
Glenapp Castle
Beneraird
1439
Carlock Hill
1046
Water of App
844
Larne
Milleur Point
Corsewall Point
324
Barnhill
North Cairn
South Cairn
Dounan Bay
Loch Connell
Kirkcolm
Ervie
Cairnryan
Main Water of Luce
Penwhirn Reservoir
Loch Ryan
Knocknain
Leswalt
Lochnaw Castle
Innermessan
Lochinch and Castle Kennedy Gardens
Black Loch
White L.
Castle Kennedy
STRANRAER
Soulseat Loch
Portslogan
Broadsea Bay
Piltanton Burn
Lochans
596
Cairn Pat
Genoch Mains
Black Head
Portpatrick
Stoneykirk
Sandhead
Cairngarroch
Dumfries
The Rhins
53
Port-patrick
Stoneykirk
Sandhead
Cairngarroch
KIRKMADRINE
Luce Bay
Ardwell Bay
Ardwell
Logan Gardens
Drumbreddan Bay
Logan Mains
Portacree
Mull of Logan
Port Logan
Terally
Clanyard Bay
Kilstay Bay
Kirkmaiden
Drummore
Laggantalluch Head
537
Damnaglaur
Cailiness Point
Crammag Head
Maryport
Maryport Bay
Cairngaan
Mull of Galloway

46
67
Va
Vb
Vc
Vd
Ve
Vf
15
16
17
18
19
Irvine
Kilmarnock
Kilmarnock
BARASSIE
TROON
Lady Isle
Loans
Symington
Craigie
Carnell
Middleyard
Millburn
Crosshands
Auchmillan
Middlefield Law
Netherwood
Muirkirk
Kames
Limmerhaugh Muir
Sorn
Mauchline
Mossgiel
Tarbolton
Failford
Catrine
MONKTON
Ayr
PRESTWICK
Ayr Bay
Airds Moss
Cronberry
Lugar
Auchinleck
Logan
HOLMHEAD
CUMNOCK
Dalblair
Glenmuirshaw
Mossblown
WHITLETTS
Annbank
Stair
Trabboch
Orchiltree
AYR
SEAFIELD
ALLOWAY
Belston
Coylton
Hillhead
Drongan
Heads of Ayr
DOONFOOT
Burns's Cottage
Fisherton
Dunure
Brown Carrick Hill
Culroy
Sauchrie
Mount Oliphant
Martnaham Loch
Sinclairston
Skares
Littlemill
Pathhead
New Cumnock
Connel Park
Drumshang
Knoweside
Minishant
Dalrymple
Rankiston
Culzean Bay
Culzean Castle
MAYBOLE
Grimmet
Polnessan
Patna
Dalleagles
Burnside
Kirkmichael
Loch Spallander Reservoir
Waterside
Maidenhead Bay
Maidens
Kirkoswald
Crossraguel Abbey
Turnberry
Crosshill
Straiton
Dalmellington
Bellsbank
Enoch Hill
Blackcraig Hill
Afton Reservoir
Matthew's Port
Dowhill
Kilkerran
Tairlaw
Big Hill of Glenmount
Carsphairn Forest
Windy Standard
Polskeoch
Colt Hill
Dailly
Old Dailly
Penkill
Penwhapple Reservoir
Garleffin Fell
Lintern Loch
Loch Bradan Reservoir
Loch Finlas
Drumjohn
Cairnsmore of Carsphairn
Corlae
GIRVAN
Woodland Bay
Mull of Miljoan
Dalquhairn
Loch Doon
Loch Doon Castle
Tormitchell
Carrick
Loch Riecawr
Carsphairn
Grey Hill
Barr
Changue Plantation
Carrick Forest
CAIRN AVEL
Knowehead
Polmaddie Hill
Meaul
Pinmore
Merkland
Loch Macaterick
Eglin Lane
Gala Lane
Dalshangan
Kendoon Loch
Castlemaddy
The Glenkens
Kirriereoch Hill
Strathclyde
Dumfries & Galloway
Merrick
Corserine
Forest Lodge
Glenhoul
Pinwherry
Bellamore
Colmonell
Glenduisk
Black Clauchrie
Loch Moan
Loch Enoch
Rhinns of Kells
Loch Harrow
Loch Dungeon
Earlstoun
Corriedoo
Ballochmorrie
Palgowan
Loch Neldricken
Loch Valley
Earlstoun Loch
St John's Town of Dalry
Drumbie
Garroch
Bogue
Barrhill
Glentrool Forest
Glen Trool
Glenlee
Balmaclellan
Lochton
Glentrool Village
Glen Trool Lodge
Loch Trool
Loch Dee
Craigencallie
Clatteringshaws Loch
New Galloway
Chirmorrie
Drumlamford Ho
Lamachan Hill
Darnaw
Clatteringshaws
Ironmacannie
Loch Dornal
Loch Ochiltree
Bargrennan
Kirroughtree Forest
Loch Maberry
Polbae
Dee or Black Water of Dee
Cairn Edward Forest
Stab Hill
STANDING STONES
Knowe
Auchinleck
Craignelder
Loch Grannoch
Fell of Fleet
Loch Fleet
Mossdale
Nat. Res.
Garlies Castle
Little Duchrae
GALLOWAY
Glenrazie
Carseriggan
Challoch
Minnigaff
NEWTON STEWART
Bargaly
Cairnsmore of Fleet
Clints of Dromore
Loch Skerrow
Woodhall Loch
Laurieston
Artfield Fell
Balminnoch
The Moors
Loch Ronald
Tarf Water
New Luce
Palnure
Barraer Fell
Kirkcowan
Loch Whinyeon
Loch Mannoch
Glengap Forest
Carscreugh
Carsegowan
Creetown
Glen
Ringford
Dunragit
Glenluce Abbey
Castle Kennedy
Glenluce
Spittal
STANDING STONES OF TORHOUSE
Dernaglar Loch
Whitefield Loch
Cairnharrow
Cardoness Castle
Anwoth
GATEHOUSE OF FLEET
Carsluith
CAIRNHOLY
Milton
Luce Sands
Castle Loch
Mochrum Loch
Bladnoch
WIGTOWN
The Machars
Wigtown Bay
Kirkdale
Sandgreen
Girthon
Twynholm
Stranraer
Stranraer
E18
77
76
70
75
719
741
734
714
765
7027
712
735
733
714
7052
7005
747
796
727
755
762
702
769
729
713
7000
741
730
742
744
743
7036
7046
765
7037
744
723

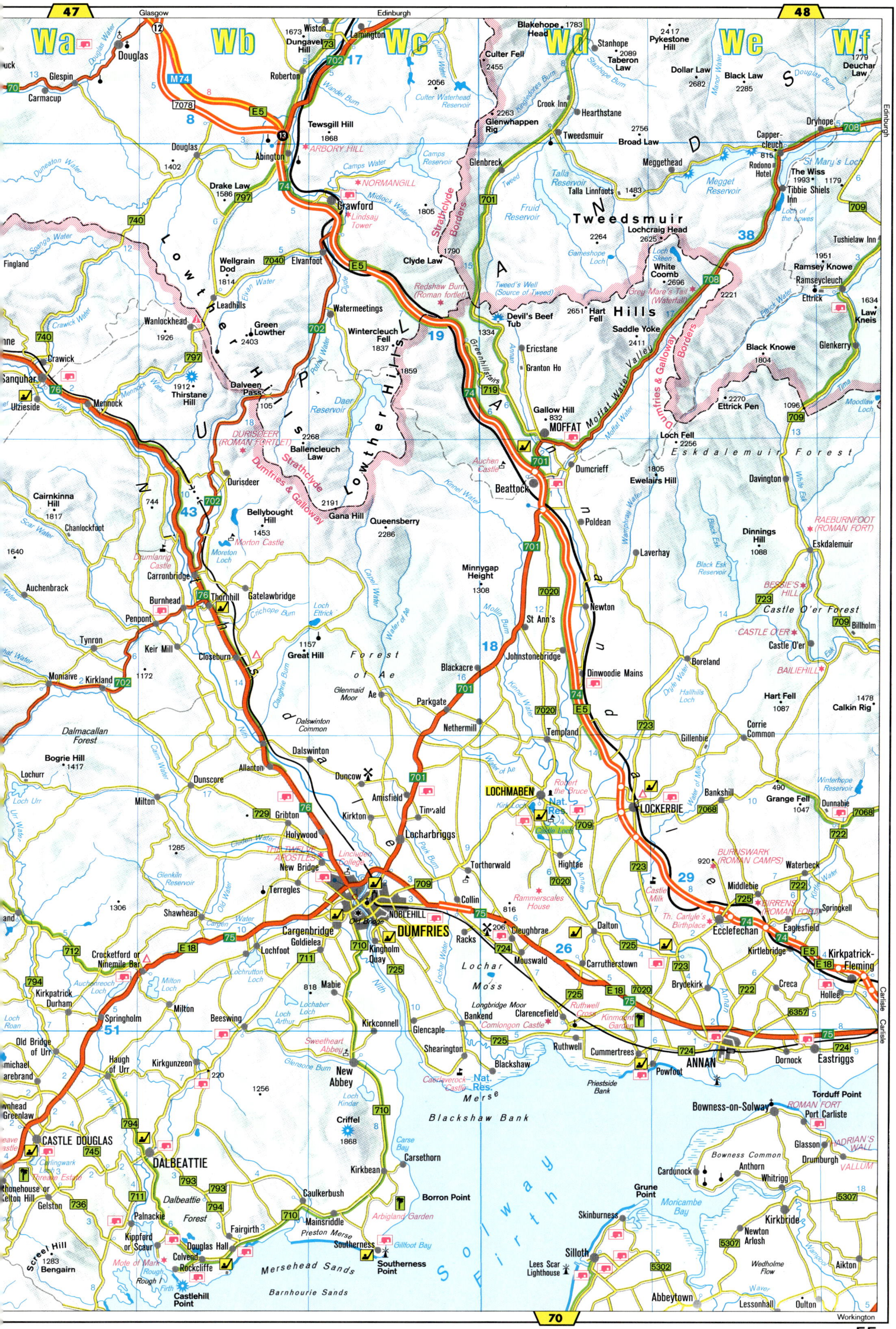
47
48
Glasgow
Edinburgh
Wa
Wb
Wc
Wd
We
Wf
Douglas
Glespin
Carmacup
M74
7078
E5
Wiston
Dungavel Hill
Lamington
Roberton
Culter Fell
Culter Waterhead Reservoir
Blakehope Head
Stanhope
Taberon Law
Pykestone Hill
Dollar Law
Black Law
Deuchar Law
Tewsgill Hill
Abington
ARBORY HILL
Camps Reservoir
Glenwhappen Rig
Hearthstane
Crook Inn
Tweedsmuir
Broad Law
Cappercleuch
Dryhope
Drake Law
NORMANGILL
Crawford
Lindsay Tower
Glenbreck
Talla Reservoir
Talla Linnfoots
Meggethead
Megget Reservoir
Rodono Hotel
St Mary's Loch
The Wiss
Tibbie Shiels Inn
Loch of the Lowes
Fruid Reservoir
Tweedsmuir
Lochcraig Head
Tushielaw Inn
Fingland
Lowther Hills
Wellgrain Dod
Elvanfoot
Clyde Law
Strathclyde
Borders
Gameshope Loch
Loch Skeen
White Coomb
Ramsey Knowe
Ramseycleuch
Ettrick
Redshaw Burn (Roman fortlet)
Tweed's Well (Source of Tweed)
Grey Mare's Tail (Waterfall)
Leadhills
Watermeetings
Devil's Beef Tub
Hart Fell
Hills
Law Kneis
Wanlockhead
Green Lowther
Wintercleuch Fell
Ericstane
Saddle Yoke
Black Knowe
Glenkerry
Crawick
Sanquhar
Ulzieside
Mennock
Thirstane Hill
Dalveen Pass
Daer Reservoir
Granton Ho
Gallow Hill
MOFFAT
Moffat Water Valley
Ettrick Pen
Dumfries & Galloway
Moodlaw Loch
DURISDEER (ROMAN FORTLET)
Ballencleuch Law
Lowther Hills
Loch Fell
Eskdalemuir Forest
Auchen Castle
Dumcrieff
Beattock
Ewelairs Hill
Davington
Durisdeer
Cairnkinna Hill
Chanlockfoot
Bellybought Hill
Gana Hill
Queensberry
Morton Castle
Poldean
RAEBURNFOOT (ROMAN FORT)
Dinnings Hill
Eskdalemuir
Laverhay
Black Esk Reservoir
Drumlanrig Castle
Moreton Loch
Carronbridge
Minnygap Height
Auchenbrack
Burnhead
Thornhill
Gatelawbridge
Loch Ettrick
Penpont
Newton
BESSIE'S HILL
Castle O'er Forest
Billholm
CASTLE O'ER
Castle O'er
Tynron
Keir Mill
Closeburn
Great Hill
Forest of Ae
St Ann's
Johnstonebridge
Boreland
BAILIEHILL
Moniaive
Kirkland
Blackacre
Dinwoodie Mains
Glenmaid Moor
Ae
Parkgate
Hart Fell
Calkin Rig
Dalmacallan Forest
Dalswinton Common
Nethermill
Templand
Gillenbie
Corrie Common
Bogrie Hill
Dalswinton
Lochurr
Allanton
Duncow
Dunscore
Amisfield
LOCHMABEN
Robert the Bruce
Bankshill
Grange Fell
Winterhope Reservoir
Dunnabie
Milton
Gribton
Kirkton
Tinwald
Nat. Res.
Castle Loch
LOCKERBIE
Holywood
Locharbriggs
Glenkiln Reservoir
THE TWELVE APOSTLES
Lincluden College
New Bridge
Torthorwald
Hightae
BURNSWARK (ROMAN CAMPS)
Waterbeck
Terregles
Middlebie
Castle Milk
BIRRENS (ROMAN FORT)
Shawhead
Collin
Rammerscales House
Springkell
NOBLEHILL
Cargenbridge
Goldielea
Old Bridge
DUMFRIES
Racks
Cleughbrae
Dalton
Th. Carlyle's Birthplace
Ecclefechan
Eaglesfield
Crocketford or Ninemile Bar
Lochfoot
Kingholm Quay
Mouswald
Carrutherstown
Kirtlebridge
Kirkpatrick-Fleming
Lochar Moss
Brydekirk
Creca
Hollee
Kirkpatrick Durham
Auchenreoch Loch
Milton Loch
Lochrutton Loch
Mabie
Longbridge Moor
Bankend
Clarencefield
Ruthwell Cross
Kinmount Gardens
Springholm
Milton
Beeswing
Lochaber Loch
Loch Arthur
Kirkconnell
Glencaple
Comlongon Castle
Old Bridge of Urr
Sweetheart Abbey
Shearington
Ruthwell
Cummertrees
ANNAN
Dornock
Eastriggs
Haugh of Urr
Kirkgunzeon
New Abbey
Blackshaw
Caerlaverock Castle
Nat. Res.
Merse
Powfoot
Priestside Bank
Torduff Point
Bowness-on-Solway
ROMAN FORT
Port Carlisle
Loch Kindar
Blackshaw Bank
Criffel
Carse Bay
Carsethorn
CASTLE DOUGLAS
DALBEATTIE
Kirkbean
Bowness Common
Anthorn
Glasson
Drumburgh
HADRIAN'S WALL
VALLUM
Cardurnock
Whitrigg
Threave Estate
Threave Castle
Gelston
Dalbeattie Forest
Caulkerbush
Borron Point
Grune Point
Moricambe Bay
Palnackie
Mainsriddle
Preston Merse
Arbigland Garden
Skinburness
Kirkbride
Newton Arlosh
Kippford or Scaur
Douglas Hall
Fairgirth
Gillfoot Bay
Southerness
Southerness Point
Silloth
Screel Hill
Bengairn
Colvend
Rockcliffe
Mote of Mark
Rough Firth
Rough Island
Mersehead Sands
Solway Firth
Lees Scar Lighthouse
Wedholme Flow
Aikton
Castlehill Point
Barnhourie Sands
Abbeytown
Lessonhall
Oulton
70
Workington
Carlisle

48
71
Edinburgh
Berwick-upon-Tweed
Darlington
Wf
Xa
Xb
Xc
Xd
15
16
17
18
19
SELKIRK
HAWICK
JEDBURGH
LANGHOLM
BRAMPTON
CARLISLE
Longtown
Gretna
Haltwhistle
Broadmeadows
Yarrow
Yarrow Feus
Mountbenger
Bowhill
Philiphaugh
Newark Castle
Bowhill House
Kirkhope
Ettrickbridge
Ettrick Forest
Black Knowe Head
Gilmanscleuch
Caver's Hill
Crosslee
Dun Knowe
Ashkirk
Woll
Clerklands
Lilliesleaf
Riddell
Midlem
Bowden
Longnewton
Belses
Ancrum
Maxton
Rutherford
Waterloo Monument
Peniel Heugh
Monteviot House
Nisbet
Crailing
Crailinghall
Eckford
Cessford
Morebattle
Linton
Linton Hill
Town Yetholm
Kirk Yetholm
Hownam Law
Mowhaugh
Howgate
Hownam
Craik Moor
Chatto
Whitton
Bonjedward
Chesters
Lanton
Jedburgh Abbey
Newton
Minto Hills
Minto
Hassendean
Horsleyhill
Knowetownhead
Denholm
Appletreehall
Hornshole Bridge
Wilton Dean
Dunion Hill
Hundalee
Mary Queen of Scots House
Ferniehirst Castle
Oxnam
Mossburnford
Swinside Hall
Rubers Law
Kirkton
Borthwickshiels
Roberton
Borthwickbrae
Buccleuch
Snoot
Burnfoot
Motte
White Hill
Branxholme
Branxholm Hall
Deanburnhaugh
Redcleuch Edge
Craik Forest
Newmill
Northhouse
Dodburn
Bonchester Bridge
Abbotrule
Bonchester Hill
Hobkirk
Chesters
Southdean
Camptown
Pennymuir (Roman Camps)
Woden Law
Beefstand Hill
Blindburn
Leithope Forest
Chew Green (Roman Camps)
Carter Bar
Arks Edge
Ravens Knowe
Roman camps
Byrness
Redesdale Forest
The Cheviot
Craik
Pike Hill
Teviothead
Skelfhill Pen
The Pike
Note o'the Gate
Wauchope Forest
Carter Fell
Catcleugh Reservoir
Kielderhead Moor
Peel Fell
Fanna Hill
Singdean
Oh Me Edge
Blackman's Law
Rochester
High Rochester (Roman)
Stock Hill
Mosspaul Hotel
Wisp Hill
Cauldcleuch Head
Tudhope Hill
Hermitage Castle
Saughtree
Larriston
Border
Emblehope Moor
Monkside
Padon Hill
Blackburn Common
Jamestown
Faw Side
Broad Head
Din Fell
Hermitage
Newlands
Roan Fell
Steele Road
Kielder
Bakethin Reservoir
Kielder Water (Reservoir)
Kielder Forest
Highgreen Manor
Black Middens Bastle House
Eskdale
Bentpath
Dumfries & Galloway
Borders
Black Edge
Liddesdale
Newcastleton
Newcastleton Forest
Larriston Fells
Black Knowe
Glendhu Hill
Rough Pike
Falstone
Greenhaugh
Tinnis Hill
Monument Sir J Malcolm
Forest Park
Bower
Hesleyside
Kershopefoot
Kershope Forest
Cumbria
Black Knowe
Sighty Crag
Paddaburn Moor
Churnside Lodge
Wark Forest
Bigholms
Auchenrivock
Caulside
Nook
Solwaybank
Hollows Tower
Rowanburn
Canonbie
Evertown
Blackpool Gate
Crossings
White Preston
Whygate
Stonehaugh
Milltown
Dumfries & Galloway
Cumbria
Chapelknowe
Haggbeck
Roughsike
Bewcastle
Roman fort
Butterburn
Black Fell
Haughton Common
The Debatable Land
Easton
Spadeadam Forest
Broomley Lough
Greenlee Lough
Vercovicium (Housesteads)
Solway Moss
Stapleton
Spadeadam
Northumberland
Thirlwall Common
Whiteside
Hadrian's Wall
Crag Lough
Boltonfellend
Kirkcambeck
West Hall
Gilsland
Thirlwall Castle
Aesica
Vindolanda (Chesterholm)
Bardon Mill
Gretna Green
Rigg
Kirklinton
Hethersgill
Camboglanna (Birdoswald)
Greenhead
Henshaw
Sarkfoot Point
Redkirk Point
Westlinton
Smithfield
Banks
Willowford
Bellister Castle
Blenkinsopp Castle
Melkridge
Willimontswick
Walton
Lanercost Priory
Tadpoles
Scaleby Hill
Scaleby
Newtown
Naworth Castle
Low Row
Denton Fell
Rockcliffe Marsh
Rockcliffe
Blackford
Harker
Irthington
Carlisle
Featherstone Castle
Rowfoot
Plenmeller Common
Hallbankgate
Tindale
Fellhouse Fell
Burgh by Sands
Beaumont
Cargo
Kingstown
Houghton
Stanwix
Low Crosby
Newby East
Talkin Tarn
Tindale Tarn
Lambley
Whitfield
Tindale Fells
Forest Head
Halton Lea Gate
Stonehouse
Bearsbridge
Thurstonfield
Moorhouse
Grinsdale
Warwick Bridge
Warwick
Hayton
Talkin
How
Heads Nook
Faugh
Castle Carrock
Cold Fell
Whitfield Moor
Kirkbampton
Great Orton
Newby West
Cathedral
Scotby
Wetheral
Great Corby
Corby Castle
Knarsdale
Ninebanks
Allen
Wiggonby
Baldwinholme
Cummersdale
Carleton
Brisco
Cumwhinton
Cumwhitton
Cumrew Fell
Slaggyford
Thursby
Durdar
Dalston
Cotehill
Hornsby
Cumrew
Kirkhaugh
Ayle
Dumfries
Glasgow
Workington

49
Edinburgh
Berwick-upon-Tweed
Xf
Ya
Yb
Yc
Yd
WOOLER
Akeld
Humbledon
Earle
Middleton Hall
Haugh Head
Lilburn Tower
Chatton
Chillingham
Greendykes
Ros Castle
Hepburn
Newtown
East Lilburn
Ilderton
Roseden
Roddam
Wooperton
Old Bewick
Bewick Moor
New Bewick
Beanley
Eglingham
West Ditchburn
Cateran Hill
Middle Moor
North Charlton
South Charlton
Newham
Newstead
Fleetham
West
Ellingham
Chathill
Preston
Preston Tower
Brownieside
Christon Bank
Swinhoe
Beadnell
Beadnell Bay
Nat. Res.
Snook Point
High Newton-by-the-Sea
St Mary's or Newton Haven
Embleton Bay
Embleton
Brunton
Dunstanburgh Castle
Dunstan
Craster
Cliffs of Cullernose
Rock
Rennington
Howick Hall
Howick
Howick Haven
Littlehoughton
Longhoughton
Boulmer
Boulmer Haven
Denwick
Lesbury
Alnmouth
Alnmouth Bay
Bilton
High Buston
Shilbottle
Eastfield Hall
Hermitage
Birling
Warkworth
Coquet Island
AMBLE-BY-THE-SEA
Hauxley
Hauxley Haven
Radcliffe
Hadston Carrs
Druridge Bay
Acklington
Togston
Broomhill
Red Row
West Chevington
Widdrington
Cresswell
The Scars
Ellington
Lynemouth
Beacon Point
Blue Holes
St Bartholomew's
NEWBIGGIN-BY-THE-SEA
ASHINGTON
Queen Elizabeth II
HIRST
Wansbeck
BLYTH
Cold Law
The Cheviot
Langleeford
Hedgehope Hill
Comb Fell
Dunmoor Hill
BROUGH LAW
GREAVE'S ASH
Ingram
Brandon
Powburn
Branton
Glanton
Bolton
Breamish
Cushat Law
Prendwick
CASTLE HILL
Alnham
Great Ryle
Whittingham
Eslington Hall
Callaly Castle
Thrunton
Thrunton Wood
Callaly
Yetlington
Scrainwood
Biddlestone
Netherton
Lorbotte
Long Crag
Edlingham
Bigges' Pillar
Hulne Park
Hulne Priory
Abbey
ALNWICK
Alnwick Moor
Newton on the Moor
Guyzance
Swarland
Old Swarland
Longframlington
Felton
Eshott
Alwinton
Harbottle
Burradon
High Trewill
Sharperton
Cartington
Warton
Snitter
Flotterton
Thropton
Rothbury
Cragside House
Shirlaw Pike
Holystone
Holystone Common
Caistron
Hepple
Newtown
Great Tosson
Nelly's Moss Lakes
Pauperhaugh
Coquetdale
LORDENSHAW
Brinkburn Priory
Coquet
Low Hesleyhurst
Tosson Hill
Forestburn Gate
Wingates
Causey Park
Longhorsley
Causey Park Bridge
Fenrother
Espley Hall
Ulgham
Tritlington
Billsmoor Park
Harwood Forest
Nunnykirk
Fontburn Reservoir
Fallowlees Burn
Rothley Lakes
Ewesley Burn
Rayburn Lake
Elsdon
Raylees
Netherwitton
Longwitton
Stanton
Pigdon
Hebron
Longhirst
Pegswood
Bothal
Stakeford
Guide Post
Hepscott
West Woodburn
HABITANCUM (ROMAN FORT)
Knowesgate
Cambo
Kirkwhelpington
Wallington Hall
Middleton
Hartburn
Meldon Park
Meldon
Mitford
Newminster Abbey
MORPETH
Tranwell
Whalton
Bolam Lake
Kirkharle
Capheaton
Sweethope Loughs
Saltwick
Stannington
BEDLINGTON
Plessey Woods
COWPEN
NEWSHAM
Cramlington
New Hartley
Seaton Delaval Hall
Hartley
Seaton
Seaton Delaval
Thockrington
Great Bavington
Colt Crag Reservoir
Belsay
Belsay Castle
Black Heddon
Ogle
Berwick Hill
Horton Grange
Dinnington
Prestwick
Kirkheaton
Hallington
Hallington Reservoir
Gunnerton
Colwell
Great Swinburne
Barrasford
Haughton Castle
Humshaugh
Chollerford
Low Brunton
Ryal
Ingoe
Milbourne
Fenwick
Stamfordham
Matfen
Heugh
Dalton
Bingfield
Great Whittington
PONTELAND
DARRAS HALL
Newcastle (Woolsington)
Woolsington
FAWDON
Wide Open
Seaton Burn
Dudley
Shiremoor
MONKSEATON
WHITLEY BAY
CULLERCOATS
TYNEMOUTH
Stavanger, Bergen
Kristiansand, Göteborg, Oslo, Esbjerg (summer only)
NORTH SHIELDS
SOUTH SHIELDS
HARTON
Marsden Bay
LONGBENTON
WILLINGTON
Jesmond Dene Park
WALLSEND
Tunnel
Northumberland
Tyne & Wear
Black Callerton
GOSFORTH
KENTON
BLAKELAW
JESMOND
HEATON
WALKER
BYKER
WALLBOTTLE
THROCKLEY
NEWBURN
NEWCASTLE UPON TYNE
HEBBURN
MONKTON
JARROW
Souter Point
Whitburn
Whitburn Bay
ROKER
Harlow Hill
Stagshaw Bank
Vallum
Wall
Fourstones
Acomb
Sandhoe
Aydon
VINDOVALA
Horsley
Wylam
Newton
Ovington
Ovingham
CRAWCROOK
RYTON
PRUDHOE
BLAYDON
Greenside
Barlow
Mickley Square
Painshawfield
Tyne Bridges
DUNSTON
GATESHEAD
FELLING
WHICKHAM
HEXHAM
Tyne Green
Corstopitum
Corbridge
Dilston
Dilston Castle
Riding Mill
Bywell
Hedley on the Hill
High Spen
ROWLANDS GILL
Gibside Chapel
Sunniside
Kibblesworth
WREKEN TON
BOLDON
Southwick
Hylton
Castletow
SOUTH HYLTON
SUNDERLAND
MONKWEARMOUTH
HENDON
NEW SILKSWORTH
RYHOPE
Dalton
Whitley Chapel
Slaley
Slaley Forest
Healey
Minsteracres
Chopwell
Hamsterley
Burnopfield
Tanfield
Tourist Railway
Tyne & Wear
BIRTLEY
WASHINGTON
Old Hall
Nat. Res.
Whittonstall
Newlands
Ebchester
Derwent Walk
Dipton
Tantobie
Beamish Hall
Beamish
STANLEY
Grange Villa
CHESTER-LE-STREET
Lumley Castle
Ouston
SHINEY ROW
HERRINGTON
HOUGHTON-LE-SPRING
Bournmoor
COLLIERY ROW
Broadwell Ho
Dukesfield Fell
Blanchland Moor
Blanchland
Kiln Pit Hill
Derwent Reservoir
Caterway Heads
SHOTLEY BRIDGE
Leadgate
BLACKHILL
CONSETT
Annfield Plain
SOUTH MOOR
Craghead
Iveston
Maiden Law
Edmondsley
Waldridge Fell
Great Lumley
Plawsworth
HETTON-LE-HOLE
Dalton-le-Dale
SEATON
SEAHAM
Edmundbyers
Pow Hill
Castleside
Knitsley
DELVES
Burnhope
Northumberland
Durham
Darlington
Durham
72
Middlesbrough

ENGLAND

The overall impression is one of rolling hills, fertile landscapes of neat fields, dotted with trees and hedgerows, interspersed with ancient forests, downland and plains. There are bleak moors in the north and west, but in general the English landscape is gentle and kind and the climate temperate. England is a heavily-populated land. With many pretty little towns and villages in between, yet there are stretches of glorious scenery – the Yorkshire Moors, Dartmoor and Exmoor, the Peak District and the Lake District, to name but a few.

Northumbria and Cumbria

The north-eastern corner of England tends to get left off the tourist trail. This leaves it unspoilt for visitors, because in addition to heavy industry there is magnificent countryside, redolent with history.

Alnwick (pronounced "Annick")

This town overlooking the River Aln boasts one of the finest castles in England. Alnwick Castle, ancestral home of the Percy family, the Dukes of Northumberland, still has its original 12th century keep and curtain wall. The Barbican and Gatehouse date from the 15th century. The early 14th-century Abbot's Tower in the Outer Bailey contains a regimental museum. The whole castle was heavily restored in the 19th century, both internally and externally, and the interior is now decorated in the style of a Renaissance palazzo. There is an impressive collection of Old Masters, including works by Tintoretto, Van Dyck, Titian and Turner. The grounds were landscaped by Capability Brown. The only relic of the medieval walls that surrounded the town is the 15th century Hotspur Gate. The Gate is named after Sir Henry Percy, son the first Earl of Northumberland, nicknamed "hotspur" for his bravery. St. Michael's Church has a battlemented tower and is said to be one of the best examples of 15th-century architecture in England. There is a rare Flemish chest in the vestry.

Bamburgh

This village was the ancient Saxon capital of the Kingdom of Bernicia and the later Kingdom of Northumbria. Bamburgh Castle is perched on a basalt crag over looking the sea and served for generations as a royal fortress. The keep is Norman and much of the curtain walling dates from c.1250. The remainder of the castle is mostly 19th century. The interior contains paintings and furniture, and the staterooms, as well as the kitchens, bakery and scullery can be visited. There is a particularly fine collection of porcelain. The local church has a 13th-century crypt and chancel. It is here that St. Ninian died, though he is buried on Holy Island. The churchyard contains the tomb of Grace Darling, the lifeboat heroine, who also has a special museum commemorating her famous rescue of the *Forfarshire*. in 1838.

Baskets woven on Lindisfarne (above).

Holy Trinity Church, Berwick upon Tweed (above right).

Durham Castle (right).

Hadrian's Wall, Northumberland (opposite above).

The White Walls across the River Tweed topped by the remains of Berwick Castle (opposite left).

Sheep grazing on the Cumbrian uplands (opposite right).

Beamish

Beamish lies between Chester-le-Street and Durham and is easily accessible from either city. It is home to an award-winning museum, The North of England Open Air Museum, which has been voted the best museum in Europe. This re-creation of what country life was like in Northern England in the early 20th century, is set in 300 acres of woodland and rolling countryside. It has a farm, a village complete with shops, a reconstructed colliery and a genuine drift mine with an engine house and winding gear. The miners' cottages have been furnished to show how miners lived at different periods. Visitors travel around the exhibits in early motor-buses or trams, some of which are London

trams, originally taken out of service in the late 1940s and brought here.

Berwick-on-Tweed

See "Excursions - The Scottish Borders"

Carlisle

The county town of Cumbria is an ancient border fortress and cathedral city. Carlisle was once surrounded by a wall of which only the West Walls survive. The Augustinian priory church was granted cathedral status in 1133 by Henry I. In 1292 there was a fire, but the re-building produced the magnificent vaulted ceiling, painted with stars in a blue sky. Each of the ceiling bosses is painted with a face. The ceiling was covered over in the 18th century, but restored to full glory in the 19th. The cathedral has witnessed many historic events. It is here that Edward I pronounced the excommunication of Robert the Bruce and Mary Queen of Scots was permitted to worship here during her brief incarceration in Carlisle Castle in 1568. Cromwell's men destroyed part of the cathedral, which has left it with a rather lopsided appearance, and robbed it of its library and treasures. The bells pealed a welcome to Bonnie Prince Charlie in 1745, and were removed after his defeat; they were not rehung until the 19th century. Sir Walter Scott was married here. Carlisle's other famous church, St. Cuthbert's, was founded in 686, but the present building dates from 1778. Carlisle Castle was originally built in 1092 but constantly rebuilt for military purposes until the 15th century. The massive Norman keep is one of the finest of its kind in England. A pleasant excursion from Carlisle is a trip on the Carlisle to Settle railway, with its many viaducts, which passes through countryside inaccessible by road, and is a brilliant feat of 19th-century engineering.

Cumbria and Northumbria

Cumbria and Northumbria in the north-eastern corner of England cover the counties of Cleveland, Durham, Northumberland and Tyne and Wear. Although parts of Tyneside and Teeside are heavily industrialised, there is also glorious countryside which contains some of Britain's most important national monuments and part of the largest official area of Outstanding Natural Beauty, the Northumberland National Park. The area is sparsely populated outside the large towns. East of the Cheviot Hills, a large triangle of upland country between Alnwick and Chollerford is dotted with ash trees and has no major roads or villages. The Cheviot Hills which form a natural border with Scotland are fairly steep and grass-covered. They blend in at their southern end at Lauriston Fells with the most northerly stretch of the heather-covered Pennines, the ridge of mountains that runs like a spine up the northern half of England. The northern part of the Northumberland coastline with its wide, sandy beaches and rugged cliffs has been declared a Heritage Coast. The Farne Islands, and Holy Island, also known as Lindisfarne, and Marsden Rock off the coast near South Shields are additional coastal attractions. Northumbria was an early centre of Christian missionary activity and has many ruined abbeys and fine churches. There are also several fine castles such as Alnwick, Bamburgh and

Information
Visitor Information Centre
Old Town Hall
Green Market
Carlisle
CA3 8JH
Tel: (0228) 512444

There are visitor information centres at most towns in Northumbria.

Northumberland
National Park
Eastburn, South Park
Hexham, NE46 1BS
Tel: (0434) 60555

National Trust
(Northumbria)
Scot's Gap
Morpeth
NE61 4EG
Tel: (0670) 74234

There are National Trust Information Centres at all National Trust properties.

Events
Alnwick Fair is held in late June and early July.

Lindisfarne. For the railway enthusiast and industrial archaeologist there is lots to see since it was in this part of the world that the railway originated. Northumbria is a wonderful destination for a motoring holiday because it is relatively uncrowded even in high summer, there is plenty of accommodation of all types and prices are extremely reasonable. The local people have a dialect and strong traditions all their own. There are many local delicacies such as the Singing Hinny, a scone baked on a griddle, and of course Newcastle Brown Ale.

Hadrian's Wall

The Roman wall runs for a distance of 73 miles from Wallsend on the Tyne to Bowness-on-Solway, West of Carlisle. It was built to keep out the Scots, the work starting in 122 a.d. after Emperor Hadrian's visit. The most interesting sights are the forts and civilian settlements at Corbridge, Chesters and Homesteads. One can follow parts of the wall by car but the best way to see it is to walk along the top of it. Much of the Wall is owned by the National Trust.

Hexham

Hexham is a beautiful town, an unspoilt corner of Northumbria with a wealth of sights to visit, including the Border History Museum, Hexham Abbey, Tynedale Park and Tynedale House and Chipchase Castle. For recreation there is the Hexham Racecourse.

Holy Island or Lindisfarne

The island is connected to the mainland by a causeway that can only be crossed at low tide. It was granted to St. Aidan by King Oswald of Northumbria in the 7th century. Nothing remains of the first monastery, in which the famous Lindisfarne Gospels, now in the British Museum, were copied and illuminated. The existing ruins are of the Benedictine Priory founded in 1083. The red sandstone church is like a small replica of the order's mother church, Durham Cathedral. Lindisfarne Castle is a 16th-century fort converted into a private residence by Sir Edward Lutyens, which has a fine collection of oak furniture and can be visited. The grounds include a beautiful walled garden. There is limited hotel accommodation on the Island.

Newcastle upon Tyne

This is the capital of the administrative district of Tyne and Wear as well as of Northumberland and the unofficial capital of the Northeast. It was originally a station on Hadrian's Wall but took its name from the castle built here in 1080 by Robert Curthose, eldest son of William the Conqueror . The city was destroyed several times by the Scots. Since Newcastle was a convenient port for open-cast mining, it was a flourishing port from early times. Coal was shipped south in barges, and the sarcastic expression "coals to Newcastle" was already common currency in the 17th century. The city expanded mightily in the late 18th and 19th centuries when huge shipyards were built and it became a centre of heavy industry. George Stephenson's "Rocket" railway engine was built in Newcastle. Not much remains of the castle because the site has been cut in two by the railway. However, there is the Black Gate, dating from 1247 with 17th century additions which houses a Bagpipe Museum, containing many Northumbrian pipes. St. Nicholas Cathedral stands between the famous landmark, the Tyne Bridge, and the central station. The interior is mainly 14th and 15th century and contains magnificent carving and stained glass, but the cathedral is famous mainly for its spire. This example of a crown spire, supported by flying butresses was the first in England and set the pattern for similar spires, notably that of St. Giles's in Edinburgh. The city contains many fine museums. These include the Museum of Science and Engineering, the Museum of Antiquities (relics from Hadrian's Wall) and the John George Joicey Museum. This last is housed in the Holy Jesus Hospital, established in 1681. It is now a museum of social history with audiovisual displays depicting the history of Tyneside. Newcastle and its twin city of Gateshead are famous for shopping and nightlife. Newcastle has a magnificent shopping centre known as Eldon Square, and Gateshead has the even bigger Metro Centre. Gateshead also has plenty of sports facilities and Metroland, Europe's only indoor theme park.

The Tyne Bridge, Newcastle (above).

Lindisfarne or Holy Island (right).

Sunderland

Sunderland has two important transport museums, the Monkwearmouth Station Museum and the North East Aircraft Museum, both containing important exhibits. It also has two art galleries, the Northern Centre for Contemporary Art and the Sunderland Museum and Art Gallery. Hylton Castle was built in the 15th century and has fine stone carvings.

Washington

The little town is famous largely for Washington Old Hall, home of the ancestors of George Washington. This ancient manor house, parts of which date from the 12th century, was restored in 1936. Washington also has a thriving Arts Centre and the F Pit a colliery turned into an industrial museum.

Xd
Xe
Xf
Ya
Yb
Yc
11
12
13
14
15
N O R T H
S E A
Barns Ness
Skateraw
Skateraw Harbour
Thorntonloch
Innerwick
Bilsdean
Reed Point
Cocklaw Hill
1046
Collegiate Church
Cockburnspath
Pease Bay
Siccar Point
Wheat Stack
Fast Castle
Telegraph Hill
Lumsdaine
EARN'S HEUGH
St Abb's Head
Nat. Res.
Northfield
St Abbs
Coldingham Loch
Coldingham Moor
Coldingham Bay
Buss Craig
Coldingham
Press
Lothian
Borders
Heart Law
1283
Ecelaw
Meickle Black Law
803
744
Blackburn Rig
Grantshouse
Houndwood
Eye Water
Cairncross
EYEMOUTH
Burnmouth
Abbey St Bathans
Ellemford
Horseley Hill
859
Reston
Ayton
Marygold
Auchencrow
EDIN'S HALL BROCH
COCKBURN LAW
Lamberton Beach
712
Lamberton
Marshall Meadows Bay
Lintlaw
Preston
Chirnside
Clappers
Halidon Hill 1333
Needles Eye
Sharper's Head
Duns Law
713
Duns Castle
Manderston House
Edrom
Whiteadder Water
Foulden
1307
Dirrington Great Law
Nat. Res.
DUNS
Allanton
Blackadder Water
Hutton
Paxton
Elizab. Ramparts
BERWICK-UPON-TWEED
Royal Border Bridge
Blackadder
TWEEDMOUTH
EAST ORD
SPITTAL
Tweed
Redshin Cove
Gavinton
Whitsome
Greenlaw Moor
Polwarth
Hule Moss
Horncliffe
Fogo
New Horndean
Murton
Scremerston
Cheswick Black Rocks
Swinton
Ladykirk
Norham Castle
Thornton
Cheswick
Greenlaw
Swintonmill
Norham
West Allerdean
Allerdean Burn
Goswick
Causeway flooded at high tide
Keel Head
Emmanuel Head
Holy Island or Lindisfarne
Simprim
Shoreswood
Shoresdean
Grindon
Ancroft
Haggerston
Beal
Causeway
Nat. Res.
Holy Island
Holy Island Sands
Lindisfarne Castle
Lindisfarne Priory
Castle Point
Leitholm
Borders
Northumberland
Felkington
Haydon Dean
Berrington
Guile Point
Fenham Flats
Lambden
The Hirsel
Duddo
Bowsden
Kyloe
Fenwick
Hume
Hume Castle
Eccles
Lennel
COLDSTREAM
Bridge
Pallinsburn Ho
Etal
Lowick
Buckton
Elwick
Ross
Longstone
Farne Nat. Res.
Farn Island
Staple Sound
Islands
Inner Sound
Bamburgh Castle
Bamburgh
Monks House Rocks
Stichill
Birgham
Carham
Wark
Learmouth
Branxton
Crookham
Ford
Kyloe Hills
Holburn
Detchant
Easington
Budle
Budle Bay
Ednam
Hadden
Tweed
Flodden Field 1513
Flodden
Kimmerston
692
St Cuthbert's Cave
Belford
Waren Mill
Burton
Spindlestone
Seahouses
Sprouston
Pressen
807
Downham
Fenton
KELSO
MAXWELLHEUGH
877
Housedon Hill
Milfield
Doddington
DODDINGTON MOOR
Nesbit
Till
655
Horton
Elford
North Sunderland
Roxburgh
Heiton
Hoselaw Loch
Pawston
Kilham
Lanton
Glen
Coupland
Warenton
Bellshill
Adderstone
Lucker
Newham
West Fleetham
Beadnell
Beadnell Bay
Teviot
Bowmont Forest
881
Linton Hill
Town Yetholm
Kirk Yetholm
Hethpool
Kirknewton
YEAVERING BELL
Akeld
Humbleton
WOOLER
547
Chatton
Greendykes
Warenford
Newstead
Swinhoe
Chathill
Nat. Res.
64
65
Newcastle-upon-Tyne
Newcastle-upon-Tyne
1
E15
A1
1107
6438
6355
6112
6437
6105
6461
6460
6470
6354
6525
6353
6350
6364
6089
697
698
6396
6352
6351
6348
6349
1342
1340
1341
688
20
30
32
12

48
Edinburgh
Edinburgh
Berwick-upon-Tweed
Wf
Xa
Xb
Xc
Xd
15
16
17
18
19
Broadmeadows
Yarrow
Yarrow Water
Newark Castle
Bowhill
Bowhill House
Philiphaugh
Sir Walter
SELKIRK
Bowden
Maxton
Rutherford
Linton Hill
Town Yetholm
Kirk Yetholm
Yarrow Feus
Mountbenger
Ettrick Water
Kirkhope
Ettrickbridge
Midlem
Longnewton
Waterloo Monument
PENIEL HEUGH
Nisbet
Eckford
Linton
Morebattle
Riddell
Lilliesleaf
Belses
Ancrum
Montevoit House
Crailing
Bonjedward
Cessford
Clerklands
Ale Water
HOWNAM LAW
Ettrick Forest
Black Knowe Head
Cavers Hill
Akermoor Loch
Ashkirk
Wolll
Minto Hills
Minto
Chesters
Lanton
Jedburgh Abbey
JEDBURGH
Crailinghall
Whitton
Mowhaugh
Gilmanscleuch
Langhope Burn
Hassendean
Newton
Mary Queen of Scots House
Howgate
Craik Moor
Shaws Under Loch
Horsleyhill
Knowetownhead
Hundalee
Oxnam
Hownam
Bowmont Water
Crosslee
Dun Knowe
Hellmoor Loch
Appletreehall
Denholm
Dunion Hill
Ferniehirst Castle
Mossburnford
Chatto
Oxnam Water
Swinside Hall
HAWICK
Wilton Dean
Hornshole Bridge
RUBERS LAW
Alemoor Loch
Borthwickshiels
Rankle Burn
Robertson
Kirkton
Camptown
Beefstand Hill
Buccleuch
Borthwickbrae
Borthwick Water
Motte
White Hill
Bonchester Bridge
Abbotrule
PENNYMUIR (ROMAN CAMPS)
WODEN LAW
Snoot
Burnfoot
Deanburnhaugh
Branxholme
Branxholm Hall
BONCHESTER HILL
Redcleuch Edge
Craik Forest
Newmill
Slitrig Water
Hobkirk
Chesters
Jed Water
Leithope Forest
CHEW GREEN (ROMAN CAMPS)
Blindburn
Kale Water
Northhouse
Dodburn
Southdean
Carter Bar
Arks Edge
Craik
Pike Hill
Teviot
Teviothead
The Pike
Note o' the Gate
Wauchope Forest
Ravens Knowe
Roman camps
Carter Fell
The Cheviot
Stock Hill
Skelfhill Pen
Allan Water
Fanna Hill
Singdean
Peel Fell
Kielderhead Moor
Catcleugh Reservoir
Redesdale Forest
Byrness
Sandy Edge
Cauldcleuch Head
Oh Me Edge
Rochester
HIGH ROCHESTER (ROMAN
Mosspaul Hotel
Wisp Hill
Tudhope Hill
Border
Blackman's Law
Rede
Meggat Water
Hermitage Castle
Liddel Water
Saughtree
Emblehope Moor
Jamestown
Faw Side
Din Fell
Hermitage Water
Monkside
Blackburn Common
Padon Hill
Broad Head
Hermitage
Newlands
Larriston
Kielder
Highgreen Manor
Ewes Water
Roan Fell
Steele Road
Larriston Fells
Bakethin Reservoir
Kielder Forest
Black Middens Bastle House
Eskdale
Black Knowe
Kielder Water (Reservoir)
Tarset Burn
Bentpath
Dumfries & Galloway
Borders
Tarras Water
Black Edge
Newcastleton
Newcastleton Forest
Liddesdale
Falstone
Greenhaugh
Lewis Burn
North Tyne
Glendhu Hill
Rough Pike
LANGHOLM
Tinnis Hill
Monument Sir J Malcolm
Kershope Burn
Cumbria
Forest Park
Bower
Hesleyside
Wauchope Water
Kershopefoot
Bigholms
Auchenrivock
Caulside
Kershope Forest
Black Lyne
Sighty Crag
Paddaburn Moor
Chirdon Burn
Blacka Burn
Nook
Hollows Tower
Rowanburn
White Lyne
Churnsike Lodge
Blackpool Gate
Solwaybank
Crossings
White Preston
Wark Forest
Whygate
Stonehaugh
Warks Burn
Evertown
Canonbie
Roughsike
Bewcastle
Roman fort
Butterburn
Milltown
Dumfries & Galloway
Cumbria
Haggbeck
Spadeadam Forest
Haughton Common
Chapelknowe
The Debatable Land
Easton
Irthing
Black Fell
Broomlee Lough
CARRAW
Stapleton
Spadeadam
Greenlee Lough
VERCOVICIUM (HOUSESTEADS)
Runaway marriages
Solway Moss
Northumberland
Thirlwall Common
Whiteside
Crag Lough
Gretna Green
Gretna
Longtown
Boltonfellend
Kirkcambeck
West Hall
HADRIAN'S WALL
Walltown Crags
Thirlwall Castle
Gilsland
AESICA
Greatchesters
VINDOLANDA (CHESTERHOLM)
Bardon Mill
Rigg
Kirklinton
Hethersgill
CAMBOGLANNA (BIRDOSWALD)
Greenhead
Stanegate
Henshaw
Sarkfoot Point
Hether Burn
Banks
King Water
Willowford
Blenkinsopp Castle
Bellister Castle
Haltwhistle
Melkridge
Willimontswick
Redkirk Point
Westlinton
Smithfield
Walton
Lanercost Priory
VALLUM
Banks East
Todhills
Rockcliffe Marsh
Scaleby Hill
Newtown
Naworth Castle
Denton Fell
South Tyne
Eden
Scaleby
BRAMPTON
Low Row
Plenmeller Common
Blackford
Irthington
Carlisle
Featherstone Castle
Rowfoot
Fellhouse Fell
Burgh Marsh
Rockcliffe
Harker
Hallbankgate
Tindale
Lambley
Burgh by Sands
Beaumont
KINGSTOWN
Houghton
Low Crosby
Newby East
Talkin Tarn
Tindale Tarn
Whitfield
Cargo
Tindale Fells
Forest Head
Halton Lea Gate
Stonehouse
Bearsbridge
Tower
Grinsdale
STANWIX
Warwick Bridge
Warwick
Hayton
Talkin
Thurstonfield
Moorhouse
How
Cold Fell
Whitfield Moor
Kirkbampton
CARLISLE
Cathedral
Heads Nook
Faugh
Castle Carrock
Knarsdale
Ninebanks
Great Orton
Newby West
Scotby
Wetheral
Great Corby
Gatehouse
Cumrew Fell
Slaggyford
Wiggonby
Cummersdale
Carleton
Corby Castle
Baldwinholme
Cumwhinton
Cumwhitton
Durdar
Brisco
Thursby
Dalston
Cotehill
Hornsby
Cumrew
Kirkhaugh
Ayle
West Allen
71
Darlington
Dumfries
Glasgow
Workington

53
Edinburgh
Berwick-upon-Tweed
Xf
Ya
Yb
Yc
Yd
WOOLER
Akeld
Humbleton
Earle
Middleton Hall
Chatton
Greendykes
Chillingham
Ros Castle
Haugh Head
Lilburn Tower
Newtown
Hepburn
Cateran Hill
Newham
Newstead
Ellingham
West Fleetham
Chathill
Swinhoe
Beadnell Bay
Nat. Res.
Snook Point
High Newton-by-the-Sea
St Mary's or Newton Haven
Embleton Bay
Preston
Preston Tower
Brownieside
Christon Bank
Brunton
Embleton
Dunstanburgh Castle
North Charlton
South Charlton
West Ditchburn
Eglingham
Old Bewick
Bewick Moor
Cold Law
1485
The Cheviot
2674
Langleeford
Hedgehope Hill
Ilderton
Roseden
Roddam
Wooperton
East Lilburn
New Bewick
Beanley
Rock
Rennington
Dunstan
Craster
Cliffs of Cullernose
Howick Hall
Howick
Howick Haven
Comb Fell
Dunmoor Hill
1860
BROUGH LAW
Ingram
GREAVE'S ASH
Breamish
Brandon
Powburn
Branton
Glanton
Bolton
Hulne Priory
Littlehoughton
Longhoughton
Boulmer
Boulmer Haven
Hulne Park
Abbey
ALNWICK
Denwick
Lesbury
Alnmouth
Alnmouth Bay
Bilton
2020
Cushat Law
Prendwick
Great Ryle
Whittingham
Eslington Hall
Thrunton
Thrunton Wood
Callaly Castle
Callaly
CASTLE HILL
Alnham
Yetlington
Scrainwood
Alnwick Moor
High Buston
Shilbottle
Edlingham
Biddlestone
Netherton
Lorbotte
Long Crag
1047
Biggés' Pillar
Eastfield Hall
Birling
Warkworth
Hermitage
Coquet Island
Newton on the Moor
Guyzance
AMBLE-BY-THE-SEA
Hauxley
Hauxley Haven
Alwinton
Harbottle
Burradon
High Trewitt
Cartington
Shirlaw Pike
Sharperton
Warton
Snitter
Cragside House
Swarland
Old Swarland
Acklington
Togston
Radcliffe
Hadston Carrs
Holystone
Holystone Common
Flotterton
Thropton
Rothbury
Newtown
Pauperhaugh
Nelly's Moss Lakes
Longframlington
Felton
Broomhill
Red Row
Druridge Bay
Caistron
Hepple
Great Tosson
LORDENSHAWS
Coquetdale
Coquet
Brinkburn Priory
Eshott
West Chevington
Widdrington
Tosson Hill
1444
Low Hesleyhurst
Rothbury Forest
Forestburn Gate
Billsmoor Park
Wingates
Causey Park
Longhorsley
Causey Park Bridge
Cresswell
The Scars
Harwood Forest
Elsdon
Fontburn Reservoir
Nunnykirk
Rayburn Lake
Fenrother
Espley Hall
Ulgham
Tritlington
Ellington
Lynemouth
Ewesley Burn
Rothley Lakes
Netherwitton
Longwitton
Stanton
Hebron
Longhirst
Beacon Point
Blue Holes
St Bartholomew's
Raylees
Pigdon
Pegswood
ASHINGTON
NEWBIGGIN-BY-THE-SEA
Queen Elizabeth II
Hart Burn
Mitford
Newminster Abbey
Bothal
HIRST
Wansbeck
Woodburn
HABITANCUM (ROMAN FORT)
Knowesgate
Cambo
Kirkwhelpington
Middleton
Hartburn
Meldon Park
Meldon
MORPETH
Guide Post
Stakeford
Hepscott
BLYTH
Tranwell
Bedlington
COWPEN
Wallington Hall
Kirkharle
Bolam Lake
Whalton
Saltwick
Sweethope Loughs
Capheaton
Blyth
Ogle
Stannington
NEWSHAM
Plessey Woods
Cramlington
New Hartley
Seaton Delaval Hall
Seaton Hartley
Thockrington
Great Bavington
Colt Crag Reservoir
Kirkheaton
Belsay
Belsay Castle
Black Heddon
Berwick Hill
Horton Grange
Dinnington
Seaton Delaval
Dudley
Northumberland
Tyne & Wear
Shiremoor
WHITLEY BAY
Milbourne
Hallington
Hallington Reservoir
Colwell
Gunnerton
Great Swinburne
Barrasford
Ryal
Ingoe
Fenwick
Prestwick
Seaton Burn
Wide Open
MONKSEATON
CULLERCOATS
TYNEMOUTH
Stavanger, Bergen
Haughton Castle
Humshaugh
Chollerford
Low Brunton
Bingfield
Great Whittington
Matfen
Stamfordham
Heugh
Dalton
PONTELAND
DARRAS HALL
Newcastle (Woolsington)
Woolsington
FAWDON
LONGBENTON
WILLINGTON
NORTH SHIELDS
Kristiansand, Göteborg, Oslo, Esbjerg (summer only)
SOUTH SHIELDS
Stagshaw Bank
Vallum
Harlow Hill
Black Callerton
GOSFORTH
KENTON
Jesmond Dene Park
WALLSEND
Wall
Fourstones
Acomb
Sandhoe
ROMAN WALL
Aydon Castle
VINDOVALA
THROCKLEY
WALL BOTTLE
BLAKELAW
JESMOND
HEATON
WALKER
Tunnel
HARTON
JARROW
Marsden Bay
Nat. Res.
HEXHAM
Corbridge
Newton
Horsley
Wylam
NEWBURN
NEWCASTLE UPON TYNE
BYKER
HEBBURN
MONKTON
Souter Point
Whitburn
Whitburn Bay
Dilston
Dilston Castle
Ovington
Ovingham
PRUDHOE
CRAWCROOK
RYTON
Tyne Bridges
DUNSTON
Tyne Green
Bywell
Mickley Square
Greenside
BLAYDON
Barlow
WHICKHAM
GATESHEAD
FELLING
BOLDON
Southwick
ROKER
Riding Mill
Painshawfield
High Spen
ROWLANDS GILL
Sunniside
WREKENTON
Hylton
Castletown
Wear
Healey
Dalton
Slaley
Hedley on the Hill
Chopwell
Gibside Chapel
Tourist railway
Kibblesworth
Old Hall
SOUTH HYLTON
MONKWEARMOUTH
SUNDERLAND
Whitley Chapel
Devil's Water
Slaley Forest
Minsteracres
Whittonstall
Hamsterley
Burnopfield
Tanfield
BIRTLEY
WASHINGTON
HENDON
NEW SILKSWORTH
Ryhope
Broadwell Ho
1171
Dukesfield Fell
Nat. Res.
Derwent Reservoir
Kiln Pit Hill
Newlands
Ebchester
Derwent Walk
Tantobie
Beamish Hall
Beamish
Ouston
SHINEY ROW
HERRINGTON
Lambton Castle
Blanchland Moor
Caterway Heads
SHOTLEY BRIDGE
Leadgate
Dipton
STANLEY
Grange Villa
Craghead
CHESTER-LE-STREET
Bournmoor
HOUGHTON-LE-SPRING
1467
Edmundbyres
Blanchland
Pow Hill
BLACKHILL
CONSETT
DELVES
Iveston
Annfield Plain
SOUTH MOOR
Maiden Law
Edmondsley
Waldridge Fell
Great Lumley
COLLIERY ROW
HETTON-LE-HOLE
SEATON
SEAHAM
Northumberland
Durham
Castleside
Knitsley
Burnhope
Plawsworth
Dalton-le-Dale
Darlington
Durham
72
Middlesbrough

The Isle of Man, Isle of the Vikings

An island in the North Sea with its own language and the oldest parliament in the world. There is lovely, unspoilt scenery, and a timeless feel to the little towns and villages that have hardly changed in 100 years.

The Isle of Man lies in the North Sea closer to Scotland than to Ireland or England, though it is linked by ferry services to the English mainland. It is considered to be geographically part of England, though it was sold to Scotland in 1266, having previously been a Viking dependency. It passed to England under Edward I. Man's political relationship with England is complex. The reigning monarch rules the Isle of Man as Lord of Man though this is not one of the official titles of the sovereign and he or she is only known by that name on the island. The title was sold to the crown in 1765 by the Duke of Atholl, the then Lord of Man. The Manx parliament, the Tynwald, reputed to be the oldest continuous parliament in the world, first sat in 979. It has two houses, the Council or Upper House and the House of Keys. The island issues its own stamps and currency, though British and Irish money are accepted. It has thus become a tax haven for British companies, a major contribution to the island's prosperity. The Isle of Man has a very curious coat of arms, consisting of three legs joined in the centre. They are supposedly the legs of the warlock Mannanin, who put a curse on the island and so was changed into this shape by St. Patrick, to which the warlock is said to have responded "Whichever way you throw me, I stand!". This motto, in Latin, appears on Manx coinage.

The island is very hilly, the highest point being Snafell (2036 feet) a favourite spot for climbers and walkers. The wealth of Norse mythology and Celtic and Viking remains make it of great historical interest. There are more runic inscriptions on the Isle of Man than in the whole of Norway. The rune stones have largely been preserved in the churches. The oldest remains date back to 3500 b.c.

Douglas has been the capital of the Isle of Man since 1869. It is also the chief holiday resort and the ferry terminal. **The Manx Museum**, on Crelin's Hill, is the national museum devoted to Manx culture and social history, and has fascinating displays including a reconstructed dairy and farmhouse. The **Legislative Buildings** (1894) in which the Manx parliament sits can be visited. Another Manx institution open to the public is the **Cattery**, where Manx cats (cats without tails) are bred. **Castletown** was the old capital. It has a 13th century castle, **Castle Rushen**, developed by successive Lords of Man. **Peel** is the most attractive village on the island, and the main centre for curing Manx kippers, the local delicacy. **Peel Castle** stands on **St. Patrick's Isle**, linked by a causeway to the western side of the harbour. It is mainly 13th century but is surrounded by a massive 16th-century wall.

Ramsey is the Isle of Man's second city, which has lovely beaches and **Grove Rural Life Museum**. Ramsey is linked to Douglas by the **Manx Electric Railway.** A ride on this 3-ft gauge track offers wonderful scenic views. The train stops on the way at **Laxey**, which has an **Industrial Archæology Park** featuring a giant water wheel used in mining operations. The mountain road that links the two main towns is used by the famous Isle of Man TT Motorcycle Race, and at the highest point on the course there is a **Motorcycle Museum**, which exhibits motor bikes and racing memorabilia. **Port St. Mary** and **Port Erin** are fishing villages and tourist resorts from which boats make day trips to the neighbouring island, the **Calf of Man.** This island is now owned by the National Trust and administered as a bird sanctuary and nature reserve. **Port Erin** has a **Railway Museum** and a **Marine Biological Station** which contains an aquarium.

Information
Isle of Man Tourist Board
13 Victoria Street
Douglas, Isle of Man
Tel: (0624) 74323

Events
On 5 July (midsummer's day by the Julian calendar) new laws promulgated by the Tynwald, the Manx Parliament are read out in the Manx language on Tynwald Hill in the centre of the island. The ceremony begins with a service at the Church of St. John the Baptist, followed by a procession.
The Isle of Man Tourist Trophy is probably the most famous motorcycle race in the world It is held in late May or early June. Other cycling and motorcycling races are held between June and September, including the Tudor Webasto Manx Car Rally.
Peel holds a Viking Festival in the first wek in July, to commemorate the Norse invasion of 798, when replica longships are launched.

The waterwheel at Laxey (top left).

Douglas, administrative offices (left).

The ferry, with Port Erin in the Background (above).

54
Stranrear
Dumfries
Vb
Vc
Vd
Ve
Vf
Wa
The Machars
Bladnoch
Kirkinner
Wigtown Bay
Kirkdale
Fleet Bay
Islands of Fleet
Girthon
Sandgreen
Knockbrex
Kirkandrews
Borgue
Borness
Ross
Little Ross
Kirkcudbright Bay
St Mary's Isle
Maclellan's Castle
KIRKCUDBRIGHT
Townhead
Balmae
Auchencairn
Kirkcarswell
Rascarrel
Dundrennan
Abbey
Orroland
Abbey Head
Castle Loch
Mochrum Loch
Culshabben
Chapel Finian
Barrachan
Elrig
Whauphill
Sorbie
Eggerness Point
Garlieston
Mochrum
Drumtroddan
STANDING STONES
Port William
White Loch
Monreith Mains
FORT
Monreith
Barsalnoch Point
Monreith Bay
Luce Bay
WHITHORN
St Ninian's Priory
Portyerrock Bay
Cairn Head
Glasserton
St Ninian's Cave
Isle of Whithorn
St Ninian's Chapel
Cuteloy
Burrow Head
20
21
22
23
24
IRISH SEA
Point of Ayre
The Ayres
Belfast
Cranstal
The Lhen
Dhowin
Bride
Andreas
Jurby West
Jurby East
Ballamoar Castle
Ballasalla
Sandygate
Regaby
St Judes
Dhoor
RAMSEY
The Cronk
The Curragh's
Sulby
Ramsey Bay
Churchtown
CRONK SUMARK
Port e Vullen
Maughold Head
Maughold
Ballaugh
North Barrule
Ballajora
Ravensdale
Kirk Michael
Corrany
Sulby Reservoir
CASHTAL YN ARD
Ballacarnane Beg
Snaefell
Barregarrow
Druidale
Dhoon
White Strand
Shoughlaige-e-Caine
Lady Isabel
KING ORRY'S GRAVE
St Patrick's Isle
Knocksharry
Cronk-y-Voddy
Injebreck
Cathedral
Peel Castle
Lambfell Moar
Colden
Laxey
Ballagyr
PEEL
Tynwald Hill
Ballig
Ballacannell
Laxey Bay
Patrick
St John's
Baldwin
Baldrine
Clay Head
Isle of Man
Glenmaye
Hillberry
Crosby
Glen Vine
Union Mills
ONCHAN
Foxdale
Garth
Dalby
SOUTH BARRULE
Eairy
Braaid
The Braaid
DOUGLAS
Douglas Bay
Niarbyl Bay
Close Clark
St Mark's
Quine's Hill
Douglas Head
Newtown
Fleetwood, Heysham
Liverpool (seasonal)
Ronague
Ballamodha
Ballaveare
Port Soderick
Lingague
BALLAKELLY
tourist railway
Fleshwick Bay
Rushen Abbey
CRONK NY MERRIU
Colby
Ballabeg
Santon Head
Dublin (seasonal)
Bradda Head
Bradda
Ballasalla
Port Erin
Balladoole
Derbyhaven
The Howe
CASTLETOWN
MULL HILL
Castle Rushen
Cregneish
Port St. Mary
Castletown Bay
Langness
Calf Sound
Nat. Res.
Spanish Head
Dreswick Point
Calf of Man
Chicken Rock

Cumbria, the Moors and Dales

Two beautiful and historic districts on either side of the Pennines, including Cumbria, part of County Durham, North Yorkshire with the North York Moors National Park and Lancashire.

Barnard Castle

This lovely little town on the north bank of the Tees is named after its ruined castle. The town and castle take their name from Bernard de Bailleul, son of Guy de Bailleul who fought at the Battle of Hastings and whom William charged with subdueing this part of the country. The original wooden fort was rebuilt by Bernard in stone c.1150. The castle later passed to Richard III and it remained a royal property until the 17th century. The last owner, Sir Henry Vane, largely dismantled it to add to his own castle at Raby, which is nearby and is well worth visiting.

Darlington

Darlington was founded by the Anglo-Saxons and flourished as a centre of the wool industry, but it was the coming of the railways that put Darlington on the map. The North Road Station, opened in 1842, is now the Darlington Railway Centre and Museum. The main attraction is *Locomotion No. 1*, the engine used to haul the world's first passenger train in 1825. The Church of St. Cuthbert has very fine Early English architecture and a magnificent rood screen.

Durham

Durham grew up around its cathedral, which dominates the city. Durham Castle is the only fortress in England which never fell to the Scots, a fact which is hardly surprising considering how impregnable it is. It was later used as a bishops' palace and then as a university college. Little of the original castle built by William the Conqueror survives, except for the chapel. The castle keep is a cunning replica built in the 19th century as student dormitories! A second chapel was added in the 16th century which has some amusing carvings, including one of a pig playing the bagpipes, a local comment on the marauding Scots! The town hall and guildhall are worth visiting as is the Old Fulling Mill. Fulling was the process of cleaning, stretching and thickening cloth. The mill now contains a museum of archæology whose exhibits include some Roman altars excavated in the district.

North York Moors National Park

The remote, wild country of the Moors is nevertheless well served with roads and has two scenic railways, the North York Moors Railway and the Middlesborough to Whitby line. Railway excursions are sometimes the best way to see landscape that is far from paved roads. There is plenty to do and see in the area, especially in the coastal resorts. The dales (valleys) within the Park are Eskdale, Farndale and Newtondale, and there are the small market towns of Helmsley, Newtondale and Pickering. Nunnington Hall (1655) near Helmsley

West Tanfield, Yorkshire (above).

The Yorkshire Dales, a typical scene (above right).

Castle Howard, one of the greatest stately homes in Britain (above far right).

The ruins of Rievaulx Abbey (right).

Robin Hood's Bay, a seaside beauty spot (opposite above).

Whitby harbour with fishing boats (opposite below).

in Ryedale is a delightful Yorkshire manor house, the home of the Graham family for nearly 400 years, which contains a unique collection of miniature rooms, each one-eighth life size. The Park contains the ruined abbeys of Rievaulx and Byland. Mount Grace Priory at Osmotherley, is a National Trust property which exhibits an interesting display of monastic life. Newborough Priory is the site of Oliver Cromwell's tomb. At Coxwold, Shandy Hall, home of the author of *Tristram Shandy*, Lawrence Sterne (1713-68), has been lovingly restored. At Hutton-le-Hole there is the Ryedale Folk Museum.

Penrith

Ruined Penrith Castle (14th-15th century) stands opposite the railway station. The 16th-century grammar school attended by William Wordsworth his sister Dorothy can be visited. The town has some interesting inns, especially the 16th-century Two Lions, once the town house of the Lowther family and the Gloucester Arms in Great Dockray which dates from 1477 and may have been a residence of Richard III.

Richmond

The town grew up around the Norman castle of Richemont, which dominates the town overlooking the River Swale. Richmond grew prosperous on the wool trade; it is largely built of stone, some of the houses even have sandstone slab roof tiles. The street called Newbiggin contains some lovely Georgian houses; at one end there is the former town gaol which is now the headquarters of the Womens Royal Voluntary Service. The Richmondshire Museum specialises in local history, including a major display devoted to the television series *All Creatures Great and Small* which was filmed in the area. The Theatre Royal was built in 1788 and restored in 1963.

Robin Hood's Bay

This famous beauty spot has the widest and sandiest beaches in the area. There is a definite link with Robin Hood who, despite his exploits in Sherwood Forest, was born a Yorkshireman.

Scarborough

Although the most popular seaside resort in the north-east and allegedly the oldest in Britain, there is more to Scarborough than fun fairs and sandy beaches. There has been a settlement since prehistoric times on the headland where the medieval Castle now stands, and the 4th-century remains of a Roman signal station are visible here. Richard III is alleged to have stayed at a house in South Bay (now a café). The town has several theatres; the playwright Alan Ayckbourne always stages the premières of his plays at the Theatre in the Round.

Stockton-on-Tees

An ancient market town which claims to have the broadest High Street in England – broad enough to have its Town Hall (1735) on an island in the centre – Stockton is the centre of heavily industrialised Teeside. The open-air market was started in 1310 and is still held on Wednesdays and Saturdays. The Stockton Heritage Centre in Green Dragon Yard off the High Street includes a Georgian theatre, museum, inn and craft shops. Stockton was the destination of the first passenger train which steamed into the town on 27 September 1825.

Whitby

This charming little seaside resort is now more notorious than famous, thanks to the fact that it is the setting for much of Bram Stoker's novel *Dracula*. The sinister-looking ruined abbey and the windswept churchyard with its crooked tombs are thought to have inspired the novelist, who stayed here frequently. The Dracula Society regularly tours the town, visiting places mentioned in the novel, and first and foremost the churchyard. Whitby is split in two by the River Esk and the harbour.

Information
Northumbria Tourist Board
Aykley Heads
Durham
DH1 5UX
Tel: (091) 384 6905

North York Moors National Park Information Service
The Old Vicarage
Bondgate, Helmsley
Tel: (0439) 70657

Tips
The North Yorkshire Moors National Park is a good place to visit in late August and September when the heather is flowering. Avoid it in winter, when travel is difficult and you could get snowed in or stranded. In very dry weather, the Danby Forest Drive is closed. Avoid the coast in July and August if you don't like crowds.

55

Wb
Wc
Wd
We
Wf
20
21
22
23
24
Solway Firth
Barnhourie Sands
Rough I
Rough Firth
Castlehill Point
Auchencairn Bay
Hestan Island
Balcary Point
Rascarrel
Wedholme Flow
Abbeytown
Oulton
Lessonhall
Baldwinholme
Thursby
Wigton
West Curthwaite
Rosley
Westward
Red Dial
Beckfoot
Pelutho
Dundraw
Blencogo
Waverton
Bromfield
Langrigg
Mawbray
Edderside
Westnewton
Dubmill Point
Allonby
Allonby Bay
Aspatria
Hayton
Blennerhasset
Mealsgate
Boltongate
Torpenhow
Caldbeck
Parkend
Hesket Newmarket
Allerby
Crosscanonby
Crosby
Plumbland
Bothel
Whitrigg
Ireby
Gilcrux
Binsey 1467
Uldale
Branthwaite
MARYPORT
Dearham
Tallentire
Sunderland
Blindcrake
Bewaldeth
Flimby
Broughton Moor
Bridekirk
Dovenby
Broughton
Knott 2329
CARROCK FELL
Seaton
Camerton
COCKERMOUTH
Castle
Embleton
Bassenthwaite
Brigham
Greysouthen
Bassenthwaite Lake
Skiddaw Forest
Skiddaw 3054
Saddleback or Blencathra 2847
WORKINGTON
Great Clifton
Bridgefoot
Eaglesfield
Deanscales
Thornthwaite Forest
Mirehouse
Moss Bay
Branthwaite
Dean
Pardshaw
Lorton
Thornthwaite
Whinlatter Pass
Applethwaite
Threlkeld
Distington
Ullock
Gilgarran
Mockerkin
Braithwaite
KESWICK
CASTLE RIGG
Lowca
Pica
Lorton Vale
Derwent Water
Parton
Morseby
Asby
Lamplugh
Loweswater
Grasmoor 2791
Stair
Little Town
Legburthwaite
Arlecdon
Derwent Fells
WHITEHAVEN
Frizington
Kirkland
Crummock Water
Buttermere
Grange
Lodore Falls
Saltom Bay
Sandwith
St Bees Head
Ennerdale Bridge
Scale Force
Buttermere Fell
Powder Stone
Rosthwaite
Thirlmere
CLEATOR MOOR
Ennerdale Water
Scarth Gap Pass
Honister Pass
Seatoller
Borrowdale
Cleator
Rottington
Nat. Res.
St Bees
EGREMONT
Ennerdale
Taylorgill Force
Seathwaite
Black Sail Pass
Great Gable 2949
Sty Head
Langdale Pikes
Haile
Nethertown
Beckermet
Wasdale Head
Copeland Forest
Wastwater
Scafell Pike 3210
Bow Fell 2960
Dungeon Ghyll Force
Grasmere
Chapel Stile
Braystones
Calder Bridge
Ponsonby
Cross
Cumbrian Mountains
Lake District National Park
Gosforth
Nether Wasdale
Hardknott Pass
Wrynose Pass
Cockley Beck
Seascale
Santon Bridge
Eskdale Green
Boot
BURNMOOR
Beckfoot
ROMAN FORT
Furness Fells
Seathwaite Tarn
Drigg
Holmrook
Eskdale
Dudden Valley
The Old Man of Coniston 2635
Coniston
Ravenglass
Nat. Res.
Muncaster Castle
ROMAN FORT
BIRKER FELL
Devoke Water
Woodend
Hall Dunnerdale
Torver
Coniston Water
Waberthwaite
Ulpha
Whitfell 1881
Tarn Bay
Hycemoor
Corney
CORNEY FELL
Broughton Mills
Woodland Fell
Water Yeat
Blawith
Satterthwaite
SWINSIDE FELL
Bootle
Duddon Bridge
Broughton in Furness
Annaside
Black Combe 1970
Hallthwaites
Whitbeck
Foxfield
Grizebeck
Lowick
Colton
Spark Bridge
Gawthwaite
Penny Bridge
Broughton Beck
Greenodd
Beck Side
Arrad Foot
The Hill
Whicham
Kirkby-in-Furness
Silecroft
Kirksanton
MILLOM
Soutergate
ULVERSTON
Haverigg
Duddon Sands
Pennington
Askam in Furness
Lindal in Furness
DALTON-IN-FURNESS
Urswick
Stainton with Adgarley
Bardsea
SUNBRICK
BARROW-IN-FURNESS
Furness Abbey
Scales
Gleaston
Baycliff
Aldingham
Isle of Walney
NORTH SCALE
Newton
Leece
Newbiggin
VICKERSTOWN
Biggar
Roosebeck
Rampside
Foulney Island
South End
Piel Island
Hilpsford Point

64
Carlisle
Carlisle
Xa
Xb
Xc
Xd
Xe
Xf
Brisco
Wreay
Cotehill
Hornsby
Cumrew
Newbiggin
Croglin Water
Croglin
Kirkhaugh
Ayle
Alston
Carr Shield
Allenheads
Coalcleugh
Nenthead
Northumberland
Durham
Rockhope
Low Hesket
Aiketgate
High Hesket
Ainstable
Armathwaite
Ruckcroft
Staffield
Renwick
Hartside Height
Gilderdale Forest
Leadgate
Bayles
Garrigill
Middlehope Moor
Cornriggs
Cowshill
Wearhead
St. John's Chapel
Westgate
Daddry Shield
Ireshopeburn
Burnhope Reservoir
Weardale
Ivegill
Low Braithwaite
Calthwaite
Hutton End
Kirkoswald
Lazonby
Gamblesby
Glassonby
Melmerby Fell
Melmerby
Inglewood Forest
Plumpton
Plumpton Head
Graet Salkeld
Little Salkeld
Hunsonby
LONG MEG & HER DAUGHTERS
Ousby
Burnhope Seat
Lamonby
Unthank
Skelton
Hutton-in-the-Forest
Catterlen
Langwathby
Winskill
Skirwith
Townhead
Cross Fell
Kirkland
Harwood
Langdon Common
Langdon Beck
Chapelfell Top
Cow Green Reservoir
Johnby
Blencow
Edenhall
Blencarn
Milburn Forest
Greystoke
Newton Reigny
PENRITH
HOGBACK STONES
Culgaith
Newbiggin
Milburn
Dufton Fell
Forest-in-Teesdale
High Force
Newbiggin
Teesdale
Berrier
Newbiggin
Penruddock
Stainton
Dacre
Dalemain
Tirril
Brougham Castle
Clifton
Temple Sowerby
Thore Kirkby
Knock
Dufton
Nat. Res.
Mickle Fell
Hutton
Great Mell Fell
Pooley Bridge
Askham
Lowther
Cliburn
Melkinthorpe
Long Marton
Brampton
High Cup Nick
Lune Forest
Wreay
Watermillock
Helton
Whale
Great Strickland
Morland
Bolton
Crackenthorpe
King's Meaburn
APPLEBY-IN-WESTMORLAND
Murton
Hilton
Grassholme
Selset Reservoir
Dockray
MOOR DIVOCK
Little Strickland
Newby
Sleagill
Colby
Hunderthwaite Moor
Clove Lodge
Sandwick
Martindale
Bampton
Reagill
Hoff
Great Ormside
Durham
Cumbria
Balderhead Reservoir
Patterdale
Dale Head
Rosgill
Shap
Keld
Abbey
Mauld's Meaburn
Drybeck
Sandford
Warcop
Helbeck
Brough
North Stainmore
Bleatarn
Great Musgrave
Bridgend
Hartsop
Haweswater Reservoir
CASTLE CRAG
Crosby Ravensworth
EWE CLOSE
Great Asby
Brough Sowerby
Kaber
Maiden Castle
Rey Cross
Stainmore Forest
Wet Sleddale Reservoir
Soulby
Winton
High Street
Shap Fells
Orton
Crosby Garrett
Waitby
Hartley
KIRKBY STEPHEN
Nateby
Harter Fell
Kentmere Reservoir
Kirkstone Pass
Raisbeck
Greenholme
Bretherdale Head
Kelleth
Newbiggin-on-Lune
Cumbria
North Yorkshire
Wansfell
Sadgill
Tebay
AMBLESIDE
Kentmere
Borrowdale
Weasdale
Ravenstonedale
Ravenseat
Rogan's Seat
West Stonesdale
Keld
Pendragon Castle
Park
Troutbeck
Forest Hall
Langdale Fell
Outhgill
Troutbeck Bridge
Low Dovengill
Mallerstang Common
Thwaite
Muker
Garnett Bridge
Watchgate
Ings
Staveley
Grayrigg
Howgill Fells
The Calf
Low Haygarth
Uldale Ho
Great Shunner Fell
Buttertubs Pass
WINDERMERE
BOWNESS-ON-WINDERMERE
Burneside
Meal Bank
Beck Foot
Cautley
Lambrigg Fell
Firbank
Grisedale
Cotterdale
Crook
KENDAL
Ingmire Hall
SEDBERGH
Baugh Fell
Garsdale Head
Hardraw Force
High Shaw
Sedbusk
Hardraw
Winster
Underbarrow
Grigghall
New Hutton
Millthrop
Garsdale
Hawes
Burtersett
Gayle
Bowland Bridge
Crosthwaite
Brigsteer
Natland
Millholme
Oxenholme
Killington Reservoir
Killington
Rise Hill
Garsdale
Widdale Fell
Yorkshire Dales
Sizergh Castle
Old Hutton
Gawthrop
Dent
Cowgill
Dentdale
Countersett
Semer Water
Marsett
The Howe
Cartmel Fell
Witherslack Hall
Levens
Sedgwick
Stainton
Gatebeck
Middleton
Stone House
Staveley-in-Cartmel
Witherslack
Endmoor
Rigmanden Park
Dodd Fell
Stalling Busk
Hincaster
Leasgill
Heversham
Crooklands
Old Town
Barbon
Crag Hill
Deepdale
National Park
Middle Tongue
Oughtershaw
Mill Side
High Newton
Milnthorpe
Lupton
Bullpot Fm
Langstrothdale Chase
Meathop
Farleton
Kearstwick
Yockenthwaite
Beckermonds
Lindale
Beetham
Casterton
Whernside
RIBBLE HEAD
Ribble Head
Upper Wharfedale
Storth
Arnside
Holme
KIRKBY LONSDALE
Ribble Head Viaduct
GRANGE-OVER-SANDS
Hutton Roof
Burton-in-Kendal
Cumbria
Lancashire
Leck
Ireby
Chapel-le-Dale
High Birkwith
Foxup
Halton Gill
Kents Bank
Yealand Redmayne
Nat. Res.
Whittington
Newton
Masongill
Selside
Silverdale
Leighton Hall
Yealand Conyers
Priest Hutton
Nether Burrow
Tunstall
Westhouse
INGLEBOROUGH
New Houses
Pen-y-ghent
Horton in Ribblesdale
Littondale
Litton
Humphrey Head Point
Warton Crag
Rectory
Borwick
Arkholme
Cantsfield
Burton in Lonsdale
Ingleton
Slaterber
Ingleborough Cave
Warton Sands
Warton
76
Preston
Lancaster
Bradford
Darlington
Darlington
Darlington

Newcastle-upon-Tyne
Sunderland
65
77
Harrogate
York
Carlisle
Penrith
Kendal
Xf
Ya
Yb
Yc
Yd
20
21
22
23
24
CONSETT
LANCHESTER
DURHAM
HETTON-LE-HOLE
SEAHAM
Easington Colliery
Horden
PETERLEE
TOW LAW
CROOK
WILLINGTON
SPENNYMOOR
Ferryhill
Sedgefield
Bishop Auckland
SHILDON
NEWTON AYCLIFFE
BILLINGHAM
STOCKTON-ON-TEES
Thornaby-on-Tees
Eaglescliffe
DARLINGTON
Hurworth-on-Tees
BARNARD CASTLE
Middleton-in-Teesdale
Stanhope
Wolsingham
Greta Bridge
Croft-on-Tees
RICHMOND
CATTERICK GARRISON
Catterick
NORTHALLERTON
Romanby
Leyburn
Middleham
Bedale
Masham
THIRSK
Sowerby
RIPON
Kirkby Malzeard
Askrigg
Bainbridge
Aysgarth
Yorkshire Dales National Park
Swaledale
Wensleydale
Coverdale
Arkengarthdale
Nidderdale
Teesside International Airport
Durham
North Yorkshire
A1 (M)
A66 (M)
E15

Yf
Za
Zb
Ze
Zf
Zc
Zd
Scarborough
Cayton Bay
23
Lebberston
FILEY
Gristhorpe
Hertford
Muston
1039
Filey Bay
Hunmanby
18
165
Reighton
Speeton
Nat. Res.
DANES' DYKE
Bempton
1229
Flamborough Head
Burton Fleming
WILLY HOWE
24
Grindale
Flamborough
1255
1259
Sewerby Hall
Sewerby
Boynton
St Mary
BRIDLINGTON
Bridlington Bay
1253
Rudston
Bessingby
Carnaby
HILDER-THORPE
Haisthorpe
166
York
Kingston-upon-Hull
Hartlepool Bay
HARTLEPOOL
Seaton Carew
Tees Bay
Tees Mouth
Coatham
REDCAR
Dormanstown
1085
174
MARSKE-BY-THE-SEA
SALTBURN-BY-THE-SEA
Skinningrove
Grangetown
Lazenby
Wilton
New Marske
Upleatham
1269
1380
Eston
793
ESTON NAB
LOFTUS
Easington
Boulby
Staithes
BROTTON
SKELTON
173
Boosbeck
Priory
GUISBOROUGH
171
Lingdale
Stanghow
Liverton
1366
Port Mulgrave
Runswick Bay
Hinderwell
Roxby
Kettleness
Goldsborough
Ellerby
Moorsholm
Scaling
1266
Lythe
Sandsend
WHITBY
Abbey
Mickleby
Newton under Roseberry
Great Ayton
Gisborough Moor
1078
Cleveland
North Yorkshire
27
Scaling Dam Reservoir
Ugthorpe
Dunsley
Newholm
Captain Cook Monument
Commondale
Little Ayton
1064
Kildale
Easby
1099
Battersby
981
Danby
Houlskye
Castleton
Leaholm
Aislaby
Sleights
Egton
Stainsacre
Hawsker
Sneaton
Ugglebarnby
Great Broughton
Ingleby Greenhow
Kirkby
Westerdale
Street
Glaisdale
Egton Bridge
Grosmont
Littlebeck
1416
Sneaton-thorpe
Fylingthorpe
Raw
Robin Hood's Bay
DANBY RIGG
HIGH BRIDESTONES
Beck Hole
945
846
1427
1422
North York Moors
Urra
1490
Westerdale Moor
1407
Glaisdale
1418
Moor
Egton High Moor
Mallyn Spout
Goathland
Ravenscar
Flask Inn
Fylingdales Moor
959
Seave Green
1410
Cockayne Ridge
Cockayne
1326
1379
Church Houses
Hunt Ho
Wheeldale Moor
Wheeldale
Rosedale
North York Moors
Staintondale
Harwood Dale
Langdale Forest
1257
The Grange
Bransdale
Thorgill
Rosedale Abbey
169
Low Mill
Cloughton Newlands
National Park
Fangdale Beck
Cropton Forest
Stape
Spaunton Moor
Cloughton
Burniston
Silpho
Langdale End
Suffield
Keldy Castle
Helmsley Moor
Lastingham
Levisham
Bridestones
Scalby Ness Rocks
Hackness
Everley
SCALBY
SCARBOROUGH
Gillamoor
Fadmoor
Hawnby
Hutton-le-Hole
Spaunton
Newton-on-Rawcliffe
Lockton
Dalby Forest
Wykeham Forest
Appleton-le-Moors
Cropton
Nat. Res.
Carlton
Pockley
Kirkbymoorside
Keldholme
Sinnington
Wrelton
Aislaby
Old Byland
Rievaulx Abbey
Rievaulx
Beadlam
Roman villa
Kirkby Mills
170
Middleton
Thornton-le-Dale
Hutton Buscel
Sawdon
Ayton
Osgodby
Cold Kirby
Helmsley
Nawton
Great Edstone
44
Ebberston Hall
Irton
Seamer
Eastfield
Cayton Bay
Castle
Wombleton
Marton
PICKERING
Wilton
Allerston
Ebberston
Snainton
Wykeham
Brompton
Cayton
Lebberston
165
Scawton
Harome
Normanby
1261
Gristhorpe
866
The Carrs
Vale of Pickering
Staxton
Willerby
Hertford
Folkton
1039
Sproxton
Salton
Little Barugh
169
Kirby Misperton
Yedingham
Ganton
Flixton
Oldstead
Wass
Byland Abbey
Ampleforth
Ampleforth College
Oswaldkirk
1257
Nunnington
Nunnington Hall
Ness
Stonegrave
Great Barugh
Brawby
Derwent
1258
Sherburn
20
East Heslerton
Hunmanby
Coxwold
Newburgh Priory
Thorpe Hall
Gilling East
Cawton
Hovingham
Butterwick
Great Habton
Ryton
Wykeham
Scampston
Knapton
64
West Heslerton
Fordon
565
1363
Howardian Hills
Slingsby
Barton-le-Street
Amotherby
Old Malton
Rye
Wintringham
Thorpe Bassett
Foxholes
Wold Newton
Burton Fleming
Husthwaite
Oulston
Yearsley
Coulton
Scackleton
Appleton-le-Street
Broughton
1257
Place Newton
Butterwick
WILLY HOWE
Brandsby
Stearsby
Coneysthorpe
MALTON
NORTON
Scagglethorpe
Helperthorpe
Weaverthorpe
Terrington
Great Lake
Settrington
Thwing
Crayke
Skewsby
Marton Abbey
Ganthorpe
Castle Howard
West Lutton
1253
Easingwold
Whenby
Huttons Ambo
1249
York
78
79

Lancashire, Yorkshire, Humberside

Despite the large population centres, there is plenty of lovely countryside in the North, plus the most popular seaside resorts in the country. The local townsfolk have been making day trips to the coast ever since the Industrial Revolution shut them inside the "dark satanic Mills".

Barrow-in-Furness and the Furness Peninsula

The main town of the peninsula, Barrow-in-Furness, has some interesting sights although it became a steel town in 1846 and now has added a gas pipeline to its industrial installations. It is connected via a bridge to Walney Island which has nature reserves. There is a ferry to Piel Island on which stands a ruined castle built in 1327. Dalton-in-Furness in the centre of the Peninsula has the 14th-century Dalton Tower, near Furness Abbey. This foundation was once second only in importance to Fountains Abbey. The infirmary chapel and choir are particularly fine examples of medieval architecture. The Bow Bridge which crosses Mill Beck outside the abbey is also medieval.

Beverley

See "Excursions"

Blackpool and the Lancashire Coast

Lancashire's "golden coast" is a string of holiday resorts of which the largest and most famous is Blackpool. For at least 100 years, this has been a place where Lancastrians, and indeed British holidaymakers from all over the country, have gone to relax, and there is every facility that a seaside resort can offer. The Golden Mile, the promenade beside the wide beach, is full of stands and booths selling souvenirs. The most northerly of the resorts is Morecambe, on Morecambe Bay. Further north still are Grange-over-Sands, Cartmel with the lovey Cartmel Priory Gatehouse, Bradford-le-Sands and Carnforth. The last has a huge collection of steam trains known as the Steamtown Railway Centre. There are regular trips down the line in the summer. Morecambe is a popular seaside resort, famous for its shrimps. Heysham, to the south of it, is a fishing village and the ferry terminal for the Isle of Man. It has an interesting church and is overlooked by the ruined St. Patrick's chapel, said to date from the 9th century. Fleetwood is one of the largest fishing ports in England, as the museum in Dock Street will testify. There is a seasonal ferry service to Douglas, Isle of Man. South of Blackpool, Lytham St. Anne's is a more "genteel" holiday resort, famous for its Royal Lytham St. Anne's Golf Club.

Bridlington

This attractive Yorkshire resort has fine sands and holds an annual regatta. The parish church is imposing, since it was originally part of an Augustinian priory founded in 1113.

Halifax

Halifax is at the heart of Calderdale on the slopes of the Hebble Valley. It is one of the most historic towns in Yorkshire, whose prosperity is based on the cloth trade. The pride of Halifax is the Piece Hall(1779), still used as a market on Fridays and Saturdays in what must be the most attractive setting in Britain. The Art Gallery and Tourist Information Centre are in the same building. Halifax has a wealth of museums, both usual and unsual. The Calderdale Industrial Museum and the Pre-Industrial Museum both trace the rise of Halifax's prosperity as a trading centre. The National Museum of the Working Horse is in the former railway goods yard. At Gibbet Street there is a replica of the notorious Halifax

Limestone "pavement", an interesting geological formation at Malham, North Yorkshire (above).

Janet's Foss, waterfall in North Yorkshire (above right).

The North Yorkshire moors near Settle (right).

The Leeds-Liverpool Canal at Gargrave, North Yorkshire (opposite).

Gibbet (as in the old saying "From Hell, Hull and Halifax, may the good Lord deliver us!"), used until 1650 for executing cloth thieves.

Harrogate

Once the premier spa town of northern England, Harrogate is now more popular for conferences than for health treatments. There are more than 90 springs, including quite separate iron and sulphur wells. The Royal Baths, Royal Pump Room and Assembly Rooms rival those of Bath (q.v.) The Royal Pump Room is now a museum; the waters can be sampled in the basement. Harrogate is a place of green lawns and beautiful gardens. These include the Valley Gardens and the Northern Horticultural Society's Harlow Car Gardens.

Ilkley

This was once another popular spa town, which stands on Ilkley Moor, made famous in the Yorkshire song. The area is rich in Bronze Age remains, including stone circles, and strange stone formations. The Manor House Museum, on the site of the Roman fort of Olicana, houses some of the archæological finds.

Kingston-upon-Hull

Generally known as Hull, never as Kingston, the town stands at the wide mouth of the Humber which is spanned by the longest suspension bridge in the world, the Humber Bridge. The ferry terminal to Rotterdam and Zeebrugge is in Hull Docks. Maister House, in the High Street, owned by the National Trust, has a fine Palladian staircase. Barton-on-Humber, a suburb of Hull, was once the port and it has many interesting buildings, including two fine churches and the 17th-century Tyrwhitt Hall.

Lancaster

The original county town of Lancashire and a university city, Lancaster has a long and glorious history. Lancaster Castle high above the river on the site of the Roman fort now includes the prison, the Shire Hall and the Crown Court. The Norman keep and gatehouse are preserved intact. Hadrian's Tower contains an exhibition of prison equipment. Of the many historic houses in the town, the Judges Lodging is probably the finest.

Leeds

As the birthplace of Henry Moore, Leeds City Art Gallery can be expected to house many of the master's works. They are in a special section of the City Museum, which also has a fine collection of modern art. The old masters are contained in the nearby stately home of Temple Newsam. Leeds has many fine buildings which attest to its prosperity, both past and present, including the Corn Exchange, Kirkgate Market and the Town Hall. The Brotherton Library is one of the largest in Britain.

Manchester

It is impossible to do justice in such a small space to this huge metropolis of 3.5 million people which has spread to cover the neighbouring towns of Oldham, Rochdale, Stockport and many others. The attractions include guided tours of the Granada Television Studios, the John Rylands Library and the City Art Gallery.

Ripon

This beautiful cathedral city and market town was granted its first charter by Alfred the Great in 886. The Cathedral is the fourth on the site. The present building was begun in the 12th century, but the Early English twin-towered façade was added in the 13th century. Only a mile outside Ripon there is the great estate of Studley Royal and Fountains Abbey. The ruins of the abbey, the largest and best preserved in Britain, are situated in the wooded valley of the Skell. Fountains was founded by Benedictines in 1132 but was taken over by the Cistercians in 1135.

York

See "Historic Cities"

Information

Lancaster Tourism
7 Dalton Square
White Cross, Lancaster
LA1 1PP
Tel: (0524) 32878

Leeds City Tourism
19 Wellington Street
Leeds
LS1 4DG
Tel: (0532) 478301

Events

There are so many events in this part of the country, it is hard to know what to recommend. In Leeds, for instance, Roundhay Park is the venue for many outdoor events, such as Bonfire Night on 5 November, the Leeds Marathon in October and the Leeds Show in August. Leeds has a Lord Mayor's Parade in June and the Leeds International Film Festival held in October. In Manchester there is the Manchester University Students' Rag Procession on Shrove Tuesday, the Manchester to Blackpool Vintage and Veteran Car Run and the Lord Mayor's Show in June, the Manchester Show in August and Castlefield Carnival in September. For more unusual celebrations, St. Wilfred's Feast is celebrated in Ripon with a procession through the streets on the first Sunday in August.

Tips

If you don't like crowds, stay away from the coasts in high summer. The hill country of Lancashire, the Penines and the Yorkshire Dales are relatively uncrowded. The large towns in this area are industrialised but have good museums and art galleries, plus plenty of accommodation at reasonable prices for tourists, since the hotels cater mainly to business visitors. All these towns have had wealthy benefactors who have donated handsome public buildings and art treasures to their cities.

Kendal
Carlisle
Kendal
71
Kendal
Wf
Xa
Xb
Xc
Xd
DALTON-IN-FURNESS
BARROW-IN-FURNESS
Stainton with Adgarley
Newton
Gleaston
Scales
Baycliff
Aldingham
Leece
Newbiggin
Roosebeck
VICKERS-TOWN
Biggar
Rampside
Foulney Island
South End
Piel Island
Isle of Walney
Hilpsford Point
Humphrey Head Point
Cartmel Wharf
Morecambe Bay
Warton Sands
Warton
CARNFORTH
Bolton-le-Sands
Nat. Res.
Hest Bank
MORECAMBE
TORRISHOLME
HEYSHAM
Heaton
LANCASTER
SCOTFORTH
Middleton
Stodday
Overton
Conder Green
Glasson
Galgate
Thurnham
Thurnham Hall
Cockersand Abbey
Cockerham
Forton
Priest Hutton
Borwick
Capernwray
Over Kellet
Nether Kellet
Arkholme
Melling
Tunstall
Cantsfield
Wennington
Burton in Lonsdale
Low Bentham
High Bentham
Ingleton
Slatenber
Newby
Clapham
Gressingham
Hornby
Tatham
Wray
Aughton
Halton
Claughton
Brookhouse
Caton
Crossgill
Quenmore
Salter
Lowgill
Moor Cock
Keasden
Thrushgill
Botton Head
Burn Moor
White Hill
Mallowdale Fell
Ward's Stone
Forest of Bowland
Tarnbrook
Lee
Abbeystead
Dolphinholme
Street
Marshaw
Trough of Bowland
Sykes
Sykes Fell
Hawthornthwaite Fell
Dunsop Bridge
Newton
Slaidburn
Whitewell
Bleasdale Moors
Oakenclough
Fair Snape Fell
BLEASDALE CIRCLE
Browsholme Hall
Grindleton
Pilling Lane
Knott End-on-Sea
Pilling
Stake Pool
Winmarleigh
Preesall
Stalmine
FLEETWOOD
THORNTON
CLEVELEYS
Hambleton
BISPHAM
Carleton
POULTON-LE-FYLDE
Singleton
BLACKPOOL
The Tower
Normoss
Staining
Weeton
GREAT MARTON
COMMON EDGE
Plumpton
Blackpool
ST ANNE'S
LYTHAM ST ANNE'S
LYTHAM
Higher Ballam
Moss Side
Wrea Green
Warton
KIRKHAM
Freckleton
Clifton
Wesham
Treales
Elswick
Great Eccleston
Out Rawcliffe
St Michael's on Wyre
Crossmoor
Inskip
Esprick
Wharles
Garstang
Nateby
Eagland Hall
Bowgreave
Churchtown
Catterall
Bilsborrow
Claughton
Inglewhite
Cuddy Hill
Barton
Newsham
Broughton
Woodplumpton
Cottam
Goosnargh
Chingle Hall
Haighton Green
Grimsargh
Beacon Fell
Chipping
Hesketh Lane
Longridge Fell
LONGRIDGE
Knowle Green
Ribchester
Bashall Eaves
Waddington
CLITHEROE
Low Moor
Walker Fold
Great Mitton
Barrow
Whalley
Hurst Green
New Row
Copster Green
Billington
GREAT HARWOOD
Langho
Salesbury
Wilpshire
Mellor Brook
Osbaldeston
Mellor
RISHTON
CHURCH
OSWALDTWISTLE
SHAROE GREEN
FULWOOD
RIBBLETON
PRESTON
Samlesbury
Samlesbury Hall
Samlesbury Bottoms
Walton-le-Dale
Higher Penwortham
Higher Walton
BLACKBURN
FENISCOWLES
Pleasington
Bamber Bridge
Hoghton
Tardy Gate
Hutton
Longton
New Longton
FARINGTON
Walmer Bridge
Much Hoole
Hesketh Bank
Hundred End
Tarleton
Banks
LEYLAND
Bretherton
Croston
Euxton
Sollom
Whittle-le-Woods
Withnell
Brindle
Tockholes
Abbey Village
Brinscall
Wheelton
Ryal Fold
Belthorn
DARWEN
Hoddlesden
White Coppice
ROUND LOAF
CHORLEY
Belmont Reservoir
Belmont
Winter Hill
Rivington
Egerton
Turton Bottoms
Toppings
SOUTHPORT
Mere Brow
Holmeswood
Rufford
Mawdesley
Eccleston
Heskin Green
Charnock Richard
Coppull
ADLINGTON
HORWICH
BOLTON
Lostock Junction
Brown Edge
Scarisbrick
Bescar
Shirdley Hill
New Lane
Burscough Bridge
Parbold
Wrightington Bar
Appley Bridge
STANDISH
Blackrod
Haigh
Aspull
AINSDALE
Halsall
Pinfold
Newburgh
Shevington
Haigh Country Park
Nat. Res.
Woodvale
FORMBY
Fromby Point
Haskayne
Great Altcar
ORMSKIRK
Westhead
Dalton
Roby Mill
UP HOLLAND
ORRELL
SKELMERSDALE
Scarth Hill
Aughton
WIGAN
Gathurst
WESTHOUGHTON
HINDLEY
ATHERTON
ABRAM
LITTLE HULTON
TYLDESLEY
LEIGH
FARNWORTH
MAGHULL
Ince Blundell
Hightown
Lunt
Sefton
Bickerstaffe
Barrow Nook
Melling Mount
BILLINGE
Bryn Gates
BRYN
ASHTON-IN-MAKERSFIELD
RAINFORD
Crank
MOSS BANK
Garswood
GOLBORNE
LOWTON COMMON
Astley Green
NETHERTON
BLUNDELLSANDS
GREAT CROSBY
LITHERLAND
CROSBY
Melling
Aintree
KIRKBY
Knowsley
ST HELENS
ECCLESTON
HAYDOCK
EARLESTOWN
NEWTON-LE-WILLOWS
LANE HEAD
Kenyon
Culcheth
Croft
IRLAM
BOOTLE
WALTON ON THE HILL
WEST DERBY
Croxteth Hall
Knowsley Hall
Liverpool Bay
Dublin, Laoghaire Belfast, Douglas
Lancashire Merseyside
Lancashire Gr. Manchester
Gr. Manchester Cheshire
N. Yorkshire Lancashire
Ribble
Lune
Wyre
Douglas
82
Warrington
Warrington
24
25
26
27
28
M6
M55
M61
M58
M57

72
83
Xe
Xf
Ya
Yb
Yc
Darlington
Sheffield
RIPON
HARROGATE
SKIPTON
Settle
ILKLEY
KEIGHLEY
BINGLEY
BRADFORD
LEEDS
HALIFAX
HUDDERSFIELD
WAKEFIELD
BARNSLEY
DEWSBURY
BATLEY
MORLEY
PUDSEY
OTLEY
SHIPLEY
BAILDON
GUISELEY
YEADON
HORSFORTH
BRIGHOUSE
CLECKHEATON
HECKMONDWIKE
MIRFIELD
OSSETT
HORBURY
ELLAND
SOWERBY BRIDGE
TODMORDEN
BACUP
RAWTENSTALL
BURNLEY
NELSON
COLNE
BARNOLDSWICK
BARROW-FORD
BRIERFIELD
PADIHAM
ROCHDALE
LITTLEBOROUGH
MILNROW
SHAW
ROYTON
OLDHAM
HEYWOOD
MIDDLETON
CHADDERTON
FAILSWORTH
BURY
RAMSBOTTOM
ASHTON-UNDER-LYNE
DROYLSDEN
DUKINFIELD
STALYBRIDGE
MOSSLEY
HYDE
DENTON
GLOSSOP
HOLMFIRTH
MELTHAM
PENISTONE
STOCKSBRIDGE
DARTON
Haworth
SILSDEN
HEBDEN BRIDGE
Yorkshire Dales National Park
THE PENNINES
Peak District National Park
Rombalds Moor
Wharfedale
Airedale
Malham Cave
Victoria Cave
Stump Cross Caverns
Fountains Abbey
Brimham Rocks
Bolton Abbey
Harewood House
Leeds and Bradford Airport
Kirkstall Abbey
Bleaklow Hill
Howden Moors
Boulsworth Hill
Heptonstall Moor
Pecket Well
York
Wetherby
Kingston-upon-Hill
Nottingham
Gatley

Darlington
72
Middlesbrough
Scarborough
73
Yd
Ye
Yf
Za
Zb
24
25
26
27
28
Castle Howard
Norton-le-Clay
Brafferton
Helperby
Raskelf
Easingwold
Crayke
Marton Abbey
Whenby
Terrington
Ganthorpe
Welburn
Huttons Ambo
Settrington
Skelton on Ure
Kirby Hill
Boroughbridge
Aldborough
Myton-on-Swale
Tholthorpe
Alne
Stillington
Farlington
Sheriff Hutton
Bulmer
Whitwell-on-the-Hill
Kirkham
Langton
Kennythorpe
Birdsall
North Grimston
Duggleby
Wharram le Street
Roecliffe
Minskip
Grafton
Flawith
Upper Dunsforth
Aldwark
Lower Dunsforth
Ouseburn
Tollerton
Youlton
Cross Lanes
Huby
Sutton-on-the-Forest
Sutton Park
West Lilling
Thornton-le-Clay
Foston
Crambe
Westow
Burythorpe
Wharram Percy Village
Staveley
Arkendale
Marton
Linton-on-Ouse
Barton-le-Willows
Flaxton
Harton
Howsham
Leavening
Acklam
Thixendale
Ferrensby
Flaxby
KNARESBOROUGH
Thorpe Underwood
Newton-on-Ouse
Strensall
Bossall
Claxton
Scrayingham
Leppington
Kirby Underdale
Fridaythorpe
Whixley
Green Hammerton
Nun Monkton
Beningbrough Hall
Shipton
Haxby
Towthorpe
Earswick
Sand Hutton
Buttercrambe
North Yorkshire
Humberside
Bugthorpe
Harrogate
Goldsborough
Moor Monkton
Nether Poppleton
Upper Poppleton
Skelton
Huntington
New Earswick
Stockton on the Forest
Warthill
Gate Helmsley
Stamford Bridge
Full Sutton
Youlthorpe
Bishop Wilton
Great Givendale
Huggate
Kirk Hammerton
Cattal
Marston Moor 1644
Hessay
Holtby
Low Catton
High Catton
Fangfoss
Little Ribston
Spofforth
Hunsingore
Tockwith
Long Marston
Knapton
Rufforth
Museum Gardens
The Minster
Castle
Murton
Dunnington
Kexby
Wilberfoss
Yapham
Millington
Warter
North Deighton
Bickerton
YORK
Heslington
Barmby Moor
Pocklington
Burnby Hall
Sicklinghall
WETHERBY
Askham Richard
Askham Bryan
Healaugh
Bilbrough
Copmanthorpe
Bishopthorpe
Crockey Hill
Newton upon Derwent
Elvington
Allerthorpe
Nunburnholme
Hayton
Thornton
Londesborough
Boston Spa
Wighill
Thorp Arch
Catterton
Acaster Malbis
Naburn
Deighton
Wheldrake
Melbourne
Bielby
Shiptonthorpe
East Keswick
Collingham
Clifford
Bramham
Newton Kyme
Tadcaster
Colton
Appleton Roebuck
Acaster Selby
Escrick
Thorganby
East Cottingwith
Everingham
Seaton Ross
Market Weighton
Bardsey
Scarcroft
Bramham Park
Thorner
Stutton
Ulleskelf
Bolton Percy
Stillingfleet
Ellerton
Laytham
Holme-on-Spalding-Moor
Towton
Ryther
Kelfield
Skipwith
Aughton
Harlthorpe
Foggathorpe
North Cliffe
South Cliffe
Barwick in Elmet
Scholes
Dykes
Barkston Ash
Church Fenton
Cawood
Riccall
North Duffield
Highfield
Willitoft
Sand Hole
Aberford
Saxton
Lotherton Hall
Wistow
Barlby
Bubwith
Spaldington
Bursea
GARFORTH
Biggin
South Duffield
Breighton
Sherburn in Elmet
Abbey Church
Cliffe
Wressle
Brind
North Cave
Temple Newsam
Micklefield
Newthorpe
Thorpe W.
SELBY
Hemingbrough
Newsholme
Eastrington
Sandholme
Newport
Swillington
Kippax
Ledsham
Steeton Hall Gateway
South Milford
Hambleton
Brayton
Barlow
Howden
Gilberdyke
Staddlethorpe
ROTHWELL
Great Preston
Ledston
Monk Fryston
Hillam
Gateforth
Burn
Long Drax
Barmby on the Marsh
Asselby
Balkholme
Woodlesford
Allerton Bywater
Burton Salmon
Birkin
West Haddlesey
Selby Canal
Camblesforth
Drax
Airmyn
Kilpin
Laxton
Broomfleet
Leeds
Methley
Brotherton
Chapel Haddlesey
Hirst Courtney
Newland
Hook
Saltmarshe
Blacktoft
Faxfleet
CASTLEFORD
KNOTTINGLEY
Kellington
Carlton
Rawcliffe
GOOLE
Reedness
Yokefleet
Ouse
Nat. Res.
Trent
Bradford
Stanley
Whitwood
FERRYBRIDGE
Eggborough
Hensall
Snaith
Swinefleet
Whitgift
Altofts
NORMANTON
Ackton
PONTEFRACT
Cridling Stubbs
Whitley
Cowick
Rawcliffe Bridge
Adlingfleet
Warmfield
FEATHERSTONE
Purston Jaglin
Darrington
Great Heck
Pollington
Garthorpe
Wakefield
Sharlston
East Hardwick
Wolmersley
Little Smeaton
Walden Stubbs
Aire and Calder Navigation
Burton upon Stather
Crofton
Nostell Priory
High Ackworth
Wentbridge
Fenwick
Sykehouse
Humberside
South Yorkshire
Luddington
Eastoft
Normanby
Walton
Fitzwilliam
Ackworth Moor Top
Badsworth
Thorpe Audlin
Norton
Moorends
Flixborough
Kinsley
Ryhill
South Hiendley
Upton
Campsall
Moss
Fishlake
Thorne
Crowle
Amcotts
Keadby
Notton
HEMSWORTH
South Elmsall
Askern
Thorpe in Balne
Kirk Bramwith
Stainforth
Stainforth and Keadby Canal
Ealand
Gunness
ROYSTON
Brierley
South Kirkby
Burghwallis
Carcroft
Hatfield
Derrythorpe
Burringham
Carlton
Shafton
Hampole
ADWICK LE STREET
Barnby Dun
Kirk Sandall
Sandtoft
Westgate
Belton
Beltoft
Butterwick
Staincross
Grimethorpe
Hooton Pagnell
Edenthorpe
Isle of Axholme
Epworth
Messingham
Cudworth
Monk Bretton Priory
Clayton
THURNSCOE
Brodsworth
Arksey
Ardsley
Great Houghton
Darfield
DEARNE
Hickleton
Marr
BENTLEY
DOCTASTER
Armthorpe
Wroot
Rectory
Low Burnham
Susworth
Scotterthorpe
BARNSLEY
WOMBWELL
GOLDTHORPE
Barnburgh
High Melton
Sprotbrough
DONCASTER
Cantley
Owston Ferry
Birdwell
Bolton upon Dearne
Adwick upon Dearne
Branton
Torne
Westwoodside
Haxey
East Ferry
HOYLAND NETHER
Jump
Elsecar
Brampton
WATH UPON DEARNE
MEXBOROUGH
Cadeby
Warmsworth
Auckley
Blaxton
Graizelound
Wildsworth
Wentworth
SWINTON
Old Denaby
Castle
CONISBROUGH
New Edlington
Finningley
Nottinghamshire
Laughton
Chapeltown
Kilnhurst
Wadworth
New Rossington
Misterton
West Stockwith
East Stockwith
Blyton
Thorpe Hesley
Nether Haugh
RAWMARSH
Hooton Roberts
Ravenfield
Thrybergh
Misson
Austerfield
Greasbrough
Braithwell
Stainton
Tickhill
Bawtry
Walkeringham
Walkerith
Morton
Pilham
Ecclesfield
DALTON
Bramley
Scraftworth
Everton
Gringley on the Hill
Beckingham
GAINSBOROUGH
SHEFFIELD
ROTHERHAM
Wickersley
MALTBY
Harworth
Scrooby
Old
Springthorpe
Nottingham
Newark-on-Trent
86
Lincoln
Huddersfield
M1
M18
M62
M180
M181
A1(M)
E15
E20
E22
E13

Zd
Ze
Zf
Aa
Ab
Flamborough Head
Bempton
DANES' DYKE
Flamborough
Sewerby Hall
Sewerby
BRIDLINGTON
Bridlington Bay
HILDER-THORPE
WILLY HOWE
Burton Fleming
Grindale
Thwing
Boynton
Rudston
Bessingby
Carnaby
Langtoft
Cowlam Manor
Kilham
Haisthorpe
DANE'S GRAVES
Burton Agnes Hall and Norman Manor House
Burton Agnes
Ruston Parva
Harpham
Lowthorpe
Fraisthorpe
Garton-on-the-Wolds
DRIFFIELD
Nafferton
Gransmoor
Barmston
Great Kelk
Lissett
Kelleythorpe
Wansford
Ulrome
Skipsea
Castle
Kirkburn
Southburn
Skerne
Foston on the Wolds
Beeford
Hutton Cranswick
Bainton
North Frodingham
Dunnington
Atwick
Rotsea
Hempholme
Watton
Bewholme
Lund
Beswick
HORNSEA
Hornsea Mere
Nat. Res.
Hornsea Pottery
Burshill
Brandesburton
Seaton
Rolston
Lockington
Catwick
Sigglesthorne
Aike
Dalton
Scorborough
Arram
Leven
Mappleton
Etton
Long Riston
Rise
Great Hatfield
Great Cowden
Cherry Burton
Leconfield
Routh
Tickton
Withernwick
BEVERLEY
Minster
Bishop Burton
Meaux
New Ellerby
Woodmansey
South Skirlaugh
Old Ellerby
West Newton
Aldbrough
Walkington
Wawne
Burton Constable Hall
Burton Constable
Bentley
Swine
Flinton
Garton
High Hunsley
Dunswell
Coniston
Sproatley
Humbleton
Skidby
COTTINGHAM
Owstwick
Little Weighton
SUTTON-ON-HULL
Bilton
Elstronwick
Tunstall
Riplingham
Preston
Burton Pidsea
Roos
Waxholme
WILLERBY
MARFLEET
Rimswell
KIRK ELLA
Trinity House
HEDON
Swanland
ANLABY
Holy Trinity
Ring of Holderness
Burstwick
WITHERNSEA
Welton
KINGSTON UPON HULL
HESSLE
Paull
Thorngumbald
Hollym
North Ferriby
Keyingham
Ottringham
Queen of Holderness
Holmpton
New Holland
Patrington
Read's I.
South Channel
Goxhill
Welwick
BARTON-UPON-HUMBER
Barrow upon Humber
South Ferriby
East Halton
Thornton Abbey
HUMBER
Sunk Island
Skeffling
Easington
Horkstow
North Killingholme
Rotterdam (Europoort), Zeebrugge
The Old Hall
Sunk Island Sands
Burnham
Thornton Curtis
Wootton
South Killingholme
Immingham
Kilnsea
Appleby
Bonby
Ulceby
Habrough
Worlaby
Elsham Hall Country Park
Elsham
Croxton
Kirmington
Healing
Santon
Melton Ross
Brocklesby
Stallingborough
GRIMSBY
Spurn Head
Humberside Airport
Great Limber
Great Coates
Bull
Wrawby
Keelby
Aylesby
CLEETHORPES
Barnetby le Wold
Riby
Laceby
Humberston
BRIGG
Bigby
Freshney
Mouth of the Humber
Bradley
SCARTHO
New Waltham
Searby
Scawby
Grasby
Barnoldby le Beck
Irby upon Humber
Tetney Lock
Howsham
Waltham
Holton le Clay
Cadney
Swallow
Brigsley
Humberside
Lincolnshire
Hibaldstow
Beelsby
North Cotes
Caistor
Cabourne
Ashby cum Fenby
Tetney
Cuxwold
Grainsby
Redbourne
North Kelsey
Rothwell
East Ravendale
Marshchapel
South Kelsey
Nettleton
North Thoresby
Eskham
Kirton in Lindsey
Moortown
Holton le Moor
Fulstow
Wragholme
Meals
North Somercotes
Grainthorpe
Waddingham
Brandy Wharf
Thoresway
Swinhope
Wold Newton
Ludborough
Covenham St Mary
Conisholme
Snitterby
North Owersby
Usselby
Claxby
Stainton le Vale
Binbrook
Utterby
Saltfleet
Bishop Norton
Osgodby
Walesby
Kirkmond le Mire
Fotherby
Yarburgh
South Somercotes
Saltfleetby St Clement
Bishopbridge
Glentham
Kirkby
North Elkington
Alvingham
North Cockerington
Caenby Corner
Middle Rasen
Market Rasen
Tealby
Ludford
Saltfleetby St Peter
Theddlethorpe St Helen
Harpswell
Caenby
West Rasen
South Cockerington
Lincoln
Louth
87

Cheshire, South York, the Peak District

Here again, glorious countryside alternates with heavy industry, in an intriguing mixture of ancient and modern at the southern end of the Pennines. Chain that divides Lancashire from Yorkshire.

Ashbourne
This attractive market town on the southern edge of the Peak District, well-known for its bottled mineral water, has wide streets and attractive architecture. St. Oswald's church, the finest in the district, has a 212-foot spire, and was dedicated in the 13th century by the Bishop of Coventry. The grammar school dates from 1585. The Green Man and Black's Head is a public house that you cannot miss because it spans the road with its gallows sign.

Burton-upon-Trent
The town is famous for its breweries which started here because of the fine quality of the water. There is a Museum of Brewing.

Buxton
This lovely spa town claims to be the highest in England. Its graceful, Georgian buildings, reminiscent of those of Bath (q.v.) were largely created by the Duke of Devonshire. The centrepiece is the handsome crescent, built over the River Wye. It was while the crescent was being built that the Roman bath and spring were discovered. The Old Hall Hotel was visited by Mary Queen of Scots during her imprisonment in Chatsworth. The Peak Rail Steam Centre is a railway buff's delight with steam trains that ran on the old line between Buxton and Matlock.

Chatsworth
One of the great stately homes of England. The house itself contains a superb collection of furniture and works by Rembrandt, Frans Hals and Van Dyck. There are painted ceilings and magnificent oak carvings. The State Room contains Mortlake Tapestries and the Music Room has a famous trompe-l'œil painting. Other rooms of note are the Oak Room, the Library, Ante-Library and Dome Room.

Chester
See "Historic Cities"

Crich
This little village has a unique collection of tramcars from all over the world. They are on display in the Crich Tramway Museum housed in a disused quarry.

Lichfield
The distinctive, three-spiered cathedral and 18th-century townscape make this the most beautiful city in the area. In the 18th century there was a particularly rich intellectual life, a fitting birthplace for the city's most famous son, Dr. Samuel Johnson (1709-84). The Johnson Birthplace Museum is on the corner of Market Street and his statue is in Market Square. At Wall, near Lichfield, English Heritage maintains the Roman Baths and Museum of Letocetum. This was a posting station on Watling Street, the great Roman road to the North. It is the most complete example of its kind in Britain. Shugborough, 18th-century home of the earls of Lichfield, near Milford, is the home of the Staffordshire County Museum. The grounds contain a working flour mill, terraces and rose gardens.

Liverpool
See "Historic Cities"

Matlock
The administrative centre of Derbyshire includes Matlock Bath. This

Magpie Mine, Monyash, in the Peak District, a disused lead mine (above).

Well-dressing at Eyam in the Peak District (above right).

Churchyard at Eyam (below right).

Sign outside the restaurant serving the original puddings in Bakewell, Derbyshire (opposite above).

Stanton Moor in the Peak District, Derbyshire (opposite below).

spa town rose to fame in the mid-19th century. The hydro is at Matlock Bank, now occupied by the County Council offices. The most famous tourist attraction is the Petrifying Wells, in which visitors hang bottles and other objects which become coated with a thin mineral crust. Derwent Gardens contain grottoes with lush vegetation. Opposite the pavillion are the Heights of Abraham, given their name by an officer who fought with General Wolfe at Quebec. Riber Castle, a famous landmark, is a 19th-century folly built for the local textile manufacturer who originally developed the spa.

Peak District

This is one of Britain most popular tourist destinations. The Peak District National Park covers Derbyshire, Staffordshire and South Yorkshire. High Peak Estate and the Hope Woodlands, only 12 miles from Sheffield, are heather-covered moorlands. The National Trust owns large tracts of the National Park as well as many of the stately homes in the area. These include such beauty spots as Dovedale, Wolfscote Dale, Biggin Dale and the South Peak Estate. Ilam Hall and Country Park are part of this last estate, from which there are magnificent views of parts of Dovedale and Thorpe Cloud. The White Peak, in the southern half of the Park, is named after the whitish limestone that lies beneath it. Caves in the area are Peak Cavern, Bagshaw Cavern and Speedwell Cavern. The scenic drive called the White Peak Scenic Route is well-signposted.

Sheffield

The steel capital of Britain was famous for its cutlery even in Chaucer's day. Flemish immigrants helped to refine the steel-making techniques and the crucible process was invented here in 1740 by Benjamin Huntsman. The City Museum has the finest collection of cutlery and Sheffield plate in the world. It is fitting that the Cathedral church of St. Peter and St. Paul should be opposite the Cutlers' Hall. Sheffield is famous for its art galleries. The Graves Gallery on the top floor of the Central Library has a fine collection of Chinese ivories and the best collection of British water colours in the country. The Mappin Art Gallery in Weston Park features English art. The Abbeydale Industrial Hamlet south-west of the city has one of the best industrial museums in Britain, featuring demonstrations of ancient cutlery-making techniques.

Stoke-on-Trent

Familiarly known as "The Five Towns", made famous by the local author, Arnold Bennett, but actually consisting of six towns, Stoke-on-Trent is synonymous with the Potteries. The towns are Longton, Fenton, Stoke-upon-Trent, Hanley, Burslem and Tunstall. Pottery was first made here in the Middle Ages, but received its real impetus from the ingenious and inventive Josiah Wedgwood, who turned a cottage industry into one of the biggest commercial ventures in Britain, and one which is still thriving. The City Museum houses the world's finest collection of Staffordshire ceramics, and there are tours of the city, the Heritage Trail and the China Service bus, which take visitors to see all the large potteries. Other museums include the Gladstone Pottery Museum and the Whitfield Mining Museum. Perhaps the pleasantest way of visiting the Five Towns is by canal boat. The canals were built to transport the china before the coming of the railways so they pass all the important potteries.

Information
Tourist Information Centre
Old Market Hall
Bridge Street
Bakewell, Derbyshire
DE4 1DS

Tourist Information Centre
The Crescent
Buxton, Derbyshire
SK17 6BQ
Tel: (0298) 25106

Events
Undoubtedly, the major events of the year in the Peak District are the Well Dressing Ceremonies, which take place in Buxton and 20 or so of the neighbouring towns and villages from May to September. The Buxton Well Dressing is in July. Flower petals are stuck on wet clay to form a picture. Dates of other well dressings from the Buxton Tourist Information Centres.
Buxton Festival of Music and Drama is held in the Opera House in July and August.

Tips
Bakewell, famous for Bakewell Tart (known locally as Bakewell Pudding), is also known for its pies, puddings and sausages, so it is a good place to stop for a meal.

76
Southport
Wigan
Manchester
92
Welshpool
Shrewsbury
Shrewsbury
Telford
Prestatyn
Abergele
Denbigh
Denbigh
Aberystwyth
Liverpool Bay
Wf
Xa
Xb
Xc
28
29
30
31
32
WALLASEY
BOOTLE
LIVERPOOL
ST HELENS
PRESCOT
HUYTON-WITH-ROBY
NEWTON-LE-WILLOW
WARRINGTON
WIDNES
RUNCORN
BIRKENHEAD
HOYLAKE
West Kirby
HESWALL
NESTON
BEBINGTON
ELLESMERE PORT
FRODSHAM
NORTHWICH
HOLYWELL
FLINT
CONNAH'S QUAY
CHESTER
MOLD
BUCKLEY
WINSFORD
CREWE
NANTWICH
WREXHAM
RHOSLLANERCHRUGOG
LLANGOLLEN
MALPAS
WHITCHURCH
OSWESTRY
MARKET DRAYTON
Mersey
Dee
Irlam
Culcheth
Lymm
Great Sankey
Tarporley
Ellesmere
Wem
Baschurch
Shawbury
Chirk
Cefn-mawr
Ruabon
Overton
Penley
Audlem
Hodnet
Child's Ercall

77
Manchester
Hollingworth
Xe
Xf
Ya
Yb
Yc
STRETFORD
DENTON
HYDE
GLOSSOP
SALE
Bredbury
STOCKPORT
ROMILEY
MARPLE
CHEADLE
GATLEY
HAZEL GROVE
CHEADLE HULME
BRAMHALL
Peak District
High Peak
Kinder Scout
2088
National Park
SHEFFIELD
STANNINGTON
High Neb
Hayfield
Edale
NEW MILLS
Chinley Head
Chinley
Castleton
Hope
Aston
Bamford
Hathersage
Dore
Totley
Manchester Int. Airport
Handforth
Styal
Poynton
Disley
Newtown
Whaley Bridge
Chapel-en-le-Frith
Sparrowpit
Bradwell
Abney
Eyam
Grindleford
Froggatt
Holmesfield
WILMSLOW
Knutsford
Alderley Edge
Adlington
Pott Shrigle
Kettleshulme
Dove Holes
Peak Forest
Peak Dale
Little Hucklow
Great Hucklow
Foolow
Tideswell
Wormhill
Stoney Middleton
Calver
Baslow
Bollington
Prestbury
Rainow
Shining Tor
Combs
Upper End
Litton
Wardlow
Nether Alderley
Monk's Heath
MACCLESFIELD
Chelford
BUXTON
King Sterndale
Blackwell
Taddington
Chelmorton
Little Longstone
Hassop
Ashford in the Water
Pilsley
Nether End
Robin Hood
Chesterfield
Henbury
Broken Cross
Macclesfield Forest
Cat and Fiddle
Harpur Hill
Sheldon
BAKEWELL
Rowsley
Beeley
Siddington
Withington Green
Warren
Sutton Lane Ends
Wildboarclough
Axe Edge
Gleadsmoss
Marton
Rodeheath
North Rode
Oakgrove
Flash
Hollinsclough
Earl Sterndale
Monyash
Over Haddon
Youlgreave
Stanton in Peak
Swettenham
Wincle
Allgreave
Bosley
Burntcliff Top
Longnor
Crowdecote
Middleton
Two Dales
Brereton Heath
Hulme Walfield
CONGLETON
Eaton
Danebridge
Newtown
Fawfieldhead
Pilsbury
Hartington
Wensley
MATLOCK
Matlock Bath
Tansley
Astbury
Timbersbrook
Bridestones
Heaton
Upper Hulme
Sheen
Biggin
Elton
Winster
Pikehall
Brightgate
Bonsall
Cromford
Brookhouse Green
Hightown
Rushton Spencer
Biddulph Moor
Meerbrook
Brund
Hulme End
Grangemill
Aldwark
Smallwood
Fourlanes End
Brownlow Heath
Thorncliffe
Upper Elkstone
Warslow
Alstonefield
Wetton
BIDDULPH
Mow Cop
Horton
Rudyard
LEEK
Butterton
Longcliffe
Middleton
Brassington
WIRKSWORTH
Scholar Green
Harriseahead
KIDSGROVE
Blackwood Hill
Brown Edge
Longsdon
Bradnop
Onecote
Grindon
Ford
Parwich
Tissington
Hopton
Radway Green
Talke
Brindley Ford
Norton in the Moors
Endon
Cheddleton
Basford Green
Waterfall
Waterhouses
Ilam
Fenny Bentley
Bradbourne
Hognaston
Kirk Ireton
Idridgehay
Shottle
AUDLEY
Butters Green
Chesterton
Halmer End
Alsagers Bank
TUNSTALL
Milton
Stanley
Wetley Rocks
Ipstones
Winkhill
Blackbank
Calton
Blore
Thorpe
Kniveton
Biggin
Shottlegate
Silverdale
Madeley Heath
Keele
HANLEY
Bucknall
Werrington
Consall
Cellarhead
Froghall
Caudon
Swinscoe
Mappleton
ASHBOURNE
Bradley
Hulland
Turnditch
Windley
NEWCASTLE-UNDER-LYME
STOKE-ON-TRENT
Kingsley
Whiston
Weaver Hills
Stanton
Hanging Bridge
Clifton
Osmaston
Mercaston
Mugginton
Madeley
Clayton
Fenton
Caverswall
Oakamoor
Ramshorn
Farley
Wootton
Wyaston
Brailsford
Kedleston
Longton
Lightwood
Dilhorne
Cheadle
Alton Towers
Alton
Ellastone
Snelston
Norbury
Shirley
Ednaston
Kedleston Hall
Whitmore
Baldwin's Gate
Trentham
Blythe Bridge
Forsbrook
Bradley in the Moors
Denstone
Croxden
Yeaveley
Rodsley
Hollington
Longlane
Kirk Langley
Hill Chorlton
Knowl Wall
Tittensor
Rough Close
Barlaston
Meir Heath
Draycott in the Moors
Upper Tean
Lower Tean
Hollington
Rocester
Alkmonton
Longford
Thurvaston
Lees
Mackworth
Chapel Chorlton
The Rowe
Beech
Fulford
Fole
Marston Montgomery
Cubley
Great Cubley
Trusley
Radbourne
Derby
Podmore
Chatcull
Cranberry
Swynnerton
Oulton
Moddershall
Cotwalton
Beamhurst
Waldley
Somersal Herbert
Boylestone
Church Broughton
Mickleover
Standon
Millmeece
Yarnfield
STONE
Hilderstone
Garshall Green
Withington
UTTOXETER
Stramshall
Doveridge
Sutton on the Hill
Etwall
Burnaston
Wetwood
Slindon
Walton
Aston-by-Stone
Milwich
Field
Bramshall
Blount's Green
Sudbury
Foston
Scropton
Hilton
Hatton
Willington
Findern
Croxton
Sugnall
Sturbridge
Pershall
Burston
Coton
Gratwich
Fradswell
Marchington
Draycott in the Clay
Coton in the Clay
Tutbury
Egginton
Rolleston
Offley
Izaak Walton's Cottage
Whitgreave
Sandon
Gayton
Stowe-by-Chartley
Grindley
Kingstone
Marchington Woodlands
Hanbury
Stretton
Repton
Eccleshall
Norton Bridge
Chebsey
Yarlet
Salt
Weston
Drointon
Newton Solney
Wootton
Great Bridgeford
Ellenhall
Marston
Hopton
Hixon
Newborough
Needwood Forest
Anslow
Anslow Gate
Horninglow
BURTON UPON TRENT
Winshill
High Offley
Woodseaves
Seighford
Ranton
Lawnhead
STAFFORD
Tixall
Abbots Bromley
Hoar Cross
Rangemore
Tatenhill
Bretby
Norbury
Coton Clanford
Derrington
Admaston
Colwich
Blithfield Reservoir
Dunstall
Newhall
SWADLINCOTE
Woodville
Gnosall
Long Compton
Haughton
Weeping Cross
Milford
Brocton
Colton
Blithbury
Hamstall Ridware
Hadley End
Yoxall
Stanton
Castle Gresley
Church Eaton
Hyde Lea
Coppenhall
Dunston
Hill Ridware
Morrey
Pipe Ridware
Barton under Needwood
Walton-on-Trent
Caldwell
Cross Bank
Linton
Overseal
Newport
Allimore Green
Bromestead
Bradley
Acton Trussell
Levedale
Bednall
RUGELEY
Cannock Chase
Brereton
Armitage
Handsacre
King's Bromley
Orgreave
Alrewas
Rosliston
Coton in the Elms
Lullington
Netherseal
Croxall
Orslow
High Onn
Mitton
Penkridge
Hednesford
Longdon
Rileyhill
Castle Ring
Birmingham
Cannock
Lichfield
93

Nottinghamshire, Lincolnshire, the Broads

This is where England flattens out and turns into fertile agricultural country. The hills and vales of Nottinghamshire become the potato-growing lands and bulb fields of Lincolnshire, and the sugar beetfields of Norfolk. The landscape is reminiscent of Holland.

Chesterfield

This town has a parish church that is famous for its twisted spire, caused by the warping of the timbers beneath the lead roofing. The Peacock Heritage Centre, in a half-timbered, 16th-century house in Low Pavement, is the local museum. George Stephenson, the railway pioneer, lived here and is buried in the churchyard. He discovered a seam of coal in the town.

Hunstanton

This little seaside town in Norfolk sells souvenirs of the sun setting in the east. Due to its position on the Wash, it is the only part of East Anglia that faces west. Old Hunstanton was the home of the le Strange family, who are commemorated in the Church of St. Mary; New Hunstanton is sometimes known as St. Edmunds, after its local 19th-century church. The resort is also famous for its striped cliff. Nearby Holme has a nature reserve and bird sanctuary. Halfway between Hunstanton and King's Lynn is Sandringham, the royal family's Norfolk estate, where they usually spend Christmas.

King's Lynn

The town was known as Bishop's Lynn until the Dissolution of the Monasteries, though the inhabitants, then as now, prefer to call it plain "Lynn". It grew up around the Saturday Market Place, where the Old Gaol House now stands. The manacles decorating the front of the building leave no doubt as to its intended purpose. Next door is one of King's Lynn's two guildhalls. The Guildhall of the Holy Trinity was originally built in 1423. It is faced with the chequerboard patterning of split flint and pale stone, typical of important buildings in East Anglia. The undercroft contains the Lynn Regalia, medieval treasures of which the greatest are King John's Loving Cup and Sword. The Guildhall of St. George was built in 1406 and has served several purposes. In Shakespeare's time it was a theatre and the bard is rumoured to have appeared here.

Lincoln

See "Historic Cities"

Market Deeping

This little town no longer holds a market. Its 13th-century parsonage is the oldest inhabited rectory in England. There are some fine old houses and the church is even older than the parsonage. Deeping St. James, to the east, has a fine 12th-century church, once part of a Benedictine priory.

Newark-on-Trent

This is an ancient town strategically placed on the junction of two Roman roads, the Fosse Way and the Great North Road. The ruined castle, which is not open to the public, is 12th-15th century, and was partly destroyed during the Civil War. King John died here in 1216. Newark's two Town Halls, the Old Town Hall (1708) and the New Town Hall (1774-76) are both in the Market Place, and are open to the public. Prince Rupert (1619-82) Count Palatine of the Rhine, grandson of James I, was living in the Governor's House in Stodman Street, when he quarrelled bitterly with Charles I whose armies he had commanded in the Civil War.

The Norfolk Broads

This area of lakeland is a triangle on the map with the apex at Norwich and the base along the coastline between Lowestoft and Sea Palling. For a long time it was thought that the Broads were formed by the flooding of a river estuary which eventually silted up, but in fact they are the result of medieval diggings for peat which became flooded. With the local navigable rivers - the Yare, the Waveney and the Bure - they provide 200 miles of navigable waters. They are extremely popular for holidays in sailing boats, motor cruisers and houseboats and there are plenty of firms who hire craft for the purpose. Small excursion steamers ply the Yare and Bure in summer but the trading wherry, the traditional vessel of the Broads, has all but disappeared.

Norwich

See "Historic Cities"

Nottingham

This city was once riven by bitter class wars, first in the Middle Ages when the Norman overlords lived cheek-by-jowl with the Saxon peasants, and in the 19th century when the Luddites wrecked the lace-making and spinning machinery that they feared would take away their livelihoods. The story of Nottingham Lace is told in the Lace Hall, renovated Unitarian chapel built in 1874. The Nottingham Story, a re-creation of the town's turbulent history is told in a 25-minute audiovisual presentation at the Tourist Information Centre. The Saxon hero, Robin Hood, who roamed Sherwood Forest robbing the rich (the Norman French) to give to the poor (the Saxons) is commemorated in a statue in the Castle grounds. In fact the name Nottingham Castle is a misnomer. The building that stands here now is not the most important castle in England erected by William the Conqueror and visited by every monarch, including Edward IV who proclaimed himself king there. That castle was utterly demolished in 1651 after it had fallen to the Roundheads during the Civil War. The present building is a mansion built by the Duke of Newcastle in 1674 though virtually destroyed by rioting in 1831. It was restored by Nottingham City Council and became the first municipal art gallery outside London. It contains a fine collection, including paintings by Picasso and Turner. Brewhouse Yard beneath the cliffs of Castle Rock once contained the castle's maltings and brewhouse. Several inns stood here, but only one remains, the Trip to Jerusalem, which dates from 1189 and claims to be the oldest public house in England. The 17th-century houses in the Yard form the Brewhouse Yard Museum.

Skegness

Lincolnshire's most popular holiday resort and the site of Billy Butlin's first holiday camp, which he opened in the 1930s. The Church Farm Museum has displays of farm life. Lord Tennyson used to enjoy a walk along the promenade. Gibraltar Point at the southern end of the beach is a Nature Reserve and Bird Sanctuary.

Wells-next the Sea

This is an attractive sea port. The nearby salt marshes are a nature reserve. Only a few miles away is Holkham Hall, seat of the Earls of Leicester. This Palladian mansion is one of the great country houses of Norfolk, famous for its magnificent art collection, with works by Van Dyck, Rubens and Gainsborough. The most interesting room is the Marble Hall lined with coloured alabaster. The second Earl was an agricultural reformer and his tenants erected a column in his honour, supported by four cows and topped by a wheatsheaf in 1845. The terraces were landscaped by Capability Brown, and the park contains a large lake.

Windmills were once as common a sight in East Anglia as in Holland (opposite left).

Poppy-field near Beeston Priory looking towards the Bump, a low hill among Norfolk's flatlands (left).

The church of St. Edmund at Acle, Norfolk, has a most unusual thatched roof (top).

Sherwod Forest in Nottinghamshire, where Robin Hood once hid from the Sheriff (above).

Information
Tourist Information Centre
The Old Gaol House
Saturday Market Place
King's Lynn
PE30 1HY
Tel: (0553) 763044

Tourist Information Centre
16 Wheeler Gate
Nottingham
NG1 2NB
Tel: (0602) 470661

Events
On Easter Monday, there is Egg Rolling in Nottingham at Wollaton Park, and the town has an Arts Festival in May. The Goose Fair is still held in Nottingham in October.
King's Lynn holds a fair called the March on St. Valentine's Day (14 February, but March 1 under the old Julian Calendar) There is a big May Day celebration. The King's Lynn Festival is held in the last week of July.

78
96
Leeds
Doncaster
Kingston-upon-Hull
Scunthorpe
Birmingham
Leicester
Oakham
Chapel-en-le-Frith
Matlock
Ashbourne
Burton-upon-Trent
Yd
Ye
Yf
Za
Zb
28
29
30
31
32
SHEFFIELD
ROTHERHAM
MALTBY
Harworth
GAINSBOROUGH
Aughton
Anston
Dinnington
WORKSOP
EAST RETFORD
DRONFIELD
Mosbrough
CHESTERFIELD
STAVELEY
BOLSOVER
Clowne
Creswell
SHIREBROOK
WARSOP
Tuxford
MANSFIELD WOODHOUSE
MANSFIELD
SUTTON IN ASHFIELD
KIRKBY IN ASHFIELD
ALFRETON
CLAY CROSS
Ollerton
Edwinstowe
Boughton
SOUTHWELL
NEWARK ON TRENT
HUCKNALL
RIPLEY
BELPER
HEANOR
EASTWOOD
ILKESTON
Kimberley
ARNOLD
CARLTON
NOTTINGHAM
BEESTON AND STAPLEFORD
WEST BRIDGFORD
LONG EATON
DERBY
Bingham
Ruddington
Keyworth
Cotgrave
Radcliffe on Trent
East Leake
Castle Donington
Melbourne
SHEPSHED
LOUGHBOROUGH
SWADLINCOTE
ASHBY-DE-LA-ZOUCH
COALVILLE
Mountsorrel
Sileby
MELTON MOWBRAY
Asfordby
Bottesford
Vale of Belvoir
Sherwood Forest
Charnwood Forest

79
Scunthorpe
Grimsby
Grimsby
Zc
Zd
Ze
Zf
Aa
Glentham
Bishop-bridge
Caenby
Caenby Corner
West Rasen
Market Rasen
Tealby
Ludford
North Elkington
Fotherby
Alvingham
North Cockerington
Saltfleetby St Peter
Theddlethorpe St Helen
Owmby-by-Spital
Toft next Newton
Newton by Toft
Middle Rasen
North Willingham
Sixhills
Burgh on Bain
Welton le Wold
South Elkington
South Cockerington
LOUTH
Grimoldby
Theddlethorpe All Saints
Linwood
Hainton
Gayton le Wold
Raithby
Legbourne
Little Carlton
Great Carlton
Ingham
Spridlington
Faldingworth
Lissington
East Torrington
West Torrington
Donington on Bain
Tathwell
Little Cawthorpe
North Reston
South Reston
Withern
Strubby
Hackthorn
Snarford
Friesthorpe
Wickenby
Holton
Benniworth
East Barkwith
Market Stainton
Haugham
Authorpe
Maltby le Marsh
Welton
Snelland
Fulnetby
Panton
Sotby
Goulceby
Scamblesby
Nat. Res.
Cawkwell
Maidenwell
Burwell
Belleau
Claythorpe
Saleby
Beesby
Dunholme
Stainton by Langworth
Wragby
Great Sturton
Ranby
Oxcombe
Ruckland
White Pit
Alford
Bilsby
Scothern
Langworth
Langton by Wragby
Hatton
Swaby
South Thoresby
Rigsby
North Carlton
Nettleham
Kingthorpe
South Ormsby
Driby
Tetford
Well
Burton
Barlings
Apley
Baumber
Hemingby
Belchford
Fulletby
Salmonby
Somersby
Brinkhill
Ulceby Cross
Ulceby
Willoughby
Reepham
Minting
Gautby
Wispington
West Ashby
Ashby Puerorum
Harrington
Claxby
Cathedral
Fiskerton
Stainfield
Edlington
Thimbleby
High Toynton
Greetham
Hagworthingham
Sausthorpe
Langton
Skendleby
Welton le Marsh
Washingborough
Witham
Heighington
Bardney
Bucknall
Horsington
HORNCASTLE
Nat. Res.
Lusby
Mavis Enderby
Raithby
Partney
Scremby
Candlesby
BOULTHAM
LINCOLN
Branston Booths
Thornton
Mareham on the Hill
Hameringham
Ashby by Partney
Gunby Hall
Branston
Potterhanworth Booths
Potterhanworth
Southrey
Dalderby
Hareby
Old Bolingbroke
Hundleby
SPILSBY
Great Steeping
Bracebridge Heath
NORTH HYKEHAM
Haltham
Moorby
East Keal
Halton Holegate
Irby in the Marsh
Nocton
WOODHALL SPA
Wood Enderby
Miningsby
West Keal
Little Steeping
Waddington
Metheringham
Kirkstead
Kirkby on Bain
Mareham le Fen
Revesby
East Kirkby
Toynton Fen Side
Aubourn
Harmston
Timberland
Stickford
Keal Coates
Fendike Corner
Martin
Dales
Wainfleet Bank
Boothby Graffoe
Blankney
Thorpe Tilney Dales
Tattershall
Tumby
Moor Side
New Bolingbroke
Midville
New Leake
Kirkby Green
Scopwick
Coningsby
Tumby Woodside
Stickney
East Fen
Friskney
Navenby
Walcott
Tattershall Bridge
Ashby de la Launde
Scrub Hill
Carrington
Billinghay
New York
Northlands
West Fen
Lade Bank
Welbourn
Digby
Chapel Hill
Leake Commonside
Wrangle Bank
Bloxholm
North Kyme
Wrangle Lowgate
Leadenham
Gipsey Bridge
Frithville
Wrangle
Fulbeck
South Kyme
Sibsey
Old Leake
Cranwell
Ruskington
Anwick
Fishtoft Drove
Leasingham
Langrick
Leverton Outgate
Ewerby Thorpe
Frith Bank
Hilldyke
Leverton
Kirkby la Thorpe
Amber Hill
Brothertoft
Benington
North Rauceby
SLEAFORD
Howell
BOSTON
Benington Sea End
Normanton
Asgarby
East Heckington
Hubbert's Bridge
Haltoft End
Carlton Scroop
Sudbrook
Heckington
Freiston
Silk Willoughby
Burton Pedwardine
Little Hale
Swineshead Bridge
Frampton West End
Fishtoft
Freiston Shore
Ancaster
Honington
Nat. Res.
Wilsford
Fenhouses
Scrane End
Barkston
Kelby
Swarby
Scredington
Helpringham
Swineshead
Kirton End
Frampton
Culverthorpe
Aswarby
Drayton
Kirton
The Haven
Nat. Res.
Belton Park
Aunsby
Spanby
Hoffleet Stow
Sandholme
Londonthorpe
Oasby
Dembleby
Osbournby
Swaton
Bicker
Wigtoft
GRANTHAM
Newton
Horbling
Donington
Sutterton
St Wulframs
Braceby
Treekingham
Bridge End
Quadring Eaudike
Ropsley
Sapperton
Pickworth
Billingborough
South Forty Foot Drain
Fosdyke
Holbeach St Matthew
Old Somerby
Folkingham
Quadring
Gosberton
Holbeach St Marks
Little Ponton
Humby
Boothby Pagnell
Pointon
Sea Bank
Westhorpe
Surfleet Seas End
Ingoldsby
Aslackby
Dowsby
Risegate
Welland
Holbeach Marsh
Lenton
Keisby
Rippingale
Surfleet
Moulton Seas End
Holbeach Clough
Holbeach Hurn
Bassingthorpe
Bitchfield
Hawthorpe
Saracen's Head
Gedney Dyke
Easton
Burton-le-Coggles
Irnham
Kirkby Underwood
Dunsby
Northgate
Pinchbeck
Loosegate
Lutton
Fleet Hargate
Chapelgate
Hacconby
Pinchbeck Bars
Weston
Stainfield
Morton
Pinchbeck West
Moulton
Whaplode
HOLBEACH
Gedney
Long Sutton
Corby Glen
Elsthorpe
Pode Hole
Springfields Gardens
Gedney Broadgate
Swinstead
Grimsthorpe
Dyke
LITTLE LONDON
SPALDING
Swayfield
Edenham
BOURNE
Twenty
Weston Hills
Sutton Crosses
North Witham
Creeton
East Glen River
West Glen River
South Witham
Whaplode St Catherine
Sutton St James
Tydd Gote
Castle Bytham
Little Bytham
Tydd St Giles
Four Gotes
Lincolnshire
Leicester
Toft
Northorpe
Cowbit
Moulton Chapel
Holbeach St Johns
Carebу
Witham on the Hill
Manthorpe
Thurlby
North Drove Drain
South Holland Main Drain
Stretton
Carlby
Deeping St Nicholas
Newton
Overton
Clipsham
Baston
Holbeach Drove
Sutton St Edmund
Fitton End
Greetham
Pickworth
Wilsthorpe
South Drove Drain
Gorefield
Leverington
Essendine
Greatford
Langtoft
MARKET DEEPING
Crowland
Shepeau Stow
Gedney Hill
Cottesmore
Barholm
Stamford
Peterborough
97
Skegness
King's Lynn
Wisbech

Ab
Ac
Ad
Ae
Af
28
29
30
31
32
22
Theddlethorpe St Helen
MARBLETHORPE
TRUSTHORPE
Thorpe
Sutton on Sea
Sutton le Marsh
Hannah
Markby
Bilsby
Huttoft
Mumby
Authorpe Row
Cumberworth
Hogsthorpe
Chapel Saint Leonards
Willoughby
Slothsby
Addlethorpe
Ingoldmells
Lincoln
Orby
Burgh le Marsh
Bratoft
Winthorpe
SKEGNESS
Thorpe St. Peter
Croft
Wainfleet Bank
Wainfleet All Saints
Steeping River
Key's Toft
Nat. Res.
Gibraltar
The Wash
Brancaster Roads
Holkham Bay
Brancaster Bay
Titchwell
Burnham Deepdale
Burnham Norton
Burnham Overy Staithe
HOLKHAM CAMP
Holkham
Holkham Hall
WELLS-NEXT-THE-SEA
Stiffkey
Warham
WARHAM CAMP
Cockthorpe
Binham
Thornham
Burnham Market
Burnham Thorpe
HUNSTANTON
Ringstead
North Creake
Summerfield
Heacham
Docking
Stanhoe
South Creake
Egmere
Wighton
Great Walsingham
Sedgeford
Slipper Chapel
Houghton St Giles
Priory
Great Snoring
Hindringham
Snettisham
Bircham Newton
Fring
Stiffkey
East Barsham
Southgate
Ingoldisthorpe
Syderstone
Sculthorpe
Little Snoring
Kettlestone
Great Bircham
Bagthorpe
Shernborne
Tattersett
Dunton
Shereford
FAKENHAM
Dersingham
Anmer
New Houghton
East Rudham
Hempton
Stibbard
Sandringham
Sandringham House
Tatterford
Wolferton
West Newton
West Rudham
Helhoughton
Toftrees
Great Ryburgh
Flitcham
Harpley
East Raynham
Colkirk
Babingley
Castle Rising
Hillington
Oxwick
Gedney Drove End
Guy's Head
Ongar Hill
North Wootton
KINGS'S LYNN
SOUTH WOOTTON
Roydon
Little Massingham
Great Massingham
South Raynham
Horningtoft
Gately
Sutton Bridge
Little London
Clenchwarton
Pott Row
Grimston
Massingham Heath
Weasenham All Saints
Weasenham St Peter
Tittleshall
Brisley
North Elmham
Terrington St Clement
West Lynn
Rougham
Stainfield
East Bilney
Spalding
Tydd Gote
Walpole St Andrew
Tilney All Saints
Gayton
Ashwicken
Mileham
Beetley
St Peter
Tilney High End
West Winch
East Winch
East Walton
Castle Acre
Castle Acre Priory
West Lexham
East Lexham
Litcham
Bittering
Gressenhall
Four Gotes
Terrington St John
Saddle Bow
Middleton
Newton
Beeston
Longham
Hoe
EAST DEREHAM
West Walton
Walton Highway
St John's Highway
Wiggenhall St Germans
Setchey
Blackborough End
West Bilney
West Acre
South Acre
Great Dunham
Wendling
Walpole Highway
St John's Fen End
Wiggenhall St Mary the Virgin
Pentney
Narborough
Nar
Little Dunham
Great Fransham
Scarning
WISBECH
WALSOKEN
Wormegay
Wiggenhall St Mary Magdalen
Watlington
Tottenhill
Marham
Great Palgrave
Little Fransham
Daffy Green
SWAFFHAM
Necton
Bradenham
East Bradenham
Whinburgh
Ely
Thetford
98

Bb
Bc
Bd
Be
SHERINGHAM
CHROMER
West Runton
Weybourne
Salthouse
Kelling
Upper Sheringham
tourist railway
Overstrand
Sidestrand
Trimingham
Mundesley
Holt
Bodham Street
West Beckham
East Beckham
Aylmerton
Fellbrick Hall
Gresham
Crossdale Street
Roughton
Gimingham
Hempstead
Baconthorpe
Bessingham
Sustead
Hanworth
Southrepps
Paston
Bacton
Keswick
Plumstead
Thurgarton
Alby Hill
Thorpe Market
Trunch
Knapton
Edgefield
Matlaske
Antingham
Bradfield
Little Barningham
Erpingham
Colby
Suffield
Swafield
Witton Bridge
Happisburgh
Calthorpe
Saxthorpe
Itteringham
NORTH WALSHAM
Spa Common
Whimpwell Green
Corpusty
Banningham
Crostwight
Hempstead
Thurning
Blickling
Blickling Hall
Felmingham
Happisburgh Common
Sea Palling
Heydon Hall
Oulton Street
Aylsham
Tuttington
Honing
East Ruston
Ingham
Waxham
Guestwick
Wood Dalling
Burgh next Aylsham
Westwick
Stalham
Worstead
Dilham
Low Street
Stalham Green
Hickling
Themelthorpe
Marsham
Swanton Abbot
Lamas
Fairstead
Sloley
Beeston St Lawrence
Hickling Heath
Horsey
Horsey Windpump
Cawston
Reepham
Booton
Eastgate
Buxton
Sco Ruston
Hickling Broad
Nat. Res.
Hevingham
Stratton
Tunstead
Beeston Hall
Neatishead
Irstead
Potter Higham
Somerton
Brandiston
Coltishall
Sparham
Bure
Bridge
Martham
Bastwick
Lenwade
Swannington
Waterloo
Horstead
Hoveton
Ludham
Hemsby
Newport
Felthorpe
Frettenham
Wroxham
Thurne
Ormesby St Margaret
Elsing
Primrose Green
Morton
Attlebridge
St Helena
Newton St Faith
Crostwick
Upper Street
Rollesby
California
Weston Longville
Horsford
Horsham St Faith
Woodbastwick
Ranworth
Ormesby
Burgh St Margaret
Broadlands Conservations Centre
Norfolk
Hockering
Weston Green
Drayton
Rackheath
Salhouse
New Rackheath
Billockby
Filby
Caister Hall
Caister-on-Sea
Taverham
Costessey
Norwich
SPROWSTON
Thorpe End Garden Village
Little Plumstead
Panxworth
South Walsham
Mautby
Upton
Runham
West Caister
Honingham
Easton
NEW COSTESSEY
THORPE ST ANDREW
Hemblington
Acle
Stokesby
East Tuddenham
Marlingford
Colton
Great Plumstead
Blofield
Lingwood
Damgate
Welbourne
Bawburgh
NORWICH
Cathedral
Brundall
Moulton St Mary
Broads
Barford
Colney
EATON
LAKENHAM
Postwick
South Burlingham
Halvergate
Breydon Water
Yarmouth Roads
99

The Midlands and the Welsh Borders

The heart of England, part of which is known as the Black Country, due to its industrialisation, nevertheless has some areas of outstanding natural beauty, and many historic towns. It includes Birmingham, England's second city, and the Shakespeare country.

Birmingham

England's second city is a vast metropolis extending as far as Wolverhampton and Walsall in the north, and West Bromwich and Dudley in the west. In the Domesday Book (1085-86) it is recorded as having just 10 inhabitants! To the English, Birmingham is famous as the first city to have a complicated road junction in the centre, known affectionately as Spaghetti Junction. It runs around the central area known as the Bull Ring and still presents problems for motorists unfamiliar with the city. Despite appearances to the contrary, this market area has been active for 900 years, and a church has been on the site of the present Church of St. Martins-in-the-Bull-Ring since that time, though the present building dates from 1873. The church has stained glass windows by Edward Burne-Jones. Gas Street Basin is at the heart of the canal system which runs through Birmingham and a canal boat trip is a pleasant way to see the city. Birmingham has excellent museums, including the City Art Gallery, and the Natural History Museum and the Museum of Science and Industry. The Black Country Museum is about 10 miles west of the city centre and is a reconstruction of a 19th-century village in the heart of industrial England.

Bourneville

This model village, described as "the Factory in a Garden" was founded by George Cadbury about five miles from Birmingham, for the workers at the family-owned Cadbury chocolate factory. Cadbury World is an exhibition devoted to chocolate which includes a visit to two areas of the factory. It is wise to avoid visiting at weekends and in high summer as, needless to say, this is an extremely popular attraction.

Cannock Chase

The lungs of the Black Country, Cannock Chase is a 30,000-acre stretch between Lichfield and Stafford which was once a royal hunting forest. It is an area of high moorland with bracken and ferns, roamed by deer. Needwood Forest is just east of the Chase. Blythefield Reservoir is a well-known beauty spot.

Great Malvern

The town takes its name from the surrounding Malvern Hills. This area is associated with the composer, Edward Elgar (1857-1934), who drew so much of his inspiration from these limestone hills which separate the Severn Plain from the rolling countryside around Hereford. An Elgar Trail map is available from the Great Malvern Heritage Centre and the Malvern Festival is devoted to his music. Elgar is buried in St. Wulfstan's Roman Catholic Church at Malvern Wells. The town has an ancient spa, supplied by the waters of St. Anne's Well, which still gush from Beacon Hill and are now bottled and sold all over Britain. The Priory Church contains much 15th-century stained glass;

Blists Hall Industrial Village at Ironbridge (above).

Great Malvern, the main square (right).

Tower overlooking the village of Broadway, in the Cotswolds (opposite top).

Roses in bloom in garden of Elgar's birthplace at Broadheath, Worcestershire (opposite centre).

The Old House, Hereford, with St. Peter's church (opposite below).

the choir screen is panelled with locally-made 15th-century tiles.

Ironbridge

This spot, just south of the new town of Telford, named after the famous engineer, is said to be the birthplace of the Industrial Revolution. It is now the best preserved industrial archæological site in the country. Three generations of the Darby family exploited the mineral wealth here, starting as early as 1709, when Abraham Darby smelted iron ore with coke in nearby Coalbrookdale. His grandson built the world's first iron bridge here, now preserved by English Heritage. The Ironbridge Gorge Museum restores and re-creates the industrial past of the area. West of the Bridge, the Severn Warehouse contains a Visitors' Information Centre. The Coalbrookedale Museum north of the bridge explores the history of iron-making on this, the site of the first blast furnace. East of the bridge are the 18th-century Bedlam Furnaces and the Jackfield Tile Gallery. The Coalport China Museum is devoted to the region's pottery industry, with displays of Coalport and Caughley china. Blist's Open Air Museum, on the Shropshire Canal, contains factories, cottages and shops.

Stratford-upon-Avon

See "Excursions"

Warwick

This ancient university town has a magnificent medieval castle, which stands on a rocky hill overlooking the River Avon. Although it has been described as one of the finest medieval fortresses in Europe, its impressive appearance owes much to the rebuilding that occurred after a serious fire in 1694. The Earls of Warwick added many features in later years, and furnished it with their treasures. The castle is now owned by the Madame Tussaud's Company which runs several other tourist attractions in Britain. It has been refurnished and nine rooms have been recreated to look as they would have done in the 19th century, when the Earl and Countess of Warwick entertained English high society. The castle is surrounded by historic buildings.

Worcester (pronounced "Wooster")

This town stands between the River Severn and the Birmingham and Worcester Canal. It is the county town of Hereford and Worcester, two former counties merged into one. Worcester was once the centre of the glove-making industry, but this has virtually disappeared. Two other industries that are still flourishing are the Royal Worcester Porcelain Factory and Lea and Perrins Worcestershire Sauce, a condiment whose origins may date back to Roman influence and which is exported all over the world. The city showed a strong loyalty to the Royalist cause during the Civil War, earning it the motto *Civitas in Bello in Pace Fidelis* (The City Loyal in War and in Peace). Thus, the statues of Charles I and Charles II have pride of place at the entrance to the Guildhall, while an effigy of Cromwell's head is nailed by the ears! Charles II held his Council of War before the Battle of Worcester in the 15th-century Commandery, with its splendid Great Hall. The Tudor House Museum, in a 500-year-old building, has room-by-room displays of the social history of the area. Greyfriars is a massive timber-framed building dating from 1480, all that remains of Greyfriars Priory. It is now owned by the National Trust and is open to the public. The Royal Worcester Porcelain Factory is the oldest in England and has a museum attached. Worcester Cathedral has a commanding view of the River Severn and its lovely tower soars over the surrounding landscape. Much of the original building, started by Bishop Wulstan in 1084, still survives. King John was buried here at his own request. The interior has benefitted (or suffered, depending on one's point of view) from the 19th-century restoration by Sir Gilbert Scott.

Information

Birmingham Convention and Visitors Bureau
2 City Arcade
Birmingham
Tel: (021) 643-2514

Cadbury World
Linden Road,
Bourneville
B30 2LD
Tel: (021) 433-4334

Events

The National Exhibition Centre, just south of Birmingham, has a constant cycle of exhibitions and shows. For details, telephone (021) 780-4141.
The Malvern Festival, Great Malvern, Worcestershire, is devoted mainly to the music of Elgar. George Bernard Shaw wrote plays especially for the first Festival, held in 1929.
The Three Counties Agricultural Show is held at the Three Counties Fairground near Malvern, in June.
At Abbots Bromley, a village in Cannock Chase, the ancient Horn Dance is held annually on the Monday following the first Sunday after 4 September.

82
102
103
Oswestry
Whitchurch
Newcastle-u.-L.
Brecon
Newport
Gloucester
Dolgellau
Newtown
Aberystwyth
Wf
Xa
Xb
Xc
32
33
34
35
36
SHREWSBURY
WELSHPOOL
TRALLWNG
TELFORD
WELLINGTON
OAKENGATES
HADLEY
DAWLEY
Coalbrookdale
Iron-Bridge
Broseley
MUCH WENLOCK
BRIDGNORTH
MONTGOMERY
TREFALDWYN
BISHOP'S CASTLE
Church Stretton
The Long Mynd
Wenlock Edge
Ape Dale
Corve Dale
Brown Clee Hill
Clee Hill
Clun Forest
Clun
Knighton
LUDLOW
Tenbury Wells
Cleobury Mortimer
PRESTEIGNE
Radnor Forest
Great Rhos
New Radnor
KINGTON
LEOMINSTER
Bromyard
HAY-ON-WYE
HEREFORD
Long Mountain
Offa's Dyke
Powys
Shropshire
Hereford and Worcester
Pontesbury
Minsterley
Stiperstones
Bayston Hill
Condover
Cressage
Craven Arms
Onibury
Bromfield
Richards Castle
Orleton
Yarpole
Kingsland
Shobdon
Pembridge
Weobley
Dilwyn
Bodenham
Wellington
Marden
Burghill
Credenhill
Kenchester
Madley
Clehonger
Lugwardine
Withington
Tarrington
Dormington
Mordiford
Ledbury
Clyro
Glasbury
Three Cocks
Llanigon
Clifford
Whitney-on-Wye
Eardisley
Kinnersley
Almeley
Lyonshall
Huntington
Gladestry
Old Radnor
Walton
Evenjobb
Norton
Whitton
Pilleth
Llangunllo
Beguildy
Felindre
Newcastle
Llanfair Waterdine
Bucknell
Brampton Bryan
Leintwardine
Wigmore
Aymestrey
Mortimer Cross
Lingen
Titley
Staunton on Arrow
Eardisland
Monkland
Ivington
Stoke Prior
Hope under Dinmore
Dinmore Manor
Sutton St Nicholas
Moreton on Lugg
Preston Wynne
Ocle Pychard
Burley Gate
Stretton Grandison
Yarkhill
Ashperton
Canon Frome
Bishop's Frome
Munderfield Stocks
Pencombe
Little Cowarne
Much Cowarne
Stoke Lacy
Bredenbury
Edvin Loach
Tedstone
Thornbury
Grendon Green
Docklow
Hatfield
Kimbolton
Middleton on the Hill
Leysters
Kyre Park
Hanley Child
Hanley William
Stanford on Teme
Rochford
Newnham
Burford
Boraston
Greete
Whitton
Nash
Milson
Neen Sollars
Mamble
Bayton
Coreley
Knowle
Hopton Wafers
Doddington
Farlow
Silvington
Neen Savage
Oreton
Catherton
Stottesdon
Burwarton
Cleobury North
Neenton
Middleton Scriven
Middleton Priors
Ditton Priors
Holdgate
Tugford
Abdon
Stanton Long
Shipton
Brockton
Easthope
Longville in the Dale
Wilderhope Manor
Rushbury
Eaton
Broadstone
Munslow
Diddlebury
Corfton
Peaton
Culmington
Seifton
Stanton Lacy
Hopton Cangeford
Stoke St Milborough
Bitterley
Middleton
Henley
Caynham
Ashford Carbonell
Ashford Bowdler
Overton
Batchcott
Elton
Burrington
Downton on the Rock
Adforton
Leinthall Starkes
Leinthall Earls
Lucton
Luston
Eyton
Eye
Berrington Hall
Ashton
Brimfield
Little Hereford
Middleton
Cardington
Enchmarsh
Plaish
Hughley
Leebotwood
Longnor
Frodesley
Acton Burnell
Pitchford
Acton Pigott
Kenley
Ruckley
Church Preen
Presthope
Bourton
Acton Round
Morville
Aston Eyre
Upton Cressett
Nordley
Tasley
Willey
Barrow
Benthall
Harley
Sheinton
Homer
Buildwas
Leighton
Eaton Constantine
Wroxeter
Atcham
Uffington
Upton Magna
Rodington
Roden
Withington
Walcot
Wrockwardine
Admaston
Longdon on Tern
High Ercall
Poynton
Haughton
Kynnersley
Preston upon the Weald Moors
Eyton upon the Weald Moors
Sleapford
Lawley
Little Wenlock
Horsehay
Rushton
Uppington
Donnington
Longwood
The Wrekin
Dryton
Berrington
Cantlop
Great Ryton
Dorrington
Stapleton
Longden
Annscroft
Great Lyth
Hanwood
Cruckmeole
Cruckton
Nox
Yockleton
Westbury
Stoney Stretton
Edge
Lea
Hinton
Pontesford
Pleasley
Farley
Asterley
Westley
Habberley
Pulverbatch
Church Pulverbatch
Snailbeach
Hope
Gravels
Pennerley
Shelve
The Bog
Bridges
Ratlinghope
Woolstaston
All Stretton
Little Stretton
Minton
Marshbrook
Whittingslow
Acton Scott
Hatton
Harton
Alcaston
Wistanstow
Horderley
Myndtown
Asterton
Norbury
Wentnor
Linley
More
Lydham
Hyssington
Snead
Church Stoke
Priest Weston
Chirbury
Marrington
Corndon Hill
The Marsh
Wotherton
Middleton
Rorrington
Marton
Betton
Trelystan
Binweston
Brockton
Rowley
Worthen
Leigh
Ploxgreen
Hope
Leighton
Buttington
Forden
Kingswood
Fron
Berriew
Llwynderw
Abermule
Llandyssil
Pentreheyling
Sarn
Glanmule
Mainstone
Cefn Einion
Colebatch
Bishop's Castle
Lea
Eyton
Lydbury North
Brockton
Walcot
Edgton
Acton
Lower Down
Bryn
Bicton
Whitcott Keysett
Hall of the Forest
Anchor
Black Mountain
Bettws-y-crwyn
Quabbs
Dutlas
Beacon Hill
Llanfair Waterdine
Lloyney
Crug
Purlogue
New Invention
Chapel Lawn
Stowe
Bedstone
Hopton Castle
Obley
Hobarris
Woodside
Llwyn
Clunton
Purslow
Clunbury
Twitchen
Broome
Clungunford
Shelderton
Aston on Clun
Hopesay
Kempton
Little Brampton
Sibdon Carwood
Cheney Longville
Halford
Norton
Vernolds Common
Lower Hayton
Hayton's Bent
Sutton
Stokesay Castle
Upper Affcot
Westhope
Woolston
Dowles
Pulverbatch
Caer Caradoc
Hope Bowdler
Ticklerton
Wall under Heywood
East Wall
Gretton
Caynham Camp
Knowbury
Hope Bagot
Farden
Cleehill
Cleeton St Mary
Titterstone Clee
Snitton
Knighton
Milebrooke
Rhôs-y-meirch
Bleddfa
Cascob
Discoed
Kinnerton
Nash
Knill
Rodd
Combe Moor
Byton
Kinsham
Stansbatch
Ledicot
Shirl Heath
Cobnash
Cholstrey
Barewood
Marston
Moorcot
Luntley
Haven
Sollers Dilwyn
Broxwood
Holme Marsh
Kingswood
Hergest
Burlingjobb
Yardro
Llanfihangel-nant-Melan
Gwaunceste Hill
Glascwm
Colva
Hengoed
Michaelchurch-on-Arrow
Newchurch
Red Hill
Bryngwyn
Doly-cannau
Rhydspence
Llanbedr
Painscastle
The Begwns
Bronydd
Llowes
Cwmbach
Tregoyd
Hardwicke
The Bage
Dorstone
Snodhill
Priory Wood
Pen-y-Park
Merbach
Bredwardine
Moccas
Blakemere
Preston on Wye
Monnington on Wye
Staunton on Wye
Norton Canon
Moorhampton
Yarsop
Yazor
Mansell Gamage
Mansell Lacy
Brinsop
Bishopstone
Tillington
Tillington Common
Wormsley
Canon Pyon
King's Pyon
Ledgemoor
Calver Hill
Norton Wood
Sarnesfield
Woonton
Upcott
Lower Welson
Brilley
Winforton
Willersley
Letton
Ailey
Weobley Marsh
Knapton Green
Birley
Aulden
Bush Bank
Westhope
Upper Hill
Brierley
Wharton
Stretford Court
Humber Court
Risbury
Marston Stannett
Hegdon Hill
Bowley
Maund Bryan
Ullingswick
Urdimarsh
Walker's Green
The Vauld
Felton
Moreton Jeffries
Westhide
Shucknall
Hagley
Prior's Frome
Checkley
Hampton Bishop
Lower Bullingham
Lower Breinton
Swainshill
Canon Bridge
Eaton Bishop
Stretton Sugwas
Holmer
Shelwick
Pipe and Lyde
Lulham
Ploughfield
Tyberton
Peterchurch
Hinton
Shenmore
Gorsty Common
Putley
Aylton
Trumpet
Munsley
Evesbatch
Lower Eggleton
Five Bridges
Acton Beauchamp
Stanford Bishop
Bromyard Downs
Collington
Wolferlow
Upper Sapey
Stoke Bliss
Broad Heath
Bank Street
Grafton
Pudleston
Steen's Bridge
Humber
Hampton Charles
Edwyn Ralph
Middleton Scriven
Glazeley
Billingsley
Chorley
Baveney Wood
Clows Top
Frith Common
Orleton
Bircher
Croft Ambrey
Croft Castle
Comberton
Orleton Common
Yatton
Lower Lye
Ongar Street
Birtley
Letton
Lingen
Wapley
Walford
Buckton
Coxall Knoll
Bucknell
Burrow Camp
Bury Ditches
Clun Castle
Caer Caradoc
Mitchell's Fold
Hampton Hall
Beacon Ring
Caus Castle
Earl's Hill
Powis Castle
Welshpool & Llanfair
Vennington
Frochas
Garreg Bank
Pool Quay
Guilsfield
Geuffordd
Trefnanney
Sarnau
Ardleen
Deuddwr
Llandrinio
Crew Green
Criggion
Middletown
Wollaston
Breidden Hill
Melverley
Pentre
Alberbury
Stanwardine
Rowton Castle
Cardeston
Stretton Heath
Wattlesborough Castle
Ford
Montford
Ensdon
Felton Butler
Forton
Fitz
Bicton
Shelton
Shoot Hill
Haughmond Abbey
Abbey Church
Castle
Market Hall
Guildhall
St Mary's
Waen-fôach
Godor
Bwlch-y-cibau
Pentre'r-beirdd
Attingham Park
Norton
Aston
Cound
Golding
Pitchford Hall
Acton Burnell Castle
Langley Chapel
Stretton Westwood
Wenlock Priory
Guildhall
Lutwyche
Shipton Hall
Millichope Park
Heath Chapel
Broncroft Castle
Nordybank
Clee St Margaret
Loughton
Norton Camp
Hereford
Burford House Gardens
Eye Manor
Hampton Court
Wall Hills
Lower Brockhampton Hall
Queenswood
Sutton Walls
Fort
Credenhill Fort
Brobury House
Arthur's Stone
The Weir
Cathedral
Burton Court
Hergest Croft Gardens
Four Stones
Burfa Camp
Offa's Dyke
Arrow
Lugg
Teme
Wye
Severn
Camlad
Corve
Onny
Clun
Redlake
Rea
Frome
Lodon
Tern
Roden
Cole Brook
92

83
Stoke-on-Trent
Stafford
Rugeley
Burton-upon-Trent
Xe
Xf
Ya
Yb
Yc
CANNOCK
LICHFIELD
WOLVERHAMPTON
WALSALL
BROWNHILLS
ALDRIDGE
TAMWORTH
SUTTON COLDFIELD
WEST BROMWICH
DUDLEY
BIRMINGHAM
SOLIHULL
STOURBRIDGE
HALESOWEN
KIDDERMINSTER
STOURPORT-ON-SEVERN
BROMSGROVE
REDDITCH
DROITWICH
WORCESTER
KENILWORTH
WARWICK
STRATFORD-UPON-AVON
Alcester
Studley
Henley-in-Arden
EVESHAM
Pershore
GREAT MALVERN
Nuneaton
Coventry
London
Banbury
Ross-on-Wye
Gloucester
Chipping Norton
Cirencester
104

Central England and East Anglia

The breadbasket of England is a prosperous area, where industrialisation has not ruined the townscapes. The coastal area is one of dykes and sea-walls and looks very much like that of the Netherlands, which faces it across the North Sea.

Aldeburgh and Snape

Aldeburgh's golf course is almost as famous as its music festival. These sandy links are just one of the recreations on offer at this peaceful seaside resort. Like many East Anglian towns perched on the shore, the sea has ravaged the town from time to time and claimed some of it for its own. The Moot Hall, a half-timbered 16th-century building which now stands among the shingle was the town hall of the old town washed away by the sea. Snape is famous for the Snape Maltings, where barley was stored for brewing in the 19th century. One of the buildings, "The Plough and Sail", is still a public house.

Banbury

Every English child knows the nursery rhyme "Ride a cock-horse to Banbury Cross, to see a fine lady ride on a white horse". The Cross was destroyed by in the religious riots of 1602 but replaced by a new one in 1859, installed to celebrate the wedding of the Princess Royal to Prince Frederick of Prussia, and later embellished with statues of Eward VII, Queen Victoria and George V. Banbury cakes, a local delicacy, are made of flaky pastry and filled with currants. The citizens of Banbury blew up their medieval church with gunpowder in 1792, commissioning a neo-classical building from the architect S.P. Cockerell. It is a curious construction with a rounded portico and pepperpot tower. The town has two fine old inns, though one of them, the Reindeer in Parsons Street, has partially dismantled its historic interior which is now in the Banbury Museum in Horsefair by the Cross. Broughton Castle, three miles south-west of the town, is probably where the "fine lady" in the rhyme lived. The Fiennes (pronounced "Fines") family have inhabited in the castle since 1451. It is only open to the public on certain days. Banbury holds one of the largest cattle markets in Europe.

Beccles and Bungay

Beccles is another East Anglian town forced to move inland due to the encroaching sea. It stands on the Waveney and is famous for its crayfish. The Perpendicular church has a detached tower. Nearby Gillingham has the finest pure Norman church in East Anglia. Beccles and Bungay are both noted for book printing; at one time, almost all the books produced in England were printed here. Bungay has a ruined Norman castle and two interesting churches, one with a pre-Norman round tower.

Bury St. Edmunds

King Sigebert founded a church and monastery in the 7th century in the town then known as Beodericsworth. In 869, Edmund, last of the kings of East Anglia, was martyred by the invading Danes for refusing to deny his Christian faith. He was buried in the monastery and such were the miracles that were allegedly wrought over his grave that the very name of the town was changed to St. Edmundsbury or Bury St. Edmunds. King Cnut (the very same Danish king who is supposed to have lost his crown in the Wash), as a gesture of goodwill to his English subjects, conferred the status of abbey upon the monastery. The second part of the town motto "Shrine of a King, Cradle of the Law" refers to the fact that on St. Edmund's Day, 20 November, 1215, 25 barons swore an oath at the altar to obtain from King John the ratification of the Magna Carta. In its heyday, the Abbey was one of the greatest churches in the country, but it is now a ruin, destroyed during the Dissolution of the Monasteries. The great arches in the ruined west front have been filled in with houses of various periods, but bells still ring out from the Norman tower designed in 1120 as both a gateway to the abbey and a belfry for the Church of St. James. The latter was made a cathedral in 1914. The parish church of St. Mary is older than St. James, and has a magnificent Perpendicular interior. Moyse's Hall which may be the oldest private dwelling in East Anglia is now the Borough Museum. Angel Corner, a Queen Ann house, contains the collection of clocks and watches donated by the musician Frederick Gershom-Parkington in memory of his son John, killed in World War II. Much of the local architecture is Georgian. The town has connections with Charles Dickens; Mr. Pickwick is supposed to have stayed at the Angel Hotel.

Cambridge

See "Historic Cities"

Coventry

Although the centre of Coventry is modern, dominated by Sir Basil

Banbury Cross in the Horsefair (above).

Cavendish, a typical Suffolk village (right).

The River Storn at Dedham, Essex (opposite top).

Firehingfield, Essex (opposite centre).

Thatching repair at Cavendish, Suffolk (opposite below).

Spence's cathedral (1954-62), the city is a very ancient one. The bombing raid of 14 November, 1940 entirely destroyed the city centre. The charred ruins of the 14th-century cathedral stand next to the new building, its air of desolation enhanced by the altar crosses made of charred roof beams and twisted nails and the Epstein statue *Ecce Homo* (1935). The Perpendicular steeple is still intact. The new cathedral makes great use of stained glass and features a huge tapestry above the altar, *Christ in Glory*, designed by Graham Sutherland. Coventry probably grew up around the Benedictine priory founded in 1043 by Leofric, Earl of Mercia, and his wife Lady Godiva. The latter has gone down in history for her famous ride naked through the city to avert her husband's wrath against the townsfolk. The story is first recorded in 1235, though the legend of Peeping Tom did not emerge until the 17th century. There is a statue to Lady Godiva by Reid Dick (1949) in Broadgate. Under the Godiva Clock there is a memorial to the 16th-century Coventry Martyrs. The Herbert Art Gallery and Museum in Jordan Well has a fine collection of Chinese art. Coventry has always been a hive of industry, most recently its products have been sewing machines, bicycles and cars. The Museum of British Road Transport is near a section of the Old City Wall (demolished in 1662).

Ipswich
Ipswich has been a busy port since Anglo-Saxon times. There are many ancient buildings, including the Sparrowe's or the Ancient House (1567), which has oriel windows and magnificent plasterwork carvings on the exterior. Christchurch Mansion (1548-50) has a large collection of local exhibits, including paintings by Gainsborough and Constable.

Leicester
This has been a prosperous settlement since Roman times. There are Roman remains at the Jewry Wall site including Roman baths and the Roman wall itself. Newarke Houses Museum in the Chantry House (1511) offers an insight into the social history of Leicester. St. Martin's Cathedral stands on the site of a Roman Temple.

Newmarket
Racing has been centred around Newmarket since the days of King Charles II. The National Stud and the Jockey Club both have their headquarters here. It is thus not surprising that there is a National Horseracing Museum in the High Street. The Devil's Ditch is a huge earthwork built by either the Angles and Mercians in the 7th century in their battles for the control of East Anglia, which local people use as a grandstand to watch the racing at Newmarket Heath.

Peterborough
The magnificent cathedral is evidence of Peterborough's importance in the past. The town grew up around a monastery founded in 650 and has been an episcopal see since the Reformation. The city owed its 19th-century development to the railways and the Nene Valley Steam Railway is evidence of this, though it is now run by enthusiastic amateurs. Near Peterborough, there is a fortified medieval mansion, Longthorpe Tower, that contains the most complete set of medieval paintings in England.

Information
Tourist Information Centre
Banbury Museum
8 The Horsefair
Banbury, Oxon.
Tel: (0295) 259855

Leicestershire Travel Trade Service
St. Martin's Square
LE1 5DG
Tel: (0533) 511333

All the towns mentioned in the article have tourist information centres, usually in the museum, town hall or central library.

Events
The Aldeburgh Festival, started by the composer Sir Benjamin Britten and the singer Peter Piers, held in late August, is one of Britain's great musical events. For information write to:

Aldeburgh Foundation,
High Street, Aldeburgh,
Suffolk IP15 5AX
Tel: (072885) 2935.

86
104
105
Ashby-de-la-Zouch
Nottingham
Newark-on-Trent
Melton Mowbray
Birmingham
Tamworth
Stratford-upon-Avon
Chipping Norton
Kidlington
London
Oxford
Milton Keynes
Charnwood Forest
COALVILLE
Ibstock
Markfield
Mountsorrel
Syston
Anstey
BIRSTALL
THURMASTON
GLENFIELD
LEICESTER
Groby
Ratby
Kirby Muxloe
BRAUNSTONE
AYLESTONE
STONEYGATE
KNIGHTON
EVINGTON
Oadby
WIGSTON
GLEN PARVA
Enderby
Narborough
Blaby
Earl Shilton
Desford
Market Bosworth
ATHERSTONE
HINCKLEY
BURBAGE
Hartshill
NUNEATON
Bedworth
Bulkington
COVENTRY
LONGFORD
FOLESHILL
WALSGRAVE ON SOWE
STOKE
BINLEY
EARLSDON
STIVICHALL
WILLENHALL
Kenilworth
Brandon
Wolston
RUGBY
BILTON
HILLMORTON
Dunchurch
Long Lawford
Newbold on Avon
LUTTERWORTH
Ullesthorpe
Misterton
Cosby
Countesthorpe
Fleckney
Kibworth Harcourt
Kibworth Beauchamp
MARKET HARBOROUGH
LITTLE BOWDEN
DESBOROUGH
ROTHWELL
Husbands Bosworth
Welford
Naseby
Yelvertoft
Crick
Kilsby
DAVENTRY
Long Buckby
Weedon Bec
Nether Heyford
NORTHAMPTON
DUSTON
KINGSTHORPE
BOOTHVILLE
BILLING
FAR COTTON
Hardingstone
Brixworth
Moulton
Lamport
Towcester
Roade
Hartwell
Salcey Forest
Blisworth
Milton Malsor
ROYAL LEAMINGTON SPA
Offchurch
WHITNASH
Southam
Napton on Hill
Harbury
Ladbroke
Priors Marston
Byfield
Woodford Halse
Kineton
Edge Hill
BANBURY
GRIMSBURY
Adderbury
Bodicote
Bloxham
Kings Sutton
Middleton Cheney
BRACKLEY
Silverstone
Helmdon
Whittlewood Forest
BUCKINGHAM
Stoney Stratford
Wolverton
Potterspury
Yardley Gobion
OAKHAM
Uppingham
Whissendine
Compton Wynyates
Northamptonshire
Buckinghamshire
Warwickshire
Oxfordshire
Leicestershire
M1
M6
M40
M45
M69
E13
E24

Grantham
Bourne
87
Spalding
Zc
Zd
Ze
Zf
Aa
Pickworth
Essendine
Greatford
Langtoft
MARKET DEEPING
Crowland
Shepeau Stow
Holbeach Drove
Gedney Hill
Gorefield
Leverington
Exton
Little Casterton
Belmesthorpe
Barholm
West Deeping
Deeping St James
Church End
Parson Drove
Whitwell
Great Casterton
Uffington
Tallington
Maxey
Peakirk
St Vincent Cross
Murrow
Wisbech St Mary
Upper Hambleton
Empingham
STAMFORD
Etton
Thorney
Tholomas Drove
Guihirn
Burghley House
Pilsgate
Barnack
Bainton
Helpston
Glinton
Newborough
Eye Green
Waterfowl Gardens
WERRINGTON
Ketton
Edith Weston
Easton on the Hill
Southorpe
Marholm
WALTON
Eye
North Level
Ring's End
Coldham
Hobbs Lots Bridge
North Luffenham
Collyweston
Wittering
PETERBOROUGH
Nat. Res.
South Luffenham
Duddington
Thornhaugh
Upton
Cathedral
North Side
Morton's Leam
Morcott
Tixover
Yarwell
Ailsworth
Castor
WHITTLESEY
Coates
Eastrea
Westry
MARCH
Wakeney
King's Cliffe
Nassington
Alwalton
ORTON LONGUEVILLE
Old Fletton
Harringworth
Laxton
Blatherwycke
Apethorpe
Chesterton
Farcet
Twenty Foot
Gretton
Bulwick
Woodnewton
Elton
Elton Hall
Haddon
Yaxley
Pondersbridge
Middle Level
Wimblington
Deene
Deene Park
Fotheringhay
Southwick
Tansor
Morborne
Norman Cross
Ramsey Mereside
Benwick
Primrose Hill
Doddington
Deene-thorpe
Rockingham Forest
Glapthorn
Warmington
Folksworth
Stilton
Ramsey St Mary's
Weldon
Upper Benefield
Lower Benefield
OUNDLE
Ashton
Lutton
Caldecote
Holme
Ramsey Forty Foot
Forty Foot or Vermuden's Drain
CHATTERIS
Horseway
Stanion
Brigstock
Stoke Doyle
Polebrooke
Glatton
Conington
Lyveden New Bield
Armston
Barnwell
Hemington
RAMSEY
Bury
Geddington
Pilton
Great Gidding
Thurning
Sawtry
Great Raveley
Wood-walton
Little Gidding
Wistow
Sudborough
Aldwincle
Achurch
Harper's Brook
Northamptonsh. Cambridgesh.
Winwick
Copping-ford
Little Raveley
Warboys
Fenton
Somersham
Sutton
Mepal
Boughton House
Grafton Underwood
Thorpe Waterville
Titchmarsh
Clopton
Hamerton
Abbots Ripton
Broughton
Slipton
Islip
THRAPSTON
Alconbury Weston
Kings Ripton
Old Hurst
Pidley
Bluntisham
Earith
KETTERING
Barton Seagrave
Cranford St Andrew
Cranford St John
Twywell
Old Weston
Buck-worth
Little Stukeley
Great Stukeley
Wood-hurst
Great Ouse
BURTON LATIMER
Great Addington
Denford
Ringstead
Keyston
Bringston
Bythorn
Leighton Bromswold
Alconbury
HUNTINGDON
ST IVES
Houghton
Little Addington
RAUNDS
Catworth
Spaldwick
Woolley
Hinchingbrooke House
Wyton
Needingworth
Finedon
Stanwick
Hargrave
Easton
Ellington
Over
Willingham
IRTHLINGBOROUGH
HIGHAM FERRERS
Covington
Stow Longa
Brampton
GODMANCHESTER
Hemingford Grey
Fenstanton
Fen Drayton
Swavesey
Rampton
Chelveston
Lower Dean
Shelton
Grafham
Grafham Water
Buckden
Boxworth End
Longstanton
Caldecott
RUSHDEN
Tilbrook
Kimbolton
Stonely
Offord Cluny
Offord Darcy
Conington
Hilton
Westwick
WELLINGBOROUGH
Newton Bromswold
Upper Dean
Swineshead
Perry
Staughton Highway
Buckden Palace
Oakington
Irchester
Melch-bourne
Pertenhall
Diddington
Great Paxton
Graveley
Yelling
Papworth Everard
Elsworth
Boxworth
Bar Hill
Histon
Girton
Wymington
Knotting
Knotting Green
Keysoe
Little Staughton
Hail Weston
Little Paxton
Southoe
Toseland
Knapwell
Dry Drayton
Wollaston
Podington
Souldrop
Top End
Keysoe Row
SAINT NEOTS
Croxton
Caxton Gibbet
Madingley
Strixton
Hinwick
Sharnbrook
Bolnhurst
Eaton Socon
Eltisley
Caxton
Caxton End
Highfields
Coton
Bozeat
Odell
Bletsoe
Thurleigh
Colmworth
Wyboston
Chawston
Little Barford
Abbotsley
Bourn
Hardwick
Toft
Comberton
Barton
Harrold
Felmersham
Pavenham
Milton Ernest
Duck's Cross
Wilden
Colesden
Langford End
Great Gransden
Little Gransden
Longstowe
Kingston
Grantchester
Chellington
Ravensden
Waresley
Great Eversden
Lavendon
Stevington
Great Ouse
Clapham
Salph End
Green End
Tempsford
Cambridgeshire Bedfordshire
Gamlingay
Little Eversden
Haslingfield
Hauxton
Cold Brayfield
Turvey
Bromham
Great Barford
Everton
Hatley St George
Wimpole Hall
Harlton
Orwell
Olney
Newton Blossomville
Willington
BEDFORD
Blunham
SANDY
East Hatley
New Wimpole
Harston
Stagsden
Box End
Biddenham
Mogerhanger
Cople
Beeston
Potton
Sutton
Wrestlingworth
Cam or Rhee
Shepreth
Foxton
Thriplow
KEMPSTON
Cardington
Hatch
Nat. Res.
Tadlow
Wendy
Shingay
Meldreth
Fowlmere
Hardmead
Astwood
Wood End
Elstow
Cotton End
Northill
Upper Caldecote
BIGGLESWADE
Eyeworth
Guilden Morden
Nort End
Kneesworth
Melbourne
Chicheley
North Crawley
Wootton
Kempston Hardwick
Old Warden
Broom
Dunton
Bassingbourn
Litlington
Upper Shelton
Bourne End
Stewartby
Herrings Green
Wilstead
Haynes
Southill
Steeple Morden
Bridgefoot
NEWPORT PAGNELL
Moulsoe
Cranfield
Lower Shelton
Houghton Conquest
Row End
Stanford
Langford
Hinxworth
Heydon
ROYSTON
Great Chishill
Marston Moretaine
Millbrook
Haynes Church End
Chicksands
Shefford
Astwick
Ashwell
Therfield
Barley
Salford
AMPTHILL
Maulden
Clophill
Clifton
Stotfold
Newnham
Little Chishill
Milton Keynes Village
Broughborough
Lidlington
Wrest Park Gardens
Meppershall
Henlow
Bygrave
Kelshall
Reed
Barkway
Ridgmont
Steppingley
Silsoe
Flitton
Upper Gravenhurst
Arlesey
Sandon
Nuthampstead
Bow Brickhill
Aspley Guise
Husborne Crawley
Flitwick
Pulloxhill
Upper Stondon
Norton
BALDOCK
Wallington
Buckland
Biggin
Woburn Sands
Zoopark
Eversholt
Westoning
Higham Gobion
Shillington
Pirton
Holwell
LETCHWORTH
Clothall
Mill End
Rushden
Chipping
Wyddial
Meesden
Woburn
Woburn Abbey
Tingrith
Dunstable
London
Luton
Stevenage
Ware
108
Wisbech
Ely
Cambridge
London
Newmarket
Buckinghamsh. Bedfordsh.
Lincolnsh. Cambridgesh.
Bedford Level

88
King's Lynn
Fakenham
Norwich
Ab
Ac
Ad
Ae
Af
WALSOKEN
WISBECH
St John's Fen End
St Mary Magdalen
Wiggenhall
Watlington
Tottenhill
Wormegay
Shouldham
Marham
SWAFFHAM
Necton
Bradenham
East Bradenham
Daffy Green
Holme Hale
Shipdham
Emneth
Marshland St James
Stowbridge
Thorpland
South Runcton
Shouldham Thorpe
Beachamwell Warren
North Pickenham
Elm
Holly End
Stow Bardolph
Fincham
Beachamwell
Cockley Cley
South Pickenham
Ashill
Cranworth
Friday Bridge
Outwell
Barroway Drove
Wimbotsham
Stradsett
Barton Bendish
Saham Toney
Ovington
Carbrooke
Southburgh
Crimplesham
DOWNHAM MARKET
Boughton
Gooderstone
Oxborough
Hilborough
Great Cressingham
Watton
Upwell
Nordelph
Denver
Wereham
Three Holes
Fordham
West Dereham
Stoke Ferry
Foulden
Bodney
Little Cressingham
North Acre
Rockland St Peter
Wretton
Whittington
Merton
Caston
Stow Bedon
Christchurch
Ten Mile Bank
Hilgay
Thompson
Lakesend
Southery
Methwold
Cranwich
Ickburgh
Breckles
Little London
Methwold Hythe
Mundford
Welney
Thetford
Great Hockham
Norfolk
Cambridgeshire
Brandon Creek
Feltwell
Breckland
Wretham
Larling
Manea
Apes Hall
Brandon Bank
Weeting
GRIME'S GRAVES
Illington
Bedford Level
Hockwold cum Wilton
Santon Downham
Croxton
Roudham
Welches Dam
Pymore
Littleport
Mile End
Brandon
Bridgham
Little Downham
Lakenheath
Brandon Park
Kilverston
Brettenham
Shadwell
Wardy Hill
South Level
Forest
THETFORD
Rushford
Coveney
Queen Adelaide
Prickwillow
Elveden
Knettishall
ELY
Cathedral
Euston
Fen Street
Witcham
Stuntney
Kenny Hill
Eriswell
Barnham
Witchford
Holywell Row
Coney Weston
Little Thetford
Beck Row
Holmsey Green
Little Fakenham
Barningham
Hill Row
Haddenham
Broad Hill
Thistley Green
Mildenhall
Honington
Bardwell
Wilburton
Stretham
Isleham
Worlington
Barton Mills
The King's Forest
Ixworth Thorpe
Stanton
Soham
Icklingham
Wordwell
Troston
Aldreth
Freckenham
Tuddenham
Lackford
West Stow
Ampton
Great Livermere
Ixworth
Fordham
Culford
Ingham
Langham
Chittering
Upware
Wicken
Chippenham
Red Lodge
Herringswell
Cavenham
Flempton
Hengrave
Fornham All Saints
Fornham St Martin
Great Barton
Pakenham
Hunston
Stanton Street
River Bank
Snailwell
Kennett
Risby
Cottenham
Landwade
Burwell
Kentford
Higham
Westley
BURY ST EDMUNDS
Thurston
Norton
Reach
Exning
Moulton
Landbeach
Swaffham Prior
Barrow
Little Saxham
Great Saxham
Horringer
Blackthorpe
Beyton
Tostock
Woolpit
Waterbeach
NEWMARKET
Swaffham Bulbeck
Anglesey Abbey
Dunstall Green
Rushbrooke
Kingshall Street
Drinkstone
Drinkstone Greene
Histon
Milton
Horningsea
Horse racing
Cheveley
Ashley
Dalham
Hargrave
Ickworth House
Bradfield St George
Rattlesden
Stow cum Quy
Ousden
Sicklesmere
Great Welnetham
Bottisham
Hargrave Green
Hawstead
Whepstead
Bradfield St Clare
Bradfield Combust
Poystreet Green
King's College Chapel
Cambridge
Teversham
Little Wilbraham
Wooditton
Saxon Street
Upend
Lady's Green
Lidgate
Depden Green
Chedburgh
Great Greene
Felsham
Great Wilbraham
Ditton Green
Stanningfield
CAMBRIDGE
CHERRY HINTON
Fulbourn
Dullingham
Westley Waterless
Kirtling
Thorns
Rede
Six Mile Bottom
Burrough End
Burrough Green
Wickhambrook
Lawshall
Brettenham
TRUMPINGTON
WANDLEBURY
Cambridgesh.
Suffolk
Cowlinge
Stradishall
Brockley Green
Cockfield
Thorpe Morieux
Lark Hall
Weston Colville
Denston
Hawkedon
Hartest
Cross Green
Hauxton
Great Shelford
Wrest Wratting
Carlton
Great Bradley
Stansfield
Shimpling
Alpheton
Preston
Stapleford
Granta
Little Thurlow
Boxted
Stanstead
Bridge Street
Bildeston
Little Shelford
Hall
Babraham
Balsham
Great Thurlow
Kentwell Hall
Lavenham
Chelsworth
Newton
Sawston
Hildersham
West Wickham
Withersfield
Great Wratting
Barnardiston
Poslingford
Glemsford
Brent Eleigh
Whittlesford
Pampisford
Great Abington
Linton
Horseheath
Little Wratting
Chilton Street
Cavendish
Melford Hall
Little Waldingfield
Milden
Thriplow
Duxford
Bartlow
HAVERHILL
Kedington
Clare
Long Melford
Acton
Great Waldingfield
Hadstock
Stoke by Clare
Foxearth
Belchamp St Paul
Borley
Gainsborough's House
Ickleton
Great Chesterford
Castle Camps
Ovington
Edwardstone
Groton
Little Chesterford
Ashdon
Cambridgesh. Essex
Helions Bumpstead
Birdbrook
Baythorn End
Puttock End
Belchamp Water
SUDBURY
GREAT CORNARD
Boxford
Steeple Bumpstead
Ridgewell
Bulmer
Little Walden
Little Yeldham
Henny Street
Sackers Green
Assington
Elmdon
Littlebury
Red Oaks Hill
Chapeland Way
Bulmer Tye
Great Henny
Hempstead
Great Yeldham
Gestingthorpe
Littlebury Green
Audley End
SAFFRON WALDEN
Sewards End
Radwinter
Cornish Hall End
Toppesfield
Pool Street
Wickham St Paul
Twinstead
Honey Tye
Bridge Green
Wimbish
Bar Hall
Highstreet Green
Castle Hedingham
Lamarsh
Bures Green
Upper Pond Street
Wendens Ambo
Great Sampford
Great Maplestead
Bures
Nayland
Howlett End
Spain's Hall
Sible Hedingham
Little Maplestead
Langley
Arkesden
Newport
Debden
Howe Street
Pebmarsh
Colne Engaine
Mount Bures
Wormingford
Little Horkesley
Wicken Bonhunt
Debden Green
Finchingfield
Clavering
Starlings Green
Rickling
Widdington
Thaxted
Little Bardfield
Great Bardfield
Wethersfield
Blackmore End
Whiteash Green
HALSTEAD
108
London
Braintree
Colchester
Peterborough
Chatteris
Saint Neots
Royston
33
34
35
36
37

89
Norwich
Ba
Bb
Bc
Bd
Be
NORWICH
Cathedral
EATON
LAKENHAM
Colton
Marlingford
Barford
Bawburgh
Colney
Great Melton
Little Melton
Cringleford
Barnham Broom
Runhal
Wramplingham
Hethersett
Carleton Forehoe
WYMONDHAM
Crownthorpe
Hackford
Morley St Botolph
Intwood
Ketteringham
East Carleton
Swardeston
Arminghall
VENTA ICENORUM
Dunston
Swainsthorpe
Silfield
Wreningham
Bracon Ash
Ashwellthorpe
Hapton
Newton Flotman
Saxlingham Thorpe
Tasburgh
Spooner Row
Besthorpe
ATTLEBOROUGH
Bunwell
Talcolneston
Forncett End
Tharston
Long Stratton
Stratton St Michael
Forncett St Peter
Carleton Rode
Hargate
Cake Street
Aslacton
Wacton
New Buckenham
Tibenham
Tivetshall St Margaret
Banham
Kenninghall
Short Green
Winfarthing
Gissing
Shelfanger
Burston
Bressingham
Roydon
Bressingham Hall Gardens
DISS
Palgrave
Scole
Stuston
Wortham
Botesdale
Burgate
Mellis
Thrandeston
Yaxley
Brome
Oakley
EYE
Thornham Magna
Braiseworth
Gislingham
Finningham
Stoke Ash
Occold
Wickham Street
Thorndon
Rishangles
Cotton
Bacton
Mendlesham
Ward Green
Mendlesham Green
Old Newton
Brockford Street
Wetherup Street
Debenham
Mickfield
Winston
Stowupland
Middlewood Green
Little Stonham
Forward Green
Stonham Aspal
Earl Stonham
Creeting St Mary
Crowfield
Pettaugh
Helmingham Hall
Needham Market
Badley
Barking
Baylham
Coddenham
Ringshall
Ringshall Stocks
Great Blakenham
Nettlestead
Offton
Claydon
Whitton
Little Blakenham
Flowton
Elmsett
Bramford
Aldham
Sproughton
Hintlesham
HADLEIGH
Chattisham
Copdock
Raydon
Capel St Mary
Great Wenham
Holton St Mary
East Bergholt
Flatford Mill
Dedham
Castle House
Lamb Corner
Lawford
Brantham
Cattawade
Manningtree
Mistley
Wrabness
Bradfield
Ramsey
HARWICH
Zeebrugge
Esbjerg, Hamburg, Hook of Holland
Colchester
109
IPSWICH
CASTLE HILL
CHANTRY
Belstead
Wherstead
Woolverstone
Holbrook
Stutton
Alton Water Reservoir
Lower Holbrook
Holbrook Bay
Stour
Harkstead
Erwarton
Shotley
Shotley Gate
Parkeston
Harwich Harbour
Nat. Res.
FELIXSTOWE
WALTON
Trimley St Mary
Trimley St Martin
Felixstoweferry
Falkenham
Kirton
Bucklesham
Newbourn
Orwell
Deben
Kesgrave
Martlesham Heath
Martlesham
Westerfield
Tuddenham
Playford
Great Bealings
Witnesham
Henley
Grundisburgh
Hasketon
Burgh
Otley
Ashbocking
Gosbeck
Hemingstone
Helmingham
Charsfield
Debach
Bredfield
Dallinghoo
Ufford
Melton
WOODBRIDGE
Sutton
Waldringfield
Shottisham
Hemley
Alderton
Bawdsey
Hollesley
Hollesley Bay
Shingle Street
Boyton
Ore
Rendlesham Forest
Eyke
Butley
Gedgrave Hall
Chillesford
Orford
Tunstall Forest
Tunstall
Campsey Ash
WICKHAM MARKET
Blaxhall
Snape
Snape Street
Aldeburgh Moot Hall
ALDEBURGH
Aldeburgh Bay
Alde
High Street
Friston
Coldfair Green
Aldringham
Thorpeness
LEISTON
Knodishall
Sternfield
Farnham
Little Glemham
Stratford St Andrew
Great Glemham
Parham
Hacheston
Easton
Kettleburgh
Monewden
Brandeston
Framsden
Earl Soham
FRAMLINGHAM
Brabling Green
Cransford
Rendham
Sweffling
SAXMUNDHAM
Kelsale
Carlton
Theberton
Eastbridge
Middleton
Westleton
Darsham
Yoxford
Sibton
Peasenhall
Heveningham
Heveningham Hall
Ubbeston Green
Badingham
Dennington
Saxtead
Saxtead Green
Post Mill
Bruisyard
Tannington
Brundish
Worlingworth
Bedfield
Southolt
Kenton
Athelington
Horham
Bedingfield
Redlingfield
Stradbroke
Wilby
Laxfield
Cratfield
Cookley
Walpole
Bramfield
Thorington
Wenhaston
Blythburgh
Walberswick
SOUTHWOLD
Reydon
Dunwich
Wangford
Uggeshall
Blyford
Holton
HALESWORTH
Chediston
Wissett
Spexhall
Westhall
Brampton
Stone Street
Cox Common
South Cove
Covehithe
Wrentham
Benacre
Henstead
Kessingland
Suffolk Wildlife Park
Rushmere
Gisleham
Carlton Colville
PAKEFIELD
KIRKLEY
OULTON BROAD
LOWESTOFT
Oulton
Corton
Hopton on Sea
GORLESTON-ON-SEA
GREAT YARMOUTH
BRADWELL
Scheveningen
Belton
Burgh Castle
Breydon Water
Halvergate
Freethorpe
Reedham
Somerleyton Hall
Herringfleet
Haddiscoe
Lound
Blundeston
Burgh St Peter
Aldeby
Gillingham
Geldeston
Ellingham
Worlingham
BECCLES
Ringsfield
Ringsfield Corner
North Cove
Mutford
Hulver Street
Ellough
Shadingfield
West End
Clay Common
Weston
Redisham
Ilketshall St Andrew
Ilketshall St Margaret
St Michael South Elmham
St Cross South Elmham
Rumburgh
St James South Elmham
Metfield
Linstead Parva
Silverley's Green
Fressingfield
Weybread
Mendham
Withersdale Street
Homersfield
Flixton
BUNGAY
Broome
Ditchingham
Hedenham
Topcroft
Woodton
Hempnall
Fritton
Hempnell Green
Shelton
Hardwick
North Green
Denton
Great Green
Piccadilly Corner
Pulham Market
Pulham St Mary
Bush Green
HARLESTON
Redenhall
Rushall
Dickleburgh
Thelveton
Brockdish
Needham
Thorpe Abbotts
Billingford
Hoxne
Wingfield
Chickering
Denham
Heckfield Green
Pixey Green
Ashfield Green
Kirstead Green
Saxlingham Green
Shotesham
Howe
Brooke
Mundham
The Laurels
Thwaite St Mary
Kirby Cane
Hales
Loddon
Ravenigham
Thurlton
Maypole Green
Thorpe
Chedgrave
Langley Street
Hellington
Framingham Earl
Poringland
Alpington
Thurton
Claxton
Bramerton
Surlingham
Kirkby Bedon
Postwick
Great Plumstead
Blofield
Brundall
Lingwood
Buckenham
Hassingham
South Burlingham
Moulton St Mary
Freethorpe Common
Norfolk
Suffolk
Waveney

The Cotswolds and the Chilterns

This is some of the most picturesque countryside in England; there are rolling hills, prosperous farmland and elegant towns and villages. Mixed farming and industrialisation kept firmly in check have helped to preserve the national beauty of the landscape.

Aylesbury

The county town of Buckinghamshire, Aylesbury has a handsome 18th century County Hall. The Bull's Head is a public house with a Victorian frontage that masks a 15th-century interior.
The former grammar school, which dates from the 15th century, is now the County Museum.
Waddesdon Manor, near Aylesbury, the home of the Rothschild family, contains one of the finest private collections of art treasures in the country.

Cheltenham

This elegant spa town became the first planned English city when a local resident found the spring in a field in 1718. The town thus has a uniformly 18th-century architecture, and prides itself on its lovely gardens and flower displays. The Promenade in the centre of town contains an elaborate fountain with Neptune at its centre. The Pittville Pump Room stands above an ornamental lake in Pittville Park. Gustav Holst was born here and there is a museum dedicated to the composer.
The local Art Gallery and Museum contains many interesting exhibits by artists in the English Arts and Crafts Movement, some of whose exponents were based in the Cotswolds.

Chipping Campden

This is one of the chief towns of the Cotswolds. The prefix "Chipping" means that this was a Saxon market town, like Chipping Sodbury and Chipping Norton. Chipping Campden has many medieval houses and most of the buildings are 18th century or earlier. An unusual feature of the town is the sundials on the walls. The town is full of historic inns, dating the time when it was an important staging post between London and the West of England. They include the Eight Bells, with its distinctive sign, the Noel Arms and the Volunteer. The Woolstaplers Hall (c. 1340) is now a museum of the wool trade which made the area wealthy. The almshouses were built in 1612 and consist of stone blocks fitted together without mortar. The chapel is open to visitors. As in many little towns whose prosperity was greatest in the Middle Ages, the parish church is of cathedral proportions. St. James's has a 120-foot tower and large panels of stained glass, much of it 15th century.

Cotswolds, The

This lovely range of hills stretches for about 40 miles between Stratford-upon-Avon and Bath, just east of the Severn valley. The area is dotted with quaint villages nestling between the rolling hills and wooded river valleys whose thatched cottages and houses of local stone have immaculate gardens. Indeed, when many people think of England, this is the picture-postcard scene that comes into their minds. Some of the prettiest villages are Bourton-on-the-Water, Broadway, Stow-on-the-Wold, Upper and Lower Slaughter, Blockley and Burford. Special places of interest include the Cotswold Wild Life Park at Burford, the Prinknash Bird Park, the Painswick Rococo Garden, the Roman villa at Chedworth, Sudley Castle, the Railway Museum at Winchcombe and Snowshill Manor.

Forest of Dean

This magnificent stretch of primæval forest on a plateau overlooking the Severn bounded by Ross-on-Wye, Cinderford, Coleford and the river. The area is rich in mineral deposits and in ancient times the forest resounded to the sounds of iron-smelting and hammering. Cinderford takes its name from the slag in the iron forges worked even before the Romans came. Coal has also been mined here for many centuries. The 13th-century St. Briavel's Castle, now a youth hostel, was once the administrative centre of the Forest. Speech House once housed the Court of the Verderers. There are marked paths and trails through the forest and demonstrations of charcoal burning and other country crafts at the Heritage Centre. The visitor to the Forest is surprised to stumble upon sheep wandering wild or even lying asleep in the roadway; the sheep of the Forest of Dean are allowed to run wild. Littledean Hall, said to be the oldest manor house in England is built on the foundations of a Roman temple and has a Saxon great hall. The house is full of secret passages and is said to be haunted.

Gloucester (pronounced "Gloster")

A lovely cathedral city in the Severn Vale and once an important port, Gloucester attracts many visitors fascinated by its medieval past. The city centre is formed of a cross of four streets. St. Michael's Tower on the south-east corner is now the Tourist Information Centre. The Cathedral is one of the best examples of Perpendicular architecture in Britain. It stands of the site of a Saxon abbey. The Norman knight Serlo built much of the nave, but the cathedral received its most glorious features in the 14th century, including the great window in the Presbytery known as the Crecy Window whose stained glass depicts the coronation of the Virgin, and the delicate fan vaulting of the Great Cloister. A favourite with visitors is the Museum of Packaging, the Robert Opie Collection, housed in one of the disused warehouses of Gloucester Docks. It displays the colourful Victorian wrappings and shop signs of bygone days.

Henley-on-Thames

This prosperous town has many timber-framed and Georgian houses. Its most outstanding feature is a beautiful bridge over the Thames, built in 1786, with sculpted masks of the Thame and Isis over the central arches. Nearby Fawley Court is a country house built by Wren in 1684 with additions by Jame Wyatt in the late 18th century. It is now a boy's school run by the Marian Fathers. Stonor Park, five miles north of Henley, is a medieval manor house which also has Roman Catholic connections, since the Jesuit martyr Edmund Campion (1540-81) set up his secret printing press here.

High Wycombe

Famous for its furniture-making industry, the church is the largest in the county. The Guildhall and Market Hall are both 18th century, by Keene and Robert Adam respectively. West Wycombe Park, only a mile and a half away, is the former home of Sir Francis Dashwood famous for his Hellfire Club. The grounds are lovely and include artificial caves used by the Club members for their revels. Nearby is Hughendon Manor, Disraeli's home, which contains many relics of the Victorian prime minister. .

Tewkesbury

This is a lovely town to stroll through, because the medieval street plan has left it with many little alleyways and courtyards. The town is very compact since it was hemmed in by rivers and monastic lands and so has only three main streets. Tewkesbury Abbey has been magnificently restored and contains memorials to the bitter fighting at the Battle of Tewkesbury between the houses of Lancaster and York during the Wars of the Roses in the late 15th century. The Old Baptist Chapel is one of the earliest in England but is housed in a 15th-century building that is even older. It is no longer in use but has been restored. Tewkesbury Museum depicts the 4000-year old history of the town. The Mill Avon is a millstream dug in the Middle Ages The huge flour mill at the northern end is still working, though now powered by electricity.

Information
Dean Heritage
Museum Trust
Camp Mill
Soudley
Cinderford,
Gloucestershire
GL14 7UG
Tel: (0594) 22170

The Heart of England
Tourist Board
2/4 Trinity Street
Worcester, WR1 1BR
Tel: (0905) 613132

Tourist Information Centre
Corn Hall,
Market Place
Cirencester, Gloucs.
GL7 2NW
Tel: (0285) 4180

Events
The Henley Royal Regatta, held in the first week of July, is one of the fashionable events of the season. The Henley Festival of Music and the Arts follows it and lasts for a week.

Henley Royal Regatta
Office
Tel: (0491) 572153

Festival Box Office
Festival Yard
42 Bell Street
Henley-on-Thames
RG9 2BG
Tel: (0491) 411353

The elaborate fountain in the Parade, Cheltenham (above).

Shipton-on-Cherwell in Oxfordshire (right).

Bradford-on-Avon in Gloucestershire (opposite right).

Sailing boats and wharves in Gloucester Docks (opposite top).

The Railway Museum at Winchcombe (opposite left top).

Aylesbury Museum and parish church (opposite left below).

145
Aberystwyth
Hereford
Wc
Wd
We
Wf
Xa
36
37
38
39
40
Brecon Beacons National Park
The Black Mountains
BRECON
Pen y Fan
Fforest Fawr
Mynydd Llangynidr
Mynydd Llangatwg
Crickhowell
Talgarth
Hay Bluff
ABERGAVENNY - Y FENNI
BRYN-MAWR
BLAENAVON
EBBW VALE
TREDEGAR
RHYMNEY
MERTHYR TYDFIL
DOWLAIS
ABERDARE
Hirwaun
Glyn Neath
Vale of Neath
Resolven
RHONDDA
TREORCHY
TREHERBERT
MOUNTAIN ASH
ABERCYNON
PONTYPRIDD
Tonyrefail
PORTH
TONYPANDY
MAESTEG
PONTYCYMER
BARGOED
BLACKWOOD
Gelligaer
YSTRAD MYNACH
CAERPHILLY
Caerphilly Castle
BEDWAS
RISCA
NEWBRIDGE
CWMBRAN
ABERCARN
ABERTILLERY
BLAINA
ABERSYCHAN
PONTYPOOL
CAERLEON
NEWPORT
MALPAS
BRIDGEND
Pencoed
PORTHCAWL
COWBRIDGE
Llantrisant
Beddau
Pontyclun
Llantwit Major
St Athan
BARRY
Rhoose
Cardiff a. Wales Airport
PENARTH
Sully
Lavernock Point
Flat Holm
Steep Holm
CARDIFF
CAERDYDD
WHITCHURCH
LLANDAFF
RUMNEY
St Mellons
Castleton
Mid Glamorgan
South Glamorgan
West Glamorgan
Gwent
Powys
M4
A627(M)
WESTON-SUPER-MARE
Brean Down
Sand Point
Mouth of the Severn
BRISTOL CHANNEL
Swansea
113

92
93

Shrewsbury
Hereford
Leominster
Worcester
Worcester
Birmingham
Evesham
Witney
Cirencester
Swindon
Calne
Devizes
Bridgewater
Bristol
Weston-super-Mare
Wells
Shepton Hallet
Warminster
Frome
Westbury
Xb
Xc
Xd
Xe
Xf
LEDBURY
TEWKESBURY
CHELTENHAM
GLOUCESTER
ROSS-ON-WYE
MONMOUTH
Cinderford
Coleford
Lydney
Newent
Newnham
STROUD
NAILSWORTH
Dursley
TETBURY
MALMESBURY
CHEPSTOW
THORNBURY
CHIPPING SODBURY
Mangotsfield
KINGSWOOD
BRISTOL
KEYNSHAM
BATH
CLEVEDON
NAILSEA
Yatton
Congresbury
CHIPPENHAM
Corsham
MELKSHAM
BRADFORD ON AVON
TROWBRIDGE
Avonmouth
Portishead
Caldicot
Forest of Dean
Severn
Vale of Berkeley
Cotswold Hills
Bishop's Cleeve
Winchcombe
Tintern Abbey
Wyndcliff
Berkeley
Sharpness
Frampton on Severn
Wotton-under-Edge
Yate
Saltford
Chew Magna
Bridgwater

116

Evesham
Evesham
93
Stratford-upon-Avon
Stratford-upon-Avon
96
Banbury
Banbury
Birmingham
Ya
Yb
Yc
Yd
36
37
38
39
40
Tewkesbury
Cheltenham
Gloucester
Gloucester
Chippenham
Bath
Chippenham
Bristol
Chippenham
WINCHCOMBE
STOW-ON-THE-WOLD
Bourton-on-the-Water
Moreton-in-Marsh
CHIPPING NORTON
CHARLBURY
WOODSTOCK
Blenheim Palace
BURFORD
WITNEY
Carterton
CIRENCESTER
FAIRFORD
LECHLADE
FARINGDON
CRICKLADE
HIGHWORTH
SWINDON
WOOTTON BASSETT
Wroughton
Lambourn
Wantage
Didcot
ABINGDON
CALNE
MARLBOROUGH
DEVIZES
Hungerford
NEWBURY
Cotswold Hills
Vale of White Horse
Vale of Pewsey
Marlborough Downs
Savernake Forest
AVEBURY CIRCLE
SILBURY HILL
ROLLRIGHT STONES
Gloucestershire
Oxfordshire
Wiltsh.
Oxfordsh.
Berksh.
Berkshire
Hampshire
M4
M40
117
Salisbury
Whitchurch

97

Brackley
Milton Keynes
Kempston
Yf
Za
Zb
Zc
Zd
BUCKINGHAM
Bletchley
Woburn Sands
Woburn
LEIGHTON BUZZARD
LUTON
DUNSTABLE
HOUGHTON REGIS
BICESTER
Steeple Claydon
Winslow
Stewkley
Wing
AYLESBURY
Waddesdon
Thame
TRING
WENDOVER
PRINCES RISBOROUGH
BERKHAMSTED
HEMEL HEMPSTEAD
Kings Langley
WATFORD
RICKMANSWORTH
CHESHAM
AMERSHAM
Chalfont St Giles
BEACONSFIELD
HIGH WYCOMBE
Chinnor
Watlington
Wheatley
Benson
WALLINGFORD
MARLOW
MAIDENHEAD
SLOUGH
ETON
WINDSOR
HENLEY-ON-THAMES
Caversham
READING
WOKINGHAM
BRACKNELL
Crowthorne
Sandhurst
CAMBERLEY
FRIMLEY
FARNBOROUGH
Yateley
Tadley
EGHAM
STAINES
SUNBURY
CHERTSEY
ADDLESTONE
WEYBRIDGE
WALTON-ON-THAMES
WOKING
Byfleet
East Horsley
GERRARDS CROSS
UXBRIDGE
HAYES
HILLINGDON
ICKENHAM
RUISLIP
FELTHAM
London (Heathrow)
BUSHEY
Basingstoke
Southampton
Aldershot
Guildford
Hitchin
St. Albans
Leatherhead

120

Essex, Hertfordshire, Surrey, West Kent

The area around London, often referred to as the Home Counties, has attractive countryside, seaside resorts and every amenity, including parks, stately homes, picturesque villages and historic towns.

Canterbury
See "Historic Cities"

Chelmsford
The county town of Essex only became an episcopal see in 1913. The church of St. Mary, now the cathedral, was built in 1424, but collapsed in 1800 and had to be rebuilt. It has a beautiful flintwork porch and a massive tower with a flèche spire (1749). The town owes its electronics industry to Marconi, inventor of the radio, who started manufacturing his products here.

Colchester
Britain's oldest recorded town and the Roman capital of Britain, ancient Camulodunum naturally has some spectacular Roman remains. Balkerne Gate, of which only two arches of the original four are left, was the entrance to the Roman town. St. Botolph's Priory is the shell of a Norman priory destroyed during the Civil War. It was the first Augustinian religious house in England. Colchester Castle has the largest keep in England, and is partly constructed from Roman bricks. An obelisk in the Bailey marks the spot where Royalist officers were executed after their defeat at the Battle of Colchester on 28 August, 1648. This was the site of the Temple of Claudius sacked by Queen Boudicca who slaughtered the population. The temple vaults are still intact. West Stockwell Street is known as the Dutch Quarter. It contains the houses of Flemish Protestants who fled from religious persecution in the 16th century, and brought their craft of weaving to the town. The former Holy Trinity Church has a Saxon tower and now houses a Museum of Social History.

Esher and Ascot
Esher is a typical Surrey town in the Stockbroker Belt. The Claremont Landscape Garden on the Portsmouth Road, just outside Esher, is the earliest surviving English landscape garden, recently restored. It was started in the early 18th century and was designed by several of the leading landscape gardeners of the day. It has a lake, grotto and amphitheatre, and is now run by the National Trust.

London
See "Historic Cities"

Maidstone
County town of Kent and a major rail junction. Leeds Castle, near Maidstone, stands on two islands in the middle of a lake in a wooded region of undulating hills. The castle has nothing to do with the city of Leeds, it is named after its founder Led, First Minister of Ethelbert IV, King of Kent, who built it in 857. The original building was torn down and replaced by a Norman castle, started in 1120 by King Edward I and Queen Eleanor of Castile. It became official crown property in 1278 when the Gloriette, the keep which rises out of the lake at the northern end, was built. The gatehouse and outer wall also date from this period. The Fountain Court was added in the reign of Edward III (mid-14th century) and the Maidens Tower was added by Henry VIII. Leeds was a royal palace for 300 years, mainly inhabited by English queens. The main part of the castle was rebuilt in 1822 and heavily restored. The Castle is now beautifully furnished with French and English medieval furniture, tapestries and paintings. There are lovely gardens, including a Culpepper herb garden. Other attractions include exotic water birds and an extraordinary collection of antique dog-collars.

The Medway Towns
The towns known by this name are those of Chatham, Gillingham and Rochester, which were once Britain's most important naval dockyards. Looking at the map, it is easy to see why, because they were protected by the Medway Estuary and were needed to protect London and the most vulnerable of Britain's coasts from invasion from the Continent. Chatham Dockyard is now open as a museum of naval history and shipbuilding. Rochester is a cathedral city. The relatively small cathedral was begun in 1077 by Bishop Gundulph who built the tower on the north side as a defence against the Saxons. Rochester Castle commands the Medway, its mighty keep towering 100 feet to the turreted crown. The Charles Dickens Centre is a memorial to Rochester's most famous son. Those of a less literary bent might prefer to visit the Motor Cycle Museum at 144, High Street.

St. Albans
This was the Roman city of Verulamium, in which Alban was put to death and became England's first Christian martyr. The Benedictine Abbey that stands on the

site of his execution was founded in 793 by Offa, King of Mercia, who is depicted with Edward the Confessor in the 15th-century altar screen of the present building. The church is a mixture of many styles, from the original Norman nave and tower to the rather unprepossessing 19th-century west front. The 275-foot nave is the longest in England. St. Albans is unique in having erected street memorials to the many local men who died in World War I. There is a medieval Clock Tower in the town centre. French Row is so-called because King John of France was imprisoned in a house here in 1356. The site is now that of the Fleur de Lys Inn (1440). The spectacular Roman remains include the Roman Theatre and relics in the Verulamium Musem.

Sevenoaks

Sadly, six of the seven ancient oaks which gave the town its name were destroyed in the great gale of 1988, though they have been replanted. The town, a dormitory town for London, has three very fine stately homes nearby. These are Knole, a magnificent medieval mansion, dating from 1456 and enlarged in 1603, Ightham Mote, a medieval moated manor house and Old Soar Manor at Plaxtol. Old Soar Manor is a 13th-century knights' solar, attached to an 18th-century house. Emmetts Garden, noted for its collection of rare trees and shrubs is also in the vicinity.

Thanet, Isle of

This peninsula contains the very popular seaside resorts of Margate, Ramsgate and Broadstairs. Margate has one of the oldest theatres in the country outside London, the Theatre Royal (1787). The resort has all the traditional seaside entertainments. An unusual attraction is the shell-studded grotto, claimed to be very old, but in fact an 18th-century folly. The old town, known as Cliftonville, has a fine flintstone church, the Church of St. John, with interesting brasses. Broadstairs is famous for its associations with Charles Dickens. The novelist lived in a house now called Bleak House after one of his novels, and the town holds a Dickens Festival every year in June. Ramsgate has chalk cliffs and is more sheltered than Margate. The Roman Catholic Church of St. Augustine is by Pugin (1845-50) who considered it his best work. He is buried here. Beside the A256, the road that runs beside Pegwell Bay, south of the town, there is a Danish longship, built and sailed in 1949 to mark the 1500th anniversary of the landing of Hengist and Horsa at Ebbsfleet.

Information

South East England Tourist Board
1 Warwick Park
Royal Tonbridge Wells,
Kent TN2 5TA
Tel: (0892) 540766

Tourist Information Centre
Pierremont Hall
67 High Street
Broadstairs, Kent
Tel: (0843) 868399

Tourist Information Centre
Whitstable, Kent
Tel: (0227) 275482

Events

The Dickens Festival at Broadstairs is held in mid- to late June. Details from the Tourist Information Centre.

Converted oasthouse in the village of Trottiscliffe, Kent (above).

Boats moored at Maldon, at the mouth of the Chelmer and Blackwater Rivers (top left).

Half-timbered houses and church at Chilham, Kent (below left).

The River Medway at Aylesford, Kent (opposite left).

The Archbishop's Palace at Maidstone, Kent, from the River Medway (opposite right).

97
Biggleswade
Royston
Cambridge
LETCHWORTH
HITCHIN
BALDOCK
Ze
Zf
Aa
Ab
Ac
Shillington
Pirton
Holwell
Ickleford
Wallington
Clothall
Weston
Graveley
William
Great Wymondley
Little Wymondley
Lilley
Great Offley
Gosmore
Preston
Cockernhoe
King's Walden
St Paul's Walden
Breachwood Green
Luton
Whitwell
The Node
Langley
Knebworth
Old Knebworth
Codicote
Kimpton
Peter's Green
Newmill End
Blackmore End
Ayot St Lawrence
Welwyn
Marshall's Heath
Shaw's Corner
The Folly
Ayot St Peter
Wheathampstead
HARPENDEN
Childwick Green
Sandridge
Lemsford
ST ALBANS
Wilkins Green
Verulamium
Cathedral
Royal National Rose Society
Potter's Crouch
Chiswell Green
Frogmore
London Colney
Colney Heath
Brookman's Park
Colney Street
Bricket Wood
Smug Oak
South Mimms
Shenleybury
Shenley
RADLETT
Letchmore Heath
BOREHAMWOOD
Elstree
Merry Hill
Bushey Heath
Bushey
STANMORE
PINNER
WEALDSTONE
HARROW
KENTON
EASTCOTE
WOOD END
NORTHOLT
WEMBLEY
Wembley Stadium
GREENFORD
SOUTHALL
PERIVALE
EALING
BRENT
WILLESDEN
NORWOOD GREEN
HOUNSLOW
HAMPTON
TWICKENHAM
RICHMOND
Richmond Park
Ham House
Kew Gardens
KINGSTON UPON THAMES
Bushy Park
Hampton Court
East Molesey
West Molesey
WALTON-ON-THAMES
ESHER
SURBITON
HOOK
Oxshott
Cobham
Stoke D'Abernon
LEATHERHEAD
FETCHAM
GREAT BOOKHAM
Effingham
EWELL
EPSOM
Headley
Walton on the Hill
Tadworth
BANSTEAD
BURGH HEATH
Kingswood
Hooley
CHIPSTEAD
WOODMANSTERNE
SUTTON
CARSHALTON
WALLINGTON
BEDDINGTON
MITCHAM
MORDEN
NEW MALDEN
MERTON
WIMBLEDON
Wimbledon Park
TOOTING
WANDSWORTH
STREATHAM
NORBURY
Crystal Palace
CROYDON
PURLEY
KENLEY
WHYTELEAFE
COULSDON
CATERHAM
Chaldon
WOODCOTE
Addington
New Addington
Farleigh
Chelsham
Biggin Hill
WARLINGHAM
Woldingham
Tatsfield
Titsy
Oxted
Limpsfield
Westerham
Bradsted
Brasted Chart
Sundridge
Dorking
Reigate
Redhill
Crawley
East Grinstead
Southborough
121
LONDON
BRIXTON
LAMBETH
SOUTHWARK
WESTMINSTER
Westminster Abbey
Buckingham Palace
KENSINGTON
Kensington Palace
Hyde Park
CHELSEA
Chiswick House
HAMMERSMITH
Fulham Palace
CAMDEN
London Zoo
Regent's Park
HAMPSTEAD
Kenwood House
Fenton House
Keat's House
HENDON
HORNSEY
Alexandra Palace
FINCHLEY
EDGWARE
BARNET
Arkley
Totteridge
EAST BARNET
FRIERN BARNET
SOUTHGATE
Winchmore Hill
ENFIELD
EDMONTON
HARINGEY
TOTTENHAM
ISLINGTON
FINSBURY
SHOREDITCH
St Paul's Cathedral
CITY OF LONDON
Tower
Tower Bridge
HACKNEY
BETHNAL GREEN
TOWER HAMLETS
LEYTON
WALTHAMSTOW
WALTHAM FOREST
WOODFORD
CHINGFORD
BUCKHURST HILL
LOUGHTON
CHIGWELL
Chigwell Row
REDBRIDGE
WANSTEAD
ILFORD
BARKING
STRATFORD
NEWHAM
London (City)
Blackwall Tunnel
Royal Naval College
GREENWICH
Queen's House
WOOLWICH
CHARLTON
LEWISHAM
CATFORD
ELTHAM
Eltham Palace
BEXLEY
SIDCUP
CHISLEHURST
BROMLEY
BECKENHAM
BICKLEY
SOUTHBOROUGH
HAYES
ORPINGTON
Keston
Downe
Chelsfield
Badgers Mount
Halstead
Knockholt Pound
Knockholt
Cudham
Shoreham
Otford
Dunton Green
SEVENOAKS
Kemsing
Seal
Knole House
EAST WICKHAM
ERITH
CRAYFORD
DARTFORD
Dartford Tunnel
Wilmington
Hextable
Swanley
Crockenhill
North Cray
Coldblow
Sutton at Hone
South Darenth
Darenth
Horton Kirby
Farningham
Eynsford
Lullingstone Castle
West Kingsdown
Romney Street
Heaverham
Wrotham
Borough Green
Ightham
Ivy Hatch
Plaxtol
Crouch
Dunks Green
Old Soar Manor
SWANSCOMBE
NORTHFLEET
GRAYS
West Thurrock
Purfleet
Aveley
Wennington
South Ockendon
North Ockendon
Orsett
UPMINSTER
CRANHAM
HORNCHURCH
HAVERING
RUMFORD
DAGENHAM
ELM PARK
West Horndon
Bulphan
BRENTWOOD
Ingrave
Great Warley
Little Warley
Herongate
South Weald
Noak Hill
Havering-atte-Bower
Stapleford Abbotts
Lambourne End
Bournebridge
Abridge
Theydon Bois
Passingford Bridge
Navestock
Navestock Side
Kelvedon Hatch
Coxtie Green
Pilgrims Hatch
Doddinghurst
Mountnessing
Fryerning
Stapleford Tawney
Toot Hill
Greensted
Greensted Log Church
CHIPPING ONGAR
Stondon Massey
Blackmore
High Ongar
Nine Ashes
Fyfield
Norton Mandeville
Clatterford End
Bobbingworth
Willingale
Shellow Bowells
Cooksmill Green
Highwood
Margaretting
Chignall Smealy
Chignall St James
Roxwell
Beauchamp Roding
Pickerells
Little Laver
Magdalen Laver
High Laver
Matching Green
Matching Tye
Abbess Roding
Leaden Roding
White Roothing or White Roding
Sheering
Hatfield Heath
Hatfield Broad Oak
High Roding
Keeres Green
High Ester
Margaret Roding
Pleshey
Great Canfield
Takeley
GREAT DUNMOW
Little Dunmow
Barnston
Broadgroves
Bishop's Green
Hounslow Green
Little Easton
Great Easton
Molehill Green
Barmbers Green
Churchend
Stebbing
Bran End
Duck End
Lindsell
Monk Street
Thaxted
Horeham Hall
Little Bardfield
Debden Green
Widdington
Henham
Broxted
Elsenham
Ugley Green
Rickling Green
Rickling
Quendon
Clavering
Meesden
Starlings Green
Stocking Pelham
East End
Manuden
STANSTED MOUNTFITCHET
Farnham
Hazelend
Birchanger
London (Stansted)
Smith Green
Great Hallingbury
Little Hallingbury
BISHOP'S STORTFORD
Bury Green
Spellbrook
SAWBRIDGEWORTH
Allens Green
High Wych
Perry Green
Little Hadham
Hadham Ford
Much Hadham
Hadham Cross
Baker's End
Widford
Gilston Park
Eastwick
Hunsdon
Stanstead Abbots
Great Amwell
WARE
Wareside
Thundridge
Sacombe
High Cross
Tonwell
Colliers End
Dane End
Nasty
Puckeridge
Standon
Albury
Patmore Heath
Furneux Pelham
Little Hormead
Brent Pelham
Hare Street
Hay Street
Great Hormead
Wyddial
Buntingford
Chipping
Biggin
Cottered
Westmill
Wood End
Haultwick
Benington
Ardeley
Walkern
Holl's Green
Cromer
Mill End
Rushden
STEVENAGE
Aston End
Hebing End
Bragbury End
BROAD WATER
Knebworth House
Datchworth Green
Burnham Green
Woolmer Green
Harmer Green
Bramfield
Tewin
Watton at Stone
Stapleford
Waterford
HERTFORD
Hertingfordbury
Little Amwell
Hertford Heath
Bayfordbury
WELWYN GARDEN CITY
Cole Green
Essendon
HATFIELD
Hatfield House
Woodside
Welham Green
Bayford
Epping Green
Camfield Place
Newgate Street
Appleby Street
Woodfield
Bell Park
Northaw
Cuffley
Goff's Oak
BROXBOURNE
HODDESDON
Roydon
Broadley Common
Nazeing
Lower Nazeing
GREAT PARNDON
HARLOW
Potter Street
Hastingwood
Foster Street
Epping Green
Bumble's Green
Epping Upland
Thornwood Common
EPPING
Upshire
North Weald Bassett
Tylers Green
Fiddlers Hamlet
CHESHUNT
WALTHAM ABBEY
Waltham Abbey
Sewardstone
High Beach
Epping Forest
PONDERS END
POTTERS BAR
Botany Bay
Forty Hill
Hemel Hempstead
Adlestone
Nat. Res.
Nat. Gallery
Old Chelsea Church
Hereford House
Temple
Clock Tower
Sion House
Charlotte's Cottage
Meridian
ROMAN VILLA
Fawkham Green
Hartley
New Ash Green
Ridgley
Culverstone Green
Fairseat
Stansted
Betsham
Southfleet
Longfield
Bean
Green Street Green
M1
M10
M11
M25
M20
M26
M41
A1 (M)
A102 (M)
E15
E30
37
38
39
40
41

98
99
Haverhill
Sudbury
Ipswich
Ad
Ae
Af
Ba
Bb
HALSTEAD
Colne Engaine
Earls Colne
Whiteash Green
Gosfield
Gosfield Hall
Colneford Hall
Beazley End
Bocking Churchstreet
High Garrett
Greenstead Green
Chappel
Great Tey
Rose Green
Fordham
West Bergholt
Eight Ash Green
Aldham
Marks Tey
Little Tey
Stisted
Pattiswick
Broad Green
BRAINTREE
Bradwell
Coggeshall
Paycock's House
Feering
Tye Green
Cressing
Black Notley
Silver End
Kelvedon
Rivenhall
White Notley
Ranks Green
Great Leighs
Fairstead
Faulkbourne
WITHAM
Terling
Fuller Street
Wormingford
Little Horkesley
Great Horkesley
Horkesley Heath
Blacksmith's Corner
Langham Moor
Lamb Corner
Castle House
Ardleigh Reservoir
Ardleigh
Mile End
COLCHESTER
Colchester Castle
Stanway
Beacon End
Heckfordbridge
Easthorpe
Hardy's Green
Messing
Inworth
Tiptree
Birch
Roman River
Layer de la Haye
Smyths Green
Layer Breton
Tower
Tolleshunt Knights
Malting Green
Abberton
Peldon
Abberton Reservoir
Great Wigborough
Salcott
Tolleshunt Major
Tolleshunt D'Arcy
Tollesbury
Great Braxted
Great Totham
Little Totham
Wickham Bishops
Hatfield Peverel
Boreham
Ulting
Langford
Heybridge
Heybridge Basin
Goldhanger
Northey Island
Osea Island
Blackwater
CHELMSFORD
Little Baddow
Danbury
Woodham Walter
MALDON
Sandon
Woodham Mortimer
Hazeleigh
Rudley Green
Mundon Hill
Bicknacre
Cock Clarks
Purleigh
Cold Norton
Latchingdon
Howe Green
East Hanningfield
West Hanningfield
Stow Maries
Woodham Ferrers
Rettendon
South Hanningfield
Rettendon Place
South Woodham Ferrers
Hullbridge
South Fambridge
Battlesbridge
Downham
RUNWELL
WICKFORD
Rawreth
Hockley
Hawkwell
ASHINGDON
Canewdon
Rochford
RAYLEIGH
Nevendon
North Benfleet
Bowers Gifford
Daws Heath
Hadleigh
Hadleigh Castle
Southend
SOUTH BENFLEET
Corringham
CANVEY ISLAND
WESTCLIFF-ON-SEA
SOUTHEND-ON-SEA
Shoebury Ness
SHOEBURYNESS
Great Wakering
Little Wakering
Barling
Great Stambridge
Potton Island
Paglesham Churchend
Paglesham Eastend
Foulness Island
Churchend
Courtsend
Foulness Point
Crouch
BURNHAM-ON-CROUCH
Stoneyhills
Ostend
Althorne
Southminster
Asheldham
Mayland
Steeple
St Lawrence
Tillingham
Bradwell-on-Sea
Bradwell Waterside
Sales Point
Manningtree
Lawford
Mistley
Bradfield
Wrabness
Ramsey
HARWICH
Little Oakley
Great Oakley
Little Bromley
Horsleycross Street
Horsley Cross
Wix
Stones Green
Hamford Water
The Naze
WALTON-ON-THE-NAZE
Kirby-le-Soken
Kirby Cross
Great Bromley
Little Bentley
Beaumont
Tendring
Weeley
Thorpe-le-Soken
Weeley Heath
Frating Green
Great Bentley
Crockleford Heath
WIVENHOE
OLD HEATH
BLACKHEATH
Rowhedge
Fingringhoe
Alresford
Thorrington
BRIGHTLINGSEA
Aingers Green
Row Heath
Little Clacton
Great Holland
FRINTON-ON-SEA
HOLLAND-ON-SEA
GREAT CLACTON
St Osyth
Jaywick
CLACTON-ON-SEA
Colne Point
Jacobs Hall
Langenhoe
East Mersea
Cudmore Grove
Mersea Island
WEST MERSEA
Nat. Res.
Colne
MARGATE
Foreness Point
North Foreland
BROADSTAIRS
Birchington
Quex Park
Isle of Thanet
Acol
Manston
St Nicholas at Wade
Sarre
Monkton
Minster
Cliffs End
RAMSGATE
Hugin
Pegwell Bay
West Stourmouth
East Stourmouth
Stour
Elmstone
Hoaden
Ash
Richborough Castle
Great Stonar
SANDWICH
St Clement
Sandwich Bay
Marshborough
Staple
Goodnestone
Chillenden
Worth
Eastry
North-bourne
Sholden
Deal Castle
The Downs
Nonington
Easole Street
Elvington
Tilmanstone
Great Mongeham
DEAL
125
109
Thames Haven
Thames
Vlissingen
Allhallows
Cliffe
Cooling
Lower Stoke
Isle of Grain
Grain
Stoke
High Halstow
Cliffe Woods
Chattenden
Kingsnorth
Hoe St Werburgh
Medway
Higham
Upnor Castle
Grange
Pentagon Shopping Center
Cathedral
GILLINGHAM
Upchurch
CHATHAM
LUTON
WIGMORE
Capstone
WALDERSLADE
Newington
Hartlip
Borstal
Wouldham
Blue Bell Hill
Snodland
Burham
Eccles
New Hythe
Aylesford
Boxley
Sandling
Royal British Legion Village
All Saints
Thurnham
Bredhurst
Stockbury
Bredgar
Hucking
Bicknor
Broad Street
Hollingbourne
Eyhorne Street
Leeds Castle
Leed
Broomfield
Langley
Otham
Bearsted
SHEPWAY
TOVIL
MAIDSTONE
East Malling
East Farleigh
West Farleigh
Teston
SHEERNESS
Wallend
Queenborough
MINSTER
Halfway Houses
Eastchurch
Warden
Leysdown-on-Sea
Isle of Sheppey
Iwade
Lower Halstow
Bobbing
The Swale
Murston
SITTINGBOURNE
Conyer
Uplees
Oare
Borden
TUNSTALL
Oad Street
Rodmersham
Bapchild
Teynham
Lynsted
Highsted
Milsted
Doddington
Newnham
Frinsted
Wormshill
Wichling
West Street
Eastling
Otterden Place
Warren Street
Lenham
Stalisfield Green
Throwley
Stone Chapel
FAVERSHAM
Whitehill
Sheldwich
Leaveland
Selling
Old Wives Lees
Shottenden
Chilham
Molash
Graveney
Goodnestone
Hernhill
Boughton Street
Dunkirk
Dargate
Yorkletts
WHITSTABLE
HERNE BAY
Reculver
Chestfield
Tyler Hill
Honey Hill
Rough Common
Sturry
Broad Oak
Hersden
Hoath
Upstreet
Westbere
Fordwich
CANTERBURY
Cathedral
Bigbury
Chartham Hatch
Chartham
Thanington
Shalmsford Street
Petham
Bridge
Lower Hardres
Bishopsbourne
Kingston
Bekesbourne
Littlebourne
Adisham
Aylesham
Womenswold
Wickhambreaux
Wingham
Preston
Marshside
Sarre
St Nicholas at Wade
Grove
West Stourmouth
East Stourmouth
Elmstone
Hoaden
Staple
Goodnestone
Chillenden
Nonington
Easole Street
Elvington
124
Folkestone
Ashford
Dover

North-east Cornwall and Devon

The eastern part of this region has the lovely Quantock Hills, Brendon Hills and Black Down Hills. Exmoor is a National Park famous for deep, wooded valleys, roamed by red deer and Exmoor ponies, cold in winter but pleasantly breezy in summer.

Barnstaple

The most important town in north Devon was a major port in the Middle Ages. The Long Bridge over the River Taw has 16 arches and was built in the 13th century, though it has since been widened. The neo-classical Guildhall (1826) houses the Pannier Market, so called because market traders sold their wares from panniers loaded on to horses or donkeys. The market is still held on Tuesdays, Thursdays (summer only), Fridays and Saturdays. The Merchant's Exchange, in the colonnaded Queen Anne's walk, was built in 1709 and is topped by a resplendent figure of Queen Anne. In seafaring times, the Tome Stone beneath the statue was used like the nails in Bristol, as a table on which to place money when a bargain was struck. The town was prosperous enough to be able to support two homes for the poor, the Horwood Almshouses and the Penrose Almshouses. The Devon Potteries use the local red clay. The wares are distinctively glazed, mainly in cream and brown, and make an unusual souvenir.

Beer

A quaint south-east Devon fishing village, once a haunt of smugglers, twinned with neighbouring Seaton only a mile away. The houses are built of rough flintstone and it is this stone that has given the village its importance throughout the ages. The old flint quarries are now open for guided tours. Beer Head is a beautiful promontory overlooking the English Channel, which can be reached by a footpath.

Bideford

Between the 16th and 18th centuries, Bideford had an important shipbuilding industry. Sir Richard Grenville obtained a charter for the town from Queen Elizabeth I, and it was from here that he sailed his ship, the *Revenge*, crewed entirely by local men. "In Flores in the Azores, Sir Richard Grenville lay" and held out against 15 Spanish ships. Bridgeland Road contains the houses of the prosperous merchants of Sir Richard's day. The bridge over the River Torridge is a 15th-century structure whose 24 arches are all of different widths.

Bude

One of the two most popular resorts on the North Cornish coast (the other is Newquay), both loved for the huge breakers that roll in over the wide sandy beaches from the exposed Atlantic coasts. However, for those who prefer to swim, Summerleaze Beach has a natural pool constantly refilled with clean water at high tide. The town itself is sheltered from the Atlantic by ridges of downland.

Clovelly

This quaint harbour in a cleft of the cliffs of Bideford Bay has been popular with visitors for more than a century. Clovelly is best reached

from Hobby Drive, a toll road open only in the summer months. It is far too steep for cars which must be left outside the village. The cobbled streets are so steep that they are stepped on places. The main street was once the bed of a stream that plunged down to the sea. The pier was built in 1587. Once the only means of transport was the donkey which carried merchandise and tourists alike. Now visitors must walk downhill to the sea but can ride back by Land Rover. The main beauty spot is Gallantry Bower, rising sheer from the sea.

Exeter

The county town of Devon, lies on a spur of the River Exe. The cathedral is particularly fine. The Romans built a fort here in 55 A.D.-60 A.D., and a Roman bathhouse was recently discovered in the cathedral precincts. Exeter Castle, a courthouse since Norman times, and the Guildhall (14th century), the oldest municipal building in Britain, are fine medieval monuments which are still in use. The medieval city walls were built on Roman foundations and are very well preserved.

The Devonians strongly resisted William the Conqueror, since they had given shelter to King Harold's mother, Gytha, who, when her son was defeated, fled to Exeter. William was forced to make a peace with honour after a long siege of the city, but he built a castle overlooking the city as a precautionary measure against future uprisings. The castle continues to be used to uphold the rule of law, since Exeter Crown Court and the magistrates' court still meet within its walls.

Exmoor

This National Park has a wide variety of scenery, from sheep-dotted moorland criss-crossed by little valleys and streams, to picturesque villages and some of the highest cliffs in England. The ancient royal hunting preserve of Exmoor Forest is now a National Park. The wild ponies that roam the hills can sometimes be glimpsed, as can the red deer for which Exmoor is famous. Dunkery Beacon is the highest point at 1705 feet with views all over the West Country and even across to Wales. The Doone Valley is the real-life setting for the novel "Lorna Doone" by R.D. Blackmore. Dulverton is where Jan Ridd first saw Lorna Doone and there is a Lorna Doone trail for visitors to follow. The pretty villages include Porlock, made famous when a "person from Porlock" interrupted Samuel Coleridge's opium-inspired musings while he was writing "Kublai Khan". Porlock Weir is a small group of whitewashed cottages clustered around a tiny harbour and a beach of purple pebbles. The poet Shelley was much taken with the Valley of the Rocks with its strange stone formations.

Ilfracombe

This popular North Devon resort is also a ferry terminal for Swansea, Cardiff, Bristol and Lundy Island, the latter a bird sanctuary owned by the National Trust. Ilfracombe is set against beautiful cliffs, and there are attractive woods and valleys inland. Immediately west of the town, Torr's Walk is a zigzag clifftop path with lovely views of the sea. Holy Trinity Church is a Norman building enlarged in 1322, with a richly-carved roof.

Lynton and Lynmouth

Lynmouth nestles below a cliff overlooking the Atlantic, with the larger town of Lymouth perched precariously 500 feet above it. They make a good base from which to explore Exmoor. The villages suffered disastrous loss of life when parts of Lynmouth fell from the clifftop into the sea and some of Lynton was swept away during the terrible summer of 1952. Watersmeet House (1832) in the valley at the confluence of the East Lyn and Hoar Oak Water is a fishing lodge and the focal point for several beautiful walks.

Information

Exmoor National Park Authority
Exmoor House
Dulverton, Somerset
TA22 9HL
Tel: (0398) 23665

Information Centre
The Crescent Car Park
Bude, Cornwall
Tel: (0752) 849526

West Country Tourist Board
60 St. David's Hill
Exeter EX4 4SY
Tel: (0392) 76351

Tourist Information Centre
The Library
Corporation Street
Taunton
TA1 4AN
Tel: (0823) 274785

Events

The Minehead and Exmoor Arts Festival is held in the last two weeks of July. Dulverton Festival is in the last two weeks of August.

Tips

The Dartington Glass factory at Great Torrington, just south of Bideford, is an interesting place to visit, and the glass makes a good souvenir. There are glass-blowing demonstrations during working hours. For information telephone Dartington Crystal on (0805) 24233

Dawn over Hartland Quay, North Devon (opposite above).

Ilfracombe, a popular seaside resort in North Devon (opposite below).

Cottages at Branscombe, North Devon (top).

Hoar Oak Water, Watersmeet, near Lynmouth (above).

The Clapper Bridge at Postbridge, one of Dartmoor's most famous landmarks (right).

151
Vc
Vd
Ve
Vf
Wa
41
42
43
44
45
A T L A N T I C
O C E A N
B R I S T
North Devon Coast
Barnstable or Bideford Bay
Cornwall Coast
Dartmoor Forest
Rat Island
Surf Point
Heddon's Mouth
Widmouth Head
Combe Martin Bay
Watermouth
ILFRACOMBE
Bull Point
Lee Bay
Rockham Bay
Morte Point
Mortehoe
Lee
Hele
Berrynarbor
Sterridge
Chambercombe Manor
Combe Martin
Heale
Parracombe
Martinhoe
Woolacombe
Morte Bay
West Down
Bittadon
Patchole
Kentisbury Ford
Arlington
Arlington Court
Blackmoor Gate
Wistlandpound Reservoir
Knightacott
East Down
Baggy Point
Pickwell
Georgeham
Croyde Bay
Croyde
Halsinger
Milltown
Muddiford
Shirwell Cross
Shirwell
Loxhore
Bratton Fleming
Stoke Rivers
Knowle
Marwood
Marwood Hill
Saunton Sands
Saunton
Braunton
Prixford
Ashford
Wrafton
Braunton Burrows
Barnstaple-Chivenor
Chivenor
PILTON
St Peter
BARNSTAPLE
NEWPORT
Northleigh
Gunn
West Buckland
East Buckland
Fremington
Bickington
Bideford Bar
Northam Burrows
Appledore
Instow
Tawstock
Bishop's Tawton
Swimbridge Newland
Swimbridge
Westward Ho!
NORTHAM
Westleigh
Tapeley Park
St John's Chapel
Castle Hill
Filleigh
Hartland Point
Windbury Point
Tichberry
Clovelly
Clovelly Bay
Abbotsham
24 arch Bridge
BIDEFORD
EAST-THE-WATER
Horwood
Newton Tracey
Alverdiscott
Herner
Cobbaton
Chittlehampton
Chapelton Sta
Umberleigh
Hartland Quay
Hartland
Buck's Mills
Horns Cross
Ford
Fairy Cross
Littleham
Woodtown
Gammaton Moor
Yarnscombe
Fishley Barton
Atherington
Langridge
Langridgeford
Warkleigh
Satterleigh
Chittlehamholt
Portsmouth Arms Sta
Head Bridge
Milford
Elmscott
Philham
Clovelly Dykes
Clovelly Cross
Buck's Cross
Parkham
Buckland Brewer
Monkleigh
Landcross
Weare Giffard
Huntshaw Cross
High Bullen
GREAT TORRINGTON
St Giles in the Wood
Kingscott
High Bickington
Tosberry
Woolfardisworthy
Cranford
Almiston Cross
Melbury
Ashmansworthy
Powler's Piece
Frithelstock Stone
Rosemoor Garden
Roborough
Burrington
King's Nympton Sta
Knaps Longpeak
Welcombe
Devon
Cornwall
Eastcott
Meddon
Northmoor
Kismeolon Bridge
Little Torrington
Villavin
Beaford
Riddlecombe
Copy Lake
Ashreigney
Eggesford Sta
Higher Sharpnose Point
Lower Sharpnose Point
Morwenstow
Shop
Woodford
Youlstone
Bradworthy
East Putford
Bulkworthy
Stibb Cross
Langtree
Peters Marland
Winswell
Nat. Res.
Dolton
Ashley
Wembworthy
Taylors Cross
Kilkhampton
Upper Tamar Lake
Lower Tamar Lake
Alfardisworthy
Brendon
Sutcombe
Venngreen
Waldon
Milton Damerel
Newton St Petrock
Merton
Dowland
Winkleigh
Bude
Stibb
Rhude Cross
Soldon Cross
Youldonmoor Cross
Thornbury
Shebbear
Buckland Filleigh
North Town
Meeth
Iddesleigh
Broadwoodkelly
Poughill
Flexbury
Stamford Hill 1643
BUDE
STRATTON
Grimscott
Chilsworthy
Holsworthy Beacon
Cookbury
Sheepwash
Ash
Hele Bridge
Monkokehampton
Bude Haven
Launcells
Pancrasweek
Red Post
HOLSWORTHY
Anvil Corner
Brandis Corner
Black Torrington
Highampton
Hatherleigh
Bondleigh
Bay
Marhamchurch
Rydon
Pyworthy
Hollacombe
Dunsland Cross
Graddon Moor
Basset's Cross
Jacobstowe
Exbourne
Sampford Courtenay
North Tawton
Widemouth Bay
Widemouth
Bridgerule
Yeomadon
Chasty
Halwill
Forest
Halwill Junction
Beaworthy
Northlew
Inwardleigh
Oak
Folly Gate
Titson
Coppathorne
Poundstock
Penfound Manor
Dizzard Point
Whitstone
Clawton
Coffcott Green
Quoditch
Broadbury
Upcott
Crackington Haven
Trewint
Week St Mary
North Tamerton
Trebarrow
Luffincott
Lana
Ashwater
Henford
Ewworthy
Boasley Cross
Hewton
Yelland
OKEHAMPTON
Taw Green
Cambeak Point
Wainhouse Corner
Crackington
Tresparrett Posts
South Wheatley
West Curry
Roadford Reservoir
Bratton Clovelly
Sticklepath
Belstone
South Zeal
Langdon
Maxworthy
Troswell
Bennacott
Northcott
Boyton
Meldon Reservoir
Cawsand Hill 1804
Throwleigh
Collamoor Head
Canworthy Water
Brazacott
Bridestowe
Sourton
High Willhays 2038
Marshgate
Warbstow
Bridgetown
Broadwoodwidger
Hallworthy
Treneglos
North Petherwin
Ladycross
Yeolmbridge
Cross Green
Stowford
Lewdown
Bridestowe and Sourton Common
Hangingstone Hill 1983
Davidstow
Tremail
Tresmeer
Egloskerry
Langore
Wortham Manor
Liftondown
Portgate
Lewtrenchard
Lydford
Downton
Cranmere Pool
Fernworthy Reservoir
Sittaford Tor
St Clether
Downhead
Piperspool
Tregadillett
LAUNCESTON
Lifton
Allerford
Lydford Gorge
Beardon
Penzance
Plymouth
131

102

Wb
Wc
Wd
We
Wf
L C H A N N E L
Steep Holm
Brean Down
Berrow Flats
Bridgwater Bay
Stert Flats
Foreland Point
Countisbury Cove
Countisbury
Old Burrow
Doone Valley
Leeford
Malmsmead
Culbone Hill
Culbone Church
Porlock Weir
Porlock Bay
Hurtstone Point
Selworthy Beacon
Allerford
North Hill
Selworthy
MINEHEAD
Marsh Street
Blue Anchor Bay
Blue Anchor
WATCHET
St Audrie's Bay
Hinkley Point
Stolford
Stockland Bristol
Steart
Lilstock
Kilton
Burton
Shurton
Stogursey
Combwich
Kilve
Stringston
Putsham
Holford
Fiddington
Nether Stowey
Coultings
Cannington
Hillsford Bridge
Cheriton
Brendon Common
South Common
Devon
Somerset
West Porlock
Porlock
Luccombe
Dunster
Dunster Castle
Carhampton
West Somerset Railway
St Decumans
Washford
Williton
Sampford Brett
West Quantoxhead
Bicknoller
Coleridge Cottage
Dowsborough
Wootton Courtenay
Timberscombe
Dunkery Beacon
Codsend Moors
Dry Hill
Exmoor
National Park
Bilbrook
Cleeve Abbey
Orchard Wyndham
Stogumber
Quantock Hills
Quantock Forest
Four Forks
Durleigh Reservoir
Durleigh
Goathurst
Simonsbath
Exford
Luckwell Bridge
Wheddon Cross
Roadwater
Kingsbridge
Treborough
Monksilver
Combe Sydenham Hall
Crowcombe
Flaxpool
Hawkridge Reservoir
Lower Aisholt
Lype Hill
Brendon Hills
Withiel Florey
Raleighs Cross
Elworthy
Willett
West Bagborough
Courtway
Broomfield
Kinsford Water
Long Holcombe
Withypool
Withypool Common
Winsford Hill
Winsford
Exton
Lydeard St Lawrence
Tolland
Cothelstone
Cushuish
Kingston St Mary
Thurloxton
North Radworthy
Dane's Brook
Liscombe
Tarr Steps
Bridgetown
Brompton Regis
Clatworthy Reservoir
Clatworthy
Pitsford Hill
Gaulden Manor
Tarr
Ford
East Combe
Bishops Lydeard
Fulford
Adsborough
West Monkton
South Radworthy
Twitchen
Molland Common
Hawkridge
Barle
Wimbleball Lake
Haddon Hill
Upton
Maundown
Heydon Hill
Wiveliscombe
Vale of Taunton Deane
Fitzhead
Halse
Monkton Heathfield
North Molton
Molland
Dulverton
Battleton
Bury
Skilgate
Chipstable
Milverton
Heathfield
Norton Fitzwarren
Oake
Ruishton
East Anstey
Nightcott
Oldways End
Exebridge
Morebath
Shillingford
Petton
Waterrow
Bathealton
Langford Budville
Chipley Park
Bishop's Hull
TAUNTON
Stoke St Mary
Bishop's Nympton
Knowstone
Nether Woodburn
Stawley
Ashbrittle
WELLINGTON
Bradford-on-Tone
Trull
Thurlbear
Ash Mill
Rose Ash
Rackenford Moor
Bampton
Huntsham
Thorne St Margaret
Greenham
Holywell Lake
Holcombe Rogus
Rockwell Green
West Buckland
Poundisford Park
Corfe
Staple Fitzpaine
Meshaw
Creacombe
Stoodleigh
Stoodleigh Beacon
Cove
Sampford Arundel
Wellington Monument
Angersleigh
Ford Street
Blagdon Hill
Luxhay Reservoir
Widcombe
Staple Hill
Rackenford
Loxbeare
Exe Valley
Knightshayes Court
Bolham
Chevithorne
Chettiscombe
Uplowman
Burlescombe
Ayshford
Wrangway
Nicholashayne
Black Down Hills
Rosemary Lane
Churchstanton
Fyfett
Buckland St Mary
Witheridge
Nomansland
Templeton Bridge
Calverleigh
TIVERTON
Canal
Sampford Peverell
Halberton
Appledore
Waterloo Cross
Uffculme
Culm Valley
Culmstock
Hemyock
Stapley
Churchinford
Bishopswood
West Worlington
East Worlington
Thelbridge Barton
Cruwys Morchard
Withleigh
Ash Thomas
Craddock
Hackpen Hill
Bolham Water
Marsh
Hele Lane
Pennymoor
Way Village
Puddington
Willand
Smithincott
Madford
Smeatharpe
Newcott
Yarcombe
Forches Cross
Bradfield
Blackborough
Sheldon
Dunkeswell
Black Dog
Poughill
Upham
Cadeleigh
Butterleigh
Cullompton
Kentisbeare
Upottery
Stockland Hill
Lapford
Kennerleigh
Bickleigh
Oldborough
Morchard Road Sta
East Village
Cheriton Fitzpaine
Bickleigh Castle
Colebrook
Dulford
Black Down
Beacon
Stockland
Cadbury
Fursdon House
Westcott
Broadhembury
Hembury
Dumpdon
Monkton
Down St Mary
Copplestone Sta
Copplestone
Barnstaple Cross
Sandford
Stockleigh Pomeroy
Thorverton
Silverton
Bradninch
Plymtree
Luton
Payhembury
Awliscombe
Dalwood
Wilmington
Killerton Gardens
Up Exe
Langford
Clyst Hydon
Aunk
Higher Tale
Talaton
Colestocks
Buckerell
HONITON
Widworthy
Nymet Tracey
Coleford
Colebrooke
Shobrooke
Efford
Budlake
Westwood
Whimple
Fairmile
Alfington
Church Green
Shute
CREDITON
Brampford Speke
Rewe
Broadclyst
Cadhay House
Farway
Seaton Junction
Whitford
Yeoford
Uton
Hookway
Newton St Cyres
Upton Pyne
Stoke Canon
Poltimore
Dog Village
OTTERY ST MARY
Colyton
Court Barton
Cowley
Rougemont Castle
Exeter Airport
Rockbeare
West Hill
Wiggaton
Broad Down
Southleigh
Farway
Hittisleigh
Tedburn St Mary
Cheriton Bishop
EXETER
WHIPTON
Clyst Honiton
Marsh Green
Tipton St John
Colyford
Axmouth
Blackbury Castle
Whitestone
St Nicholas Priory
Cathedral
Aylesbeare
Sidbury
Harcombe
Crockernwell
Longdown
ALPHINGTON
Countess Wear
Clyst St Mary
Nat. Res.
Harpford
Bowd
Weston
SEATON
Seaton Bay
Beer
Beer Head
Branscombe
Prestonbury Castle
Dunsford
Cranbrook Castle
Ide
Shillingford St George
Topsham
Clyst St George
Hawkerland
Colaton Raleigh
Newton Poppleford
Salcombe Regis
SIDFORD
SIDMOUTH
Pinn
Bridford
Dunchideock
Exminster
Ebford
Exton
Woodbury
Bicton Gardens
Black Hill
Yettington
Otterton
Doccombe
Doddiscombsleigh
Higher Ashton
Kenn
Powderham
Lympstone
La Ronde House
Knowle
Kennick Reservoir
Manor House
Combe
Lower Ashton
Kenton
Powderham Castle
Trenchford Reservoir
Tottiford Reservoir
North Bovey
Starcross
Cockwood
EXMOUTH
BUDLEIGH SALTERTON
Plymouth
Torbay
Bridgwater
Bristol
Yeovil
Dorchester
M5

132

West Hampshire, Wiltshire, Dorset

A fascinating and extremely varied area of the country, including some of England's greatest natural wonders, from the harbours and seaside resorts of Hampshire and Dorset, through the beauties of the New Forest to the mysterious limestone caves of Cheddar and Wookey.

Axminster

Famous for its carpet-weaving factory, which was re-established in 1937 after a gap of a century, Axminster is a prosperous town with attractive Georgian architecture and an elm-shaded Green in the centre is shaded by elms, cedars and yews. The church at Musbury, two miles south-west of the town, contains a monument to Sir Francis Drake.

Blandford Forum

The town has uniformly Georgian architecture, the result of a great fire that devasted the town in 1731, after which it was rebuilt, thanks to generous donations from all over the county. The new houses were largely the work of two local architects, John and William Bastard. A classical portico by the churchyard commemorates "God's dreadful visitation by fire". The bridge over the River Stour bears the inscription that anyone "wilfully injuring" it is "liable to be transported for life". One of the houses that survived the fire is the Old House, built by a German family in c. 1630.

Bournemouth and Christchurch

This seaside resort did not exist until the early 19th century, so it has few monuments of interest, but it is set on steep cliffs, in which there are three clefts, known in these parts as chines, Branksome Chine, Middle Chine and Durley Chine. There are lovely views of the Isle of Wight from the clifftop Esplanade. The town has a pier, a pavilion and winter gardens and excellent shopping. The neighbouring town of Christchurch, on the other hand, is much older, dating back to at least 900 A.D. and has a church that is one of the most magnificent in Dorset. There is a curious story behind the town's name. It was originally called Twynham, but when the church was being built on St. Catherine's Hill, the work kept being undone again and when a beam that had been cut was mysteriously lengthened by a stranger, it was decided that Christ himself had come down to intervene, so both the site of the church and the name of the town were changed. The beam is visible, high in the wall above the choir. The church was built in the 11th century by Bishop Flambard and it became an Augustinian priory in c.1150. The castle remains stand in the grounds of the King's Arms Hotel.

Cadbury Castle

This ancient earthwork, rising steep-sided from lowlands south of the A303 is believed by some to be the site of King Arthur's Camelot. It has been partially excavated and remains found of what may be a cruciform church. At any event, it was defended in the Neolithic and Iron Ages, then by the Romans and later by the Anglo-Saxons. To the north-east is Cadbury House, an Elizabethan mansion.

Cerne Abbas

This village is famous (or notorious!) all over Britain for the giant

Vicar's Close in Wells, said to be the most perfect medieval street in Europe (above).

Glastonbury Tor, reputed to be a magical site (top right).

The moat around the Bishop's Palace in Wells (below right).

Quay Hill, Lymington, Hampshire (opposite top).

The quay at Wareham, Dorset (opposite below).

male figure with a rampant sexual organ cut out of the chalk face on the side of the hill above the village. It is now National Trust property. The village has a ruined Benedictine Abbey and a particularly beautiful 15th-century church which was restored in the 1960s.

Cheddar Caves, Cheddar Gorge and Wookey Hole

The Cheddar Caves and Wookey Hole are a network of limestone caves which permeate the Mendip Hills and are one of the great natural wonders of the world. Until relatively recently, the caves were inhabited. Now visitors come to admire the stalactites and stalagmites in the larger caves and enthusiastic speleologists explore those that are still flooded. Wookey Hole, closer to Wells, has been heavily commercialised since it was acquired by the Madame Tussaud's Wax Museum company. Cheddar Gorge is a deep cleft in the Mendip Hills. The town of Cheddar, famous for its cheese, also specialises in the growing of strawberries and anemones on the sheltered slopes of the Hills.

Dorchester

The county town of Dorset stands on the site of the Roman town of Durnovaria, built in the first century after the defeat of the Durotriges at nearby Maiden Castle (see below). Many relics from Maiden Castle are to be found in the Dorset County Museum, itself a magnificent Victorian building. Dorchester has a Dinosaur Museum, one of the finest in the country, with specimens of the many prehistoric creatures that have been found in this area, including Tyrannosaurus Rex and Megalosaurus. Maumbury Rings just south of the town centre was once a Neolithic stone circle, then a Roman amphitheatre and was later used for public executions. Other grim reminders of rough justice are the Old Crown Court, where the Tolpuddle Martyrs were sentenced in 1834 to transportation for seven years as a punishment for starting a trade union and Judge Jeffries Lodgings. Judge Jeffries, known as "the Hanging Judge", came to try citizens who took part in the rebellion against the Duke of Monmouth at "the Bloody Assizes". The heads of those he condemned to death were impaled on the railings of St. Peter's Church in the High Street. Dorchester is the Casterbridge of Thomas Hardy's novels. Hardy lived in the town and there is a statue to him here. His study at Max Gate is re-created in the museum. He was born two miles away in a thatched cottage at Higher Bockhampton.

Glastonbury

It is still believed that the original Glastonbury Abbey was founded by Joseph of Arimathea and that he buried the Holy Grail beneath it. The monastery was in fact founded by King Ine in 688 and was one of the finest in the country. King Arthur and Queen Guinevere are rumoured to be buried in the abbey precincts. The other main sight of Glastonbury is the Tor, a landmark from which there is a magnificent view for miles around.

Lyme Regis

This attractive port with its distinctive Cobb, a stone jetty in the harbour, which was the setting for much of the novel and film, *The French Lieutenant's Woman* , was once a fashionable seaside resort, the haunt of Jane Austen and the dandies of Bath. It is one of the settings for Jane Austen's *Persuasion*. The 15th-century church, built on three levels, is said to be sliding down the hill. Part of the town is indeed collapsing into the sea and the coastline round the River Axe is definitely changing. A walk to the cliff edge is not recommended.

Maiden Castle

This is the finest pre-Roman fortress in Britain, probably dug by invaders from Britanny in the first century B.C. The Romans attacked and conquered the later inhabitants, and extended the fortifications, which now extend over 120 acres.

Salisbury and Stonehenge

See "Excursions"

Wells

This tiny city has hardly grown since the Middle Ages, as if life had passed it by. It has a magnificent medieval cathedral and the Bishop of Bath and Wells still lives in the bishop's palace some of which dates from 1230. Vicar's Close is a street of 14th-century houses which is said to be the oldest in Europe.

Information

Tourist Information Centre
Marsh and Ham Car Park
West Street
Blandford Forum
Dorset DT11 7AW
Tel: (0258) 451989

Tourist Information Centre
1 Acland Road
Dorchester
DT1 1EF
Tel: (0305) 67992

Events

A two-day fair is held at Crewkerne during the first week of September. The South of England Town Criers' Content is held in Blandford Forum on Spring Bank Holiday (early May). Dorchester Carnival is in June and the Dorchester Show is in September.

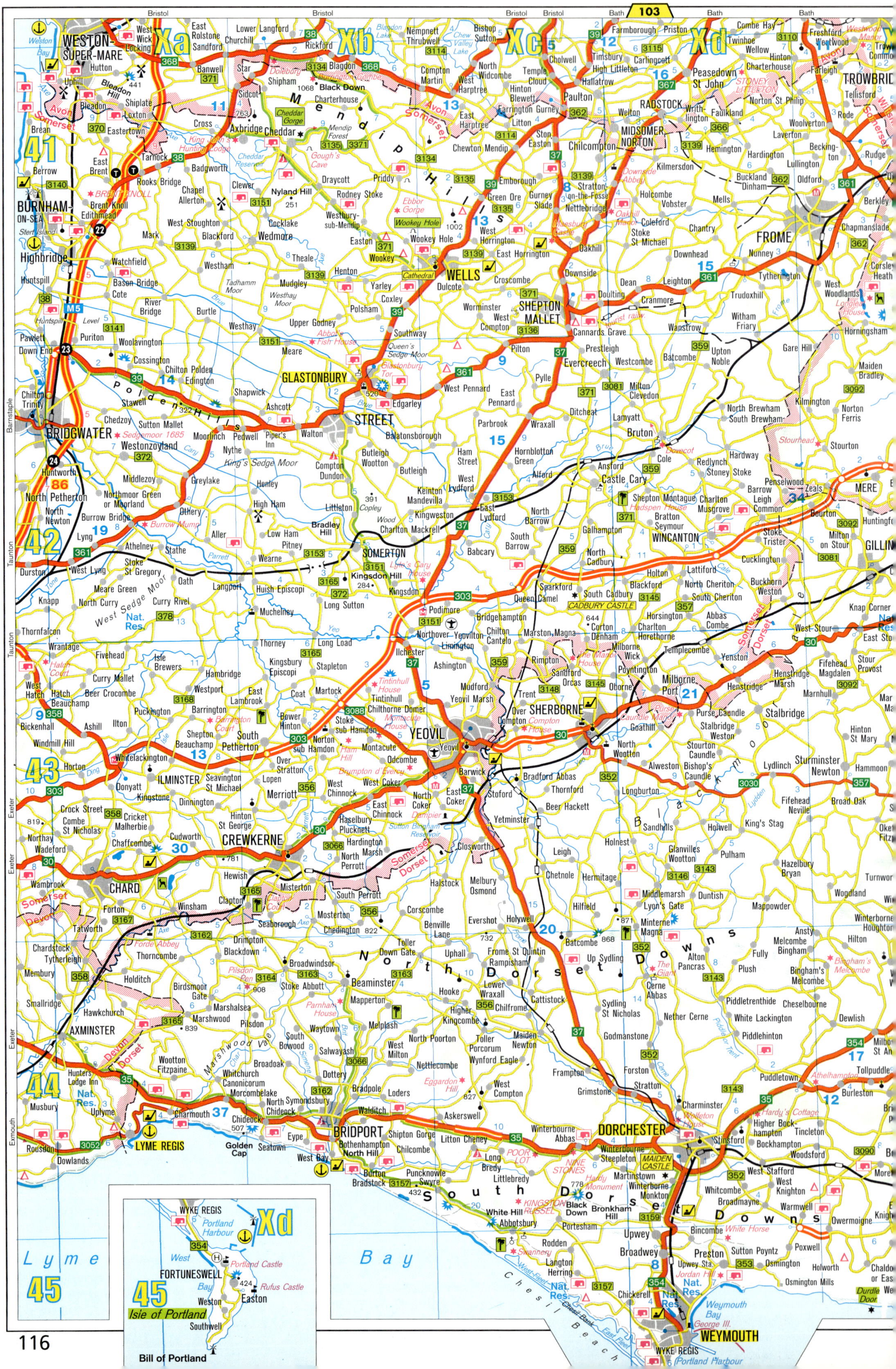
103
Bristol
Bath
Xa
Xb
Xc
Xd
41
42
43
44
45
WESTON-SUPER-MARE
Uphill
Hutton
Bleadon
Banwell
Churchill
Sandford
East Rolstone
Lower Langford
Rickford
Blagdon
Blagdon Lake
Nempnett Thrubwell
Chew Valley Lake
Bishop Sutton
Compton Martin
West Harptree
East Harptree
North Widcombe
Temple Cloud
Hinton Blewett
Farrington Gurney
Cholwell
Clutton
Timsbury
High Littleton
Hallatrow
Paulton
Farmborough
Priston
Carlingcott
Peasedown St John
Combe Hay
Twinhoe
Wellow
Hinton Charterhouse
Norton St Philip
Freshford
Westwood
Farleigh
TROWBRIDGE
Tellisford
Rode
Woolverton
Laverton
Faulkland
RADSTOCK
MIDSOMER NORTON
Welton
Writhlington
Hemington
Hardington
Lullington
Beckington
Rudge
Kilmersdon
Buckland Dinham
Oldford
Mells
Vobster
Holcombe
Coleford
Chantry
Stoke St Michael
Downhead
FROME
Nunney
Tytherington
Trudoxhill
Witham Friary
Berkley
Chapmanslade
Corsley Heath
West Woodlands
Longleat House
Horningsham
Gare Hill
Maiden Bradley
Kilmington
Norton Ferris
Stourton
Stourhead
Zeals
MERE
Penselwood
Bourton
Milton on Stour
GILLINGHAM
Knap Corner
West Stour
East Stour
Fifehead Magdalen
Stour Provost
Marnhull
Hinton St Mary
Hammoon
Sturminster Newton
Lydlinch
Broad Oak
Fifehead Neville
King's Stag
Hazelbury Bryan
Turnworth
Woodland
Mappowder
Winterborne Houghton
Ansty
Melcombe Bingham
Bingham's Melcombe
Hilton
Fully
Plush
Cheselbourne
Dewlish
Piddletrenthide
White Lackington
Piddlehinton
Puddletown
Athelhampton
Tolpuddle
Burleston
Hardy's Cottage
Higher Bockhampton
Bockhampton
Tincleton
Woodsford
Stinsford
DORCHESTER
West Stafford
West Knighton
Warmwell
Owermoigne
Broadmayne
Whitcombe
White Horse
Poxwell
Osmington
Osmington Mills
Holworth
Preston
Sutton Poyntz
Jordan Hill
Upwey Sta.
Bincombe
Broadwey
Upwey
WEYMOUTH
Weymouth Bay
WYKE REGIS
Portland Harbour
Chickerell
Nat. Res.
Chesil Beach
East Fleet
West Fleet
Langton Herring
Rodden
Swannery
Portesham
Abbotsbury
White Hill
Kingston Russell
Black Down
Hardy Monument
Bronkham Hill
Martinstown
Winterborne Monkton
Winterborne Steepleton
Maiden Castle
Winterbourne Abbas
Nine Stones
Littlebredy
Long Bredy
Poor Lot
Litton Cheney
Puncknowle
Swyre
Burton Bradstock
Shipton Gorge
Chilcombe
Bothenhampton
North Hill
West Bay
BRIDPORT
Walditch
Askerswell
Loders
Eggardon Hill
West Compton
Bradpole
Dottery
Salwayash
Melplash
Mapperton
Parnham House
Beaminster
Stoke Abbott
Broadwindsor
Drimpton
Blackdown
Pilsdon Pen
Pilsdon
Birdsmoor Gate
Marshalsea
Marshwood
Marshwood Vale
Broadoak
Whitchurch Canonicorum
Morcombelake
North Chideock
Chideock
Symondsbury
Eype
Seatown
Golden Cap
Charmouth
LYME REGIS
Uplyme
Hunters Lodge Inn
Musbury
Rousdon
Dowlands
Wootton Fitzpaine
Hawkchurch
AXMINSTER
Smallridge
Membury
Holditch
Thorncombe
Forde Abbey
Chardstock
Tytherleigh
Tatworth
Forton
CHARD
Wambrook
Wadeford
Chaffcombe
Cricket Malherbie
Combe St Nicholas
Crock Street
Donyatt
Kingstone
ILMINSTER
Whitelackington
Dinnington
Seavington St Michael
Hinton St George
Cudworth
CREWKERNE
Hewish
Misterton
Clapton
Winsham
Seaborough
South Perrott
Mosterton
Chedington
Corscombe
Halstock
Closworth
Sutton Bingham Reservoir
East Chinnock
West Chinnock
Haselbury Plucknett
Hardington Marsh
North Perrott
Merriott
Lopen
Over Stratton
South Petherton
Shepton Beauchamp
Barrington
Barrington Court
Puckington
Ilton
Ashill
Bickenhall
Windmill Hill
Horton
West Hatch
Hatch Beauchamp
Beer Crocombe
Curry Mallet
Fivehead
Isle Brewers
Hambridge
Westport
East Lambrook
Kingsbury Episcopi
Stapleton
Martock
Coat
Bower Hinton
Stoke sub Hamdon
Norton sub Hamdon
Ham Hill
Montacute
Montacute House
Tintinhull
Tintinhull House
Chilthorne Domer
Ilchester
Ashington
Mudford
Yeovil Marsh
YEOVIL
Brympton d'Evercy
Odcombe
West Coker
East Coker
North Coker
Barwick
Stoford
Yetminster
Bradford Abbas
Thornford
Beer Hackett
Over Compton
Compton House
Trent
SHERBORNE
Nether Compton
North Wootton
Longburton
Holnest
Leigh
Chetnole
Melbury Osmond
Evershot
Holywell
Hermitage
Hilfield
Batcombe
Frome St Quintin
Rampisham
Benville Lane
Uphall
Toller Down Gate
Hooke
Lower Wraxall
Chilfrome
Cattistock
Higher Kingcombe
Toller Porcorum
Maiden Newton
Wynford Eagle
North Poorton
West Milton
Nettlecombe
South Bowood
Waytown
Frampton
Grimstone
Stratton
Charminster
Wolfeton House
Forston
Godmanstone
Sydling St Nicholas
Up Sydling
Cerne Abbas
The Giant
Nether Cerne
Alton Pancras
Minterne Magna
Lyon's Gate
Middlemarsh
Glanvilles Wootton
Duntish
Pulham
Holwell
Sandhills
Blackmoor
Caundle Marsh
Goathill
Stourton Caundle
Bishop's Caundle
Alweston
Purse Caundle
Stalbridge
Stalbridge Weston
Henstridge
Henstridge Marsh
Milborne Port
Milborne Wick
Oborne
Poyntington
Sandford Orcas
Rimpton
Marston Magna
Corton Denham
Charlton Horethorne
Horsington
Templecombe
Abbas Combe
Yenston
South Cheriton
North Cheriton
Blackford
Holton
Lattiford
Buckhorn Weston
Cucklington
Stoke Trister
WINCANTON
Bratton Seymour
Shepton Montague
Charlton Musgrove
Barrow
Leigh Common
Stoney Stoke
Redlynch
Hardway
Cole
Bruton
Dovecot
Lamyatt
Ansford
Castle Cary
Hadspen House
Galhampton
North Cadbury
South Cadbury
CADBURY CASTLE
Sparkford
Queen Camel
West Camel
Bridgehampton
Chilton Cantelo
Yeovilton
Limington
Northover
Podimore
Kingsdon
Kingsdon Hill
Long Sutton
Long Load
Muchelney
Huish Episcopi
Langport
Thorney
Drayton
SOMERTON
Lytes Cary House
Charlton Mackrell
Kingweston
Keinton Mandeville
Babcary
East Lydford
West Lydford
Alford
North Barrow
South Barrow
Hornblotton Green
Wraxall
Ditcheat
Pylle
Milton Clevedon
Evercreech
Prestleigh
Westcombe
Batcombe
Upton Noble
North Brewham
South Brewham
Wanstrow
Cranmore
Doulting
Cannards Grave
SHEPTON MALLET
Croscombe
Dinder
Dulcote
WELLS
Cathedral
Wookey
Wookey Hole
Ebbor Gorge
Easton
Westbury-sub-Mendip
Rodney Stoke
Draycott
Priddy
Cheddar
Cheddar Gorge
Cheddar Reservoir
Axbridge
Cross
King John's Hunting Lodge
Sidcot
Shipham
Star
Charterhouse
Black Down
Mendip Hills
Mendip Forest
Gough's Cave
Chewton Mendip
Litton
Ston Easton
Chilcompton
Emborough
Green Ore
Gurney Slade
Stratton-on-the-Fosse
Nettlebridge
Downside Abbey
Oakhill
Oakhill Manor
Binegar
Masbury Castle
West Horrington
East Horrington
Downside
Dean
Leighton
Dinder
Worminster
West Compton
Pilton
East Pennard
West Pennard
Parbrook
Baltonsborough
Butleigh
Butleigh Wootton
Ham Street
Edgarley
GLASTONBURY
Glastonbury Tor
Queen's Sedge Moor
STREET
Walton
Compton Dundon
Littleton
Copley Wood
Bradley Hill
Pitney
Wearne
Low Ham
High Ham
Henley
King's Sedge Moor
Greylake
Othery
Aller
Burrow Mump
Burrow Bridge
Stathe
Athelney
Lyng
East Lyng
West Lyng
Stoke St Gregory
Oath
Curry Rivel
West Sedge Moor
Nat. Res.
Meare Green
North Curry
Knapp
Thornfalcon
Wrantage
Hatch Court
Durston
North Newton
North Petherton
Northmoor Green or Moorland
Middlezoy
Westonzoyland
Sedgemoor 1685
Chedzoy
Sutton Mallet
Moorlinch
Pedwell
Nythe
Piper's Inn
Ashcott
Shapwick
Stawell
Polden Hills
Cossington
Chilton Polden
Edington
Woolavington
Puriton
Pawlett
Down End
Chilton Trinity
BRIDGWATER
Huntworth
Huntspill
Level
Bason Bridge
Cote
River Bridge
Burtle
Westhay
Westhay Moor
Mudgley
Tadhamm Moor
Meare
Upper Godney
Abbot's Fish House
Polsham
Coxley
Yarley
Henton
Theale
Wedmore
Blackford
Mark
Westham
Watchfield
Highbridge
BURNHAM-ON-SEA
Stert Island
Edithmead
Brent Knoll
BRENT KNOLL
Rooks Bridge
Chapel Allerton
West Stoughton
Cocklake
Clewer
Nyland Hill
Badgworth
Tarnock
East Brent
Berrow
Brean
Eastertown
Loxton
Shiplate
Bleadon Hill
Weston Bay
Avon
Somerset
Dorset
Devon
Lyme Bay
Exeter
Exmouth
Taunton
Barnstaple
North Dorset Downs
South Dorset Downs
WYKE REGIS
Portland Harbour
West Bay
FORTUNESWELL
Portland Castle
Weston
Easton
Rufus Castle
Southwell
Isle of Portland
Bill of Portland
Durdle Door
Chaldon or East

Chippenham
Marlborough
Xf
Ya
Yb
Yc
Yd
Basingstoke
Winchester
Eastleigh
S a l i s b u r y
P l a i n
WARMINSTER
SALISBURY
ANDOVER
Amesbury
Durrington
Larkhill
Bulford
North Tidworth
South Tidworth
Ludgershall
Upavon
Pewsey
Westbury
Bratton
Edington
Erlestoke
Market Lavington
West Lavington
Potterne
Worton
Urchfont
Chirton
Patney
Stert
Poulshot
Bulkington
Keevil
Great Hinton
Steeple Ashton
Ashton Common
Coulston
Little Cheverell
Littleton Panell
Eastcott
Wedhampton
Beechingstoke
Hilcott
Manningford Bruce
Manningford Bohune
Rushall
East Chisenbury
Enford
Fittleton
Everleigh
Collingbourne Kingston
Collingbourne Ducis
Sidbury Hill
Fosbury
Vernham Street
Vernham Holt
Linkenholt
Faccombe
Ashmansworth
Crux Easton
Upton
Ibthorpe
Hurstbourne Tarrant
Tangley
Hatherden
Wildhern
Enham Alamein
Smannell
Charlton
Penton Mewsey
Weyhill
Appleshaw
Clanville
Kimpton
Thruxton
Monxton
Abbots Ann
Quarley
Upper Clatford
Goodworth Clatford
Picket Piece
Andover Down
Middleton
Wherwell
Chilbolton
Newton Stacey
Fullerton
Leckford
Longstock
Stockbridge
Danebury
Nether Wallop
Middle Wallop
Over Wallop
Palestine
Chilmark
Stonehenge
Woodhenge
Shrewton
Orcheston
Chitterne
Codford
Heytesbury
Knook
Tytherington
Corton
Sherrington
Stockton
Wylye
Steeple Langford
Hanging Langford
Little Langford
Stapleford
Winterbourne Stoke
Berwick St James
Deptford
Fisherton de la Mere
Stoford
South Newton
Great Wishford
Lower Woodford
Middle Woodford
Wilsford
Lake
West Amesbury
Great Durnford
Netton
Winterbourne Dauntsey
Winterbourne Earls
Boscombe
Allington
Idmiston
Porton
Figsbury Ring
Winterslow
Old Sarum
Wilton
Wilton House
Barford St Martin
Baverstock
Dinton
Teffont Magna
Teffont Evias
Fonthill Bishop
Fonthill Gifford
Hindon
Chicklade
Tisbury
East Knoyle
Semley
Ansty
Wardour Castle
Swallowcliffe
Sutton Mandeville
Fovant
Compton Chamberlayne
Burcombe
Netherhampton
Harnham
Coombe Bissett
Homington
Stratford Tony
Bishopstone
Fifield Bavant
Ebbesbourne Wake
Broad Chalke
Mead End
Bowerchalke
Alvediston
Donhead St Andrew
Shaftesbury
Ludwell
Berwick St John
Winkelbury
Cann Common
Melbury Abbas
Ashmore
Tollard Royal
Deanland
Sixpenny Handley
Woodyates
Pentridge
Martin
Martin Drove End
Tidpit
Whitsbury
Rockbourne
Damerham
Sandleheath
Ashford
Fordingbridge
Castle Ditches
Breamore House
Breamore
Upper Street
Woodgreen
Hale
Godshill
Stuckton
Blissford
Frogham
Bickton
Gorley
Ibsley
Harbridge
Ellingham
Blashford
Linwood
Linford
Ringwood
Picket Post
Burley Street
Burley Lodge
Burley
Bisterne
Bisterne Close
Kingston
Avon
Avon Castle
St Ives
Ashley Heath
St Leonards
West Moors
Three Legged Cross
Verwood
Woodlands
Horton
Knowlton
Sutton Holms
Edmondsham
Cranborne
Cranborne Manor
Boveridge
Wimborne St Giles
Monkton Up Wimborne
Gussage All Saints
Gussage St Michael
Cashmoor
Chettle
Chettle House
Farnham
Tarrant Gunville
Stubhampton
Tarrant Hinton
Tarrant Launceston
Tarrant Monkton
Pimperne
Blandford Forum
Blandford Camp
Tarrant Rawston
Langton Long Blandford
Tarrant Keyneston
Tarrant Crawford
Badbury Rings
Witchampton
Moor Crichel
Long Crichel
Manswood
Hinton Martell
Gaunt's Common
Holt
Holt Heath
Broom Hill
Mannington
Uppington
Stanbridge
Clapgate
Tadden
Wimborne Minster
Pamphill
Sturminster Marshall
Spetisbury
Charlton Marshall
Almer
Winterborne Zelston
Anderson
Morden
Bloxworth
East Morden
Lytchett Matravers
Lytchett Minster
Upton
Poole
Hamworthy
Canford Magna
Broadstone
Stapehill
Hampreston
Longham
Ferndown
Parley Cross
Bournemouth Airport (Hurn)
Hurn
Sopley
Winkton
Ripley
Shirley
Bransgore
Thorney Hill
Neacroft
Hinton
Christchurch
Christchurch Bay
Highcliffe
New Milton
Barton on Sea
Bashley
Wootton
Tiptoe
Sway
Hordle
Everton
Downton
Milford on Sea
Keyhaven
Hurst Castle
Lymore
Lymington
Lower Pennington
Walhampton
Boldre
Battramsley
Setley
Brockenhurst
Balmerlawn
Lyndhurst
Bank
Emery Down
Newtown
Bolderwood
Stoney Cross
Fritham
Bramshaw
Brook
Rufus Stone
Furzey
Minstead
Cadnam
Woodlands
Bartley
Ashurst
Colbury
Netley Marsh
Totton
Eling
Marchwood
Pooksgreen
Dibden
Hythe
Hill Top
Beaulieu
Palace House
East Boldre
Bucklers Hard
Pilley Bailey
East End
St Leonards Grange
Portmore
Copythorne
Ower
Canada
Landford
Nomansland
Plaitford
Lover
Hamptworth
Sherfield English
East Wellow
West Wellow
Abbey Church
Romsey
North Baddesley
Chilworth
Toothill
Rownhams
Lee
Broadlands House
Ampfield
Timsbury
Braishfield
Awbridge
Kent's Oak
Michelmersh
Mottisfont
Mottisfont Abbey
Lockerley
East Tytherley
West Tytherley
West Dean
East Dean
Whiteparish
Carter's Clay
Newton
West Grimstead
East Grimstead
Farley
Pitton
Laverstock
Alderbury
Whaddon
Charlton-All-Saints
Downton
Nunton
Wick
Woodfalls
Redlynch
West Winterslow
The Common
Lopcombe Corner
Broughton
Houghton
Bossington
Horsebridge
King's Somborne
Little Somborne
Ashley
Farley Mount
Southampton
New Forest
Bournemouth
Boscombe
Branksome
Compton Acres Gardens
Brownsea Island
Poole Harbour
Poole Bay
Hengistbury Head
Jersey, Guernsey
Isle of Purbeck
Isle of Wight
The Needles
Alum Bay
Totland
Norton Green
Yarmouth
Freshwater
Hamstead
Ningwood
Shalcombe
Mottistone
Brook
Compton Bay
Easton
Wareham
Stoborough
Stoborough Green
Sandford
Holton Heath
Arne
Stokeford
East Stoke
West Holme
East Creech
Creech Grange
Norden
Corfe Castle
Church Knowle
Kimmeridge
Smedmore
East Lulworth
Steeple
Tyneham
Studland
Old Harry Rocks
Ulwell
Swanage
Harman's Cross
Langton Matravers
Worth Matravers
Durlston Head
St Aldhelm's Head
Nat. Res.

The South Country and the South Coast

This area, where many Londoners take their holidays, contains some of the most popular seaside resorts, with sheltered, though not always sandy, beaches and warm weather. Inland, there are the rolling hills of the North and South Downs, and the farmlands and orchards of Sussex and Surrey.

Arundel

The town grew up around the castle which is still the residence of the premier Roman Catholic family of England, the Fitzalan Howards, earls of Arundel and dukes of Norfolk. Arundel Castle is perched on a hill overlooking the water meadows of the River Arun and when viewed from the distance has all the splendour of a fairytale castle. The Norman castle was largely laid waste during the Civil War in 1643-44, but was rebuilt in the 18th and 19th centuries. The Castle Keep and the Bevis Tower are 11th century. The church in the grounds, St. Nicholas, is both the Anglican parish church of Arundel and the Roman Catholic Fitzallan Chapel with separate entrances for each. The magnificent castle grounds consist mainly of beechwoods. Nearby is the Wildfowl Trust. Bignor, near Arundel, has one of the finest Roman villas in England.

Bodiam Castle

This castle stands in lovely countryside near the Cinque Ports of Rye and Winchelsea, both now miles from the sea, and thus able to preserve all their historic beauty. The castle is in an almost fairytale setting, surrounded by a moat covered in lush waterlilies. It was built in 1385 as protection against a French invasion which never happened. Although it has not been inhabited since the 17th century, it remains the best example of its kind in the country. There is an audio-visual presentation for visitors.

Brighton

See "Historic Cities"

Chichester

The Roman town of Noviomagus is now a cathedral city and the administrative centre of West Sussex. The centre of the town is the Market Cross, donated in 1501 by Bishop Edward Story. The Market House or Butter Market (1807) was designed by John Nash. The two most important buildings in Chichester are the cathedral and the Festival Theatre. Chichester Cathedral was first consecrated in 1184, but has been considerably added to since, especially after 1861 when the tower and spire crashed into the nave during a storm. The bell tower is detached from the cathedral, the only example of its kind in the country. The Lady Chapel and Retrochoir are the oldest parts of the Cathedral. Among the modern features there is a John Piper tapestry created in 1966, a bright splash of colour over the altar, and a stained glass window by Marc Chagall. The cathedral close, bishop's palace and its surrounding walls, part of the old city wall, are well worth a visit. Chichester Festival Theatre is a theatre-in-the-round which is one of the most important venues outside London. Among the many places of interest near Chichester are Goodwood House, Goodwood Race Course and the Roman palace at Fishbourne.

Guildford

This ancient town has the first entirely new cathedral to be built since the Reformation. The Cathedral of the Holy Spirit was consecrated in 1961. It is now surrounded by the equally new University of Surrey. Guildford stands beside the River Wey. The town has many old buildings, including the Guildhall, whose large, gilded clock, dated 1683, juts out over the street and is a famous landmark. The panelled Council Chamber contains a 16th-century German sword which is carried before the Mayor in formal processions. Other old buildings in the town include the Royal Grammar School (late 16th century), Guildford

House (1660) and the Abbot's Hospital (1619).

Herstmonceaux
This medieval fortified castle surrounded by a moat is now the home of the Royal Greenwich Observatory. Most of the castle is not open to the public but the grounds can be visited as can the Isaac Newton Telescope Building erected nearby.

Isle of Wight
This popular holiday destination which lies just outside Southampton Water is quite different from the nearby mainland. The scenery, particularly at Alum Bay and at the southern tip, where the rocks called the Needles are a famous landmark, is dramatic, the green-topped white cliffs dropping sheer to the sea. Inland there are rolling hills. Carisbrooke Castle is on the site of a Roman fortress. It is here that Charles I was imprisoned for a time and his daughter Elizabeth died here. There is a monument to her in the church in the nearby town of Newport. Ventnor, Shanklin and Sandown on the south-east coast are all pretty seaside resorts. The other important stately home on the island is Osborne, Queen Victoria's favourite residence, and the place where she died. Two houses with literary associations are now hotels. Faringford once belonged to Alfred Lord Tennyson and Winterbourne was home to Charles Dickens who called it "the prettiest place I ever saw in my life, at home or abroad".

Portsmouth
Britain's chief naval base since Tudor times lies on a peninsula known as Portsea Island. It is a striking contrast of old and new. In the new harbour modern warships lie at anchor, their upper decks bristling with communications and sonar equipment, but only a few miles away are the docks that have been left much as they were in Lord Nelson's day. The Naval Base, which can be visited, is an area of 62 acres of docks, including 15 dry docks. The Royal Naval Museum has a multitude of fascinating exhibits including the weathervane that once graced Portsmouth Cathedral. King Charles Dock (1648) now houses the *Victory*, restored and fitted out as it looked at the Battle of Trafalgar. Even older is the *Mary Rose*, the flagship of Henry VIII's navy, which sank off Portsmouth in 1545. The hull was raised in 1982. Nearby Southsea and Gosport both have interesting museums. Porchester Castle, just west of the town, is a medieval fortress that is well worth visiting.

Singleton
The Open Air Downland Museum in this lovely part of West Sussex, is full of buildings brought here to illustrate life in the Middle Ages in Sussex and the Weald of Kent. There are many craft demonstrations, including charcoal-burning and wood-carving. There are lovely woodland walks.

Winchester
One of the great cathedral cities and capital of the Saxon kingdom of Wessex, Winchester was joint capital of England with London until the 12th century. This greatness is reflected in the fine buildings, culminating in the Cathedral, the longest medieval building in the world. Construction started in 1079. The Saxon kings lie buried here as does William Rufus, son of William the Conqueror who was killed while hunting in the New Forest. The cathedral was sinking into the mud in the early 20th century and the diver William Walker singlehandedly saved it by replacing a million bricks with his own hands. He has a memorial in the cathedral. Other interesting sights in Winchester include the Great Hall, all that remains of Winchester Castle, and Wolvesely Castle home of the bishops of Winchester.

Penshurst Place, Kent, one of the country's lovely stately homes (opposite).

Fishing boats in Portsmouth Harbour (top left).

Leonardslee Gardens, Lower Beeding, West Sussex (above left).

Seven Sisters on the East Sussex coast (above).

The River Arun with Arundel Castle in the background (left).

Information
Tourist Information Centre
St. Peter's Market
West Street
Chichester, PO19 1AH
Tel: (0243) 775888

There are also tourist information centres in all the main towns.

Events
During Corpus Christi, in June, the Fitzalan Chapel in Arundel is decorated with a carpet of flowers. Arundel Festival is held for two weeks in August. Shakespeare Plays are often performed in the keep of Arundel Castle.
Cowes Week, the yachting regatta off the Isle of Wight is held in the first week of August.
The Haslemere Festival is held in July, and was inspired by the Dolmetsch Family. It is devoted to pre-classical music, played on ancient instruments.

Newbury
Reading
Camberley
105
London
Yd
Ye
Yf
Za
Zb
41
42
43
44
45
Kingsclere
Basing
BASINGSTOKE
Overton
Whitchurch
Oakley
Hook
FLEET
FARNBOROUGH
ALDERSHOT
Odiham
Tongham
North Downs
FARNHAM
GODALMING
Milford
Elstead
Hindhead
Haslemere
HASLEMERE
ALTON
Bordon Camp
Liphook
Liss
Headley
Grayshott
Medstead
Four Marks
New Alresford
Alresford
WINCHESTER
Kings Worthy
Twyford
Shawford
EASTLEIGH
Bishopstoke
CHANDLER'S FORD
SOUTHAMPTON
Bishop's Waltham
Wickham
Botley
Hedge End
Petersfield
PETERSFIELD
Midhurst
MIDHURST
Clanfield
Horndean
WATERLOOVILLE
Forest of Bere
HAVANT
Emsworth
Cosham
FAREHAM
Portchester
Titchfield
Stubbington
Lee-on-the-Solent
GOSPORT
PORTSMOUTH
SOUTHSEA
Portsea Island
HAYLING ISLAND
South Downs
CHICHESTER
Bosham
Selsey
Selsey Bill
East Wittering
West Wittering
BOGNOR REGIS
Hythe
Fawley
Calshot
Hamble
Netley
Sarisbury
Locks Heath
The Solent
Spithead
Caen, Cherbourg, Le Havre
St. Malo
COWES
EAST COWES
Osborne House
RYDE
NEWPORT
Isle of Wight
Carisbrooke Castle
Brading
Bembridge
Foreland
SANDOWN
SHANKLIN
Shanklin Chine
VENTNOR
Dunnose
Niton
St Lawrence
St Catherine's Point
Godshill
Yarmouth
Freshwater
Brighstone Bay
M3
M27
M275
A3(M)

108
Cobham
London
London
London
Dartford
Dartford
Zd
Ze
Zf
Aa
Ab
LEATHERHEAD
REIGATE
REDHILL
DORKING
CRAWLEY
HORSHAM
EAST GRINSTEAD
CROW-BOROUGH
SEVENOAKS
Oxted
Godstone
Edenbridge
Lingfield
Horley
Salfords
Cranleigh
BILLINGSHURST
HAYWARDS HEATH
BURGESS HILL
Uckfield
LEWES
BRIGHTON
HOVE
PORTSLADE-BY-SEA
SOUTHWICK
SHOREHAM-BY-SEA
WORTHING
LITTLEHAMPTON
ARUNDEL
Storrington
Steyning
Henfield
Cuckfield
Hurstpierpoint
Keymer
Peacehaven
NEWHAVEN
SEAFORD
Rottingdean
Saltdean
Lancing
Sompting
Angmering
Ferring
Pulborough
THREE BRIDGES
POUND HILL
IFIELD
FOREST ROW
Maresfield
Crowborough
Forest Row
Ashdown Forest
London (Gatwick)
M25
M23
North Downs
South Downs
The Weald
St Leonards Forest
Dieppe
Surrey
Kent
East Sussex
West Sussex
Nat. Res.
ENGLISH CHANNEL

The Kent Coast and the Channel Islands

The Channel Islands lie much closer to the coast of France than they do to England, nor are they part of the United Kingdom. The south-east corner of England, where Britain's only two conquerors – William and Caesar – landed, is full of historic sites.

The South-east coast of England has been the gateway to Britain even since before Julius Caesar said "Veni, vidi, vici" (I came, I saw, I conquered). The Channel Islands are only eight miles from the French coast and are not part of the United Kingdom of Great Britain and Northern Ireland. Although they are quasi-independent, they are ruled by the Duke of Normandy, who happens to be the reigning monarch of Great Britain, so they consider themselves British. Indeed, in every way, the Islands are far more British than French, since the main language is English, the currency is sterling and the way of life infinitely more English than anything else, especially since a large number of wealthy British tax exiles make the islands their home. The local dialect, which is fast dying out, is based on Norman French and varies from island to island.
There are six inhabited Channel Islands, Jersey, Guernsey, Alderney, Sark, Herm and Jethou, in order of size, each of which is self-governing. Jersey and Guernsey each have a parliament, known as the States. In the past, the islanders made a nice profit from smuggling and salvaging the wrecks of ships that washed ashore on the rocky coasts. Nowadays, the islands prosper mightily as much from the amazingly mild climate that attracts English tourists in their hordes as from the Islands' status as a tax haven. Office buildings in the town centres of St. Helier and St. Peter Port are festooned with nameplates of British and foreign companies who have their registered offices here. Farming still occupies an important place in the economy of the islands. Jersey and Guernsey dairy cattle are famous throughout Britain for their rich creamy milk and Jersey vegetables and flowers are in season long before the mainland crops. Some places of interest are listed here, taking the islands in order of size.

Jersey
This is the largest of the islands, a rectangle 9 by 5 miles. It has lovely beaches, ranging in size from secluded coves, such as **Portelet Bay** to the huge sweep of **St. Ouen's Bay,** from whose magnificent cliffs there are views of France and of the other islands. Jersey was frequently attacked and thus has many fortifications. **Montorgeuil Castle** was built in the Middle Ages to defend Jersey from the French; it is five miles outside St. Helier at the village of **Gorey**. **Elizabeth Castle** was built in the 16th century by Sir Walter Raleigh, then governor of Jersey, who named it after Queen Elizabeth I. The Napoleonic **Fort Regent** has been converted into a sports and leisure centre. There are several Norman churches on the island, but the **Glass Church** at Milbrook is of special interest because it is decorated by René Lalique. **St. Peter's Bunker** in the centre of the island is a museum of the German Occupation during World War II.

Guernsey
The capital is **St. Peter Port** is a quaint little town dominated by **St. Peter's Church,** known as the Cathedral of the Channel Islands and by the fortress of **Castle Cornet**. The latter withstood a nine-year siege during the Civil war, finally surrendering in 1651. The most famous sight on the island is **Hauteville House**, the home of Victor Hugo during his years of exile between 1855 and 1870. The house, now a museum, belongs to the City of Paris.

Alderney
This island has a small scenic railway and a little harbour at **St. Anne**. It is popular for swimming and water sports. It also has grim fortifications, a relic of German Occupation in World War II.

Sark
The island is ruled by a feudal lord, known as the Seigneur. Divorce, cars, adoption and income tax are all banned here. The **Seigneurie**, the lord's official residence and the two-man **prison** can be visited.

Herm
The only other island open to visitors is famous for its **Shell Beach**. The entire beach consists of shells brought by the Gulf Stream, some from as far away as the Caribbean. Jethou is a privately-owned island and cannot be visited.

Battle
The Battle of Hastings in fact took place here, six miles inland from Hastings. William the Conqueror promised to erect an abbey if he won the battle. He built St. Mar-

Beachy Head, East Sussex (top).

Carpet Gardens in the resort of Eastbourne (left).

The Pantiles, Royal Tunbridge Wells, Kent, once a spa (above).

Cherry Orchard in the Weald of Kent (opposite above).

Scotney Castle, Kent, in the spring (opposite below).

tin's Abbey four years later. The grounds can be visited, though not the Abbey itself which is an exclusive girls' public school. Next to Battle Abbey, in Wealden Hall House, there is an exhibition entitled Yesterday's World of live in 19th-century Sussex.

Bexhill

This quiet seaside resort is a favourite with English pensioners who want to retire to the country. The De La Warr Pavilion (1935) on the sea is considered to be one of the best examples of Art Deco architecture in Britain.

Dover

Dominated by Dover Castle, the main Channel port (France is only 17 miles away across the Straits) has always been a bulkhead against invasion, which may account for its rather grim appearance. It has not been a naval dockyard since 1923. Dover is the chief of the Cinque Ports (prounced "Sink Ports"), a defence system modelled on Roman lines. The ports were granted their first charter in 1278. The other four were Sandwich, Hythe, Romney and Hastings. Rye and Winchelsea were added later as "ancient towns". Dover is actually the only one which is still a flourishing harbour. The White Cliffs Experience is an audio-visual display in the Market Square.

Eastbourne

This placid seaside resort has always been a favourite for English people to retire by the sea. Right next door is one of England's most famous landmarks, the great white cliff known as Beachy Head, and the cliffs known as the Seven Sisters. The Redoubt, built to repell a feared Napoleonic invasion, is one of two military museums.

Hastings

The old harbour was built by William the Conqueror as the main Cinque Port (see above under "Dover"). When the encroaching sea destroyed the harbour, Hastings remained a flourishing fishing port. The Old Town still has a fishing village atmosphere, with the Fishmarket,the tall black storing-sheds for nets and the fisherman's church of St. Clement. The Old Town Hall is now a museum of local history. Hastings was never such a fashionable resort as neighbouring St. Leonards, where the Duke of Wellington spent his honeymoon.

Hythe

This little town, once a flourishing port, is split in two by the Royal Military Canal. Shorncliffe Camp, still a major military installation, was first built in the Napoleonic era, as were the three Martello Towers on the front. The Early English church contains 500 skulls and bones beleived to have brought form the old churchyard. The Romney, Hythe and Dimchurch Railway is a steam railway that is a big tourist attraction.

Royal Tunbridge Wells

This was the first spa town in England, started when Lord North discovered the chalybeate springs here in 1606. The town reached the zenith of its popularity in the mid-eighteenth century. This is when souvenirs in the form of Tunbridge ware were most popular. The Chalybeat Spring stil stands in the Pantiles, a covered arcade laid out in 1638 and named for the orignal tile paving, though this has now been replaced with Purbeck stone. The Town Hall, Assembly Hall, Library and Museum, the latter with the finest collection of Tunbridge ware in the country, are in the town centre. There is an audio-visual display entitled A Day at the Wells in the Corn Exchange in the Pantiles.

Information
States of Jersey Tourist Committee
Weighbridge Street
St. Helier, Jersey
Tel: (0534) 78000

States of Guernsey Tourist Board
P.O.Box 23
St. Peter Port, Guernsey
Tel: (0481) 23552

Alderney Recreation and Tourism Committee
States Office,
St. Anne's, Alderney
Tel: (0481) 822994

Battle Tourist Information Centre
Battle, E. Sussex
Tel: (04246) 3721

Herm Island Administrative Office
Tel: (0481) 22377

Events
The Battle of the Flowers is held on Jersey in August.

Tips
The Islands can be very crowded in the summer and during the Battle of the Flowers, so it is important to book accommodation if you intend to visit them at that time of year..
The thick-knit fishermen's jerseys or guernseys, with their distinctive shoulder patterns make wonderful souvenirs. The traditional colour is dark blue, but they are made in a wide range of other colours.

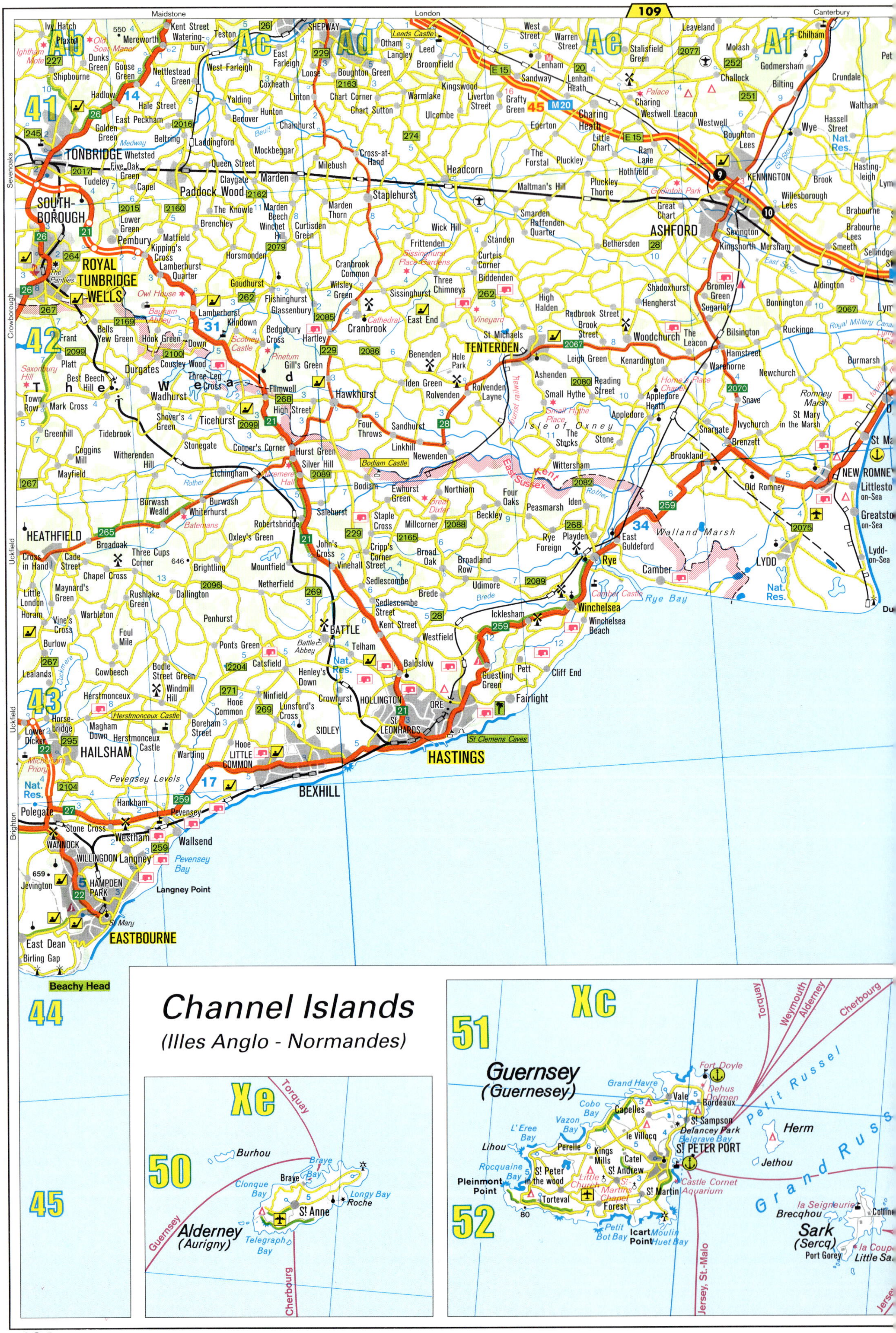

109
Maidstone
London
Canterbury
Sevenoaks
Crowborough
Uckfield
Brighton
Ab
Ac
Ad
Ae
Af
41
42
43
44
45
TONBRIDGE
SOUTH-BOROUGH
ROYAL TUNBRIDGE WELLS
Paddock Wood
Marden
Staplehurst
Headcorn
Cranbrook
Hawkhurst
Charing
Lenham
ASHFORD
KENNINGTON
Wye
TENTERDEN
Woodchurch
Hamstreet
NEW ROMNEY
Littlestone-on-Sea
Greatstone-on-Sea
LYDD
Rye
Winchelsea
Rye Bay
Camber
Walland Marsh
Romney Marsh
Isle of Oxney
Wadhurst
Ticehurst
Etchingham
Robertsbridge
HEATHFIELD
BATTLE
HASTINGS
ST LEONARDS
BEXHILL
HAILSHAM
Pevensey
Westham
Polegate
WILLINGDON
Langney
Pevensey Bay
Langney Point
EASTBOURNE
East Dean
Birling Gap
Beachy Head
Fairlight
Cliff End
Leeds Castle
Bodiam Castle
Herstmonceux Castle
St Clemens Caves
Camber Castle
M20
E15
Channel Islands
(Illes Anglo - Normandes)
Xe
Xc
50
51
52
Burhou
Braye
Braye Bay
Clonque Bay
Longy Bay
Roche
St Anne
Alderney
(Aurigny)
Telegraph Bay
Torquay
Guernsey
Cherbourg
Guernsey
(Guernesey)
Grand Havre
Fort Doyle
Vale
Bordeaux
Cobo Bay
Capelles
St Sampson
Delancey Park
Belgrave Bay
Vazon Bay
L'Eree Bay
le Villocq
Perelle
Kings Mills
Lihou
ST PETER PORT
Rocquaine Bay
St Peter in the wood
Catel
St Andrew
Castle Cornet
Aquarium
Pleinmont Point
Torteval
Forest
St Martin
Petit Bot Bay
Icart Point
Moulin Huet Bay
Herm
Jethou
Petit Russel
Grand Russel
Brecqhou
Sark
(Sercq)
Port Gorey
Little Sark
la Seigneurie
Jersey, St-Malo
Weymouth
Alderney
Torquay
Cherbourg

Bb
Bc
Bd
Be
Bf
Xe
Xf
Canterbury
Staple
Goodnestone
Eastry
Worth
Adisham
Chillenden
Aylesham
Nonington
Bishopsbourne
North-bourne
Sholden
Deal Castle
The Downs
DEAL
Kingston
Womenswold
Easole Street
Tilmanstone
Great Mongeham
Elvington
East Studdal
Ripple
WALMER
Walmer Castle
Barham
Barfrestone
Eythorne
West Langdon
Sutton
Kingsdown
Woolage Green
Shepherdswell or Sibertswold
Ringwould
Denton
Whitfield
East Langdon
Wootton
Lydden
Guston
St Margaret's at Cliffe
Elham
TEMPLE EWELL
BUCKLAND
St Margaret's Bay
Swingfield Minnis
St Radigund's Abbey
St Mary in Castro
Dover Castle
Alkham
DOVER
Lyminge
Densole
West Hougham
Chalk Cliffs
Hawkinge
Etching-hill
Paddlesworth
Capel-le-Ferne
Newington
East Wear Bay
FOLKESTONE
Castle of Saltwood
SALTWOOD
SANDGATE
HYTHE
Zeebrugge
Oostende
Calais (hovercraft)
Calais
Strait of Dover
Pas de Calais
Railway tunnel (under construction)
Tunnel ferroviaire (en construction)
Côte d'Opal
Blériot-Plage
Calais
Sangatte
Moulin
Coquelles
Cap Blanc-Nez
Escalles
Peuplingues
Frethun
Nielles-lès-Calais
St. Tricat
Ramsault
Wissant
Sombre
Hervelinghen
Bonningues-lès-Calais
Hames-Boucres
Anc. Cap Romain
Saint-Inglevert
Pihen-les-Guînes
Alenthum
le Châtelet
Audembert
Base V2
Cap Gris-Nez
Framzelle
Tardinghen
Landrethun-le-Nord
Château de Blacourt
Leubringhen
Cran-aux-Œufs
Audinghen
Caffiers
Bernes
Ferques
Fiennes
Audresselles
Bazinghen
Leulinghen
Elinghen
Locquinghen
Raventhun
MARQUISE
Rinxent
Hardinghen
Ambleteuse
Réty
Slack
Beuvrequen
Parc
Wierre-Effroy
Mont Cornet
Wacquinghen
Offrethun
Chât. de la Briamerie
Maninghen-Henne
Hesdres
Wimereux
Pittefaux
Pernes-lès-Boulogne
Wimille
Belle-et-Houllefort
Colonne de la G. de Armée
Souverain Moulin
le Wast
St. Omer
Rupembert
Conteville-lès-Boulogne
BOULOGNE-sur-Mer
la Capelle-lès-Boulogne
Alincthun
Bellebrune
Saint-Martin-Boulogne
Maquinghen
Forêt de Boulogne
Liane
Échinghen
Baincthun
le Possart
Crémarest
le Portel
Cap d'Alprech
OUTREAU
Saint-Léonard
Questinghen
Wirwignes
Régional
Saint-Étienne-au-Mont
Hesdin-l'Abbé
Isques
Questrecques
le Marais
Equihen-Plage
Hesdigneul-lès-Boulogne
Longfossé
Ecault
Wierre-au-Bois
Carly
le Choquel
Condette
Boulonnais
Auchel
le Château Hardelot
SAMER
Verlincthun
Menty
Tingry
Hardelot-Plage
Nesles
Haut-Pichot
Dalles
Mt. Saint Frieux
Haut Tingry
Séquières
Neufchâtel-Hardelot
Dunes
Halinghen
la Vertevoie
Thubeauville
Lacres
Cité l'Abeille
Widehem
Dannes
le Turne
Hubersent
Equinehaut
Plage-Sainte-Cécile
Frencq
Cormont
Bernieulles
Lydd
Camiers
Beussent
Inxent
Embouchure de la Canche
Longvillers
Lefaux
Maresville
le Touquet-Paris-Plage
ÉTAPLES
Recques-sur-Course
Tubersent
le Touquet
Bréxent-Enocq
Estréelles
Enocq
Canche
Trépied
Beutin
Attin
Stella-Plage
Villiers
Valencendre
Neuville-sous-Montreuil
le Moulinel
la Calotterie
Berck-Plage
Abbeville
Montreuil
Plémont Point
Grosnez Point
Plémont
Sorel Point
Grosnez Castle
Belle Hogue Point
Devil's Hole
St-John
l' Etacq
Philis-Léoville
Boulay Bay
Rozel Bay
Ste-Mary
Trinity
St-Ouen
Carrefour Selous
La Coupe Point
Rozel
la Hague
St.-Ouens Bay
St-Lawrence
Jersey
St-Peter
Augrès
St-Martin
St. Catherine Bay
Ville es Nouaux
Beaumont
Tumulus
Hogue-Bie
Gorey
la Pulente
St-Aubin
St-Savoir
Montorgueil
Corbière Point
St-Brelade
St-Helier
St-Aubin's Bay
Grouville
St-Clément
Elisabeth Castle
Noirmont Point
la Rocque
le Croc
St. Clement's Bay
la Rocque Point
Sark, Guernsey
St-Malo
Granville

West Devon, Cornwall and the Scillies

The peninsula of Devon and Cornwall, with the Scilly Isles beyond, is one of the most beautiful parts of the British Isles, unspoiled by the rampant industrialisation of the last century. The Land of King Arthur has a character all of its own, making it unlike anywhere else in Britain.

The peninsula of Devon and Cornwall is a visitor's paradise of picturesque villages and wild and rocky coasts, desolate moorland, rolling hills, cosy harbours and quiet, sandy coves. There are 450 miles of coastline from the Atlantic to the English Channel, a lacework of coves and inlets, interspersed with quaint fishing villages and harbours, right down to the fearsome crags of Land's End. The quality of the local food is also famous. Devon cheese, cider and Devonshire cream are reputedly the best in Britain.

The Isles of Scilly, also known as Scillonia or the Scillies, lie 28 miles south-west of the tip of Cornwall. The archipelago contains 150 islands of which only five – St. Mary's, Tresco, Bryher, St. Agnes and St.Martin's – are inhabited. The total population is about 2000. The actual Scilly Isle itself is one of the smaller, uninhabited islands. According to legend, the Scillies are all that remain of King Arthur's mythical kingdom, Lyonesse, which is supposed to lie beneath the sea between the Islands and the Cornish mainland.

Bodmin and Bodmin Moor

Bodmin is the county town of Cornwall, and at its geographical centre. Bodmin Gaol, which was still in operation until quite recently, is open to the public, who can view the dungeon and the execution block. St Petroc's Church, the largest parish church in Cornwall is named after its local founder whose bones are said to repose inside an ivory casket displayed in the church. The present Perpendicular building replaces the original construction and dates from 1469-72. Lanhydrock, a 17th-century country house standing in magnificent grounds, is 2 ½ miles southeast of Bodmin. The house and its ornamental gateway were completed in 1658. Bodmin stands in the middle of a desolate and beautiful moor, a sort of Dartmoor in miniature, which has many sites of archaeological interest. The Cheesewring on Stowe's Hill is a circle of huge granite slabs in strange formations which are natural, though an artificial support has recently been added to prevent the group toppling. The hill itself affords magnificent views across both coasts of Cornwall. South of the Hill is another stone ring, the Hurlers, but these were definitely placed there by human hands, and were probably connected with some pre-Christian rite.

Bovey Tracey

This village at the gateway to Dartmoor has a fine medieval church (14th and 15th centuries). Parke Rare Breeds Farm in the village has woodland walks as well as rare domesticated animals. Part of the building is the headquarters of the Dartmoor National Park Authority.

Brixham

Brixham occupies a special place in English history. King William of Orange landed here on 5 November, 1688 with a huge army, and successfully defeated James II. The so-called Glorious Revolution crushed the autocratic Stuarts forever. The inscription below the King's statue in harbour repeats William's pledge "The liberties of England and the Protestant religion I will maintain". Berry Head, a nature reserve and country park, a promontory on the eastern side of the harbour, protects Brixham from the full force of the Channel, as does the breakwater that extends nearly half a mile out to sea. A full-size replica of *The Golden Hind*, the ship in which Sir Francis Drake sailed around the world between 1577 and 1580 is anchored in Brixham Harbour.

Buckfast Abbey

Buckfast Abbey is one of the very few examples in Britain of a foundation that has been re-established on a site suppressed at the Dissolution of the Monasteries. The original Benedictine abbey was founded in 1018. In 1147, it was handed over to the Cistercians. After the Dissolution of the Monasteries in 1539, the building changed hands several times; the last owner decided it was beyond repair and pulled it down to use the stones for a Gothic mansion he built on the site. In 1882, the site was sold again, this time to a group of French Benedictines exiled in Ireland. They re-founded the abbey and in 1907 set about building a new home for it. The work has continued ever since, all of it the labour of the monks themselves, with the only outside help coming from the architect.

Buckfastleigh

This busy little town has many old textile mills and workshops that process the wool from Dartmoor sheep. The churchyard contains an extraordinary tomb with an iron grille over it. It is the grave of Sir Richard Cubell, said to be so wicked that the villagers built this contraption over the grave to stop his ghost escaping to haunt them! The Dart Valley Railway has a station at Buckfastleigh, decorated in 1920s and 1930s style. Hembury Castle is just a mile away. Hembury Hill is topped with an Iron Age fortress from which there are magnificent views.

Cotehele House

Cornwall's foremost stately home, and the first-ever National Trust property, is mainly 15th and 16th century, with a tower added in 1627. Cotehele stands near the River Tamar in eastern Cornwall, not far from Calstock, overlooking the river estuary. The house contains original furniture, armour and needlework. The gardens are terraced on several levels and there is a medieval dovecote. The outbuildings include Cotehele Mill which is in working order, Cotehele Quay on the Tamar and the restored sailing barge, the *Shamrock*.

Dartmoor

Dartmoor, declared a National Park in 1951, is the last great wilderness in southern England. It covers an area of 365 square miles and rises to a height of over 2,000 feet. Dartmoor Prison has greatly contributed to the notoriety of the Moor. It was originally built in the early 19th century to house French prisoners captured in the Napoleonic Wars. Not until nearly half a century later did it house criminals, who worked the local quarries. In World War I conscientious objectors were sent here and the prison is still in use, rising gloomily out of the mists that predominate in this lonely place. Dartmoor is full of remains of the country's earliest inhabitants, the Neolithic and Bronze Age peoples, in the form of barrows, cairns, stone circles and menhirs. The wild Dartmoor ponies have roamed the moor since at least the 10th century. They are rounded up once a year in the autumn and branded, but otherwise they manage to survive even during the dreadful winter weather. The native sheep have largely been replaced by Blackface and Cheviot breeds.

Dartmouth

The port at the mouth of the River Dart is the home of the Britannia Royal Naval College, established in 1905. It has many old buildings. These include two 14th-century houses, Agincourt House in Lower Ferry and The Cherub in Higher Street. The Butterwalk is an arcaded street of 16th and 17th century merchants' houses and shops. It was badly damaged in World War II but has been restored. The harbour, known as the New Quay

Buckfast Abbey, newly rebuilt by its monks (top).

Boscastle harbour, Cornwall (above).

The ruins of a tin-mining engine house near Redruth (opposite left).

Hound Tor, Dartmoor (left).

and built in the 16th century, and the 17th-century New Ground, north of the harbour, were protected by a now-ruined 16th-century fort and the 15th-century Dartmouth Castle. Bayards Cove has a picturesque cobbled quay.

Devonport

See "Plymouth"

Falmouth

The largest town in Cornwall has two separate bays, one an important fishing harbour, with quays, a dockyard and a yachting centre, and the other a seaside resort with the usual beach attractions. The sea approaches to the port, known as the Carrick Roads, are among the largest and finest open anchorages in the world.

Helston

A Saxon market town and one of the Stannary Towns, where the locally-mined tin was weighed and stamped before sale, Helston lies 12 miles east of Penzance and is the largest town in the Lizard Peninsula. It was a port until the River Cober became blocked in the 14th century and the town had to open a new harbour at Gweek. The beer served in Helston pubs enjoys a high reputation, as it is brewed on the premises using the purest water. Each public house has its own well. Two miles south of the town is Loe Pool, the largest natural lake in Cornwall, said to be the water into which King Arthur threw his sword, Excalibur. A sandbar, Looe Bar, divides the pool from the Atlantic.

Land's End

The tip of mainland Britain is a famous beauty spot, where visitors can watch the breakers dashing against the high granite cliffs and the rocks below. There is a lighthouse. The Land's End peninsula has 50 miles of spectacular coastline on which there are many resort towns, including St. Ives and Penzance.

The Lizard

This is the name of the Peninsula that juts southwards like a heel on the "toe" of Cornwall. It is laced with coves, with exciting names such as Dollar Cove, reputed to be the place where a Spanish treasure ship was wrecked in 1807. It has never been found. Gunwalloe Church, in the Cove of the same name, is the oldest in Cornwall, dating from 570 A.D. It stands only yards from the Atlantic breakers. The high ground of the peninsula is ideal for siting communications equipment. It was from Poldhu Cliffs that Marconi, then in Newfoundland, first received a trans-Atlantic wireless signal in 1901. A monument at Mullion marks the spot from which the morse transmission was made. Goonhilly Down, further inland, is dotted with mysterious dish antennae and other receiving equipment for monitoring communications, both public and secret. The Lizard lighthouse at Lizard Point is a famous landmark.

Plymouth

Perhaps the most famous port in England and the largest metropolis in the south-west, Plymouth consists of three towns, Plymouth, Stonehouse and Plymouth Dock, now known as Devonport. The port rose to prominence in the 16th century, mainly through its most famous son, Sir Francis Drake. Plymouth was a major port for exploration and colonisation. The Hoe is a limestone promontory between the inlets of Sutton Harbour and Millbay. The sea road facing the docks is known as Plymouth Sound. The Barbican, the old quarter of Plymouth, contains many picturesque inns.

Polperro

A typically picturesque Cornish fishing village and a former haven for smugglers. The village is closed to cars, so visitors travel by horse-drawn cart or use the shuttle minibus.

Princetown

The main settlement on Dartmoor began as an agricultural colony and despite its grand name is not a town but a village, 1400 feet above sea level. The Plume of Feathers Inn survives from the time of its founder, Sir Thomas Tyrwhitt, Secretary to the Prince of Wales. The land was donated by the then Prince of Wales, one of whose titles is Duke of Cornwall, much of the moorland being owned by the Duchy of Cornwall. The parish church was originally built by French and American prisoners, but has since undergone extensive rebuilding. Many of the Dartmoor prison warders live in the village.

The picturesque Cornish fishing village of Polperro (above).

Peninnis Head, St. Mary's, Isles of Scilly (right).

Plymouth Sound (far right, above).

St. Mary's in the Isles of Scilly (far right, below).

A summer's day at low tide, St. Mary's, Isles of Scilly (opposite).

St. Agnes

The Western Rocks off this island in the Scillies are famous for their wrecks. Ships that met their doom here include the flotilla of five vessels under Admiral Sir Cloudesley Shovel which foundered in 1707 with the loss of 2,000 men and the *Earl of Lonsdale*, wrecked in 1885. Many treasures have been recovered from the wrecks, including those from the *Hollandia* which sank off Gunner's Rock in 1743. The ship was located by divers in 1971 and the booty included valuable porcelain used as a ballast and rare gold Spanish-American coins The salvage from a French ship that ran aground in 1685 paid for the building of the church on St. Agnes. The ship's bell is the church bell. Bishop Rock Lighthouse was built in the mid-19th century and is still in use to prevent ships coming too near the coast. At low tide, the island is connected by a sand bar to the island of Gugh (pronounced "Hugh"). There are many standing stones (megaliths) on Gugh, the biggest of which is known as The Old Man of Gugh. Though Gugh is technically uninhabited, it has a post office, which it claims is the smallest in the world, and it issues its own stamps whose only practical use is as a surcharge to cover underpaid mail to St. Agnes. St. Agnes also boasts a sacred well called Sancta Warna.

St. Ives

A fishing port and market town on the Land's End Peninsula which has developed into a popular resort. It has an artists' colony, whose members have included the world-famous potter, Bernard Leach, and the sculptress Barbara Hepworth. The town also boasts the Barnes Cinematograph Museum, a major repository of early cinema history.

St. Mary's

The largest of the Scillies is only about two miles in diameter. Hugh Town is a haven for shipping from the fierce winds that blow through the area. It lies between the mid-18th-century Garrison and the main land mass. Star Castle, built for Sir Francis Godolphin in 1593 for the bargain price of under £1000, is now a hotel. The New Inn in Hugh Town has a map on the wall charting the wrecks of 2,000 ships known to have foundered on the treacherous rocks of the Scillies. The Longstone Heritage Centre on St. Mary's is an interesting guide to the history of the islands. Old Town Bay contains the graves of 120 people who lost their lives in the wreck of the *Schiller* in 1875.

St. Michael's Mount

This granite island lies in Mount's Bay, opposite Marazion, and rises 200 feet above sea level. It is about 20 acres in size and bears a striking resemblance to its counterpart in Normandy, the Mont St. Michel. The island is still inhabited by the St. Aubyn family who bought it in 1659, although it belongs to the National Trust. Most of the buildings are open to the public.

Saltram House

The largest historic home in Devon now belongs to the National Trust. It is mostly 18th-century, although there are traces of Tudor architecture. The main rooms were designed by Robert Adam, and the carpets for these rooms were woven locally at Axminster. There are many paintings by Sir Joshua Reynolds, who lived locally and was a friend of the Parker family who owned it.

Tintagel

A favourite spot for tourists, mainly due to its connection with the semi-legendary King Arthur. A path from the village leads to a headland whose cliffs rise 250 feet sheer above the Atlantic, and it was here that the castle is alleged to have been built, on an "island", which is actually a promontory connected to the mainland by a narrow isthmus. The Old Post Office is actually a rare example of a medieval domestic building and is now owned by the National Trust.

Torquay and the English Riviera

Torquay has been popular as a seaside resort, particularly with the elderly and retired, for more than a century. Nowadays, it is also noto-

Information

English Riviera Information Line
(Brixham, Paignton, Torbay, Torquay)
Tel: (0803) 211211

Cornwall Tourist Board
59 Lemon Street
Truro, Cornwall
TR1 2SY
Tel: (0872) 74057

The National Trust
Lanhydrock
Bodmin
PL30 4DE
Tel: (0208) 74281

Events

The festival season starts in Devon and Cornwall in late spring and continues right through the autumn. Activities range from county agricultural shows to village carnivals and fetes. In Devon, there is the Devon County Show in Exeter in early May and the Exeter Festival held in late May or early June.
The big event on Dartmoor, one made famous in an old folk song, is Widecombe Fair, held at Widecombe-in-the-Moor on Exmoor. You can join Old Uncle Tom Cobbleigh and all in the village on the second Tuesday in September.
Cornwall's best-known celebration is Flora Day in Helston, on 8 May, when the famous Flora or Floral Dance is danced through the streets and in and out of the houses and shops.

48 Td Te Tf Ua Ub
49
Uf
Ub Uc Ud Ue
46
47
48
49
ATLANTIC OCEAN
Seven Stones
Isles of Scilly
Round Island
St Helen
White Island
St Martin's
Cromwell's Castle
Bryher
New Grimsby
Higher Town
Tresco
Great Arthur
Great Canilly
North West Passage
Abbey Gardens
Eastern Isles
BANT'S CARN
Crow Sound
Samson
INNISIDGEN
HUGH TOWN
St Mary's
Star Castle
PORTH HELLICK
Scilly Isles-St Mary
Penzance
Broad Sound
St Mary's Sound
Annet
Smith Sound
Gugh
St Agnes
Western Rocks
Whitesand Bay
MAEN CASTLE
Longships
Sennen Cove
Sennen
Land's End
Gwennap Head
Trevose Head
Park Head
Bedruthan Steps
Mawgan Porth
Berryl's Point
Watergate Bay
Tregurrian
Trevelgue Head
Towan Head
Newquay Bay
Fistral Bay
NEWQUAY
ST COLUMB MINOR
Kelsey Head
West Pentire
Holywell Bay
Crantock
Trerice Manor
Penhale Point
Holywell
Cubert
St Newlyn East
Ligger or Perran Bay
Penhale Sands
Rejerrah
St Piran's Oratory
Perranporth
Rose
Newlyn Downs
Goonhavern
Bawden Rocks or Man and his man
Trevellas
Perranzabuloe
Zelah
St Agnes Head
St Agnes
Penhallow
Callestick
St Allen
The Beacon
Mithian
Mount Hawke
Tregavethan
Shortlanesend
Cornwall Coast
Porthtowan
Blackwater
TRURO
Portreath
Navax Point
Crane Islands
Reskajeage Cliffs
Illogan
Scorrier
Chacewater
Threemilestone
Godrevy Island
Twelveheads
Baldhu
Bissoe
Playing Place
REDRUTH
Kehelland
Gwithian
CARN BREA
Carharrack
Carnon Downs
St Ives Bay
The Island
ST IVES
CARBIS BAY
Connor Downs
Roseworthy
CAMBORNE
Lanner
Devoran
Feock
Perranarworthal
Angarrack
Barripper
Troon
Four Lanes
Penhalvean
Ponsanooth
Mylor Bridge
PENRYN
Hayle
Gwinear
Carnhell Green
Wendron Moors
Crowan Beacon
Stithians
Stithians Reservoir
Mylor
Carn Naun Point
The Carracks
Trendrine Hill
Halsetown
Gurnard's Head
Zennor
Towednack
Lelant
Trencrom Hill
Canonstown
Porthmeor
Cripplesease
Pendeen Watch
Morvah
MULFRA QUOIT
CHYSAUSTER
Bojewyan
MEN-AN-TOL
New Mill
Trewellard
CHUN CASTLE
LANYON QUOIT
Ludgvan
Crowlas
St Erth
St Erth Praze
Townshend
Leedstown
Praze-an-Beeble
Longdowns
Mabe Burnthouse
Rame
Edgcumbe
Porkellis
FALMOUTH
Penjerrick
Pendennis Castle
Falmouth Bay
Carnyorth
Trengwainton Gardens
Newbridge
Tremethick Cross
Botallack Mine
Cape Cornwall
St Just
Godolphin Cross
Godolphin House
Nancegollan
Poldark Mining & Wendron Forge
Relubbus
St Hilary
Longrock
St Michael's Mount
Marazion
Trescowe
Tregonning Hill
Crowntown
Wendron
Treverva
Penjerrick Gardens
Mawnan Smith
Glendurgan
Rosemullion Head
The Brisons
BALLOWALL BARROW (CARN GLOOSE)
CARN EUNY
Drift Reservoir
Drift
Kelynack
Land's End-St Just
Sancreed
Catchall
PENZANCE
NEWLYN
Perranuthnoe
Ashton
Breage
Brill
Porth Navas
Helford River
Mawnan
St Anthony-in-Meneage
Paul
Mousehole
St Clement's Isle
Cudden Point
Praa Sands
HELSTON
Gweek
Crows-an-wra
St Buryan
The Stone
Welloe
Trewavas Head
Flambards
Culdrose
Mawgan
Helford
Nare Point
MERRY MAIDENS
Boleigh
Porthleven
Loe Pool
Manaccan
Porthallow
TREGIFFIAN
Treen
Lamorna Cove
Mount's Bay
Garras
HALLIGGYE
Lizard
Newtown-in-St-Martin
Manacle Point
St Levan
Logan Rock
Berepper
Traboe
St Keverne
Runnel Stone
Cury
Cury Cross
Goonhilly Downs Earth Station
Goonhilly Downs
Lowland Point
Poldhu Cove
Poldhu Point
Mullion
Peninsula
Porth Mellin
Mullion Cove
Gwenter
Coverack
Mullion Island
Predannack Wollas
Ruan Major
Ruan Minor
Black Head
Vellan Head
Cadgwith
Kynance Cove
Lizard Town
Hot Point
Lizard Point
Hugh Town (Isles of Scilly)

Barnstaple
112
Va
Vb
Vc
Vd
Ve
Cornwall Coast
Tintagel
King Arthur's Castle
Trevalga
Boscastle
Marshgate
Bossiney
Trewarmett
Rockhead
Camelford
Davidstow
Tremail
Hallworthy
Treneglos
Warbstow
Canworthy Water
Troswell
Bennacott
Boyton
Brazacott
Bridgetown
North Petherwin
Ladycross
Yeolmbridge
Egloskerry
Langore
Launceston
Tresmeer
Downhead
St Clether
Trewen
Tregadillett
Piperspool
Polyphant
Lawhitton
Lifton
Liftonduwn
Wortham Manor
Cross Green
Broadwoodwidger
Stowford
Portgate
Allerford
Marystow
Chillaton
Kelly
Felldownhead
Milton Abbot
Dunterton
Longcross
Sydenham Damerel
Horsebridge
Latchley
Chilsworthy
Gunnislake
Calstock
Tavistock
Devon
Cornwall
Tamar
Roadford Reservoir
Newpark
Crowdy Reservoir
Lower Moor
Rough Tor
Rough Tor
Buttern Hill
Brown Willy
Altarnun
Five Lanes
Lewannick
South Petherwin
Lezant
Trebullett
Treburley
Coad's Green
Wesley's Cottage
Codda
Bodmin Moor
Bolventor
Trebartha
Kilmar Tor
Smallacombe
Downs
Dozmary Pool
Stowe's Pound
(The Cheesewring)
The Hurlers
Siblyback Lake Reservoir
Henwood
Rilla Mill
Upton Cross
Caradon Hill
Pensilva
Common Moor
Darite
Bray Shop
Linkinhorne
South Hill
Kelly Bray
Kit Hill
Stoke Climsland
Luckett
St Ann's Chapel
Dupath Well House
Cotehele House
Callington
Trevigro
Ashton
St Dominick
Newbridge
St Mellion
St Ive
Trethevy Quoit
St Cleer
Berry Castle
Warleggan
St Neot
Temple
Colliford Lake Reservoir
Cardinham Moor
Maidenwell
Blisland
St Breward
St Tudy
St Teath
Helstone
Trewalder
Tresinney
Treligga
Port Isaac Bay
Port Isaac
Portquin
Port Quin Bay
The Mouls
The Rumps
Rumps Point
Pentire Point
Long Cross Victorian Gardens
Trelights
Pendoggett
Tregeare Rounds
St Kew
St Kew Highway
Polzeath
St Endellion
St Minver
Pityme
Rock
Chapel Amble
Padstow
Padstow Bay
Hayle Bay
Camel
Kelly
Bodieve
Royal Cornwall
Egloshayle
Wadebridge
St Breock
St Mabyn
Pencarrow House
Helland
Bodmin
Cardinham
Mount
Ley
Doublebois
Dobwalls
Dobwalls Theme Park
Liskeard
Merrymeet
Quethiock
Menheniot
Blunts
Little Petherick
St Issey
Tredinnick
The Longstone
St Breock Downs
Nine Maidens
Winnards Perch
Burlawn
Lane-end
Dunmere
St Petrock
Rutherbridge
Nanstallon
Withiel
Lanivet
Lanhydrock House
West Taphouse
East Taphouse
Tregonetha
Castle-an-Dinas
Columb Major
Belowda
Black Cross
Lockengate
Trebyan
Nat. Res.
Restormel Castle
Redmoor
Lostwithiel
Bridgend
Couchsmill
Herodsfoot
St Keyne
Horningtops
Duloe Circle
Duloe
Bylane End
Widegates
Trerule Foot
Tideford
Landrake
Trematon Castle
Landulph
Carkeel
Trematon
Saltash
St Germans
St Stephens
Plymouth
Hessenford
Polbathic
Sheviock
Antony
Torpoint
St John
Millbrook
Whitsand Bay
Cawsand
Rame
Rame Head
Antony House
Crafthole
Downderry
St Martin
Sandplace
Muchlarnick
Pelynt
Lanreath
East Looe
West Looe
Looe
Looe Bay
Looe Island
St George's or Looe Island
Talland Bay
Polperro
Porthallow
Trenewan
St Veep
Penpoll
Lerryn
Golant
Tywardreath
Lescrow
Fowey
Bodinnick
Polruan
Lantivet Bay
Pencarrow Head
Gribbin Head
Menabilly
St Austell Bay
Carlyon Bay
Par
St Blazey
Penwithick
Ruddlemoor
Stenalees
Penpillick
Luxulyan
Lanlivery
Bilberry
Roche
Bugle
St Michael
Hensbarrow Downs
Indian Queens
Fraddon
Blackmoor
Nanpean
Treviscoe
Brighton
St Stephen
High Street
St Austell
St Mewan
Charlestown
Porthpean
Coombe
New Mills
Ladock
Sticker
Hewas Water
Grampound Road
Grampound
County Demonstration Garden & Arboretum
Black Head
Pentewan
Mevagissey
Mevagissey Bay
Penare Point
Chapel Point
Polmassick
Tregony
Trewarthenick
Trevarrick
Gorran Churchtown
Gorran Haven
St Michael Caerhays
Boswinger
Maenease Point
Ruan Lanihorne
Veryan
Veryan Bay
Penare
Dodman Point
Carne
Portloe
Gerrans Bay
Nare Head
Eddystone Rocks
English Channel
(La Manche)

113
Exeter
Vf
Wa
Wb
Wc
44
45
46
47
48
Bridestowe
Sourton
Lewdown
Lewtrenchard
Lydford
Downton
Beardon
North Brentor
Brent Tor
Black Down
South Brentor
Mary Tavy
Willsworthy
Lynch Tor
Horndon
WHITE TOR
Peter Tavy
Great Mis Tor
Cox Tor
MERRIVALE
Merrivale
Lamerton
TAVISTOCK
Gulworthy
Sampford Spiney
Huckworthy Bridge
Higher Walreddon
Horrabridge
Dousland
Buckland Monachorum
Buckland Abbey
Yelverton
Sheepstor
Burrator Reservoir
Meavy
Bere Alston
Milton Combe
Bere Ferrers
Maristow
Clearbrook
Shaugh Bridge
Bickleigh
Lee Moor
Roborough
Tamerton Foliot
Plymouth-Roborough Airport
CROWNHILL
Plym Forest
ST BUDEAUX
DEVONPORT
STONEHOUSE
Cremyll
Hoe
Drake's Island
The Sound
Mt Edgcumbe House
Cawsand Bay
Plymouth Breakwater
Penlee Point
PLYMOUTH
PLYMSTOCK
HOOE
PLYMPTON
Saltram House
Down Thomas
Wembury
Wembury Bay
Great Mew Stone
Gara Point
Knighton
Newton Ferrers
Noss Mayo
Netton
Stoke Point
Beacon Point
Brixton
Yealmpton
Kitley Caves
Dunstone
Torr
Sequer's Bridge
Modbury
Ford
Battisborough Cross
Santander
Roscoff
Dartmoor
Dartmoor Forest
National Park
Dartmoor Wildlife Park
Hemerdon House
Sparkwell
Lee Mill
Lutton
Cornwood
Ivybridge
Harford
Ugborough Beacon
Bittaford
Westlake
Ermington
High Willhays
Hangingstone Hill
Cawsand Hill
Sourton Common
Cranmere Pool
Cut Hill
Sittaford Tor
Fernworthy Reservoir
Princetown
Dartmoor Prison
Walkhampton Common
Two Bridges
Wistman's Wood Nat. Res.
Postbridge
Bellever
Babeny
Hexworthy
Dartmeet
Corndon Tor
Venford Reservoir
Cater's Beam
Ryder's Hill
Dean Moor
Shell Top
Plym Ridge
GREEN HILL ROW
Abbot's Way
Penn Moor
Stall Moor
Shiple Bridge
Brent Moor
Ugborough Moor
Avon Dam Reservoir
South Brent
Harbourneford
Throwleigh
Wonson
Gidleigh
Murchington
Drewsteignton
Castle Drogo
Teign
PRESTONBURY CASTLE
CRANBROOK CASTLE
Easton
Chagford
Moretonhampstead
Frenchbeer
Lettaford
North Bovey
Manor House
GRIMSPOUND
Hameldown Tor
Warren House Inn
Widecombe in the Moor
Church House
Bonehill Down
Manaton
Becka Falls
Haytor Rocks
Haytor Vale
Rippon Tor
Buckland in the Moor
Poundsgate
Horridge
Ashburton
Holne
River Dart
Buckfast Abbey
Buckfast
BUCKFASTLEIGH
Dean Prior
Landscove
Broadhempston
Staverton
Dartington
Dartington Hall
Shinner's Bridge
Tigley
Belsford
Harberton
Avonwick
Lincombe
Diptford
Harbertonford
Bickham Bridge
Crabaton
Gara Bridge
Moreleigh
Halwell
Washbourne
Topsham Bridge
Brownston
Dunsford
Doccombe
Bridford
Dunchideock
Doddiscombsleigh
Higher Ashton
Kennick Reservoir
Tottiford Reservoir
Trenchford Reservoir
Combe
Lower Ashton
Hennock
Whiteway House
Lustleigh
Bovey Tracey
Nat. Res.
Brimley
Chudleigh
Chudleigh Knighton
Heathfield
Ugbrooke House
Ideford
Luton
Stover
Drumbridge
Teigngrace
Kingsteignton
Bickington
Sigford
Caton
Rew
Woodland
NEWTON ABBOT
Bradley Manor
Wolborough
West Ogwell
Denbury
Abbotskerswell
Kingskerswell
Ipplepen
Compton
Compton Castle
Marldon
Red Post
Berry Pomeroy
Berry Pomeroy Castle
Blagdon
TOTNES
Collaton St Mary
Ashprington
Cornworthy
Stoke Gabriel
Galmpton
Dittisham
Downton
Hemborough Post
Britannia Royal Naval College
Blackawton
DARTMOUTH
Kingswear
Dartmouth Castle
Coleton Fishacre
Mew Stone
Stoke Fleming
Strete
Slapton
Slapton Ley Nat. Res.
Stokenham
Start Bay
Torcross
Beesands
Hallsands
Start Point
Bowden
Cole's Cross
Merrifield
East Allington
Woodleigh
Loddiswell
Ashford
Aveton Gifford
Goveton
KINGSBRIDGE
Sherford
Chillington
Frogmore
West Charleton
Kingsbridge Estuary
West Alvington
Churchstow
South Pool
Ford
Kellaton
East Portlemouth
East Prawle
Lannacombe Bay
Prawle Point
Bolt Head
SALCOMBE
Sharpitor House
Malborough
Bolberry
Hope
Bolt Tail
BOLT TAIL
South Huish
Thurlestone
Buckland
Upton
Bigbury-on-Sea
Burgh Island
Bigbury Bay
Bigbury
St Ann's Chapel
Kingston
Ringmore
Ide
Shillingford St George
Countess Wear
Clyst
Topsham
Ebford
Exminster
Kenn
Kenton
Powderham
Powderham Castle
Starcross
Mamhead
Ashcombe
Cockwood
Langdon House
Little Haldon
Dawlish Warren
DAWLISH
Holcombe
Bishopsteignton
TEIGNMOUTH
Shaldon
Combeinteignhead
MILBER
Stokeinteignhead
Coffinswell
Babbacombe
BARTON
BABBACOMBE
TORQUAY
Kent's Cavern
Hope's Nose
Torre Abbey
COCKINGTON
Kirkham House
TORBAY
PAIGNTON
Oldway Mansion
Tor Bay
Nat. Res.
Goodrington
Alderney, Jersey Guernsey (seasonal)
Berry Head
BRIXHAM
St Mary Bay
Sharkham Point
Churston Ferrers
Raddicombe
Boohay
Scabbacombe Head
ENGLISH CHANNEL
(LA MANCHE)
Liskeard
Bodmin

rious as the setting for the dreadful hotel featured in the television comedy series "Fawlty Towers". Much of the architecture is 19th century, since the town was popularised by the Victorians. Alfred Lord Tennyson considered it to be "the loveliest sea-village in England". It has a rather continental air, with its many palm trees, and likes to be compared to Monte Carlo.

Tresco

This is also the most interesting of the Scillies as well as the most sheltered island, protected from the fierce Atlantic winds by the island of Bryher. King Charles Castle is a ruin, of which only a few stones remain. Cromwell's Castle stands on a rocky promontory in the north-west of the island. Tresco owes its development to an eccentric Englishman called Augustus John Smith who moved here in 1834 and immediately set himself up as a sort of dictator. Smith was an enthusiastic botanist and gardener and he set about taming the wild vegetation of the island, as well as the local inhabitants. He created the magnificent Abbey Gardens, a 12-acre sub-tropical paradise amid the romantic ruins of a Benedictine Abbey, containing as many as 4,000 varieties of exotic plants from all over the world. Smith also founded the Valhalla Museum of ship's figureheads. The nearby island of Samson, now uninhabited, was once a prison colony. St. Martin's, north-east of Tresco, is famous for its fine beaches and its Bronze and Iron Age remains. The disused Bryher Lighthouse is one of the earliest ever built, erected in 1680. Its fire basket is in the Abbey Gardens, on Tresco. Bryher has no paved roads and only one hotel in the quaintly-named Hell Bay, as well as beautiful secluded beaches.

Truro

A cathedral city and the administrative centre of Cornwall. This was once a Stannary town and a busy port until its trade was taken over by Falmouth. There are handsome Georgian thoroughfares, interspersed with narrow alleys through which rivulets run (one of them is named Squeezeguts!). Truro Cathedral is less than 100 years old. The foundation stone was laid in 1880 and the church was only completed in 1910. However, parts of the 16th-century parish church of St. Mary, which was pulled down to make way for it, have been incorporated into the building.

Sub-tropical vegetation in the Abbey Gardens, Tresco, Isles of Scilly (top left).

Figureheads at the museum in the Abbey Gardens, Tresco (top right).

Tintagel, the path to Arthur's Seat (above).

Truro cathedral, Cornwall (left).

WALES

North Wales is famous for its mountainous peaks and rugged landscapes, for Snowdonia and the slate quarries. South Wales has the Valleys, where the slag heaps and rusting pit-head gear of the coal mines still dominate the landscape. South Wales also has its scenic beauties, the Black Mountains and the Gower Peninsula. Between North and South, there are the Welsh Borders, whose rushing streams and lush vegetation have created so many beauty spots.

North Wales: Anglesey and Snowdonia

This area covers Britain's oldest and largest National Park, which includes the most beautiful mountain scenery in Wales, as well as Mount Snowdon, the highest mountain in Britain. There are attractions for everyone, from seasoned mountain-climbers to young children.

North Wales, with the Snowdonia National Park at its heart, is a wonderful place for activity holidays, from guided walks and rambles to pony-trekking, angling, riding and rock-climbing. There is plenty for children to do and the local people are very friendly. Although the locals speak English, for many it is a second language. Most place names are in Welsh. It is advisable to learn basic Welsh pronunciation, so that you know how to say the place-names for when you have to ask directions!

Anglesey

Much of this beautiful island, including the coastline at Plas Newydd, home of the Marquess of Anglesey, is a Conservation Area, administered by the National Trust. The island is connected to the mainland via two bridges which span the Menai Straits, both of which are miracles of engineering, so they are a sight in themselves. The Menai Suspension Bridge is one of two in Wales built by Thomas Telford in 1819-26. This was the only link with the mainland until Robert Stephenson built the Britannia Railway bridge in 1850. The bridge was reconstructed in 1938-41 but the original graceful design was adhered to. Menai Bridge is a little town on the Anglesey side of the bridge which has a lovely Museum of Childhood. Church Island, which is reached by a causeway, contains the church of St. Tysilio, built in the 14th century on the site of one founded by the saint in 630. This church features in the name of the nearby village of Llanfairpwllgwyngyll or Llanfair P.G. as it is usually called on maps, which has the longest name of any place in Britain (and maybe in the world!). The full name is Llanfairpwllgwyngyllgogerychwyrndrobwllllanty silogogogoch and was probably invented as a joke! Trains no longer serve the village railway station, with its station sign that runs the length of the platform, but it is now the tourist information centre for Anglesey. The village's other claim to fame is that the Women's Institute movement was founded here in 1915. Beaumaris Castle, around which the town of Beaumaris is built, overlooks the Menai Straits. The castle was built in 1295 and is considered to be one of the finest examples of medieval military architecture in Europe. The Timelock Exhibition in Beaumaris is a fascinating display illustrating the history of Anglesey and Beaumaris.

Bangor

This university town, home of the University College of Wales, boasts the oldest cathedral in Britain. The Cathedral of St. Deniol, which is only the size of a parish church, was founded in 525 A.D. but fell into disrepair in the 12th century. It was largely restored in the 19th century by Sir Gilbert Scott. Nearby, there is the Bible Garden, which contains every tree, shrub and flower mentioned in the Bible that can withstand the Welsh climate. The Museum of Welsh Antiquities illustrates the history of North Wales.

Betws-y-Coed

This famous beauty spot in the Gwydr Forest is sometimes choked with visitors in the summer. They come to visit the Fairy Glen and the waterfalls of Swallow and Conwy. The bridges over the Conwy are spectacular, especially Thomas Telford's suspension bridge. Nearby is Gwydr Castle, a 16th century Tudor mansion. The beautiful gardens contain many exotic birds. The chapel roof is covered with unusual paintings.

Blaenau Ffestiniog

Famous for its slate quarries, which are a popular tourist attraction, this is a hive of industry in the heart of Snowdonia. The Gloddfa Canol Mountain Tourist Centre uses the world's largest slate mine to illustrate aspects of the mining industry. The town also has a popular narrow gauge railway which links it to the seaside resort of Porthmadog.

Caernarfon (Caernarvon)

The historic capital of Wales is dominated by the magnificent castle overlooking the bay. It was one of the many built by Edward I in his conquest of Wales. Work started in 1283 and the building took 40 years to complete. It is here that Edward proclaimed his son the first Prince of Wales in 1301 and Prince Charles was also invested with the title here in 1969. In 1660, Charles II ordered Caernarvon Castle to be demolished so the building is now little more than a shell. The town walls of Caernarfon are almost complete. To the south-east of Castle Square stands the Roman Fort of Segontium, to which a museum is

attached, tracing the history of the Roman occupation of Wales.

Chirk Castle

Chirk is a magnificent medieval castle, completed in 1310. It was built to guard the Shropshire borders against invasion from Wales, but is now in the Welsh county of Clwyd, on the Wrexham to Oswestry road. The interiors and the beautiful gardens are 18th-century.

Holyhead

The capital of Anglesey stands on an island of its own, Holy Island, reached across a causeway 1200 yards long. Holyhead is ferry terminal for Dún Laoghaire (pronounced "Dunleery"), the port for Dublin, so much traffic passes through it. The Roman fort of Caer Gybi dates from the 3rd and 4th century, but is now part of the church of Caer Gybi founded by St. Gybi in the 6th century. Most of the present church dates from the 13th and 15th centuries. Holy Island itself has beautiful scenery and many ancient monuments.

Holywell

This industrialised border town near Chester contains the Well of St. Winefride whose allegedly curative powers have attracted pilgrims for 1300 years. The chapel, built in 1480, contains the waters; it is administered by the Roman Catholic Church.

Prestatyn and Rhyl

The two of the most popular holiday resorts in Wales are packed in summer with holidaymakers from Cheshire and Lancashire. Just south of Prestatyn is the beauty spot of Graig Fawr, a large limestone hill, which is covered in spring and summer with wildflowers that love limestone soil. It is administered by the National Trust.

St. Asaph

This is the smallest city in Britain and fittingly also has the smallest cathedral. The Cathedral is of rather plain design and is 13th and 14th century for the most part, though the tower was rebuilt in 1715. The Chapter Museum contains some very rare bibles and religious works, including Bishop Morgan's Bible and a Welsh-Greek-Hebrew dictionary, written by a local prodigy called Dic Aberdaron who is buried in the parish churchyard.

Snowdonia

This area of outstanding natural beauty, carved from extinct volcanos and ancient glaciers, has 14 peaks that are higher than 3000 feet, including Mount Snowdon, the highest peak in Britain. The national park extends for 50 miles from the coast to the River Dovey. The visitors centre at Penrhyndeudraeth provides useful information on hiking, rock climbing and other activities as can the National Trust centres in the National Park.

Wrexham

Wrexham is a border town and so largely English-speaking. The church of St. Giles is mainly 16th and 17th century and is very fine. Erddig, a handsome manor house near Wrexham, has most of its original furniture as well as interesting outbuildings and a walled garden. Erddig is outstanding for its authenticity. Few of the rooms have electric light and the Tapestry and Chinese rooms are only open on Wednesdays and Saturdays due to the extreme fragility of the silk and wool hangings. The Erddig Visitors Centre holds open days which include craft demonstrations in the summer.

Caernarfon Castle in the historic capital of Wales (opposite left).

Conwy Castle, once one of the most powerful fortification in Europe (opposite right).

Henrhyd Falls, one of many lovely waterfalls in North Wales (above).

The grim fortress of Beaumaris Castle (right).

Information

The Snowdonia National Park Office
Penrhyndeudraeth
Gwynedd LL48 6LS
Tel: (0766) 770274

The daily weather forecast for Snowdonia can be dialled on:
Tel: (0286) 870120

Celtica Tourist Information Centre
The Station
Llanfairpwll, Gwynedd
LL61 5UJ
Tel: (0248) 713177

Canolfan Aberconwy Centre
Promenade
Llandudnno, Gwynedd
LL30 1BB

Events

Wales is known as "The Land of Song", so it is hardly surprising that most of the festivals in the calendar are centered around music. This is just a sample of summer events in North Wales.

The Llangollen International Eisteddfod is held annually in July. Details from:

The Eisteddfod Office
Llangollen, Clwyd
Tel: (0978) 860236

Gwyl Beaumaris Festival of Music is held in late May and June at Beaumaris Castle, Anglesey. There is a Menai Straits Regatta and Beaumaris Castle Medieval Fair in July and August.

Tips

It is advisable to stay in a coastal resort, such as Barmouth, Porthmaddog (Portmaddoc) or the north coast resorts, as accommodation within Snowdonia is limited. However, there are plenty of youth hostels in the mountains (see General Information on the Youth Hostel Association). The narrow roads become choked with cars in the high summer, and parking is very difficult around Betws-y-Coed, Beddgelert, Llanberis, Blaenau Ffestiniog and the beauty spots.

Va
Vb
Vc
Vd
Ve
28
29
30
31
32
Dublin, Laoghaire
The Skerries
West Mouse
Middle Mouse
Carmel Head
Cemlyn Bay
Cemaes Bay
Llanbadrig
Porthllechog
Bull Bay
Amlwch Port
Point Lynas
Tregele
Cemaes
AMLWCH
Pengorffwysfa
Llaneilian
Llanfechell
Llanfairynghornwy
Bodewryd
Penysarn
Rhosgoch
Gadfa
Dulas
Dulas Bay
Llanrhyddlad
Carreglefn
Rhydwyn
Llanfflewyn
Rhosybol
City Dulas
Capel Parc
Brynrefail
Moelfre
DIN LLIGWY
BURIAL CHAMBER
Holyhead Bay
Llanfaethlu
Llanbabo
Llyn Alaw
Ceidio
Llanallgo
Llandyfrydog
Marian-glas
Benllech
Elim
Llanerchymedd
Maenaddwyn
Llanfwrog
Llanddeusant
North Stack
Holyhead Mountain
South Stack
Llaingoch
St Cybi
HOLYHEAD
Salt I
KINGSLAND
CAERGYBI
TY MAWR STANDING STONES
Penrhyn Mawr
Llanfachraeth
STANDING STONE
Llantrisant
Pen-llyn
Carmel
Capel Coch
Brynteg
Red Wharf Bay
Red Wharf Bay
Llanynghenedl
Llanfigael
BURIAL CHAMBER
Llechcynfarwy
Llanbedrgoch
Penrhos
Bodedern
Trefor
Tregaian
Dyffryn
Caergeiliog
Anglesey
Llangwyllog
Rhosmeirch
Pentraeth
Trearddur
Four Mile Bridge
Bryngwran
Llynfaes
Cefni Reservoir
Llanddyfnan
Pen-y-Garnedd
Rhoscefnhir
Holy Island
Bodior
Llanfihangel yn Nhowyn
Llanfairyneubwll
Bodffordd
Heneglwys
Talwrn
Llansadwrn
Rhoscolyn
Capel Gwyn
Gwalchmai
LLANGEFNI
Manor House
Penmynydd
Valley
Cymyran Bay
BURIAL CHAMBER
Ceint
Llandegfan
Rhosneigr
Cerrigceinwen
Llangristiolus
Llanfairpwllgwyngyll
MENAI BRIDGE
BURIAL CHAMBER
Pentre Berw
Menai Suspension Bridge
Malltraeth Marsh
Gaerwen
Llanddaniel Fab
BURIAL CHAMBER
Bethel
Trefdraeth
CHAMBERED CAIRN
Vaynol Hall
St Cwyfan
Llangadwaladr
PLAS NEWYDD
Waen-wen
Aberffraw
Hermon
Malltraeth
Llangaffo
Brynsiencyn
Y Felinheli
Llanddeiniolen
Bodorgan
Dwyran
Bethel
Penisa'r Waun
Niwbwrch
CASTELL BRYN GWYN
Menai Strait
Pont-rug
Llanrug
Malltraeth Bay
Newborough Warren
Nat. Res.
Llanddwyn I
Caernarfon Castle
CAERNARFON
Abermenai Point
Roman fort
Caeathro
Cwm-y-glo
Llanberis
Llanfaglan
Foryd Bay
Bontnewydd
Waunfawr
Caernarfon Bay
Llanwnda
Rhostryfan
Moel Eilio
2382
Betws Garmon
DINAS DINLLE
Llandwrog
Rhosgadfan
Groeslon
Carmel
Talysarn
Nantlle
2209
Llyn Cwellyn
Penygroes
Llyn Nantlle Uchaf
Pontllyfni
Llanllyfni
Garnedd-goch
2408
Nebo
Tai'n Lôn
Nasareth
Clynnog-fawr
Capeluchaf
CAERAU
Pant Glâs
Trefor
1712
Gyrn Ddu
Bwlch-derwin
TRE'R CEIRI
1837
Yr Eifl
Llanaelhaearn
Cennin
Bryncir
1190
Garn Dolbenmaen
Llanfihangel-y-pennant
Moel Hebog
2566
Pen-sarn
Llithfaen
Cefn-caer-Ferch
Golan
Dolbenmaen
CARN PENTYRCH
Carreg Ddu
Pistyll
Porth Dinllaen
Llwyndyrys
Llangybi
Rhoslan
Tremadog
Morfa Nefyn
Nefyn
GARN BODUAN
Fron
Llanarmon
Gell
Penmorfa
Edern
Boduan
Lleyn Peninsula
Rhos-fawr
Y Ffôr
Chwilog
Llanystumdwy
PORTHMADOG
Morfa Bychan
CRICCIETH
Borth-y-Gest
Rhos-y-Llan
Tudweiliog
Llannor
Abererch
Dinas
CAER CARADOG
Efailnewydd
Pen-ychain
1218
Garn
Rhyd-y-clafdy
PWLLHELI
Tremadog Bay
Penllech
Llaniestyn
Penrhos
Y Gamlas
Llangwnnadl
Sarn Meyllteyrn
Rhedyn
Nanhoron
Mynytho
Llanbedrog
Tŷ-hen
Bryncroes
Botwnnog
Nethlern
Rhydlios
Whistling Sands
Llandegwning
Inscribed stone
Rhoshirwaun
999
Llangian
St Tudwal's Road
Capel Carmel
CASTELL ODO
Llawr Dref
Abersoch
Llanengan
Rhiw
Rhydolion
Llwchmynydd
Aberdaron
Llanfaelrhys
Porth Neigwl Hell's Mouth
Sarn Bach
Bwlchtocyn
St Tudwal's Islands
Braich y Pwll
Uwchmynydd
Cilan Uchaf
Trwyn yr Wylfa
CARDIGAN BAY
Pen y Cil
Trwyn Cilan
Bardsey Sound
St Mary's Abbey
548
Bardsey Island Ynys Enlli
Dyffryn Ardudwy
Harlech
144

Wa
Wb
Wc
Wd
We
Great Ormes Head
Great Orme
St Tudno
Gogarth Abbey
LLANDUDNO
Puffin Island
Conwy Bay
Conwy Sands
Little Ormes Head
Penrhyn Bay
Penrhynside
RHÔS-ON-SEA
Penrhyn Old Hall
COLWYN BAY
Llanrhos
Tywyn
Llandudno Junction
Old Colwyn
Mochdre
Llansantffraid Glan Conwy
CONWY
Conwy Castle
PENMAENMAWR
Dwygyfylchi
Byffin
DRUIDS' CIRCLE
LLANFAIRFECHAN
Henryd
Roewen
Ty'n-y-groes
Abergwyngregyn
Crymlyn
Aber Falls
Llanbedr-y-cennin
Tal-y-Bont
Dolgarrog
Foel-Fras
Pont Dolgarrog
Carnedd Llewelyn
Llyn Eigiau Reservoir
Carnedd Dafydd
Trefriw
Llewelyn's Old Church
Llanrhychwyn
LLANRWST
Gwydir Castle
Capel Curig
Snowdonia
Swallow Falls
Nat. Res.
Devil's Kitchen
Pass of Llanberis
Carnedd Moel-siabod
Pont Cyfyng
BETWS-Y-COED
Pont-y-pant
Dolwyddelan
Dolwyddelan Castle
Forest
Conwy Falls
Ty Mawr
Inscribed stones
Penmachno
Park
Glanaber Terrace
Rhiwbryfdir
BLAENAU FFESTINIOG
Moelwyn Mawr
Tanygrisiau Reservoir
Bethania
FFESTINIOG
Rhaeadr Cynfal
Gellilydan
Amphitheatre
Migneint
Arenig Fawr
National
Llyn Celyn
Frongoch
Arenig Fach
Llyn Trawsfynydd
Trawsfynydd
Moel Ysgyfarnogod
Bronaber
Rhinog Fawr
Park
Coed y Brenin Forest
Y Llethr
Ganllwyd
Y Garn
Rhobell Fawr
Llanfachreth
Precipice Walk
Cymmer Abbey
Llanelltyd
Nannau
Penmaenpool
Bontddu
Caerdeon
Abergwynant
Cutiau
DOLGELLAU DOLGELLEY
Brithdir
Rhydymain
Oerddrws Pass
Aberystwyth
Welshpool
Bryn-y-maen
Llanelian-yn-Rhôs
Dolwen
Pentrefelin
Dawn
Betws-yn-Rhos
Graig
Bodnant Gardens
Eglwysbach
Gell
Pentre Isaf
Llangernyw
Rhos-y-mawn
Wenlli
Llanddoged
Pandy Tudur
Pentre-tafarn-y-fedw
Gwytherin
Melin-y-coed
Moel Seisiog
Oaklands
Nebo
Capel Garmon
CHAMBERED CAIRN
Fairy Glen
Glan Conwy
Pentrefoelas
Rhydlydan
CAMBRIAN MOUNTAINS
Gwynedd
Clwyd
Ysbyty Ifan
Carnedd y Filiast
Llysfaen
Llanddulas
Gwrych Castle
Rhyd-foel
PEN Y CORDDYN
Garthewin
Llanfair Talhaiarn
Llansannan
Plasisaf
Tan-y-fron
Bylchau
Aled Isaf Reservoir
Llyn Aled
Llyn Alwen
Mynydd Hiraethog
Alwen Reservoir
Hafod-Dinbych
Glasfryn
Cefn-brith
Cerrigydrudion
Ty Mawr Cwm
Gellioedd
Llangwm
Foel Goch
Glan-yr-afon
Cefn-ddwysarn
Rhiwlas
Sarnau
BALA
Llanfor
Llanycil
Bala Lake
Llyn Tegid
Rhos-y-gwaliau
Aberhirnant Forest
Cyffdy Farm Park
Mynydd Bryn-llech
Llanuwchllyn
Pont Rhyd-sarn
Bryn
Cwm Cynllwyd
Ty-nant
Aran Fawddwy
Llanymawddwy
Powys
Gwynedd
Kinmel Bay
RHYL
PRESTATYN
Meliden
Gronant
Gwaenysgor
Gwespyr
Talacre
Point of Ayr
Hilbre Island
Pen-y-ffordd
Llanasa
Mostyn
Glan-y-don
Trelogan
Gop Hill
Trelawnyd
Dyserth
MOEL HIRADDUG
Bodrhyddan Hall
Whitford
Downing
Mertyn
Carmel
Gorsedd
HOLYWELL
Brynford
Towyn
ABERGELE
Abergele Roads
Rhuddlan
Castle
Cwm
Rhuallt
St George
Bodelwyddan
Pengwern
Glascoed
St Asaph
Cathedral
Tremeirchion
Pen-y-cefn
Babell
Caerwys
Halkyn Mtn
Ysceifiog
Lixwm
Groesffordd Marli
Llannefydd
Bont-newydd
Trefnant
Graig
Afon-wen
Odol
Nannerch
Bodfari
Cefn Berain
Henllan
DENBIGH
St Marcella
Castle
PEN Y CLODDIAU
Llangwyfan
Waen
Llandyrnog
Cilcain
Ffordd-las
Llangynhafal
Moel Famau
Clwydian Range
Gellifor
Hirwaen
MOEL Y GAER
FOEL FENLLI
Groes
Llanrhaeadr
Pentre
Llanynys
Pant-pastynog
Meifod
Rhewl
Llanbedr-Dyffryn-Clwyd
RUTHIN
Cyffylliog
Bontuchel
BRENIG
Llyn Brenig
Nilig
Efenechtyd
Llanfair-Dyffryn-Clwyd
Graig-fechan
Clocaenog
Clocaenog Forest
Pentre-celyn
Pentre-llyn-cymmer
Clawdd-newydd
Derwen
Cross
Llanelidan
Llanfihangel Glyn Myfyr
Melin-y-Wig
Betws Gwerfil Goch
Gwyddelwern
Bryneglwys
Llantysilio Mtn
CAER DREWYN
Corwen
Carrog
Ty-nant
Maerdy
Druid
Glan-y-afon
Four Crosses
Plas Isaf
Glyndyfrdwy
Wenallt
Cynwyd
Moel Fferna
Llandderfel
Llandrillo
Pôlas Nantyr
Bryn Du
Berwyn
Pale
Pentre
Foel Wen
Llanarmon Dyffryn Ceiriog
Tyn-y-ffridd
Moel Sych
Milltir Cerrig Pass
Tan-y-pistyll
Pistyll Rhaeadr (Waterfall)
Y Clogydd
CRAIG RHIWARTH
St Melangell's
Pennant-Melangell
Llangynog
Pentre
Llanrhaeadr-ym-Mochnant
Tai-bach
Cefn Coch
Pentrefelin
Penybontfawr
Penygarnedd
Rhos-y-brithdir
Alltforgan
Cedig
Hirnant
Abernaint
Ty-uchaf
Llyn Efyrnwy Nat. Res.
Llanwddyn
Abertridwr
Tycrwyn
LLANFYLLIN
Llanfihangel-yng-Ngwynfa
Dyfnant Forest
Flint
Chester
Buckley
Wrexham
145

76
Southport
Wigan
Liverpool Bay
WALLASEY
BOOTLE
LIVERPOOL
ST HELENS
NEWTON-LE-WILLOWS
PRESCOT
HUYTON-WITH-ROBY
WARRINGTON
WIDNES
RUNCORN
BIRKENHEAD
HOYLAKE
West Kirby
HESWALL
BEBINGTON
ELLESMERE PORT
FRODSHAM
NESTON
HOLYWELL
FLINT
CONNAH'S QUAY
CHESTER
BUCKLEY
MOLD
NORTHWICH
WINSFORD
CREWE
NANTWICH
WREXHAM
RHOSLLANERCHRUGOG
LLANGOLLEN
Chirk
OSWESTRY
WHITCHURCH
MARKET DRAYTON
Ellesmere
Wem
MALPAS
Tarporley
LYMM
Great Sankey
Culcheth
Cadishead
Delamere Forest
Cheshire
Shropshire
Clwyd
Merseyside
Manchester Ship Canal
Dee
Mersey
Wf
Xa
Xb
Xc
28
29
30
31
32
Shrewsbury
Welshpool
Telford
146

Manchester
Hollingworth
77
Xe
Xf
Ya
Yb
Yc
TRETFORD
SALE
GATLEY
CHEADLE
CHEADLE HULME
BRAMHALL
DENTON
HYDE
Bredbury
ROMILEY
STOCKPORT
HAZEL GROVE
MARPLE
Disley
Compstall
Charlesworth
Chisworth
Broadbottom
Mellor
GLOSSOP
Chunal
Peak District National Park
High Peak
Kinder Scout
2088
Hayfield
Birch Vale
NEW MILLS
Chinley Head
Chinley
Edale
Barber Booth
MAM TOR
Speedwell Mine
Peak Cavern
Peveril Castle
Castleton
Hope
Aston
Bamford
Brough
Hathersage
High Neb
Redmires Reservoirs
Ladybower Reservoir
Derwent Reservoir
Howden Reservoir
Margery Hill
1765
Derwent Dale
Ashop
High Bradfield
Low Bradfield
Oughtibridge
GRENOSIDE
Worrall
SHEFFIELD
STANNINGTON
Dore
Totley
CARL WARK
Manchester Int. Airport
HANDFORTH
Styal
Woodford
Poynton
Higher Poynton
Newtown
Whaley Bridge
Chapel-en-le-Frith
Slackhall
Sparrowpit
Lyme Hall
Morley Green
WILMSLOW
Dean Row
Adlington
Adlington Hall
Pott Shrigle
Knolls Green
ALDERLEY EDGE
Nether Alderley
KNUTSFORD
Kirkleyditch
Prestbury
BOLLINGTON
Kettleshulme
Fernilee
Combs
BULL RING
Peak Forest
Dove Holes
Peake Dale
Upper End
Little Hucklow
Great Hucklow
Abney
EYAM MOOR
Foolow
Grindleford
Eyam
Froggatt
Nether Padley
Longshaw Country Park
Holmesfield
Moorhall
Wheston
Tideswell
Litton
Stoney Middleton
Calver
Wardlow
Ollerton
Marthall
Chelford
Monk's Heath
MACCLESFIELD
Rainow
Lamaload Reservoir
Shining Tor
1834
Errwood Reservoir
BUXTON
Wormhill
Miller's Dale
Blackwell
Little Longstone
Hassop
Baslow
Nether End
Wadshelf
Robin Hood
Chatsworth House
Hob Hurst's House
East Moor
Pilsley
Badgerbank
Capesthorne
Henbury
BROKEN CROSS
Macclesfield Forest
Sutton Lane Ends
Cat and Fiddle
Axe Edge
Harpur Hill
King Sterndale
Taddington
Chelmorton
Ashford in the Water
Sheldon
BAKEWELL
Haddon Hall
Rowsley
Beeley
Siddington
Withington Green
Warren
Highlane
Oakgrove
Wildboarclough
1659
Withington
Gleadsmoss
Marton
Rodeheath
North Rode
Flash
Hollinsclough
Earl Sterndale
Monyash
Over Haddon
Youlgreave
Stanton in Peak
Swettenham
Brereton Green
Brereton Heath
Hulme Walfield
CONGLETON
Eaton
Bosley
Wincle
Allgreave
Danebridge
Burntcliff Top
Longnor
Fawfieldhead
Crowdecote
Pilsbury
ARBOR LOW
Middleton
NINE LADIES
Two Dales
Arclid Green
Brookhouse Green
Astbury
Timbersbrook
Key Green
BRIDESTONES
Bridestones
Hightown
Rushton Spencer
Heaton
Upper Hulme
Newtown
Sheen
Hartington
Biggin
Elton
Winster
Wensley
MATLOCK
Matlock Bath
Tansley
Fourlanes End
Brownlow Heath
Little Moreton Old Hall
Cheshire
Staffordshire
Biddulph Moor
Rudyard Reservoir
Meerbrook
Tittesworth Reservoir
Thorncliffe
Upper Elkstone
Warslow
Hulme End
Pikehall
Brightgate
Bonsall
Grangemill
Cromford
Derbyshire
Hassall Green
Rode Heath
Scholar Green
BIDDULPH
Mow Cop
Harriseahead
Hurlton
Rudyard
LEEK
Butterton
Wetton
Alstonefield
Aldwark
Longcliffe
Bolehill
Middleton
Brassington
Hopton
WIRKSWORTH
Alderwasley
KIDSGROVE
Blackwood Hill
Brown Edge
Brindley Ford
Bradnop
Onecote
Grindon
Parwich
Tissington
Carsington Reservoir
Radway Green
AUDLEY
Talke
Norton in the Moors
Endon
Cheddleton
Longsdon
Ford
Waterfall
Ilam
Fenny Bentley
Bradbourne
Hognaston
Shottle
Butters Green
CHESTERTON
TUNSTALL
Stanley
Nat. Res.
Basford Green
Ipstones
Winkhill
Waterhouses
Calton
Blore
Thorpe
Kniveton
Kirk Ireton
Idridgehay
Halmer End
MILTON
HANLEY
Wetley Rocks
Blackbank
Cauldon
Atlow
Biggin
Shottlegate
Alsagers Bank
BUCKNALL
Werrington
Cellarhead
Consall
Froghall
Swinscoe
Mappleton
ASHBOURNE
Bradley
Hulland
Cross o'the Hands
Turnditch
Windley
Silverdale
Madeley Heath
STOKE-ON-TRENT
Kingsley
Whiston
Near Cotton
Weaver Hills
1220
Stanton
Hanging Bridge
Clifton
Keele
NEWCASTLE-UNDER-LYME
Madeley
CLAYTON
FENTON
Caverswall
Dilhorne
Oakamoor
Cheadle
Ramshorn
Farley
Alton Towers
Wootton
Snelston
Osmaston
Wyaston
Mercaston
Brailsford
Mugginton
LONGTON
LIGHTWOOD
Forsbrook
Blythe Bridge
Bradley in the Moors
Alton
Ellastone
Norbury
Shirley
Ednaston
Kedleston
Kedleston Hall
Whitmore
Baldwin's Gate
Trentham
Meir Heath
Rough Close
Barlaston
Draycott in the Moors
Upper Tean
Lower Tean
Denstone
Croxden
Rocester
Yeaveley
Alkmonton
Rodsley
Hollington
Longlane
Kirk Langley
Hill Chorlton
Knowl Wall
Tittensor
The Rowe
Beech
Fulford
Hollington
Fole
Marston Montgomery
Great Cubley
Longford
Thurvaston
Lees
Mackworth
Chapel Chorlton
Cranberry
Moddershall
Beamhurst
Waldley
Somersal Herbert
Boylestone
Church Broughton
Trusley
Radbourne
MICKLEOVER
Oulton
Stramshall
Cotwalton
Withington
UTTOXETER
Doveridge
Sutton on the Hill
Etwall
Burnaston
Podmore
Chatcull
Swynnerton
Standon
Millmeece
Yarnfield
Hilderstone
STONE
Garshall Green
Field
Bramshall
Blount's Green
Marchington
Sudbury
Sudbury Hall
Foston
Scropton
Hilton
Hatton
Willington
Findern
Wetwood
Slindon
WALTON
Aston-by-Stone
Milwich
Gratwich
Draycott in the Clay
Coton in the Clay
Tutbury
Egginton
Rolleston
Croxton
Sugnall
Sturbridge
Burston
Coton
Fradswell
Stowe-by-Chartley
Grindley
Kingstone
Marchington Woodlands
Hanbury
Stretton
Repton
Offley
Norton Bridge
Izaak Walton's Cottage
Whitgreave
Yarlet
Sandon
Gayton
Drointon
Newborough
Needwood Forest
Anslow
Anslow Gate
Horninglow
Newton Solney
Eccleshall
Chebsey
Salt
Weston
Abbots Bromley
Rangemore
BURTON UPON TRENT
WINSHILL
Bretby
Adbaston
High Offley
Wootton
Great Bridgeford
Marston
Hixon
Blithfield Reservoir
Tatenhill
Woodseaves
Ellenhall
Hopton
Seighford
Ranton
STAFFORD
Tixall
Admaston
Hoar Cross
Dunstall
NEWHALL
SWADLINCOTE
WOODVILLE
Norbury
Lawnhead
Coton Clanford
Derrington
Colwich
Colton
Blithbury
Hamstall Ridware
Hadley End
Yoxall
Stanton
Gnosall
Long Compton
Haughton
Allimore Green
Hyde Lea
Weeping Cross
Milford
Brocton
Nat. Res.
RUGELEY
Hill Ridware
Pipe Ridware
Morrey
King's Bromley
Barton under Needwood
Walton-on-Trent
Castle Gresley
High Cross Bank
Caldwell
Rosliston
Linton
Overseal
NEWPORT
Bromestead
Church Eaton
Coppenhall
Dunston
Bradley
Acton Trussell
Bednall
Cannock Chase
BRERETON
Handsacre
Orgreave
Armitage
Rileyhill
Alrewas
Croxton
Coton in the Elms
Lullington
Netherseal
Orslow
High Onn
Mitton
Levedale
Penkridge
HEDNESFORD
Longdon
CASTLE RING
Birmingham
Cannock
147
Lichfield
Birmingham
Chesterfield
Belper
Derby
Derby

Mid-Wales and the Welsh Marches

This is where the wild scenery of the north meets the rolling hills and valleys of the south. The landscape varies greatly from the wide sweep of Cardigan Bay to the grey slate quarries of Dolgellau and the wooded glades and quaint little tours of the Wye Valley.

The mid-Wales area of the Cambrian Mountains contains some of the remotest country in the British isles. untouched by road or human habitation. Also included in this section are the Welsh Marches, now the western strip of the English counties of Cheshire, Salop, and Hereford and Worcester. The word "March" is a Norse word, used by the Normans (who were of Nordic origin) to denote the border. William the Conqueror appointed Lords Marcher, loyal followers who became the earls of Chester, Shrewsbury and Hereford, to rule this part of the land. They only lost their autonomy in 1536 but the Council of Marches continued to function at Ludlow until 1689.

Aberystwyth

Home of the National Library of Wales and one of the seats of the University College of Wales, Aberystwyth was founded in 1277, when Edmund of Lancaster built a fortress here. It came into its own in the 18th century, when a spa was created after the discovery of sulphur springs. The castle is now a ruin, having been attacked and taken at least seven times by the Welsh. The National Library is open to the public and contains more than a million books. A funicular railway runs up Constitution Hill. Aberystwyth is the terminal for the Vale of Rheidol Railway, the only narrow gauge steam railway operated by British Rail, which runs between Aberystwyth and the Devil's Bridge, great fun for a day excursion.

Barmouth

This popular seaside resort, which has the longest beach and promenade in Britain, is a good centre for exploring the hinterland of Snowdonia. It came into its own in the 19th century and is a typical British seaside town. The panorama walk above the town has spectacular views over Barmouth Bay.

Builth Wells

This market town in the Wye Valley, once famous for its mineral springs, has a ruined Norman castle. This is where the Wye joins the Irfon; there are a number of rapids near the town centre.

Cader Idris

The isolated peak in the southernmost part of Snowdonia is a great favourite with visitors, including rock climbers, because of its unusual shape. It descends steeply on the south side to the geological fault which created the Bala Lake and Tal-y-Llyn. There are five recognised ascents. A good short route from Dolgellau is to ascend by the Bridal Path and descend by the Fox's Path. The Aran Route is a longer pathway along the ridge.

Cardigan Bay

The magnificent sweep of this bay is dotted with holiday resorts, such as Llanrhystyd, with its shingle beach, and Aberaeron. The latter is an elegant town of Regency houses with a sheltered yacht harbour. New Quay has a large sandy bay and plenty of caravan and camp sites. There is a wonderful view from New Quay Head. Cardigan itself, at the mouth of the Teifi, is a very old settlement. It was once a prosperous port until the river silted up in the 19th century.

Dolgellau (pronounced "Dol-gech-li")

This little town at the foot of Cader Idris has the typical grey walls and grey slate roofs of Wales. The seven-arched bridge over the river Wnion dates from 1638. The church of St. Mary is 14th century.

Devil's Bridge
The River Mynach enters a deep, wooded gorge here, creating a series of waterfalls, considered to be one of the finest beauty spots in Britain. The waters are spanned by three superimposed bridges. The topmost, iron bridge (1901) surmounts the stone bridge built in 1753. The lowest is the original Devil's Bridge, built not by the devil but probably by the monks of Strata Florida in the 11th century or earlier.

Hay-on-Wye
Most of this little town is just inside Wales, though the river that separates the two countries runs through it. It has been a market town since 1233, and holds cattle and sheep auctions. The town is famous, however, not for sheep but for bookshops. Hay boasts the largest second-hand bookshop in the world, scattered throughout the town, and there are many other second-hand book dealers here, making it the centre for the European antiquarian book trade.

Llandryndod Wells
This lovely spa town has been famous for its waters since the 17th century, but was at the height of its popularity in the 19th century. Sadly, the Pump Room closed in the 1960s, but the spa is now a National Health treatment centre. The lovely strawberry-pink and white buildings are a welcome relief from the drabness of so much Welsh slate-and-stone architecture The town is now a popular centre for conferences and is the administrative centre of the county of Powys.

Montgomery
This little town has predominantly Georgian architecture. It stands in the shadow of its ruined castle. The castle church was rebuilt in the 19th century.

Presteigne
This lovely town of old half-timbered houses on the River Lugg is often by-passed by tourists, but it is well worth seeing, since so much of its architecture is 16th and 17th century. Parts of the church are pre-Norman.

Welshpool
Despite its name, Welshpool is a very English-looking town of red brick buildings. Nearby Powis Castle was built in the 13th century by Welsh princes, but was heavily restored in the 17th century. Now administered by the National Trust, it has the finest collection of furniture and paintings outside museums in Wales. The gardens are particularly magnificent, with their four terraces and orangery.

Information
Tourism Development Office
Montgomeryshire Council
Severn Road
Welshpool, Montgomeryshire
SY21 7AS
Tel: (0938) 551255

Ceredigion
Marketing Dept.,
Lisburne House
Terrace Road
Aberystwyth
SY23 2AG
Tel: (0970) 612125

Tourism Office
Randorshire District Council
Gwalia
Llandrindod Wells, Powys
LD1 6AA
Tel: (0597) 823737

Events
The Royal National Eisteddfod of Wales is held at Builth Wells in the summer, and is one of the great cultural events of Europe. The same town is host to the Royal Welsh Agricultural Winter Fair in December. The Cilgerran Coracle Races are held on the River Teifi at Cilgerran in August.

Cilgerran Castle and the River Teifi (opposite).

The ruins of Strata Florida Abbey, near the Devil's Bridge (top).

Sign near the River Usk in Powys (above).

Cardigan Bay with Llangranog Cave, Dyfed (right).

138
Va
Vb
Vc
Vd
Ve
32
33
34
35
36
Bardsey Island
Ynys Enlli
548
Barmo
C A R D I G A N
B A Y
Llangelynr
Llanfendigaid
ABERYST
Llanrhystud
16
Llansantffraed
Llanon
Aberarth
4577
Pennant
ABERAERON
Monachty
4337
Foss-y-ffin
761
Cilcennin
NEW QUAY
CEINEWYDD
Llwyn-onn
Llwyncelyn
Oakford
Ciliau-Aeron
5342
Gilfachreda
Cross Inn
Llanarth
482
Brynog
Tal-sarn
Nanternis
Dihewyd
Ystrad Aeron
4342
Ynys-Lochtyn
Llwyndafydd
486
Mydroilyn
Temple Bar
Synod Inn
Llangranog
21
487
Caledrhydiau
Pont Creuddyn
Penbryn
Pentregat
4334
Plwmp
Cardigan I
Tresaith
Sarnau
4338
Cribyn
Gorsgoch
Parcllyn
Talgarreg
4337
Cemaes Head
Aberporth
Inscribed stone
Brynhoffnant
1062
Gwbert
Bwlch-y-fadfa
Aber
Capel Cynon
Verwig
Blaenannerch
Glynarthen
Castell Howell
Cwrtnewydd
Tan-y-Groes
Tremain
Rhydlewis
4459
Llanwnnen
Blaenporth
Ffostrasol
Pont-Siân
Cwmsychbant
Dre-fach
475
Alltyblaca
Penparc
4333
Betws Ifan
CARDIGAN
475
St Dogmaels
Pantgwyn
Troedyraur
Tre-groes
Rhydowen
Llanwenog
4338
Penc
Llanybydd
Beulah
Penrhiwpal
486
Moylcrove
Abbey
Llangoedmor
Ponthirwaun
Brongest
Maesllyn
487
4570
Prengwyn
478
Llechryd
Capel Tygwydd
4334
Capel Dewi
Monington
Castle
Llandygwydd
4541
Horeb
Trwyn y Bwa
645
4582
Cwm-Cou
Aber-banc
Maesycrugiau
Abergiar
Dinas Head
Tredrissi
Bridell
Cilgerran
Inscribed stone
NEWCASTLE EMLYN
Llandyfriog
Penrhiw-llan
CRAIG GWRTHEYRN
485
Mynydd Llanbyther
Trewllym
Llantood
Abercych
484
Pentre-cagal
Henllan
Llandysul
Llanllwni
1339
150
Milford Haven
Tenby
Carmarthen

139

Llandudno
Wrexham
Llanymawddwy
Wa
Wb
Wc
Wd
We
DOLGELLAU
DOLGELLEY
Penmaenpool
Abergwynant
Oerddrws Pass
Brithdir
Bontddu
Caerdeon
Cutiau
Arthog
Cadair Idris
Cae Afon
2213
Aberangell
Dinas Mawddwy
Minllyn
Cwm-Cewydd
Mallwyd
Waun-oer
2197
Dovey Forest
Minffordd
Aberllefenni
Corris
Corris Uchaf
Tal-y-llyn
Tal-y-llyn Lake
Nat. Res.
2928
2040
Llanfihangel-y-pennant
Castell-y-Bere
Abergynolwyn
Dolgoch
Tarrenhendre
2076
2189
Pantperthog
Garneddwen
Esgairgeiliog
Plâs Llwyngwern
Llanwrin
Cemmaes
Cemmaes Road
Dol fôr
Cwm-Llinau
Esgair Ddu
1523
Mynydd y Cemais
Dol Fawr
Pentre-celyn
Plas-rhiw-Saeson
Pandy
Llanbrynmair
Commins Coch
Abergwydol
Abercegir
Darowen
Tal-y-Wern
Penegoes
MACHYNLLETH
Plâs Machynlleth
Pennal
Cwrt
Derwenlas
Glaspwll
Pant-glâs
Aberhosan
Llyfnant Valley
Eglwys Fach
Cwm Einion
Dovey
Dyfi
Tre'r-ddôl
BEDD TALIESIN
Llancynfelyn
Tre Taliesin
Moel-y-Llyn
1708
Dolybont
Tal-y-bont
Nant-y-moch Reservoir
Drosgol
1806
Bont-goch (Elerch)
Bow Street
Salem
Penrhyn-coch
Pen-bont
Cwmerfyn
Capel Dewi
Capel Bangor
Goginan
Ponterwyd
Cwmbrwyno
1304
DOLGAMFA
Rheidol Falls
Capel Seion
Nanteos
Gors
New Cross
Llanfihangel-y-Creuddyn
Devil's Bridge
Mynach Falls
Cnwch Coch
Llanafan
Pont-rhyd-y-groes
Ysbyty Ystwyth
Lledrod
Tynygraig
1092
Trawsallt
1944
Ffair Rhos
Bronnant
Ystradmeurig
Swyddffynnon
Pontrhydfendigaid
Strata Florida
Abbey
Dibyn Du
1738
Llyn Teifi
Tregaron
1668
NANT-Y-MAEN
Bryn Crwn
1732
INSCRIBED STONE
Llanddewi Brefi
Bryn Brawd
1589
Llanfair Clydogau
Pen y Gurnos
1497
Llyn Brianne Reservoir
1445
Cellan
Pont-faen
CAER CADWGAN
Llanycrwys
Ffarmers
Mynydd Mallaen
1515
Ffaldybrenin
Pumsaint
Caio
Roman mines
Llandre
Cilycwm
Rhandirmwyn
Ystradffin
1120
Swansea
Pen Plynlimon Fawr
2467
Plynlimon
Eisteddfa Gurig
Source of Wye
1909
Hafren Forest
1488
PEN Y GAER
Geufron
Pant Mawr
Llangurig
1350
Bryn Garw
2003
Cwmystwyth
Geifas
1873
1798
Powys
Dyfed
Elan Valley
CAMBRIAN MOUNTAINS
Rheidol Valley
1758
Craig Goch Reservoir
Penygarreg Reservoir
Garreg-ddu Reservoir
Claerwen Reservoir
1827
1799
Drygarn Fawr
2104
Llanerch-yrfa
1644
1588
Abergwesyn
Tywi Forest
Cwm Irfon
1599
Mynydd Trawsnant
1695
Llanwrtyd
LLANWRTYD WELLS
CAE'R MAEN
Cynghordy
Crychan Forest
Tirabad
Llanwrthwl
Dylife
Pont Crugnant
Staylittle
Llawryglyn
Trannon
Pennant
Bont Dolgadfan
Llan
Bryn Amlwg
1602
1537
Talerddig
Plas Llysyn
Carno
Foel
Llangadfan
Dyfnant Forest
Llanwddyn
Abertridwr
Llanerfyl
Dolwen
1715
Nant yr Eira
Mynydd Waun Fawr
1444
Rhyd
1590
Y Fan
Llanidloes
Cwmbelan
Tylwch
Dolfach
Hirddywel
1921
1634
Pant-y-dwr
St Harmon
Rhayader
Gwastedyn Hill
1566
Llansantffraed-Cwmdeuddwr
1633
657
Elan Village
Nant Glâs
Llanyre
Castell Collen
1448
Drum Ddu
1761
Gorllwyn
2010
1572
Llanafan-fawr
Pentre-llwyn-llwyd
Llwyn Madoc
Beulah
Garth
Llanfechan
Cilmery
Tyn-y-graig
1448
Maesmynis
Llangammarch Wells
Cefngorwydd
Drum Ddu
1554
Mynydd Eppynt
Pentre Dolau Honddu
1559
1519
1419
Upper Chapel
Llaneglwys
Caerswys
Caersws
Maesmawr Hall
Trefeglwys
Cefn Carnedd
1007
Oakley Park
Llandinam
1692
Pentre
Mochdre
NEWTOWN
Y DRENEWYDD
Llanllwchaiarn
Llanmerewig
Kerry
Dolfor
1022
Cilfaesty Hill
1732
Llaithddu
Llanbadarn Fynydd
1736
1618
CASTELL TINBOETH
Bwlch-y-sarnau
Llanbister
Brynmelyn
Abbeycwmhir
Abbey
1657
Camlo Hill
1670
Llanddewi Ystradenni
Nantmel
Gwystre
Fron
Dolau
Llanfihangel Rhydithon
Crossgates
Penybont
Llandegley
LLANDRINDOD WELLS
1431
Howey
Disserth
Newbridge-on-Wye
Crossway
1440
Betws Disserth
Llansantffraed-in-Elwel
Hundred House
Cwmbach
Builth Road
Llanelwedd
Cregrina
BUILTH WELLS
Llanfaredd
1481
Rhulen
Llanbadarn-y-garreg
Llanddewi'r Cwm
1549
Alltmawr
Pencaerreg
1571
Aberedw
Llanbedr
Llandeilo Graban
TWYN Y GARTH
Erwood
Gwenddwr
Llanstephan
Crickedarn
Boughrood
Newport
1532
Llanwnog
869
Bwlch-y-ffridd
Bettws Cedewain
Dolforwyn
Tregynon
Brooks
Mynydd Clogau
New Mills
Llanwyddelan
Adfa
Llanllugan
Manafon
Pant-y-ffridd
Castle Caereinion
1193
Llanfair Caereinion
Melin-y-ddôl
Melin-y-grug
Four Crosses
Glascoed
Cyfronydd
1419
Dolanog
1084
Pontrobert
Meifod
Llanfihangel-yng-Ngwynfa
Pont Llogel
Tycrwyn
1168
Pen-y-Lan
Welshpool
Shrewsbury
Leominster
1806
1183
Bach
Tregaron
Capel Betws-Lleucu

152

140
Oswestry
Whitchurch
Newcastle-u.-L.
SHREWSBURY
TELFORD
WELSHPOOL
TRALLWNG
MONTGOMERY
TREFALDWYN
BISHOP'S CASTLE
Church Stretton
MUCH WENLOCK
Craven Arms
LUDLOW
KNIGHTON
PRESTEIGNE
KINGTON
LEOMINSTER
Tenbury Wells
HAY-ON-WYE
HEREFORD
Bromyard
Cleobury Mortimer
Clun Forest
Radnor Forest
The Long Mynd
Wenlock Edge
Brown Clee Hill
Shropshire
Powys
Hereford and Worcester
Dolgellau
Newtown
Aberystwyth
Brecon
Newport
Gloucester
152
103

Stoke-on-Trent
Stafford
141
Rugeley
Burton-upon-Trent
Burton-upon-Trent
Xe
Xf
Ya
Yb
Yc
CANNOCK
LICHFIELD
BROWNHILLS
ALDRIDGE
TAMWORTH
WOLVERHAMPTON
WALSALL
SUTTON COLDFIELD
WEST BROMWICH
DUDLEY
BIRMINGHAM
STOURBRIDGE
HALESOWEN
SOLIHULL
KIDDERMINSTER
STOURPORT-ON-SEVERN
BROMSGROVE
REDDITCH
KENILWORTH
WARWICK
DROITWICH
WORCESTER
STRATFORD-UPON-AVON
GREAT MALVERN
EVESHAM
Pershore
Alcester
Studley
Henley-in-Arden
Chipping Campden
Broadway
Ross-on-Wye
Gloucester
Chipping Norton
104
Cirencester
Chipping Norton
Nuneaton
Coventry
Coventry
London
Banbury

Pembrokeshire and South Wales

In South Wales, dramatic and deserted landscapes alternate with heavily industrialised areas. From the wild coasts of Pembrokeshire in the west to the Valleys of Gwent on the English borders, this is a land of sharp contrasts.

Abergavenny
The remains of Abergavenny Castle are south-west of the town. It was attacked several times, the last time in 1645. The town museum is situated in the Castle grounds. The Old Court is a house dating from 1500 and built into the town walls. St. Mary's Church in Monk Street was originally founded as a Benedictine Priory in the 11th century. The church contains many interesting features, including a 13th-century tomb of a knight, bearing his effigy.

The Black Mountains
This area of high moorland is part of the Brecon Beacons National Park. It extends southwards to end at the Sugar Loaf above Abergavenny. A network of paths extends over the mountains. Enthusiastic walkers can use the signposted paths to get as far as the Malvern Hills in England.

Brecon Beacons
These mountains , the newest of Britain's National Parks, are largely owned by the National Trust. The town of Brecon itself in the heart of the park is a good place to start the visit. It has an interesting church part of a priory which has been skillfully restored. The Brecon Beacons Mountain Centre, just off the A470 at Libanus, contains an exhibition and information on pathways, rock climbs and sporting facilities in the area. The Beacons themselves are best approached from Mountain Centre or from the A470. On clear days, the view from the top of Pen-y-fan is breathtaking.

Bridgend
This town at the gateway to Wales is a busy industrial centre. The most interesting feature is the Norman gateway. The prisoner-of-war camp hit the headlines in March, 1945 when 67 German officers managed to escape, though they were soon recaptured.

Cardiff
See "Historic Cities"

Gower Peninsula
One of the loveliest parts of Wales, the peninsula projects into the Bristol Channel from Swansea. Much of it is part of the Gower Coast Nature Reserve which belongs to the National Trust and Nature Conservancy Council. The Mumbles are two islets accessible at low water beyond Oystermouth. The Peninsula contains many caves in which the bones of prehistoric animals have been found.

Haverfordwest
The town is rather English in character, spreading along the slopes of a hill. The castle was built about 1120 A.D. for the Earl of Pembroke and was the scene of many battles. It has been used as a prison and a police station, but now houses the County Museum and Art Gallery.

The parish church of St. Mary (13th-15th century) is one of the three interesting churches in the city. The 18th-century Old Quays are well worth a visit.

Llantwit Major

This little village was once the most important centre of learning in British christendom. St. Illtyd founded a monastic school here which was attended by Christian luminaries of his own and succeeding generations, including St. David, St. Samson, Taliesin and Gildas. Llantwit's monastery was turned by the Normans into a cell of Tewksbury Abbey. The Church of St. Illtyd is most unusual in that it is actually two churches joined together The Old Church was rebuilt in the 15th century on the foundations of a medieval building and contains some Norman features. It contains a collection of Celtic Stones. The New Church has a 14th-century stone rood screen and a unique carving of Jesse and the Tree of David, showing how Christ is descended from King David. The town itself is full of old buildings, including Ty Mawr, a Tudor house.

Monmouth

The historic town, founded by the Romans, is an excellent centre for

Tenby, Pembrokeshire (opposite).

Monorbier Castle in Pembrokeshire (top).

The Dynosaur Park is a popular attraction at Dan-y-Ogof (above).

The Brecon Mountain Railway offers scenic tours of the Brecon Beacons (left).

Aberystwyth
Ue
Uf
Va
Vb
Vc
36
37
38
39
40
Rosslare
Strumble Head
Dinas Head
Trwyn y Bwa
Newport Bay
Tresinwen
Pen Caer
Llanwnda
Trefasser
GOODWICK
Fishguard Bay
FISHGUARD
Manorowen
St Nicholas
Brynhenllan
Dinas Cross
Llanychaer
Cil-rhedyn Bridge
Parrog
Newport
Berry Hill
Nevern
Tredrissi
St Brynach's
Felindre Farchog
CASTELL HENLLYS
CARN INGLI
PENTRE IFAN
Cilgwyn
Llantood
Trewllym
Bridell
Cilgerran
Castle
Rhos Hill
Newchapel
Abercych
Eglwyswrw
Llanfair-Nant-Gwyn
Boncath
Cilwendeg
Blaenffos
Bwlchygroes
Eglwyswen
Crosswell
Brynberian
Star
Mynydd Preselie
Nyfer
FOEL DRYGARN
Crymych
Tegryn
Foel Cwmcerwyn
Mynachlog-ddu
Hermon
Llanfyrnach
Pentre-galar
Panteg
Granston
Scleddau
PARC Y MEIRW
Pontfaen
Trecwn
Pembrokeshire
Abercastle
Porthgain
Trevine
Mathry
Castlemorris
Abereiddy
Llanrhian
Square and Compass
Letterston
Little Newcastle
Puncheston
CAS-FUWCH
Rosebush
GORS FAWR
Glandwr
Coast
Berea
Croes-goch
Treglemais
Treffynnon
Castlebythe
Tufton
WARRIOR'S DYKE
St David's Head
Whitesands Bay
Treleddyd-fawr
Tretio
Carnhedryn
Solva
Bishop's Palace
Whit-church
Middle Mill
Cathedral
Ramsey Island
Rhosson
St David's
Ramsey Sound
Nat. Res.
Abbey
CASTELL HEINIF
National
Welsh Hook
Wolf's Castle
Hayscastle Cross
Hayscastle
Llandeloy
Ambleston
Wallis
Rinaston
Reservoir
Maenclochog
Llangolman
New Moat
Llanglydwen
Cefn-y-pant
Cwm Mynach
Efailwen
Login
Llanboidy
Lys-y-frân
Llanycefn
Treffgarne
Spittal
Walton East
Penffordd
Pencwm
Newgale
Roch Castle
Wolfsdale
Leweston
Scolton
Inscribed stones
Llandissilio
Crosshands
Clarbeston
Bletherston
Henllan Amgoed
Roch
Folly
Rudbaxton
Clarbeston Road
Llanfallteg
St Brides
Park
Sompson Cross
Keeston
Camrose
Pelcomb Cross
Crundale
Gelli
Bethesda
Clunderwen
Llanddewi Velfrey
Cwmfelin Boeth
Whitland Abbey
Whitland
Llangynin
Nolton
Lambston
Wiston
Llawhaden
Castle
Robeston Wathen
CAERAU GAER
Druidston
Portfield Gate
Castle
St Mary's
HAVERFORDWEST
Uzmaston
The Rhos
Picton Castle
NARBERTH
Crinow
Lampeter Velfrey
Bay
Haroldston West
Dreenhill
Oakwood Adventure and Leisure Park
Cold Blow
Tavernspite
Llanddowror
Broad Haven
MERLIN'S BRIDGE
Boulston
Minwear
Templeton
Princes Gate
Red Roses
Little Haven
Walton West
Ludchurch
Talbenny
ROMANS CASTLE
Freystrop
Hook
Landshipping
Martletwy
Llanteg
Marros
TOWER POINT
Martin's Haven
Rose-pool
Walwyn's Castle
Tiers Cross
Yerbeston
Reynalton
Skomer Island
St Brides
Hasguard
Robeston Cross
Johnston
Llangwm
Loveston
Colby Lodge
THE LONG STONE
Rosemarket
Begelly
Kilgetty
Stepa-cide
Amroth
Marloes
Sandy Haven
Herbrand-ston
Steynton
Hill Mountain
Cresswell Quay
Cresselly
Jeffreyston
Broad Sound
Saint Ishmael's
Waterston
Houghton
Lawrenny
Pentlepoir
Saundersfoot
Westdale Bay
Dale
MILFORD HAVEN
NEYLAND
Burton
Upton Castle
West Williamston
Redberth
East Williamston
Skokholm Island
Milford Haven
Llanstadwell
Cosheston
Carew Castle
Sageston
New Hedges
St Ann's Head
PEMBROKE DOCK
Pwllcrochan
Carew
TENBY
Carma
Angle
Angle Bay
Rhoscrowther
Monkton Priory
Pembroke Castle
Palace
Gumfreston
St Mary's
Rosslare
Hungleton
Lamphey
St Florence
Tudor Merchants House
Penally
Cross
Freshwater West
PEMBROKE
PENFRO
Hodgeston
Jameston
Castlemartin
Freshwater East
Castle
Manorbier
Lydstep
Caldey Sound
Warren
St Twynnells
St Petrox
Cheriton
Monastery and Priory
Caldey Island
Merrion
HAROLD STONE
Stackpole
Linney Head
Crow Rock
Stacks Rocks
Bosherston
St Govan's Chapel
St Govan's Head
St Gowan
A T L A N T I C
O C E A N

144
145
112
Aberystwyth
Aberystwyth
Newton
Vd
Ve
Vf
Wa
Wb
Cwm-Cou
Llandyfriog
Aberbanc
Horeb
Capel Dewi
Maesycrugiau
Abergiar
Penrhiw-llan
Henllan
Llandysul
CRAIG GWRTHEYRN
NEWCASTLE EMLYN
Pentre-cagal
Llangeler
Pentre-cwrt
Llanfihangel-ar-arth
Llanllwni
Mynydd Llanybydder
Rhydcymerau
Llidiad-Nenog
Felindre
Saron
Bancyffordd
New Inn
Capel Iwan
Moelfre
Cwmpengraig
Pencader
Gwyddgrug
Gwernogle
Abergorlech
Rhos
Dolgran
Forest of Brechfa
Cwm Morgan
Alltwalis
Cwmduad
Hermon
Llanllawddog
Brechfa
Llanfynydd
Esgair
Llanpumsaint
Pontarsais
Horeb
Plas
Capel Isaac
Pen-y-bont
Blaen-y-coed
Cynwyl Elfed
Rhydargaeau
Pentglas Hall
Talog
Bwlchnewydd
Newchurch
Bronwydd Arms
tourist rlw.
Felingwmuchaf
Llanfihangel-uwch-Gwili
Abernant
Ffynnon-ddrain
Capel Gwyn
Pontargothi
Court Henry
Broadoak
Pentrefelin
Abergwili
Nantgaredig
Felindre
Llangathen
Merthyr
CARMARTHEN CAERFYRDDIN
St Peters
Llangunnor
Capel Dewi
Llanegwad
Dryslwyn
Castle
Llanarthney
Golden Grove
Gelli Aur
Paxton's Tower
Bron y-Gaer
Sarnau
Pensarn
Bancyfelin
Llanllwch
Cwmffrwd
Croesyceilog
Llanddarog
Porthyrhyd
Maesybont
Carmel
Pentre-Gwenlais
Llandybie
Llangynog
Llangain
Cwmisfael
Llangendeirne
Heol-ddu
Cefneithin
Gorslas
Pen-y-groes
Crwbin
Drefach
MYNYDD LLANGYNDEYRN
Cross Hands
AMMANFORD
Tycroes
Llanybri
Llandefaelog
Pontantwn
Pontyberem
Tumble
Capel Hendre
Llanstephan
Castle
Ferryside
Meinciau
Broadway
Broadway
St Ishmael
Llansaint
Pontyates
Pont Henri
Llannon
Sylen
Cynheidre
KIDWELLY
Castle
Gwendraeth
Carway
Trimsaran
Five Roads
Cefn Sidan Sands
Pembrey Forest
Pembrey
BURRY PORT
Pwll
Felinfoel
Llangennech
LLANELLI
Bynea
Bryn
GORSEINON
Gorseinon
Hendy
Fforest
Pontardulais
Pentrebach
Grovesend
Pontlliw
Penllergaer
Whiteford Point
Loughor Llwchwr
Crofty
Pen-clawdd
Gowerton
FFOREST-FACH
Llanmorlais
Three Crosses
Dunvant
Waunarlwydd
Llanmadoc
Cheriton
Landimore
SAMPSON'S JACK
FORT
Llanrhidian
Burry Holms
Llangennith
Burry Green
Oldwalls
Rhossili
Bay
G
o
w
e
r
ARTHUR'S STONE
LONG CAIRN
Ilston
Upper Killay
Llanddewi
Reynoldston
Parkmill
Bishopston
Rhossili
Middleton
Knelston
Oystermouth Castle
Worms Head Penrhyn-gwyr
Nat. Res.
Sourlage
Penrice
Nicholaston
Southgate
Newton
Mewstade Bay
Paviland Caves
Port-Eynon
Horton
Oxwich
Oxwich Bay
Nat. Res.
Culver Hole
Port-Eynon Point
SKETTY
Clyne Gardens
Guildhall
SWANSEA ABERTAWE
Black Pill
West Cross
The Mumbles
Swansea Bay
Nat. Res.
The Mumbles
Cork
Pumsaint
Roman mines
Caio
Llandre
Cilycwm
Aber Bowlan
Porthyrhyd
Crugybar
Llansawel
Siloh
LLANDOVERY
Cynghordy
Pentre-ty-gwyn
Babel
Edwinsford
Talley
Abbey
Halfway
Llanwrda
Cwmdu
Llansadwrn
Halfway
Cilgwyn
Myddfai
Llangadog
Glan-Sefin
Felindre
Abermarlais
Usk Reservoir
Dyfed
Powys
Manordeilo
Dyffryn Ceidrych
Bethlehem
Twynllanan
Llanddeusant
Salem
Rhosmaen
CARN GOCH
Penybanc
Dyffryn Tywi
LLANDEILO
Capel Gwynfe
Fan Brycheiniog
Ffairfach
Dynevor Castle
The Black Mountain
Trapp
Carreg Cennen Castle
Llandyfan
Brynamman
Glanaman
Garnant
Pontamman
Betws
Lower Brynamman
Gwaun-Cae-Gurwen
Cwmllynfell
Cwmgiedd
Cwm-twrch Isaf
Caer-Lan
Abercraf
Caehopkin
Ystradgynlais
Gwmgors
Pantyffynnon
Dyfed
West Glamorgan
Ystalyfera
Gurnos
CARN LLECHART
Godre'r-graig
Swansea Valley
Seven Sisters
Rhyd-y-fro
Llangiwg
Pontardawe
Cilybebyll
Crynant
Alltwen
Rhos
Craigcefnparc
Felindre
Vale of Neath
Resolven
Melincourt
Clydach
Vardre
Ynystawe
Glais
Cilfrew
Pant-lasau
Llangyfelach
Bryn-coch
RHYDDING
Birchgrove
Tonna
Llansamlet
SKEWEN
Abbey
NEATH
Tonmawr
Pentre-dwr
Cwm
Bon-y-maen
Briton Ferry
Baglan
Pwll-y-glaw
Afan Argoed
Cwmafan
Bryn
PORT TALBOT
ABERAVON
Margam
Margam Park
Eglwys Nunydd Reservoir
Nat. Res.
Cornelly
Kenfig
PORTHCAWL
Brecon
Brecon
Merthyr Tydfil
Bridgend
Bridgend
B R I S T O L   C H A N N E L
Carmarthen Bay
M4
E30
M4
A40
A48
A483
A484
A465
A4067
A4070
A4118
A4138
A4242
A4296
A4300
A4301
A4306
A4308
A4309
A4310
A4317
A4069
A4068
A4109
A4107
A4287
A4282
A4302
A4337
A4336
A4333
A4459
A4484
A475
A476
A477
A482
A485
A474
A4066
A4298
A4312
A4297
A4271
A4247
A4436
A4291
A4434
1339
1070
1173
1042
955
1079
1120
1207
1443
1360
2630
2076
1617
1580
2022
1832
861
895
933
1226
1113
1370
1121
632
617
1100
1030

145
146
113
Wc
Wd
We
Wf
Xa
36
37
38
39
40
Aberystwyth
Hereford
Swansea
Tirabad
Upper Chapel
Merthyr Cynog
Llaneglwys
Boughrood
Llyswen
Cwmbach
Glasbury
Three Cocks
Llanigon
Hinton
Peterchurch
Vowchurch
Turnastone
Hay Bluff
Craswall
Blaendyryn
Llanfihangel Nant Brân
Pont-faen
Lower Chapel
Ponde
Llandefalle
Bronllys
Velindre
Tregoyd
Twmpa
Llanelieu
Talgarth
Rhos Dirion
Capel-y-ffin
Michaelchurch Escley
Upper Maes-coed
Middle Maes-coed
St Margarets
Bacton
Lower Maes-coed
Llandeilo'r-Fan
Pentre-bach
Pwllgloyw
Garthbrengy
Llandefaelog
Talachddu
Felinfach
Llanfilo
Trefeca
Llanddew
Battle
Tredomen
Llandefaelog-tre'r-graig
Pengenffordd
CASTELL DINAS
Llanveynoe
Longtown
Clodock
The Black Mountains
Mynydd Bwlch-Groes
Llywel
Trecastle
Sennybridge
Defynnog
Pentre'r-felin
Trallong
Aberscir
PEN Y CRUG Gaer
BRECON
Llechfaen
Llanywern
Llangorse
Waun Fâch
Llanthony
Rowlestone
Llanspyddid
Ffrwdgrech
Cefn Cantref
Llanfrynach
Scethrog
Talyllyn
Llangorse Lake
Llangasty-Talyllin
Cathedine
Walterstone
Oldcastle
Gwmyoy
Pandy
Libanus
Pencelli
ALLT YR ESGAIR
Llansantffraed
Bwlch
Cwmdu
Pen Cerrig-calch
TWYN Y GAER
Partrishaw
Pont Newydd
Llanbedr
Heol Senni
Crai
Glasfynydd Forest
Cray Reservoir
Brecon Beacons
Pen y Fan
Bryn
Aber Village
Talybont-on-Usk
Gaer
Tretower
CRUG HYWEL
Stranton
Forest Coal Pit
Llanvihangel Crucorney
Llangattock Lingoed
Brecon Beacons National Park
CERRIG DUON
Forest Fawr
MAEN LLIA
Fan Fawr
Ystradfellte Reservoir
Neuadd Reservoirs
Talybont Reservoir
Abercynafon
Llangynidr
Crickhowell
Llangenny
Ffawyddog
Llangattock
Bettws
Ysgyryd Fawr
Llanvetherine
ABERGAVENNY Y-FENNI
Dan-yr-Ogof
Penwyllt
Craig-y-nos
Pen-y-cae
Aber-Llia
Ystradfellte
Mynydd Llangynidr
Mynydd Llangatwg
Gilwern
Croes Hywel
Llanddewi Rhydderch
Llanvapley
Henrhyd Falls
Porth yr Ogof
Pontsticill Reservoir
Trefil
Clydach
Llanelly
Blackrock
Govilon
Llanfoist
Coed Morgan
Coelbren
Pontneathvaughan
Llwyn-on Reservoir
Pontsticill
Vaynor
Tafarnaubach
Llechryd
Rassau
Beaufort
BRYN-MAWR
NANTYGLO
BLAENAVON
Llanellen
Llanover
Llanvihangel Gobion
Dyffryn Cellwen
Pontneddfechan
Glyn Neath
Aber pergwm
Vale of Neath
Penderyn
Hirwaun
Cefn-coed-y-cymmer
DOWLAIS
MERTHYR TYDFIL
RHYMNEY
TREDEGAR
EBBW VALE
BLAINA
Coity Mountain
Rhyd-y-meirch
Nant-y-derry
Bettws Newydd
Pontlottyn
Abertysswg
New-Tredegar
Cwm
ABERTILLERY
Varteg
Pont Walby
Blaengwrach
Cwmgwrach
Rhigos
Ochr-y-mynydd
Fochriw
Pentrebach
CARN BUGAIL
Manmoel
ABERSYCHAN
Penperlleni
Croes y pant
Monkswood
Resolven
Cwmdare
Llwydcoed
Aber-nant
Abercanaid
Troedyrhiw
Bedlinog
Deri
Hollybush
Cwm Frrwd-oer
Trevethin
ABERDARE ABERDAR
ABERAMAN
CWMBACH
Aberfan
Saint Illtyd
Llanhilleth
Little Mill
Glascoed
PONTYPOOL
Glyncorrwg
Tynewydd
Cwmaman
Merthyr Vale
BARGOED
ABER-BARGOED
Argoed
OAKDALE
Trinant
GRIFFITHS-TOWN
Llanbadoc
TREHERBERT
Maerdy
MOUNTAIN ASH
FERNDALE
GILFACH
BLACKWOOD
Crumlin
Mynydd Maen
NEWBRIDGE
Coed-y-paen
Llangybi
Llandegveth
Cymmer
Blaengwynfi
Abergwynfi
CRUG YR AFAN
TREORCHY
RHONDDA
Treharris
Trelewis
Gelligaer
Hengoed
Nelson
Llanwonno
ABERCYNON
PONTLLAN-FRAITH
CWMBRAN
ABERCARN
Henllys
Llanfrechfa
Ponthir
Tredunnock
Duffryn
Croeserw
Caerau
Dyffryn
Nantyffyllon
Blaengarw
Nant-y-moel
Cwmparc
LLWYNYPIA
YSTRAD
CLYDACH VALE
TONYPANDY
Tylorstown
Wattstown
Ynyshir
PORTH
Ynysybwl
Llanfabon
YSTRAD MYNACH
Maesycwmmer
Croes-y-mwyalch
Castel-y-bwch
RISCA
BETTWS
CAERLEON
Roman Fort
Amphitheatre
MALPAS
PONTYCYMER
MAESTEG
Price Town
Aber
Ogmore Vale
PENYGRAIG
Ogmore Forest
Gilfach Goch
HOPKINS-TOWN
COEDPEN-MAEN
Trehafod
PONTYPRIDD
Tonyrefail
TREFOREST
GLYNTAFF
Cilfynydd
Senghenydd
Llanbradach
Abertridwr
Ynysddu
Cwmfelinfach
Wattsville
BEDWAS
MACHEN
Lower Machen
Llangynwyd
Pont Rhyd-y-cyff
Llangeinor
Blackmill
Glynogwr
RHYDYFELIN
Nant-garw
CAERPHILLY
Caerphilly Castle
Draethen
Rhiwderin
Bassaleg
NEWPORT
Cathedral
BWLWARCAU
Betws
Coytrahen
Bryncethin
Brynmenyn
Heol-y-cyw
Brynna
Coedely
Beddau
Castellau
Pen-y-coedcae
Church Village
Efail Isaf
Gwaelod-y-Garth
Rudry
Parc Cefn Onn
Thornhill
Cefn Mably
Ruperra Castle
Michaelstone-y-Fedw
Duffryn
Coedkernew
Pye Corner
Nash
Goldcliff
Aberkenfig
Tondu
Cefn Cross
Pyle
Cefn Cribwr
Pen-y-fai
Tre-groes
Pencoed
Llanilid
Llanharry
Brynnae
Llanharan
Tyle-garw
Llantrisant
Cross Inn
Pontyclun
Miskin
Creigiau
Pentyrch
Castell Coch
Tongwynlais
Castleton
Marshfield
Llanrumney
St Mellons
St Brides Wentlooge
Peterstone Wentlooge
Laleston
Coity
BRIDGEND
Groes-faen
Radyr
WHITCHURCH
RUMNEY
South Glamorgan
Tythegston
St Mary Hill
Graig Penllyn
Treoes
Llangan
Llansannor
Penllyn
Ystradowen
Maendy
St Brides-super-Ely
Pendoylan
St Fagans
LLANDAFF
Cathedral
ROATH
City Hall
CARDIFF
CAERDYDD
Merthyr Mawr
Ewenny
Norman church
PORTHCAWL
Ogmore
Ogmore-by-Sea
Southerndown
St Bride's Major
Colwinston
COWBRIDGE
Walsh St Donats
Bonvilston
St George's
TRE-HILL
CAERAU
Fort
Castle
Llysworney
Llandow
Wick
Llanblethian
Llandough
St Hilary
Beaupre Castle
TINKINSWOOD
St Nicholas
St Lythans
Dyffryn
Michaelston-le-Pit
Wenvoe
Dinas Powys
PENARTH
Llanmihangel
St Mary Church
Tre-guff
Llantrithyd
LONG CAIRN
St Andrews Major
Monknash
Marcross
Flemingston
Llanmaes
Llanbethery
Llancarfan
Eglwys-Brewis
St Athan
BARRY
Lavernock
Lavernock Point
Nash Point
St Donats
Castle Ditches
Llantwit Major
Gileston
East Aberthaw
Breksea Point
Cardiff a. Wales Airport
Rhoose
Penmark
Porthkerry
Cold Knap
Sully
Sully Island
Flat Holm
Mouth of the Severn
Woodspring Priory
Langford Grounds
Wick St Lawrence
Sand Point
Sand Bay
Kewstoke
Worlebury
WORLE
MILTON
WESTON-SUPER-MARE
Brean Down
Weston Bay
Locking
Steep Holm
BRISTOL CHANNEL
Powys
Gwent
Mid Glamorgan
West Glamorgan

exploring the many local beauty spots and places of interest, which include Symonds Yat Rock, a beauty spot on the River Wye, King Arthur's Cave right on the English border, Raglan castle to the west and Tintern Abbey. Monmouth has a unique fortified 13th-century bridge. The street plan has remained virtually unchanged since 1450, so the town is full of interest. The Shire Hall (1724) in Agincourt Square contains a statue of Henry V. It is outside this building that the Chartists were tried in 1839. On the eastern side of the bridge, the Church of St. Thomas Becket has many Norman features, though the porch is a 19th-century imitation.

Newport

Not to be confused with Newport in Dyfed, Newport, Gwent on the Usk, near the English border, is an important river port. The castle was built in 1171, rebuilt in the 14th century but destroyed in the Civil War. The town has an important Museum and Art Gallery which contains works by Epstein and Rodin. The Civic Centre in Clytha Park contains murals by Hans Feibush, telling the story of Monmouthshire (1961-64).

Pembrokeshire Coast National Park

This is the only one of Britain's 11 national parks which is predominantly coastal. It is also the smallest in area, though it covers a long stretch of coastline, from Poppit Sands near St. Dogmaels to Amroth in the south. There is a 450-mile Coastal Path along the whole stretch. The Presely Hills, the only inland section, south of Fishguard, are full of standing stones and other prehistoric monuments. Milford Haven Waterway (the Daugleddau), by contrast, is a landscape of mudflats and wildfowl. Other interesting sights are Carew Castle, Upton Castle and the Tidal Mill at Carew. The only towns within the National Park are Tenby and St. David's, but there are plenty of convenient centres nearby, such as Fishguard, Haverforwest, Pembroke and Milford Haven.

Pontyprydd

This is the southernmost end of the Rhondda Valley, the mining district of Wales so seriously hit by the pit closures and resulting unemployment. The town itself is named after the bridge built over the Taff in 1756 by William Edwards. It has a single span and is considered a masterpiece of its kind, but is now disused. Ynysangharad Park in the centre of town contains statues by the Welsh sculptor Goscombe John.

Ross-on-Wye

Ross-on-Wye is a market town on a hill overlooking the lovely Wye Valley, which for much of its length constitutes the border between England and Wales. The Market House (1660-74) has a medallion of Charles II on its eastern wall and a monogram on the south wall. The town had a great benefactor, John Kyrle (1637-1724) who spent enormous sums of money and much time in adding new buildings to the town and refurbishing old ones, including the 13th-century church.

St. David's

The town, a gateway to the Pembrokeshire Coast National Park district, is notable for its cathedral, probably the finest church in Wales. The interior is largely 12th century and the exterior 14th century. The west front was rebuilt by John Nash in the 18th century and Sir Gilbert Scott rebuilt the west front in what is thought to be the original design.

Swansea

The main commercial centre of south-west Wales has a large harbour. The city suffered badly from bombing during World War II and the centre has been entirely rebuilt. The remains of the Castle are largely those of the fortified manor house erected on the site of the castle in 1330-32 by Bishop Gower. The Glyn Vivian Art Gallery holds interesting contemporary exhibitions and has many fine works by modern artists. The most interesting museum is the Maritime and Industrial Museum, opened in 1977 in the disused South Dock, is a lively exhibition on a grand scale of the history of Swansea docks. It includes a 200-ton tugboat, a lightship and the Abbey Woollen Mill, transported from Neath, which is in full production.

Information:
Pembrokeshire Coast
National Park
County Offices
Haverfordwest, Dyfed
SA61 1QZ
Tel: (0437) 766141
There are also information centres in Kilgetty, Pembroke, Tenby, St. David's, Newport, Broad Haven and Saundersfoot.

Brecon Beacons
Information Centre
Monk Street
Abergavenny
Tel: (0873) 858618

For information about facilities in the forests:
Forestry Commission
Wentwood
Llanfaches, Newport
Gwent
NP6 3AZ
Tel: (0633) 400205

Gower Peninsula:
Rhossili Visitor Centre
Gower
Tel: (0792) 390707

Aberdulais Falls
Visitor Centre
Aberdulais, nr. Neath
Tel: (0639) 56674

Tretower Castle, a ruined Norman fortress (left).

NORTHERN IRELAND

Lovely scenery, dominated by the loughs and mountains, is characteristic of the Province of Northern Ireland, where even the most impressive sights – the Giant's Causeway and the Mountains of Mourne – remain unspoiled. With the exception of Belfast, the capital, the towns and cities are small and the atmosphere rural.

Northern Donegal, Antrim, Londonderry

The northern part of Ireland is a wonderful land of glens, mountains and lakes, dotted with castles and cottages. The coastal scenery is inspiring and there are many offshore islands with a culture all of their own.

The far north of Ireland is split between County Donegal in the west and the counties of Londonderry, Tyrone and Antrim. Ireland is full of spectacular scenery and this part of Ireland is no exception.

Glens of Antrim

This series of valleys between Larne and Ballycastle is among the most beautiful scenery in Ireland. The Glens resemble those of Lowland Scotland, which can be glimpsed across the sea from those closest to the coast. They can conveniently be visited from Larne, Antrim, Cushendell or Balymena. The Glens contain two important nature reserves, Slieveanorra Forest and Glenariff Forest Park. The footpath along the north-east coast, known as the Ulster Way passes, through the Antrim Gorges.

Aran Islands

These are three islands off the coast of Galway in the west of Ireland. The Islands are famous for their prehistoric forts of dry stone masonry and for the traditional Irish way of life that the local inhabitants still preserve. The people speak mainly Irish, though they will speak English to visitors. They build the traditional currach boats which they use for fishing and wear local traditional dress, which includes a leather "pampootie" (a jerkin) and a coloured woolen girdle known as a "crio". The handwoven Aran sweaters of undyed wool are famous the world over.

Ballycastle

This Ballycastle is not to be confused with the town of the same name in County Mayo in the south. Ballycastle in Antrim is a market town and seaside resort. It takes its name from the castle founded by Sir Randall MacDonnell, second Earl of Antrim, which is now in ruins. A second Macdonnell castle, also in ruins, lies off the shore of Kinbane The ruins of Bunamargy Friary stand one mile east of the town. Ballycastle is a convenient starting point for visiting both the Glens of Antrim to the west and the Giant's Causeway to the east, since it lies between the two.

Castlerock

Castlerock is an attractive coastal resort, which is almost contiguous with Portstewart and Portrush. It contains the most easterly of a string of golf links which stretch along the coast. Hezlett House at Castlerock is a National Trust property, a long, low thatched rectory built in the 17th century. The cruck-truss roof was built by balancing curved timbers, or crucks, in pairs to form a series of arches and building the house around this frame. Just east of Castlerock is Downhill Castle. This 18th century estate was laid out by the Earl Bishop, Frederick Hervey who was both Bishop of Derry and Earl of Bristol. It includes Mussenden Temple, a domed rotunda which the Bishop used as his summer library. The estate has extensive grounds with panoramic views of Ireland's north coast and a visit is highly recommended.

Giant's Causeway

See "Excursions"

Letterkenny

This is the cathedral town of the Catholic diocese of Raphoe in County Donegal and one of the County's two administrative cen-

The seaside resort of Portstewart in Londonderry (above).

Ballintoy, County Antrim (above right).

Gray's Printing Shop in Strabane, now owned by the National Trust (below right).

Rathlin Island, County Antrim (opposite above).

Downhill Castle, County Londonderry (opposite below).

tres, the other being Lifford. St Eunan's Cathedral is of late 19th-century construction with a Romanesque interior. Just two miles west is the site of an ancient monastery, including a parish church, a holy well and two carved cross-pillars.

Limavady

This attractive market town on the Roe river was created by Sir Thomas Phillips. It is commemorated in a poem by Thackeray, *Sweet Peg of Limavady,*, since the poet stayed here in 1842 at an inn where Peg was barmaid. The *Londonderry Air* was noted down here when Jane Ross (1810-79) heard this traditional tune being played by a fiddler. There is a plaque on the house in which she lived.

Londonderry

County Londonderry (or Derry as the Catholic Irish prefer to call it) has magnificent forests on the eastern side of the county. There are Springwell and Cam forests and to the south near the Tyrone border, the forests of Glenshane, Banagher and Moydamiaght. Dungliven Priory contains O'Cahan's Tomb, the finest medieval tomb in Ulster. The Roe Valley Country Park has some lovely walks, particularly for those interested in industrial archæology. The city of Londonderry is the second-largest in the province of Northern Ireland. It is encircled by sturdy 17th-century ramparts which have withstood heavy sieges in the various Irish uprisings, including the famous siege of 1688 when the Apprentice Boys of Derry locked the gates against the army of James II. The Apprentice Boys March to commemorate the occasion is an annual Derry event. The heavy cannons still sit on the ramparts; the most notorious of these, known as Roaring Meg, was built in 1642 and is mounted at Double Bastion. There is a beautiful fountain in the historic city centre. The Guildhall has dozens of stained glass windows illustrating almost every episode in Derry history and is a good place to start a tour of the city. Other interesting buildings are the Irish Society House and the former Bishop's Palace. St Columb's Anglican Cathedral, built in 1633, is yet another of the city's monuments made possibly by donations from the city of London, hence the city's name. A stone inscription, preserved in the porch as a mark of gratitude, records the fact.

Rathlin Island

This island off the north-west coast, easily reached by ferry from Ballycastle, has been claimed by Scotland, though a 17th-century court case confirmed its Irishness once and for all. The island has one rough road, few cars and no mains electricity. The most famous sight is Bruce's Cave, the cave in which Robert the Bruce hid from the English in 1306 after losing the Battle of Perth and watched as a spider tried again and again to build its web. The creature's perseverence inspired Bruce to fight the English again and, of course, this time he won. There are two attractive churches on the island, one Catholic the other Protestant. Fish are still plentiful around the island, so fishing and tourism are the main occupations.

Springhill House

This National Trust property near Moneymore, County Londonderry is claimed to be the prettiest house in Ulster. The 17th-century house has been home to ten generations of the same family and contains family furniture, paintings, ornaments and curios. There is a costume museum in the large outbuildings. The grounds are extensive and have walled gardens and woodland walks.

Information

Tourist Information Office
Railway Road Coleraine,
Co. Londonderry
Tel: (0265) 44723

Irish Tourist Board
Derry Road
Letterkenny
Tel: (010) 353 74 21160

Events

In Londonderry, the Apprentice Boys' March is held on 12 August to celebrate the efforts of the Apprentice Boys in withstanding the siege of 1688.

In Portstewart, County Londonderry, the North-west 200, the fastest motor cycle race in Britain, is held in May.

In Donegal, in the Republic of Ireland, the Mary from Dungloe International Festival is held at Dungloe, in late July or early August. It is attended by emigrants from the county who come from all over the world.

Rc
Rd
Re
Rf
Sa
16
17
18
19
20
Tory Island
Camusmore Bay
282
East Town
Tory Sound
Inishbeg
Inishdooey
Inishbofin
Horn Head
835
Claggan
Dunfanaghy
Dooros Point
Sheep Haven
Breaghy Head
Fionnachaidh
Faugher
Ballymore
Ards Forest Park
Cashelmore
Doe Castle
Creeslough
Cashel
Rinnafaghla Point
Doagh
Rosguill
Derrycassan
Mulroy Bay
Island Roy
Carrickart
Gortnabrade
Glenree
Greevagh
Tullagh
Glen
Glen L.
Derrylaggy
Loughsalt Mtn.
1546
L. Salt
1160
L. Greenan
L. Nacreaght
946
Termon
15
Kilmacrenan
Cottian
Treantagh
Spring Vale
Rathdonnel Ho.
Ellist
Killyclug
Glendoon Hill
Rashedoge
499
Letterleague
Melmore Head
Ballyhoorisky Point
Mulroy Ho.
Bloody Foreland
Knockfola
Bloody Foreland
1036
Meenaclady
Rocking Stone
Aninver
Cloghaneely
Corveen
L. Lagha
Stranabrooey
Gweedore
Tievealehid
1413
Derrybeg
Cronalaght
1335
Bunbeg
Dore
Gweedore
Meenacung
36
56
72
Ballynes
Ballynes Bay
Falcarragh
Millmount
Carowcanon
Moyra
Ray
Corcreggan
Drumdoo
Port L.
Sessiagh L.
Shanbally
Crockglass
Croaghlosky
Agher L.
Gortahork
Beltany
Tullaghobegly
Meendarragh
Cashelnagor
Mukish Mtn.
2197
Aghla Beg
1860
Crocknalaragagh
1554
792
Altan L.
Errigal Mtn.
2466
Dooish
2147
Derryveagh Mtns
Glenveagh Castle and Gardens
L. Beagh
L. Inshagh
Glenveagh Deer Forest
Staghall
1599 Mtn.
1589
Red Deer Park
Glenveagh National Park
1461
Gartan L.
Church Hill
Churchill Forest
Glendowan
Glendowan Mtns.
Moylenanav
1771
Slieve Snaght
2240
Dunlewy
Dunlewy L.
Lough Nacung
Inishsirrer
Inishmeane
Umfin Island
Gola Island
The Stag Rocks
Inishinny
Gweedore Bay
Inishfree Lower
Owey Island
Inishfree Bay
Cruit Island
Carrick Finn
Lough Fadda
Crolla
Annagary
Mullaghderg Lough
Torneady Point
Rinrawros Point
Aran Island
730
Eighter I.
Inishcop
Aphort
Ballintra
Burtonport
Rutland I.
Inishal
Inishkeeragh
Inishfree Upper
The Rosses
Inishinny
Rosses Bay
Waskel L.
Meela L.
Loughanure
L. Anure
Parknatomogard
Inishene
Dunglow
Dunglow L.
Craghy L.
1038
1488
Glentornan L.
1707
Crocknafarragh
Crocknasharragh
1636
L. Croangar
L. Barra
Commeen
1379
L. Muck
1112
Altadush
Altinierin
940
Meenirroy Forest
28
Cronamuck
1134
L. Deele
Cark Mountain
1205
Cark
Stralongfort
Meenasrona
Three Tops
1181
Geological Interest
Crohy Head
Maghery
L. Illion
Nageeragh L.
L. Aleck More
Aghnish L.
808
L. Salt
Meenacross
Derrydruel
Meenlecknalore
L. Gannivegil
L. Nanuarragh
882
Doocharry
Trawenagh Bay
17
Croaghleheen
1257
Drumnaha
Roaninish
Dooey Point
Gweebarra Bay
Inishkeel
Ballincrick
578
Machugh
Derry Loughlan Forest
L. Finn
L. Muck
Glashagh
Cloghan
Lettermacaward
Dunmore Head
Dawros Head
113
Portnoo
Naran
Clooney
Doon L.
L. Kiltooris
Rossbeg
Sheskinmore
Loughros More Bay
Glendorragha
Cloghboy
Cranaogeboy
Sandfield
Derryness
Tully More
Crockaslowra
782
Derkbeg Hill
1100
L. Nacroaghy
Clooney Forest
Maas
L. Derryduff
333
L. Fad
L. Adery
Machugh
L. Anamma
Glenties
Meenachallow
Shallogan
1481
Aghla Mtn.
1961
Knockletteragh
Boultypatrick
1415
1266
Graffy
Tievelough
Mullanmore
Tangaveane
L. Ea
Croveenananta
1568
Reelan
Gaugin Mtn.
1865
L. Anna
Maghrath
Commeen
Altnapaste
Welchtown
Stranorlar
Ballybofey
Cappry
Woodlands
Mullaghaga Forest
Cloghroe
Drumgumber
Dunnacross
Aughagault
Corranagh
Drumbologe
Owencarrow
Akibbon L.
13
Donegal
164
Donegal

Sc
Sd
Se
Sf
Ta
Inishtrahull Sound
Garvan Isles
Malin Head
Ballyhillin
Ballygorman
935
Culoort
Keenagh
Meedanmore
Urbalreagh
Glentooskert
Glengad Head
Glashedy Island
809
856
Glacknabrade
Ballagh
Portaleen
Tullagh Point
Pollan Bay
Lagacurry
Doagh Isle
Malin
Corthage Ho.
Dunmore Head
Culdaff
Fanad Head
Dunaff Head
690
Dunaff
Kindrohid
830
Bunacrick
Ballyliffin
Trawbreaga Bay
Drumaville
Rock Tunnel
Claggan
Straid
Raghtin More
1657
Clonmany
Clagan
Clogherny
Kindroghed
Drumaville
Ballymagaraghy
Carrowmenagh
Doagh Beg
Lenan Head
Gap of Mamore
Cloghfin
Cabadooey Hill
625
St. Patrick's Cross
Carndonagh
Gorey
Crockaughrim
Turraboy
Straruddan
Ballintroohan
Seven Arches
1381
Effishmore
L. Fad
Gleneely
Crocknamerragh
Crocknasmug
1076
Urris Hills
1379
Clogfiglass
Hollymount
Milltown
Craignamaddy
1054
Crocknabronta
Stroove
Inishowen Head
Garryblagh
Dunree Head
Carha
Magherabane
Old Mountain
Muineagh
Glasmullan
Mintiaghs L.
Inishnaneill
Cashel
Glentogher
Crockbrack
Claggan
Greencastle
Magilligan Pt.
32
Meenaward
Slieve Snaght
2019
Whitefield
21
L. Fad
L. Inn
Moville
Inishowen
Glebe
Linsford
Town
1198
Glenvar
Lough
Garrynabolloge
1253
Kinnagoe
Turk
Stranagappoge
Glencaw Hill
1123
Pensylvania
34
Lough
Leherdan
Buncrana Castle
Clonblock
Ballymagan
Craha
Illies
Srath
BUNCRANA
BUN CRANNCHA
Creehennan
White Castle
20
Magilligan Sta.
Mussenden Temple
Coleraine
Lurganboy
Killygarvan Point
Hill Head
Tullydush
1309
Cabry
Hells Hole
Lower Ballyleighery
Croaghan Hill
1137
1008
Drumhallagh Ho.
Swilly
Luddan
Dunerun
Binevenagh
1260
Grange Park Wood
Rathmullan
Rathmullan Wood
Fahan
Aught Upper
Foyle
Scone
Formoyle
Town
Inch Top
732
Strahack
Moress
Sealp Mtn.
1589
1377
Granias Gap
Carrowreagh
Crindle
Aghanloo
Coleraine
Ray
Inch I.
Inch
Tompsons Town
Muff
Oatlands
Bolea
13
Springwell Forest
Ardnaree
Aughnish Isle
Whale Head
Carnaghan
Tieveborne
Soppog
Burnfoot
Lenamore
Culmore
Rush Hall
Keady Mtn.
1101
Castlequarter
Ballynagart
Ballyarnet
Orchards Town
Ballymoney
Gortaway
Speenoge
Bridge End
Grianan of Aileach
Galliagh
Coolkeeragh
Cregan
Tullyverry
Ballykelly
LIMAVADY
LEIM an MHADAIDH
Whitehill
Stewart
Shellbrook
Milltown
Broad Br.
17
Bresteel
Eglinton
Killylane
Roe Valley
Clagan
Ardmore
Cam Forest
Drumboy
22
Bohullion
City Walls and Gates Guildhall
Killylane Upper
Drumraighland
Ballydarrog
Glenhead
Killyverry
Gortlush
LONDONDERRY
DERRY DOIRE
Gortnessy Hill
Gortnessy
Moys
Lislane
Ballylawn
Newton Cunningham
Bogay
Gorticross
Highmoor
Terrydremont
Craiggore
Gortree
20
Killea
Drumahoe
Gortica Hill
Loughermore
1298
Baranailt
Carrick Rocks
1318
Drumsurn
1280
Magherabeg
Glensmill
Listacall
Imlick
Corrody
Ardbrook
Ardmore
Straw Ho.
Legavannon
Drumgravenny
Manorcunningham
Dooish Mountain
Church Town
Carrigans
Foyle
New Buildings
Gortgranagh
Slaghtmanus
Altahullion Hill
914
Gortscanlan
Owenbeg
Boyevagh
Ballyriess
Gortnamoyagh Forest
Drumoghill
Lismoghry
Donegal
Tyrone
Meenaghill
Magheramason
Disertown
Gosheden
E 16
Scriggan
1535
17
Castledowey
Treantagh
Saint Johnstown
13
Heatheryhill
Tullyowen
Bready
The Ness Ervey Wood
963
Holly Hill
Bawn
Dungiven
Sheskinapoll
Whitehill
Cullion
Carrickatane
Glenmangoorland
Glenlough
19
Claudy
Letterlogher
Hass Upper
Carn Hill
1479
Ballylennan
Stony Hill
Mountcastle
Glebe
Turmeel
Derrychrier
Boviel
Carn
13
Raspberry Hill
Fawney
Glenshane Pass
Drumbeg
Tullyrap
Milltown
Loughneas
Glencosh
Tullintrain
The Glen
Straidarran
Feeny
Fairy Lo.
Raphoe
Ballylaw
Windy Hill
Dunnamanagh
Ballyneaner
Carnanbanc
Straid Hill
1002
Fincarn
Glenshane Forest
Beltany Stone Circle
Ballymagorry
Artigarvan
Ballynacross
Curradrolan Hill
Moneyhoghan
Learmount Forest
Learmount
Ballydonegan
Glenshane
Cloghfin
Rossgeir
Ballee
Silver Brook
Banagher Forest
Glenshane Mtn.
Ballindrait
Deele
Lifford
Castletown
L. Ash
Carnanreagh
Stranagalwilly
Dreen
Mullaghmore
1825
STRABANE
AN STRATH BAN
Altishahe
Ballynamallaght
Nat. Res.
Moydamlaght Forest
Ardnaglass
Milltown Lo.
Moor L.
Craig
Sperrin Mountains
Londonderry
Tyrone
2070
Castlefinn
Ballard
Owenreagh Hill
1344
Stroanbrack
2240
Sawel Mtn.
Black Fort
Clady
Edymore
Mullaghclogha
2088
Moneyneany
Belfast
Omagh
165
168

44
15
16
17
18
19
Tb
Tc
Td
Te
Tf
Rathlin Island
Bull Point
Crockantirrive
Ballyconagan
Robert the Bruce's Cave
Church Bay
Rue Point
Antrim Coast
Rathlin Sound
Benbane Head
Giant's Causeway
Tonduff
Dunseverick
Rope Bridge
Sheep I.
White Park Bay
Ballintoy
Kinbane or White Head
Benmore or Fair Head
Views to Scotland
Murlough Bay
The Skerries
Ramore Head
Dunluce Castle
PORTRUSH
PORT ROIS
Bushmills
Ballyallagnt
Lisnaguogue
Fallgarrive
Magherintendry
Ballycastle Bay
Clare Wood
BALLYCASTLE
BAILE an CHAISTIL
Ballycastle Forest
Craigfad
Torr Head
Carnanmore
1253
Runabay Head
PORTSTEWART
PORT STÍOBHAIRD
Castlerock
The Ulster Way
COLERAINE
CUIL RAITHIN
Knocklayd
1695
Ballypatrick Forest
Crockaneel
1321
Cushendun
Antrim Gorges
Armoy
Natur Reserve Breen Wood
Croghan
1368
Agangarrive Hill
1225
Antrim Mountains
BALLYMONEY
BAILE MONAIDH
Garry Wood
African Game Reserve
Ossan's Grave
Cushendall
Red Arch
Red Bay
Glenariff or Waterfoot
Milltown
Natur Reserve Slieveanorra Forest
Trostan
1817
Slievenanee
1782
Knockore
Garron Point
Garron Twr.
Glens of Antrim
Glenariff Forest Park Nat. Res.
Waterfalls
Carnlough
Carnlough Bay
Collin Top
1426
Soarns Hill
1326
Cranny Falls
Garvagh
Garvagh Forest
Kilrea
Rasharkin
Craigs Wood
L. Naroon
Clogh
Dunloy
Loughguile
Portglenore
Ahoghill
Gracehill
Broughshane
Slemish Mountain
1446
BALLYMENA
Douglas Top
1325
Maghera
Swatragh
Carntogher
1521
Cam Forest
Cookstown
Antrim
Larne
168
169
Londonderry

53

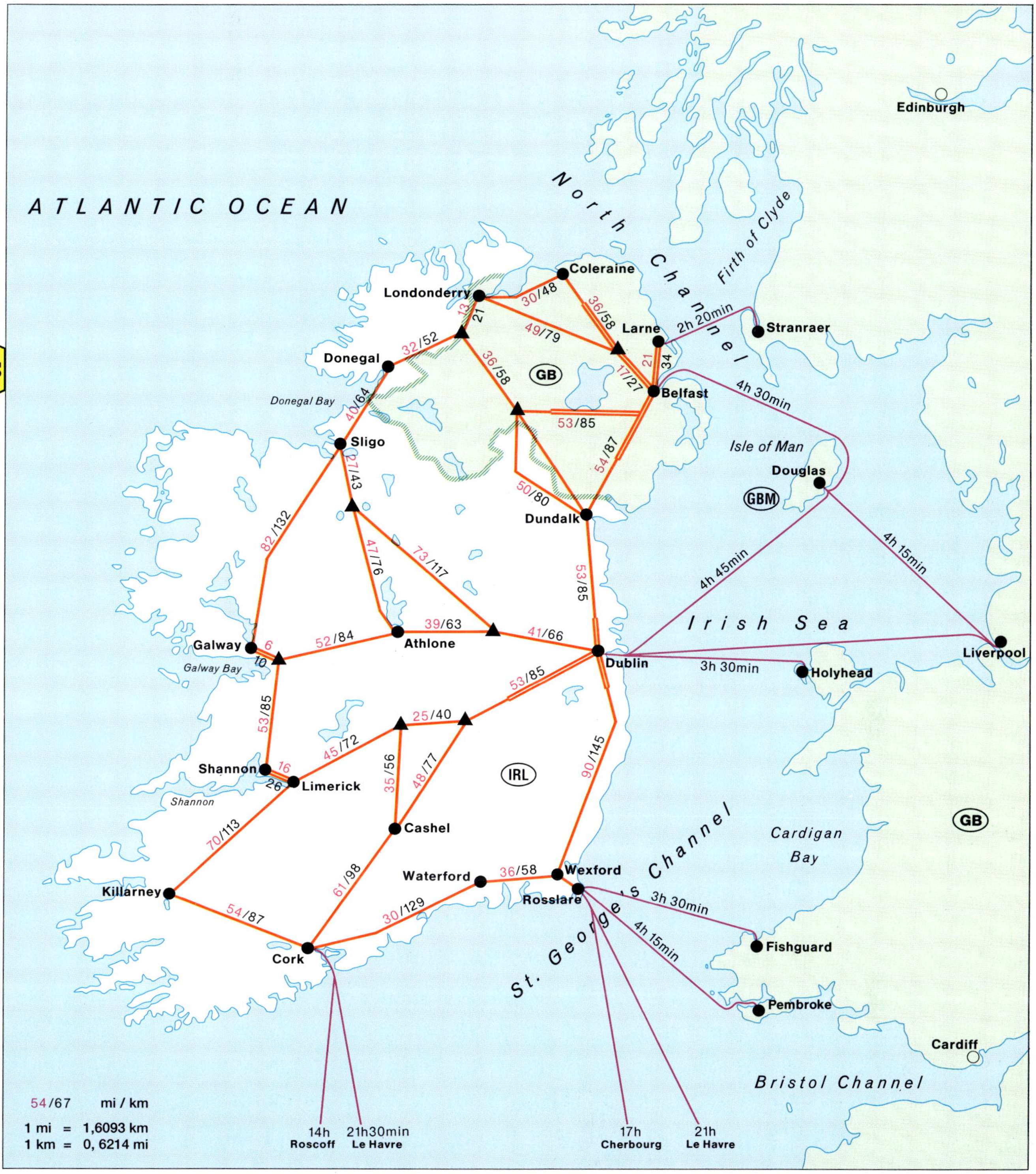
ATLANTIC OCEAN
North Channel
Firth of Clyde
Edinburgh
Coleraine
Londonderry
Larne
Stranraer
2h 20min
Donegal
Donegal Bay
Belfast
4h 30min
Sligo
Isle of Man
Douglas
GB
GBM
Dundalk
4h 15min
4h 45min
Irish Sea
Galway
Galway Bay
Athlone
Dublin
3h 30min
Holyhead
Liverpool
Shannon
Limerick
IRL
Cashel
St. George's Channel
Cardigan Bay
Waterford
Wexford
Rosslare
Killarney
Cork
3h 30min
4h 15min
Fishguard
Pembroke
Cardiff
Bristol Channel
54/67 mi / km
1 mi = 1,6093 km
1 km = 0, 6214 mi
14h Roscoff
21h30min Le Havre
17h Cherbourg
21h Le Havre

Ub

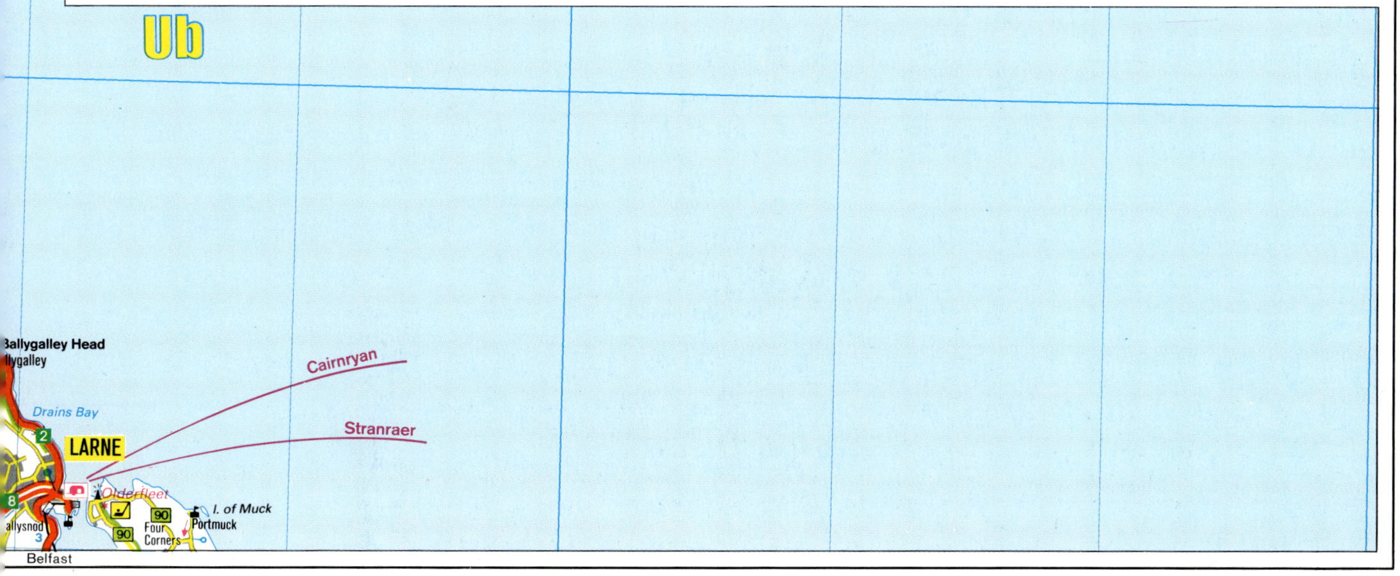
Ballygalley Head
Cairnryan
Drains Bay
LARNE
Stranraer
I. of Muck
Portmuck
Four Corners
Belfast

South Donegal, Fermanagh and Tyrone

Fermanagh's lakeland is an undiscovered tourist paradise which is still agreeably free of crowds even in high summer. Lough Erne, a magnificent expanse of water, has probably fewer boats on it than any other lake in Europe.

Ballyshannon
This seaport and market town at the head of the Erne estuary has always been of great strategic importance. It is now the headquarters of Ireland's massive Erne Hydroelectric Scheme and the dams and generating equipment are interesting to visit. The river Erne is a famous salmon-fishing river and special provision has been made for the fish to ensure that they still spawn in peace. St. Anne's Protestant church north of the town occupies the traditional site of the Conaill Gulban, King of Tara. The poet William Allingham (1824-89) is buried in the churchyard. Just outside the town, four miles to the north-west, is the prehistoric Two Mile Stone. There are also remains of ring forts and ancients earthworks connected with them. In the same general direction is Giant's Grave, a prehistoric chamber tomb.

Clogher Valley
This peaceful part of County Tyrone is dotted with villages along the Blackwater River. The river is fast-flowing and has good facilities for canoeists and others who want to brave the whitewater rapids. It includes the town of Moy, with its magnificent 18th century architecture, laid out by James Caulfield, Earl of Charlemont. The four churches are 19th century. The rectangular marketplace was inspired by the square at Marengo in Italy, which the Earl had seen when he was making the Grand Tour. Benburb Castle and Priory is a ruined castle overlooking Blackwater, in the grounds of a Servite priory. This was the first community of the order in Ireland, established as recently as 1948 in a red-brick Victorian mansion. The priory contains an art gallery which is open to the public. The priory is entirely self-sufficient, the monks even having built their own electricity generating plant on the Blackwater River. A ruined castle stands on a rock overlooking the little town of Benburb. Inside its massive walls there is a little village, built in the 17th century, which is still a flourishing community.

Mellon home in the Folk Park near Omagh (above).

County Doun, with the Mountains of Mourne (left).

The Watergate of Enniskillen Castle (opposite).

Donegal
County Donegal is part of the Republic of Ireland. The county town, Donegal, is a market town and small seaport on Donegal Bay. The name means "fort of the foreigners" because it was founded by the Vikings. Donegal boasts a fine castle built by Red Hugh II O'Donnell in 1505 and added to by Sir Basil Brooke in 1610. The banqueting hall is particularly magnificent, a rare example in a castle of this late period. Donegal Abbey, as it is known, is really a Franciscan friary, founded by the father of the castle builder, Hugh I O'Donnell, in 1474. The founder is buried here with his wife. The friary was attacked several times by the English, who eventually took it in 1601. In the course of this battle, the English ammunition store blew up and wrecked the buildings. The ruined friary was granted to Sir Basil Brooke, the church and cloisters remaining in good condition. The Franciscan friars were scattered troughout the region but managed to cling to their order. In Bundrowes, the Four Masters, who were members of the order, compiled a diary of their wanderings, entitled *Annals*, between 1630 and 1636.

Enniskillen
This is the county town of Fermanagh, in a beautiful location on an islet in the River Erne. This is where the main highway between north and south crossed Lough Erne. It is an ideal centre from which to explore the lakes of Fermanagh, including Lough Erne. The countryside is rich in ancient monuments. The town has always been a stronghold of Protestant settlers who rallied to the cause of William of Orange in his quelling of the Irish rebellions of 1641 and 1689. The Protestant cathedral was only built in 1840, but it incorporates a

17th-century tower. Enniskillen Castle is a fine example of 16th-century fortifications. Despite constant battles to gain possession of it, much of it remains, including a fine watergate (1580-90). The Royal School, Inniskillen, founded in 1626 by Charles I is a handsome 18th-century building.

Gortin Glen Forest

This is a National Park with wonderful scenic drives around Mullaghcarn Mountain, Gortin and Plumbridge on the Glenelly River. At Gortin, there is a History Park. Plumbridge has a cattle market and is also the centre for gold-prospecting, recently revived in the area. There is irish gold in the royal regalia.

Lough Derg

This Lough is in County Donegal in the Republic of Ireland, in the heart of the Mountains of Donegal. Its importance lies in its being the site of St. Patrick's Purgatory, a cave on Saint's Island where he is supposed to have fasted for 40 days and to have had terrifying visions. It was said that pilgrims would behold the same visions if they visited the cave. Oliver Cromwell's men blocked up the entrance and subsequently destroyed it, but the lake is still the most important pilgrimage centre of Ireland. Pilgrims come between 1 June and 15 August to Station Island and perform the "stations", including walking barefoot around the crosses of St. Patrick and St. Brigid. They subsist on one meal a day, consisting of coarse bread and black tea.

Lough Erne

In the Middle Ages there was a chain of island monasteries down the lake, which were convenient stopping places for the faithful on their way to St. Patrick's Purgatory on Lough Derg. On Devenish Island, there are the remains of the monastery and church founded in the 6th century by St. Mo-Laisse (or Molaise). The church, originally a small, stone-roofed Romanesque oratory, has since been added to. North of Devenish in Killadeas graveyard, there are three early Christian carved monuments with traces of Irish inscriptions. The perfect round tower was used as sanctuary by the monks into which they could flee when attacked.

Lough Eske

This beautiful lake at the foot of the Bluestack Mountains is well-stocked with fish. At the western end, there are two romantic castles, Lough Eske Castle and Ardnamona. O'Donnell Castle stands on an islet in the centre. Just north of the lake there is the waterfall of Eas Dúnan on the Corraber River. The isolated lough, ringed with cliffs, is difficult of access.

Omagh

The county town of County Tyrone in Northern Ireland, on the Strabane-Monaghan road. The Ulster-American Folk Park is a record of Ulster's links with the early American settlers. Omagh is a convenient base for touring the beauties of the Munterlony and the South Sperrins. One of the best circular tours is to Curraghchosaly and Mullaghcarn via the Gortin Gap, then eastwards via the Drumlea Bridge and up the north-eastern side of the Owenreagh Valley to Sheskinshule, then south to Creggan and west to Mountfield and finally back to Omagh.

Information
Lakeland Visitor Centre
Enniskillen
Tel: (0365) 23110

The centre supplies information about the whole of Fermanagh, including details of boat trips and boat hire.

Events
The Sealink Classic Fishing Festival is held in Fermanagh in mid-May. Details from the Northern Ireland Tourist Board or from the Enniskillen Lakeland Visitor Centre.

158
Dunglow
Rb
Rc
Rd
Re
Rf
20
21
22
23
24
Rossbeg
Loughros More Bay
Sheskinmore
Sandfield
Clooney Forest
Maas
Machugh
L. Ananima
Glenties
Mullanmore
Tangaveane
Knockletteragh
Boultypatrick
1415
1481
Graffy
Tievelough
Croveenananta
1568
Gaugin
1865
Loughros Point
Loughros Beg Bay
Glendorragha
Cloghboy
Crannogeboy
Crumlin
Tormore Island
Slievetooey
1458
Croaghballaghdown
Ardara
Crockaslowra
Meenachallow
L. Anna
Tullyhonwar
Silver Hill
1979
Lavagh More
2211
2219
2118
Blue Stack Mtn.
Sturall
Port
L. Annaffrin
Straboy
Crockuna
1268
L. Naloghraman
Aighe
Monargan Glebe
Cronkeeran
Carnaween
1713
Meenaguse Lough
Croaghaniw
Glen Head
Pre and Early Christian Remains
Kinnakillew
Kilgoly
Glencolumbkille
1230
Meenacross
Meenadreen
Lergynasearhagh
Neck of the Ballagh
Glengesh Pass
Mulmosog Mtn.
1042
1157
Binbane
1493
Waterfall
Rossan Point
Doonalt
Malin More
Folk Village
Malin Bay
Meenaneary
Crove
Crocknapeast
1649
Meenybraddan
L. Meenybraddan
Meenataggart
Banagher Hill
1268
Straleel
Molnanaff
1551
Balbane
L. Namanfin
Malin Beg
L. Auva
L. Unna
Clonasillagh Forest
White Hill
Meenagolan
Croagh
Carraduffy
Letterbarra
Lackrom Forest
L. Esk
Rathlin O'Birne Island
Slieve League
Carrick
Meenychanon
748
Limestone Brook Br.
Winterhill
1273
1621
Crownarad
Crocknasharragh
Frosses
Red Bridges
Teelin
Derrylahan
Kilcar
Largy
Calhame
Lisaveddy
Inver
Mountcharles
Donegal
Drummenny
Milltown
Milltown
The Hall
Donegal Castle
Carrigan Head
Donegal Tweed
Cashel
Tawny
Shalwy
Fintragh Bay
Killybegs Harbour
Dunkineely
Ballyboyle I.
Copany
Drumbar
Carntullagh
Mc Swyne's Bay
Castle Murray
217
Inver Bay
Drumgorman
Rooney's I.
Muckros
Muckros Head
Drumanoo
Drumanoo Head
Carntullagh Head
Ballyederlan
Tullyvoos
Doorin Rock
Strand Forest
Rossilybeg
Laghy
Oughtdarnid
898
Inishduff
Pound Point
Ackle Back
Doorin Point
Mullanasole
Killultan
The Pullans
Mullanacross
Shannagh
St. John's Point
Donegal Bay
Durnesh
Ballintra
Drumlins and Pullans
Rossnowlagh Lower
Cashel
Golagh
Kildoney Point
Kildoney
Tullymore
Breesy Hill
855
Croagh
321
Ballyshannon
Beal Atha Seanaidh
Tully
Aughrus Pt.
Knader Forest
Belleek
Mullagmore Head
Tullaghan
Bundoran
Bun Dobhrain
Fort William
Rowantreehill Ho.
Magherameenagh Castle
Castle Caldwell
Roskeeragh Pt.
Ward Ho.
Castlegal
Ashbrook
Gubacreeny
Askill
Inishmurray
Monastic Enclosure
Creevykeel Cross Rds.
Creevykeel Court Cairn
Agharroo
Kinlough
Lough Melvin
Rosska I.
Killy Beg
Cliffony
Balloor
Unshinagh
Inishtemple
Dernish I.
Cartronplank
Fermanagh
Leitrim
Streedagh Pt.
Conors I.
Ballaghnatrillick Br.
Largydonell
1720
Garrison
Grange
1702
Eagles Rock
Truskmore
2120
L. Aganny
1609
Lissiniska
Cloonagh
Breaghwy
Ballyconell
Ballinphull
Benbulbin
1730
Glenade
Rossinver
Roskeeragh Pt.
Cloghboley
Lissadell House
Cashelgarran
Kings Mtn.
1527
Dartry Mts.
Ballagh Cott.
Glenade L.
Carney
Yeat's Grave
Glencar Waterfalls
Kiltyclogher
Rughly
Drumcliff Bay
Drumcliff
Faughary
Black Rock
Ballybeg
Rosses Point
1527
Gurteen
Dough Mtn.
1515
Corracloona
Sligo Bay
Drum
Milltown Forest
Oyster I.
Coney I.
Dorrins Strand
Aughris Head
Auburn Ho.
Keelogyboy
1446
Manorhamilton
Thur Mtn.
1425
Cummeen Strand
St. John's Cathedral
Colgagh
Ballyglass Ho.
Benbo
1367
Glenboy
Glenfarne Forest
Kilrusheighter
Carrowcaslan
Strandhill
Strandhill Ho.
Sligo
Sligeach
Ardogelly
Carrowreagh
Knocknarea
1083
Queen Maeve's Grave
Magheraboy
Church I.
Park's Castle
Leckaun
Brockagh
Deep Chasm
Carrowmore
Carrowmore
L. Gill
Carrigeencor L.
Skreen
Dromard
Ballysadare Bay
Breeoge
Slish
970
Wood
Stonepark
Dromahair
L. Klo
1451
Naglog
Carrowculleen Ho.
Beltra
Belladrihid
Castle-dargan Forest
905
Creevelea Friary
Killarga
1476
Chapel Street
Ballysadare
Correagh Forest
Gowlaun
Knockalongy
1786
Glen Wood
896
Ballintogher
Tober
Mullagh L.
Collooney
Ballygawley
Lisacoghil
Coolaney
Owenbeg
Castle Neynoe
Killavoggy
Dowra
Rockfield
Carrownacarrick
Cloghtin
Tullynasereen
Drumkeeran
Lavan Forest
Killadiskert
Carrowneden
Coola Cross Rds.
Aghoo
Leitrim
Sligo
Ballinaglera
Killoran
Carrowntawy
Gortnadrass
910
Carrigans
Riverstown
1503
Knockateean Forest
Lough Allen
164
Iron Mountains
Cloonacod
Lavagh
Falnasoogaun or Roperfield
Knockadalteen
Drumdoney
1385
Templehouse L.
Kilmorgan
Ballinphull
Ballina
Castlebar
Boyle
Carrick

159
Letterkenny
Londonderry
STRABANE
AN STRATH BAN
Stranorlar
Ballybofey
Castlefinn
Lifford
Sion Mills
Clady
Killygordon
Curradrolan Hill
Sperrin Mtn.
Mullaghclogha
2088
Mullaghclogher
1896
Owenreagh Hill
1344
Plumbridge
Craignamaddy
1264
Glenelly Valley
Gortin
Rousky
Curraghchosaly Mtn.
1372
Gortin Glen Forest Park
Ulster American Folk Park
Mullaghcarn
1778
Newtown Steward
Ardstraw
Baronscourt Forest
Barons Court
Bessy Bell
1387
Castlederg
Killeter Forest
Killeter
Mullyfa
812
Croaghanierin
912
Meenglass Forest
L. Mourne
Fearn Hill
755
Mountjoy
Mountfield
OMAGH
AN OMAIGH
Drumquin
Bin Mtn.
Balaght Mtn.
1073
Lough Bradan Forest
Tappaghan Mtn.
1112
Crockkinnagoe
1194
L. Derg
Pettigo
Boa I.
Kesh
Ederny
Lower Lough Erne
Irvinestown
Dromore
Fintona
Clanabogan
Seskinore
Beragh
Sixmilecross
Garvaghy
Newtownsaville
Eskragh
Trillick
Brougher Mtn.
1048
Ballinamallard
Duross Pt.
Castle Archdale Forest
Inishmakill
Inishmassaint
Inish Fowar
Inish Lougher
Cullen Hill
Ely Lodge Forest
Monea
Monea Plantation Castle
Devenish
Tempo
Clabby
Fivemiletown
Clogher
Augher
Slieve Beagh
1255
Jenkin Hill
972
Mullaghfad Forest
ENNISKILLEN
INIS CEITHLEANN
Tamlaght
Lisbellaw
Belmore Mtn.
1316
Belmore Forest
Boho Caves Systems
Letterbreen
Belcoo
L. Macnean Lower
Marble Arch Boat Caves
Florence Court Forest Park
Mullalean
1400
Benauahlin
1221
Tiltinbane
1949
Cuilcagh Mountains
Cuilcagh
2188
Swanlinbar
Maguiresbridge
Brookeborough
Lisnaskea Forest
Upper Lough Erne
LISNASKEA
LIOS na SCEITHE
Derrylin
Kinawley
Donagh
Newtownbutler
Crom Castle
CLONES
CLUAIN EOIS
Rosslea
Rosslea Forest
Smithborough
Slieve Rushen
1331
Source of the Shannon
Benbrack
1632
Belturbet
Cavan
170
Cookstown
Dungannon
Armagh
Monaghan
Tyrone
Fermanagh
Donegal

County Down, St. Patrick's Country

Central Northern Ireland is St. Patrick's own country. There are shrines to the Saint and the city where he founded his first church. There are to found two of Ireland's most famous sights, Carrickfergus Castle and the Mountains of Mourne.

Antrim
The county town boasts a fine 10th-century round tower in Steeple Park a mile from the centre, which belonged to a 6th-century monastery. Antrim Castle was burned down in 1922 but has a magnificent gateway and the grounds are now a public park. The stables and coach house are used as an arts centre. Pogue's Entry is a narrow alley off Church Street that contains a restored 18th-century cottage, the birthplace of the American author, Alexander Irvine.

Armagh
The spiritual capital of Ireland for 1500 years, Armagh has both Anglican and Roman Catholic cathedrals. The Anglican cathedral is built on the site of a stone church erected on the orders of St. Patrick in 445. The Mall was once the city's racecourse and is surrounded by many fine houses whose front windows would have afforded a grandstand view. Archbishop Richard Robinson disapproved and turned the racecourse into a street. The Sovereign's House in the north-east corner of the Armagh County Museum contains the museum of the Royal Irish Fusiliers. Armagh boasts a planetarium and an observatory, the latter founded in 1790 by the same Archbishop Robinson.

The Ards
The entrance to this curved peninsula west of Belfast contains two of Northern Ireland's largest cities, Bangor and Newtownards. Bangor is a coastal resort with pleasant marine gardens and sandy beaches. Local pasttimes are yachting, sea-angling and golfing. Bangor Abbey was established in the 16th century, as were the three other abbeys on the peninsula, Grey Abbey, Movilla at Newtownards and Holywood Abbey. The Ulster Folk and Transport Museum, between Belfast and Bangor, has been developed since the 1950s, by bringing typical buildings from all over the Province. There are two main areas, a small Ulster town and a rural section, including a flax mill from County Tyrone and a blacksmith's forge from Fermanagh. There are demonstrations of traditional crafts. Many buildings in Newtownards, including the Town Hall, are 16th and 17th century. The Peninsula can be toured starting at either Newtownards or Bangor and taking the road that almost completely encircles it, passing through Portaterry in the south.

Belfast
See "Historic Cities"

Carrickfergus
The town grew up around the massive Anglo-Norman castle built by John de Courcy in 1180 to guard the approach to Belfast Lough. The castle has been of great strategic importance to Ulster. It was here that William of Orange landed in 1690, on his way to the Battle of the Boyne, at which the Old Pretender James II was finally defeated. This is the battle commemorated by Irish Protestants on 12 July annually. The town walls were built in the 17th century. Despite these massive fortifications, Carrickfergus suffered at the hands of the French who captured it in 1760. St. Nicholas church is a 12th-century building like the castle, though the chancel was finished in 1305 and is out of alignment with the nave. The building was much restored in 1614. North of Carrickfergus is the peninsula called Islandmagee. Facing the top of the peninsula across narrow straits is Larne, the ferry terminal for Stranraer in Scotland.

Downpatrick

This is the heart of St. Patrick's Country and the site of St. Patrick's Grave. Various abbeys and churches have been built here thanks to the connection with St. Patrick, and many were subsequently destroyed. The present cathedral was rebuilt on several occasions, and was restored in the late 18th and early 19th centuries, though the tower was not added until 1829. Outside the cathedral there is a 10th-century cross. The former county gaol in English Street now houses the Down Museum, which has a section devoted to St. Patrick. Thomas Russell was executed here for his part in two success Irish uprisings; he is buried in the local churchyard. North of Downpatrick are the ruins of Inch Abbey overlooking the Quoile River. The Mound of Down is a huge prehistoric earthwork near the Quoile Marshes. Castle Ward, near Downpatrick, is an 18th-century mansion whose different façades reflect the two conflicting styles of the period, since the west front is neo-classical and the east front in the Gothick taste. There is a theatre in the stable yard and a collection of wildfowl in a walled garden. The property is now run by the National Trust.

Mourne Mountains

The Mountains of Mourne do indeed sweep down to the sea, as claimed in the song. The compact range is only 15 miles long and eight miles wide, and few of the peaks rise above 2,000 feet but their position right by the sea gives them a dramatic quality. The ancient Kingdom of Mourne was hidden away behind these steep hills. The largest town in the area is Newcastle. At its south end, it is squeezed on to a mountain ledge, with barely room for the road. Near Newcastle is the 12th-century Dundrum Castle which majestically dominates Dundrum Bay. It has a massive circular keep built into the curtain wall and is one of the string of castles that controlled this coast from Greencastle on Carlingford Lough to Carrickfergus. There is a large population of wild birds. Seals bask on the beaches, seemingly unaffected by the rifle range across the narrow channel at Ballykinler. Beyond Dundrum village there is a dolmen at Sidderyford

Cultra, the folk museum at Donn, a schoolroom (top right).

Pogue's Entry, Antrim (above).

St. Patrick's Grave at Donnpatrick, County Donn (top).

Portaferry, sea port in County Donn (opposite left).

Grey Abbey, County Donn (left).

Newry

This town, named after a yew tree allegedly planted by St. Patrick himself, is at the head of the "Gap of the North", the pass between two ranges of hills, one in Ulster, the other in Leinster. It straddles two counties, Down and Armagh and the town hall is built right on the border. The Poor Clares convent in the High Street has a garden that almost encircles the burail ground of the town's first Presbyterian Church. The first Protestant church (1578) to be built in Ireland is also in Newry and the first canal ever built in the British Isles (1730) runs through Newry. The local museum contains a wealth of exhibits of local history, and there is an arts centre attached to it which holds regular exhibitions of the work of local artists.

Sieve Gullion Forest Park, five miles south-west of Newry, is on rugged terrain roamed by wild goats. The Park contains an interesting Neolithic passage grave. Bessbrook model village, three miles from Newry, was once linked to it by tram. This was one of the first model communities of its kind, built for linen workers, and those in England – such as Bourneville and Port Sunlight – are modelled on it.

Information

Oxford Island Nature Reserve, Lough Neagh
Tel: (07622) 22205

Down Museum and St. Patrick Heritage Centre Downpatrick
Tel: (0396) 5218

Events

Bangor Game and Country Fair is held in late June.
In Portadown, the International Rose trials are held between July and September and Rose Week the finals for catalogued roses is in late July.
Lughanasa (Lammas) Medieval Fair is held in late July at Carrickfergus Castle.
Newtownards Harvest Fair is held in September and has been a regular event since 1613.

159
160
170
Londonderry
Coleraine
Coleraine
Coleraine
Omagh
Omagh
Enniskillen
Enniskillen
Lisnaskea
Navan
Dundalk
Dundalk
Dundalk
Dundalk
Warrenpoint
Sf
Ta
Tb
Tc
Td
20
21
22
23
24
Sperrin Mountains
Sawel Mtn.
Banagher Forest
Glenshane Mtn.
Mullaghmore
Moydamlaght Forest
Maghera
Portglenore
Gracehill
Ahoghill
Draperstown
Tobermore
Desertmartin
Magherafelt
Castledawson
Toome
RANDALSTOWN
Goles Forest
Spaltindoagh
Slieve Gallion
Davagh Forest Park
Fir Mtn.
Moneymore
Springhill House
Ballyronan
Lough Neagh
COOKSTOWN
AN CHORR CHRÍOCHACH
Black Bog
Creggan
Drum Manor Forest Park
Coagh
Ardboe Cross
Pomeroy
Stewartstown
Washing Bay
Coney I.
DUNGANNON
DÚN GEANAINN
Moygashel
Ballyreagh
Peatlands
Lady Bay
Sandy Bay
Rams I.
Gartree P.
Tolan P.
Oxford I.
Castor B.
LURGAN
AN LORGAIN
CRAIGAVON
PORTADOWN
Port an Dúnáin
Moy
The Argory
Ardress House
AUGHNACLOY
ACHADH na CLOICHE
Benburb
Blackwatertown
ARMAGH
ARD MHACHA
Navan Fort
Rich Hill
Hamilton's Bawn
GILFORD
ATH MHIC GIOLLA
TANDRAGEE
TÓIN re GAOITH
BANBRIDGE
DROICHEAD
Caledon
Emyvale
Glaslough
Castle Leslie
Middletown
Gosford Castle Forest Park
Markethill
MONAGHAN
MUINEACHÁN
Rossmore Forest Park
KEADY
AN CÉIDE
Darkley
Newtownhamilton
Bessbrook
NEWRY
AN tIÚR
Camlough Mtn.
Mt. Kearney
Poyntz Pass
Scarva
Loughbrickland
Clontibret
Castleshane Forest
Tynan
Lisnagreeve
Forkhill
Annayalla
Creevagh

161
Carnlough
Tf
Ua
Ub
Uc
Ud
Slemish Mountain
LARNE
Stranraer
Island Magee
The Gobbins
Black Head
WHITEHEAD
Douglas
CARRICKFERGUS
Carrickfergus Castle
Town Walls, Castle
GREENISLAND
Belfast Lough
NEWTOWNABBEY
BALLYCLARE
Ballynure
Ballyeaston
Doagh
Straid
Carn Hill
Woodburn and North Carn Forest
Light House Island
Mew Island
Copeland Island
GROOMSPORT
BANGOR
Grey P.
Helen's Bay
Foreland P.
DONAGHADEE
Millisle
Ballycopeland Windmill
HOLYWOOD
BELFAST
Cairn Wood
NEWTOWNARDS
Mt. Stewart Gardens
Mt. Stewart Ho. and Garden
Ballyferis Pt.
Ards Peninsula
Ballywalter
Greyabbey
Grey Abbey
COMBER
The Ulster Way
Strangford Lough
Nendrum Castle
Mahee I.
Kircubbin
Portavogie
Ringboy Pt.
Cloghy Bay
Kearney Pt.
Coastguard Lookout
Ballyquintin Pt.
Strangford
Audley's Castle
Killyleagh
Ringburr Pt.
I. Taggart
Portaferry
Killard Pt.
Guns I.
Ardglass
Jordan's Castle
Ringfad Pt.
St. John's Pt.
Dundrum Bay
Murlough Nat.Res.
DOWNPATRICK
DUN PADRIG
Inch Abbey
St. Patrick Shrine
Saintfield
Ballygowan
Carryduff
Moneyreagh
LISBURN
Hillsborough
DROMORE
BALLYNAHINCH
Castlewellan
Castlewellan Forest Park
Dundrum
NEWCASTLE
AN CAISLEAN NUA
Tollymore Forest Park
Mourne Mountains
Slieve Donard
2796
Slieve Bearnagh
2394
Slieve Muck
2198
Donard Cave
Warrenpoint
171

Enniskillen
Clones
165
Monoghan
168
Sc
Sd
Se
Sf
Ta
24
25
26
27
28
Bawnboy Ho.
Moher
Ballyconnell
Slieve Russell Ho.
Gortmullan
Cloncoohy
Killycluggin
Fartrin Cross Rds.
Callaghs
Ardlougher
BELTURBET
BEAL TAIRBIRT
Milltown
Drumlane Abbey
Derrygoss
Butler's Bridge
Clonnaroo
Annies Br.
Redhills
Scotshouse
Corraskea
Crossbane
Lisnalee
Rockfield
Newbliss
Aghabog
Annaghmakerrig Forest
Rectory
Rockcorry
Dromore
Corvoy
Creevaghy
BALLYBAY
BEAL ATHA na BEITHE
Edenaneane
Creevelands
Magherashaghryl
Coppanagh Mills
Monaghan
Cavan
Bellamont and Darty Forest
COOTEHILL
MUINCHILLE
Latton
Loughmorne
Shantonagh
Fort Henry
Tullyvin
Drumliff
Ballyhaise
Duley
Drung
Cornagall
Kill
Corgreagh
Binbane
Killyvahan
Coskemduff
Lisnadarragh
Doogary
Raleagh
Killegar
Killeshandra
Killykeen Forest Park
Killykeen
Garthrattan
Danesfort
Drumgor
CAVAN
AN CABHAN
St. Patrick's College
Stragellif
Artonagh Ho.
Stradone
Carrickallen
Mountain Lodge
Drutamon
Canningstown
Corraneary
Knockbride
Shercock
Corvally
Carrigallen
Derrylane
Drumcrow South
Lisnamandra
Crossdoney
Lisduff
Moynehall
Lisreagh
Corraweelis
Killyconnah
Clifferna
Beehive
Tonyduff
Corravilla
Cornafean
Bruse Hill
Drumcrow
Bellananagh
Carrickaboy
Mullymagowan
Knocknagillagh
Drumnaveagh
Waterloo
Drumanespick
Beglieve
Nolagh
Crocknahattni
Arvagh
Moyne
Rosduff
Losset
Aghaconny
Cross Keys
Lurganamre
Derryhum Cross Rds.
Termon Cross Rds.
Baileborough
Braeklin
Cornasaus
Loughanlea
Mohercrom
Drumacarrow Ho.
Galbolie
Knockagby
Ballytrust
Carrigan
Drumbarry
Shannow
Ranrenagh
New Inn
Billis Br.
Cargagh
Killinkere
Fartadreen
Teevurcher
Corfree
Loch Gowna
Loughduff
Mullaghboy
Teedehan
Crosserlough
Derrylurgan
Ballyjamesduff
Annagharnet Ho.
Fertagh
Aghnacliff
Woodville
Larkfield
Cloonagh
Callagh
Aghaloory
Kilnaleck
Killykeen
Kildorragh
Kilquilly
Cuilcagh Ho.
Corboggy
Ash Field
Cormeen Cross Rds.
Newcastle
Virginia
Cloncovet
Ballyheelan
Fortland
Fourhalf Moons
Castlerahan
Dring
Clooneen
Moynagh
Kinahard Ho.
Lough Sheelin
Mount Nugent
Eighter
Corronagh
Lough Ramor
The Gates of Mullagh Cross Rds.
Annesbrook
Ballymakane
Ardmaghbreen
Hill Town
Rathbrackan
Bracklagh
Ross Ho.
Ross
Dungummin Cross Rds.
Knockatemple
Woods Cross Rds.
Maghera Cross Rds.
Lisduff
Mullagh
Carrickspringan
Moata Fm.
Kilshruley Manor
Ballynamona
GRANARD
Finnea
Dungummin Ho.
Ryefield
Ballaghdorragh
Fartagh Cross Rds.
Leitrim
Walterstown Ho.
Moynalty
Ballynasraw Cross Rds.
Clonbroney Cross Rds.
Corbeagh Ho.
Brownes Cross Rds.
Abbeylara
Ramogue
Fernsborough
Castlecor
Fennor Cross Rds.
Carroll's Cross Rds.
O'Dalys Br.
Billywood Cross Rds.
Horath Cross Rds.
Mossvale
Moorhill Ho.
Toneen Lo.
Derrycrave
Castletown
Ballynacree
Moat View
Oldcastle
Virginia Road
Rahendrick
Cloonagrouna Ho.
Togherstown
Mahonston Ho.
Firmount
Castle Nugent
New Grove
Millbrook
Slieve na Calliagh
Stonefield Ho.
Carnaross
Dulane
Carlanstown
Lisryan
Killasong
The Rock of Curry
Whitegate
The Hill of Mael
Baltrasna Ho.
Naper's Dome
Ballinlough
Castlekeeran
Maudlin Br.
Collamber Manor
Lismacaffry
Float
Newcastle
Ballycomoyle
Drumone
Seymourstown
Ballally
CEANANNAS
Sedenrath
Lisnageeragh
Edgeworthstown House
Edgeworthstown
Kildevin
Coole
Turbotston
Coole Upper
Freaghmore
Corbally
Knocklough Cross Rds.
Crossakeel
Boltown Ho.
Roachtown
Clonwhelan
Street
Coolnagun
Simonstown Ho.
Tullynally Castle
Srunahella
Fore Priory
Ballinlough Lo.
Lakefield Ho.
Rathniska
Kilskeer
Robinstown
Grangegoddan Glebe
Bohernacross
Lissanure
Newpass
Barratogher Ho.
Coolure
Castlepollard
Lough Park Ho.
Fore
Ben of Fore
Cross Keys
King's Cross Rds.
Scurlockstown
Millton Ho.
Cortown
Rathowen
Lough Derravaragh
Kiltoom
Grangestown
Old Court
Lough Lene
Fore Antiquities
Glenidan Cross Rds.
Killallon
Clonmellon
Girley
Tordstown
Balrathboyne Glebe
Killeen
Clontymullan
Lackan
Donore
Faughalstown
Collinstown
Lough Adeel
Scurlockstown Cross Rds.
Fax Hall
Legan or Lenamore
Ballinacloon
Ten Acres
Multyfarnham
Rathbrack
Knockeyon
Drumcree
Ballinlough Castle
Cloran Cross Rds.
Grennanstown Ho.
Athboy
Tullaghanstown
Emper
Baronstown
Lough Iron
Bunbrosna
Franciscan College
Patrick
Garlandstown Ho.
Devlin
Delvin
Rath Cain
Emper Lo.
Willifield Ho.
Grange Hall
Blind Key
Ballynafid
Crookedwood
Lough Analla
Cumminstown
Kelly's Br.
Lodge
Ballynacarrigy
Mount Murray
Portnashangan
Rectory
Monkstown
Fennor
Rockview Ho.
Clonleame Cross Rds.
Ballynadrimna Cross Rds.
Moyme
Piercetown
Sonna Ho.
Monroe
Lough Owel
Portloman
Ballynagall
Monilea
Knockdrin Castle
Knockdrin
Lough Drin
Crazy Corner
Graffanstown
Sallyview
Robbersbush
Kildalkey
Tullyard
Fairy Mount
Tullaghan
Levington Park
Pass if you can
Tevrin
Sion Hill
Scarden Ho.
Craddanstown
Corballis Br.
Milltown
Skeagh
Rathconrath
Ardonagh Cross Rds.
MULLINGAR
AN MUILEANN gCEARR
Rathconnell Court
Clogham
Drumman
Clonlost
Craddanstown Lo.
Grange More Ho.
Belvue
Ballivor
BAILE ÁT
Dalystown House
Glascorn Ho.
Loughazon Hall
Kenny
Walshestown South
Raharney
Ratrass
Clonycavan
Muchwood Ho.
Darlingstown Ho.
Clonown
Balrath Lo.
King Tuathal's Palace
Uisneach
Milltown
Ladestown Ho.
Lynn Cross Rds.
Plodstown
Greatdown
Kinnegad
Russellstown
Killucan
Rathwire
Riverdale Ho.
Tinkerslane
Kilmur Ho.
Dalystown Ho.
Killare Ho.
Killare
Lunestown Ho.
Loughanavally
Gainestown
Larkfield Ho.
Thomastown
Cara
Dysart
Tudenbam Park
Tallyho
Gaybrook
Violetstown Ho.
Knockaville
Heathstown
Ballinla
Coralstown
Cloncrave
Hill of Down
Ardanew
Kilballyporter
Killaroo
Rathnamuddagh Ho.
Kilcooley Ho.
Lough Ennell
Belvedere
Anneville Ho.
Gaybrook Ho.
Lemongrove Ho.
Aghamore
Togher
Freagh
Streamstown
Adamstown
Castletown Geoghean
Lilliput Ho.
Dunboden Park
Kinnegad
Longwood
Rathcore
Garhy
Middleton Ho.
Baughna
Milltownpass
Heatherville
Ballynakill Cross Rds.
Perth Ho.
Ballynabarna Cross
Cloonagh Ho.
Ticroghan
Mulphedder
Kilbeggan
Kilbeggan
Dublin

169

Armagh
Newry
Camlough
NEWRY
AN IUBHAR
Mourne Mountains
Slieve Muck
2198
Slieve Binnian
2449
Annalong Wood
Silent Valley Reservoir
Crossmaglen
Slieve Gullion
1893
Slieve Gullion Forest Park
Forkill
Jonesborough
Omeath Park
WARRENPOINT
AN POINTE
Omeath
Rostrevor
Rostrevor Forest Nat. Res.
Carlingford Lough
Carlingford
Slieve Foye
1935
Greenore
Cranfield Pt.
KILKEEL
CILL CHAOIL
Mourne Park
Ballymartin
Riverside
DUNDALK
DÚN DEALGAN
Dundalk Harbour
Slievenaglogh
1027
Ballagan Pt.
Whites Town
White Ho.Pt.
Cooley Pt.
CARRICKMACROSS
CARRAIG MHACHAIRE
Inniskeen
Knockbridge
Louth
Blackrock
Clermont Park
Marsh Fm.
Dromiskin
Castlebellingham
Annagassan
Dunany Point
ARDEE
BAILE ÁTHA FHIRDHIA
Tullydonnell Hill
218
Clonmore
Togher
Port
Slieve Donard
2796
Donard Cave
Mullartown
Annalong
Ballyveagh
Ballinran
Ballymartin
KILKEEL
CILL CHAOIL
Derryoge
Mount Oriel
810
Collon
Clogher Head
Monasterboice High Crosses and Rd.Tower
Monasterboice
Termonfeckin
Mellifont Abbey
DROGHEDA
DROICHEAD ÁTHA
Baltray
Hill of Slane
Slane
New Grange
Dowth Tombs
Mornington
Bettystown
Laytown
NAVAN
AN UAIMH
Duleek
Julianstown
Mosney
Gormanstown
Kilberry
Boyne Towpath
Athlumney
Raths of Tara
BALBRIGGAN
BAILE BRIGÍN
Rockabill
St. Patrick's Island
SKERRIES
NA SCEIRÍ
Shenick's Island
Loughshinny
Rush
Lusk
Portraine
Donabate
The Nose
418
Lambay Island
Ratoath
Ashbourne
Dunshaughlin
Fairyhouse Race Course
Swords
MALAHIDE
MULLACH ÍDE
Dublin
Dublin
Dublin

IRELAND (ÉIRE) 174 Galway Galway

KINTYRE
Southend
Mull of Kintyre
Sanda
Malin Head
Trawbreaga Bay
Glengad Head
Malin
Culdaff
Fanad Head
Seven Arches
Portsalon
Clonmany
Carndonagh
Carn Domhnaigh
Inishowen
Slieve Snaght
2019
Moville
(Bun an Phobail)
Inishowen Head
Greencastle
Rathlin I.
NORTH CHANNEL
Giant's Causeway
Dunluce Castle
Portstewart
Portrush
Bushmills
Ballintoy
Carrick-a-Rede
Ballycastle
Ballyvoy
Torr Head
Downhill
COLERAINE
Macosquin
Derrykeighan
Ballybogy
Armoy
Cushendun
Antrim Gorges
Cushendall
Trostan
1817
Waterfoot
(Glenariff)
Garron Tower Hotel
Carnlough
Glenarm
Antrim Mts.
Stranraer (2)
The Maidens
Buncrana
(Bun Crannaighe)
Carrowkeel
Lough Foyle
Rosapenna
Carrickart
Glen
Milford
Rathmullan
Inch Island
Fahan
Muff
GRIANAN OF AILEACH
Bridgend
Rathmelton
Eglinton
LONDONDERRY
Limavady
Ringsend
Ballymoney
Drones
Killagan
Cloghmills
Newtown Crommelin
Clogh
The Sheddings
Carncastle
LARNE
Island Magee
The Goblins
Gransha
Newtown Cunningham
Carrigans
Kildrum
St Johnstown
Raphoe
Convoy
CARVINGS
Lifford
(Leithbhear)
Stranorlar
(Srath an Urláir)
Ballybofey
Castlefinn
Strabane
Clady
Dunnamanagh
Claudy
Feeny
Park
Five Cross Road
Garvagh
Kilrea
Dungiven
Carn
Glenshane Pass
1774
Swatragh
Cullybackey
Portglenone
Maghera
Tobermore
Ahoghill
Ballymena
Broughshane
The Battery
Moorfields
Kells
Ballyclare
Doagh
Ballynure
Whitehead
Eden
Carrickfergus
Carrickfergus Castle
Liverpool (9)
Sperrin Mts
2240
Mount Hamilton
Moneyneany
Desertmartin
Bellaghy
Magherafelt
Randalstown
Toome
Round Tower
Antrim
Templepatrick
Whiteabbey
Bangor
Mew I.
Copeland I.
Donaghadee
Millisle
Castlederg
Killeter
Ardstraw
Newton Stewart
Gortin
Plumbridge
Gortin Glen
Mullaghcarn
1778
Forest Park
NORTHERN
IRELAND
Ballyronan
Moneymore
Springhill House
Cookstown
Coagh
Lough Neagh
Belfast International Airport
Nutts Corner
Newtownabbey
BELFAST
Holywood
Newtownards
Glenavy
Hannastown
Dundonald
Comber
Mt. Stewart Gardens
Greyabbey
Ballywalter
Omagh
Drumquin
Drumskinny
Lack
Clanabogan
Carrickmore
Pomeroy
Stewartstown
Newport Trench
Ederny
Beragh
Dromore
Fintona
Irvinestown
Dungannon
Coalisland
Maghery
Aghalee
Lisburn
Carryduff
Nendrum Castle
Ballygowan
Kirkcubbin
Ballyhalbert
Trillick
Ballinamallard
Ballygawley
Moy
Portadown
Lurgan
Magheralin
Waringstown
Hillsborough
The Temple
Saintfield
Gardens of Rowallane
Ardkeen
Ards Penins.
Cloghy
Killadeas
Augher
Clogher
Aughnacloy
Dyan
Caledon
Tempo
Fivemiletown
ARMAGH
Clare
Lawrencetown
Dromore
Ballynahinch
Crossgar
Killyleagh
Portaferry
Kearney
Strangford Lough
Strangford
Enniskillen
Castlecoole House
Lisbellaw
Brookeborough
Slieve Beagh
1221
Emyvale
Killylea
Hamiltons Bawn
Gosford Castle
Gosford Park
Markethill
Poyntzpass
Scarva
Gilford
Banbridge
Loughbrickland
Dromara
Katesbridge
Ballyward
Clough
Downpatrick
Kilclief
Maguiresbridge
Upper Lough Erne
Lisnaskea
Rosslea
Monaghan
(Muineachán)
Middletown
Keady
Ballyroney
Castlewellan
Tyrella
Jordan's Castle
Ardglass
Killough
Mullan
Newtown Butler
Clontivrim Bridge
Clones
Carnagh
Newton Hamilton
Derrymore
Camlough
Rathfriland
Dundrum
Dundrum Bay
Newcastle
Slieve Donard Hotel
Slieve Donard
2796
Ballyconnell
Belturbet
Legakelly
Newbliss
Corvoy
Ballybay
Tullynagrow
Belleek
NEWRY
Hilltown
Mourne Mountains
Glasdrumman
Annalong
Bawnboy
Rockcorry
Castleblaney
Upper Fathom
Warrenpoint
Rostrevor
Lisnacree
Kilkeel
Newton Gore
Butlers Bridge
Drum
Cootehill
Culaville
Tullydonnell
Carrickcarnon
O'Meath
Flurry Bridge
Carlingford
Greencastle
Greenore
Killashandra
Ballyhaise
Shantonagh
Drumbilla
DUNDALK
(Dún Dealgan)
Riverstown
Carrigallen
Crossdoney
Cavan
(An Cabhán)
Stradone
Shercock
Carrickmacross
(Carraig Mhachaire Rois)
Sandymount
Arvagh
Bellananagh
Bailieborough
Louth
Dundalk Bay
Moyne
Scrabby
Kingscourt
Castlebellingham
IRISH SEA
Greengates
Kilnaleck
Ballyjamesduff
Virginia
Ardee
(Ath Fhirdia)
Annagassan
Dunany Point
Drumcondrath
Dromin
Togher
Dring
Granard
Nobber
Dunleer
Grangebellew
Ballinalee
Finnea
Lough Sheelin
Mullagh
Moynalty
Woodtown
Newtown Monasterboice
Clogherhead
Abbeylara
Oldcastle
Carlanstown
Collon
Monasterboice
Lisryan
Ceanannus Mor
(Kells)
Wilkinstown
Mellifont Abbey
Termonfeckin
Coole
Castlepollard
Fore
Crossakeel
Kilberry
Slane
DROGHEDA
(Droichead Átha)
Rathowen
Clonmellon
Fordstown
Newgrange Tumulus
Laytown
Ballinalack
Drumcree
Navan
(An Uaim)
Dunmoe Castle
Duleek
Julianstown
Mosney
Bunbrosna
Crookedwood
Athboy
Kentstown
Gormanston
Delvin
Ardcath
Naul
Balbriggan
(Baile Brigin)
Ballynacarrigy
Kildalkey
Bective
Tara
Rockabill
Rathconrath
RATHS OF TARA
Garristown
Balrothery
Skerries
Mullingar
(An Muileann Cearr)
Ballivor
Trim
Killucan
Raharney
Dunsany Castle
Dunshaughlin
Ashbourne
Lusk
Rush
Gaybrook
Royal Canal
Rathmolyon
Drumree Hotel
Ratoath
Ballyboghil
Lambay I.
Castletown
Dalystown
Kinnegad
(Ceann Átha Gad)
Longwood
Rathoan
Kilbride
Swords
Donabate
Ballynagore
Rochfortbridge
Castlejordan
Innfield
(An Bóthar Buidhe)
Moyvalley
Dunboyne
Malahide
Portmarnock
Kilbeggan
175
Dublin
IRELAND (ÉIRE)
Dublin

172
Castlebar, Sligo

Boyle, Sligo
Mullingar
Mullingar
173
Dundalk, Belfast
Lambay
ATHLONE (Áth Luain)
Bellaugh
Moyvoughly
Moate (An Móta)
Castletown
Ballynagore
Dalystown
Kinnegad (Ceann Átha Gad)
Longwood
Rathoan
Royal Canal
Kilbride
Donabate
Swords
Malahide
Portmarnock
Ireland's Eye
Howth
Baldoyle
Santry
Dundonnell
Ballinasloe (Béal Átha na Sluagh)
Cornafulla
Clara
Kilbeggan (Cill Bheaga'in)
Tyrrellspass
Rochfortbridge
Castlejordan
Moyvalley
Johnstown
Innfield (An Bóthar Buidhe)
Kilcock
Dunboyne
Carton
Clonee
Maynooth
Leixlip
Lucan
Celbridge
Clondalkin
DUBLIN (BAILE ATHA CLIATH)
DUN LAOGHAIRE (DUNLEARY)
Dalkey
Killiney
Douglas [4 3/4]
Liverpool [8]
Clonmacnoise
HIGH CROSS
Ballycumber
Derrygolan
Derrygrogan
Road
Killiane
Edenderry (Eadan Doire)
Carbury
Derrycrib
Shannonbridge
Ferbane
Gallen Priory
Tullamore (Tulach Mhór)
Grand Canal
Daingean
Ballinagar
Allenwood
Prosperous
Clane
Newcastle
Rathcoole
Mt. Seskin
Tallaght
Dundrum
Cathedral
Clonfert
Eyrecourt
Banagher
Clonbullogue
Geashill
Killeigh
Robertstown
Kilmeage
Sallins
Boston
Rathangan
Kill
Naas (Nás)
Kilteel
Brittas
Kilbride
Bray (Bri Chualann)
Bray Head
Enniskerry
Powerscourt Gardens
Greystones
Clogham
Frankford (Kilcormac)
Cushina
Clonygowan
Portarlington (Cúl-an-t-Súdaira)
Milltown
Blessington
Droichead Nua
Kildare
Shannon
Little Brosna
Portumna (Port Omna)
Rath
Clonaslee
Rosenallis
Jamestown
Monasterevin
Japan Gardens
Kildoon
Kilcullen
Ballymore Eustace
Poulaphuca Falls
Athgreany Piper's Stones
Hollywood
Mullaghcleevaun 2783
Newtown M. Kennedy
Kinnitty
Birr (Biorra)
Killyon
Claree
Ballingarry
Slieve Bloom Mountains
Mountmellick
Ballybrittas
Museum
Longford
1734
Ballyfin
Portlaoise
Stradbally
Fontstown
Narraghmore
Ardscull
Ballitore
Crookstown
Dunlavin
Roundwood
Ashford
Mount Usher Gardens
Ballinalea
Rathnew
Wicklow (Cill Mhanntá'in)
Wicklow Head
Newcastle
Glendalough
Laragh
Boheraphuca
Mt. St. Josephs Abbey
Roscrea (Ros Cré)
Shinrone
Mountrath
Castletown
Borris in Ossory
Athy (A'th 1)
RATH OF MULLAMAST
Timolin
Moone
Stratford-on-Slaney
Lugnaquilla Mt. 3039
Deputy's Pass
Rathdrum
Glenealy
Beehive
Ardcrony
Cloughjordan
Dunkerrin
Ballyroan
Abbeyleix (Mainistir Laoise)
Timahoe
Ballylynan
Arless
Baltinglass
Castledermot
Kiltegan
Aghavannagh
Brittas Bay
Nenagh (Aonach Urmhumhan)
Toomyvara
Moneygall
Errill
Donaghmore
Rathdowney
Durrow (Darú)
Ballinakill
Clogh
Graigue
CARLOW (Ceatharlach)
Rathvilly
BIG TREE RATH
Hacketstown
Wicklow Mountains
Aughrim
Avondale Forest Park
Avoca
Woodenbridge
Mizen Head
Templemore
Templetouhy
Castlecomer
Clonmore
Tullow (Tulach Ua bhFeidhlimidh)
Tinahely
Croghan Mt. 1993
ARKLOW (AN TINBHEAR MÓR)
Borrisoleigh
Johnstown
Urlingford (A'th na nUrlainn)
Freshford
Ballyragget
835
Leighlinbridge
Upperchurch
Milestone
Thurles
Cistercian Abbey
Littleton
Twomileborris
Kilcooley Abbey
Slieveardagh Hills
Dunmore Caves
Clara Castle
Whitehall or Paulstown
Bagenalstown
Ballon
Myshall
Clonegal
Shillelagh
Carnew
Inch
Gorey (Guaire)
IRELAND (ÉIRE)
Holycross
Kilkenny (Cill Chainnigh)
Kilmanagh
Ballingarry
Gowran
Bunclody (Bun Clo'idi)
Clogh
Courton Harbour
Riverchapel
Ballagh
Dundrum
Rock of Cashel
Cashel (Caiseal)
Killenaule
Burnchurch
Callan
Bennettsbridge
Dungarvan
Borris
Leinster Mt. 2610
Kiltealy
Camolin
Ballycanew
Ferns
Golden
Kells
Graiguenamanagh
Enniscorthy (Inis Córthe)
Monamolin
Cahore Point
Bansha
Rosegreen
Mullinahone
Jerpoint Abbey
Thomastown
Knocktopher
Killane
Ford
Newinn
Fethard
Cloneen
Inistioge
Ballyhale
Oulart
Kilmuckridge
Blackwater
Mountains
Cahir (Cathair Dún Iascaigh)
Ninemilehouse
Kilmaganny
Clonroche
Oilgate
Clonmel (Cluain Meala)
Kilsheelan
Carrick-on-Suir
Piltown
Fiddown
Mullinavat
Glenmore
Rosbercon
New Ross (Ros Mhic Treoin)
Adamstown
Camaross
Castlebridge
Curracloe
Wexford Bay
WEXFORD (Loch Garman)
Ardfinnan
Comeragh Mountains
Clogheen
Knockmealdown Mountains
2609
Ballymacarbry
2478
Curraghmore House
Portlaw
Clonea
Granny Castle
John F. Kennedy Memorial Park
Dunbrody Abbey
Taghmon
Johnstown Castle
Rathmacknee Castle
Bridgetown
Rosslare (Ros La'ire)
Rosslare Harbour
Fishguard [3 1/2]
Ballinamult
Mt. Melleray Monastery
Monavullagh Mountains
2387
Kilmacthomas
The Sweep
WATERFORD (Port Láirge)
Cheekpoint
Passage East
Arthurstown
Coolhull Castle
Duncormick
Killinick
Tagoat
Tuskar Rock
Churchtown
Carnsore Point
Ballyduff
Cappoquin
Lismore
Tallowbridge
Tallow
Kill
Bunmahon
Tramore (Tráig Mór)
Dunmore
Fethard
Ballyteige Bay
Kilmore Quay
Saltee I.
Conna
Stradbally
Annestown
Waterford Harbour
Churchtown
Hook Head
Pembroke [4]
Aglish
Strancally Castle
Blackwater
Dungarvan (Dún Garbhán)
Ringville
Clashmore
Mine Head
Killeagh
Round Tower
Youghal (Eochaill)
Ardmore
Castlemartyr
Youghal Bay
Ballymacoda
Ballycotton Bay
Swansea [10]
Roscoff [45]
Le Havre [21 1/2]
Cherbourg [17]
Le Havre [21]

HISTORIC CITIES

Great Britain has more than its fair share of historic cities, in a land which has been safe from conquest for nearly 1,000 years and has thus been able to preserve so much of its historic past. Every town and city in the country has its medieval street plan, its rows of elegant, Georgian houses, and can boast a church or cathedral in the great styles of English architecture. The British townscape is unique and distinctive, it is an open invitation to exploration.

Aberdeen The Granite City

John Betjeman described Aberdeen as "a strange, textured place... so remote, so windswept and of such a solid, grey strangeness". Scotland's third-largest city is the centre of Britain's oil-drilling industry.

Aberdeen is the third-largest city in Scotland. It is the capital of the Grampian region, the north-eastern corner of Scotland that is not technically part of the Highlands, but a region all on its own. Aberdeen is not only the oil capital of Great Britain and a major fishing port, it is also a Scots holiday resort with sandy beaches, excellent golf links and a mild climate. The first impression of Aberdeen is of overwhelming cleanliness. Aberdeen is a city built on and of grey granite, and this gives the buildings their rather stark aspect, especially in overcast weather.

Information
City of Aberdeen Tourist Information Centre
St. Nicholas House
Broad Street
Aberdeen
Tel: (0224) 632727

Events
The Aberdeen Alternative Festival is held in October, and combines traditional Scottish culture (pipe bands, Scottish fiddlers, Scottish folksongs) with music, dance and drama from all over the world. There is usually an entry from Aberdeen's twin city, Bulawayo in Zimbabwe. Many of the events are free.
The Fish Festival in August features ways in which to cook and serve fish.
The Clydesdale Horse Show features those famous carthorses with their lovely "feathered" feet. There are plenty of opportunities for pony rides for children.

Tips
Aberdeen is now quite a cosmopolitan city, thanks to the oil boom, one of the few places in Scotland where you are likely to find good continental food. There are plenty of attractions that will amuse and interest children. The city centre is fairly accessible by car, and there are plenty of local excursions, especially for people who like visiting castles of which there are at least 150 on Deeside!

History

Despite the fact that Aberdeen is built on a convenient stretch of beach between two rivers, the Dee and the Don, there does not appear to have been a settlement here until relatively recently. A town was founded in the 12th century, which was granted a series of charters in the 13th century, giving it the status of a Royal Burgh. In 1308, the English occupied the town but the Aberdonians won it back attacking the castle using as their battle cry the French phrase "Bon Accord" which remains the city's motto. Unfortunately, the English returned in 1336 when they practically razed Aberdeen to the ground; the castle was never rebuilt. This why the St. Machar's Cathedral is so heavily fortified. Aberdeen is divided into "old" and "new" towns, though as usual, the "new" is not new at all. "Old" Aberdeen was once known as the Kirktoun of Seaton; it is the area closest to the River Don, and is popularly referred to as Aulton. It was in Old Aberdeen that the university was founded when a papal bull was granted to Bishop Elphinstone in 1494 to establish Kings College. After the Reformation, the Protestants, not to be outdone, founded their own university in New Aberdeen, known as Marischal College. The two were merged in 1860 and became the University of Aberdeen. The city's first shipyard was built in 1753, but Aberdeen shipping reached its zenith in the era of the tea clippers and the whaling ships. The fishing industry has always been important. The catch was originally whales, then it became herring and now it is white fish – cod and haddock. Despite the serious decline in fishing, due most recently to EC quotas, Aberdeen remains Scotland's leading fishing port.

St. Machar's Cathedral, looking towards the altar (above, far right).

Marischal College, part of the University of Aberdeen (above left).

Provost Skene's House, in typical Scottish baronial style (far right).

St. Machar's viewed from the gate (above right).

Tourist Attractions

Much of Aberdeen including the long, straight Union Street in the centre of town, was built in the early 19th century. Its elegant Georgian buildings have been compared with those of Edinburgh's New Town. However a few medieval buildings have survived.

The Old Tollbooth and Aberdeen Town House. The first tollbooth on this site at the corner of Broad Street and Castle Street was erected in the 15th century, though this one dates from 1627. The tower and steeple of the Tollbooth now form part of a newer building, the Abderdeen Town House, which is the headquarters of the City Council. The Town House part of the building is in typical 19th-century Scottish baronial style. Aberdeen's **Mercat Cross**, generally considered to be finest in Scotland, dates from 1686. It stands in the centre of the **Castle-**

gate in Castle Street, at the eastern end of Union Street. The cross is heavily decorated with portraits of the Stuart kings and surmounted with a unicorn. **Provost Skene's House** was built in the mid 16th century but was extensively refurbished a century later. It is named after Sir George Skeen, who was Provost (mayor) of Aberdeen. The Duke of Cumberland lodged here before going off to defeat the Bonnie Prince Charlie's army at Culloden in 1746, ending forever the Stuart claims to the throne of Britain. The house is now a museum and features a magnificent painted ceiling dating from 1630. Another provost's house is also a museum. **Provost Ross's House** (1593) is now the **Aberdeen Maritime Museum.** The museum contains models of famous tea clippers built in the Aberdeen shipyards. The **Aberdeen Art Gallery** exhibits a permanent collection of the works of Scottish artists as well as some fine French Impressionist paintings. There is also an important collection of applied arts including Scottish silverware and glassware.

King's College In Old Aberdeen is the complex of buildings now part of the University of Aberdeen which have been added to since their foundation in 1495. **King's College Chapel** (1501) boasts a tower surmounted by a crown. It is interesting to compare the King's College buildings with those of **Marischal** (pronounced "Marshall") **College** in the city centre. Marischal was founded on the site of a Greyfriars' monastery of which one gable has been incorporated into **Greyfriars' Church**, completed in 1903. Although almost all the buildings are 19th-century, their imaginative use of the local granite has been much admired.

St. Machar's Cathedral is considered to be one of the finest examples of a fortified church in western Europe. According to legend, it was founded by Machar, a missionary from Iona who was instructed by St. Columba to go northwards through the land of the Picts until he found a place where the river curved like a bishop's crozier. The present church was founded in 1357 and contains 15th- and 16th-century additions of which the most striking is the magnificent painted ceiling (1520). North of the cathedral is the **Wallace Tower**, also known as **Benholme's Lodging**, a 16th-century tower-castle. The Wallace in question is Sir William Wallace, the famous Scottish patriot, though no connection has been established between him and the tower.

Aberdeen has no fewer than three ancient bridges which are still in use. **The Old Bridge of Don**, also known as **Brig o'Balgownie**, is a magnificently-preserved medieval bridge It was begun in 1286 and completed in 1329. The second bridge, **The Bridge of Dee** was built between 1520 and 1527 by Bishop Dunbar, who was also responsible for the cathedral's painted ceiling. The third bridge is the three-arched **Ruthrieston Pack Horse Bridge**, just upstream of the Bridge of Dee (1693-94), which was built on the orders of the Town Council to carry the South Road right into the city centre.

Aberdeen Fish Market in **Aberdeen Docks** is a very special sight which has to be seen when in full swing, at about 6.30 a.m. The fishwives are notorious for their antics and if you can understand their broad Scots accents and Aberdonian dialect a visit to the fish market is as good as watching a comedy show.

Edinburgh "Scotia's darling seat"

Scotland's capital, known as "The Athens of the North" for its learning, or to the inhabitants "Auld Reekie" (Old Smoky) for its smog-filled atmosphere, is built around five extinct volcanoes and two lochs.

The dramatic landscape of Edinburgh is dominated by five extinct volcanos, including Arthur's Seat and Salisbury Crags, which lie within the city limits. Edinburgh's older buildings are built of this grey volcanic stone. The Scottish architectural style of steeply-pitched roofs, narrow windows, towers and turrets and the winding lanes which in Edinburgh are called "wynds", give the city centre its medieval air. Edinburgh is divided into two sections, the central historic Old Town, dominated by Edinburgh Castle, and the New Town, facing it across the valley, with Princes Street. as the dividing line. As usual in Britain, the New Town is far from new, having been built in the late 18th and early 19th centuries. Newtown has spacious streets, crescents, circles and squares, laid out in a grid pattern. The stone-faced buildings were designed and built by the greatest architects of the day, making New Town one the great cityscapes of the Age of Enlightenment.

History

The Celts and Picts held the Castle Rock, the fortress site on which Edinburgh Castle now stands, while the Romans preferred to linger in the lowlands, in the ports of Cramond and Inveresk. King David I (c. 1085-1153) built St. Margaret's Chapel on Castle Rock and several abbeys, thus expanding the city, but Edinburgh did not become the capital of Scotland until the mid-14th century when James II moved his parliament here from nearby Dunfermeline.
Edinburgh flourished, becoming so crowded that rich and poor huddled together in the maze of streets at the foot of the Castle. They crammed into buildings as high as 10 stories which a 17th-century visitor described as "the tallest in the world". The town did not have a proper sewage system and by the 18th century it had become so unpleasant to live in that the City Council was forced to act. The waters of the Nor' Loch, a pool at the edge of the city centre, were drained, and the hill on the other side of the valley was laid out in a pattern of spacious squares and streets, many named in honour of the Hanoverian monarchs.

The visit to Edinburgh of King George IV, in 1822, was such a momentous occasion that the 1.00 p.m. gun fired from Edinburgh Castle in his honour is still fired at the same time today. The Lord Provost (lord mayor) of the time, George Drummond, was successful in urging his fellow citizens to leave the cramped Old Town for the open spaces of the New. This was the period of Edinburgh's great glory, when it was known as "the Athens of the North". The New Town swiftly attracted such eminent inhabitants as James Young Simpson, who discovered anaesthetics and Joseph Lister, who discovered antiseptics, both of whom practised at the Edinburgh Royal Infirmary and taught at Edinburgh University. Sir Walter Scott, Robert Louis Stevenson, David Hume and Adam Smith were writing in Edinburgh at this time, and famous visitors flocked to the city, including Count Bismarck, Felix Mendelssohn and Hans Christian Andersen.

Typical New Town architecture (above).

The Grassmarket in Old Town (above right).

The Forth Road Bridge (above far right).

Ramsey Gardens with the Tollbooth St. John Church in the background (below right).

View of Edinburgh Castle and the Old Town (below far right).

The people of Edinburgh have been accused by other Scots of being "anglicised", partly because of their bitter opposition to Bonnie Prince Charlie, who stayed briefly in the city in 1745, after he had defeated the English at the Battle of Prestonpans.

Tourist Attractions

Any tour of Edinburgh has to begin in Princes Street, at the foot of Edinburgh Castle. This street was once so crowded that there was no room for proper shops and goods were sold from little sheds called luckenbooths ("locked booths"). Princes Street is still the main shopping street in Edinburgh. It has magnificent views of the Castle which overlooks it on one side; on the other there are the lovely Princes Street Gardens. The gardens are laid out over what was once the Nor'Loch, the lake drained when the New Town was built. Starting from the Waverley Station, the Waverley Market built over the station contains many elegant boutiques. The clock in the clocktower of the **North British Hotel**, an Edinburgh landmark, is always three minutes fast to ensure that hotel guests do not miss their trains! The nearby **Register House**, Scotland's public record office, was designed by Robert Adam in 1774. Outside it there is an equestrian statue of the **Duke of Wellington**, and facing it on the opposite corner of the street, a statue of **David Livingstone** (1813-1873), the explorer. The most famous statue in all Scotland is the **Scott Monument**. This elaborate memorial in high Victorian gothic style was created by a local man, George Meikle Kemp, in honour of Edinburgh's most famous son, the novelist Sir Walter Scott. Its 287 steps can be climbed for a magnificent view of the city.

If shopping is more to your taste than climbing, **Jenners**, an elegant department store built in 1895, is on the opposite side of the street. Further along are the **Royal Scottish Academy** and the **National Gallery of Scotland**. Both massive neo-classical buildings were designed by the Scottish architect William Playfair in the early 19th century. The Academy is a school of art which fosters avant-garde painting and holds frequent exhibitions. The collection in the National Gallery is world-famous, and includes the works of major British painters, including Scotland's own Raeburn, as well as Old Masters. Through the Maitland Bequest in 1960 the Gallery received a fine collection of French Impressionist paintings. The city has several other art galleries, including the **Talbot Rice Art Centre** (part of Edinburgh University) the **City Arts Centre** and the **Fruit Market Gallery**, the latter facing each other in Market Street. The **Floral Clock** in the gardens nearby is the oldest in the world, dating from 1903. Just below it is Edinburgh's newest monument, **The Scots Grey**, commemorating the soldiers of the Regiment of the Royal Scots Greys who fell in the Boer War (1899-1902). Edinburgh is a city of statues and memorials to its beloved citizens. Others honoured in this way in Princes Street are **Thomas Guthrie**, a temperance reformer and **James Young Simpson** the discoverer of the anæsthetic chloroform.

Edinburgh Castle is a mighty fortress which dominates the skyline of the city and is still garrisoned by soldiers on active service. It houses Scotland's crown jewels, the **Honours of Scotland**., consisting of the Crown, the Sceptre and the Sword of State. The castle buildings have been erected over the centuries, and many have been destroyed again, since they have been besieged many times in Scotland's turbulent history. The last time was during the 1745 Rebellion when the castle garrison was loyal to the Hanoverians and withstood the siege by Bonnie Prince Charlie's men. The most important buildings in the Castle are David's Tower, built in 1367 and the Half-Moon Battery built in 1574. The Castle **Esplanade** is the setting for the annual **Edinburgh Military Tattoo**, the display which accompanies the **Edinburgh Festival**. The Esplanade marks the beginning of the **Royal Mile**, stretching from Edinburgh Castle to the Palace of Holyroodhouse. At the entrance to the Esplanade, a plaque commemorates the fact that more witch-burnings took place here than anywhere else in Scotland. Just off **Castle Hill** is **Ramsay Gardens**, a collection of 16th-century turretted houses. The nearby **Outlook Tower** has a magnificent view of the city and contains a **Camera Obscura**, installed by an optician named Maria Short in 1853. The Gothic **Tollbooth St. John Church** has the tallest spire in the city. One of the older houses in this area, the 17th-century **Gladstone's Land**, is open to the public and has been refurnished in period style. **Lady Stair's House** (1622) is preserved as a museum and contains relics of Robert Burns (who lived briefly in the close nearby), Sir Walter Scott and Robert Louis Stevenson. A taste of what Edinburgh life used to be like is afforded by **Riddle's Court**, once the home of Bailie

Information
Scottish Travel Centre
South St. Andrews Street
Edinburgh
Tel: (031) 332 2433

Tourist Information and
Accommodation Centre
Waverley Market
Princes Street
Edinburgh
EH2 2QP
Tel: (031) 333 2167

Events
The Edinburgh Festival, the world-famous event whose official name is the Edinburgh International Festival of Music, Drama and Art, and the Military Tattoo, were once part of the same festive occasion. They are now considered as separate events. They are held from mid-August to early September. If you do not want to attend them, it is wise to avoid Edinburgh during this period as naturally it is hard to find accommodation. Book a place to stay well in advance.

Tips
The best way to arrive in Edinburgh is by train, since Waverley Station is right in the heart of the Old City, near Princes Street.
Edinburgh is not an easy city in which to drive. Parking is expensive and hard to find, and the combination of very steep hills and narrow streets is a difficult one. On the other hand, there are plenty of buses and walking is very pleasant; even in the rain there is always somewhere to shelter. It is a good idea to rent a car in Edinburgh and use the city as a centre from which to explore the surrounding area, for there are lots of interesting day excursions.

MacMorran who tried to restore order when rioting broke out in the High School because holidays were to be shortened. The schoolboys shot him dead!
Two of Edinburgh's infamous residents were Burke and Hare, the bodysnatchers, who started by robbing graveyards and digging up corpses to sell to the medical school for experiments but who "graduated" to murdering tramps just to sell the bodies. They were publicly hanged in 1828 at the intersection between George IV Street and Bank Street; a brass plaque marks the spot. Many Edinburgh graves of the period have iron railings and padlocked gates to prevent the bodies being snatched. **Parliament House**, in Parliament Square now houses the **High Court**, the **Court of Session** and the **Signet Library**. The interiors are magnificent and can be visited. There is statue of Charles II on horseback in the square which is said to be the oldest equestrian statue in Britain, completed in 1685. Charles II was the last monarch to have a separate Scottish coronation. A heart-shaped pattern in the west side of the square, known as the **Heart of Midlothian**, marks the site of the **Old Tollbooth**, demolished in 1817. In contrast to the neo-classical parliament buildings of the square, **St. Giles Church** is Gothic in style. It is often referred to as a cathedral, a status bestowed on it by Charles II in 1633, but strictly speaking it is a High Kirk, since it is not the see of a Bishop. Its 15th-century crown tower is one of the city's landmarks; the rest of the exterior was heavily restored in the 19th century. Three of the chapels date from 1387. St Giles has had a turbulent history, having frequently been attacked, first by the English and later by the Scottish Dissenters. The Protestant reformer John Knox preached a sermon here in 1560 denouncing Mary Queen of Scots and her mother, Mary of Guise, for their religious tolerance. The **John Knox House** is now a museum in the High Street and his statue, in a typical ranting pose, stands outside the **Assembly Hall**. The 17th-century **Tron Church**, also in the High Street, has a distinctive spire. The original steeple was burned down in the Great Fire of Edinburgh in 1824 and had to be replaced. It has not been used for worship since 1952. The 16th-century **Huntly House** in Canongate is a fascinating museum of local history. Among its relics is the National Covenant signed in Greyfriars Churchyard in 1638. The 16th-century **Canongate Tollbooth** is also a museum. The **Canongate Church**, built in 1688, was used as a prison for English soldiers by

Princes Street (top).

Street performers in the Edinburgh Festival (above).

The opening parade of the Edinburgh Festival passes the Royal Museum of Scotland above right).

The Edinburgh Castle as seen from the Princes Street (right).

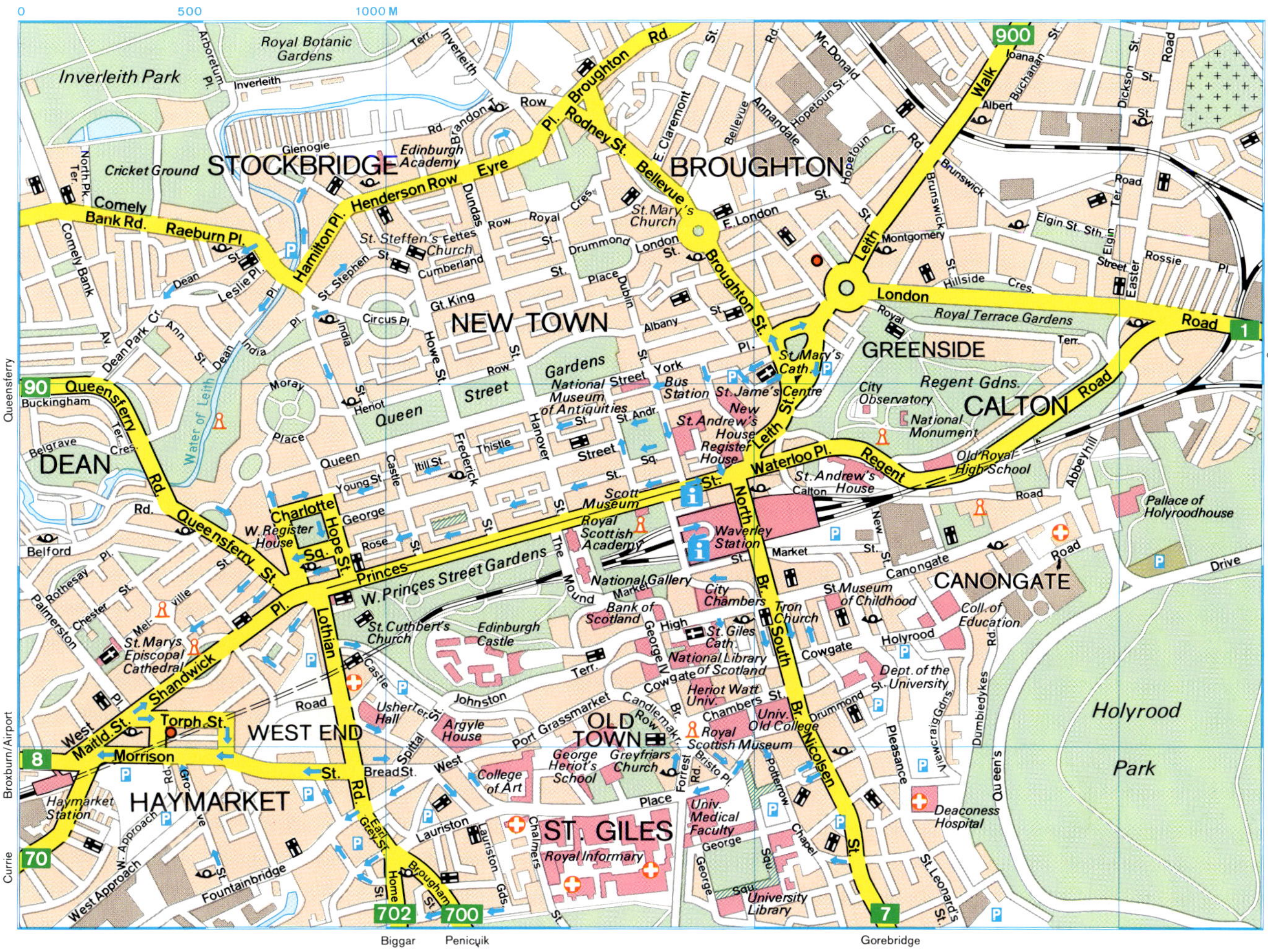

Bonnie Prince Charlie's army. Robert Fergusson, the Scottish poet, is buried in the graveyard.

At the end of the Royal Mile stands the **Palace of Holyroodhouse**. The grounds are known as **Holyrood Park,** a former royal hunting preserve which also contains **Arthur's Seat**, one of Edinburgh's extinct volcanos. There is evidence of a prehistoric hill fort on the site. The Palace itself is the official residence of the monarchy in Scotland though little used by the Royal Family. This is fortunate for visitors, as it can only be toured when royalty is not in residence. It is built on the ruins of the abbey founded by King David I, of which only the roofless nave remains. Much of the fabric of the building is medieval, though restoration and rebuilding were carried out in the 17th and 18th centuries. In the Audience Chamber of the Palace, Mary Queen of Scots argued with her sworn enemy John Knox. It was at Holyroodhouse that Mary married her second husband, Lord Darnley, and here that her secretary, David Rizzio, was murdered. The rooms are magnificently furnished and there is a fine collection of paintings of Scottish monarchs.

Edinburgh has several bridges which are actually viaducts. The **National Library of Scotland**, which contains every book published in the U.K., stands at one end of the **George IV Bridge.** Nearby are the **Edinburgh Central Library** and the **Royal Museum of Scotland.** This museum, one of the largest in Europe, has a magnificent collection of every type of historical artefact. It is a soaring 19th-century glass-and-steel structure. The **North Bridge** spans the valley through which the Nor' Loch once flowed.

Calton Cemetery and **Calton Hill** contain monuments to many famous people, including **Abraham Lincoln** and **David Hume**, the philosopher. The most distinctive monument is that of **Dugald Stewart**, a professor of philosophy. It is based on the Lysicrates monument in Athens. At the top of the hill there is a curious structure consisting of 12 classical columns. It was intended to be the **National Monument**, a replica of the Parthenon in Athens but was never finished.

The **Nelson Monument** (1815), which looks like an upended telescope, was built after the Battle of Trafalgar in 1805. When the 1.00 p.m. gun is fired at Edinburgh Castle, a ball drops from the top of this Monument. Every year on Trafalgar Day on 21 October, the Monument is bedecked in the flags with which Nelson signalled the fleet reading "England Expects Every Man to Do his Duty".

Greyfriars Church stands on the site of a Franciscan monastery. It is here that the National Covenant was signed in 1638, leading to religious wars between the Presbyterians and the established Church. Greyfriars was destroyed several times and finally rebuilt and restored in 1845. **Greyfriars Churchyard** has a unique collection of magnificent memorials, including those to Sir Walter Scott's father and to James Douglas, Earl of Morton, executed in 1581 for his part in the murder of Lord Darnley. The most famous monument however, is that of **Greyfriars Bobby**, the Scots' terrier who watched over his master's grave in the churchyard for 14 years until he himself died.

Edinburgh's **New Town** is as gracious and elegant as ever it was when first inhabited by the intellectuals and middle classes of the city, for it is still the preserve of advocates (Scottish lawyers) and doctors. Many of the buildings were designed by the brothers John and Robert Adam, who were responsible for so many handsome buildings in London. **The Georgian House** at 7 Charlotte Square, has been preserved by the National Trust for Scotland and recreates the decor and furnishings of the house when it was new in 1800. The dark stone and sombre classicism of the buildings are a reinforcement of Edinburgh's rather austere and intellectual image in the eyes of the world. North of New Town, the **Royal Botanic Garden** contains spacious hothouses full of tropical vegetation, and there are frequent special exhibitions at **Inverleith House.**

The only large stretch of water left in Edinburgh is the **Water of Leith**, a little river running west of the city from the moors to the sea at Leith, Edinburgh's harbour. There is riverside path, and a summer stroll along it is a pleasant way of spending the long, bright evenings. There are plenty of opportunities for rest and refreshment in Leith's waterfront cafés and restaurants.

Glasgow – "The pride of the Clyde"

The largest city in Scotland and birthplace of the Industrial Revolution, Glasgow is shedding its image of "the dear, dirty city" and cleaning up its act, particularly since it became European City of Culture for 1990.

Glasgow is the hub of the metropolis along the River Clyde, which includes Paisley, famous for its textiles and East Kilbride, Scotland's "silicon glen" where there is a burgeoning computer industry. Glaswegians are famous for being short, tough and heavy drinkers. This last trait is encouraged by the generous measures of whisky, known locally as "a wee goldie", served in the innumerable public houses. Glasgow is the birthplace of the Industrial Revolution, which in Britain began as early as the mid-18th century. Well before that date, the city and surrounding villages had a flourishing weaving industry. Then, in 1765, James Watt of Greenock, a Glasgow suburb, invented the steam engine and the hand-powered looms were converted to steam. The weavers moved out of their homes and into the mills. Glasgow's other claim to fame is that it is the only city in Britain to be at the centre of an artistic movement, that of Art Nouveau, as propounded by Charles Rennie Mackintosh.

History

Even when the Clyde was a narrow stream suitable mainly for salmon-fishing, Glasgow was a busy place. Roman legions were stationed here during Rome's disastrous attempt to conquer Scotland. The Romans soon retreated, beaten by a combination of the harshness of the Scottish climate and the equally harsh local inhabitants. Ironically, Glasgow now has a large Italian population, though most came this century. They include such famous names as the hotel owner, Charles Forte and the actor Tom Conti. Once the Romans left, nothing was heard of Glasgow until 400 A. D. when St. Ninian is said to have set up the first cross in Glasgow.

Glasgow's prosperity is based on the Clyde. In the Middle Ages, merchants could sail their ships right up the Firth of Clyde (the Clyde Estuary) to dock outside their houses; later the narrow channel of the river was made deep enough for the launch of the luxury liners built in the Clydeside shipyards in the 1920s, 1930s and 1940s, such as the *Queen Mary*, the biggest ship in the world at the time, and the *Queen Elizabeth*. Unfortunately, the great shipyards of Govan, Renfrew and Greenock no longer resound to the riveter's hammer, as shipbuilding is in massive decline. All over the city, the opulently extravagant buildings point to Glasgow's prosperity in the 19th century and the first half of the 20th century, when it was known as the Second City of the Empire and flourished as the greatest industrial centre in Britain.

Tourist Attractions

Although Glasgow is a very ancient settlement, dating from pre-Roman times, no building which survives is older than the 12th century. Of the medieval buildings that remain, **Glasgow Cathedral**, in the High Street, is a fine example of the style known as Early English. It is the only large Scottish church (apart from St. Magnus cathedral in Orkney) to have come through the Reformation intact and is also the only pre-Reformation church in the city. The church, which is divided into two parts, an upper church and a lower church, is dedicated to Glasgow's patron saint, St. Kentigern, who is rather confusingly referred to on his tomb in the Cathedral and elsewhere as St. Mungo. That is because "kentigern" means "chief lord" but this compassionate man was so loved that he was nicknamed Mungo "the dear one". As well as being patron saint of Glasgow, St. Mungo is patron saint of the poor and homeless everywhere. The tomb is alleged to date from 603, and is inside the crypt of the lower church, which itself dates from 1197. The tapestry and murals depicting the life of St. Mungo which decorate the tomb are of even more recent date, but the building itself is said to be on the site of the church St. Mungo himself founded. It

took 300 years to complete the building of the cathedral. It was threatened with destruction during the Reformation, but was defended by local residents who formed an armed guard against the Protestant zealots. It now observes the Church of Scotland rite, and there are two Sunday services and one on Wednesday mornings. The choir stalls were heavily restored in 1957 and these and the pews are dedicated to the various guilds and professional bodies who contributed to their restoration. Next to the cathedral is the **Necropolis**, a burial ground containing many elaborate 18th and 19th century tombs, as well as earlier ones such as that of John Knox (c. 1505-1572), the fiery Protestant reformer. Knox's statue appears to be shaking his fist at the Cathedral, which in his day was Roman Catholic. In Castle Street, a continuation of the High Street, there is a museum in the little house known as **Provand's Lordship**, probably the oldest house in Scotland. The Scottish monarchs, James II, James IV and Mary Queen of Scots are believed to have lodged here briefly. It was here that Mary Queen of Scots, whom John Knox did much to destroy, is supposed to have written the so-called Casket Letter which led to her downfall. The letter was intercepted, she was accused of high treason and forced to flee the country. High Street and Castle Street are probably the oldest streets in Scotland, since there is a record of them in a document which dates from 540.

Glasgow is unusual in that the city, instead of growing up around the original settlement, actually moved away from it and the present city centre is away to the south-west of the Cathedral. Modern Glasgow starts at **George Square**, the main square of the city, which is surrounded by magnificent examples of 18th-century architecture and statues including those of Sir Walter Scott and Robert Burns who lived nearby in Ayr. The city is built on the grid system like New York, and this fact, plus the tenements, the tall, narrow blocks of flats which were a feature of Scottish urban architecture long before they were introduced into England, give the city its unique aspect. A **Tenement House** of the 1890s has been preserved in Buccleuch Street as a museum of Victorian Glaswegian life. Glasgow is the shopping centre for a large part of Scotland. The main shopping streets are **Sauchiehall Street**, **Queen Street** and **Nelson Mandela Place** (formerly St. George's Place). A proportion of Glasgow's wealth traditionally came from tobacco trading with the New World, a fact commemorated by the name Virginia Street. This street contains the **Tobacco Exchange**, now part of an antiques market. Glasgow has some excellent markets, including the Barras (Burrows) in the East End and Candleriggs, an indoor market. After a tiring day's shopping, it is a good idea to drop into a tearoom such as the **Willow Tearooms** on Sauchiehall Street, another of Charles Rennie Mackintosh's masterpieces, though the restaurant itself is now confined to an upper floor. Another historic restaurant in the city is **Sloan's** in the elegant **Argyll Arcade**, between Argyle Street and Buchanan Street. This was the first of the glassed-in arcades, built in 1827 by a wealthy timber importer, and the restaurant contains the original mahogany staircase. The shops, which are decorated with the badges of the leading Scottish clans and families, specialise in gold, silver and jewellery.

Glasgow has many excellent museums and art galleries. One of the most central is the **Annan Gallery** in West Campbell Street, which has a wonderful collection of photographs, prints and paintings from Glasgow's past. The gallery is still owned by the family which founded it in 1855. The **Pollok House** is a handsome 18th-century mansion which is also a museum, and exhibits paintings by Goya and El Greco. The **Hunteri-**

A fierce lion guards George Square (far left).

West George Street (above left).

South Queensferry and bridge over the Clyde (left).

Clydeside (above).

Information
Greater Glasgow Tourist Information Centre
35-39, St. Vincent Place
Glasgow G1 2ER
Tel: (041) 2274894

Travel Information Centre:
St. Enoch Square,
Glasgow G1 4BW
Tel: (041) 226 4826

Events
The biggest annual event in Glasgow is the Mayfest, an international festival of music, poetry and dance.
For more information:
Mayfest Office
Tel: (041) 22755

Glasgow is a busy, vibrant city, in which there is always something happening. Here is a sampler of some other Glasgow events:
The Paisley Festival, a festival of music, is held in May. In June there is a Jazz Festival and the Glasgow Show, as well as the Lord Provosts's Procession (the Lord Provost is the Scottish equivalent of the mayor). In July, there is a Glasgow Folk Festival on Glasgow Green, and in August, the World Pipe Band Championship is held in Bellahouston Park, and the Glasgow Marathon in September.

Tips
It is probably easier to get around Glasgow by car than to travel in other big cities. However, taxis are inexpensive and there are plenty of buses, though since the bus service was deregulated, it is sometimes hard to know where they are going and when they will arrive. The Glasgow Underground, affectionately known as "The Clockwork Orange", is an eight-station railway, originally built in the 19th century, and is worth travelling on for the experience alone. In true Scottish tradition, it is closed on Sundays. There are excellent guided bus tours of Glasgow starting from St. Enoch's Square. Details are available from either of the Information Centres.

an Art Gallery belongs to **Glasgow University**, the second-oldest university in Scotland, founded in 1451 though transplanted to its present site in the mid-19th century. The collection is housed in the Tower, built in 1980. It includes paintings by Whistler, plus Old Masters and works by British artists. The **Mackintosh Wing** contains a reconstruction of Mackintosh's home. The Tower can be climbed for a view of Glasgow, though permission is needed in order to do so. **The People's Palace**, by the River Clyde, is a handsome red sandstone building, with a permanent exhibit devoted to the history of Glasgow, told in tableaux and artefacts. Next to it is the **Winter Garden**, a greenhouse of glass and wrought iron full of huge palm trees. They both stand on **Glasgow Green,** one of the oldest public green spaces in Europe. **Nelson's Column on the Green** was the first monument to be erected to the national hero, long before the one in Trafalgar Square, London. It was dedicated in 1807. The list of Nelson's victories over the armies of Napoleon is carved around the base. Nearby is a boulder with an inscription commemorating the invention of the steam engine by James Watt. The Green overlooks the River Clyde at a point where it is much used by rowing clubs in the summer, so it is a pleasant place to linger in the long summer evenings. On the far side of the Green is the building now known as the **Templeton Business Centre.** William Templeton was a carpet manufacturer, who owned a site on the Green. The City Council would not allow a factory to be built in such a prominent place, so Templeton hired an architect to create a replica of the Palace of the Doges in Venice, though faced with glazed bricks and tiles instead of Italianate marble. While it was being built in 1889, part of it collapsed killing 29 women who were working in a weaving-shed below. Not far from the Green is **Glasgow Cross**, the intersection which once marked the centre of a busy marketplace. The only building to survive from those days is the **Tollbooth Steeple** (1626). The original Tollbooth functioned as both courthouse and jail and public executions and floggings were conducted at its foot. The unicorn-topped **Mercat** (Market) **Cross** which stands at the spot was erected as recently as 1929, to mark the site of the original cross. The nearby **Briggait Centre** is a handsome shopping mall converted from the fish market that once occupied this city centre site.

North-east of the centre is the **Glasgow School of Art**, designed by Charles Rennie Mackintosh, which has become a place of pilgrimage for lovers of his distinctive style of Art Nouveau. Mackintosh was virtually unknown in his home city during his lifetime, but in their fervour to make amends, the City Council has commissioned lamp-posts in the Mackintosh style which now grace the city centre. There is also a **Mackintosh Centre** in Queen's Cross church, Garscube Street, the only church designed by the Art Nouveau master. The congregation of the church has moved to a nearby venue, and the building has been acquired by the Charles Rennie Mackintosh Society which has carefully renovated it.

The **Kelvingrove Art Gallery and Museum** is on the edge of another green space, **Kelvingrove Park**. Downstairs there is a Scottish Natural History section and a small armory. Upstairs, there is a fine collection of Dutch, Flemish, French and Italian Old Masters. Of the sites on the opposite bank of the Clyde, perhaps the most fascinating is **Hagg's Castle**, a little house built c. 1580 for the Maxwells of Pollok, which is now a museum owned by Glasgow Corporation. The museum caters specially to children who have the run of the place. It is mainly an educational centre, teaching the young about life in Glasgow's past, by showing them how to try their hand at such old-fashioned pursuits as cheese-making, butter-churning and sewing rag dolls. There is a lovely garden where horticulture is taught. The **Burrell Collection** in nearby **Pollok Park** contains more than 8,000 exhibits, originally owned by Sir William Burrell, including Chinese pottery and porcelain, medieval stained glass and French 19th-century paintings. The Collection easily rivals the City Museum and Art Gallery in scope and quality. It is now housed in a modern building which can display the collection to its best advantage.

The only castle in Glasgow classified as an Ancient Monument is **Crookston Castle**, four miles from the centre of town in the direction of Paisley. Perched on a hill, the castle affords lovely views of the city and of the Renfrew Moors. It has associations with Mary Queen of Scots, because it was built by the Stewarts of Darnley in the 15th century, and

The magnificent glass roof of the Winter Gardens with the People's Palace behind it (top).

The gothick splendour of the Necropolis with Victorian tombs (above).

Shopping Mall, Princes Square (above right).

George Square with equestrian statues (right).

Glasgow Cathedral (opposite)

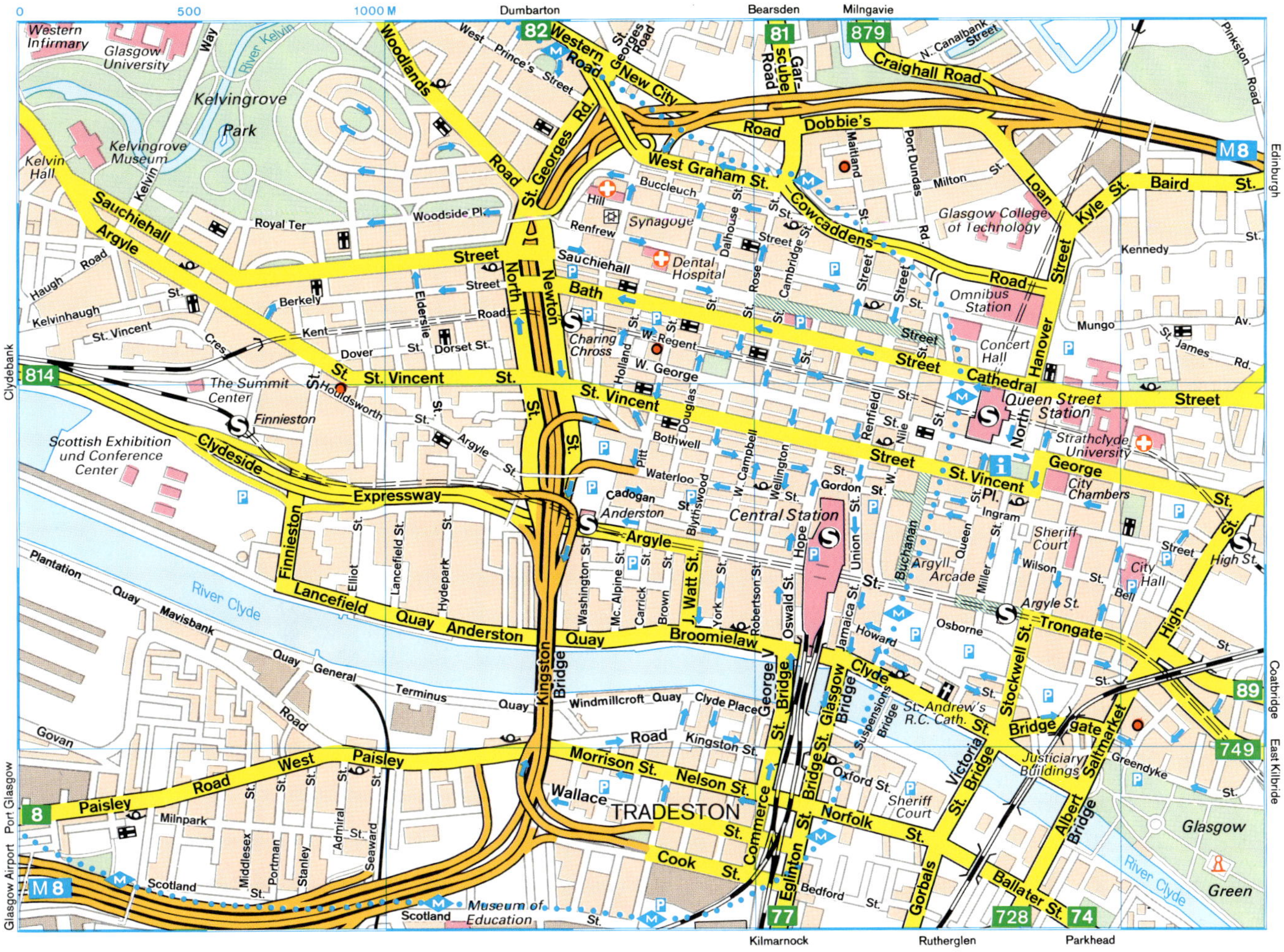

Lord Darnley became Mary's husband. The couple spent some time in the castle in 1567, before they moved to Edinburgh, where Darnley was murdered.
West of the city in the direction of Dumbarton lies the **Kelvin Hall**, once Glasgow's major exhibition centre but now converted into a huge indoor sports centre and home of Glasgow's **Transport Museum**, one of the best collections of vehicles in the country. The neighbouring **Kelvingrove Park** was laid out by Sir Joseph Paxton, designer of the Crystal Palace in London, in the mid-19th century.The park contains the main **City Art Gallery and Museum**, which has a huge variety of exhibits, ranging from ancient Scottish arms and armaments, archæology and the work of local artists. The main attraction, in the art gallery on the upper floor, is Salvador Dali's "Christ of St. John of the Cross", since it was the subject of a scandal. The then director of the museum, Dr. Tom Honeyman, used money from a discretionary fund to buy the painting in 1957 for the huge sum of £8,200. The city councillors were outraged, but

Honeyman's idea of charging admission to see the painting meant that it paid for itself several times over in the first year. Another Glasgow landmark in the general direction of the River Kelvin is the **Mitchell Library**, the largest reference library in Europe and headquarters for Glasgow's excellent public library system with its 43 branches. Nearby are the **Botanic Gardens**, which are successors to the ancient Physick Garden planted by the university professors. The Gardens were moved here in 1842. They contain many hothouses full of rare plants, the most notable and extraordinary of which is known as the Kibble Palace. It has a main dome surrounded by several sattelite houses linked by glassed passages and was designed by an excentric engineer named John Kibble. It contains some magnificent tree-ferns and other beautiful tropical vegetation.
Glasgow becomes more beautiful as more of it is constantly being restored, revived and modernised. It also has more parks and open spaces than any other city in Europe, so that the population density is surprisingly low.

Belfast – Metropolis of the North

Towns and cities are small in Ireland, so Belfast is huge compared with the North, Londonderry. It expanded quickly in the 19th century, its prosperity founded on the linen trade and shipbuilding.

Belfast is the capital of Northern Ireland and the second-largest city in Ireland after Dublin. One third of the population of the province of Northern Ireland lives within ten miles of the city centre. The spirit of the city is epitomised in the statue of Queen Victoria in front of Belfast City Hall, since the town owes its growth, size and prosperity to the 19th-century Industrial Revolution. Belfast is a Protestant and a Roman Catholic see, since both sects have cathedrals in the city.

History

Belfast was founded round a crossing place on the River Lagan which flows into Belfast Lough (pronounced "loch" as in Scotland) a deep inlet of the sea rather than a lake. The city has since grown around the Lough. John de Courcy, a Norman knight sent by Henry II to quell the rebellious Irish, built a castle here in 1177, but the fortress and the settlement around it were destroyed in 1315 after the invasion of Edward Bruce. Belfast then passed into the hands of the O'Neills of Clandeboye. During the Plantation of Ulster in the 17th century, when Northern Ireland was heavily colonised by the English and Scots, Belfast was granted to Sir Arthur Chichester. A new castle was built on the site of the old, though it was later demolished. In 1613, Belfast was granted a charter by King James I. After the Revocation of the Edict of Nantes in 1685, when French Protestants were denied the right to their beliefs, many Huguenots settled in the Belfast area. They brought their weaving trade to the area, thus providing the foundation for much of the wealth of the province. The importance of the linen industry to Northern Ireland is symbolised by the flax plant which is depicted on the reverse side of the Northern Ireland £1 coin. The linen industry reached its zenith in the 18th century. In the 19th century heavy industry came to Belfast, the only town in Northern Ireland to be affected by the Industrial Revolution. When poverty and famine in Ireland were at their height and thousands were emigrating, Belfast continued to prosper mightily from its shipbuilding industry, supplemented by rope-making and tobacco. In the 20th century, it became a centre of the aircraft industry. The population mushroomed from 20,000 in 1800 to 438,000 in 1939. The decline of heavy industry and even of the linen trade has left Belfast with a huge unemployment problem. The gap has been partially

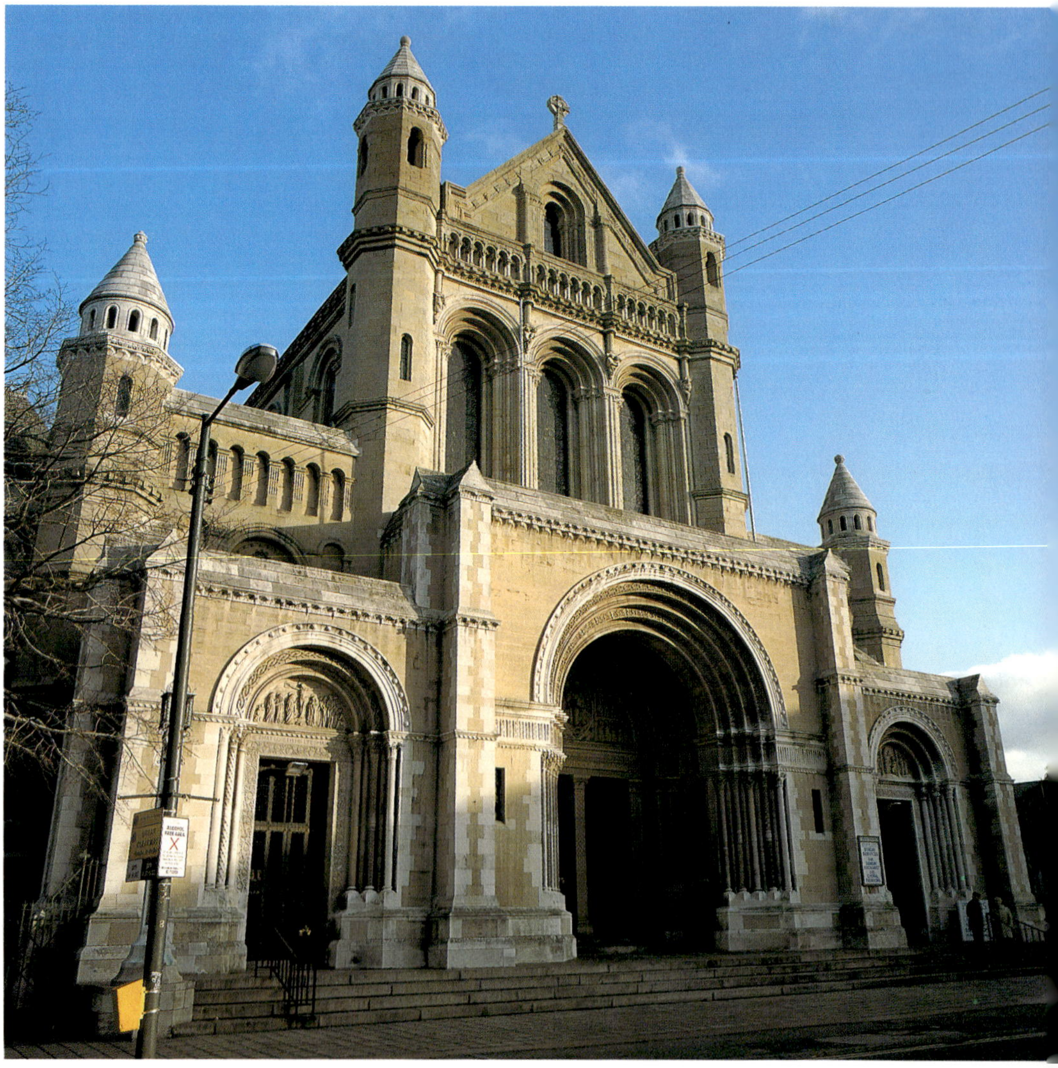

The Croun Bar, a historic Belfast public house (above).

Royal Avenue, Belfast (top).

St. Anne's Cathedral, Belfast (right).

The Stormont, just outside Belfast (opposite above).

Belfast City Hall at night (opposite below).

filled by firms making textile machinery, electronics and electrical goods and by a revival of the linen mills.

Tourist Attractions

By far the majority of Belfast's public buildings date from its heyday in the 19th century. The Victorian taste for opulence caused some fine old buildings to be demolished. When Belfast officially became a city in 1888, the City Fathers decided that the old White Linen Hall, built in 1784, which served as the town hall, was unworthy of the new status and tore it down to build a new **City Hall** of gigantic proportions. The building, which was completed in 1906, now covers one whole side of **Donegall Square** in the city centre. The main façade is 300 feet long, and it has a green copper dome rising to a height of 173 feet, as well as a turret on each corner of the building. The architect, Brumwell Thomas, nevertheless had to sue Belfast Corporation to get his fees! The interior of the building is lined with Italian marble, there is an oak-panelled **Banqueting Hall** and a **Great Hall**. The Great Hall was destroyed in the Blitz in 1941, but was rebuilt in time for the visit paid by Queen Elizabeth II to the province of Northern Ireland in1953. The first Northern Ireland parliament was opened in City Hall by King George V in 1921.

A statue of **Sir Edward Harland** stands in front of the city hall This industrialist came to Belfast from Yorkshire in the 1850s and was a founder of Harland and Wolff, the city's biggest shipbuilder's and one source of its wealth. This was the shipyard which built the *Titanic*, which sank in 1912 on its maiden voyage. The tragic event is commemorated by a marble statue also in front of City Hall. Of course, Harland and Wolff have built many of Britain's greatest ships, including the *Canberra*, a P & O Steamship Company ocean liner (1960), and the oil tanker *Myrina*, the biggest ever built in Europe (1967). Despite the decline in shipbuilding, the shipyard's two giant cranes, known as **Samson** and **Goliath**, still dominate the city skyline. Although the Hall itself has gone, the **Linen Hall Library** stands in the square opposite City Hall. The library was established in 1788 by public subscription and is still maintained in this way. It contains an important collection of books on Irish history. The first librarian, Thomas Russell, was a strong advocate of Irish separatism and was executed in 1803 as a supporter of Emmett's Rising. The other important civic building in the area is the 19th-century **Opera House** which was recently restored. It has a particularly opulent interior, including painted ceilings.

Information

Northern Ireland Tourist Board
48 High Street
Belfast, BT1 2DS
Tel: (0232) 231221

Belfast Tourist Information Centre
48 High Street
Belfast, BT1 2DS
Tel: (0232) 246609

Events

The main annual event in Belfast, as in other parts of Protestant Northern Ireland, is the Orangemen's March, the march to commemorate the Battle of the Boyne, when the Protestant King William II overthrew the Catholic James II. The March takes place on the anniversary of the Battle, 12 July. In Belfast as many as 80,000 men take part. They dress in a "uniform" of bowler hats, dark suits and white gloves. The members of the Orange Lodge, a freemason-like society, wear an orange sash diagonally over the chest.
The Catholics try to rival the Protestants with their march on the Feast of the Assumption on 15 August. The Hibernians wear green sashes, no bowler hats and no white gloves, but other than that the two marches are very similar in style.

Tips

Despite the widely-publicised stories of violence, Belfast is no more violent than any other major city, less in some ways because of the strict security. However, you will have to get used to the regular security checks, especially when shopping in the City centre.

Royal Avenue, the city's main shopping street, leads off from the north side of Donegall Square. **St. Anne's Cathedral**, the Romanesque-style Protestant cathedral which was begun in 1898 and is still unfinished, is in nearby Donegall Street. The cathedral is decorated with many beautiful mosaics. Other churches of particular interest are the **First Presbyterian Church** in Rosemary Street, built in 1783 and much admired by John Wesley who preached there, and the **Sinclair Seamen's Church** (1857). The latter church in the docks area is full of nautical themes; the organ is fitted with port and starboard lights and the pulpit is actually formed from a ship's prow. Nearby is the **Albert Memorial Clock Tower**, Belfast's answer to both Big Ben and the Leaning Tower of Pisa, since subsidence has made it tilt sideways at more than three feet from the vertical. **The Harbour Office** in North Belfast, across the river from **Short's Aircraft Factory**, is now a museum, a fascinating record of the history of Belfast as a port, once the third-largest in Britain. The exhibits include paintings, sculpture and stained glass.

The Roman Catholic cathedral of **St. Malachy** was opened in 1844. It has a beautiful fan-vaulted ceiling and other attractive embellishments in the early Victorian Gothic style.

Belfast is very definitely the seat of learning in Northern Ireland. **The Royal Belfast Academical Institution**, popularly known as the "Inst." is housed in a handsome building built in 1808-10 by the famous English architect, Sir John Soane. Its most illustrious alumnus is Lord Kelvin (1824-1907), whose father taught mathematics here. Kelvin is the inventor of the Kelvin Scale, the absolute scale of thermodynamics. **Queen's University, Belfast** (1849) was founded as one of three non-sectarian Irish colleges, the other two being in Galway and Cork. The University is famous for its science departments. The area around the University is one of the pleasantest in the city, and contains small art galleries and theatres as well as moderately-priced restaurants. Belfast's **Botanic Gardens**, next door to the University, is a focal point of the city. These lovely gardens are famous for the **Palm House**, one of the finest examples of early glass-and-iron constructions in Europe. It was built by Richard Turner of Dublin between 1839 and 1852. Opposite the Palm House is the **Tropical Ravine**, in which exotic species are grown. The **Ulster Museum**, formerly known as the Belfast Museum and Art Gallery, stands amidst the gardens. It has sections devoted to Natural History, Archæology, Ethnography and Applied Arts, including a fine collection of Irish furniture and china. The archæology section specialises in the history of the Armada, the ill-fated Spanish mission to destroy England which set sail in 1588, many of whose ships foundred off the Irish coast. Scholars come from all over the world to study the finds displayed here which include gold and silver jewellery from the Spanish galleon *Girona*, salvaged in 1967-69 by Belgian divers off the Antrim Coast near the Giant's Causeway. The art gallery section contains paintings by local artists, including Sir John Lavery and Andrew Nicholl. The Museum also boasts a valuable coin collection. Ulster's other important museum is the **Transport Museum** in East Belfast, near Glentoran Football Ground. The exhibits cover 200 years of Irish transport and include **Old Maeve,** the biggest steam locomotive built in Ireland, as well as trams, buses, early fire engines, penny-farthing bicycles and vintage cars.

Cave Hill in North Belfast is a steep cliff on whose lower slopes a later Earl of Donegall chose to erect his own "castle" in 1870. **Belfast Castle** is built in 19th-century Scottish baronial style with turrets. It has a square, six-storey tower with an external baroque staircase. The Castle was presented to the nation in 1924, and is open to the public. Part of it is now a restaurant. The grounds are beautifully landscaped. Cave Hill is topped by **McArt's Fort**, the remains of medieval fortifications. Man-made Neolithic caves are in the vicinity. It is here that the United Irishmen, led by Wolfe Tone, plotted rebellion in 1795. On the other side of Cave Hill is **Belfast Zoo**, which also contains a **crannog,** an artificial island which early Christian settlers used as a defence. Cave Hill is 1200 feet high and a good spot from which to view the city, ringed by hills, the highest of which is **Divis Mountain** (1600 feet).

The **Stormont,** four miles east of Belfast, is another building generally associated with the capital. This is the parliament building of Northern Ireland and its Royal Courts of Justice. Despite the grandiose scale and neo-classical style of the building, Stormont itself was only built in 1932 and the Law Courts added in the following year. Both may be visited.

As elsewhere in Ireland, Belfast has even more public houses than churches. Many of Belfast's historic drinking dens are to be found in the "entries", the narrow passageways leading off the **High Street**. Two which are of particular interest are the **Crown Liquor Saloon** in Great Victoria Street near the Opera House and **White's Tavern,** the latter being the city's oldest public house. The Crown Liquor Saloon has been restored by the National Trust to its full 19th century glory, including gas lighting. **Kelly's Cellars** in Bank Street was the headquarters of the United Irishmen who led the Rebellion of 1798; it is now a lively place at night and a popular place to hear traditional Irish music.

The Linenhall Library, Donegall Square, Belfast (above).

Belfast's magnificent Botanic Gardens (left).

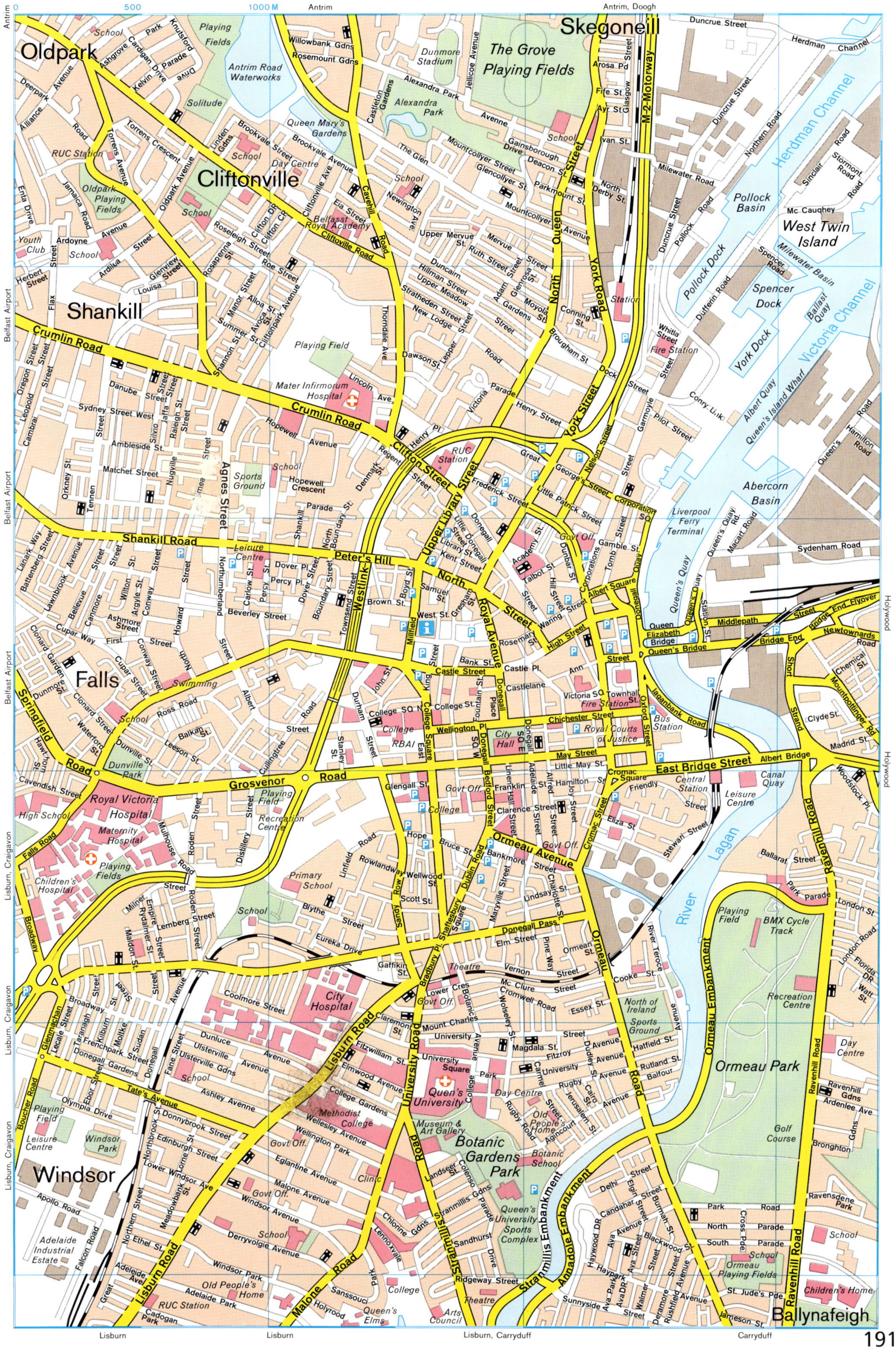
0
500
1000 M
Antrim
Antrim, Doogh
Oldpark
Skegoneill
The Grove Playing Fields
Cliftonville
Shankill
Falls
Windsor
Ballynafeigh
Herdman Channel
Victoria Channel
West Twin Island
Pollock Basin
Pollock Dock
Spencer Dock
York Dock
Abercorn Basin
Liverpool Ferry Terminal
Crumlin Road
Shankill Road
Springfield Road
Grosvenor Road
Antrim Road Waterworks
Mater Infirmorum Hospital
Royal Victoria Hospital
Maternity Hospital
Children's Hospital
City Hospital
City Hall
Royal Courts of Justice
Queen's University
Botanic Gardens Park
Museum & Art Gallery
Ormeau Park
Ormeau Road
Ravenhill Road
Lisburn Road
Malone Road
Stranmillis Road
University Road
Ormeau Embankment
Stranmillis Embankment
Annadale Embankment
River Lagan
North Queen Street
York Road
M 2 Motorway
Westlink
Royal Avenue
East Bridge Street
Albert Bridge
Queen Elizabeth Bridge
Queen's Bridge
Sydenham Road
Central Station
Belfast Airport
Lisburn, Craigavon
Lisburn
Lisburn, Carryduff
Carryduff
Holywood

York – Historic City par excellence

York has preserved a better record of its 1900 years of history than any other British city. "The history of York is the history of England" according to the late King George.

York, at the confluence of the Ouse and the Foss, was for a large part of its history the second-most important city in Britain. Fortunately, it has preserved the relics of its fascinating past. In the 19th century, York successfully avoided the depradations of the Industrial Revolution which blighted so many Yorkshire towns and cities. As the county town of Yorkshire, it remained an important centre, its prosperity resting largely on its confectionery industry and the railways.

History

An Iron Age settlement probably existed here when the Romans founded the garrison of Eboracum in 71 a.d. This became the headquarters of the 6th Legion and the capital of Lower Britain (the Roman name for northern England). The first stone walls were built in the 2nd century a.d. The Emperor Hadrian visited York in 121 A. D. and the Emperor Septimius Severus died here in 211 A. D. This is where Constantine the Great was proclaimed Emperor on the death in the city of Constantius Chlorus in 306, the only instance of a Roman being proclaimed emperor in Britain. The Romans left in 407 and the Saxon town of Eoforwic emerged. The town was a bridgehead for the spread of Christianity and it was here that the missionary Paulinus baptised King Edwin of Northumbria in 627. The city was captured by the Danes in 867, who renamed it Jorvik (hence the modern name) and made it their chief trading centre. William the Conqueror built two wooden castles here. The City walls were started by the Romans but assumed their present shape in the 12th and 13th centuries. There are four gates in the walls which are called Bars; in York, the word "gate" is used in its Norse sense of "street". Medieval York thrived on the wool trade. During the Reformation, the City was plagued by religious strife. In 1586, Margaret Clitherow, the wife of a local butcher, was executed for harbouring Catholic priests; she was canonised as St. Margaret of York in 1970. Another native of York, Guy Fawkes, tried to blow up the Houses of Parliament in 1605, as part of a Roman Catholic plot. Another notorious resident of York was the highwayman Dick Turpin, executed here in 1739. In the Georgian period, York was a centre of fashion and it was also in this period that its main industry – confectionery – emerged. The factories were started by Quakers who were attempting to wean working people away from alcoholic drink and on to sweets and confectionery which they judged to be healthier; the factories are still thriving today. York also became an important railway centre thanks largely to George Hudson, "The Railway King" who made York the headquarters of his North-Eastern Railway.

Tourist attractions

The first thing that strikes one about York is that the walled city happily bestrides the River Ouse and does not confine itself to one bank. The cathedral, **York Minster**, is in the eastern corner of the city and stands on the site of the Roman garrison. It is the

Information
Tourist Information Centre
De Grey Rooms
Exhibition Square
York
YO1 2HB
Tel: (0904) 21756/7

The York Association of Voluntary Guides offers free walking tours of the city.

Events
There is a York Festival every four years, when the York Cycle of Mystery Plays is performed in the ruins of St. Mary's Abbey. York Festival of Early Music is held in July. Race meetings are held between May and October.

Tips
York becomes very crowded in summer so try if possible to visit it out of season. Do not bring a car inside the city walls, the centre of York is much better explored on foot. It makes an excellent centre for touring the Yorkshire Dales by car.

largest Gothic cathedral in Europe north of the Alps, and second in importance only to Canterbury. Its official name is the Cathedral and Metropolitical Church of St. Peter in York. The name "minster", means that it was a centre for missionary activity. The first church on the site was a wooden chapel built for the baptism of King Edwin of Northumbria in 627. The Norman church was gradually replaced by the present structure, a process which took 250 years, starting in the early 12th century. Unfortunately, the Minster has been badly damaged three times by fire, the first time being in 1829 when it was attacked by a madman. In 1840 a candle carelessly dropped burned down the wooden nave and in 1984 lightening destroyed the central vault of the South Transept, the oldest part of the cathedral. As a result, the Minster is guarded night and day by its own 11-man police force, probably the only ecclesiastical institution to have its own police outside the Vatican. Fortunately, many of the Minster's treasures have survived intact. The stained glass windows are famous. They include the **Rose Window**, the work of 16th-century Flemish painters, in the South Transept, and the **Five Sisters Window**, the largest piece of grisaille glass in existence, which is in the North Transept. The Five Sisters are set in huge lancet windows 53 feet long which date from 1260.

The **South Transept** contains the Tomb of Archbishop Walter de Grey who was largely responsible for building this part of the cathedral, designing it on this grandiose scale. When de Grey's tomb was opened in 1968 during restoration work, a painting of him was found inside it, together with his chalice, patten and crozier which are all now on display in the **Undercroft**, along with other Minster treasures. **The Treasurer's House** (c. 1100) stands in the Minster Yard. The Treasurer was responsible for the financial administration of the Cathedral until the Dissolution of the Monasteries. The house deteriorated over the years, but was rescued by a 19th-century philanthropist who used it to house a fine collection of china and furniture. It is now owned by the National Trust.

The story of Viking York is told vividly in the award-winning exhibition called the **Jorvik Viking Centre**, which aims to bring the past to life. Visitors are transported in "time-cars" through a series of tableaux of Viking life, complete with sounds and smells. At the end of the tour, there is a chance to visit the Viking excavations in the Coppergate. Another museum that is fun for all ages is the **Castle Museum**. The Museum is contained in three buildings which surround a grassy circle known as "The Eye of York". They are the castle bailey, known as **Clifford's Tower** (1245), and the three imposing neo-classical structures which were once the Women's Prison, the Debtors' Prison and the Assize Courts, all built in the 18th century. Clifford's Tower is notorious for the massacre of the Jews of York who took refuge in the Tower and were burned to death by the local people in 1190. The tower was later rebuilt though it is no longer used. The Museum exhibits consist of a number of reconstructed streets, furnished with shops containing "bygones", based around the collection of a country doctor called John Lamplugh Kirk who lived on the North Yorkshire Moors. He approached several cities, and finally York agreed to house the museum and accepted his advice on how to display it. The Castle Museum thus became the first folk museum in the country and one of the first in the world.

The Minster viewed from the Close (far left).

Tableau of Viking craftsmen at work in the Jorvik Viking Centre (above left).

Scene in the Shambles, a medieval street perfectly preserved (below left).

Street artist at work on a spring morning outside the Minster (above right).

The most famous street in York is the medieval alleyway known as the **Shambles**. The houses project so far over the pavement that the upper storeys almost touch each other on either side of the street. The Shambles is just one of the quaint passageways of which York is full and which are generally called **Snickelways**. Shambles is a corruption of "fleshammels" – butchers. This may seem a strange name, but it is nothing to the names of some of the snickelways, which include **Mucky Peg Lane**, **Mad Alice Lane**, **Pope's Head Alley**, **Little Thief Lane**, **Hole-in-the-Wall Passageway** and York's shortest street, **Whip-ma-whop-ma Gate**. A stroll through these narrow passageways is a fascinating way to spend an afternoon.

Another way to see York is to walk along the top of the 14th-century walls, a 2 1/2 mile stroll If you only want to walk part of the way. The best part is probably between **Bootham Bar** and **Monk Bar**, via **Mickelgate Bar**, one of the original four gates to the city. The circuit of the Wall is not continuous however, because the area between the 16th-century **Red Tower** and **Layerthorpe Bridge** had the natural protection of a marsh so did not need a wall.

York has many Roman remains. **The Roman Bath Inn**, a modern public house, displays the Baths discovered in 1930 and now glassed in. In the Minster Yard there is a 30-foot **Roman Column** dating from the 4th century a.d. and placed on its present site by the York Civic Trust in 1971 to mark the 1900th annversary of the founding of the city. The most spectacular Roman building is the **Multangular Tower**, which formed the south-western corner of the Roman fortress and which contains various Roman finds. It stands in the Museum Gardens, the grounds of the **Yorkshire Museum**, set in 10 acres of botanical gardens. The Museum is built into the remains of **St. Mary's Abbey,** which was partially destroyed at the Dissolution of the Monasteries and the stones later used for other buildings. Excavations have uncovered the Norman abbey church with its seven apses. The Museum itself, a neo-classical building, was originally built to house a collection of fossils. It now has some excellent specialist collections, including one of optical instruments. The **King's Manor**, originally the Abbot's Lodging, is next door. Most of the building [illegible] 15th century. It now belongs [illegible] the University of York but is open to the public. The oldest residence in York is the **Twelfth Century House** in the Stonegate which dates from c. 1180, is partially ruined. The neighbouring **City Art Gallery** which dominates Exhibition Square has a fine collection of paintings dating from the 14th century to the present day.

Terry's of York, one of the three big confectionery firms, have been responsible for two major bequests to the city. The first is the reconstruction of Joseph Terry's original sweetshop in the Castle Museum and the other is the **Terry Collection** of paintings and furniture, donated to the city and now housed in **Fairfax House**, an 18th century mansion restored by the York Civic Trust.

Railway enthusiasts will find their interests well catered for in York, the home of the **National Railway Museum**, one of the most popular museums in the North. The exhibits here include restored locomotives dating from 1829 onwards and carriages dating from 1797. Several royal carriages are on display, including Queen Victoria's private carriage. **York Railway Station** is a sight to see in itself, its opulence being due to the profligacy of its original owner, George Hudson, three times Lord Mayor and York and known as "the Railway King". York also has a model r[illegible] museum, **Rail Riders'** [illegible] situated between the [illegible]on and the Royal York Hotel. [illegible]ere are two detailed railway layouts, one of which shows a German town at night, lit by hundreds of tiny lights.

York boasts a particularly fine **Assembly Rooms**, built in 1730 by Richard Boyle, and one of the earliest neo-classical buildings in Europe. The main hall is in Egyptian style and is edged with 48 Corinthian columns.

These are just a foretaste of the delights of York, a city packed with ancient churches, inns, restaurants and tearooms, elegant Georgian residences and opulent 19th-century mansions.

The city walls with the Minster in the background (above).

Pleasure boat on the River Ouse (right).

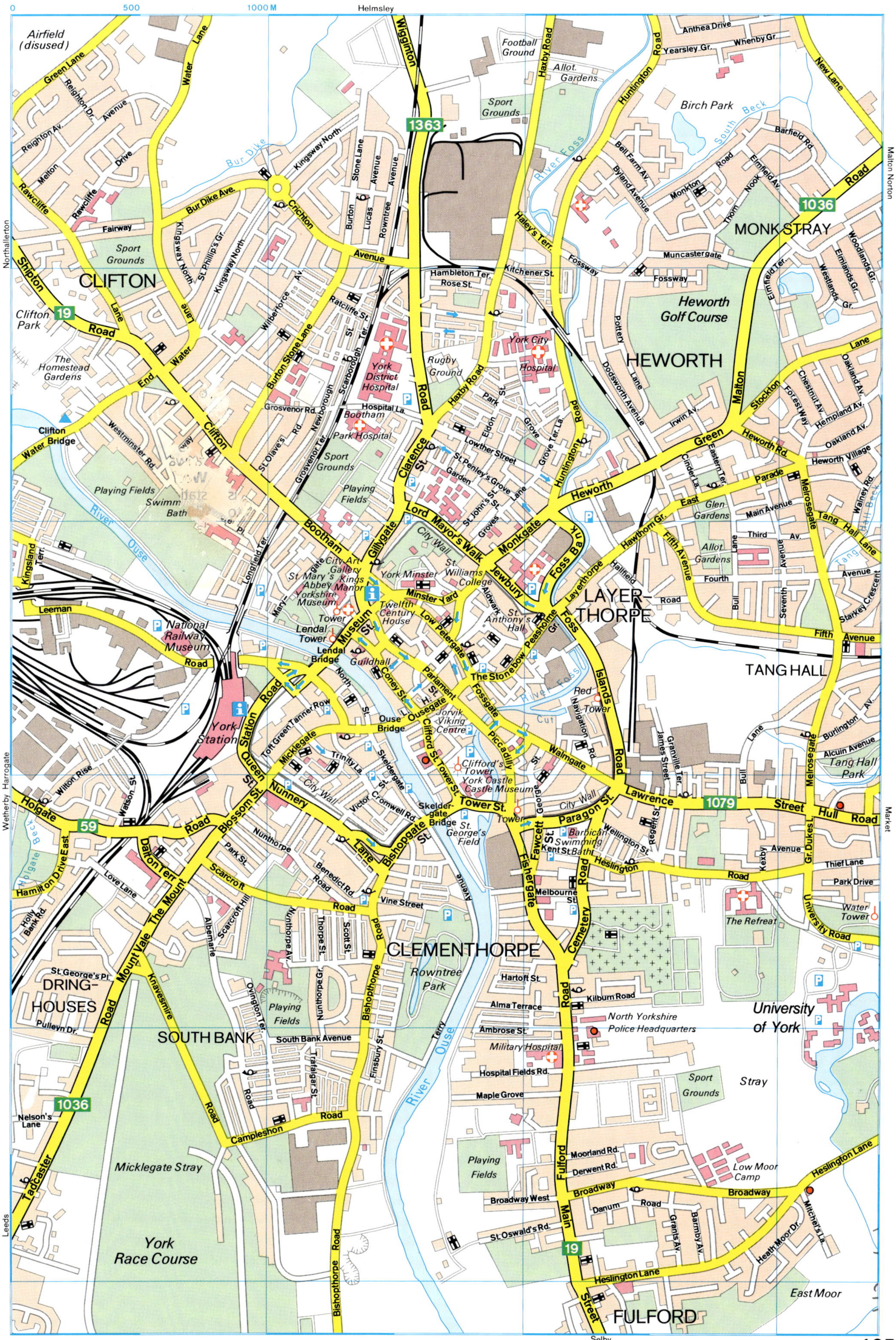
0
500
1000 M
Helmsley
Airfield (disused)
Green Lane
Water Lane
Wigginton
Haxby Road
Football Ground
Allot. Gardens
Sport Grounds
1363
Huntington Road
Anthea Drive
Yearsley Gr.
Whenby Gr.
New Lane
Birch Park
South Beck
Barfield Rd.
Bur Dike
Kingsway North
Bur Dike Ave.
Crichton Avenue
Stone Lane
Burton
Lucas
Rowntree
Avenue
River Foss
Haley's Terr.
Bell Farm Av.
Byland Avenue
Monkton Road
Elmfield Av.
Thorn Nook
1036
Road
MONK STRAY
Rawcliffe
Reighton Av.
Reighton Dr.
Melton
Drive
Fairway
Sport Grounds
CLIFTON
Shipton Road
Clifton Park
19
Hambleton Ter.
Rose St.
Kitchener St.
Fossway
Muncastergate
Heworth Golf Course
Woodlands Gr.
Elmlands Gr.
Westlands Gr.
Eastfield Ter.
Kingsway North
St. Philip's Gr.
Wilberforce Av.
Burton Stone Lane
Ratcliffe St.
Scarborough Ter.
York District Hospital
Rugby Ground
Haxby Road
York City Hospital
Pottery Lane
HEWORTH
Stockton Lane
Malton
Lane
Oakland Av.
Chestnut Av.
Forest Way
Hempland Av.
The Homestead Gardens
Clifton
Water End
Grosvenor Rd.
Newborough
Hospital La.
Bootham Park Hospital
Eldon St.
Park Gr.
Dodsworth Avenue
Irwin Av.
Clifton Bridge
Westminster Rd.
St. Olave's Rd.
Grosvenor Ter.
Sport Grounds
Clarence St.
Lowther Street
Grove Ter. La.
Huntington Road
Green
Heworth Rd
Heworth Village
Playing Fields
Swimm Bath
Playing Fields
St. Penley's Grove St.
Garden St.
St. John's St.
Heworth
East Parade
Eastern Ter.
Cinder La.
Glen Gardens
Main Avenue
Melrosegate
Tang Hall Lane
Walney Rd
River Ouse
Bootham
Lord Mayor's Walk
Groves La.
Monkgate
Foss Bank
Hawthorn Gr.
Fifth Avenue
Third Av.
Allot Gardens
Kingsland Terr.
Gillygate
City Wall
City Art Gallery
King's Manor
St. Mary's Abbey
Yorkshire Museum
York Minster
St. Williams College
Jewbury
Layerthorpe
Hallfield Road
LAYERTHORPE
Fourth Avenue
Bull Lane
Seventh Avenue
Starkey Crescent
Leeman Road
National Railway Museum
Marygate
Lendal Tower
Twelfth Century House
Minster Yard
Low Petergate
Aldwark
St. Anthony's Hall
Peasholme Gr.
Foss Islands Road
Fifth Avenue
TANG HALL
Lendal Bridge
Museum St.
Guildhall
North St.
Coney St.
Parliament St.
Fossgate
The Stonebow
River Foss
Red Tower
Navigation Rd.
York Station
Station Road
Toft Green
Tanner Row
Ouse Bridge
Ousegate
Jorvik Viking Centre
Clifford St.
Foss Cut
Walmgate
Granville Ter.
James Street
Bull Lane
Burlington Av.
Alcuin Avenue
Tang Hall Park
Wilton Rise
Watson St.
Micklegate
Trinity La.
Skeldergate
City Wall
Tower St.
Clifford's Tower
York Castle Museum
Piccadilly
George St.
Lawrence Street
1079
Hull Road
Holgate Road
59
Queen St.
Blossom St.
Nunnery Lane
Victor St.
Cromwell Rd.
Skeldergate Bridge
St. George's Field
Paragon St.
Barbican Swimming Bath
Kent St.
Wellington St.
Regent St.
Heslington Road
Kexby Avenue
Gr. Dukes L.
Thief Lane
Park Drive
Hamilton Drive East
Holgate Beck
Love Lane
Dalton Terr.
The Mount
Park St.
Nunthorpe
Benedict Rd.
Bishopgate St.
Scarcroft Road
Vine Street
Fawcett St.
Fishergate
Melbourne St.
Cemetery Road
The Retreat
Water Tower
University Road
Holly Bank Rd.
Albemarle
Scarcroft Hill
Nunthorpe Av.
Thorpe St.
Scott St.
Bishopthorpe Road
CLEMENTHORPE
Rowntree Park
Hartoft St.
Kilburn Road
St. George's Pl.
DRINGHOUSES
Mount Vale
Knavesmire
Ortington Ter.
Playing Fields
Nunthorpe Gr.
Alma Terrace
North Yorkshire Police Headquarters
University of York
Pulleyn Dr.
Road
SOUTH BANK
South Bank Avenue
Trafalgar St.
Finsbury St.
Terry Avenue
Ambrose St.
Military Hospital
Hospital Fields Rd.
Maple Grove
Sport Grounds
Stray
1036
Nelson's Lane
Road
Campleshon Road
River Ouse
Playing Fields
Moorland Rd.
Derwent Rd.
Low Moor Camp
Heslington Lane
Tadcaster
Micklegate Stray
Broadway West
Broadway
Danum Road
Fulford
Main
Grants Av.
Barmby Av.
Mitchel's La.
Heath Moor Dr.
St. Oswald's Rd.
York Race Course
Bishopthorpe Road
19
Heslington Lane
Street
FULFORD
East Moor
Selby
Leeds
Wetherby Harrogate
Northallerton
Malton Norton
Market

Liverpool – Metropolis on the Mersey

The gateway to the Mersey has a remarkable architectural heritage and some fascinating museums. The city which saw the birth of the Beatles has figured largely, in Britain's trading history, the great sailing days are over.

Liverpool's waterfront has the largest collection of Grade 1 listed buildings in Europe, over 1,000 of them. In the 19th and early 20th centuries, Liverpool was the gateway to the world. Liverpudlians are famous for their distinctive accent, their toughness in the face of adversity and offbeat sense of humour. They are often referred to as "Scouse" or "Scousers". Scouse is a local dish, a stew which is a variation of the Norwegian *lobskaus*, introduced to the city by Scandinavian sailors.

Liverpool's strong musical tradition goes way back before the Beatles, as is evidenced by the number of folk songs which mention the city. The city has its own Royal Liverpool Philharmonic Orchestra. Greater Liverpool covers both sides of the Mersey. The opposite side is called Birkenhead which is on the Wirral, a peninsula west of the city in Cheshire. Also included are the Lancashire suburbs of Kirby and Bootle.

History

Liverpool has always been a convenient port for Ireland, especially in the days when Wales was hostile territory as far as the English were concerned. In the early 13th century, King John built a small port in the natural harbour formed by the estuary of the River Mersey. The ferry service to Ireland is as busy as ever. However, Liverpool really came into its own in the 17th century, a prosperity that lasted until only recently.

The city's wealth was founded on trade with the Americas, especially Virginia and the West Indies, in rum, sugar, tobacco – and, of course, slaves. The first dock opened in 1715 and it was not long before the port covered a long stretch of coastline, right from Liverpool Airport in the south to Blundell Sands in the north. Liverpool's famous residents include the scientist and philosopher Sir Francis Bacon (1561-1669) and the statesman William Ewart Gladstone (1809 - 1898).

Tourist Attractions

The biggest tourist attraction in Liverpool is **Albert Dock.** It was opened in 1845 and closed to shipping in the 1970s. This was once the preserve of sailors, slave-traders, pirates and the press gangs, who "pressed" unwilling volunteers into the Navy. One of the warehouses contains the **Tate Gallery of the North**, a new permanent home for some of the Tate's best modern paintings and sculpture and the finest gallery of modern art outside London.

The other star attraction is the **Merseyside Maritime Museum**, probably the best museum of shipping in the country. Among the most popular exhibits are a builder's model of the *Titanic*, and an exhibition entitled "Emigrants to the New World", including a reconstructed dockland peopled with actors in

period costume. It is those would-be emigrants who never managed to make it past the docks that give Liverpool its cosmopolitan air today. The city has always had a constant influx of foreigners mainly from Central Europe and the Orient. It has the oldest-established Chinatown and the biggest in Britain after London.

Popular culture is represented in Albert Dock by **The Beatles Story**, featuring tableaux of the Fab Four, including a mock-up of the Star-Club in the St. Pauli district of Hamburg where they made their first professional appearance. The original Cavern Club where the Beatles once played and where so many other pop stars were discovered, has now gone. In its place there is a shopping mall, **Cavern Walks**, one of the many in Liverpool's revitalised city centre. A sta[illegible] of [illegible] Four stands in the cen[illegible] shopping mall, and t[illegible] new **Cavern Club** in th[illegible]ment. On Matthew Street is a **John Lennon Memo[illegible] Club**, but the best Beatles show is **Beatle City**, in Seel Street, an award-winning exhibition which contains a multitude of Beatles memorabilia.

For lovers of classical art, the **Walker Gallery** has the largest collection of Old Masters in the North including particularly fine Flemish and Italian paintings. The Gallery contains Rembrandt's "Self-Portrait as a Young Man".

The building is linked to the **Liverpool Museum** through the **County Libraries** (1875-79), which contain an exceptionally fine circular reading room, the **Picton Reading Room**. The Liverpool Museum has a very varied collection, including an aquarium and vivarium, a transport gallery and an area devoted to the social history of Merseyside. However, for the best in social history, there is the **Museum of Labour History**, depicting working-class life in the 19th century and boasting a very fine collection of trades union banners.

Liverpool has more than its fair share of unusual museums of a type that will enthrall even the most hardened disliker of glass cases, but the most fascinating is undoubtedly the **Large Object Collection** in the Princes Dock. The Collection contains such huge structures as a tunnel-cleaning machine, a satellite rocket launcher and a two-ton telescope.

Bluecoat Chambers, (1717), the oldest building in the city centre, was built by a wealthy merchant as [illegible] school for poor children, but is now an arts centre with a permanent exhibition of British crafts. The building also contains a concert hall, café and restaurant.

Liverpool has two cathedrals, the **Liverpool Anglican cathedral** and the Roman Catholic **Metropolitan Cathedral of Christ the King.** The Anglican cathedral was only started in 1903 and finally completed in 1978. It overlooks the city on St. James Mount. It is the work of Sir Giles Gilbert Scott, a vast construction of local red sandstone, the largest cathedral in Britain and the second-largest in the world after St. Peter's in Rome. The design represents a resolute attempt to turn back the clock architecturally, in stark contrast to the Roman Catholic structure, which is resolutely post-modernist. It consists of a circle of concrete flying buttresses surmounted by a glass-walled lantern tower and has been variously dubbed by the locals "The Mersey Funnel" (as opposed to the **Mersey Tunnel**, the road link between Liverpool and Birkenhead) and "Paddy's Wigwam", due to the wigwam-like appearance of the tower and the preponderance of Liverpool Irish among the faithful. For best effect, it is advisable to visit both buildings on the same day.

No visit to Liverpool would be complete without a trip on the **Mersey Ferry**, from which the most spectacular view of the port is obtained. The ferry leaves from the **Pier Head**.

Distinctive features of the port include the **Liver Building**, headquarters of the Royal Liver Insurance Company topped by the Liver Birds, the solid neo-classicism of the **Adelphi Hotel**, **St. George's Hall** and **Liverpool Town Hall** (1754) surmounted by a golden dome. St. George's Hall was built to be both law courts and a concert hall.

Liverpool is one the few cities in Britain which has no large central parks, but it has the **Festival Gardens** a few miles south of the city centre, beside the waterfront. There are 75 acres of landscaped gardens with fountains and a Japanese garden. For children, there is a model of the Beatles' Yellow Submarine to play on. The Gardens were created for Britain's first International Garden Festival in 1984.

Information

Merseyside Welcome Centre
Merside Tourism Board
Clayton Square
Liverpool L1 1QR
Tel: (051) 709 3631

Events

The Grand National, the world's most famous steeplechase, is run on the course at Aintree, a suburb of Liverpool. "The National" is run in late March or early April.

The Mersey River Festival is held in June,and there are tall ships' races in some years, the last being for the 500th anniversary of Christopher Columbus' discovery of America in 1992.

The Mersey Beatle Convention is a two-day event held in late August or September, which gives Beatlemaniacs a chance to indulge in their favourite pasttime.

Tips

Like most big cities, Liverpool is crowded with traffic in the city centre, and besides, many of the sights are in pedestrian precincts, so it is a good idea to find a car park and move around the dock area on foot or by bus. A car is very useful for travelling further afield. A trip through the Mersey Tunnel is a must.

The famous Lion Building, topped with the Liver birds (left).

The Maritime Museum on Albert Dock (opposite top).

Liverpool's waterfront at night (opposite below).

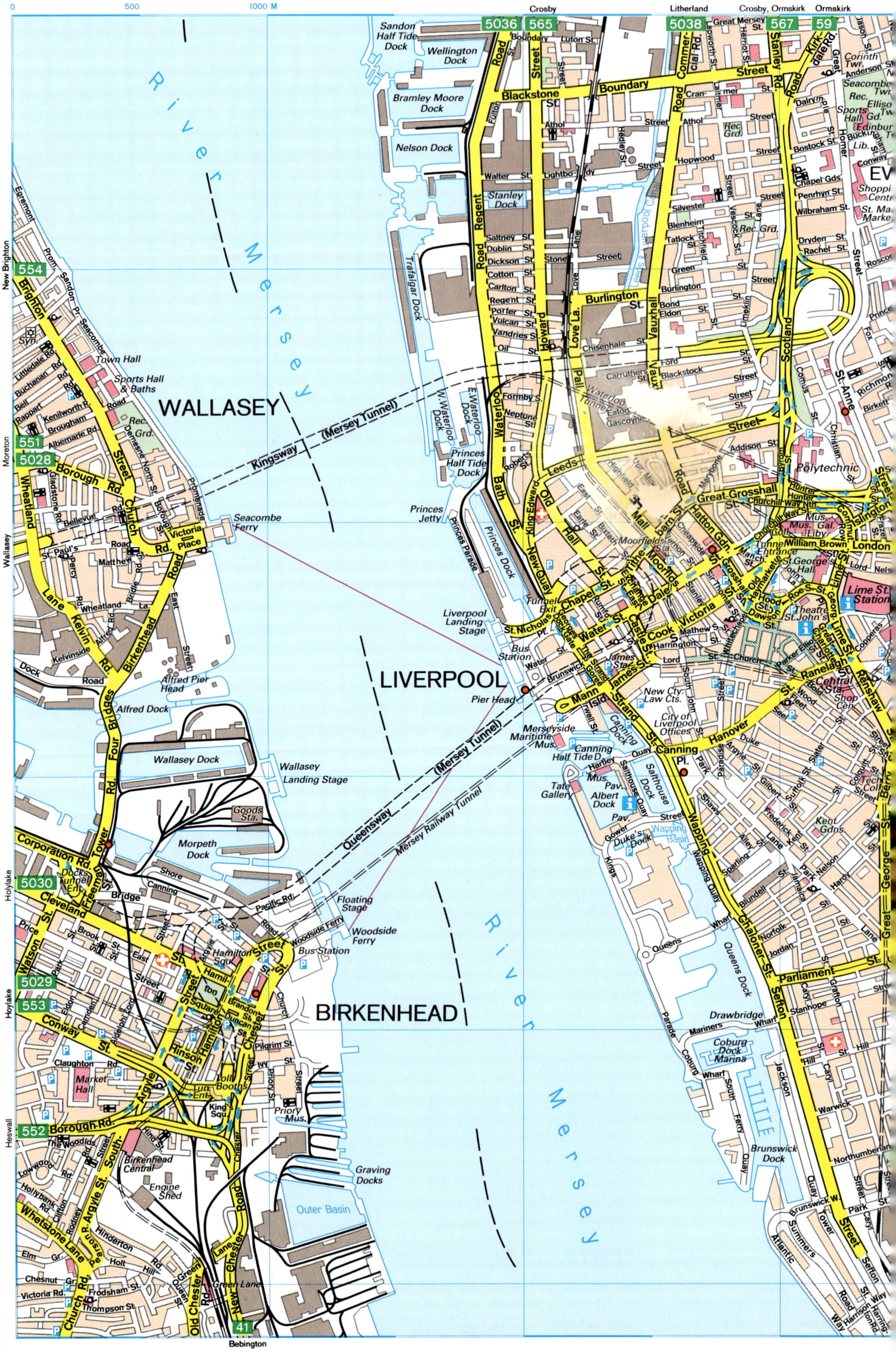
0
500
1000 M
Crosby
Litherland
Crosby, Ormskirk
Ormskirk
New Brighton
Moreton
Wallasey
Holylake
Hoylake
Heswall
Bebington
River Mersey
WALLASEY
LIVERPOOL
BIRKENHEAD
Sandon Half Tide Dock
Wellington Dock
Bramley Moore Dock
Nelson Dock
Stanley Dock
Trafalgar Dock
E. Waterloo Dock
W. Waterloo Dock
Princes Half Tide Dock
Princes Jetty
Princes Dock
Princes Parade
Liverpool Landing Stage
Pier Head
Bus Station
Merseyside Maritime Mus.
Canning Half Tide D.
Canning Dock
Salthouse Dock
Albert Dock
Tate Gallery
Duke's Dock
Wapping Basin
Queens Dock
Coburg Dock Marina
Brunswick Dock
Kingsway
(Mersey Tunnel)
Queensway
Mersey Railway Tunnel
Seacombe Ferry
Town Hall
Sports Hall & Baths
Alfred Pier Head
Alfred Dock
Wallasey Dock
Wallasey Landing Stage
Goods Sta.
Morpeth Dock
Floating Stage
Woodside Ferry
Bus Station
Hamilton Squ.
Market Hall
Birkenhead Central
Engine Shed
Priory Mus.
Graving Docks
Outer Basin
Polytechnic
Lime St. Station
St. George's Hall
Theatre
Central Sta.
New Cty. Law Cts.
City of Liverpool Offices
Kent Gdns.
Blackstone St.
Boundary Street
Regent Road
Great Howard St.
Vauxhall Road
Scotland Road
Leeds St.
Old Hall St.
Tithebarn St.
Dale St.
Victoria St.
Hanover St.
Wapping
Chaloner St.
Sefton St.
Parliament St.
Great George St.
Borough Rd.
Conway St.
Cleveland St.
Corporation Rd.
Four Bridges
Birkenhead Road
Church St.
Whetstone Lane
Chester St.
New Chester Road
Old Chester Rd.
5036
565
5038
567
59
554
551
5028
5030
5029
553
552
41

Ormskirk, Manchester
St. Helens / Manchester
Ormskirk, St. Helens
St. Helens
Prescot
Manchester
Widnes
Huyton
Liverpool Airport / Widnes
Widnes
5089
580
5049
57
5047
562
5058
561
CABBAGE HALL
Pavillon Recreation Ground
Anfield Boys Sec. Sch.
Newsham Park
Newsham House
FAIRFIELD
ELM PARK
STANLEY
KENSINGTON
EDGE HILL
SANDOWN PARK
WAVERTREE
PRINCES PARK
SEFTON PARK
Sefton Park
Princes Park
Botanic Gardens
Wavertree Park
Wavertree Technology Park
Wavertree Playground
Toxteth Park Cemetery
Sefton General Hospital
Royal Liverpool Hospital
Dental Infirmary
University
Cathedral (R.C.)
Stanley Industrial Estate
Stanley Abattoir
Bus Depot
Millbank College of Commerce
Wavertree Trading Estate
Liverpool Coll. Playing Fields
Greenbank Park
Prescot Road
West Derby Road
Edge Lane
Smithdown Road
Picton Road
Wavertree Road
Queens Drive Mossley Hill

Lincoln – "The finest cathedral in England"

Once England's second city, Lincoln is now far enough off the beaten track to have plenty of room for visitors, even in high summer. It has all the classic attractions of a historic English city – a cathedral, a castle and narrow, cobbled streets.

Lincoln, the county town of Lincolnshire, is in the centre of a largely agricultural county, to the east of the industrialised heart of England. It is the perfect place for a quiet weekend break, picturesque and easily accessible from the main centres.

History

Lincoln occupies a strategic position on a hill, so it is not surprising that the site has been inhabited since ancient times. The Romans, who called it Lindum, from the Saxon name Lindon, established a garrison here in 48 AD. The fort of Lindum stood at the meeting point of two great Roman roads, Ermine Street and the Fosse Way, the latter still travelled and known today as the Great North Road or the A1. The Romans later built a wall around the fort and made it into a Colonia or chartered city. William the Conqueror decided to make Lincoln into the local bishopric. In medieval times, Lincoln was the centre of the wool trade which turned England into the most prosperous land in Europe. The city was famous for its Lincoln Green cloth. Several parliaments were held in the cathedral Chapter House in the Middle Ages, where some of the Knights Templar were put on trial in 1310. With the decline of the river ports and the opening of alternative road and sea routes, Lincoln lost its importance and gradually dwindled into a little market town, reviving briefly as a centre for small industry during the 19th century.

Information
Tourist Information Centre
9 Castle Hill, Lincoln
Tel: (0522) 529828

Festival Calendar
The Lincoln Festival is held in the first three weeks in May. The Lincoln Carnival is held in the first weekend in June and is followed by a wine festival. In early July, there is a weekend celebration of Medieval Lincoln with jousting and banquets. The Lincoln Community Play is performed starting in late July.

Tips
Getting there: Lincoln is about two hours by rail from London (King's Cross), though there are very few direct trains and you may have to change at Newark. It takes about two hours by coach from Victoria Coach Station. By car from London, simply follow the signs for the A1 (the Great North Road) and turn off at Stamford, Grantham or Newark.
Lincoln's steep hills are difficult of access for the disabled, and the streets around the cathedral are traffic-restricted. The city can be seen by car, and there are plenty of local car hire firms, but the guided walking tours of the City are highly recommended. Contact the Tourist Information Centre for details.

Places of interest

The whole city seems to rise up towards the cathedral which dominates the surrounding landscape. John Ruskin went so far as to describe Lincoln Cathedral as "out and out the most precious piece of architecture in the British Isles". The cathedral was founded in 1072, when Bishop Remigius, whose tomb is in the nave, became bishop of Lincoln. He built the Exchequer Gate on the west front, now surrounded by Early English arcades which were added later. The Norman church was seriously damaged by fire in 1141 but the third bishop, Alexander, restored the West Front. The cathedral was greatly enlarged by the much-revered Bishop Hugh of Avalon, after an earthquake in 1185. Hugh appointed a brilliant builder and architect, Geoffrey de Noiers, who introduced many innovations, later copied by other English cathedrals. Hugh of Avalon was canonised in 1220. His statue tops one of the spires on the west side of the church. Another spire is topped by the Swineherd of Stow who amassed silver pennies all his life to help pay for the rebuilding. The shrine of St. Hugh dominates the cathedral nave. The tomb once attracted [illegible] many pilgrims that the a[illegible] around it had to be enlarge[illegible] accommodate them. A famous feature of the cathedral is the 12th-century Angel Choir so named because of the angel carved over the stalls. The strange little stone carving known as the Lincoln Imp is to be found on a corbel here. Another glory of the interior is the rose window known as the Dean's Eye (c. 1220) which still has its original stained glass and is best viewed from under the vault of central tower. Cloisters were added to the Cathedral in about 1290, although it was never a monastery. The cloisters link the Cathedral to the Chapter House, the first ever built in this country and the only one with ten sides. The original cathedral library burned down and a new one was designed by Christopher Wren in 1674, which is rather Italianate Renaissance in appearance. The library contains a copy of the Magna Carta, one of only four in England, and some valuable first editions. It is worth climbing the 335 steps of the central tower (only open at certain times) to see the magnificent view over the city. It is something of an irony that most of the money for building Lincoln cathedral was raised by a Jew, Aaron of Lincoln, the richest man in England and treasurer to Henry II, then the most powerful monarch in Europe. Aaron was leader of the local Jewish community, the second-largest in England after London. A medieval stone house is,reputed to have been Aaron's home, but there is no proof of this. However, two houses on the aptly-named Steep Hill, the oldest stone houses in England, certainly did belong to Jews. The Jew's House was built around 1180 and was owned by a woman called Bellaset. Next door is a house called Jews' Court, which was probably a synagogue. Both buildings are owned by the Diocese of Lincoln. Jews Court is now a Regional Crafts Centre, the first to be established in Britain. St. Hugh of Lincoln is not to be confused with Little "saint" Hugh. In 1255, a boy named Hugh disappeared from Dernstall, the district in which most of Lincoln's sizeable Jewish population was concentrated. His body was discovered some days later in a well and the local Jewish community were blamed for the death. The inevitable pogrom ensued. Despite numerous denunciations by eminent clerics throughout the ages, the legend persisted until well into [illegible]ury.

[illegible] Castle, which stands [illegible] the Cathedral, was built [illegible]m the Conqueror. It was a [illegible]n Victorian times and the [illegible]hapel is well worth a visit. [illegible] long the castle battle[illegible] gives you splendid views of [illegible] city. Bailgate, once the main street of the castle's outer bailey is now a shopping street, which leads to the Newport Arch, the only Roman arch in Britain through which traffic still passes. The Bishop's Palace is near the cathedral, though no bishop has lived there since 1548, and Oliver Cromwell

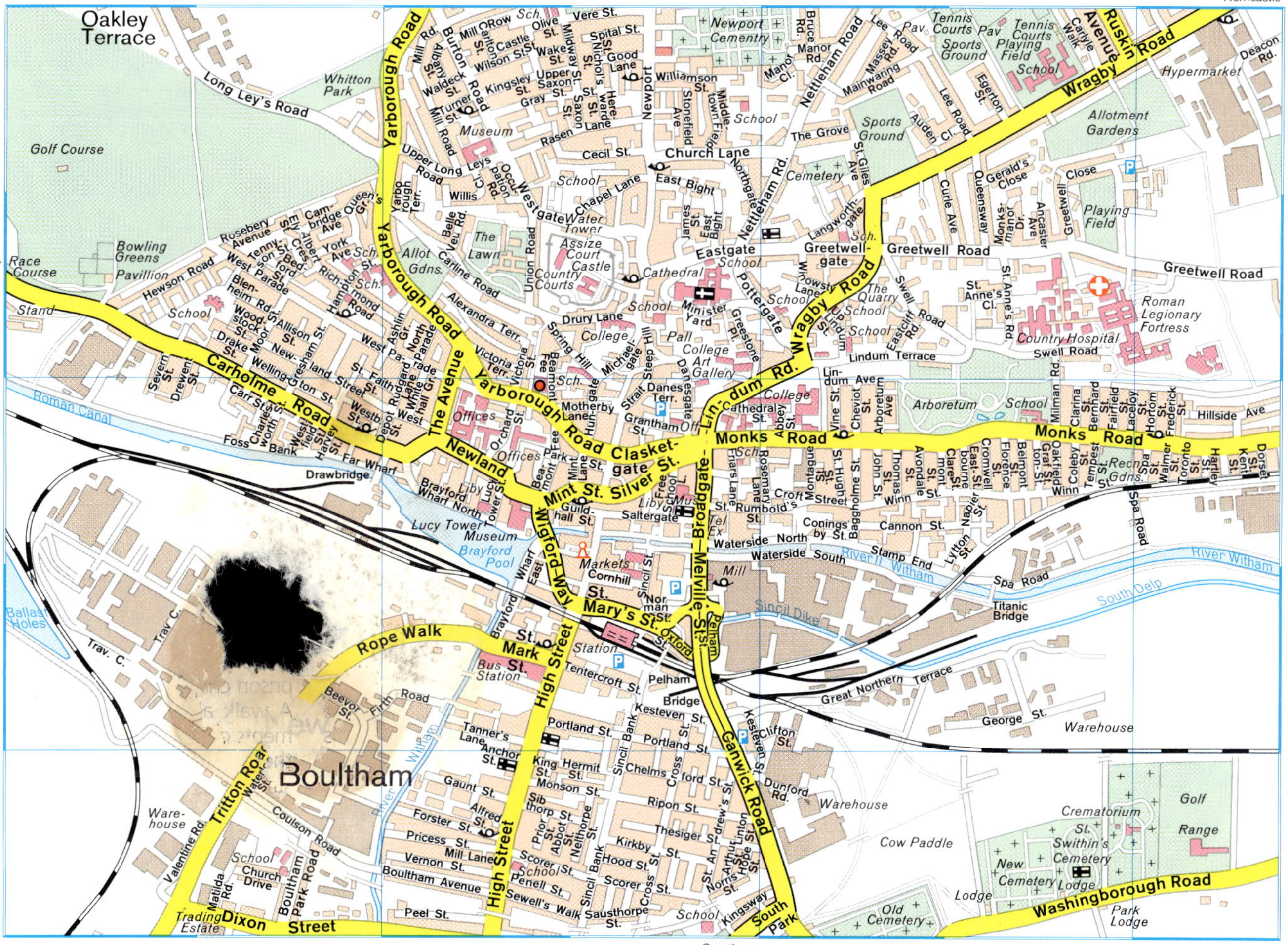

had it partially dismantled. The original medieval building has been excavated by the Department of the Environment. The River Witham encircles the city on three sides. It was once a major artery before the waterways were superseded by road and rail transport. Unfortunately, ugly office buildings have replaced many of the tall Victorian waterside warehouses, but a few relics of the past survive. The High Bridge over the river is the oldest in Britain still to have houses on it. One of these is the public house called The Glory Hole, an ideal place to sit on a summer's day, watching the swans sail majestically downstream from Brayford Pool, the inland port built by the Romans.

Lincoln "below hill" is a hodgepodge of supermarkets and chain stores, though here and there some of the old buildings can be glimpsed behind car parks and ugly access roads. There are some remains of the old Roman wall and the medieval St. Mary's Guildhall graces the High Street. Lincoln boasts two important museums, the National Cycle Museum on the roof of a supermarket in Brayford Wharf North and the Usher Gallery on Lindum Road, which has the best collection of clocks and watches in England. The Exley Collection of ceramics and glass is also of interest. The upper rooms are devoted to memorabilia of Alfred Lord Tennyson, the poet, who lived in Lincoln for a time and was born in Lincolnshire. There is a Tennyson Research Centre at the Central Library on Free School Lane. The Museum of Lincolnshire Life, a folk museum housed in a converted army barracks, contains interesting displays of rural life.

The rose window ("Bishop's Eye"), Lincoln Cathedral (above).

The keep, Lincoln Castle (left).

Lincoln Cathedral, view of the nave (opposite top).

Steep Hill (opposite below).

Chester
Fortress on the Dee

James Boswell, Dr. Johnson's biographer, wrote in 1779, "Chester pleases my fancy more than any town I ever saw". Chester remains as pleasing as ever, with its ancient buildings and city walls.

History

Chester, the county town of Cheshire, grew from a crossing-point on the River Dee into a flourishing trading centre. The Romans settled here in 48 a.d. and made it the headquarters of the XXth Legion. They named it either Castra Devana (the camp on the Dee) or Castra Legionum (camp of the legions) which the Welsh shortened to Caerleon. The Romans left in about 380, after which Chester was fought over by the Welsh, Saxons and Danes, since it was in a strategic position, protecting England from invasion from the Welsh on the land side and from other marauders who might arrive from the sea, across the Sands of Dee. Chester was able to resist the Norman Conquest for longer than any other city in England but it eventually fell to William the Conqueror in 1070. William handed it over to his nephew, Hugh Lupus, dubbing him Earl of Chester. The title reverted to the Crown in 1237 and has since belonged to the sovereign's eldest son, so the Prince of Wales is also the Earl of Chester. The town was a prosperous river port in the Middle Ages, trading between England and Wales, but the Sands of Dee, which had done so much to protect it from attack, began to silt up the river channel in the 15th and 16th century, and the town stagnated, with commerce switching to nearby Liverpool. It is thanks to this phenomenon, unfortunate for local traders but fortunate for tourists, that so much of the medieval and Elizabethan townscape has been preserved.

Tourist Attractions

The main attraction of Chester [illegible] undoubtedly the **Rows**, the gall[illegible]ies which form continuous pa[illegible]es along the upper floors of half-timbered houses and shops, [illegible] sort of medieval shopping mall [illegible] two levels. The Rows were begun in the 13th century but no one is quite sure why they were built like this. One theory is that they were erected over Roman remains which blocked the streets at ground level. The Rows are built around the **Cross**, at the centre of Chester. The present cross is relatively recent, its 15th-century predecessor having been destroyed during the Civil War. Not all of the buildings in the Rows are genuinely ancient, several were added as recently as the 19th century, but these blend in well with the others. Every kind of merchandise is available in the Rows which are by no means mere tourist attractions but serve the usual purpose of a commercial centre. Chester's department store, **Brown's of Chester**, uses its 13th century basement as a sales floor and several shops, in[illegible] bookshop, are housed in [illegible] buildings. One of the [illegible]g ways of enjoying the [illegible] on a pub crawl visit[illegible]s, most of which are [illegible] buildings that contain [illegible] where the fabric of the [illegible] is not original, there is [illegible]d to have been a public house on the site from an early date. One exception is the **Beare and Billet Inn**, near Bridgegate, which until the 19th century was the town house of the Earls of Shrewsbury. Other public houses include the **Boot Inn**, **Ye Olde King's Head** in Lower Bridge Street and the **Pied Bull Inn** in Northgate Street. The German composer, George Frederick Handel, stayed at the **Falcon Inn** in Lower Bridge Street in 1741. One old inn, the **Blue Bell Inn** in Northgate, has been converted into a restaurant.

Chester is a city of towers and fortifications, still surrounded by the rectangular **City Walls**. The two-mile walk along the top of the walls is a must for the visitor. The walls were originally built by the Romans who created them first of turf and later of local red sand-

The cross, with the Rows in the background (above).

King Charles' Tower in the city walls (right).

The Jubilee Clock at Eastgate (opposite).

Information
Chester Information Centre
Vicars Lane
Chester
Tel: (0244) 324324

Chester Tourist Information Centre
Town Hall
Northgate Street
Chester
Tel: (0244) 351609

Events
Chester has almost as many traditional ceremonies as London. There is the miltary ceremony of Beating the Retreat at Chester Castle, and the ritual locking of the Chester Cathedral's Kaleyard Gate at curfew bell, which has taken place since the 13th century.

Tips
Chester is a medieval city and it is choked with traffic, so it is a good idea to leave the car at one of the many car parks just outside the city walls and visit the centre on foot.
Chester Zoo makes a delightful family outing. It is the biggest zoo in Great Britain and is only two miles north of the city centre.

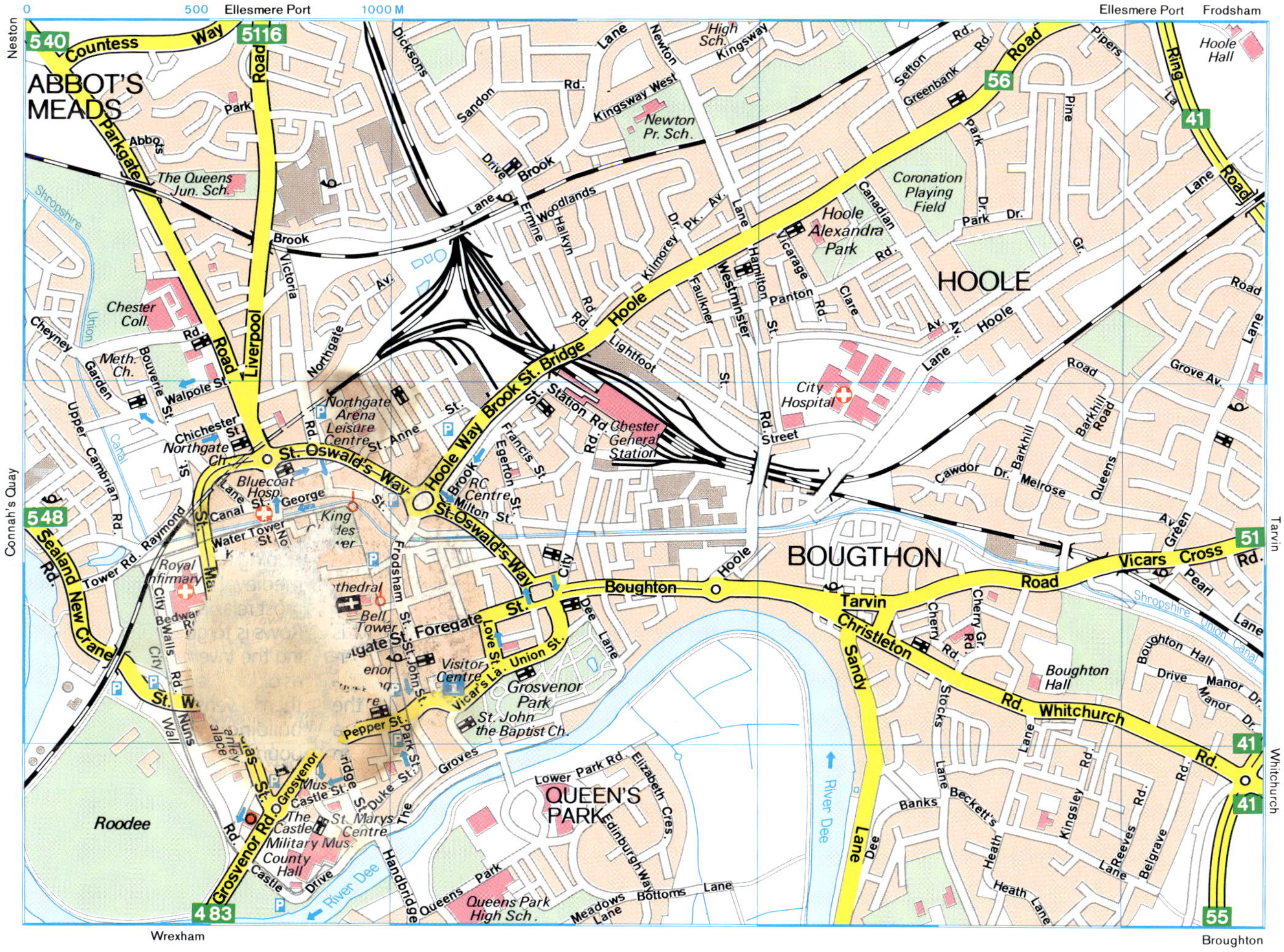

stone. Towers were added much later, in the 13th and 14th centuries. Most of the surviving wall is medieval although there are Roman remains on the north and east sides. There are eight gates in the walls, some of which were added recently to relieve traffic congestion. **Eastgate** is now topped by an ornate clock erected to commemorate Queen Victoria's Jubilee. North of Eastgate is **Kaleyard Gate** at the end of Abbey Street. Nearby is **King Charles's Tower**, so called because King Charles I watched from this tower as his troops were defeated at the Battle of Rowton Moor in 1643 during the Civil War. The tower contains a small museum of the Civil War. **Northgate,** which was rebuilt in 1808, has the best view of the Roman parts of the wall. Unusually for Britain, **Newgate** is indeed new, built in 1932 as an alternative to the narrow **Wolfgate.** Newgate and Wolfgate overlook the **Roman Gardens** outside the wall which contain Roman remains. The **Roman Amphitheatre**, just beyond the Gardens, is the largest in Britain, with room for 9,000 spectators. The **Grosvenor Museum** in Grosvenor Street contains more Roman artefacts and much else from Chester's history. **Bridge Gate** in the south opens on to the **Old Dee Bridge**, a seven-arched medieval bridge widened in the 19th century. North of Bridge Gate in Bridge Street there is the **Chester Heritage Centre**, housed the former **St. Michael's Church** in the Rows. The **Toy Museum**, also on Bridge Street, has the largest collection of Dinky and Lesney model cars in the world. **Watergate** in the west is so named because it is by the **Water Tower**, built to defend the port area in 1322. Just outside the Watergate is the oddly-named open space called the **Roodee**, encircled by **Chester Race Course**, the oldest in Britain, where horses have been raced since 1540. **St. Martin's Gate** nearby was cut into the north wall as recently as 1966 to the relieve the congestion on North Gate. One of the most interesting of the towers in the wall is **Morgan's Mount**, a square building with a magnificent view of the Welsh Hills, and built for precisely that reason, to repel the Welsh marauders, who would periodically attack and plunder the city from Roman times until well into the Middle Ages.

Chester's other two great glories are the castle and the cathedral. All that remains of the original **Chester Castle**, built by Hugh Lupus in 1070, are parts of the inner bailey wall. There is also a 12th-century tower, but most of the buildings are late 18th century, designed by Thomas Harrison in neo-classical style. The north-east corner of the castle contains the **Cheshire Military Museum**, displaying relics of the Cheshire Regiment, one of the most distinguished in the British Army. The Castle now houses public buildings such as the Assizes (law courts) and County Hall, and these sections can be visited when they are not being used for official purposes.

Chester Cathedral is the most handsome church in north-western England. It was founded by St. Werburgh in the 7th century. Hugh Lupus, Earl of Chester, refounded it as a Benedictine abbey in 1092. After the Reformation it became the cathedral of the new diocese of Chester. The cathedral is built of the local red sandstone. Much of the Norman church remains, including the Lady Chapel (1259-75) and the choir which was built by Richard of Chester in c.1300. The Cloisters were largely rebuilt in the mid-16th century, though some medieval traces remain, but the Chapter House and Refectory (now used as a cafeteria) are original 13th century constructions. Many of the cathedral buildings were restored in the 19th century by Sir Gilbert Scott, who also built the organ.

Norwich The Fine City

Regional capital of East Anglia and county town of Norfolk, Norwich was once the second city of England, as can be seen from its fine15th-century buildings.

History

Norwich is situated near a ford over the River Wensum (where the Fye Bridge now stands) above its confluence with the River Yare. The city's proximity to the east coast, and thence to the Netherlands and Germany, made it an ideal spot for both trading and invading. It was a flourishing Saxon burgh when it was destroyed by Sweyn Forkbeard in the 9th century, but it was rebuilt and by the time of the Norman Invasion (1066) Norwich was one of the largest towns in England. William the Conqueror soon rid himself of the city's Saxon ruler Gyrth Godwinsson (as he did of 90 per cent of the Saxon nobility of England) and installed a Norman knight as Earl of East Anglia. A castle was swiftly built from which to rule over the English. When Bishop Losinga decided to build his cathedral in the city in 1094, he demolished most of the Saxon dwellings in order to do so. A wall was built around the city in the 13th century which compares in size with that of London. The Black Death decimated the population in the 14th century, but it revived when immigrant weavers from Flanders made Norwich a centre of the weaving trade, using the wool from sheep flocks reared in the area. The Society of Friends (Quakers) were powerful in Norwich, which is the birthplace of the Quaker pr[illegible] former, Elizabeth Fry (1780-[illegible] The Industrial Revolution p[illegible] Norwich by, as it did the [illegible] East Anglia, leaving it unsp[illegible] The city has a few traditi[illegible] dustries such as brewin[illegible] tionery and Colman's [illegible] The wool trade has gone, [illegible] East Anglian agriculture is no[illegible] primarily cereal-based.

Tourist Attractions

The centre of Norwich is small enough to be crossed on foot in 15 minutes if you are in a hurry. It is a maze of quaint narrow streets and alleys laid out according to the Saxon town plan. Norwich once had more churches than in any other city in Europe. Few of them still perform their religious functions, most have been put to other uses, such as community centres, a brass-rubbing centre, etc. Some churches are closed, but can be visited by arrangement with the Tourist Information Centre. **St. John's Cathedral** is the focal point of Norwich, though it stands on low-lying ground by the river. The building material is Caen stone brought over from France by its founder Bishop Losinga, who started the works in 1096. The Clerestory was rebuilt in Decorative style in the mid 14th century, and the Cloisters and Spire – the [illegible]cond-highest in England – were [illegible]lly completed with the rest of [illegible] building in the 15th century. [illegible]rman style predominates [illegible] church. The roof-bosses [illegible] of the Bible but be[illegible]re so high up and thus [illegible]e, mirrored trolleys are [illegible] enable visitors to view [illegible] better. The Bishop's Throne [illegible]nd the altar predates the

Information

Tourist Information Centre
Guildhall
Gaol Hill
Norwich NR2 1NF
Tel: (0603) 666071

The Norwich Official Guide is on sale locally and provides information about guided walks of the City and local events.

Events

The Royal Norfolk Show is held in June or early July. The Lord Mayor's Procession is held in July. The parade is followed in the evening by a firework display. The Norfolk and Norwich Festival is a cultural festival held every three years.

Tips

Norwich is famous for having a large number of theatres for such a small town. There are the Theatre Royal, the Maddermarket Theatre, the Sewell Barn Theatre and the Whiffler, an open-air theatre which only puts on performances in Summer. Furthermore, Norwich is one of the few places to have a permanent puppet theatre, The Norwich Puppet Theatre is housed in a former church, St. James Whitefriars.
The Maid's Head Hotel, whose restaurant is open to non-residents, is the oldest continuously-operated hotel in Britain. It first opened its doors in 1272. Four of the rooms have four-poster beds.

Norwich Cathedral seen from Almary Green (left).

The moat at Norwich Castle on a fine spring day (above).

Houses in Norwich Cathedral Close (top).

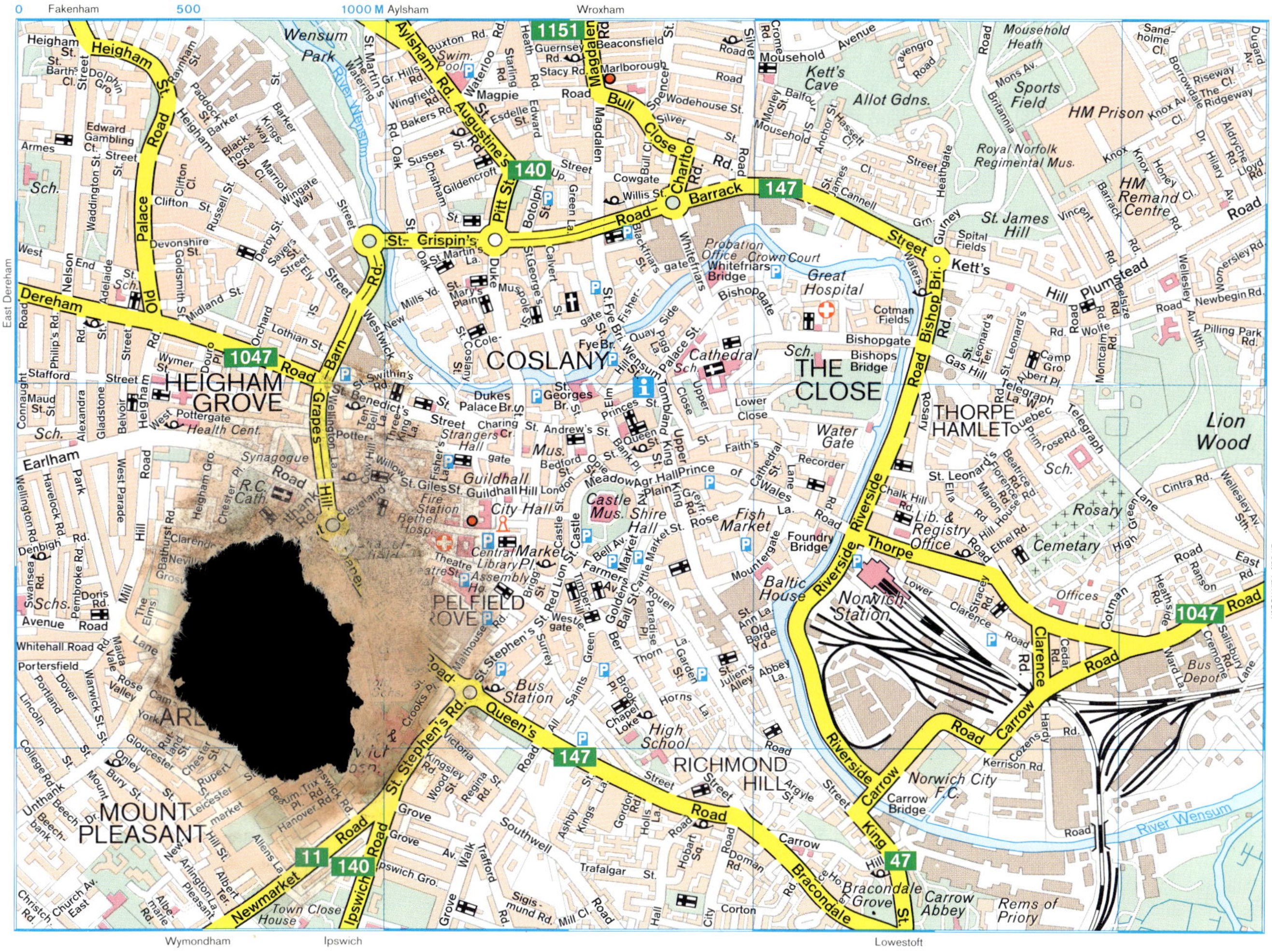

church and may have been brought from Thetford, the former see, or from the Saxon cathedral at Dunwich. The painted panels in St. Saviour's Chapel and the painted retable in St. Luke's Chapel are rare surviving examples of the East Anglian School of painting. The Cathedral has the only two-storied monastic cloister in England.

Just outside the Cathedral by the entrance to the **Bishop's Palace** is the **Church of St. Martin-at-Palace**, which dates mainly from the 14th century. Opposite is **Cotman House**, home of the great British landscape painter J. S. Cotman. **The Erpingham Gate** (1420) leads into the **Cathedral Close**, a cluster of quaint, ivy-covered Georgian houses, a world away from the bustle of the 20th century. The Close also contains a statue of Lord Nelson and the grave of Nurse Edith Cavell, shot by the Germans in Belgium in 1915.

Norwich Castle is only 500 yards away from the Cathedral on man-made **Castle Mound**, which in East Anglian terms is a veritable mountain! The Mound looks particularly lovely in spring when covered in daffodils. The original castle was probably made of wood. All that remains of the later structure is the castle keep built in the reign of Henry I, in the early 12th century, but refaced with Bath stone in 1834. The castle was used as a prison right up until the 19th century. The battlements, from which there is an excellent view of the city, and the dungeons, containing various gruesome relics, are open to the public. The rest of the castle contains the **Castle Museum**, which has an exceptionally fine range of paintings of the Norwich School of 19th-century landscape painters and a collection of china, including 600 teapots.

St. Georges Tombland is a 15th-century church with a lofty tower in the strangely-named Tombland, which was the marketplace in Saxon times. **St. Peter Hungate** stands on **Elm Hill**, one of the finest examples of a medieval street in Britain. The church was rebuilt in 1460, with a cruciform hammer-beam roof. It is now a museum of church art and contains some exceptional examples of medieval woodwork and illuminated manuscripts.

Norwich Market is the largest daily market in England. A sea of striped awnings (known as "tilts") covers the Market Place, which is surrounded by many buildings of historic interest. The great parish church of **St. Peter Mancroft** is on the south side. While much of the church is in the Perpendicular style and dates from the 16th century, there are some 18th and 19th century additions. The sequence bell-ringing known as "Ringing the changes" is a unique feature of English church bells. The church bells were the first in the country to ring the entire cycle of 5040 changes, in 1715.The Sacristy contains illuminated manuscripts.

The **Royal Arcade**, a covered shopping arcade in elegant late-19th century style, in the manner of the arcades of London and Paris, leads off the marketplace. The **Guildhall** (1407-13) in the square has a distinctive chequered gable, added in 1535, which has almost become a Norwich hallmark. **Strangers Hall** (the "Strangers" were emigrant Flemish weavers) in the Maddermarket, is a guildhall which has been turned into a museum devoted to English domestic life. The Georgian **Assembly Rooms**, near the Theatre Royal are open to the public. The ballroom is an excellent place to have tea and there are evening concerts. The Riverside Walk along the Wensum from Carrow Bascule Bridge to Hellesdon makes for a delightful evening stroll. If the whole five-mile walk is too much, you can always leave it at one of the numerous bridges. There are also riverbus cruises in the summer that leave from Roaches Court or outside Thorpe Station.

A visit to Norwich must take in one of the most unusual museums in the country, the **Mustard Museum** attached to the **Mustard Shop**. Colman's Mustard, a local industry, almost has a monopoly in Britain. Mustard tastings are held by arrangement. **Bridewell Museum**, which is devoted to local crafts and industries, also has a display of mustard-making, as well as clock-making, boot-making and printing. This 14th-century merchant's house was once a prison, as can be seen from the graffiti scratched on the walls. The **Sainsbury Centre for Visual Arts**, part of the University of East Anglia, just outside the city centre, contains an extensive collection of modern art, including ethnic art, as well as examples of works by Picasso and Henry Moore.

Information
Tourist Information Centre
Wheeler Street
Cambridge
CB2 3QB
Tel: (0223) 322640

The Festival Administrator
Mandela House
Regent Street
Cambridge
CB2 1BY
Tel: (0223) 358977

Festival Box Office
The Corn Exchange
Wheeler Street
Cambridge
CB2 3QB

Festivals
There are lots of student festivities, including "May Week" in June, a season of parties and dances to mark the end of the annual examinations.
Midsummer Fair is held in late June and is opened at noon by the Mayor. Midsummer Fair is a university festival however. The town of Cambridge has its own fair, the two-week Cambridge Festival, in late July.

Tips
The best time to visit Cambridge is in the warmer months, when the bitter wind that blows across the flat lands of Cambridgeshire is likely to be stilled. Try and avoid May, because this is examination time when an ominous quiet hangs over the city, and high summer, when the students are on holiday and only your fellow-tourists are about. However, if you are in Cambridge at Christmas, the event to attend is the Festival of Nine Lessons and Carols on Christmas Eve at King's College Chapel. Admission is free but long queues form as it is, of course, a very popular event.
Cambridge is small enough for all these attractions to be visited on foot, though it would take more than a flying visit to see them and the many other beauties of the city. Another, more relaxing, way of seeing the Cambridge colleges is from the river in a punt.

Cambridge – The great seat of learning

Capital of the Fenland, Cambridge, once a Roman fortress, is a placid market town of great beauty, whose greatest architecture is that of the colleges of the University.

Cambridge is at the southern end of what was once a marshland crisscrossed with canals and rivers called the Fens. The Fens are now the richest wheatfields in Britain.

History

Unlike Oxford, a city which grew up around the university, there was a flourishing trading centre at this point on the River Cam for at least 1,000 years before the students arrived. When the Romans left the fortress they built here, the town was largely abandoned until the Danish invasions of the 6th and 7th centuries. Under the Treaty of Wedmore, which Alfred the Great signed with the Danes in 878, the town became part of the Danelaw, the area of England under Danish rule. The Danes made Cambridge a river trading port, building a Great Bridge roughly where Magdalene Bridge stands today. The Normans built a wooden fortress to ward off attacks by the English rebel, Hereward the Wake, who could escape his Norman pursuers by using secret paths through the Fens, wh[illegible] were then treacherous pe[illegible] Cambridge University ma[illegible] grown up earlier than th[illegible] century, around the various [illegible] and priories, but the officia[illegible] its foundation is 1209, w[illegible] group of students from C[illegible] fled here to escape the riots. [illegible] relationship between Town and Gown in Cambridge has been as bitter as at Oxford. In both cases, the town resented the rights and privileges of the university. The mayor of Cambridge had to swear an oath of loyalty to the University and yield to the Vice-Chancellor on every occasion. At least one Cambridge college was burned to the ground during the Peasants' Revolt of 1381 and King Richard II punished the town heavily as a result. The only event of national importance that occurred at Cambridge was the proclamation by the Duke of Northumberland in Kings College Chapel of Lady Jane Grey as Queen of England in 1553. She was beheaded nine days later and he was arrested and executed as well. Cambridge escaped the Industrial Revolution, since it had no particular advantages as a manufacturing town. However, the university has always been famous for producing mathematicians and scientists and of late Cambridge and its surrounding area have become home to many hi-tech industries, especially in the computer field.

Tourist Attractions

Cambridge University has 25 colleges and about 9000 students. The oldest, which is also the smallest college, is known as **Peter-**[illegible] (1281-84), though its cor[illegible] St. Peter's College. It [illegible] graduates. The col[illegible] ill substantially the [illegible] g. The Gothic chap[illegible] nd the Old Library [illegible] visiting. The same [illegible] ington Street, con[illegible] 14th-century church of [illegible] **the Less**, whose elegant architecture is still pre-

Market Hill, showing the Church of St. Mary the Great (top).

King's College Chapel from the Backs (above).

Punts passing under the Bridge of Sighs on a summer's day (left).

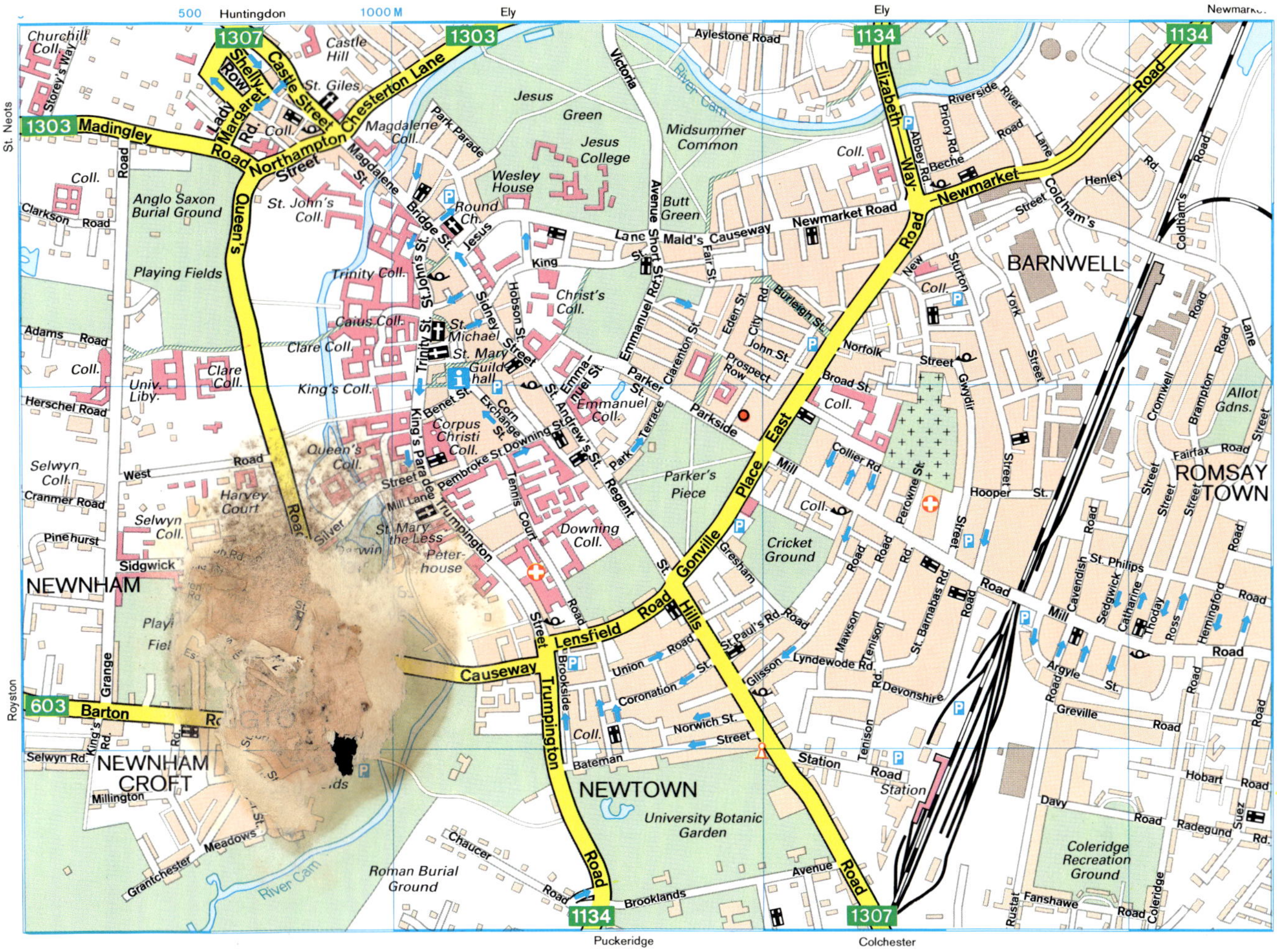

served. Just beyond Peterhouse stands the **Fitzwilliam Museum**, designed in the 19th century to house the priceless collection left to the university by Viscount Fitzwilliam The museum is vast and its treasures too numerous to mention, ranging from South American folk art to Impressionist paintings. The centre of Cambridge is called **Market Hill**, thought it is not a hill at all (the highest point in Cambridge is 50 feet above sea level!) but a square in which a lively open market is still held regularly In one corner of the square stands the church of **St. Mary the Great**, the parish church of Cambridge, which is also the University Church. There has been a church on this site since the 12th century, but most of the present building is 15th to17th century. Opposite the tower end of the church stands the **Senate House** (1722-30), a handsome, neo-classical building in which degrees are awarded. Near the Senate House are the **Old Schools**, once lecture rooms, now used as offices. They are on King's Parade, facing **King's College**, the most imposing of the colleges. King's College was founded as the College of Our Lady and St. Nicholas by Henry VI in 1441. Despite their ancient look, the college buildings are 19th century. They surround the huge quadrangle known as **The Great Court**, with its central fountain. On the north side of the court is **Kings College Chapel**, the most magnificent building in Cambridge. The church was begun by Henry VI in 1446 and continued under successive monarchs, bridging the medieval and the Renaissance periods. The interior is richly decorated, the woodwork being Tudor, and heavily carved with Tudor roses. The church is famous for its 25 16th-century stained-glass windows and its fan-vaulted roof. The altarpiece is *The Adoration of the Magi* by Peter-Paul Rubens. A choir school is attached to the Chapel, whose boys still dress in a uniform of top hats, Eton jackets and striped trousers. Kings College Choir is world-famous, and a choral service in the chapel is not to be missed.

All that remains of **Cambridge Castle**, built by the Normans, is an earth mound in the grounds of the **Shire Hall**. However, since the mound is the highest point in the city, it is worth climbing it for a view of Cambridge. Castle Street contains the **Folk Museum**, housed in the former White Horse Inn. North of Market Hill is **Gonville and Caius** (pronounced "keys") **College**, on the wall of which is a plaque to mark the spot where Sir William Harvey discovered that blood circulates around the body. The college has a handsome **Gate of Honour** (1575) leading to the Senate House Passage. **Trinity College** is the largest college in either Cambridge or Oxford, with 600 graduates. It was founded by King Henry VIII in 1546. **St John's** is the second-largest college. Its magnificent 16th- and 17th-century buildings form a series of courts on either side of the River Cam. The bridge which links the old and the new courts was built in 1831 and is a replica of the bridge in Venice known as **The Bridge of Sighs.** The first bridge over the Cam was built in 875 near **Magdalene** (pronounced "mawdlen") **College.** This College had a famous undergraduate, Samuel Pepys (d. 1702), the diarist, who left it his extensive library. The **Pepys Library** (c. 1640-1700) was built to house the collection. The present **Magdalene Bridge** dates from 1823 and was strengthened in the 1970s. It has an unusual three-pin, cast iron arch. Even more unusual is the **Mathematical Bridge**, a wooden bridge originally built in 1750 when it was known as Queen's Bridge. It is supposed to have been built by interlocking straight pieces of wood in such a way that no nails or bolts were needed to hold it together. However, according to legend, when students got drunk they were in the habit of dismantling it and in their inebriated condition could not put it back together again! This is all highly unlikely, but just in case, the present copy, which dates from 1902, is securely bolted in place. The oldest bridge is **Clare Bridge** (1638-40), by **Clare College**, (founded in 1326).

Another famous Cambridge sight is the Church of the Holy Sepulchre, known as the **Round Church**. Only four Norman round churches survive in England. This one was built in 1130. The round churches are supposedly reproductions of the Church of the Holy Sepulchre in Jerusalem which crusaders built after their return from the Holy Land.

Oxford "The Dreaming Spires"

This great university city is also a hive of industry, as famous as the birthplace of Britain's car industry as it is as a seat of learning. There is a sharp contrast between the calm of the colleges and the bustle of the busy main streets of the city.

History

Strangely, although Oxford was obviously a convenient place for crossing the River Cherwell, a tributary of the Thames (Oxford = Oxenford) there is no record of any settlement here until 912 a.d. No one actually knows how or when the University came to be founded, though there is a legend that it was started by Alfred the Great (848 -c.900), a scholar-king who did much to shape the English language. The University is first mentioned in the 12th century. In 1214, Pope Pandulf granted it immunity from lay jurisdiction, a separation from local affairs that was the origin of the later bitter battles between the city and the university, known respectively as Town and Gown. During the Civil War, the University and the City were firmly on opposing sides, the city not surprisingly favouring the Roundhead cause. The city of Oxford is famous as the birthplace of British car industry. In 1910, William Morris, who made bicycles, began manufacturing a small, cheap car from his factory in Cowley, a suburb of Oxford. By the 1920s, the Morris Oxford was the most popular British car, and Oxford, which had escaped the worst effects of the Industrial Revolution, became a manufacturing city.

Information
Oxford Information Centre
6 St. Aldate's
Oxford OX1 1DY
Tel: (0865) 726871
There is also an information centre inside Oxford Railway Station.

Festivals
Oxford is a great place for celebrations. May Morning, May 1, is a medieval tradition still celebrated with great enthusiasm in Oxford. Citizens and students gather at the foot of Magdalen Tower to hear choristers sing hymns from the top at 6.00 a.m. before they celebrate with Morris dancing and other junketing.
Ascension Day – Beating the Bounds. This ceremony which is a tradition in many parts of England, is still celebrated in Oxford, when choirboys and girls armed with rods, beat a route along the boundaries of the city.
St. Giles Fair is the great annual celebration, named after the city's patron saint. It is held on the first Monday and Tuesday after the first Sunday in September, except when September 1 falls on a Sunday.

Tips
Avoid taking a car into the city centre and if travelling from north to south avoid doing so through the centre of town, which like most of Britain's cities is incredibly crowded. There are good park-and-ride facilities.

Tourist Attractions

Oxford University consists of 35 colleges, of which 28 admit both undergraduates and graduates. The colleges consist of rooms in which students live and are generally closed to the public during term time, but can be visited in the holidays, especially in the "long vac." in summer. Oxford is small enough for the most interesting colleges to be visited on foot, starting at the city's central crossroads, known as **Carfax**. The 14[illegible] century clocktower at the corne[illegible] of Carfax is all that remains of S[illegible] Martin's Church. It has Sha[illegible]spearian connections, in t[illegible] Shakespeare is said to have a[illegible]tended the baptism of William Davenant, whose father was landlord of the Crown Inn which is now No. 3 Carfax. The **Painted Room** of the inn, where Shakespeare is said to have stayed, is open to the public. **Pembroke College** in Broadgate was founded in 1624. Its graduates include Dr. Samuel Johnson who was here between 1728 and 1729, and James Smithson, founder of the Smithsonian Institute in Washingdon, D.C. **Christ Church**, known familiarly as "The House", is the largest of all the colleges. It was founded by Cardinal Wolsey in 1525, on the remains of the Priory of St. Frideswide. By a unique arrangement, the priory church became **Oxford Cathedral**, the smallest cathedral in England. The Cathedral has some interesting Norman pillars, alternately round and octagonal, and the roof is 16th century. The spire, unusually squat and low for an English church, is 13th century. The west end of the cathedral opens into the **Great Quadrangle** or **Tom Quad**, overlooked by **Tom Tower**, a famous Oxford landmark. Lewis Caroll, who wrote *Alice in Wonderland* and *Alice through the Looking Glass,* was a don at Christ Church, and Oxford landmarks feature in both his stories about Alice. **Oriel College**, another beautiful college well worth vis[illegible]ing, was founded in 1324, [illegible] the buildings are 17th-[illegible]othic. The Hall has a fine [illegible]erbeam roof. Its famous un[illegible]duates include two of the [illegible]mous British explorers, Sir [illegible] Raleigh and Cecil Rhodes. [illegible]e oddly-named **Radcliffe Camera** is a handsome baroque rotunda with a dome rising from an

Oriel College (top).

Oxford's own version of the Bridge of Sighs (above).

The Radcliffe Camera, where examinations are held (left).

The Bodleian Library (right).

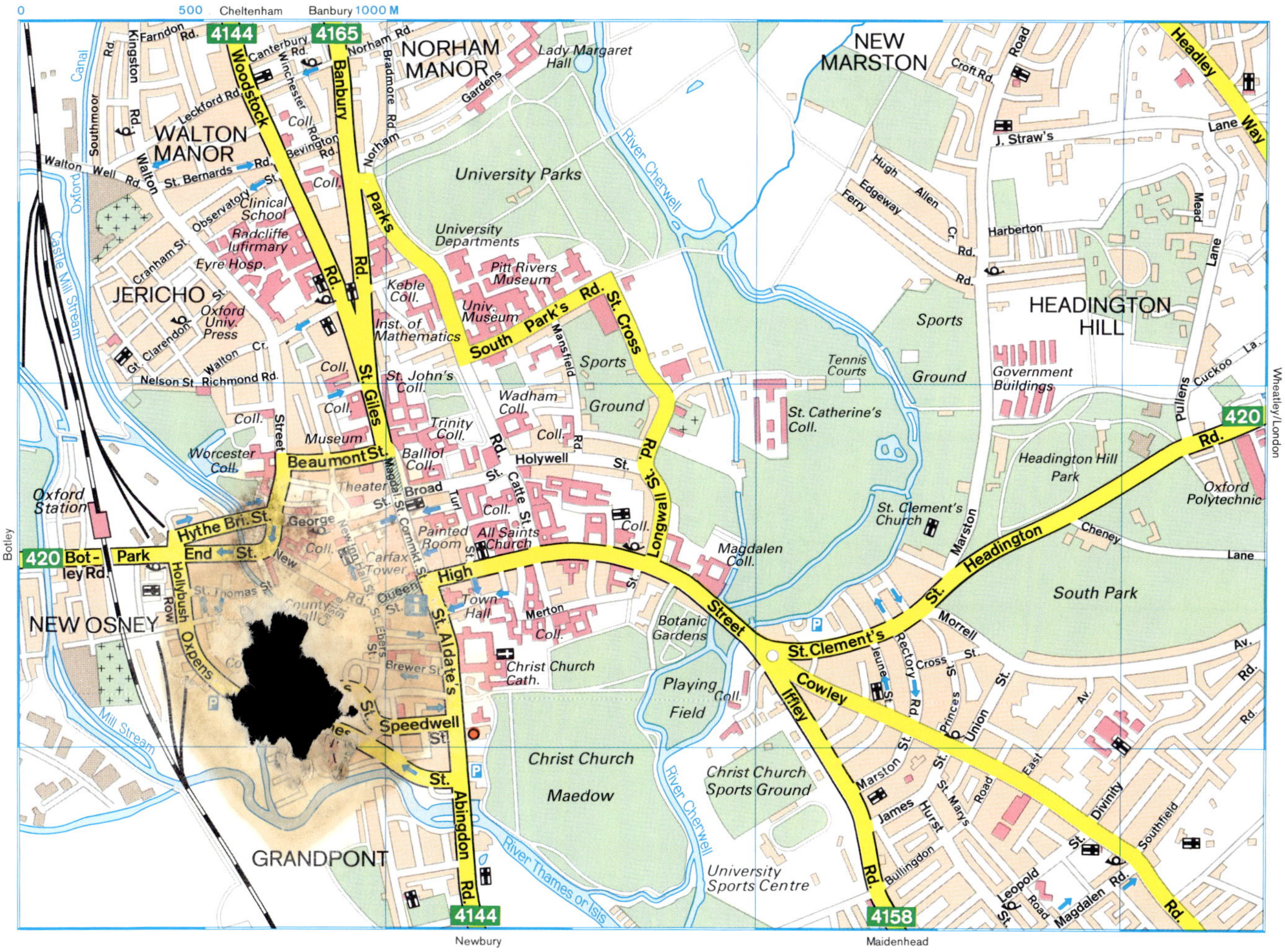

octagonal base. It is used as an examination hall and is not open to the public. It was built to house Dr. Radcliffe's science library, and has long been part of the **Bodleian Library.** The Bodleian periodically holds exhibitions of the manuscripts and rare books in its collection. **University College,** which stands on **Oxford High Street**, familiarly known as "The High", is the oldest of the Oxford Colleges, founded in 1249, though the buildings are mainly 17th century. The Front Quad was built by the famous architect, Nicholas Hawksmoor **Magdalen College** (pronounced "Mawdlen") is probably the most beautiful of all the Oxford colleges. It was founded in 1458 by William of Waynflete who eventually became Lord Chancellor. Magdalen's most interesting feature is the Tower in the Perpendicular style, built in 1492-1505, supposedly by Cardinal Wolsey who was then college bursar. St. John's Quad is surrounded by buildings of even earlier date. The chapel is open to the public and is particularly worth visiting for the choral services held during term time. To the right of the college, **Magdalen Bridge** crosses the River Cherwell, leading to a meadow containing the lovely riverside **Water Walks**. Opposite Magdalen is the **Botanic Garden**, the oldest in England, founded in 1621, and still containing a fascinating variety of medicinal plants growing outdoors and in greenhouses. **Balliol College** in Broad Street is another of the early colleges, founded in 1266 by John de Balliol, father of the King of Scotland, supposedly as a penance for insulting the Bishop of Durham! The college boasts a host of famous alumni, including John Wyclif (1320-1384), who translated the Bible into English and was denounced as a heretic, and who was master here. Other famous graduates include Sir John Evelyn, Adam Smith, Gerard Manley Hopkins, King Olav of Norway, Aldous and Julian Huxley and Graham Greene. As a counterpoint, **Lincoln College**, the best preserved of the late medieval colleges was founded in 1427 by Bishop Fleming of Lincoln to train clergy to refute the Wyclifian heresy! The **Sheldonian Theatre**, Sir Christopher Wren's first public building, was built in 1663-1669 at the expense of Archbishop Sheldon, to be used for ceremonial occasions. This is where the degrees are awarded. The design is based on the Theatre of Marcellus in Rome. Typical of Oxford (where North Parade is south of South Parade!) **New College** is one of the oldest of the Oxford colleges. Most of the buildings were completed in about 1386 and remain a superb example of Perpendicular architecture. Fortunately for the students, a modern wing built in the 1970s provides more comfortable accommodation. The Hall adjoining the chapel is the oldest in Oxford with early 16th century linenfold panelling. The **Ashmolean Museum** is one of the finest museums in Britain and has a magnificent collection of art and archaeology.

Cardiff – Europe's Youngest Capital

A castle, a river and parkland – all in the very centre of the City. Cardiff is one of the few English cities to have a planned civic centre laid out amid spacious lawns. It is also Europe's newest capital.

Although Cardiff has been the administrative centre of Wales for centuries, and the headquarters of the Welsh Office, it was only officially made the capital in 1955. This makes Cardiff the youngest capital city in Europe. Cardiff has no cathedral of its own, and was only granted the official status of city in 1905. However, it acquired an "instant" cathedral, when Llandaff was incorporated within the city boundaries in 1922. Cardiff has a compact but beautiful city centre which makes it easy to tour. It is twinned with Nantes in France and Stuttgart in Germany.

History

The Romans established a fortress here beside the River Taff in c.76 a.d., but little is known about it and the next event in Cardiff history is the arrival of the Norman knight Robert FitzHamon, who built his castle on top of the Roman stone fortifications. In 1158, the castle was stormed by Ifor Bach, ruler of Senghenydd, north of Cardiff. It fell briefly to Owen Glendower, who led a revolt against the English in 1404. In 1490, the castle was granted to Jasper Tudor, uncle of Henry VII, the first of the Tudor kings. A settlement had grown up around the castle, which received a series of charters. In 1551, Edward VI awarded Cardiff Castle to Sir William Herbert, and it has remained in the hands of his descendants, the Marquesses of Bute. It was the Industrial Revolution that changed Cardiff from a remote village to a thriving city. Suddenly, its geographical location made it the ideal place from which to export coal and iron mined in the neighbouring valleys. The population mushroomed, especially after the docks were opened. The first dock was excavated on the initiative and at the expense of the Marquess of Bute in 1839 and the second dock opened in 1860. In the meantime, the railways had come to Cardiff. The docks were badly damaged in the air raids of World War II. When coal exports declined, the port was modernised for container shipping and now handles oil [illegible]kers, timber and general cargo.

Tourist Attractions

Cardiff Castle in the city ce[illegible] was officially handed over to th[illegible] City in 1948 by the fifth Marqu[illegible] of Bute. The Norman castle keep has remained virtually intact on its mound throughout centuries of attack and is one of the finest examples of its kind in Britain. Much of it is the work of Robert of Gloucester, an illegitimate son of Henry I. Gilbert de Clare added the **Black Tower**, now used as the entrance, in the late 13th century. There have been many later additions, especially in the late 18th century. Between the mid- and the late 19th century, the third Marquess of Bute rebuilt the entire south-western end, added a spire to the **Octagonal Tower** and erected the **Clock Tower**. He also redecorated the interior in a uniquely flamboyant style. The Clock Tower can be climbed and affords a magnificent view of Cardiff. The interior of Cardiff Castle has a wealth of exotic features, including an **Arab Room**, decorated in gold leaf, white marble and lapis lazuli, a **Chaucer Room**, and in the **Banqueting Room** a [illegible] with a hole in the centre [illegible]gh which a vine grows. **The** [illegible] **Tower** [illegible]s topped by a roof [illegible] another Victorian conceit, [illegible] is open to the public in the [illegible]mer. Part of the castle is used the [illegible]official receptions and banquets. It also houses the **Museum of the Welch Regiment.**

Cardiff Castle, clocktower (opposite).

Cardiff Castle (above right).

Cardiff's city centre, an aerial view (right).

Cardiff City Hall (above).

Information
Wales Tourist Board
Brunel House
2 Fitzalan Road
Cardiff CF2 1UY
Tel: (0222) 499909

8-14 Bridge Street
Cardiff
Tel: (0222) 227281

Public Relations Office
Cardiff City Hall
Cardiff
Tel: (0222) 822000

Tips
Cardiff is a compact city with just a few tourist attractions, all of which are very special. It is easy to get around on foot, but not too crowded in the City centre.

Local dishes
Visit the Victorian indoor market and try local specialities, such as Welsh lamb, the currant cake called Bara Brith, and laver bread, seaweed usually fried with bacon, black pudding and fried bread in a traditional Welsh breakfast.

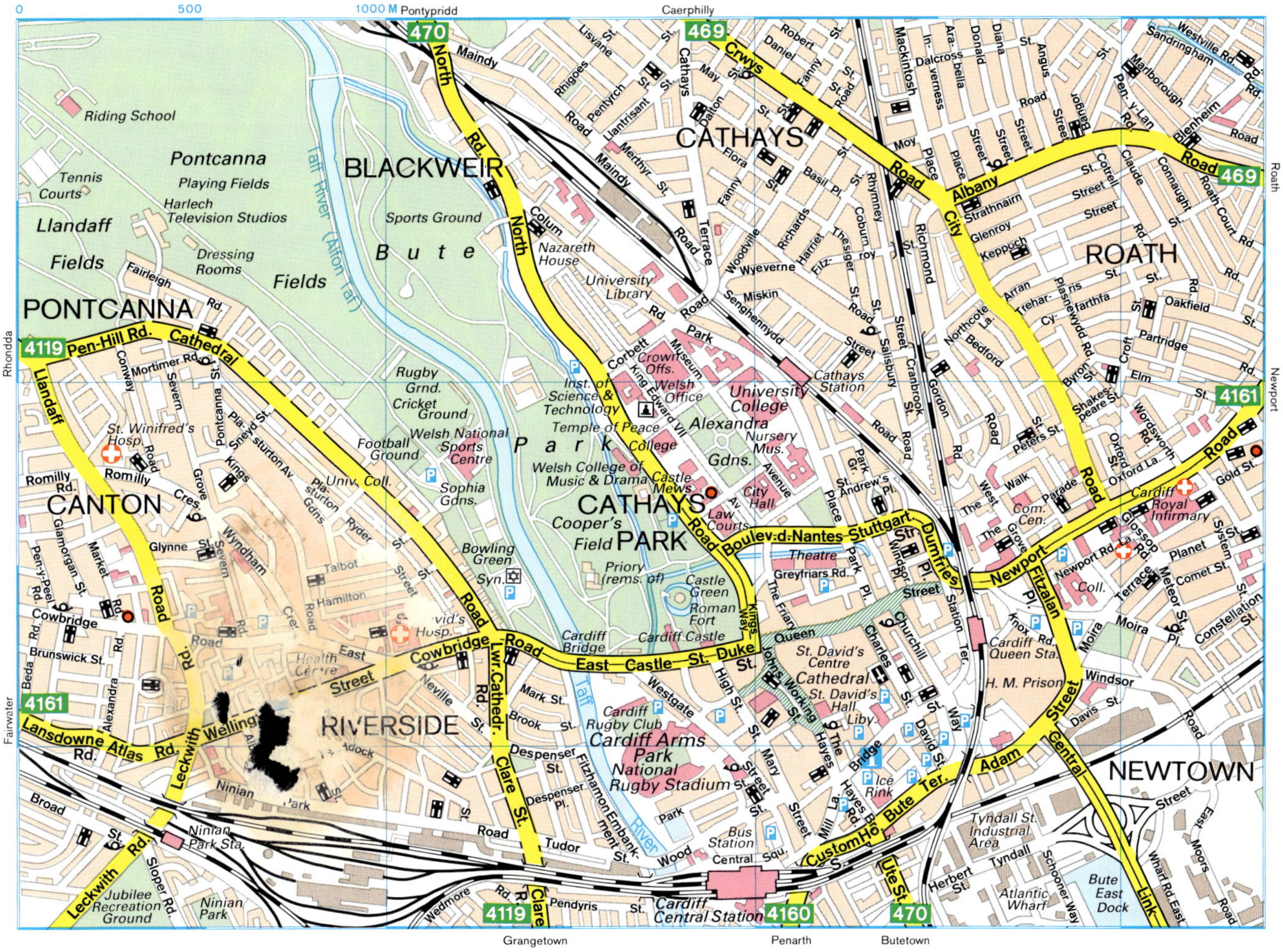

Cardiff Arms Park which is due south of the castle is the Rugby football ground, where the Welsh indulge in their national sport. To the east is the **Victorian Market**. Further east is **St. John's church**, the parish church of Cardiff, which dates mainly from the mid-15th century. **Cathays** (pronounced "Catt-hays") **Park**, north of the castle, is an expanse of wide lawns and magnificent avenues lined with the city's main public buildings, including the **Temple of Peace** (1938), built as a headquarters for international organisations and Cardiff's **City Hall**, a white marble edifice erected in 1905. The fountains in front of City Hall were installed for the investiture of Prince Charles as Prince of Wales in 1969. Inside the hall, a series of statues depicts heroes from Welsh history, including Owen Glendower who did his best to destroy the city!

To the right of the City Hall, is the **National Museum of Wales**, one of Britain's largest museums. Whilst the emphasis is on the history and natural history of Wales, there are also paintings and sculptures including works by Augustus John and Gwen John and many works by the French Impressionists. The Science Galleries contain working models and an environmental picture of the Welsh countryside, as well as fossils and a collection of Welsh standing stones.

The **Welsh Industrial and Maritime Museum** is set in what was once the notorious **Tiger Bay** area, which the residents prefer to call by its original name, **Butetown**. The museum covers four acres of dockland and traces the history of Welsh industry and shipping.

The village of **Llandaff** and **Llandaff Cathedral** are reached by crossing the **Llandaff Fields**, where cricket is played in summer. The founding of the church is linked to St. Teilo, who was Bishop of South Wales in the mid-6th century. The earliest existing parts of the Cathedral are the Norman arch dividing the presbytery from the Lady Chapel and some traces of blocked windows in the South Wall of the Presbytery, dating from c.1120. Much of the rest of the Cathedral dates from the 13th century, including the Lady Chapel (1266), although additional building work was completed in the 14th century. The Cathedral was subsequently virutally abandoned and fell into dangerous disrepair. Cromwell's soldiers used it as a tavern, turning the font into a pig trough, and they ceremonially burned the Cathedral records. The south-west tower and the roof of the nave collapsed in the hurricanes which swept Britain in 1703 and 1723. The rebuilding took the extraordinary form of an Italianate temple designed by John Wood, the architect responsible for most of the city of Bath. However, true restoration was undertaken in 1835 by Precentor Douglas who had Wood's temple removed (all that remains are a couple of urns); Douglas and his successors carefully restored the Cathedral to its medieval glory. All their years of painstaking work was destroyed in 1941 when a landmine virtually demolished the Cathedral. However, when rebuilding started it was decided to recreate the previous building. The work was supervised mainly by the architect George Pace, who also added the parabolic concrete arch which is a feature of the present Cathedral. Another modern addition is the huge (and controversial) statue of **Christ in Majesty** by Jacob Epstein in unpolished aluminium.

No visit to Cardiff would be complete without a trip to the **Welsh Folk Museum** at St. Fagan's, a branch of the National Museum of Wales. The museum centres around **St. Fagan's Castle**, which was given to the nation in 1946 by the Earl of Plymouth. The castle grounds contain fully-furnished farmhouses, cottages and craft shops all brought from other parts of Wales to be re-erected here.

Bristol An Historic Port

"Shipshape and Bristol fashion" and "on the nail" are two old sayings that show how important Bristol has been as a port and trading centre. The port has moved downstream, but Bristol is still the biggest manufacturing centre in the West Country.

Bristol, capital of the West Country, stands on the river Avon, seven miles from the Bristol Channel. For centuries it afforded a safe harbour for vessels on the west coast of Britain. However, Bristol Docks were completely destroyed during the Second World War, and the harbour has now moved down to Avonmouth, where the harbour is wide and deep enough to take container ships.

History

Bristol became wealthy and powerful by importing three commodities – wine, tobacco and slaves. The city is recorded as importing wine from Bordeaux in the 12th century, and from Spain, Portugal and the Americas thereafter. In medieval times, Bristol was a prosperous city, since ships could sail right up the Avon and dock outside the merchants' houses. It was from here that John and Sebastian Cabot sailed in 1497 to discover the mainland of North America, whose east coast they later explored. Until the late 19th century, when it was overtaken by Liverpool, Bristol was the premier port for the Americas, and its tobacco industry started as a consequence of this. The tobacco tycoon, H.O. Wills, whose company long dominated the cheaper end of the cigarette market, made many generous donations to the city and its university. Much of Bristol's wealth has even more sinister origins. The traders and owners of the slave-ships, which plied between Britain and Africa and between Africa and the Americas, built themselves luxurious mansions in the suburb of Clifton. Bristol became a gateway for British exports during the Industrial Revolution, largely through the efforts of the great engineer, Isambard Kingdom Brunel. Today, Bristol is the only industrial centre in the west of England, its main products being confectionery and aircraft. The first British plane, the Bristol Boxkite was made here in 1910 and British Aerospace built the prototype Anglo-French Concorde in Bristol in 1969.

Tourist Attractions

Driving into the city from the London end, one crosses the Floating Harbour, created in 1803-1809 by diverting part of the Avon into a new channel. This is the site of the church of **St. Mary Redcliffe**, which Queen Elizabeth I described as "the fairest, the goodliest and most famous parish church in England". The fabric of the building dates back mostly to the late 15th century, but was heavily restored in 1933. The church contains many monuments to 17th century worthies, including Admiral Sir William Penn (died 1670) who was the father of the founder of Pennsylvania. The church has an American chapel and beautiful stained-glass windows.

The Bristol Docks area has been extensively restored and made into public leisure facilities. These include the **Arnolfini Arts Centre**, where there are regular events and exhibitions, mainly of contemporary arts and crafts and the **Bristol Exhibition Centre,** where international trade fairs are held, many of which are open to the public. Prince's Wharf contains the **National Lifeboat Museum** and [illegible]**stol Industrial Museum.** [illegible]er contains examples of [illegible] aircraft manufactured in the

[illegible]**S. Great Britain** was one of [illegible] first iron ships, a Transatlantic

> **Information**
> Bristol Tourist Information Office
> Narrow Quay
> Tel: (0272) 260767
>
> **Festivals**
> Bristol Eisteddfod, based on the Welsh festivals of poetry, drama, song and dance is held in late March and early April. Many ensembles are invited from abroad to perform here.
> A new annual event in Bristol is the World Wine Fair and Festival, held in July in the Bristol Exhibition Centre. Many other events are held in the Centre.
> Tel: (0272) 298630.
> Fax (0272) 215386.
> There are always important art and cultural exhibitions at the Arnolfini Arts Centre, Narrow Qay.
> Tel: (0272) 299191
>
> **Tips**
> A unique way in which to see Bristol and the magnificent surrounding countryside is by balloon, from Bristol Balloons. The River Avon's gorges cause rising currents of hot air, making the Bristol area particularly suitable for ballooning.
> **Museums and Theatre:** For information about the Bristol City Council Museums and Art Gallery telephone (0272)223571. Admission is free. To reserve seats for the Bristol Old Vic, King Street.
> Tel: (0272) 250250.

The Clifton Suspension Bridge spanning the Avon (above).

Bristol Docks are now a recreation area (above right).

Wills Tower, part of Bristol University, is a Victorian gothic endowment by a tobacco baron (below right).

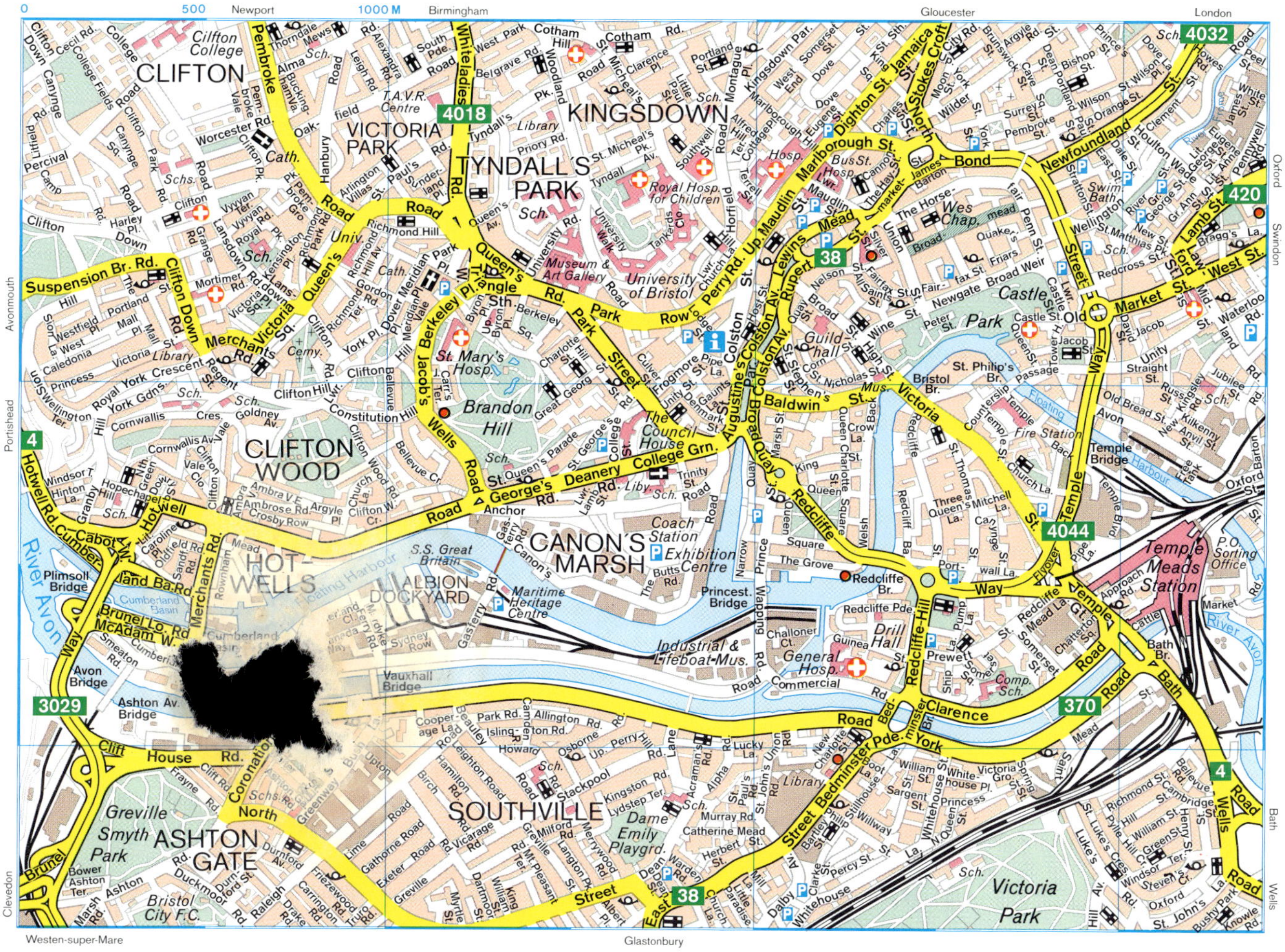

luxury liner and the first ocean-going vessel to have screw propulsion. She was the invention of the great Victorian engineer, Isambard Kingdom Brunel (1806-1859), who in his short life substantially altered the face of Britain and made a major contribution to public transport. The ship made her maiden voyage from Bristol to New York in 1845. She was rescued from a watery grave in the Falkland Islands in 1970 and towed back to Britain to be restored and put on show in the **Western Docks**. **King Street** in the centre of the dock area managed to escape much of the wartime bombing. This is the site of the Merchants' Almshouses, built in 1699 by the Merchant Venturers Society, which traces its history back to a charter granted by Henry II. The **Theatre Royal** in King Street is modelled on the Theatre Royal, Drury Lane in London. It opened in 1766 and since 1946, has been home to the Bristol Old Vic, one of the most important theatre companies based outside London. Handily opposite the theatre is one of Britain's most famous public houses, the **Llandoger Trow**. This splendid 17th-century tavern is said to be the original of the Admiral Benbow, in which the pirates met to plot their dirty deeds in Robert Louis Stevenson's *Treasure Island*.

Bristol Cathedral is not a very imposing church from the outside. It lacks a steeple, the nave is Victorian gothic and the church is a so-called "hall church", whose aisles, choir and nave are all the same height. However, it has a beautiful interior and an ancient history. The cathedral is said to stand on the site of St. Augustine's Oak, where the saint held a meeting with British Christians in 603. It was founded in 1148 as an abbey church , and became a cathedral in 1542 after Henry VIII's Dissolution of the Monasteries. The chapterhouse and gateways are of Norman origin and the choir was rebuilt in the late 13th and early 14th centuries. The central tower is also 14th century. Of particular interest is the choir, which is in an Early Decorative style unparalleled elsewhere in England. Bristol boasts another important place of worship, the "New Room", built by John Wesley in 1739, the first Methodist Chapel in the world. Wesley lived "over the shop" and his statue now stands in the courtyard. The chapel is opposite the **Broadmead Shopping Centre**, a good place to look around on a rainy day if the museums do not appeal.

Bristol City Museum and Art Gallery, in Queen's Road has a large collection of decorative and applied art. A highlight of the collection is a series of Assyrian carvings dating from the 8th century b.c., but the museum is best known for its valuable and extensive collection of glassware. Bristol was once famous for its dark blue glass, similar to Bohemian glass, and the museum has an extensive collection of Bristol glass as well as products from neighbouring Nailsea, where decorative glass of the Murano type was blown in the 19th century. The museum boasts the largest collection of Chinese glass outside China. Glassware, of another type, whose contents are more valuable than the containers, is displayed at **Harvey's Wine Museum**. Harvey's, the biggest sherry importers in the world, are headquartered in Bristol, hence the name of one of their leading brands, Bristol Cream. Harvey's cellars are open to the public and there are exhibits of 18th-century English drinking glasses and other wine-related artefacts. Tastings can be arranged by appointment.

The Exchange (1743) near the old city centre in Corn Street, is now a bustling covered market for household goods, but it was once the place where merchants bought and sold whole cargoes. In front of the Exchange, in the open air, stand four bronze tables with central depressions. These are the famous "nails". If the sample of grain placed by the seller into the central depression in the table looked good to the buyer, he would put his cash "on the nail".

The suburb of Clifton is full of 18th- and 19th-century houses decorated with elegant wrought ironwork, many of which once belonged to slave- traders. Clifton also has a landmark that is as closely associated with Bristol as the Eiffel Tower is with Paris. It is Isambard Kingdom Brunel's **Clifton Suspension Bridge** (1831-1864) over the Avon.On the Bristol side of the bridge there is an **Observatory** containing a camera obscura. From the same end of the bridge a footpath descends to **Hotwells**, a spa which attracted many visitors in the 18th century.

Bath
World Heritage City

Bath is a watchword for elegance, a city created by and for fashionable people. There are more phrases connected with Bath in English than with any other city, showing how popular and important it was as a health resort.

History
Bath's historic importance stems from its hot springs, which for thousands of years have attracted visitors who believed in their curative powers. When the Romans came, they named the place Aquae Sulis, "Aquae" meaning waters and Sulis being a local goddess, though they later re-dedicated the Baths to Minerva. In the Middle Ages, Bath was the centre of cloth trade. Then in the mid-18th century, it suddenly became the most fashionable place in Britain. This was the era of the English dandy, known as a "beau". Bath became the first holiday resort. Richard Nash, known as Beau Nash, was Master of Ceremonies at Bath and persuaded the rich and famous to take the waters, and disport themselves afterwards at dances in the Assembly Rooms. An entrepreneur named Ralph Allen persuaded the architects John Wood the Elder and his son John Wood the Younger to rebuild the city in neo-classical style, using the lovely honey-coloured local stone. Bath is now an enduring monument to Palladian elegance, with its squares, gardens and crescents. Anyone who was anyone in Georgian England visited Bath when Beau Nash and Beau Brummel presided over the festivities.

Information
Tourist Information Centre
The Colonnades
Bath Street
Bath BA1 1SW
Tel: (0225) 462831

Events
Mid-Somerset Festival: Early spring fesival of arts, crafts and music. International Contemporary Art Fair held in late May, the biggest showcase for contemporary art outside London. Bath International Festival: Late May/Early June, a music festival concentrating on classical music and jazz. Collectors and Antique Fairs are held regularly throughout the summer, usually in the vicinity of the Abbey and in the Covered Market.

Tips
The best way to see Bath is on a walking tour organised by Bath Parade Guides., 33 Priory Close, Bath
Tel: (0225) 832642.

Tourist Attractions
The Baths themselves are, of course, the major attraction in Bath. The warm waters are unusual in that they do not contain minerals. In fact, their origin remained a mystery until the 1970s, when it was discovered that they are the result of rainwater gradually filtering down towards the earth's core then welling up again through the porous local limestone. It takes a raindrop 10,000 years from the time it falls on Bath to the time it emerges again inside the hot springs at a temperature of exactly 46.8 °C. An even more extraordinary fact is that the elaborate baths built by the Romans fell into disuse, were covered by rubble and remained completely hidden until the late 19th century. When the Georgians were building their own facilities, they had no idea that a magnificent Roman bathing complex was there right under their feet! The **Roman Baths** which are the centrepiece of the **Roman Baths and Museum** were not properly excavated until 1878. Work has continued to uncover the most elaborate complex of Roman Baths in Europe, and these and various later medieval and Georgian installations are on view, together with Roman artefacts discovered elsewhere in the city, such as the magnificent head of Minerva, found in the High Street. Next to the Roman Baths there is the **Pump Room** (1792-96). Inside this Georgian edifice, the famous waters are freely available from a fountain, sometimes served by ladies in period costume. Two sedan chairs have been preserved here. These were Bath's form of public transport in the days of Beau Nash, whose statue now presides over the proceedings. Morning coffee and after- [illegible] are served to the strains of

Bath Abbey in summer (top right).

Royal Crescent from Royal Victoria Park (top left).

Pulteney Bridge in winter (above).

The Roman Baths overlooked by the Abbey (right).

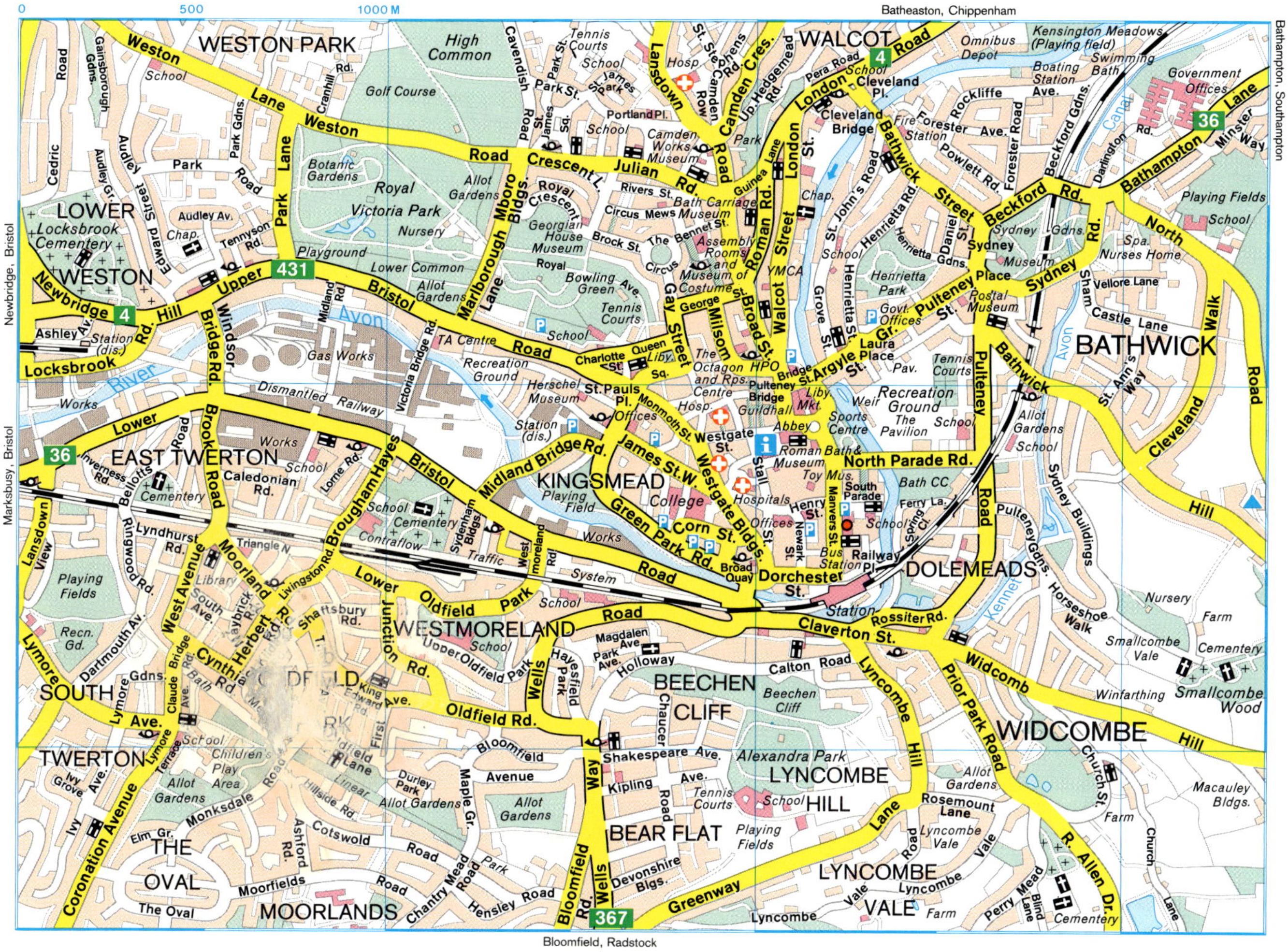

the Pump Room Trio. The architrave over the entrance to the Pump Room bears the inscription in Greek" Water is Best". This theme is continued outside **Bath Abbey**, where there is a statue to the Temperance Movement, a reminder of the fact that so many came to take the waters as a cure for their overindulgence in alcohol. The Abbey itself was the last great church to be built in England before the Reformation. It is in Perpendicular style throughout with handsome flying buttresses and impressive stained glass windows on the West front, flanked by turrets carved with angels ascending and descending a ladder, representing Jacob's Dream. Opposite the Abbey there are beautiful gardens down to the Avon. Another feature of Bath is its wealth of beautifully-kept parks and gardens. The **Assemby Rooms**, just around the corner, were built by John Wood the Younger in 1771. They now house the **Museum of Costume**, probably the finest museum of its kind in Britain.

Bath's architecture is best appreciated on foot. Among the finest examples of the work of the Woods, father and son, are **The Circus**, **Queen Square** and the **Parades**, culminating in the magnificent **Royal Crescent**, a semi-circle of terraced houses on a hill overlooking the **Royal Victoria Park,** which has a **Botanical Garden**. **No 1 Royal Crescent** is now open as a museum furnished in period style.

Bath has been called a city of museums, and has exhibitions for all tastes. **The Bath Industrial Heritage Centre** is based on two former industries, a Victorian brass foundry and Mr Bowler's Mineral Water Manufactory which made soft drinks. **Bath City Art Gallery** contains works by the European Old Masters, as well as British paintings, many of which feature Bath as their subject-matter. The **Building of Bath Museum** is housed in the Countess of Huntingdon's Chapel in the Vineyards, the Paragon. It traces the story of how Bath became the most fashionable city in 18th-century England. For those interested in philately, Bath has an important **Postal Museum**; the first known posting of a Penny Black, the first postage stamp, was from this very building. Just beyond the Postal Museum, there is the **Holburne of Menstrie Museum**, housed in a late 18th-century building. It exhibits the fine collection of English paintings which were the bequest of Sir Thomas Holburne (d. 1874). The emphasis is on British painters, including Raeburn, Gainsborough and Stubbs, though there are also examples of European bronzes and ceramics. A **Crafts Study Centre** opened here in 1977. There is another unusual museum, the **American Museum** at Claverton Manor, just outside the city. It is famous for its unique collection of early American folk art, including period furniture, patchwork quilts, pewter and silver.

After a tiring day out at the museums, the visitor can eat, drink and rest – at another museum! **Sally Lunn's Refreshment House and Museum** is housed in the oldest building in the city, containing the remains of the Roman, Saxon and medieval buildings that occupied the site, before Sally Lunn made it her bakehouse. The good lady laboured here from 1680, to produce the substantial bun that bears her name, though it is supposedly a version of the French "soleil-lune". You can enjoy a Sally Lunn and much more besides at this delightful restaurant. Bath is still famous for its good food, so it is not surprising that many English delicacies take their name from this city – the Bath bun, Bath chaps (breaded pig's cheek), and the Bath Oliver (a dry biscuit). In the evening, it is a good idea to attend a performance at the **Theatre Royal**, with its magnificent interior, which was another fashionable place to see and be seen for the 18th-century *beau monde*. Beau Nash's house is almost opposite the theatre; it is now a restaurant.

Bath is an excellent place to shop, with its own large department store, **Jolly's**, numerous antique shops and fashionable boutiques. There are lovely speciality shops, especially those on and around the **Pulteney Bridge** over the Avon, built by the famous Robert Adam and lined with shops like the Ponte Vecchio in Florence on which it is modelled. Boat trips along the **Kennet and Avon Canal** are organised from Pulteney Bridge. **The Boathouse** in Forester Road is another living museum, a Victorian boating station with tea gardens and restaurant, at which wooden skiffs, punts and canoes can be hired for a day out on the river.

London – Capital of the Kingdom

"There is in London all that life can afford" wrote Dr. Samuel Johnson. That is as true today as it was when he wrote it, 200 years ago. The city is four times the size it was in Dr. Johnson's day, and much of the activity has shifted westwards.

London is much more than the capital of England, or even of Great Britain. It is the mother city of the Commonwealth, the heir to the British Empire "on which the sun never set". That is why there is more to do and see in London than in any other capital city in the world. For one thing, for the past 1,000 years London has been not one city but two – the City of London and the City of Westminster. Over the centuries, many surrounding villages have been absorbed into the metropolis. Greater London covers an area of 625 square miles and consists of 33 separate boroughs, with a total population of about seven million. While many big cities have grown large relatively recently, Londoners started living outside the city walls almost as soon as the Romans built them, so London has been in a state of constant expansion, helped by its position in the centre of the shallow clay basin of the Thames Valley. Central London has a lower population density than most other European capitals, because most people work in the West End or the City and live in the suburbs. Another reason is that London is full of parks and green spaces, ranging in size from small private gardens and gardens in the London squares to which residents have the key, to vast open spaces such as Regents Park, Hyde Park and Hampstead Heath.

History

Ten thousand years ago, the land bridge that existed between Britain and the Continent sank, creating the English Channel. From then onwards the easiest way to enter England was by sailing up the Thames which lay more or less opposite the River Rhine. At London, the Thames was shallow and could easily be forded. This is how the Belgae, the Angles and the Saxons came to settle here. Evidence of their presence has been found, including a huge wooden temple at Heston, near the present London Airport. For centuries before the Romans invaded Britain in 43 a.d., the Thames was the frontier between warring tribes. The Romans made Camulodium (Colchester) in Essex their capital, as it had been the capital of the British kings who ruled before they came. However, Londinium, as the Romans called it, continued to grow. There is evidence that the Romans built a bridge across the Thames almost as soon as they arrived, which boosted the growth of Southwark, on the opposite bank. The first written mention of London is by the Roman historian Tacitus. He records the destruction of the city in 60 a.d. by Queen Boudicca (Boadicæa) who sacked Londinium and razed it to the ground in

her revolt against Roman rule. Many Roman artefacts have been recovered in London, especially in the rivers, such as the Walbrook and the Fleet, once tributaries of the Thames but now covered over and used as sewers. They include a magnificent head of the Emperor Hadrian, probably cast to commemorate his visit to the city in 122 a.d. It can be seen in the Museum of London. London continued to grow and by the time the Romans left Britain in the 5th century, it was the biggest city in Britain. During the ensuing Dark Ages, Celts, Saxons and Danes used London as a battleground, causing it to be largely abandoned by human habitation. In 604, Ethelbert, the first Christian king of Kent, founded St. Paul's Cathedral. In 1060, King Edward the Confessor founded an abbey west of the city, which became known as Westminster Abbey, and built himself a palace nearby. This is

The Thames at night with the Royal Festival Hall (top above).

The Thames Barrier, the futuristic Gloodgates protecting London from her river (above).

Aerial view of Tower Bridge with the Tower of London (opposite left).

Albert Bridge which spans the river from the Chelsea Embarkment to Battersea (opposite top).

Information
Tourist Information Centres are at the following locations:

Victoria Station Forecourt
London SW1

Harrods
Knightsbridge
London SW1

Heathrow International Airport

Selfridges
Oxford Street W1

Telephone Information Service: (071) 730 3488

Written enquiries:
London Tourist Board
26 Grosvenor Gardens
London SW1 0DU

Events
To find out what is happening in London, buy one of the weekly listings magazines, such as *Time Out*, *City Limits* or *What's On in London.*
Annual events are as follows: the Oxford and Cambridge boat race, rowed on the Thames from Putney to Mortlake in late March or early April; the Chelsea Flower Show and the (football) Cup Final in May, the Trooping of the Colour on the Queen's official birthday in early June, the Royal Tournament in July, the Notting Hill Carnival on August Bank Holiday (late August), State Opening of Parliament in October and on the second Saturday in November, the Lord Mayor's Show.

Tips
Remember when driving into London the signs that say "West End" actually mean the Oxford Street area which most people consider to be the centre of London and "City" means the City of London which is to the east of the centre. A short journey for three or more people is actually cheaper by taxi than by underground train. In the suburbs there are minicabs, which cannot be hailed in the street like taxis but must be booked by telephone.

how London came to have a twin city, Westminster, so early in its history. When William the Conqueror arrived in England in 1066 he built the mighty fortress known as the Tower of London just east of the city walls. The city was granted the right to appoint its own mayor and corporation (town council) under King John in 1215. They ran the city so efficiently that its administration was taken as a model for other cities in England. London suffered badly under King Henry VIII when the monasteries were dissolved and the currency debased, both of which caused great unemployment and hardship. Sir Thomas Gresham, who founded the Royal Exchange and promoted foreign trade on a scale unknown anywhere else in the world, was instrumental in creating a spectacular recovery. This was also the time of the great playwrights, when Christopher Marlowe, Ben Jonson and William Shakespeare were staging their plays and performing in them on the South Bank. London's prosperity lasted until the Great Plague of 1665 and the Fire of London of 1666. The Fire destroyed many fine buildings, including St. Paul's Cathedral but it was not entirely harmful. It exterminated the plague-carrying Norwegian brown rat so that the disease never recurred in London. Even more important, it gave the city the chance to rebuild along modern lines, introducing spacious avenues and squares. Inigo Jones, a Londoner born and bred, was the city's first town-planner. Sir Christopher Wren, the Surveyor-General, had produced an ambitious plan for London which was rejected, but he was able to build 52 London churches, the Royal Hospital at Chelsea and St. Paul's Cathedral. The late 18th and early 19th centuries were the heyday of Georgian architecture, of which the best examples are Regent Street and Regent's Park. These were created by John Nash, who built Buckingham Palace and also designed the elegant Georgian terraces which surround Regents Park. The brothers Adam designed the Adelphi, a complex of residential apartments and shops, off the Strand. The Industrial Revolution, which hit London in the mid-19th century, radically changed its face forever. Expansion had to be ruthless to accommodate the millions who had flocked to the capital. Thousands of identical rows of houses covered what was once fertile farmland and lovely countryside, all thrown up to house the workers. However, the Victorians also made significant contributions to the well-being of Londoners, adding public buildings and major public works. The most important was the sewage system, built by Thomas Cubitt the speculative builder and Joseph Bazalguette the architect. Bazalguette also built the Thames Embankment where his statue has been erected, and several Thames pumping stations. This was also the era of the railway, when Sherlock Holmes and his faithful Dr. Watson were able to slip away to investigate dirty deeds in the heart of rural England, thanks to their proximity to the Marylebone station and its excellent connections to all parts of England. Large swathes of London were demolished in the second half of the century in order to construct the best railway system in Europe. The 1920s and 1930s saw the extension of the London Underground (known as "the tube"), the world's first underground railway, out into the countryside. Mass transport and mass-produced cars meant that it was now possible for Londoners to live even further from the centre. Strings of "bijou residences" in a cottagey, mock-Tudor style sprang up along the railway and overground tube lines. Then came the devastation caused by World War II and the Blitz. Huge areas of the London Docks and the City of London were destroyed. In the second half of the 20th century, two big arts complexes have been built, the South Bank Arts Complex and the Barbican Centre. New wings have been added to the Tate Gallery and the National Gallery and Shakespeare's Globe Theatre has been rebuilt on the

Docklands from the air (left).

The Houses of Parliament from the Thames (top above).

The new yachtmarina in the Docklands development (above).

Big Ben, whose chimes echo across the world (opposite left).

Harrods department store by night (opposite right).

South Bank. The latest attempt to stop the Thames engulfing London, the Thames Flood Barrier, erected after the disastrous flood of 1972, was completed in 1982.

Tourist Attractions – The West End

Central London is now generally accepted to mean what Londoners call the West End, which roughly covers the City of Westminster and parts of the London Boroughs of Camden and Islington. In the heart of the city of Westminster lies the church which belonged to the Benedictine Abbey founded by King Edward the Confessor. Traces of Edward's church have been found beneath the nave of **Westminster Abbey**. The king died only eight days after it was consecrated and was buried before the High Altar. When King Edward was canonised, successive monarchs wanted to be associated with the saint and showered gifts upon the Abbey. Most of the current building was erected on the orders of Henry III in the 13th century. The design is heavily influenced by French architecture of the time. William the Conqueror started a tradition by being crowned in the Abbey and all successive sovereigns have held their coronations here. The custom of burying famous commoners in the Abbey was begun by Richard II in the late 14th century. This has made the graves in Westminster Abbey like a roll-call of famous characters from British history. The area known as **Poet's Corner** was inaugurated with the tomb of one of the greatest writers in English history, and a native Londoner, Geoffrey Chaucer, author of *The Canterbury Tales* who died in 1400. Many writers and poets who are buried elsewhere – Shakespeare, Jane Austen, the Brontë Sisters – have memorials here. Other parts of the Abbey that are well worth visiting include the **Undercroft Museum**, which contains wax effigies of the monarchs carried in funeral processions during the Middle Ages, the **Chapel of the Pyx** and the **Cloisters**. **Westminster School**, once the choir school for the Abbey, now a famous public school, is just round the corner from the Abbey, in Little Dean's Yard. **St. Margaret's Westminster**, a church in the Abbey grounds, was built in the late 15th and early 16th centuries and heavily rebuilt thereafter. It has traditionally been the favourite place for society weddings. Samuel Pepys the diarist was married here and Sir Walter Raleigh is buried here.

The corner of Westminster Abbey looks on to **Parliament Square**, on the opposite side of which are the **Houses of Parliament**, officially known as the **Palace of Westminster**, since it was on this site that Edward the Confessor built his palace. The oldest remaining part of the Palace is **Westminster Hall**, built in the 11th century by William Rufus. It has a magnificent hammerbeam roof. It was in this hall that the Model Parliament was held by Edward I and here that Charles I was condemned to death; a plaque marks the spot. In the cellars beneath the palace, Guy Fawkes and his fellow Roman Catholic conspirators were caught trying to blow up parliament on 5th November, 1605. The event is still celebrated throughout Britain with fireworks and bonfires on which a "guy" is burned in effigy. Parliament has suffered much damage over the centuries. The two worst incidents were a fire of 1834, after which the buildings were rebuilt in Victorian Gothic style by Charles Barry, aided by Augustus Pugin. Thus although they are medieval in style, the Houses of Parliament are much younger than they look. The chamber of the **House of Commons** was badly damaged by fire bombs on 10 May, 1941 but have been restored. At one end of the Houses of Parliament, next to the House of Lords is the **Victoria Tower**, completed in 1858, and at the other, St. Stephen's Tower which contains the famous clock, **Big Ben**. Thanks to the power of radio and television the clock chimes are heard worldwide before the radio and television news broadcasts.

The street leading off Parliament Square to the north-west is Victo-

ria Street. Just behind it, in the Broadway is **New Scotland Yard**, the headquarters of the Metropolitan Police. This is a new building, erected in 1967. The former Scotland Yard building, much featured in old British detective films, is now used as offices for members of parliament and has been renamed the **Norman Shaw Building** after its architect. The police headquarters were so named because they stand on the site of the palace once used by the kings of Scotland on ceremonial visits to London. On the opposite side of Victoria Street, linked to the street by a piazza, is the Roman Catholic **Westminster Cathedral**, whose official name is the Cathedral of the Precious Blood of Our Lord Jesus Christ. The building is in Byzantine style, built of brick with bands of Portland stone. The exterior was completed in 1903, but for the sake of economy, it was decided to leave the decoration of the interior to future generations and this is an ongoing process.

Nearby is **Victoria Station**, the busiest railway station in the world. The inscription among the elaborate statuary over the entrance proclaims it to be the "Gateway to the Continent", but it is fast losing this accolade to **Waterloo Station** on the opposite side of the Thames which is the Eurostar Channel Tunnel terminus. Victoria Station lies behind the spacious grounds of **Buckingham Palace**, the official home of the monarch. It was built in 1703 as a mansion for the Duke of Buckingham, but vastly expanded by George IV in 1825 who squeezed the money out of a reluctant Parliament and demanded that John Nash, the leading architect of the day, be commissioned to convert what had previously been a relatively modest dwelling into the present vast edifice. The Palace proved to be uncomfortable to live in and subsequent monarchs hated it. However, Queen Victoria redesigned and rehabilitated it and it has been used as the official residence ever since. Buckingham Palace has 600 rooms, as well as a covered swimming pool and 45 acres of grounds, in which a series of Royal Garden Parties are held every year for about 8,000 specially invited guests. The **Queen's Gallery** of paintings and the **Royal Mews,** which houses royal carriages, are open to the general public. The Palace faces **The Mall**, a handsome avenue leading up to **Admiralty Arch**, off **Trafalgar Square**, in the centre of which stands **Nelson's Column.** The Square was built in 1835, but was added to even as recently as 1939.

The National Gallery is on the north side of the square. It contains an unparalleled collection of Renaissance paintings, and holds special exhibitions from time to time. The architecture of the new wing, the **Sainsbury Wing**, has been the subject of much controversy as it is so resolutely traditionalist in style. **The Tate Gallery**, the major London art gallery which specialises in modern art, is also near Buckingham Palace, but in the opposite direction, westwards along the Thames. It contains paintings from the 19th century onwards, and it also has a new wing, the **Clore Gallery,** which is devoted to the works of Turner, perhaps Britain's greatest painter, the son of a Covent Garden barber. Other important art galleries in the West End are the **Wallace Collection** in Manchester Square, famous for its French and Dutch paintings and the **Royal Academy**, in **Burlington House**, Piccadilly.

The West End is also the premier shopping area of London. The streets, bounded by Park Lane in the West, Piccadilly in the south, Regent Street in the east and Wigmore Street in the north, are world-famous for their fashionable shops and boutiques .There are major department stores, such as **Selfridges** in Oxford Street, Britain's first department store, **Fortnum and Mason** in Piccadilly, famous for food and fashion and **Hamleys** a toy shop on four floors which claims to be the largest in the world. Bond Street, which runs north from Piccadilly, is famous for its exclusive boutiques selling jewellery and antiques, including **Aspreys**, a very exclusive jewellery and fashion department store.

On the other side of Regent Street lies the other face of the West End, the area known as **Soho**. There are two faces to Soho, the bustling, busy, cosmopolitan aspect visible mainly by day, and the seedy side which comes out mainly at night. Soho has plenty of strip clubs, peep shows and similar entertainments that do a brisk trade at all hours of the day and night. The live music scene, of which Soho was the heart in the 1950s and 1960s, has dwindled to a couple of jazz clubs, though Soho still holds a summer Jazz Festival. Soho was once the only cosmopolitan neighbourhood in London and still has many speciality food stores selling exotic ingredients, as well as the lively **Berwick Street Market**. For this reason, it is still famous for its restaurants. Soho has recently seen a large influx of Chinese, turning what was once a tiny **Chinatown** into the second-largest in Britain. The Chinese restaurants are reputed to serve food as good as any in Hong Kong. Piccadilly starts at **Piccadilly Circus**, in the centre of which is the statue known as Eros, which is really supposed to be the angel of Christian charity, though its popular name is far more appropriate, considering its surroundings. The Circus is brilliantly lit at night with neon signs. The **Trocadero** in Piccadilly Circus is a former restaurant which now houses the **Guinness World of Records Exhibition**, a series of exhibits and tableaux illustrating the Guinness Book of Records. Just around the corner is **The London Experience**, housed in the London Pavilion, once a theatre. This is a combined shopping centre and café, which serves a variety of exciting ethnic dishes from booths around a central courtyard in the basement. The West End is the heart of **Theatreland**, where

two-thirds of London's thirty or more theatres are to be found. Piccadilly ends at **Hyde Park Corner**, which has the distinctive **Constitution Arch** and statue of the **Duke of Wellington** in its centre. The Duke's London home, **Apsley House**, whose official address is No.1 London, faces the arch. It is open to the public as a museum of Wellington memorabilia and the Napoleonic Wars.

West of the West End

Grouped around Hyde Park and its westward extension, **Kensington Gardens**, are the elegant districts of **Chelsea**, **Knightsbridge** and **Kensington**. **Chelsea** was once the artists' quarter of London, in which **Cheyne Walk** was the address of more famous writers and artists than any street in London, including George Eliot and Oscar Wilde, but Chelsea is now far too expensive for all but the most affluent residents. T**he King's Road** in Chelsea is well-known for its avant-garde fashion boutiques, and is said to be where punk rock fashions originated. The mid-17th century **Royal Hospital, Chelsea**, designed by Sir Christopher Wren as a home and hospital for old soldiers, still serves that purpose today. The inmates, known as Chelsea Pensioners, wear a distinctive red and blue uniform. The hospital was commissioned by Charles II who is depicted on horseback in a magnificent painting in the Great Hall and in a statue in the courtyard. The **Chelsea Flower Show** is held in the Hospital grounds, which were once the **Ranelagh Pleasure Gardens**. Part of the Hospital now houses the **National Army Museum**, which tells the story of the life of the British soldier through the centuries**.** Knightsbridge is famous for **Harrods** department store, and behind it **Beauchamp** (pronounced "Beecham") **Place** with its smart dress shops. Kensington, west of Knightsbridge, boasts another royal residence, **Kensington Palace**, where several members of the Royal Family have apartments, though the **State Apartments** can be visited as well as the **Royal Ceremonial Dress Collection.** In nearby **Kensington Gardens**, a favourite place for nannies to take children, there is the pretty little monument to **Peter Pan**, hero of the play by J.M. Barrie, and the **Albert Memorial**, a Gothic monstrosity containing the statue of Prince Albert of Saxe-Coburg-Gotha, Queen Victoria's beloved husband. The statue faces the **Albert Hall** (1871), a circular concert hall, originally designed as a Hall for the Arts and Sciences, and the brainchild of Prince Albert. The **Brompton Oratory**, a Roman Catholic church of magnificent proportions built in 1878 boasts a magnificent Italian altarpiece; the high altar is from St. Servatius, Maastricht. Just west of this church, in Cromwell Road, South Kensington, are the museums, which are offshoots of the British Museum. The **Victoria and Albert Museum** is Britain's premier museum of the decorative arts with magnificent collections of English furniture (including the Great Bed of Ware, an Elizabethan four-poster big enough to sleep 11 people!) costumes and jewellery, and frequent exhibitions devoted to modern British design. Next to it is the **Natural History Museum**, famous for its reconstructions of dinosaurs. Behind them, the **Science Museum** has plenty of interesting working models, especially in the Children's Gallery. **The Geological Museum** has examples of every type of rock and gemstone and there is a simulation of an earthquake.

The **British Museum** itself is to be found in a district known as **Bloomsbury**, north-east of Oxford Street. Bloomsbury was once famous for its intellectuals, such as Virginia Woolf, and something of the atmosphere persists with many publishing houses and bookshops grouped around the neo-classical façade of the Museum. The British Museum's collection of exhibits is almost legendary, but it is worth mentioning the **Elgin Marbles** taken from the Parthenon, the Egyptian relics including the **Rosetta Stone**, the

Summer lunchtime in Soho Square (opposite left).

Piccadilly Circus at night, "the heart of London" (opposite right).

Guard on duty at Houseguards Parade (above left).

Christmas lights in Regent Street (above right).

Lively Berwick Street Market, Soho (left).

Trafalgar Square at night (right).

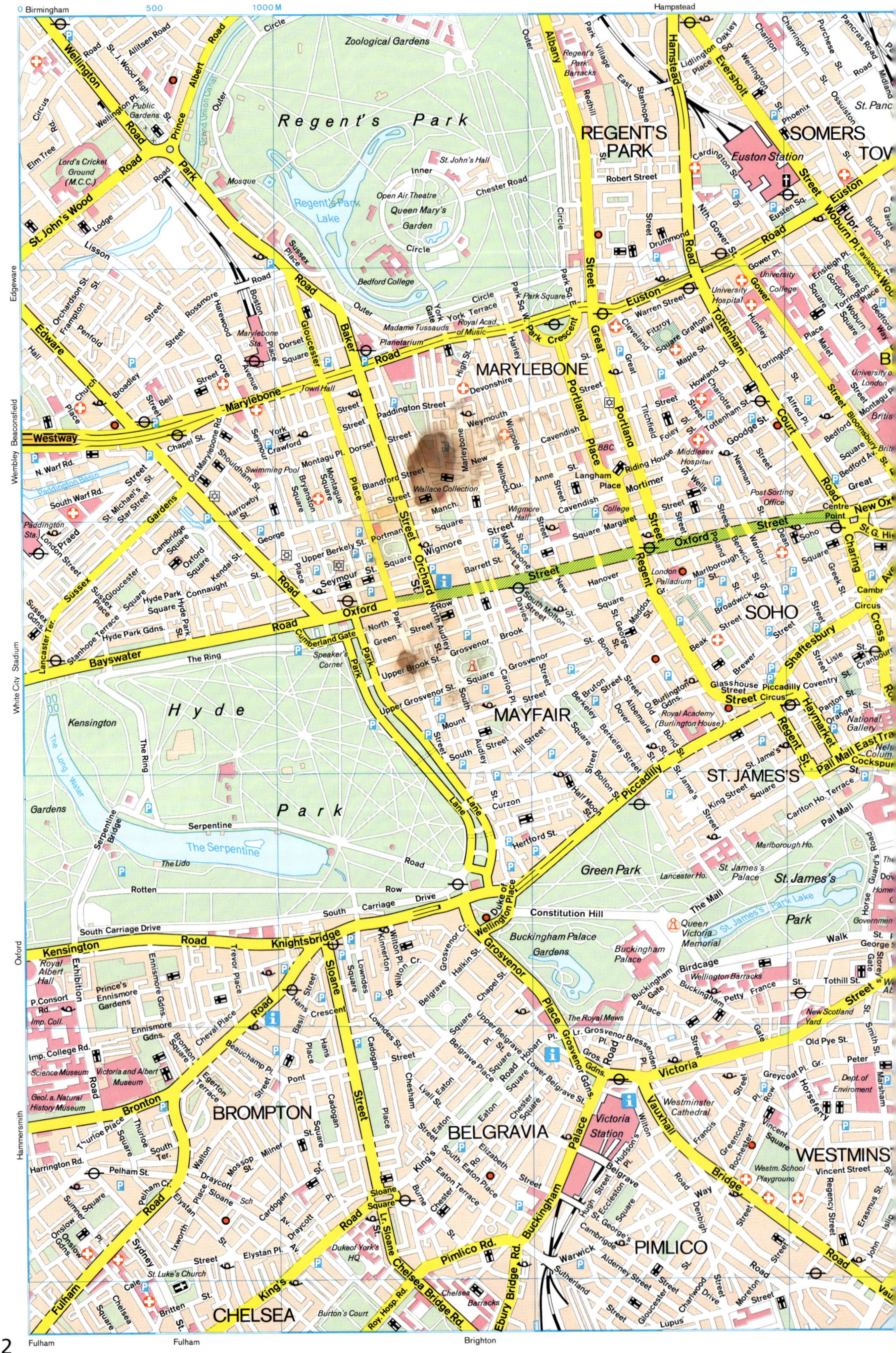
0 Birmingham
500
1000 M
Hampstead
Edgeware
Wembley Beaconsfield
White City Stadium
Oxford
Hammersmith
Fulham
Fulham
Brighton
Regent's Park
Zoological Gardens
Regent's Park Lake
Queen Mary's Garden
Open Air Theatre
St. John's Hall
Bedford College
Mosque
Lord's Cricket Ground (M.C.C.)
REGENT'S PARK
Euston Station
SOMERS TOWN
University College
University Hospital
MARYLEBONE
Madame Tussauds
Planetarium
Royal Acad. of Music
Wallace Collection
Paddington Sta.
Paddington Basin
Westway
Marylebone
Euston Road
Oxford Street
BBC
Post Sorting Office
Middlesex Hospital
London Palladium
SOHO
Shaftesbury
Piccadilly Circus
MAYFAIR
Royal Academy (Burlington House)
National Gallery
ST. JAMES'S
Hyde Park
Kensington Gardens
The Long Water
The Serpentine
The Lido
Speaker's Corner
Cumberland Gate
Bayswater Road
Park Lane
Piccadilly
Green Park
Constitution Hill
St. James's Palace
St. James's Park
St. James's Park Lake
Lancaster Ho.
Marlborough Ho.
The Mall
Queen Victoria Memorial
Buckingham Palace
Buckingham Palace Gardens
Wellington Barracks
The Royal Mews
New Scotland Yard
Dept. of Environment
Kensington Road
Knightsbridge
Royal Albert Hall
Imp. Coll.
Science Museum
Victoria and Albert Museum
Geol. a. Natural History Museum
BROMPTON
BELGRAVIA
Victoria Station
Westminster Cathedral
WESTMINSTER
Westm. School Playground
PIMLICO
CHELSEA
Chelsea Barracks
Dukeof York's HQ
Burton's Court
St. Luke's Church
King's Road
Sloane Square
Pimlico Rd.
Chelsea Bridge Rd.
Ebury Bridge Rd.
Buckingham Palace Road
Vauxhall Bridge Road
Victoria Street

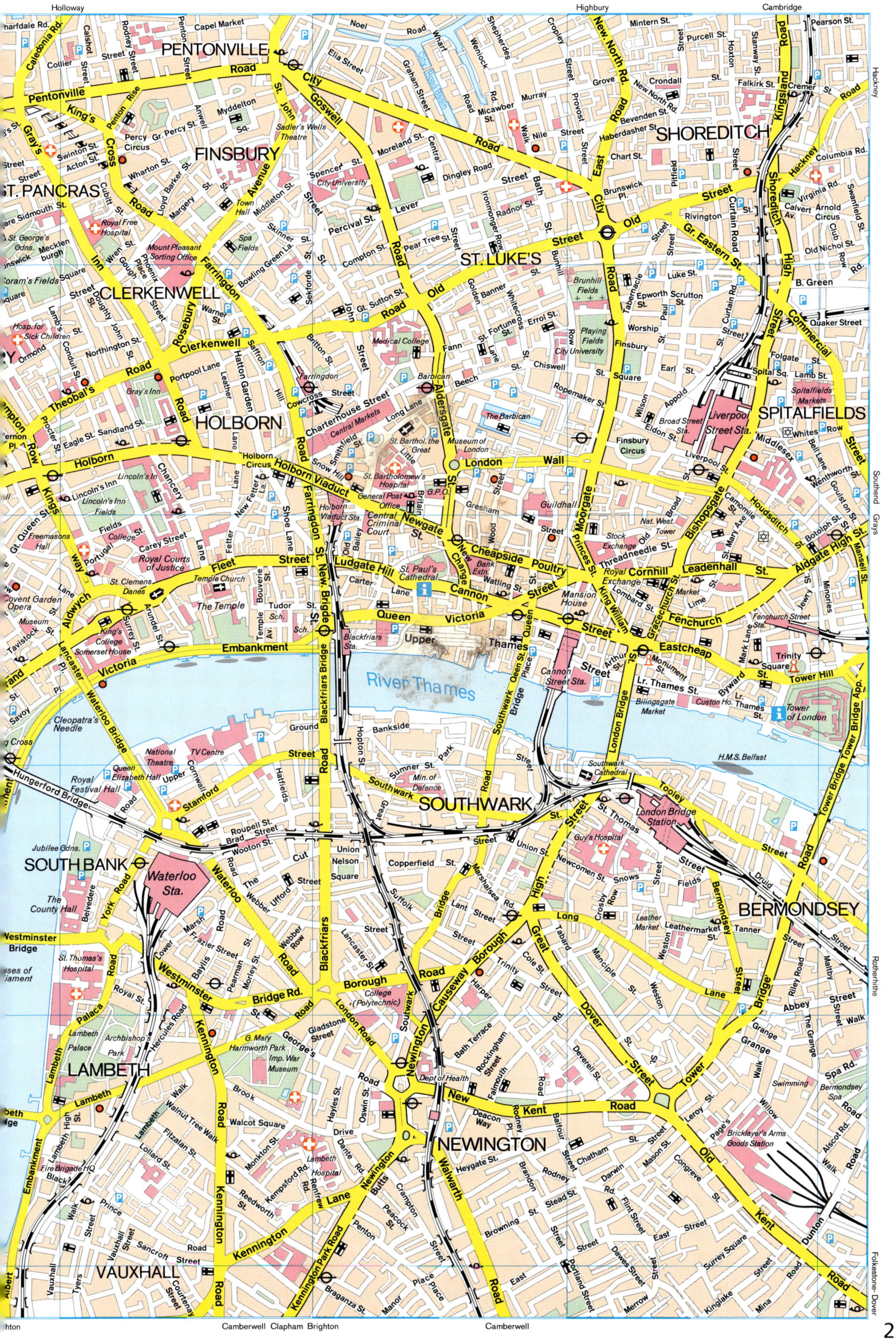
Holloway
Highbury
Cambridge
Hackney
Southend
Grays
Rotherhithe
Folkestone Dover
Camberwell Clapham Brighton
Camberwell
PENTONVILLE
Pentonville Road
FINSBURY
ST. PANCRAS
CLERKENWELL
HOLBORN
SHOREDITCH
ST. LUKE'S
SPITALFIELDS
SOUTHWARK
SOUTH BANK
BERMONDSEY
LAMBETH
NEWINGTON
VAUXHALL
City Road
Goswell Road
Old Street
Farringdon Road
Clerkenwell Road
Theobald's Road
Holborn
Holborn Viaduct
London Wall
Cheapside
Poultry
Cornhill
Leadenhall St.
Fenchurch Street
Eastcheap
Cannon Street
Queen Victoria Street
Upper Thames Street
Fleet Street
Ludgate Hill
Newgate St.
Aldersgate St.
Moorgate
Bishopsgate
Aldwych
Kingsway
Victoria Embankment
River Thames
Waterloo Bridge
Blackfriars Bridge
Southwark Bridge
London Bridge
Tower Bridge
Hungerford Bridge
Waterloo Sta.
London Bridge Station
Cannon Street Sta.
Liverpool Street Sta.
Fenchurch Street Sta.
Blackfriars Sta.
Holborn Viaduct Sta.
Tower of London
Trinity Square
Tower Hill
H.M.S. Belfast
Monument
St. Paul's Cathedral
Southwark Cathedral
Guildhall
The Barbican
Museum of London
St. Bartholomew's Hospital
Central Criminal Court
Royal Courts of Justice
The Temple
Temple Church
Somerset House
King's College
Covent Garden Opera
Cleopatra's Needle
National Theatre
Royal Festival Hall
Queen Elizabeth Hall
TV Centre
The County Hall
St. Thomas's Hospital
Houses of Parliament
Lambeth Palace
Archbishop's Park
Imperial War Museum
G. Mary Harmworth Park
Guy's Hospital
Bricklayer's Arms Goods Station
Mount Pleasant Sorting Office
Royal Free Hospital
Hosp. for Sick Children
City University
Finsbury Circus
Finsbury Square
Bunhill Fields
Stock Exchange
Bank of England
Mansion House
Royal Exchange
Billingsgate Market
Custom Ho.
Smithfield Central Markets
Spitalfields Markets
Blackfriars Road
Borough High Street
Great Dover Street
Old Kent Road
New Kent Road
Tower Bridge Road
Long Lane
Tooley Street
Southwark Street
Stamford Street
Westminster Bridge Road
Kennington Road
Kennington Lane
Kennington Park Road
Walworth Road
Newington Butts
Lambeth Road
Borough Road
London Road
Elephant and Castle
Commercial Street
Shoreditch High Street
Kingsland Road
Hackney Road
Great Eastern St.
Aldgate High St.
Minories
Lower Thames St.

stamp collection and the medieval illuminated manuscripts and oriental prints. The British Museum is within walking distance of **Covent Garden**. This was once London's wholesale fruit and vegetable market. The flower market,, designed by Inigo Jones, but covered over in Victorian times, has been imaginatively converted into a craft market, museum complex and speciality shops. The area contains dance studios, gymnasiums and cosy restaurants and cafés, the whole dominated by the **Royal Opera House**, with the **Theatre Royal, Drury Lane** (where Charles I met his mistress Nell Gwynne) just around the corner. The **London Transport Museum** with its working buses, trams and tube trains and the **Theatre Museum** are two of the museums in Covent Garden.

Three of the greatest attractions in London lie just to the north of the West End. The first of these is **Madame Tussaud's**, the wax museum which is the single most profitable tourist attraction in Britain. Madame Tussaud was a refugee from the French Revolution and the collection boasts a couple of her original models. There are life-sized representations of almost every famous person, including film and rock stars and all the kings and queens of England. The most popular attraction is the Chamber of Horrors which not only contains wax effigies of murderers and their victims, but some authentic artefacts from murders. Enthusiasts of this type of grisly show will find more exhibits to their taste in the **London Bridge** area beside the Thames, at the **London Dungeon** in Tooley Street. Next door to Madame Tussaud's is the **London Planetarium** which stages daily shows depicting the night sky. **Regent's Park** is just behind the Planetarium. It is a well-kept park with a large lake and banks of flowers, especially in **Queen Mary's Rose Garden**, in the centre. **London Zoo**, whose attractions include the elegant aviary designed by Lord Snowdon, the Penguin Pool and Pets' Corner where children can play with the animals, is on the eastern side of the Park.

The **Regent's Canal**, the name that the **Grand Union Canal** takes here, runs south of the Zoo and Regents Park. In the summer, there are rides in gaily-coloured barges from Little Venice, Camden Lock and the Caledonian Road. For those who like the water, there are many river trips on offer along the Thames. River buses ply between London City Airport and the City of London, and there are excursions to **Greenwich** to see the magnificent **Royal Naval College**, the **Royal Observatory**, where Greenwich Mean Time originated, and which is now a museum of astronomy. Two famous ships are moored at Greenwich, the tea clipper the **Cutty Sark** and **Gipsy Moth IV** in which Sir Francis Chichester made the first solo circumnavigation of the globe. Further downstream, at North Woolwich, is the **Thames Barrier**, the system of floodgates designed to stop the Thames engulfing London. The south-east of England is sinking at the rate of two feet a century! Other ships moored in the Thames which can be visited are the **HMS Belfast**, a huge grey battleship and the **Kathleen & May**, a wooden topsail schooner, moored almost opposite each other, the former by the South Bank at Southwark, the latter by the Tower of London in **St. Katharine's Dock**, which is now a yacht marina. For those who prefer dry land, the Thames can be admired from its many bridges, though the finest view is undoubtedly from the glassed-in upper floor of **Tower Bridge**, whose twin towers contain a museum. Tower Bridge stands next to the grim fortress, which has been a royal residence and a state prison, known as the **Tower of London.** A visit to the Tower is a must, though it is very crowded in the height of the season. The Crown Jewels are kept in the **Jewel House**. The list of prisoners held here ranges from Lady Jane Grey, Queen of England for nine days before she was beheaded in 1554,

to Rudolf Hess held here in 1941 after his flight to England. The Tower is still a garrison with an arsenal. The **Changing of the Guard** takes place here daily at 11.00 a.m., just as it does at Buckingham Palace at 11.30 a.m. The **White Tower** was the first of the buildings, and was erected by William the Conqueror. Most of the other buildings are medieval or Tudor. The Tower has a magnificent collection of arms and armour from all over the world, including the Far East. Very close to the Tower is one of the oldest churches in Britain, **All Hallows by the Tower**, most of which was built in Saxon times. The brick tower is 17th century, and it was from here that Samuel Pepys watched the Fire of London in 1666.

The Tower of London lies between the **City of London** and the **East End**. The best way to see the City is to start with a visit to the **Museum of London** in the **Barbican**, which will explain the background to the story of the City of London, or the Square Mile, as it is known, since that is the area it covers. The Barbican is a residential complex incorporating an **Arts Centre**, whose theatre is now the Royal Shakespeare Company's London address, with a concert hall and exhibition centre. Sections of the old Roman Wall have been unearthed nearby, next to the church of **St. Giles Cripplegate Without** (the "without" refers to the fact that the church stood outside the walls). The outstanding sight in the City is **St. Paul's Cathedral**, modelled by Sir Christopher Wren on St. Peter's in Rome and famous for its Whispering Gallery. Many famous men are buried in the Crypt, including Lord Nelson who lies beneath the dome and Wren himself, whose tomb is inscribed "*Lector, si monumentum requiris, circumspice*" (Reader, if you seek a monument, look around you). The City of London contains many other churches designed by Wren, including **St. Bride's** of Fleet Street and **St. Stephen's Walbrook**. Fleet Street is no longer home to the great British daily newspapers, many of which have moved into Docklands, but there are still plenty of souvenirs of their presence, including **The Olde Cheshire Cheese**, a public house with a restaurant that was rebuilt in 1667 after the Great Fire, which was once Dr. Samuel Johnson's local pub. The **Inns of Court**, where solicitors and barristers have their chambers, are nearby, so the drinking dens, such as **El Vino's,** so beloved of printers and journalists, are now mostly frequented by lawyers. The City is best explored at weekends when the office workers have deserted it and it is quieter than any suburb. The narrow alleys and streets with names such as Cheapside, Milk Street and Bread Street are reminders that this was where London's street markets were held. London is famous for its street markets, of which there is one in almost every neighbourhood. The main market in the city is **Leather Lane** on the western edge of the city.

The East End

Two of London's most famous street markets lie east of the City in the area known as the **East End**. These are **Petticoat Lane Market** centred on Middlesex Street and **Brick Lane Market**, both of them open only on Sunday mornings. The East End, near what were once London Docks, has traditionally been a cosmopolitan neighbourhood peopled by recent immigrants. For the first half of the century, the newcomers were mainly from eastern and central Europe and were mostly Jewish. Now they are largely Bengalis, Pakistanis and Cypriots. Small craftsmen still ply their trades in the local sweatshops, working all hours to eke out a miserable living making clothes and leather goods though the furniture trade which once flourished in the area has now gone. The East End has been been irrevocably associated with crime, from Jack the Ripper to the Kray Twins. This has become one of its great tourist attractions, and there are walking tours through the streets where the dirty deeds were committed. Two places of interest face each other incongruously across the Whitechapel Road. The **Whitechapel Art Gallery** holds

The unmistakeable silhouette of Tower Bridge (above).

The Piazza between the old Flower Market and St. Paul's church, Covent Garden, is a favourite spot for street theatre (left and right).

The City of London with the Tower of London in the foreground (opposite).

exhibitions of contemporary art and the **Whitechapel Bell Foundry** is still casting bells, one of only two such foundries left in the country. The Foundry was established in 1420 in nearby Houndsditch but moved to the present site in 1583. It cast the bells for Westminster Abbey, Big Ben and the Liberty Bell in Philadelphia, U.S.A.

The docklands of the East End have been transformed from the traditional sleaziness of a port area into 14 square miles of brand-new tower blocks, offices and homes. Before World War II, the London Docks handled 25 per cent of Britain's imports, but thanks to the ravages of wartime bombing and the introduction of containerisation, the docks moved to Tilbury at the mouth of the Thames and much of the area became derelict. Docklands includes the land enclosed in a meander in the River Thames known as the **Isle of Dogs** (since it is where the Royal hunting dogs were once kept) and stretches east as far as the Thames Barrier at North Woolwich. The site is dominated by the massive tower of **Canary Wharf**, the tallest building in Europe, which can be visited for a wonderful view of London. Erected hastily in the 1980s without much thought for amenities or local residents, and riding roughshod over planning considerations, a question mark hangs over the future of Docklands. The best way to see it is by taking a trip on the **Docklands Light Railway,** since the track is elevated and gives a good view of the area, as well as some lovely views of the River Thames. The trip should be made in daylight as Docklands, despite its newness, is poorly-lit at night.

The South Bank

Facing the East End across the water, the south bank of the Thames is also undergoing its own regeneration, but a much more sensitive one, with the restoration of old buildings and the creation of new attractions. Londoners once crossed the river to indulge in such forbidden pleasures as the theatre (banned in the city under Oliver Cromwell). Around **London Bridge Station** there are many speciality shops and restaurants, especially in **Hay's Galleria**, created out of the twin warehouses of Hays Wharf. Downstream, at **Butler's Wharf, Shad Thames**, is the **Design Museum**, London's most recent major museum. The oldest part of the South Bank is **Southwark**, where Chaucer stayed at the Tabard Inn (the Inn has gone but **Tabard Street** remains) before setting out on the pilgrimage to Canterbury in 1383. The nearby **George** in Borough High Street, is an inn with literary connections, which is mentioned in Charles Dickens' *Little Dorrit*. Shakespearean plays are performed in the courtyard in summer. The present building dates from 1676. The **Imperial War Museum** is housed in the building (1815) which formerly housed Bedlam, the popular name for the Royal Bethlehem Hospital, an institution for the insane. The Museum has a valuable collection of war memorabilia. Nearby **Lambeth Palace** is the only surviving bishops' palace in London, the official residence of the Archbishop of Canterbury. It has been heavily restored, but the **Crypt** and distinctive **Gatehouse** are medieval. The **Great Hall** had to be rebuilt in 1660, after it was burned down during the Civil War. There is a valuable library of ecclesiastical books. Next to the Palace, the church of **St. Mary-at-Lambeth**, restored after its virtual destruction during World War II, contains the graves of Captain Bligh, of "Mutiny on the Bounty" fame and the botanist John Tradescant, both of whom lived locally. The little houses in this neighbourhood are dwarfed by **Southwark Cathedral**, the oldest Gothic church in London (1207), which received cathedral status in 1903. It contains a Harvard Chapel in honour of the theologian John Harvard, who in 1636 founded the American university that bears his name. The memorial to Shakespeare marks the close association with the Bard, who acted at theatres in nearby **Bankside**, including the **Rose Theatre** (recently excavated during rebuilding work and now on view) and the rebuilt **Globe Theatre**. The **Shakespeare Globe Theatre Museum** is devoted to the history of Bankside, and also includes a full working model of the Cockpit Theatre. Further west, almost opposite Waterloo Station, is another theatre associated with Shakespeare, the **Old Vic** (short for Old Victoria) **Theatre**, a converted music hall which was the temporary home of the National Theatre before it had a permanent building of its own on the South Bank. The **South Bank** Complex was started on a derelict site after World War II, when the government attempted to revive Britain's bankrupt economy and flagging spirits by inaugurating the Festival of Britain in 1951. The first two permanent buildings on the site were the **Royal Festival Hall**, a concert hall, and the **National Film Thea-**

tre, which was enlarged in 1956. A smaller concert hall, the Queen Elizabeth Hall (1967) and an art gallery, the **Hayward Gallery** were added later. The **National Theatre** opened in 1976, under the direction of the great actor, Laurence Olivier. The most recent addition to the Complex is the **Museum of the Moving Image**, opened by Prince Charles in 1988. This is a history of film and television, presented imaginatively and with plenty of hands-on exhibits that make it enjoyable for young and old alike. The South Bank Complex is a wonderful place to spend a weekend afternoon, wandering among the impromptu stalls selling crafts and second-hand books before visiting exhibitions, which include displays and popular music concerts frequently held in the spacious foyers of the halls.

The Inner Suburbs – Hampstead, Richmond, Kew

Not all the important sights of London are in the centre. Bus and tube connections are excellent and it is worth exploring further afield, at least as far as the inner suburbs. Hampstead, in north-west London, is one of the most attractive of these. This little village grew apace when health-giving springs were discovered in the early 19th century. Many famous people have lived in the area, as witnessed by the lovely 18th- and 19th-century houses in Hampstead Village, several of which bear the distinctive blue plaques that in London indicate that the house was occupied by a famous person. Well-known residents of Hampstead include the Indian poet, Rabindranath Tagore who lived in the group of cottages on the Heath called the **Vale of Health**, the writer Leigh Hunt, the painter George Romney, the novelist John Galsworthy and the poet John Keats, whose house is open as a museum. One could do worse than patronise the local pub used by all these artists, the **Spaniards' Inn**, founded in the 16th century. The building opposite the Inn was once a tollbooth, and virtually blocks the road at that point. This is where Dick Turpin, the notorious highwayman, is reputed to have started his ride from London to York; alas, it is only a legend. **Kenwood House** is a 17th-century mansion north-east of the Heath, with interiors designed by Robert Adam, including the magnificent Library. The house was bought by the Earl of Iveagh who bequeathed his priceless collection of paintings to the nation in 1927, and they are now on view in the house. There are works by English, Flemish and Dutch artists, including a Rembrandt self-portrait. The beautiful grounds are notable for the artificial bridge over the lake, which is one-sided like a piece of scenery. Open-air concerts are held here in the summer. North of the Heath is **Highgate Cemetery**, in which the most famous grave is that of Karl Marx.

Another pleasant excursion, this time to the south-west, is to the south bank of the Thames at Richmond and Kew. **Richmond Park**, once a royal hunting preserve, is famous for its deer. Nearby are **Kew Gardens**, which contains the **Royal Botanic Gardens,** and the **Palace of Kew**. The latter, once known as the Dutch House, because of its Dutch-influenced architecture, is the only survivor of a group of palaces that once stood around Kew Green. It was the favourite home of George II, known contemptuously to his subjects as "Farmer George" because his modest lifestyle was considered to be unworthy of a monarch. The present Palace Garden is laid out in 17th-century style with a herb garden. The surrounding Royal Botanic Gardens, which cover 300 acres (121 hectares), were once a pleasure garden started by Frederick, Prince of Wales, son of George II. His widow, Augusta, created the original botanical gardens on a nine-acre site. They were improved and expanded by the famous landscape gardener, Lancelot "Capability" Brown in 1770. In 1841, Kew Gardens were handed over to the nation. The Gardens contain many interesting buildings, including the **Orangery**, **The Prince of Wales Conservatory**, a recent addition in which modern technology has created different climatic zones, and a series of handsome glasshouses, many of them dating from the 19th century, of which the **Palm House** is the most spectacular.

This is just a sample of the delights of London, which has something to offer every age group, every pocket (many of the museums do not charge admission) and every taste – and which can be enjoyed whatever the weather.

Tombs in Highgate Cemetery, (above).

Docklands, old and new (top right).

HMS Belfast moored in the River Thames (right).

The Pagoda in Kew Gardens (opposite left, top).

The Grand Union Canal in the suburb (opposite left).

The London „village" of Blackheath (opposite right).

Canterbury Centre of Christianity

Historic Canterbury, seat of the primate of the Church of England, has retained its magnificent Cathedral and its historic importance. It is set in lovely countryside within easy reach of London.

History

Canterbury is situated at a crossing-point on the River Stour between London and the most important English Channel port, Dover, so it has always been of strategic importance. The name Canterbury comes from *Cantwarabyrig,* meaning "fortress of the men of Kent". Canterbury was an important Roman settlement called Durovernum, later becoming the capital of the Saxon Kingdom of the Cantii. When St. Augustine, the missionary, first arrived in 597 he found Christian worship already in progress at St. Martin's church, probably the oldest Christian place of worship in Britain. Augustine founded a Benedictine monastery which became known later as St. Augustine's Abbey and was the traditional burial place for the early English kings and nobility. Augustine later returned to England and founded another church which became the cathedral. He turned Canterbury into the centre of English Christendom, and made its Archbishop the head of the British arm of the church. However, the cathedral and the city which grew up around it gained in importance after the murder inside the Cathedral of the Archbishop Thomas à Becket in 1170. The archbishop had been a childhood friend of King Henry II who had ordered his assassination. Thomas was canonised three years after his death and Henry II himself did penance for his deed. Pilgrims flocked to Canterbury from all over the Christian world. They even included King Louis VII of France. The event has had a lasting effect on English literature. Geoffrey Chaucer's "Canterbury Tales", written c. 1387 and "Murder in the Cathedral" by T.S. Eliot (1935), who was himself educated at King's School, Canterbury, are just two works which take their theme from it. The shrine of St. Thomas allegedly had miraculous powers. It was destroyed by Henry VIII in 1538. The Elizabethan playwright Christopher Marlowe (1564-93) lived in Canterbury, but his house was destroyed during World War II along with much else of historic Canterbury.

Tourist Attractions

Naturally, Canterbury's main attraction is the **Cathedral**. The best way to reach it is from the High Street along Mercery Lane, where pilgrimage souvenirs (Holy Water, medallions of St. Thomas and other trinkets) were once sold to pilgrims. The main entrance is **Christ Church Gate**, built in 1517 in memory of Arthur, Prince of Wales (1486-1502), though the gates themselves are 17th century. Although a church has occupied this site for 1000 years, the fabric of the cathedral dates mainly from two periods, 1070-1184 and 1391-1505. It is hard to say which is the more magnificent, the beautiful exterior, built largely of grey Caen stone or the richly-adorned interior. The exterior is equally impressive whether seen close up or from the opposite side of the Stour.

The main entrance to the Cathedral, the South Porch (1418), was probably built to commemorate the victory at Agincourt (1415). Much of the carved wood of the interior, including the "Corinthian Throne" was produced by Grinling Gibbons in c. 1704. The nave is the longest in England. It was built by Henry Yevele as was the West Transept in c. 1391. The main work on the cathedral was finished when the central tower, known as Bell Harry, was completed in 1505. The spot where St. Thomas is alleged to have fallen is marked with a plaque in the floor in the north-west transept. The adjoining **Lady Chapel** (1449-68) is one of the finest in England, noted for its late Perpendicular fan-vaulted ceiling. The Choir, also extremely long, was built by William de Sens in the late 12th century in a mixture of Norman and Early English styles, and the side-chapels are Norman. The **Trinity Chapel** has magnificent stained glass windows (much other stained glass has been lost from the cathedral). Immediately behind the high altar, is **St. Augustine's Chair**, on which archbishops of Canterbury have traditionally been enthroned. This chapel contains the tombs of The Black Prince (d. 1376) and King Henry IV (d. 1413), buried with his second wife, Joan of Navarre. **The Crypt** has some magnificent Norman stonework carved in the time of the original builders of the Cathedral, the priors Ernulf and Conrad (1096-1130).

In the town itself, **Queen Elizabeth's Guest Chamber**, a Tudor house built in 1573, is now a restaurant, so it is possible to eat, drink and see the sights simultaneously. A disused church in St. Margaret's Street contains an exhibit in the form of a series of tableaux called **The Canterbury Tales: A Medieval Adventure** which recreates the story of the Canterbury Tales. The **Museum of Canterbury's Heritage**, housed in the **Poor Priests' Hospital**, a lovely medieval building, has exhibits ranging from Roman artefacts to Stephenson's Invicta steam engine used on the Canterbury to Whitstable railway until 1830. Canterbury has several other important museums, of which the foremost is the **Beaney Institute,** in the High Street, which houses the **Royal Museum and Art Gallery**. The displays include fine examples of Roman glass, found locally. The building is mock-Tudor Victorian. The **Westgate**, is the only surviving city gate, a massive fortification once used as the city prison and built c. 1380. It contains a fine collection of arms and armour, including a bridle for nagging wives and fetters; the condemned cell can be visited. The **Canterbury Centre** in **St. Alphege's Church** is used for occasional exhibitions.

The Weavers' Houses is a group of Elizabethan houses in the very centre of town which have now been converted into shops. They are named after the Huguenot weavers who lived in them after fleeing from persecution in France. Close by is the **Hospital of St. Thomas**, also known as the **Eastbridge Hospital** founded in 1180 for poor pilgrims. It contains a "Christ in Majesty" painted in the early 13th century.

It is typically English that a city so closely associated with the Church of England, should freely allow churches of other denominations within its walls. There is a Roman Catholic church in the south-east corner and the refectory and undercroft of **Blackfriars** in Best Lane is now a Christian Science

Information
Tourist Information Centre
34, St. Margaret's Street
Canterbury
Tel: (0227) 766567

What's On in Canterbury
Tel: (0227) 67744

Events
Canterbury Festival is a three-week international arts festival held in September and October. There is music, dancing, drama and art exhibitions. For further information:

Canterbury Festival
59 Ivy Lane
Canterbury CT1 1TV
Tel: (0027) 452853

The anniversary of the death of St. Thomas à Becket, on 29 December is commemorated in the Cathedral every year.

Tips
Canterbury is rather too full of tourists in high summer, so the best time to visit is out of season, though try and make it the school holidays, when it is easier to visit the Benedictine Abbey inside King's School.
Like all walled cities, Canterbury becomes choked with traffic though there is plenty of parking outside the walls.

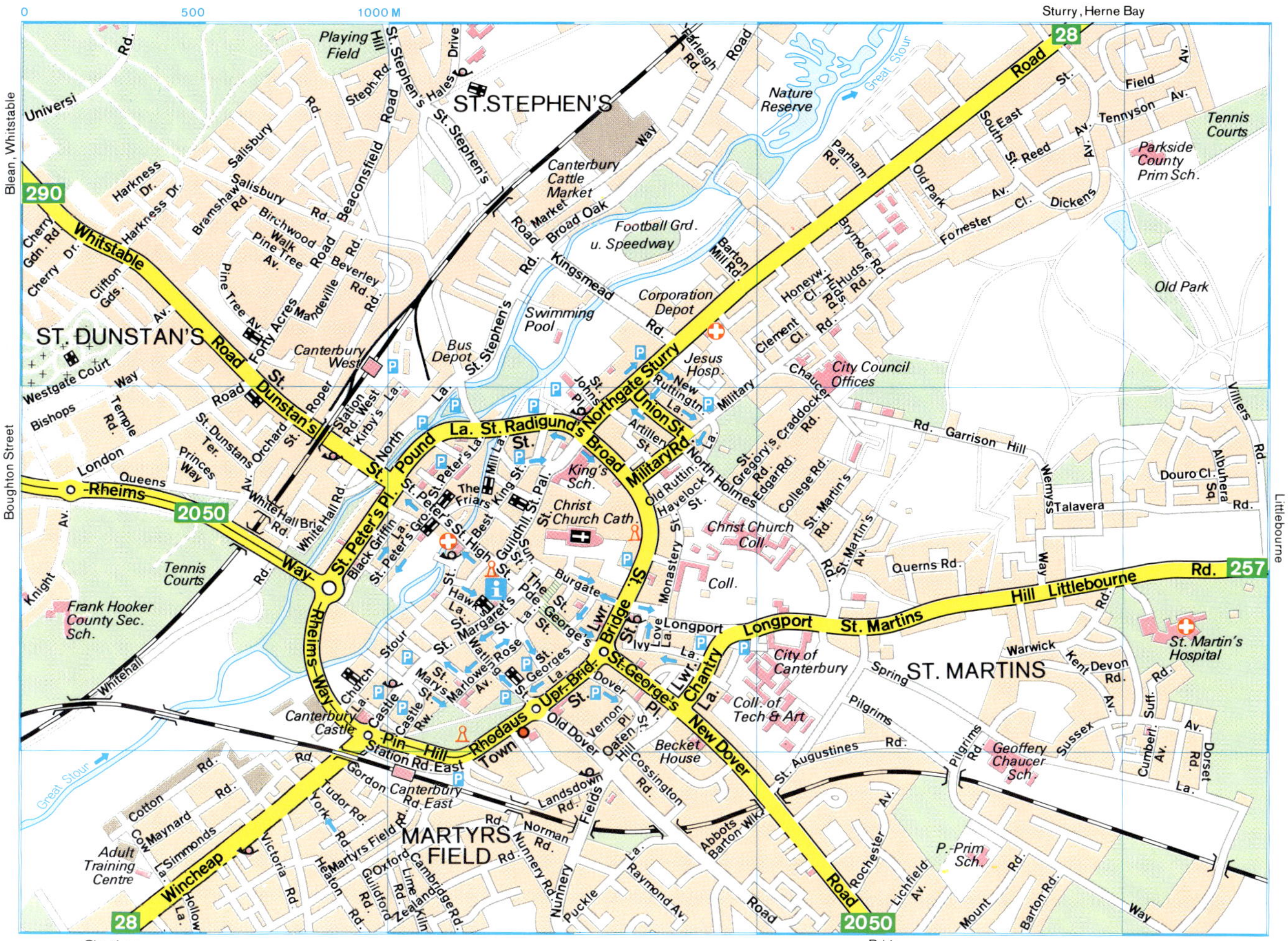

church. For a time, the Refectory was a Baptist chapel at which the writer Daniel Defoe is said to have preached.

St. Augustine's Abbey is outside the **City Walls**. Much of its original architecture is 14th century. Excavated ruins of the Abbey churches and cloisters can be visited but some of the grounds and buildings are occupied by **King's School**, one of England's leading public schools, founded as a monastic institution of learning in the 7th century, but moved to this site by King Henry VIII. The boys wear traditional 19th-century dress similar to that of Eton. Many famous Englishmen were pupils at the school, including Somerset Maugham, William Harvey (who discovered the circulation of blood) and Christopher Marlowe. Nearby is **St. Martin's Church**, used for Christian worship even before the coming of St. Augustine. The oldest parts of the present church are part of the south wall of the chancel and the base of the font. The rest of the church is 13th and 14th century. There is a 16th-century carving of St. Martin on the north wall.

Canterbury Cathedral at night (above).

West front of the cathedral (left).

The Weavers Houses, built by Huguenots (opposite).

Salisbury and Stonehenge

This city set in a valley surrounded by mysterious ancient monuments is the perfect place from which to set out to see the greatest prehistoric monument in Europe. Salisbury Plain is a high plateau littered with relics of prehistoric England.

History

Despite its many old buildings, and the medieval layout of the area around the market place, Salisbury only came into being in 1220 when Bishop Poore moved his see here from nearby Old Sarum. The settlement grew rapidly, thanks to its location in a sheltered valley, which is the meeting-point of three rivers, the Avon, the Bourne and the Nadder. Salisbury was a centre of the cloth trade in the Middle Ages and is still a flourishing market town; market days are Tuesdays and Saturdays. The view of Salisbury in the distance, with the great cathedral spire rising above the water meadows, has been a favourite theme for English painters.

Tourist Attractions

Salisbury Cathedral has the tallest spire in England (404 feet) and is the only English cathedral to be in uniform Early English style. It was designed in the 13th century though the spire was added a century later. It has the highest apex of any cathedral in England. Although the church is non-monastic, it has fine cloisters and a Chapter House in which one of the three examples of the Magna Carta is on display, as well as other cathedral treasures. The cathedral clock dates from c. 1386 and is the oldest in Britain, possibly the oldest working clock in Europe.

The best way to approach the Cathedral is through the 14th-century **St. Anne's Gate**. The other gate in the cathedral wall is **Harnham Gate** by the fish pond. **The Queen Elizabeth Gardens** by the River Nadder also give a good view of the Cathedral. Salisbury Cathedral suffered much from insensitive restoration in the late 18th century, when rood screens were removed to give a supposedly better vista of whole nave. However, the interior was not completely ruined and it contains some interesting tombs, including a diminutive statue of Bishop Poore which probably contains his heart. The medieval tombs have been repainted recently in their original gaudy colours. Salisbury's **Cathedral Close** is the largest in Britain and contains some imposing mansions, built largely from stone quarried locally or brought from Old Sarum. One of the fine houses in the Close that can be visited is **Mompesson House**, built in 1701. It contains decorative plasterwork and elegant woodwork, and has an attractive walled garden. The house

Information
Tourist Information Centre
Fish Row
Salisbury, Wilts.
SP1 1EJ
Tel: (0722) 334956

Mompesson House
The Close
Salisbury, SP1 2EL
Tel: (0722) 335659

National Trust Administration
Stonehenge
Amesbury, Nr. Salisbury
SP4 7DE
Tel: (0980) 623108

Events
The Salisbury Fesival is a two-week cultural event held in September For information:
Salisbury Festival
The King's House
The Close
Salisbury, Wilts SP1 2EN
Tel: (0722) 23883

Tips
The best time to see Stonehenge is outside the summer months and at dawn or dusk, if possible.

Salisbury's magnificent spire seen from the cloisters (top).

The church rises above the plain to dominate the city (above).

Salisbury Cathedral's five cloisters (left).

Stonehenge (opposite).

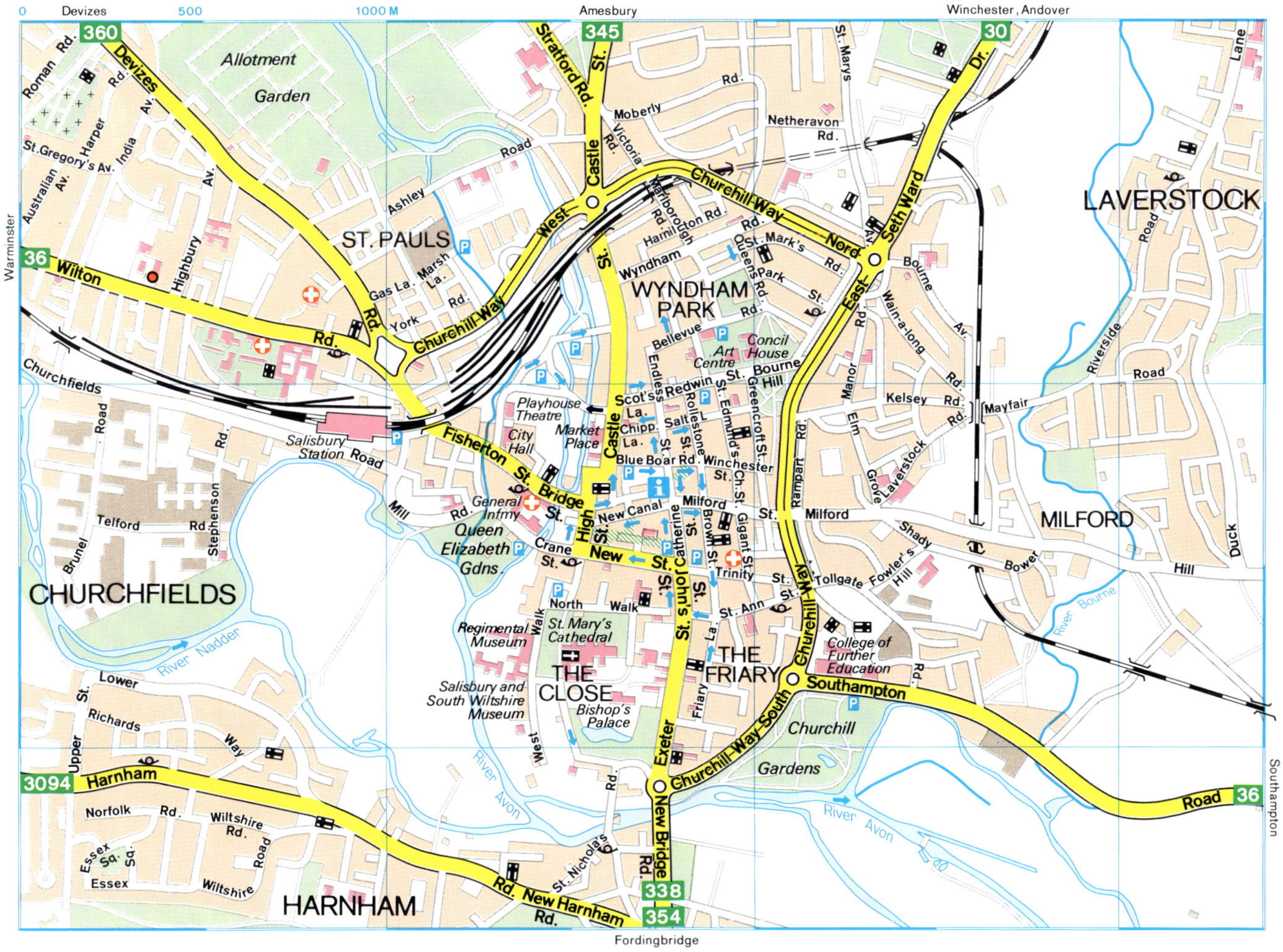

houses the **Turnbull Collection** of 18th-century English drinking glasses. The nearby **Riverside Gardens** are open in summer. The Close also contains the late 14th-century **King's House** which contains the **Salisbury and South Wiltshire Museum**. This museum is a must for archaeology buffs. It contains finds from Stonehenge and the numerous prehistoric remains in the area. The **Pitt-Rivers Collection** illustrates the history of Salisbury and Old Sarum with photographs and prints.

The area around the Market Place, known as **The Chequer** has many medieval and Renaissance houses. They include the **Joiner's Hall** (c. 1550), with its handsome façade and the **College of Matrons** (1682). Two public houses of particular interest are. the **King's Arms**, in which the Royalists plotted the escape of Charles II after the Battle of Worcester during the Civil War, and the **Old George**, an inn in which Samuel Pepys once spent the night. Near the 15th-century **Poultry Cross** is the church of **St. Thomas**, also 15th century, which contains a fine painting of The Last Judgement. The 18th century **Guildhall** boasts a painting of the Marquess of Queensbury by Raeburn.

Britain is full of strange stone monuments, known variously as menhirs, dolmens or standing stones. Most of them are in exposed places where they can be seen from afar, such as Dartmoor or Exmoor. **Salisbury Plain** is dotted with such monuments, as well as with barrows, ancient burial mounds, but none is as spectacular as **Stonehenge**. Stonehenge is the best known ancient monument in Britain, the first to be officially protected by the British government (it is now run by National Heritage) and probably the most famous pre-historic site in the world. This huge group of stones stands alone, silhouetted against the skyline, on the high, treeless plateau of Salisbury Plain and can be seen for miles around. The great mystery of Stonehenge is how and why the stones were brought here all those centuries ago. The monument consists of two concentric rings of stones arranged in pairs with lintel stones as crossbars linking them together and forming a continuous ring. The lintels are held in place by mortice-and-tenon joints. There is a third, outermost ring beside a moat or ditch, consisting of about 30 small upright stones. The circle of 60 uprights about 5 feet above ground, of which only six are still standing, was supplemented with a horseshoe arrangement. The large circle and horseshoe are of sarsen, a local sandstone which is very hard and which occurs naturally in outcrops in the area. There is a central altar stone, which now lies flat but was once an upright.

Stonehenge was constructed in stages beginning in about 3000 b.c. and ending in about 1000 b.c. The two central stone rings, which date from about 2000 b.c. are unique in Europe. It is assumed that this stone circle was used for worship since it is oriented towards the north-east where the sun rises on Midsummers's Day and the south-west where it sets in midwinter. It has been claimed as a Druidic shrine, but experts are divided as to who the original worshippers were. Their engineering expertise is all the more astonishing when it is realised that all the lintel stones are level with each other although the ground slopes, so that the standing stones are of different heights and the lintels of different thicknesses.

Brighton "London by the sea"

"Where they say such things and they do such things". Brighton's naughtiness has been immortalised in song as the place where Londoners go to do what they wouldn't dare to at home, taking their cue from the Prince Regent and many prominent people subsequently.

Brighton is the largest town in south-eastern England after London, and also its most popular seaside resort, which is quite surprising considering the beach is covered with pebbles and the climate is very windy – though the locals call it "bracing"! Brighton lies 60 miles almost due south of London on the chalk escarpment of the South Downs. Lumps of pure chalk are often to be found on the beach.

Information
Brighton Tourist
Information Centre
Marlborough House
54 Old Steine
Brighton
Tel: (0273) 23755

Brighton Arts
Information Centre
111 Church Street
Brighton, East Sussex
BN1 1EQ
Tel: (0273) 676926

Events
The Brighton Festival, in the first three weeks of May, is a national and international cultural event, featuring poetry, drama, song and dance. If you want to visit during this time and the town is fully booked, there are plenty of places to stay nearby along the coast, or you could always drive down from London for the day (about 1-1 1/2 hours, depending on the time of day and where you start from). Further information is available from the Brighton Arts Information Centre.

Brighton Races
Brighton race week is in early August, during the so-called "Sussex Fortnight", the first week of which is racing at Goodwood, in West Sussex.

Tips
Unlike most seaside towns in Britain, Brighton is quite lively even out of season, due to the large number of students who come here to learn English at the various colleges dotted all over the town. Most of the attractions therefore stay open year round.

History

The little village of Brighthelmstone, as Brighton was originally called, is mentioned in the Domesday Book but remained totally obscure until Dr. Richard Russell of Lewes recommended its "bracing air and sea-bathing" to his patients in the mid-18th century. A tablet in memory of Brighton's, benefactor can be found on the wall of the Albion Hotel. Brighton started to become fashionable in the late 17th century, but it really came into its own when the Prince Regent, later George IV, made it his home in 1786. Other famous residents of Brighton include William Frieze Greene, inventor of the first movie camera; in fact, Brighton was a centre of British filmmaking in the 1920s.

Tourist Attractions

The centre of Brighton is the Old Steine (pronounced "Steen"), a spacious green surrounded by houses which may take its name from the stones on which fishermen spread their nets to dry. On the west side at No. 55 lived Maria Fitzherbert, King George IV's mistress whom he later married in a morganatic (secret) marriage. He could not marry her openly since she was both a commoner and a Roman Catholic. The Steine is dominated by the **Royal Pavilion**, built by the King when he was the Prince Regent, as a love-nest for the two of them. The king rented a "superior farmhouse" in 1786, which he subsequently bought. It was then enlarged by Henry Holland into a neo-classical building, but John Nash, who built the neoclassical Nash Terraces in London, enlarged and embellished it (1815-1822) into the extraordinary edifice it is today. The building's domes and minarets dominate the landscape; a casual visitor would assume it was the property of some oriental potentate. In fact, the Royal Pavilion is an expression of everything that the Georgians considered "exotic" in its day, a fantasmagoria in the Indian, Chinese and Egyptian taste. During the summer season, the Pavilion interior is kept fully furnished in the period Regency style, including the kitchen which has a large, stuffed rat running across the floor! Every item of furniture, however oriental-looking – the Chinese tea-caddies, the bed in Mrs. Fitzherbert's room upstairs, the painted wallpaper, and the Indian furnishings and brassware – was made in Britain, in the newly-emerging industrial centres such as Manchester and Birmingham. The music room, with its harp, lavish chandeliers and elegant draperies, is particularly beautiful. What were once the Royal Stables, with their distinctive dome, are now the **Dome Theatre**. Nearby there is the **Public Library, Museum and Art Gallery**. The Museum has a Sussex Room containing much information about local Sussex history. The Art Gallery has some fine paintings as well as 18th century furniture.

The Old Town, between West Street and North Street, contains **The Lanes**, a maze of little streets that are now a pedestrian precinct. They have been famous for a century or more for their antique shops and they now also contain fashionable boutiques.

Of course, Brighton's main attraction is the seaside. Brighton has a handsome **Esplanade** along the seafront, lined with elegant hotels, such as the Albion, the Metropole and the Palace, as well as two piers, the **West Pier** and the **Palace Pier**. The Palace Pier replaces the old Brighton Chain Pier, the very first pier ever, built in 1823,

but destroyed in a storm in 1896. The West Pier is currently closed for redecoration, but the Palace Pier has all the traditional seaside amusements. If the weather is too cold for sea bathing and you do not fancy walking over the pebbles to the sea, there are the **King Alfred Baths**, a newly-refurbished leisure centre with indoor swimming pools and other sports facilities. A statue of Queen Victoria facing the sea at the end of Montpelier Road separates Brighton from its twin city, **Hove**. Hove, west of Brighton, was always the more respectable residential area, famous for its Georgian terraces and squares, such as Brunswick Terrace and Brunswick Square. **Hove Museum and Art Gallery** contains furniture and paintings, including an allegorical painting of Brighton featuring "prinny", as the Prince Regent was dubbed. Hove also has a museum which will fascinate anyone interested in applied science, the **Engineerium**, which contains hundreds of model and full-sized working engines. **Kemp Town**, one mile east of the town centre, boasts another of Brighton's big attractions, **Volk's Electric Railway,** the first electrified track in Britain, built in 1883. The railway runs from the **Aquarium** to the **Marina,** the biggest yacht harbour in Europe. **Brighton Aquarium and Dolphinarium** contains an interesting display of marine life and the dolphins put on frequent displays in the summer. There is also an aircraft simulator. Young children will enjoy the Pirates' Deep play area.

Overlooking Brighton, there is a deep, natural hollow in the South Downs known as **Devil's Dyke**, a beauty spot which belongs to the city. From the top of Dyke's Hill (697 feet) there is an excellent view of the city and the surrounding area, as far west as Worthing and east to Beachy Head. **The Booth Museum of Natural History**, on Dyke Road is famous for its collection of birds and of butterflies. The village of Rottingdean contains a lovely toy museum, **The Grange**, which also displays Rudyard Kipling memorabilia, since Kipling was a local resident.

Two views of Brighton's seafront, including shops selling the famous candy known as Brighton Rock (above and right).

Brighton Marina, Britain's biggest yacht harbour (opposite).

EXCURSIONS

The following are excursions to some of Great Britain and Ireland's most popular attractions, including Scotland's Border Country, great parks and gardens and cathedrals and abbeys. They vary from the serene beauty of the Lake District, the quaint cottages of Stratford-upon-Avon and the majesty of Windsor Castle, to the wild landscape of the Ring of Kerry and the romantic setting of Rievaulx Abbey.

Giant's Causeway and Antrim

One of the natural wonders of the world, and now on the UNESCO World Heritage List, the Giant's Causeway is connected with many Irish legends. It is situated on the coast of Antrim, Ireland's northernmost county.

The Giant's Causeway is a mass of basalt crystallised in the shape of curiously angular columns packed tightly together. It is the result of the volcanic rock contracting as it cooled. The tops of the columns form stepping stones which appear to lead from the base of the cliff beneath which they stand and right into the sea. Thus the name Giant's Causeway, as if a giant had used them to cross the narrow stretch of sea between the North Antrim coast of Ireland and the coast of Scotland facing it. Indeed, the geological phenomenon does stretch right across to the west coast of Scotland to the isle of Staffa, where it is clearly visible in the rock formations of Fingal's Cave, which was visited by Felix Mendelssohn and immortalised in his music.

This being Ireland, the Causeway is linked to many legends. It is supposed to have been built by the giant named Finn McCool, the Ulster warrior and commander of the King of Ireland's armies, who fell in love with a lady giant, who lived on the Island of Staffa. Finn (which is actually the same name as Fingal) built a pathway across the sea so that he could visit her easily.

The Causeway consists of about 40,000 columns some as high as 40 feet (12 metres). Most are hexagonal, others have seven or eight sides. The cliffs above them along the Antrim coast are of great geological interest because the flows of molten lava buried many older rocks and protected them from erosion and their strata are now visible along the edge of the plateau. There are bands of red sandstone, lignite (coal), blue clay, iron ore and black basalt. **Fair Head**, the cliff at the eastern end, has as many as sixteen different strata.

This remote area was completely neglected until a description of the Causeway was published by the Royal Society in 1693. Ever since, people have flocked to see it. The 18th-century artist, Susanna Drury, did much to popularise the Causeway. Some of her paintings are in the Ulster Museum in Belfast. The whole area is one of outstanding beauty which should be toured by car, or on foot along the **North Antrim Cliff Path**. It has been saved from being spoiled since it was taken over by the National Trust which maintains the Visitors Centre, now the nearest access to the site for private cars. The Visitors Centre has all the usual facilities, including a snack bar, and lots of interesting displays, as well as a 25-minute film, explaining the history and geology, flora and fauna of the Causeway and its surrounding rock formations. A tramway to the Causeway was opened in 1883, the first hydroelectric tram in Europe, which ran on a narrow-gauge railway from the nearest large town, **Portrush**, to the Causeway. The tram service was discontinued in 1949 but one of the carriages is on display at the Visitor Centre.

A five-mile circular walk starting at the Centre descends to the **Grand Causeway**, past rock formations with names like **The Organ** and **The Harp**, up a wooden flight of steps to Burbane Head and back along the cliff top. There is also a two-mile walk for those who are less energetic. Near the car park there is a little whitewashed church that looks as though it belonged in central Europe. It was

built by Clough Williams-Ellis in 1915.

At nearby **Port-na-Spaniagh**, the wreck of the *Girona* is on view. This is the Spanish Armada galleass built and launched in 1588 which foundered on the rocks off the Antrim Coast during the ill-fated attempted invasion. The ship was only salvaged in 1967 by a team of Belgian divers. The gold and silver treasures found on the ship are now in the Ulster Museum, Belfast.

Another major attraction in this part of the world is the **Bushmills Whiskey Distillery**, only four miles south of the Causeway. This was traditionally the last stop on the coach ride to the Causeway and the first on the way back, where visitors from Belfast refreshed themselves before and after the trip with "a drop o' the hard stuff". It is the oldest legal distillery in the world, having received a charter in 1608. There is a visitors centre where souvenirs can be bought and the whiskey can be sampled. The village of Bushmills itself is one of quaint houses surrounding a square containing a Victorian clock tower. The National Trust owns 104 acres of the coastline between the Giant's Causeway and **Dunseverick Castle**. This ruined castle, of which only the gatehouse remains, has a long and noble history. Dunseverick was the capital of the ancient kingdom of Dalriada and was the destination of one of the five great highways from Tara, near Drogheda, with the best access to Scotland. Irishmen had established a colony on the Argyll coast by the 5th century a.d. Dunseverick also features in Ireland's oldest love story called "The Fate of the Children of Uisneach" as the landing place of Deirdre of the Sorrows and the sons of Uisneach. East of Dunseverick are the pale golden sands and low chalk cliffs of **Whitepark Bay**. West of the Bay is the little hamlet of **Portbraddan**, which contains the smallest church in Ireland, only 12 feet by 6 1/2 feet. The beach has caves which can be explored and in which prehistoric flint tools have been found. **Ballintoy** is a little fishing village with a picturesque harbour, in which it is pleasant to stop for a snack. The road to the harbour passes an isolated little white 16th-century church with a tapered square tower. The local Protestants took refuge here in 1641 when they were under siege and were rescued by the Earl of Antrim.

Fishermen are happy to take visitors out fishing or for trips along the Antrim coast. **Sheep Island** is a basalt outcrop covered in turf 500 yards offshore, which has a large colony of cormorants and other seabirds. There were also puffins, those penguin-like birds native only to the British Isles, but they were killed off by rats. However, the rats have been exterminated and there are signs that the puffins are re-establishing themselves. Ballintoy once had a castle, but it was dismantled, and the oak panelling and staircase are now installed in Downing College, Cambridge. Beyond the harbour, a stack of basalt forms a tiny island which in summer is connected to the mainland by the **Carrick-a-Rede Rope Bridge** which swings precariously 80 feet above the waves. The name means "Rock in the Road", the road being the searoad taken by the salmon returning from the Atlantic Ocean to spawn in the rivers of Ireland. There is a commercial salmon fishery on the south-east side of the island. Salmon are trapped in a series of underwater nets. Both bridge and fishery have existed for at least 350 years. The bridge is taken away in winter, when the waters are too rough for fishing. Access to the bridge is from **Larrybane Head**, also owned by the National Trust, which maintains an information centre, an aquarium and a teashop here. The lime kiln on the headland is a relic of the abandoned limestone quarry.

Information
Giant's Causeway Visitor Centre
Bushmills, Co. Antrim
BT57 8SU
Tel: (02657) 31582

Tips
Cars cannot drive right to the Causeway itself, but must be parked at the Visitor Centre. A bus takes visitors to the site, or you can walk there through the beautiful scenery.
The Giant's Causeway could be the focal point of a tour of northern Ulster, starting and finishing in Belfast. On the other hand, if you intend to visit Bushmills Whiskey Distillery and sample the local brew, you could leave the car behind and take a coach trip from Belfast or Antrim.

A closeup of Finn McCool's stepping stones (opposite).

General view of the Causeway (above).

The cliff and North Antrim coast (left).

The Scottish Borders, Berwick-on-Tweed

Ideal for touring by car, the Scottish Borders is an area of lovely countryside, with plentyto do and see. The turbulent history of this part of the world has left plenty of historic ruins.

The Scottish Borders consist of four counties – Berwickshire, Roxburghshire, Peeblesshire and Selkirkshire – through which the River Tweed runs its 100-mile course. The landscape is very varied, consisting of rugged peaks in the west and gentle, green valleys in the east, dotted with ruined castles and abbeys. This was the land inhabited by the wild and lawless Borderers depicted in the novels of Sir Walter Scott. Black Douglas and his men no longer roam the land stealing cattle, indeed one of his descendants (Lord Home) is a recent prime minister, so the Borders have been well and truly tamed.

History

The Borders have changed hands between England and Scotland throughout their history. Berwick-on-Tweed, now in England, was a Scottish town six times and an English one seven times, between 1200 and 1600 alone! The towns of the borders are small, and there are many villages, so the area is quite heavily populated.
Before the Industrial Revolution there were many spinners, knitters and weavers who worked in their own homes and these industries have remained small. The main product of the Borders is still high quality woollens – tweed, of course, cashmere and other types of cloth. Many of the top names in Scottish knitwear have their factories at Hawick.

Tourist Attractions

The best way to see the borders is to begin in the east, where the River Tweed forms the border with England, and travel through the lowlands of the Merse to the more mountainous western region,via the populated central region which has many historic houses and abbeys.
If you are coming from the south, the first village you will encounter is **Coldstream.** Despite the absence of any frontier posts, you will know that you are in Scotland immediately. The dialect, the cakes and buns in the bakeries and the Scottish banknotes are immediate indications (English money is accepted). There is a lovely country house to visit at Coldstream known as the **Hirsel**. It belonged to the former prime minister, Lord Home, and has a homestead museum and woodland walks around a lake. From the **Eildon Hills** north of Coldstream, **Flodden Field** is just visible three miles over the Scottish Border in England. A tablet in the town of **Selkirk** commemorates the fact that of 100 Scottish soldiers sent to the terrible battle of Flodden, only one returned. The battle took place in 1513, and it was the last of the bitter fights between the two countries before they united. Selkirk has a very interesting town museum in a historic building called **Halliwell's House**.
Kelso grew up around **Kelso Abbey**, founded by David I The **Kelso Museum** has particularly interesting exhibits of daily life as it used to be lived in the town and abbey. **Floors Castle** at Kelso is the magnificent home of the Dukes of Roxburghe and contains fine French furniture and paintings.
Ferniehurst Castle, near **Jedburgh**, the home of the Kerr (Carr) clan, is now open to the public. It was once a border fortress, and has many mementos of clan history. The **Castle Gaol and Museum** at **Jedburgh** are actual-

Border Sign at Coldstream (above).

Caldon Hills and the River Tweed (top right).

Jedburgh Abbey from the south (right).

Kelso Abbey, a view from the gardens (opposite).

ly 19th century replicas of the original buildings which were destroyed in 1409 by the townspeople to keep them out of English hands. The Castle served as a prison until 1886; it is now a museum of prison life and of the history of Jedburgh. **Mary, Queen of Scot's House** is a 16th-century fortified house of a type frequently seen in the Border Country. Mary stayed here in 1556. **The Woodland Centre** not only has woodland trails but a collection of treen and giant wooden games to play. Jedburgh has a special delicacy, a kind of boiled sweet called a Jethart Snail, which may first have been made by a French prisoner during the Napoleonic Wars Jedburgh has one of the three famous ruined abbeys of the Border country; the others are at **Dryburgh** and **Melrose**. Dryburgh Abbey, which stands in a meander of the Tweed is also the site of the graves of Field Marshal Haig and Sir Walter Scott. **Melrose Abbey** a huge foundation is a ruin run by the National Trust for Scotland.

The **Merkat Cross** at **Peebles** is carved with the town's emblem – three salmon – indicating the importance of the fish to the local community. The main square, **Parliament Square**, takes its name from the meeting of the Scottish parliament held here in 1346, after the Scottish king David II was captured by the English. The **Chambers Institute** is a 16th-century building which now houses the Tweeddale Museum and Art Gallery. The museum has a very fine geological collection. **Neidpath Castle**, overlooking the Tweed, is also worth a visit. **Kailzie Gardens** a beautiful garden and woodland area contains a bird sanctuary.

Berwick-on-Tweed, though now considered to be in England, is actually north of the Tweed. It has been so hotly contested over the centuries that although it was finally surrendered to the English crown in 1482, it seems that even then the British government was not quite sure in which country it belonged! Old Acts of Parliament mention "England, Scotland, Ireland and our town of Berwick-on-Tweed", and Berwick's status as a semi-independent Royal Burgh lasted until the 19th century. Although the inhabitants have repeatedly voted to stay English, the local accent and the fact that haggis, the national dish of Scotland, features on the menus of local cafés is proof of a lingering affection for north of the Border. Even the local football team plays in the Scottish league. Given its history, it is not surprising that the town has sturdy **ramparts** around it. These were started by Edward I and Edward II but strengthened considerably by Queen Elizabeth I in 1555. The views from these fortifications is spectacular, both across the Tweed and over the sands out to sea, with Holy Island (Lindisfarne) in the distance; a walk along the top of the ramparts is strongly recommended. **Berwick Castle**, now dominated by a railway arch, is a ruin. It was begun by Edward I in 1297, but many stones were plundered to build the town, and the final damage was done when most of it was demolished to build the railway station. The **Town Hall**, in Marygate (here the word "gate" has its Norse meaning of "street") was once an 18th-century Guildhall. It has a bell-tower with a curfew bell which is still rung at 8.00 p.m. every evening. The first floor was used as a prison. Drunken prisoners were hauled up through a trap-door in the bell-tower; those awaiting transportation to Botany Bay in Australia were shackled to the walls. Occasionally, privileged visitors are allowed to ring the bells, two of which actually belong to the church of Holy Trinity, which has no bell tower of its own. The **Cow Port** is the only surviving original gate in the ramparts**. Holy Trinity Church** (1648-52), owes its distinctive architecture to the fact that it is one of the few churches in England built during the Commonwealth, when the country was ruled by Oliver Cromwell. Berwick has a **Wine and Spirits Museum**, at which you can also view the making of the local Lindisfarne pottery.

Information
The Scottish Borders Tourist Board
Municipal Buildings
High Street
Selkirk
TD7 4JX
Tel: (0750) 20555

Tourist Information Centre
Castlegate Car Park
Berwick-on-Tweed
TD15 1JS
Tel: (0289) 330733

There are tourist information offices in all the main towns. For information on guided walks, picnic sites and trails through beautiful scenery:

The Countryside Ranger Service
Borders Regional Council
Regional Headquarters
Newtown St. Boswells
TD6 4SA
Tel: (0835) 23301

Events
The Great Tweed Raft Race, starting at Kelso, is held on a Sunday in late May. The Braw Lads Gathering in Galashiels is in the last week of June. The Melrose Summer Festival is also held in June. The Borders Festival of Ballads and Legends is held from September to mid-October, with many performances in historic houses. Details are available from the Visitor Information Centres.

The Lake District A National Park

This area of steep hills, cliffs and lakes only 30 miles across and just an hour from the industrial centres of Northern England, is Britain's favourite National Park, closely associated with the great poet, Wordsworth.

The Lake District is the favourite countryside tourism destination for Britons themselves, and has been for the past 200 years. Written guides to the Lake District abound, one of them by the area's most famous native son, the poet William Wordsworth. Many other writers have spent time in this beautiful region, which now attracts 12 million visitors a year. The lakes were formed from melting glaciers cutting deep valleys into this area which was originally much higher than the surrounding hills. Each lake has a different character and shape, some are wooded, at others the hills descend straight into the water, at yet others there is a gentle slope to the shore. The weather can be very changeable, but many landscape painters have found this a bonus. The British artist William Turner was among the many who spent much time here, trying to capture the light as it falls on the becks (streams) and fells (hills) the rain and the mists. The Lake District is a paradise for climbers and hill walkers. There are 1,500 miles of paths and bridleways. The most popular climbs are up **Scafell** and **Skiddaw**.

The largest of the lakes is **Windermere**, over 10 miles long. It has a steamer service and is very popular for water sports. **Bowness-on-Windermere**, a small town about half-way down this long narrow lake, is the largest in the Lake District. Bowness is rather commercialised but there are pleasant places to stay on the outskirts. It has a **Steamboat Museum**, containing Victorian and Edwardian pleasure craft, lovingly restored to working order. The western shore of the lake is the least crowded. West of Windermere is the peaceful **Esthwaite Water**. Footpaths lead to the largest area of woodland in the Lake District, **Grizedale Forest**, on the eastern shore of **Coniston Water**. This is the lake on which Duncan Campbell made many attempts to break the world speed record on water; he died trying to do so in 1967. There is a restored Victorian steam yacht, the *Gondola*, built in 1859, which runs excursions on the lake. The vast **Monk Coniston Estate** is run by the National Trust and includes the cottage known as **Tarn Hows**, that was once owned by the children's novelist and artist Beatrix Potter. **Hawkshead,** a quaint little village in which motor vehicles are not allowed, contains the **Beatrix Potter Gallery** where a selection of her lifelike water colours of subjects from nature are displayed. The author's first home in the Lake District, **Hill Top**, near **Sawry**, is also open to visitors. **Brantwood**, on Coniston Water, was the home of John Ruskin. It has a lovely garden.

Wasdale in the Lake District. The area is very popular with ramblers (top).

Another view of Wasdale (above).

Typical Lake District view (left).

Ambleside is an attractive village with interesting shops at the northern end of Lake Windermere. **Grassmere** is the lake beside which William Wordsworth and his sister, Dorothy, lived at **Dove Cottage** between 1799 and 1808. The tiny museum next door contains many memorabilia, including a pair of the poet's socks! The other Wordsworth home open to the public is **Rydal** at **Rydal Mount**, a much larger building, which contains more artefacts and painted portraits. North of Rydal is **Haweswater**, which is very remote and secluded and used as a reservoir to supply water to the Manchester area. Neighbouring, **Ullswater**, one of the most beautiful of the lakes, is also popular with pleasure craft, though a 10 m.p.h. speed limit keeps water-skiers away. Two miles north of the lake at Dalemain, there is a medieval mansion, **Dacre**, that is open to the public and contains period furniture and portraits, as well as a museum of agricultural implements. There is a famous waterfall near here called **Aira Force**. It is by this lakeside that Wordsworth came across the daffodils that are the subject of his most famous poem. The poet was born north of here at **Cockermouth**, where the **Wordsworth House** is open to the public. The town of Cockermouth itself is worth visiting, especially on a Monday, which is market day. **Muncaster Castle,** just outside it, is a 14th-century building with later additions, restored in the 19th century, and furnished in 16th- and 17th-century style. From the terrace, there is a wonderful view over **Eskdale**. There is a bird garden in the spacious grounds. Nearby **Muncaster Mill** is a restored 18th-century water mill which produces stone-ground flour for sale.

The River Derwent winds its way up to **Derwentwater**, a lake with several wooded islands in the centre. The largest island is known as **Derwent Island**; a colony of German miners established itself here in the 16th century. This island, and the other islands, **Lord's Island**, **Rampsholme** and **St. Herbert's Island** all belong to the National Trust and can be visited. This lake is familiar to most British schoolchildren through the Lakeland Pencil Company, which has been making coloured pencils here since the 16th century and features the lake on its pencil boxes. The **Pencil Museum** is in nearby **Keswick** and shows how the "lead" (plumbago, a type of soft slate) for the pencils was mined here. Other articles made of the soft green lakeland slate are for sale. The village of Keswick is a popular tourist centre. The buildings are mainly early 19th century, and there are many mementoes of the poets and writers who lived here, who include Southey, Coleridge and Shelley. Hugh Walpole is buried in St. John's churchyard. **Castlerigg Stone Circle**, off the road from Keswick to Grasmere, is one of the mysterious monuments that are dotted over many parts of western England. At Derwentwater, there are the **Lingholm Gardens**, formal and woodland gardens laid out below the fells west of the lake. The Skiddaw range rises north of Keswick. Skiddaw itself is the highest peak in the Lake District, rising to 3054 feet, and overlooking **Bassenthwaite Lake.** The small manor house on the eastern shore of Bassenthwaite, called **Mirehouse**, has associations with Wordsworth and Alfred Lord Tennyson. It has attractive gardens, including a nature trail. The marshy southern end of the lake is a nature reserve for water fowl.

There are a couple of steam railways that run through the Lake District and a trip on them makes a pleasant family outing. The **Lakeside and Haverthwaite Railway** is a standard gauge steam railway which runs through the **Leaven Valley** for three and a half miles. The engines and carriages are kept at Haverthwaite and can be inspected. **Ravenglass and Eskdale Railway** is a seven-mile narrow-gauge track which once linked the mines and quarries of the area with the coast. The locomotives are either diesel or steam. The village of Ravenglass has a **Railway Museum** with models and an audio-visual display.

Thanks to the large number of tourists, the Lake District has more hotels of all types and sizes than any other National Park in Britain. They range from the expensive Miller Howe Hotel, whose owner is an internationally-famous chef, to Youth Hostels which are situated in some of the most beautiful countryside.

The Ravinglass and Eskdale steam railway, making its way to the coast (above).

Descendants of the daffodils that inspired Wordsworth beside Ullswater (right).

Information

A large part of the Lake District is owned and administered by the National Trust and the Countryside Commission.

The Cumbria Tourist Board
Ashleigh Holly Road
Windermere, Cumbria
LA23 2AQ
Tel: (05394) 44444

The National Park Information Centre
Brockhole
Windermere, Cumbria
LA23 1LJ
Tel: (05394) 42231

The Forestry Commission
1a Grosvenor Terrace
York, YO3 7BD
Tel: (0904) 20221

Tips

The Lake District can be very crowded in high summer, when it is a good idea to avoid busy centres like Bowness and sights like Dove Cottage, but there is always plenty of room to be alone in the remoter parts.

Stratford-upon-Avon Shakespeare Country

Shakespeare was born in one of the most beautiful parts of England. His birthplace and childhood surroundings have been lovingly preserved in a town which was a triving community long before he was born.

Stratford-upon-Avon is a small market town midway between Birmingham and the Welsh Marches, and although very attractive it would never have hit the headlines were it not for its most famous son, William Shakespeare. It is fortunate that this part of the country has always remained rural and was never touched by the Industrial Revolution, because this has meant that both those buildings associated with the Bard as well as other ancient structures have remained unchanged. Stratford is full of quaint old buildings, even some of the local hotels are at least 150 years old (though modernised!). The river winding through the town is a lovely place to linger on a warm summer's day, and punts and rowing-boats can be hired for the afternoon.

Stratford received its Royal Market Charter in 1196. Before that it was a Celtic settlement (the word "Avon" means "river" in Celtic, the town's name meaning "the place where the street fords the river"). The 13th century saw the formation of the Guild of the Holy Cross which fostered local industry and founded the school, the **King Edward VI Grammar School**, which Shakespeare attended and which is still going strong. John de Stratford became Archbishop of Canterbury in the 14th century, but he did not forget his home town and built additions to Holy Trinity Church, where Shakespeare's children were baptised and where he himself is buried. Hugh Clopton, who was Lord Mayor of London in the late 15th century, built the 14-arch **Clopton Bridge** which still spans the Avon at the entrance to the town.

The spiritual centre of Stratford is **Shakespeare's Birthplace**, in Henley Street, two half-timbered Tudor cottages knocked into one, originally part of a row, in which Shakespeare was born on or about 23 April, 1564 (only the date of his christening, 26 April, is known for certain). Shakespeare is presumed to have been born in the west half, which is furnished in period style. The window panes of the room upstairs in which Shakespeare is assumed to have been born has been incised with the names of famous visitors, including Sir Walter Scott, Alfred Lord Tennyson and Ellen Terry. Half a million people tramp through these rooms annually! The other half of the house is a museum, displaying contemporary artefacts as well as a collection of costumes used in BBC productions of Shakespearian drama. Behind the house there is an Elizabethan-style garden, planted with flowers and herbs mentioned in the plays. The site of Shakespeare's house at **New Place** can also be visited, but unfortunately it has been demolished, the owner being so irritated by the hordes of visitors that he tore it down in 1759! The garden is very attractive, laid out as an Elizabethan knot garden. Next door is **Nash's House**, the home of Shakespeare's granddaughter, Elizabeth Nash née Hall, which now houses the **New Place Museum**, an archæological museum containing local finds. **Hall's Croft**, the home of Shakespeare's eldest daughter, Susanna and her husband John, stands in the street known as Old Town. They lived here from 1607 to 1616. This house is also furnished in period style, with the bonus of a Jacobean doctor's surgery and dispensary, complete with jars of herbs and potions. The large, walled garden behind the house is used to grow some of the herbs that would have been used in the medicines.

Shakespeare's mother, Mary Arden, came from Wilmcote, three miles from Stratford. **Mary Arden's House,** a farmhouse with farm outbuildings is now a museum devoted to agriculture and local crafts. It can be reached by road, rail or even by boat along the **Stratford-upon-Avon Canal**. The Canal is now open for pleasure craft. It was built in 1793-1816 and joins the Worcester and Birmingham Canal at King's Norton.

Perhaps **Ann Hathaway's Cottage** is even more famous than Shakespeare's birthplace itself, since it has a picture postcard charm, and is not part of a row of houses. This lovely thatched cottage, the home of Shakespeare's wife is in the village of Shottery, only a mile away from Shakespeare's home, and is best reached by footpath from Evesham Place. The cottage is also furnished in period style and has a delightful garden full of scented flowers. **Holy Trinity Church**, the 13th-century parish church on the banks of the Avon in Old Town, contains Shakespeare's grave. The present spire was erected in 1765 to replace a wooden one. Photocopies of the parish register, showing the dates of the Bard's baptism and burial are on display. The font at which Shakespeare was christened is at the west end of the north aisle. The bust of Shakespeare which his family erected as a memorial in 1623 is on the north wall. The King Edward VI Grammar School,

Shakespeare's birthplace at Stratford-upon-Avon (above).

Old Town, Hall's Croft (left).

The Elizabethan garden at New Place (opposite).

which is housed in the former **Guildhall**, can only be visited outside term-time since the very classroom to which Shakespeare went "creeping like snail unwillingly to school" is still in use. Next door there are the **Almshouses** built at the same time as the school. The **Guild Chapel**, on the corner of Chapel Lane and Church Street, has a late 13th-century chancel. The nave was rebuilt by the Stratford benefactor, Sir Hugh Clopton, in 1495. The chapel contains a Renaissance painting of the Last Judgement (c. 1500). There is a **Brass Rubbing Centre** in Stratford at the Royal Shakespeare Theatre Summer House where replicas of brasses from the two churches can be rubbed. Paper and wax are supplied as part of the admission charge. **The World of Shakespeare** is a 25-minute sound and light show, illustrating contemporary events such as a bear-baiting contest, the Plague, and a Royal procession.

Shakespeare's parents were married at the church at **Aston Cantelow**, about five miles northwest of Stratford. It is worth visiting for its 13th century chancel. Legend has it that Shakespeare was forced to leave Stratford in his youth when caught poaching in the grounds of **Charlecote House**. This Tudor mansion still stands five miles outside the town. It was owned in Shakespeare's day by the Lucy family, many of whose members are buried in the nearby church. Both buildings were heavily restored in the 19th century and the interiors are now Victorian.

No visit to Stratford-upon-Avon and its surroundings is complete without a visit to the theatre, and Stratford now has three of them. There is the original **Shakespeare Memorial Theatre**, the provincial home of the Royal Shakespeare Company. The original theatre was made possible through a gift from a Stratford resident, Charles Edward Flower, in 1877. It opened in 1879, but was gutted by fire in 1926. It is designed along the lines of an Elizabethan theatre. His grandson, Sir Archibald Flower, made the largest contribution to the building of the present Theatre, erected in 1932.

The Swan Theatre was opened in 1986 in the shell of the old Memorial Theatre. It now houses the Royal Shakespeare Collection of props, costumes and other memorabilia. Backstage tours of the Royal Shakespeare Company, lasting 45 minutes, are held regularly and can be booked. The other theatre is **The Other Place** in which a variety of classical and contemporary plays are performed.

Information

Heart of England Tourist Board
Old Bank House
Bank Street
Worcester, WR1 2EW
Tel: (0905) 613132

Guide Friday
Stratford Centre for Tourism
Civic Hall
The Market Place
14/15 Rother Street
Stratford-upon-Avon
CV37 6LU
Tel: (0789) 294466

Bookings for the Royal Shakespeare Theatre (season lasts from April to the end of January):
The Box Office
Royal Shakespeare Theatre
Stratford-upon-Avon
Warwicks. CV37 6BB
Tel: (0789) 295623

Events

The Stratford-upon-Avon Festival, which combines a carnival with poetry readings and other performances, takes place in the second half of July.

Tips

Stratford-upon-Avon is the biggest foreign tourist attraction in Britain and is always packed with coaches, even in the depths of winter. However, it is still a good place to visit while touring this lovely part of England, completing the trip with a performance at the Royal Shakespeare Theatre.

Hampton Court and Windsor Castle

These two royal residences recently suffered serious damage by fire, but both have been restored to their former glory. They are conveniently close to London, so are excellent destinations for a day excursion. Both are situated in an attractive riparian landscape.

Both **Hampton Court Palace** and **Windsor Castle** are on the banks of the River Thames, west of London. Both are surrounded by lovely countryside and there are many other places of interest nearby, so they are ideally situated as destinations for day excursions from London.

Hampton Court, south-west of London on the north bank of the Thames, is the finest example of Tudor architecture in Britain. It was built in 1515 by Cardinal Wolsey, Lord Chancellor of England, who intended to make it the largest private residence in the country. He bought the site from the Order of St. John of Jerusalem, a year before he became cardinal. When Wolsey fell from grace, he presented the palace to Henry VIII in a vain attempt to win favour. The gift was accepted, but Wolsey's fate was sealed nevertheless. In 1529, all his property was confiscated. The king was furious at Wolsey's lavish lifestyle and the magnificence of his hospitality which was the talk of Europe. Henry moved into the palace at once, making many alterations to erase traces of the original owner. Hampton Court remained a royal residence until the 18th century, but is now lived in mainly by privileged subjects of the Queen who are granted "grace-and-favour" residence, meaning free accommodation on royal property. Most of the building is built of mellow red brick. The Great Gatehouse, the Base Court and the Clock Court are part of the original building. Henry VIII added **Anne Boleyn's Gateway**, with its lovely fan-vaulted ceiling and the unusual **Astronomical Clock**, which is still in working order. Anne Boleyn was Henry's second wife, who was eventually beheaded. Her coat-of-arms can be seen among the carvings in the **Great Hall** (1531-36) which has a hammerbeam roof. and which Henry built to replace Wolsey's smaller one. Five of Henry VIII's six wives spent some time here. This is where his favourite wife, Jane Seymour, died while giving birth to his only legitimate heir, Edward VI. Jane and Catherine Howard, his fifth wife, whom he had beheaded in 1542, are even alleged to haunt the place! Sir Christopher Wren added the east and south wings for William III, destroying several Tudor courtyards in the process, but retaining the Tudor kitchens which are open to the public. The **Formal Gardens** in the Dutch style were laid out for William and Mary (late 17th century), who made many improvements to the buildings and took great personal interest in the works. The gardens have two unique attractions, the **Great Vine**, planted by Capability Brown in 1769 and still yielding grapes, and the **Maz**e, which was planted in the reign of Queen Anne. The **Banqueting Hall** stands apart from the rest of the palace, and is the work of Sir Christopher Wren, who used bricks from Cardinal Wolsey's original hall. The **Royal Chapel** was built by Wolsey and embellished by Henry VIII, as were the **Watching Chamber** and the **Old Tennis Court**. Henry was an

Information
Hampton Court
Hampton, Middlesex
KT8 9AU
Tel: (089) 977 8441

Windsor Castle
Windsor, Berks SL4 1NJ
Tel: (0753) 868286.

Events
It is interesting to watch Real Tennis being played in the court built for Henry VIII and polo being played at Smith's Lawn. The two-week Windsor Festival centres on the Theatre Royal, Windsor, with concerts in St. George's Chapel and in Eton College. It is held in September. There are musical events, concerts, exhibitions of paintings and other events. For details:

Windsor Festival
Dial House
Englefield Green
Surrey, TW20 0DU
Tel: (0784) 32618

enthusiastic player of the game known as Real Tennis, which is played indoors. In 1986, a disastrous fire destroyed much of the fabric of the main building of the Palace, including the Great Hall, though fortunately the magnificent tapestries and Renaissance paintings were saved and Hampton Court has now been restored to its former glory.
There has been a palace in the Windsor area since the days of the Saxon kings, but it was William the Conqueror who founded **Windsor Castle**, on the south bank of the Thames, when he built a wooden fortress there in 1066. Windsor is now the oldest and the largest inhabited castle in the world. This vast, rambling 13-acre fortress is encircled by a medieval wall. Its most distinctive feature is the central **Round Tower** (1170), which contains the **Queen's Private Apartments** (not open to the public). The castle is divided into three Wards, the public entrance being through the Lower Ward. The buildings here are all medieval. The **Curfew Tower** contains an unusual clock which chimes every three hours. **St. George's Chapel**, is considered to be one of the finest examples of Perpendicular architecture in Britain. It was built for Edward IV (1478-1511). This is where the knights are invested with Britain's highest honour, the Order of the Garter. The whole castle is closed to visitors on Garter Day, a date in June. Several kings of England are buried in the chapel, including Henry VIII, with his beloved Jane Seymour, Charles I and all the kings of England since Edward VII. The **Bray Chapel** contains the remains of the Prince Imperial, son of Napoleon III, who was killed in the Boer War in 1879. Windsor is surrounded by other attractions. The **Albert Memorial Chapel** was originally built by Henry VII in the early 16th century, but was converted by Queen Victoria into a memorial for her husband, Prince Albert, who died in 1861. The nearby **Winchester Tower** may have been lived in by Geoffrey Chaucer when he was Master of Works at Windsor in 1390.
Windsor Castle suffered a terrible fire in1992 which destroyed the Queen's private chapel and some neighbouring rooms in the Round Tower, but fortunately did not damage the **State Apartments** in the North Wing of the Upper Ward. This series of rooms contains the Castle's greatest treasures, including furniture, china, and paintings. There are also drawings from the Royal Collection, including cartoons by Leonardo Da Vinci and Raphael. Another favourite attraction at Windsor is **Queen Mary's Dolls' House**, created by the former Princess May of Teck, wife of King George V. **Frogmore House** in the grounds of the castle has a **Mausoleum** attached which contains the tombs of Queen Victoria and Prince Albert, as well as those of the Duke of Windsor (who reigned briefly as Edward VIII) and his wife, the former Mrs. Simpson. It is only open occasionally to the public.
Windsor Castle is set in the beautiful grounds of **Windsor Great Park**, which has beautiful walks, such as the **Long Walk**, planted with trees by Charles II, from which there is a magnificent view. The **Savill Garden** is 20 acres of woodland and beyond **Smith's Lawn**, a polo ground, there are the **Valley Gardens**. The town of **Windsor** itself is also worth visiting. The railway station, **Windsor and Eton Central**, boasts a special **Royal Waiting Room**, built for Queen Victoria, which is now an exhibition hall devoted to **Windsor, Royalty and Empire**, on the theme of Queen Victoria's Diamond Jubilee celebrations. Just over the footbridge across the Thames lies the little town of **Eton**, famous for its public school, **Eton College**, which has produced more heads of state, prime ministers and leading politicians of all nationalities than any other school in Britain and perhaps the world. It was founded by Henry IV in 1440. The 16th- and 17th-century **School Yard**, whose dormitories are exclusively inhabited by scholarship pupils, the medieval **Chapel** and the **Cloisters** can be visited. During term time, the school can only be visited in the afternoons.
One of the pleasantest ways to see both Hampton Court and Windsor Castle and their surroundings is by boat. There are day trips to Hampton Court from Westminster Pier in London, and to Windsor from Reading.

The grapevine planted by Capability Brown in 1769 (opposite above).

The main entrance to Hampton Court Palace (opposite below).

The Long Walk looking towards Windsor Castle (above).

A fine summer's day on the Thames at Hampton Court (right).

Cathedrals, Churches and Abbeys

British church architecture is unique in style but very varied. Monateries and abbeys are few and most are in ruins, due to Henry VIII's break with Rome and the subsequent Reformation. Catholics were not allowed to build new houses of worship until the 19th century.

British insularity, its safety from invasion for nearly 1,000 years and the variations in royal attitudes to religion are the main reasons for the unique ecclesiastic architecture. The strongest foreign influence on British architecture is the Romanesque style known as Norman, brought here by William the Conqueror and his followers, which was rapidly superseded by native styles. It is helpful to list briefly the main styles of English church-building, as they appear over and over again in descriptions.

First there is the Saxon style (c.400-1066) which still shows traces of the Roman occupation, with round arches and square towers. This was superseded by the Norman style which lasted for about 100 years after the Norman invasion (1066), a Romanesque style with round arches, frieze decorations and square towers. Then came the Transitional style, in which the Norman was combined with features which were later to become typical of English church architecture, such as pointed arches combined with rounded ones. Early English (c.1150-1280) is a style which retains the dogtooth moulding of earlier periods but introduces new elements such as flying butresses and rib vaulting. Decorated style lasted until 1380; as the name implies, the basic features differed little from the previous style but it was more ornate, with finials, bosses and other heavily carved capitals. Elaborate tombs and monuments appeared in churches. The last phase of Gothic architecture in Britain was the Perpendicular style, which is characterised by the stress on verticals and horizontals and delicately fan-vaulted ceilings. After the Reformation, fewer churches were built, but they are characterised by larger windows (thanks to improved glass-making techniques) and simpler decoration as befits the Protestant ethic. The style known as English Baroque is typified by the work of Sir Christopher Wren, John Wood and their contemporaries, a mixture of the classicism of Palladio with remnants of the flamboyance of the medieval. The style is echoed in the Greek Revival of the mid-18th to mid-19th centuries. Similarly Gothic architecture was revived twice, once in the so-called "gothick" of the 18th and early 19th centuries, which was almost a pastiche and once flmaboyantly in the 19th century, when architects like Pugin and Scott made cathedrals look like railway stations and railway stations like cathedrals (St. Pancras Station in London is a good example of the latter).

While churches of all denominations proliferate in Britain, abbeys are few and far between. When Henry VIII broke with the Church of Rome in 1534, he began the Dissolution of the Monasteries, which lasted until 1540. These institutions were disbanded and their buildings either destroyed, or donated as gifts to those who found favour with the monarch. A few abbey churches survived with cloister and chapter house intact, but without the attendant monks. However, there are a several modern Roman Catholic monasteries and convents, founded since the Catholic Emancipation in 1829.

Many English and Welsh churches suffered during the Civil War and afterwards from attacks by the Roundheads; Scottish churches were attacked by Dissenters, Protestants who considered that the the statues of saints and beautiful stained glass smacked of "popery". Many churches fell into disrepair during the 16th and 17th centuries for this reason, as well as due

Interior of Lincoln Cathedral (left).

Detail of a column in Durham Cathedral (above).

Ruins of Tintern Abbey (top right).

Lincoln Cathedral towers over the city (below right).

The nave of Durham Cathedral (opposite right).

Gargoyle in the parish church of St. Peter, Winchcombe, Gloucester (opposite centre).

to the great catastrophes such as the Black Death. World War II also took its toll, notably of Coventry, Exeter and Llandaff Cathedrals.
The following are just a few British churches and abbeys, chosen for the beauty of their architecture. They are in alphabetical order and are drawn as far as possible from all parts of the country.
Very large churches are often to be found in which what are now small towns or even villages. This is because the places in question have lost the importance they once had. This is the case with Beverley in Humberside, once capital of the East Riding of Yorkshire. **Beverley Minster** has been described as larger than many cathedrals in size and outstripping most in splendour. Its stone carvings represent the finest work in each of the main periods of English medieval church architecture. The present building was started in 1213 and took two centuries to complete. The west front with its twin towers was finished in 1420. Nicholas Hawksmoor's sensitive restoration saved the church from ruin in the 18th century, and further restoration took place in the 19th and 20th centuries.
Buckfast Abbey, on the edge of Dartmoor, is one of the very few abbeys in Britain occupied by a monastic order. Buckfast was founded by King Canute in 1018, then refounded by French Cistercians in 1147. It fell into disrepair when the monks were expelled at the Dissolution of the Monasteries, but refounded for the second time in 1882. The French Benedictine monks rebuilt the monastery with their own hands on the old foundations between 1907 and 1938. The interior is Romanesque with some interesting mosaics.
The spire of **Chichester Cathedral**, on the Sussex-Hampshire borders is said to be the only cathedral spire visible from the sea. Much of the building is Norman. It was consecrated in 1075, and the later additions are in Early English style. The composer Gustav Holst (1874-1934) is buried here. The cathedral is unique in having the only detached belfry in an ancient English cathedral. Although the architectural style is early medieval, Chichester has several modern decorative features, notably a brightly-coloured tapestry by John Piper (1966) over the altar screen and a window by Marc Chagall (1978) in the North Transept.
Durham Cathedral, near the Scottish border, is the greatest Norman cathedral in the British Isles. It stands on a hill, dominating the surrounding countryside and the town around it. The cathedral was founded by monks from Lindisfarne, and has a friary, most of which has been preserved. The Venerable Bede and St. Cuthbert are buried here. The Galilee Chapel, added in the 12th and early 13th century, with its rows of columns is one of the gems of English architecture.
Fountains Abbey, near Ripon, Yorkshire is one of the best preserved and the largest of England's ruined abbeys. It is now administered by the National Trust and is surrounded by a magnificent garden, **Studeley Royal**. The abbey was founded by Cistercian monks in 1135, and there are various additions, such as the perpendicular tower of the church added between 1498 and 1526.
In stark contrast to these, **St. Paul's Church, Covent Garden**, in Central London must be one of the plainest churches in England. It was built in neo-classical Italianate style by Inigo Jones, who also designed the Flower Market hall, for the miserly fourth Duke of Bedford, in 1631-33. This was the first Anglican church to be built after the Reformation. The Duke ordered the architect not to "go to any considerable expense. In short I would not have it much better than a barn". Hence the plainness of the exterior, though the interior was later refaced with stone. The church had to be completely rebuilt after a fire in 1795, but remains true to the original design. The main entrance overlooking the Covent Garden Piazza cannot be used because it faces east, and the Bishop of London decreed that the altar must be placed there. A host of famous people are buried here and almost every leading figure in show business has been commemorated at St. Paul's by a memorial service. There is also a special annual service for puppeteers.

Information
Visitors who have not come to pray are discouraged, though not forbidden, during services. Those unfamiliar with the Church of England will be surprised at the variation in the amount of decoration in church interiors, which vary from Roman Catholic extravagance to Low Church austerity. Services are always in English. Some large churches and most cathedrals make a charge for visiting the undercroft or crypt where the treasures are stored. The most beautiful services to attend are carol services at Christmastime and Evensong at 3.00 p.m. or 4.00 p.m. Details are available from notices posted outside the churches.

Parks and Gardens Jewels in the Landscape

The English are world-famous for their beautiful parks and gardens that range from carefully-tended lawns to magnificent wildernesses. In various parts of the country there are gardens of special interest.

The English are world-famous for their gardens and there are enthusiastic gardeners all over Britain. Even the most modest suburban home can blossom with elaborate topiary work or a carefully-cultivated wilderness. Under the National Gardens Scheme, even ordinary people open their gardens to the public every year in exchange for a small payment which goes to charity. If you want to see local gardens, check with the Tourist Information Centre or the regional Tourist Board in the area you want to visit.
The latest innovation in English gardens is the Butterfly Farm, where varieties of these beautiful insects – of which many species are under threat due to the use of insecticides – are encouraged to breed by being provided with suitable vegetation and the right environment. In addition to beautiful gardens of all kinds Britain has many public parks, including Country Parks full of outdoor recreational facilities, Wildfowl Trusts, city parks and National Parks such as Snowdonia in Wales and the Lake District. This category also includes parks which foster rare breeds of animal and plant and the parks which are the grounds of stately homes.
Below are just a few of the gardens and parks of all kinds in various parts of the country which are of special interest.
Athelhampton is a medieval manor house near Dorchester in Dorset, whose formal gardens were laid out in the 19th century and are enclosed by a wall. There are water gardens and a herb garden.
The gardens at **Chatsworth**, in Derbyshire, the ancestral home of the Duke of Devonshire, are famous for the magnificent **Water Garden**, the work of the head gardener Joseph Paxton, who under the guidance of the Duke tamed the copious waters of the nearby canal into a series of cascades that sweep down in glittering staircase. The Emperor Fountain is a single jet of water capable of shooting 267 feet into the air. The grounds are huge, covering 105 acres, and are full of exciting things for children to do.
The Chalk Garden at **Highdown Manor**, the former home of Colonel and Lady Stern on the downs above Goring-by-Sea in West Sussex, contains plants imported from all over the world that will flourish on chalk, the most inhospitable type of soil. These include the handkerchief tree from South Africa and many colourful sub-tropical and temperate plants. There are also plenty of ornamental fish-ponds.
The **Chelsea Physic Garden**, in Chelsea, London is the second-oldest physic garden in the country, the first having been founded at Oxford in 1621. It was established by the Apothecaries' Company in 1676. In 1683, the first cedar trees to be grown in England were planted here. The first heated greenhouse in Britain was built here in 1681. In 1732, Egyptian cotton seed sent from here to America established the first cotton plantations in the New World. The garden contains many exotic plants and shrubs including the largest olive tree in Britain, which bears edible fruit.
Dawyck on the River Tweed, near Peebles in the Scottish Borders, has a collection of trees and shrubs unequalled in the country. There are also many flowering plants.
A very different type of garden is to be found at Findhorn, near Forres in the Highlands of Scotland, where the **Findhorn Foundation** has established a farming community. Thanks to the mild climate created by the Gulf Stream, the residents have been able to cultivate sub-tropical vegetation in this northern clime, and their achievements in horticulture are unmatched anywhere in the country.

Glendurgan Garden, nr. Falmouth in Cornwall is administered by the National Trust. It is a valley garden of great beauty with subtropical vegetation, walled gardens, a water garden and a wooded valley running down to a little village.

Mount Stewart House, Garden and Temple of the Winds in County Down, Northern Ireland, was the home of Lord Castlereagh (1769-1822), who was Foreign Secretary during the Napoleonic Wars. It is an 18th-century house with 19th-century additions. The beautiful gardens were largely created by Edith, 7th Marchioness of Londonderry, starting in 1921. The collection of plants is unrivalled and the setting is incredibly beautiful with magnificent vistas of Strangford Lough. There is a Shamrock Garden containing lovely topiary work including a representation of an Irish harp and a Red Hand of Ulster (Ulster's heraldic crest) consisting of red-leaved plants. The stone figures of various mythical creatures on the terraces were carved to amuse Lady Londonderry's children. The house and gardens are administered by the National Trust who rank it among the six top gardens in Great Britain under their care. The Temple of the Winds is an octagonal gazebo in the grounds built in 1780.

Rievaulx Terrace, near Helmsley, North Yorkshire is unlike the other parks and formal gardens, in that it is a half-mile stretch of grass-covered terrace with carefully planned vistas of the ruined **Rievaulx Abbey** and the **Hambleton Hills**. At each end of the Terrace there is a classical rotunda. An Ionic Temple formerly used as a dining room, has an exhibition of landscape design in the basement.

Rutland Water is a manmade reservoir in Leicestershire, which now has a Nature Reserve with a Butterfly and Aquatic Centre, and two birdwatching centres. There are plenty of water sports of all kinds, including sailing, windsurfing and fishing.

The **Stackpole Estate** in Dyfed, Wales, administered by the National Trust, is a 2,000-acre park four miles south of Pembroke. There are eight miles of cliffs as well as beaches and a tiny harbour, farmland and sand dunes. The series of freshwater lakes are thick with waterlilies. The Trust administers similar estates nearby along the Pembrokeshire coast.

Tatton Park, near Knutsford, Cheshire, one of Britain's favourite tourist destinations, stands in 2,000 acres of deer park and 54 acres of ornamental gardens, laid out by Humphrey Repton. There is an authentic Japanese garden, an Italian garden, an orangery, a fernery, a rose garden and an arboretum. Banks of rhododendrons and azaleas flower in season. There is also a farm run in 1930s style and many varieties of wildfowl. Tatton Park is close to Chester and Liverpool.

The **Wildfowl and Wetlands Trust** at Slimbridge, Gloucestershire was the first of eight such conservation areas in Britain. The whole project was begun by the naturalist and artist Sir Peter Scott, who founded the Slimbridge Centre in 1946. There are now seven others, at **Castle Espie** in Northern Ireland, **Caerlaverrock** in Scotland, **Washington** in north-eastern England, **Martin Mere** north of Liverpool, **Welney** in Norfolk, **Llanelli** in Wales and **Arundel** in West Sussex. They not only protect wild birds but they also bring in waterfowl that have become extinct in Britain, in order to encourage them to breed again here. Slimbridge has over 200 species of bird, including Flamingoes , the Ruddy Duck and the Australian Freckled Duck, on an 880-acre site. There is a tropical aviary containing humming-birds.

The Royal Horticultural Society has its own gardens at **Wisley**, Surrey, within easy reach of London. They are full of exotic species, and there are large banks of rhodedendrons, hydrangeas, etc. The gardens were donated to the Society by Sir Thomas Hanbury in 1903. This is a good place to get advice on how to look after your own garden.

Information

The National Gardens Scheme arranges the opening for charity of gardens not usually open to the public. A booklet is published every March which is available from newsagents or from:

The National Gardens Scheme
57 Lower Belgrave Street
London S W 1W 0LR

Stourhead Garden, Wiltshire (opposite above).

Sissinghurst Gardens from top of Tower Kent (opposite left).

Wisley Gardens (opposite right).

Flowers in the Harewood House and gardens, Yorkshire (right).

The Republic of Ireland

The Republic of Ireland is more rural and sparsely populated than Britain; the population is welcoming, the scenery glorious and the food and drink especially delicious.

Ireland is ideal for touring by car because it is the least populated country in the European Community, so there are stretches of road on which there is no human habitation. The similarities with England are clear immediately to the foreigner, though the Irish would deny them strenuously! Still, the British ruled with a rod of iron for 800 years, so some influence was bound to rub off. It is there in the language, for instance. Everyone in Ireland speaks English but by no means all Irish speak their native language, Irish, also known as Erse or Gaelic, which is related to Scots Gaelic and Welsh, but written in its own alphabet. The currency, the Irish pound, is known as the punt and no longer identical in value to the pound sterling. The most telling relic of English domination is the fact that the great cathedrals and churches, as well as the great country houses are still in Protestant hands in this overwhelmingly Roman Catholic country..

Dublin, the capital, is a city whose centre is famous for its elegant Georgian architecture, notably St. Stephen's Green, Merriam Square and Parnell Square. One of the main sights of Dublin is the **General Post Office** in **O'Connell Street**, scene of the rioting in 1916 which led to home rule for Ireland and eventually to Irish independence. **Grafton Street** is an elegant shopping street of early 19th-century houses with many literary associations. **Trinity College**, the only college of the University of Dublin, was founded in 1591 by Queen Elizabeth I, at the behest of Archbishop of Dublin, then a Protestant. The first buildings were erected in 1593. Roman Catholics were not allowed to receive degrees until 1793 and could not win scholarships or hold office in the university until 1873. The university was Protestant in spirit until very recently. It is the third-largest university in Ireland. The **Great Library** (1712 -32) contains many valuable manuscripts, including the **Book of Kells**, a beautifully illuminated codex of the Bible dating from the 8th century. It is reputed to have been written and painted at the Columban monastery of Iona, the oldest in Scotland. **Dublin Castle**, behind **City Hall**, was the official seat of British rule, where the Lord Lieutenant resided. Although founded in the early 13th century, the Castle has been heavily rebuilt and most of the present building dates from the 18th century. The **State Apartments** are open to the public, as is the **Genealogical Office and Heraldic Museum.** The **Guiness Brewery** is a Dublin landmark of very different kind. There are conducted tours of the brewery at which free samples are distributed.

St. Patrick's Cathedral is the cathedral church of the Protestant Church of Ireland, and the largest church in the country. It has had a chequered career as a cathedral, since it had a rival for the title in the form of **Christchurch Cathedral**, now cathedral of the Protestant archdiocese of Dublin and Glendalough. Both cathedrals have magnificent monuments. **The National Library of Ireland** and the **National Museum of Ireland** stand side by side next to **Leinster House**, headquarters of the **Royal Dublin Society**. The Museum has the finest collection of Irish relics anywhere in the world.

The most famous tourist attraction outside Dublin is **Blarney Castle**, County Cork. The legend that kissing the Blarney Stone gave one the "gift of the gab" grew from Queen Elizabeth I's irritation with the loquacious Lord Blarney. The stone is set in a wall in the top of the 15th-century battlements, from which there is a fine view of the surrounding countryside.

The Cliffs of Moher, are a spectacular natural phenomenon, southern Ireland's answer to the Giant's Causeway. These gigantic cliffs opposite the **Aran Isles** rise sheer out of the water to a height of 600 feet or more. On the very top there is a turreted tower,

O'Brien's Tower, which looks medieval but is in fact a 19th-century folly.
The **Ring of Kerry**, a circular tour through around the coast of Kerry, starting and ending at Killarney, is one of the best ways to see the beauties of western Ireland. **Killarney** is a cathedral city and market town at the heart of a region renowned for its wealth of flora, including rare species. **St. Mary's Catholic Cathedral** (1842-1855) was built by Augustus Pugin, and is considered to be one of the finest examples of Gothic Revival in the country. There is a monument to four of Kerry's Gaelic poets in College Street. Killarney is near the eastern shore of **Lough Leane**. Lough Leane is divided by spurs of land into three parts, the **Lower Lake**, **Muckross Lake**, also known as the **Middle Lake** and the most southerly part, known as **Upper Lake**. Ruined **Ross Castle** stands on **Ross Island** in the Lough. **Governor's Rock Headland** is a nature preserve. At **Killegy**, there is a small church with an 18th-century belltower. The churchyard contains the grave of Rudolf Ehrich Raspe (1737-94) the author of *The Travels and Adventures of Baron Münchhausen*. Raspe was invited to Ireland to help work the copper mines on Ross Island and at Muckross. **Dunloe Castle**, on the western shores of Lough Leane, opposite Killarney, is an excellent point from which to see the **Gap of Dunloe**. This narrow pass through the Macgillycuddy Reeks is too narrow for cars, but ponies may be hired at the local public house, known as **Kate Kearney's Cottage.** Kate Kearney was a 19th-century innkeeper who sold strong liquor to tourists. The promontory that separates the Middle and Upper Lakes is the Bourne-Vincent Memorial Park, formerly **Muckross Abbey**. The abbey is, in fact, a priory, founded in 1448 by Observantine Friars. The friars kept the priory going until they were finally evicted by Cromwell's men in 1652. The extensive gardens of **Muckross House** can be visited and contain beautiful shrubs. Nearby is the **Devil's Punchbowl**, a two-mile hike from Mangerton peak (2,756 feet) to Stoompa (2,281 feet) along the crest of the Cirque of Gleann na Capall, taking in views of the Loughs **Erhugh**, **Managh** and **Garogarry**, makes a pleasant outing. Another famous Killarney beauty spot is the **Torc Falls**, one of a series of waterfalls between the Middle and Upper Lakes. The grounds of **Kenmare House** lie between Killarney and Lough Leane. The house itself was destroyed by fire in 1913 and most of the grounds now form part of the **Killarney Golf Club**. **Cahirsiveen** is a small at the tip of the Kerry peninsula beside the Valencia River. The Spanish-sounding name of the river and the nearby island is actually a corruption of Béal Inse, the name of the adjacent stretch of water. Nearby are the ruins of **Carhan House**, birthplace of the great Irish liberator, Daniel O'Connell. North of the town there is an ancient anchoritic site called Killobarnaum or Killavaraun. To the west are the ruins of the 15th-century **Ballycarbery Castle** owned by the Mac Carthy Mór family, the ancient rulers of Kerry. **Leacanabuile**, an ancient ring-fort, is a national monument, next to which is the large, stone ringfort of **Cathair na Cat**. There are other ancient forts and earthworks in the vicinity.
Tralee is the county town and as famous for its bacon-curing as for *The Rose of Tralee Festival*.

The Old Library, Trinity College, Dublin (top).

Aran Island, Irishmaan (above).

St. Stephen's Green, Dublin (right).

Dromoland Castle, County Clare (opposite right).

Merrion Square (opposite left).

Information
Irish Tourist Board
Ireland House
150 New Bond Street
London Q1Y 9FE
Tel: (071) 493 3201

Irish Tourist Board
Baggot's Street Bridge
Dublin 2
Tel: (010) 3531765871

Events
There are St. Patrick's Day parades all over Ireland, and music festivals abound in the summer months. In the Ring of Kerry, the Puck Fair is held in mid-August in Killorglin. A feature of the fair is the merrymaking connected with the Puck, a large, beribboned, male goat. Another popular event is the Rose of Tralee International Festival, at which talented and beautiful girls whose ancestors emigrated from Ireland compete for the title. It is held in August or the first week of September.

TRAVEL INFORMATION

The United Kingdom of Great Britain and Northern Ireland is very different to the rest of Europe, due to its long isolation from the mainland and the closer ties it has developed with the other English-speaking countries. The British way of life therefore differs substantially from that of the rest of Europe. It is worth studying local customs beforehand in order to find one's bearings.

An international, U.S. or EC driving licence that is valid for at least one year from date of arrival in the country is valid for driving in Britain.

Driving is on the left-hand side of the road. Drivers should buy a copy of the Highway Code (latest edition published in 1993) upon arrival, available from all booksellers and newsagents, to familiarise themselves with the rules of the road. Road signs and signposts usually conform to international standards on major roads, though not on country roads. A few road signs at the ports are multilingual, and they are bi-lingual (English and Welsh) in Wales. Roads are categorised as motorways (the road number preceded by an M), A-roads which are major or arterial roads, B-roads and unclassified roads. Many major roads are dual carriageways, i.e. traffic is separated by a central barrier or reservation. All distances are given in miles; a kilometre is approximately five-eighths of a mile. Petrol (gasoline) is sold either by the gallon or by the litre; the British gallon is the imperial gallon, equivalent to 1.75 litres, not the American gallon which is equivalent to one litre. The Republic of Ireland is in the process of converting to both kilometres and litres.

Roads in both parts of Ireland are not as well-made as those in Britain, and as the distances between settlements is greater, it is wise to take precautions before travelling to ensure that breakdowns are avoided.

If you are travelling in your own car, it is a good idea before starting on a tour to obtain membership of one of the two British motoring organisations, the AA (Automobile Association) or the RAC (Royal Automobile Club). Hire cars will usually have membership already, but it is best to inquire. British motoring organisations tend to send help to repair a car on the spot in case of a breakdown, rather than have the car towed away. The AA has offices in most towns, always at an address known as Fanum House. The head offices of the motoring organisations are:

Automobile Association
Fanum House
Basing View
Basingstoke, Hants. RG21 2EA
Tel: (0256) 20123

Royal Automobile Club
83-85 Pall Mall
London S W 1Y 5HW
Tel: (071) 839 7050

Accommodation

There is no official hotel classification or government approval of hotels in Great Britain, as there are in some European countries. The English Tourist Board, however, inspects 17,000 hotels, guesthouses, inns, bed and breakfast accommodation, and farmhouses every year. It publishes a free list of the approved ones called *Let's Go*, which is available from Tourist Information Centres or you can order it by telephoning (0272) 217917. The Welsh Tourist Board has a free publication called *Great Little Breaks*, and the Scottish Tourist Board publishes *Autumn, Winter, Spring Breaks*. The British Tourist Authority has a booklet of recommended accommodation called *Commended Country Hotels, Guesthouses and Restaurants*, which can be bought at newsagents all over the country. Several other organisations inspect hotels and give their seals of approval. These include the AA (Automobile Association), the RAC (Royal Automobile Club), the Consumers' Association and several travel guide publishers, as well as the various regional and national tourist boards.

English Tourist Board
Thames Tower - Blacks Road
London W 6

Welsh Tourist Board
Brunel House
2 Fitzalan Road
Cardiff CF2 1UY

Scottish Tourist Board
P.O. Box 15
Edinburgh EH1 1UY

Camping and caravanning is the cheapest form of do-it-yourself lodging. Youth Hostels are the cheapest form of accommodation, all you need to bring with you is a sleeping bag and sheets or a sheet sleeping-bag. However, most will not accept non-members or even a non-member accompanied by a member. If you intend to stay at Youth Hostels, it is advisable to join in your own country before setting out. Most hostels restrict stays to three nights. For information about hostels, contact

Youth Hostel Association
Trevelyan House
8 St. Stephen's Hill
St. Albans, Herts. AL1 2DY

The Scottish Youth Hostels Association
7 Glebe Crescent
Stirling FK8 2JA

The YHA also has a shop in London, the Adventure Centre, at 14, Southampton Street, WC2E 7HY, just off the Strand (nearest tube stations Charing Cross or Covent Garden), where you can join the Association, buy equipment, maps and the current guide to YHA accommodation.

Bed and breakfast accommodation is the next cheapest. London hotels are much more expensive than elsewhere, but even here there are often cheap rates to be had for weekend stays out of season.

It is great fun to stay at a country inn or a farmhouse. Many inns and public houses have accommodation, some of it to a very high standard. Many such hostelries have been in existence since the 17th century and even earlier. For farmhouse accommodation, it is best to reserve in advance. Farmhouses can be found through British or Irish Tourist Authority offices abroad or the relevant Tourist Boards in Britain or Ireland, as well as through weekly publications devoted exclusively to advertisements, such as Dalton's Weekly and the Loot. (in London).

For information about camping and caravanning in Britain, write to:

The National Caravan Council Catherine House
Victoria Road
Aldershot, Hants. GU11 1SS

The Camping and Caravanning Club
11 Lower Grosvenor Place
London S W 1W 0EY

The Caravan Club
East Grinstead House
East Grinstead, West Sussex
RH19 1UA

Eating Out

Great Britain is more notorious than famous in the food department, and quality varies enormously. Restaurants may receive an approval from the Good Food Guide or other guidebooks and some display favourable reviews from newspapers in their windows. The best that can be said is that even in the suburbs it is possible to get take away or restaurant meals in the evening, even in quite remote places, though don't count on being fed after 10.00 p.m. The best British meals are breakfast and tea. To find out what the local specialities are, tour the local food markets and see what people are buying. However, in the big towns especially, the sort of food people are eating in their own homes is hard to come by in restaurants. Britain has always had more foreign restaurants than any other kind, and traditionally they have been Italian, Chinese and Indian. Here too, quality and price vary, but the food in these is generally of a better standard. The food in public houses can be very elaborate restaurant standard or can be pie-and-chips standard.

Using the Telephone

Although British Telecom no longer has an official monopoly, most public telephones in the street are owned by BT. It is advisable to buy a BT phone card for calls. In London, there are Mercury telephones, which are cheaper but can only be operated with a Mercury card. Many card phones of both types take credit cards but there is a 50p minimum charge on such calls. The country code for Great Britain is 44.

Events

The following is a list of public holidays and events celebrated throughout Great Britain and Northern Ireland:

Public Holidays and Special Days in Great Britain and Ireland

The name for public holidays in Great Britain is a bank holiday. On a bank holiday, banks, schools and some shops are closed. The only public holiday on which everything is closed and there is no public transport is Christmas Day. Although the banks are shut, it is usually possible to find a bureau de change for changing money in the cities.

1 January – New Year's Day bank holiday
First Monday after New Year's Day – Bank Holiday (Scotland only)
St. David's Day – 1 March (Wales only)
St. Patrick's Day – 17 March (Northern Ireland and Republic of Ireland only)
Mothering Sunday – Third Sunday in March
Good Friday – Bank holiday
Easter Monday – Bank holiday (not Scotland)
May Day holiday – First Monday in May (not Scotland)
Spring Bank holiday – Last Monday in May
Pentecost – First Monday in June (Republic of Ireland only)
Orange Day – 12 July (Northern Ireland only)
August Bank Holiday – First Monday in August (Scotland and Ireland only)
August Bank Holiday – Last Monday in August (not in Scotland)
Bank Holiday – 25 October (Republic of Ireland only)
Halloween – 31st October
Guy Fawkes Day – 5th November (not Republic of Ireland)*
St Andrews Day – 30 November (Scotland only)
Christmas Day – 25 December
Boxing Day – 26 December (UK and Northern Ireland)
St. Stephen's Day – 26 December (Ireland)

*This is the anniversary of the Gunpowder Plot of 1605, a Roman Catholic-inspired plot to blow up the Houses of Parliament. All over Britain there are firework displays, both public and private, and in many places Bonfire Societies prepare all year for the great event. Children make a "guy" a doll to be burned on top of the bonfire, supposedly an effigy of Guy Fawkes, and beg for pennies in the street to pay for their fireworks, asking "a penny for the guy". As a result, Halloween which falls so close to Guy Fawkes night, is not as widely celebrated in Britain as elsewhere in the English-speaking world. However, there are halloween parties, masks and lights made from hollowed-out pumpkins and games such as bob-apple are played. In some places, children dress up in masks and fancy dress and go out "trick or treating", a custom revived in Britain by immigrants from the Caribbean.

Useful Addresses

British Tourist Authority
64 St. James Street
London S W 1.

This is the address for correspondence. The Authority publishes a monthly journal entitled *In Britain*, which is available at British embassies.

For leaflets, pamphlets and guides, the Authority runs a shop at:

12 Lower Regent Street
London S W 1
(nearest tube station: Piccadilly Circus).

The English Tourist Board
Thames Tower,
Black's Road
London W 6 9EL
Tel:071 -846 9000

London Visitor and Convention Bureau
26 Grosvenor Gardens
London S W 1 0DU
Tel: 071 -730 -3488

The Scottish Tourist Board
19 Cockspur Street
London S W 1Y 5BL
Tel:(071)930 8661

23 Ravelston Terrace
Edinburgh EH4 3EU
Tel: (031)332 2433

Scottish Travel Centre
14 South Street
EH2 2AZ
Tel: (031)332 2433

Wales Tourist Board
2 Fitzalan Road
Cardiff CF2 1UY
Tel: (0222)49909

The National Trust

The National Trust and the National Trust for Scotland administer places of historic interest in Great Britain and Northern Ireland. It is easy to become a member, and membership offers free or reduced price entry into all the Trusts' properties. Visitors to Britain who are interested in historic houses and gardens are strongly advised to join.

The National Trust
42 Queen Anne's Gate
London S W 1H

Travellers with disabilities should ask for advice from the following organisation, which publishes an excellent booklet, *Holidays for Disabled People*.

The Royal Association for Disability and Rehabilitation (RADAR)
25 Mortimer Street
London W 1N 8AB
Tel: (071) 637 5400

Index of Place Names
Instructions for Use

Oxford	ENG	62	Ye 38
①	②	③	④

GB ① Place name ② Country or province ③ Page number ④ Grid search reference

②
ENG England
ISL Island Areas (Isles of Scilly, Orkney, Shetland Western Isles)
NIR Northern Ireland
SCO Scotland
WAL Wales

GBA Alderney
GBG Guernsey
GBJ Jersey
GBM Isle of Man

A

B

C

G

H

I

J

K

L

M

O

S

U

V

W